# China's Economic Transformation

*To Paula*

# China's Economic Transformation

## Second Edition

Gregory C. Chow

**Blackwell**
Publishing

BLACKWELL PUBLISHING

350 Main Street, Malden, MA 02148-5020, USA
9600 Garsington Road, Oxford OX4 2DQ, UK
550 Swanston Street, Carlton, Victoria 3053, Australia

First edition published 2002 by Blackwell Publishing Ltd
Second edition published 2007

1   2007

*Library of Congress Cataloging-in-Publication Data*

Chow, Gregory C., 1929–
China's economic transformation / Gregory C. Chow. — 2nd ed.
p. cm.
Includes bibliographical references and index.
ISBN-13: 978-1-4051-5624-0 (pbk. : alk. paper)   1. China—Economic
conditions—1976–2000.   2. China—Economic policy—1976–2000.
3. China—Economic conditions—2000–   4. China—Economic policy—
2000–   5. China—Politics and government—1976–2002.   6. China—Politics
and government—2002–   7. China—Social conditions.   I. Title.

HC427.92.C4782 2007
338.951—dc21
2006034587

A catalogue record for this title is available from the British Library.

Set in 10/12pt Times
by Graphicraft Limited, Hong Kong
Printed and bound in the United Kingdom
by TJ International Ltd, Padstow, Cornwall

The publisher's policy is to use permanent paper from mills that operate a
sustainable forestry policy, and which has been manufactured from pulp processed
using acid-free and elementary chlorine-free practices. Furthermore, the publisher
ensures that the text paper and cover board used have met acceptable environmental
accreditation standards.

For further information on
Blackwell Publishing, visit our website:
www.blackwellpublishing.com

# Contents

Preface                                                                 x
Preface to the Second Edition                                        xiii
Introduction: The Transformation of China's Economy                     1

## Part I: Historical Background and General Survey                      7

**1**  Economic Lessons from History                                    9
  1.1  Introduction                                                      9
  1.2  Significant Events in Major Historical Dynasties                 10
  1.3  The Republic of China, 1911–                                     16
  1.4  Summary of Historical Lessons                                    21

**2**  Experiments with Planning and Economic Disruptions              24
  2.1  The Communist Party Rises to Power                               24
  2.2  Historical Review: 1949–78                                       26
  2.3  A Model of the Chinese Planned Economy                           29
  2.4  The Behavior of Economic Units in a Planned Economy              33
  2.5  Output Planning in Theory and Practice                           36
  2.6  Organization and Administration of Economic Planning             41

**3**  Economic Reform up to the Mid-1990s                             47
  3.1  Why Economic Reform Started in 1978                              47
  3.2  Agriculture                                                      49
  3.3  Reform of State-owned Enterprises                                50
  3.4  Price Reform                                                     52
  3.5  The Banking System                                              54
  3.6  Foreign Trade and Investment                                     54
  3.7  The Nonstate Sectors                                            55

3.8     Institutional Infrastructure                                      56
3.9     Reform Policies Similar to Those of Taiwan                        57
3.10    Reasons for the Success of China's Economic Reform               60
3.11    Summary                                                          64
        Appendix: China's Geography                                      65

**4**   Further Reform: Problems and Prospects                           69
4.1     Introduction                                                     69
4.2     Enterprise Reform                                                69
4.3     Banking Reform                                                   72
4.4     Foreign Trade and Investment during the Asian Financial Crisis  76
4.5     The Impact of WTO Membership                                     78
4.6     Agriculture and Rural Poverty                                    85
4.7     Prospects for Reform                                             87

**Part II: Analysis of the Macroeconomy**                               **91**

**5**   Economic Growth                                                  93
5.1     The Neoclassical Model of Economic Growth                        93
5.2     Data on Output, Capital, and Labor                               94
5.3     A Review of Regression Analysis                                  99
5.4     Estimating Production Functions for China                       101
5.5     Use of the Neoclassical Growth Model to Forecast GDP            104
5.6     How Large will the Chinese Economy be in 2020?                  107

**6**   Economic Fluctuations                                            110
6.1     The Multiplier-Accelerator Model of Economic Fluctuations       110
6.2     Dynamic Properties of the Multiplier-Accelerator Model          113
6.3     An Econometric Method for Estimating Parameters of Linear
        Stochastic Equations                                            115
6.4     Estimating a Multiplier-Accelerator Model of the Chinese
        Economy                                                         116
6.5     A Vector Autoregression (VAR) System                            119
6.6     Econometric Models of the Chinese Economy                       120

**7**   Macroeconomic Policies                                           124
7.1     Introduction                                                     124
7.2     Monetary Policy                                                  126
7.3     An Econometric Analysis of Inflation and of Monetary Policy
        in China                                                        133
7.4     Basic Facts about Government Revenue and Expenditure            136
7.5     Fiscal Policy                                                    136

**8**  The Effects of Political Movements on the Macroeconomy            142
    8.1   Specification of a Dynamic Optimization Model of the
          Chinese Economy                                                  142
    8.2   The Solution of the Dynamic Optimization Problem                 145
    8.3   Statistical Estimation                                           147
    8.4   Measuring the Effects of Two Political Events                    150
    8.5   Conclusions                                                     156

**Part III: Topics in Economic Development**                            **159**

**9**  Consumption                                                        161
    9.1   Trends in Per Capita Consumption                                 161
    9.2   Household Expenditure Patterns                                   165
    9.3   Rural Per Capita Consumption Expenditures in 1998 by Province    172
    9.4   Consumption of Housing in Rural and Urban Areas                  174

**10**  Western Development and Environmental Policies                    177
    10.1   Inequality in Per Capita Consumption and East–West Disparity    178
    10.2   Developing the Western Part of China                            179
    10.3   Environmental Policies                                          187
    10.4   A Study of Industrial Pollution                                 189

**11**  Population                                                        193
    11.1   The Role of Population and Human Capital in Economic
           Development                                                   193
    11.2   The Chinese Population and its Rate of Growth                   195
    11.3   Population Policy                                               198
    11.4   Evaluation of China's Population Policy                         202
    11.5   Economic Explanation of the Birth Rate                          204

**12**  Human Capital                                                     207
    12.1   The Importance of Human Capital and its Measurement             207
    12.2   Labor Supply and Demand                                        209
    12.3   Investment in Human Capital                                    216
    12.4   Measuring the Rates of Return to Schooling in China            224
    12.5   Health Services                                                226
    12.6   The Social Welfare System                                      229

**Part IV: Analysis of Individual Sectors**                             **233**

**13**  The Banking and Financial System                                 235
    13.1   Commercial Banks                                               235

13.2   The People's Bank                                                237
13.3   Factors Affecting the Functioning of the Banking System          239
13.4   Possible Weaknesses of the System                                242
13.5   Possible Directions of Reform                                    243
13.6   The Financial Condition of Commercial Banks and
       the Bad-loan Problem                                             245
13.7   Other Financial Institutions                                     247
13.8   The Role of the Chinese Government in Reforming the
       Financial System                                                 251

14   Shanghai Stock Price Determination                                 255
14.1   Introduction                                                     255
14.2   A Model of Stock Price Determination                             256
14.3   Empirical Findings from the Shanghai Stock Exchange              259
14.4   Comparison with Findings for Hong Kong and New York Stocks       263
14.5   Concluding Comments                                              264

15   The Behavior of State Enterprises                                   267
15.1   Organization of a State Enterprise under Central Planning        267
15.2   Planning and Operations of a Large-scale State Enterprise        271
15.3   A Simple Model of a State Enterprise under Central Planning      275
15.4   A Simple Model of a State Enterprise after Initial Reform        278
15.5   State Enterprise Restructuring in the Late 1990s and its Effects
       on Enterprise Behavior                                           281

16   The Nonstate Sectors                                               286
16.1   Relative Growth of Nonstate Sectors                             286
16.2   Private Enterprises Prior to 1949                               288
16.3   Economic Conditions for the Growth of Township and
       Village Enterprises                                              288
16.4   Econometric Measurement of the Relative Efficiency of State
       Enterprises and TVEs                                            291
16.5   Characteristics of a Free-market Economy                        293
16.6   Characteristics of the Chinese Market Economy                   295

17   Foreign Trade                                                      299
17.1   Some Statistics of China's Foreign Trade                        299
17.2   Explanation of Trading Patterns under Free Trade                301
17.3   The Determination of Foreign Exchange Rates                     307
17.4   China's Foreign Trade Policy                                     313
17.5   Problems in Implementing Foreign Trade Policies in the
       Early 1980s                                                      316
17.6   Protectionism in the United States                              322

**18** Foreign Investment 326
   18.1 The Role of Foreign Investment 326
   18.2 Historical Developments 328
   18.3 The State of Foreign Direct Investment (FDI) as of 2002 329
   18.4 Policies for the Regulation of Foreign Investment 332
   18.5 Opportunities and Problems for Foreign Investors 334
   18.6 How Attractive is China for Foreign Investment? 338
   18.7 The Impact of WTO Membership on Foreign Investment 339
   18.8 A Proposal to Increase Foreign Investment from Taiwan 342

**Part V: Studies of Economic Institutions and Infrastructure** 345

**19** Corruption and Misuse of Assets 347
   19.1 Introduction 347
   19.2 Laws of Asset Management 349
   19.3 Managing One's Own Person 352
   19.4 Managing Physical Assets 354
   19.5 Managing Collections of Assets under the Responsibility System 356
   19.6 The Misuse of Collectively Owned Land 359
   19.7 Corruption and Economic Reform 360
   19.8 Concluding Comments 364

**20** The Legal System and the Role of Government 366
   20.1 The Legal System prior to 1949 366
   20.2 The Legal System since 1949 368
   20.3 The Role of the Legal System in a Market Economy 371
   20.4 The Economic Role of Government 373
   20.5 The Role of Planning in China's Market Economy 377
   20.6 The Government's Decision Process 381

**21** The Education System and Policy 385
   21.1 The Education System prior to 1949 385
   21.2 The Education System after 1949 387
   21.3 Education Policy 387
   21.4 Economics Education 391
   21.5 Demand for Education 399
   21.6 Concluding Comments 403

**22** Taking Stock and Looking Ahead 405
   22.1 Taking Stock 405
   22.2 Prospects for the Chinese Economy up to 2020 417

Conclusion: Lessons for the Study of Economic Transformation 425

Index 433

# Preface

In the twenty-first century, economic integration and the increase in the economic and political influence of Asian countries relative to the rest of the world are two important driving forces shaping world events. China plays a very important role in both developments mainly because of the increasing size of its economy. It is therefore necessary for anyone concerned with the development of the world to understand China's economy.

The purpose of this book is to introduce the reader to the workings of the Chinese economy. It is written both for undergraduate and graduate students as a textbook and for the general reader who wishes to understand the Chinese economy. It describes the process of economic transformation in China in its various aspects. Understanding this transformation process is essential to understanding the current economy of China.

I combine historical-institutional and theoretical-quantitative approaches to study China's economy because neither one by itself can provide a complete picture. The former approach is favored by area specialists and historians. The latter is familiar to economists. These approaches complement each other. Without a solid understanding of the historical-institutional background, one can make serious errors in applying a theoretical-quantitative model to the Chinese economy. On the other hand, understanding the history and institutions without the benefits of a theoretical and/or quantitative analysis is not sufficient either. The first four chapters of this book provide a historical-institutional background, while many of the remaining chapters are theoretical and quantitative, including chapters 5–9, 11, 12, 14, 15, 17, and 19. Chapters 7, 9, 10, 11, 13, and 15–22 contain historical-institutional material as well. Hence the two approaches are integrated in this book. By studying the Chinese economy in this way, one forms a clear picture of the dynamic and continuing process of transformation from a planned economy to a market economy.

Historians and area specialists have raised objections to those economists who believe in universal laws in economics and apply them to the study of the economies of all countries alike, without regard to the special historical and cultural setting. Economists have expressed disappointment at area studies that fail to take advantage of the powerful tools of economic analysis. In this book I suggest that economic tools can be applied to

China provided that the researcher carefully examines whether the basic assumptions are consistent with the realities of Chinese society. Examples of integrating institutional material with theoretical or quantitative analysis are provided in chapters 2, 5–9, 11, 14, 16, 17, and 19. Nor can economic tools be properly applied without considering the institutional setting. One hopes that the application of economic tools to China and other countries with non-Western cultural-institutional settings will help extend the field of economics by suggesting new tools and concepts of analysis when existing ones are found to be inadequate. This topic is discussed in chapter 22.

Because this book deals with the process of economic transformation it is of interest to readers studying transitional economics. Perhaps the word "transformation" better describes the economic changes in China than the word "transition." The latter word may imply that the process will reach a definite, terminal state, whereas in the Chinese case the final form that the economic system will take remains unknown. Chinese government officials have guided the reform process in steps, determining one step after observing the result of the previous step. Unlike most studies in economics, this book pays special attention to changes in economic institutions. Economic transformation and transition have attracted general attention since economic reforms started in China in the late 1970s and in eastern Europe and the former Soviet Union in the early 1990s. Historically, institutional changes have come about when the same profit motive and economic self-interest that explain behavior under a given set of institutions have also motivated the design of new institutions to make more money. However, the economic transformation that has taken place in China is to a significant extent an act of the Chinese government aimed at modernizing the Chinese economy, although private profit motives also play a role. In chapters 2, 3, and 4 respectively we study China's planning system, the economic reform process, and the problems in reforming the state sectors. Economic transformations are also discussed in chapters 10, 20, and 21, which deal respectively with the government's effort to develop the western region and to set environmental policies, to build the institutions of a modern legal system, and to improve the educational system. In chapter 16, we study the nonstate sectors including the township and village enterprises that have evolved through profit motives in a Chinese institutional setting.

Theoretical-quantitative analysis is applied to the study of economic growth (chapter 5), economic fluctuations (chapter 6), macroeconomic policies (chapter 7), economic effects of the Great Leap Forward and the Cultural Revolution (chapter 8), consumption (chapter 9), population (chapter 11), human capital (chapter 12), the banking and financial system (chapter 13), Shanghai stock price determination (chapter 14), the behavior of state enterprises (chapter 15), the nonstate sectors (chapter 16), foreign trade (chapter 17), and foreign investment (chapter 18). Chapter 22 concludes by summarizing several important institutional characteristics of the Chinese economic system that are different from those of a Western market economy, providing challenges for further study. It also discusses the prospects of continued economic growth in the twenty-first century based on the momentum of historical forces.

This book is based on my study of the subject since 1980 through research, teaching, and working with Chinese educators, economists, and government officials. I have used the material in an undergraduate course on the Chinese economy at Princeton University.

The course started in 1986 when it covered only the topics of chapter 2 and parts of chapters 3, 9, 11, 12, 17, and 18, as contained in my *The Chinese Economy* (1985). The remaining material draws on my research since, as partially reported in *Understanding China's Economy* (1994) and in more recent writings cited in the references. In writing this book I have benefited from questions and critical comments from students through the years. About 20 percent of the material (including parts of chapters 5, 6, 8, and 14 in particular) is technical and mathematical. The general reader can skip the technical material and read the text only.

I would like to thank Patrick Bolton, Simon Chen, Paula Chow, Vida Chu, Shouwei Hu, D. Gale Johnson, Lawrence Klein, and Chia Yu Shen for reading parts of the manuscript, and especially Kan Chen for reading the entire manuscript and making suggestions for improvement. The remaining errors are my own responsibility. Annamarie Scarpati has assisted in many respects in the preparation of the manuscript with skill, efficiency, and enthusiasm. It has been a pleasure to work with Al Bruckner of Blackwell Publishers, who has handled the publication of this manuscript at all stages with a remarkable professionalism that is based on his vast knowledge and experience. Financial support from the Gregory C. Chow Econometric Research Program of the Department of Economics at Princeton University is gratefully acknowledged.

Gregory Chow
Princeton, NJ
May 2001

# Preface to the Second Edition

Since the first edition was published in 2002 the major economic trends and economic institutions described here have remained essentially unchanged, while China's economic development has received much more attention because of its rapid growth. The economic trends have remained unchanged because the three fundamentals mentioned in the book continue to operate. Inertia and vested economic interests (corruption included) have made the change in economic institutions a slow process, in spite of the Chinese government's serious attempts to push economic reform forward.

Although trends of economic growth and economic reform have remained about the same as described in the first edition, the Chinese people and government are starting to use their new wealth to confront poverty and inequality. As China becomes richer and economic growth, driven by rapid development in the coastal provinces, is assured, attention is shifting to the problems of the environment and the poor. Attention of the government has shifted to rural development, the alleviation of poverty, social security, healthcare, and education. In the meantime, as wealth has accumulated, the government bureaucracy has had more opportunity for corruption and has become more difficult to manage. With these issues in the background, this second edition has added new materials in sections 4.6 on agriculture and rural poverty, 6.5 on vector autoregression VAR with an application to the study of the effects of monetary policy in China, 7.3 on econometric analysis of inflation and of monetary policy, 10.2.4 on rural development policies, 12.5 and 12.6 on healthcare and social insurance, 19.6 on the misuse of land, 19.7 on corruption and economic reform, 20.5 on the role of planning in China's market economy, 21.5 on the demand for education. It also updates the statistical tables, describes more recent developments in various sectors, and adds recent material to previous discussions on many topics.

The author would like to thank Bert Horwitz for his careful reading of the first edition and for providing detailed comments; the students at Princeton University and Oberlin College, who raised interesting questions to sharpen my thinking of the subject; and the Gregory C. Chow Econometric Research Program at Princeton University and the

Department of Economics and Finance at the City University of Hong Kong, for providing research support and a pleasant environment to study the Chinese economy.

Gregory C. Chow
Princeton University
October 2006
gchow@princeton.edu

# Introduction: The Transformation of China's Economy

This book is about the transformation of China's economy into a market economy with its special characteristics. It deals with the process of transformation and the special features of the Chinese economy. It contains much of what I have discovered about China's economy and the economics of institutional transformation from research, teaching, traveling, working with Chinese educators and government officials, and observing the Chinese society simply by talking to Chinese friends and citizens since 1980. As an introduction I would like to make three sets of observations. The first is about the economics of institutional changes. The second is about China's government, and third about China's historical and cultural traditions. In the remainder of this book the reader will find these observations elaborated upon in more detail.

In the study of economic transformation, the role of the government needs to be stressed. Thomas Jefferson has aptly remarked that the government is the best which governs the least. However, in the process of an economic transformation promoted by government, the government has to play an important role, even if Jefferson's statement is valid when a set of economic institutions is well established. The economics of transformation is related to the economics of transition, since both deal with changes in economic institutions. A possible difference is that the latter conveys a notion that the economy is in a temporary state of transition to some ideal state, such as a special form of market economy. The former does not carry a notion of a known final stage of transformation. It studies the process of economic transformation without a definite statement regarding the final state.

Secondly, besides understanding the important role of the government it is important to understand the role of the remaining sectors which may support or reject the reform measures introduced by the government. These sectors may also play an important role in initiating reform of their own, sometimes even guiding government reform policies, and sometimes serving as a supplement to government reform. The former is illustrated by the introduction of the household responsibility system in Chinese agriculture from the grassroots, and the latter by the rapid growth of township and village enterprises in China as a supplement to state-owned enterprises.

Thirdly, if one is to understand the important roles of the government and the nongovernment sectors and their interaction in shaping the transformation of an economy, it is necessary to understand the historical, cultural, and institutional factors that affect the actions of government officials and the people. Government officials and the important players in the nongovernment sectors are guided in their behavior by historical and cultural factors, in addition to economic calculations. Economic reform in China and Russia has taken different directions partly because of the differences in historical and institutional factors. For example, China's reform in the agricultural sector succeeded because Chinese farmers in 1978 still remembered private farming – the commune system was introduced in China only in 1958. Collectivization of agriculture in the Soviet Union took place in the early 1930s and Russian farmers in the early 1990s did not know how to operate as private farmers. It was difficult to privatize the agricultural sector in Russia. The success of agricultural reform in China provided the economic foundation for reform in other sectors.

Concerning the historical institutions of China, there is a long tradition of the use of social networking known as *guanxi*. *Guanxi* determines many social interactions, including economic transactions. It affects the reform of the legal system, as we will see in chapter 20. There is also an established bureaucratic tradition which affects the behavior of government officials and of state-owned enterprise managers. This tradition, further modified and developed under the government of the People's Republic of China, affects the reform of the banking and financial system, of state-owned enterprises, and of the nonstate sectors, as we will see in chapters 13, 15, and 16 respectively.

A fourth feature of the economics of transformation is that, since the government plays such an important role and the government's reform policies depend on historical and institutional factors, many aspects of the transformation process need to be studied as isolated events. Economists, following the lead of natural scientists, would like to find general laws that can be applied to explain economic behavior in general, regardless of time and space. There are such laws in economics, some of which will be illustrated in this book. However, while laws can explain economic behavior under a given set of economic institutions and may even be valid for a variety of economic institutions, they do not as a rule explain why economic reform started in China in 1978 and why it proceeded the way it did. The explanation has to rely on the historical circumstances in 1978. The nature of the economic reform that followed was subject to the constraints of the historical, institutional, and political factors affecting the actions of the Chinese Communist Party leaders. It also depended on the personal characteristics of the leader, Deng Xiaoping, himself.

The discussion of China's historical tradition in chapter 1, of its planning system in chapter 2, its general reform process in chapters 3 and 4, and the transformation of the individual sectors later on in this book illustrates the above important features in the study of the economics of institutional transformation. The individual sectors include consumption in chapter 9, western development in chapter 10, population policies in chapter 11, human capital in chapter 12, the banking and financial system in chapter 13, state enterprises and the nonstate sectors in chapters 15 and 16, foreign trade and foreign investment in chapters 17 and 18, and the legal system and the education system in chapters 20 and 21. These chapters emphasize in many places the important role of the government and of the historical and institutional factors affecting the reform process. Many take into account the interaction of government and nongovernment influences, and the nature of Chinese society, including bureaucratic behavior. Such are the important considerations in the study of the economics of institutional transformation.

In this book traditional economic tools are also applied to study the Chinese economy. Examples are a model of aggregate economic growth in chapter 5, theories of economic fluctuations in chapter 6, macroeconomic policies in chapter 7, an econometric study of the macroeconomic effects of the Great Leap Forward movement and the Cultural Revolution in chapter 8, analysis of consumer behavior in chapter 9, population growth and investment in human capital in chapters 11 and 12, and an economic analysis of behavior of individuals controlling state-owned assets in chapter 19. Even if the important concepts of economic incentives and self-interest cannot explain the transformation of economic institutions as isolated events influenced by historical circumstances and political considerations, these concepts can be applied in evaluating the incentive effects and economic efficiency of particular reform measures. Such applications can be found in many places in this book.

What remain to be discussed in this introduction are the nature of China's government and its historical and cultural tradition. People outside China today still think of it as essentially a Communist country having the typical characteristics associated with Communism as it was understood during the period up to 1980. These characteristics include a totalitarian regime in which government leaders attempt to manipulate the people as Chairman Mao did. There is no freedom. There are many labor camps. The government can change public opinion at will by controlling the press and the TV stations. That it is oppressive is evidenced by, for example, the tragic event on June 4, 1989, in Tiananmen Square.

In fact, the Chinese Communist Party and the Chinese government have changed a great deal since 1978. Economic reform has led to openness and more freedom. The Communist Party officially accepted "a socialist market economy" for China in 1992. Although the country is still ruled by the Communist Party, the current characteristics of China's political and economic system are very different from those listed in the last paragraph. Since economic reform started in 1978, the Chinese people have continually gained economic freedom. Economic freedom and economic wealth obtained through the market have given the Chinese people much more political power than before. Foreign trade and foreign investment promoted by the open-door policy have increased the contact of the Chinese people and government officials with the outside world. Both ordinary people and government officials are exposed to modern concepts of law and democracy. Some are even convinced of the virtues of many of these ideas. The government has instituted significant reform of China's legal system, as I shall describe in chapter 19.

Three issues often appear in the Western press when the topic of China comes up. These are the treatment of Tibet, Falung Gong, and certain political dissidents. On Tibet, most Chinese citizens (Han being the vast majority) side with the government in making sure that Tibet remains a part of China. Some Han Chinese believe that certain religious leaders in Tibet use the issue of religious freedom as a means to promote political independence. I may add that some Chinese citizens believe that China should have more religious freedom than the government allows, even when Christian church attendance has been allowed to increase rapidly in recent years. The vast majority of educated Chinese citizens, including those studying and working in the United States, believe that Falun Gong (a "new religion" in China) is a cult and a menace to society. They tend to support the government in taking punitive actions. On the treatment of political dissidents, it depends on which political dissidents and under what circumstances.

China has its own form of representative government. In the selection of representatives to China's legislature, members of the People's Congress are indirectly elected by representatives at the level immediately below, until public election determines the representatives at the lowest street district or village level. Unlike the situation before the 1980s. when members of the People's Congress only rubber-stamped legislation proposed to them by the State Council at the direction of the Communist Party, members of the People's Congress today are educated and vote according to their own opinion. Truly democratic public elections are held in villages all over China to elect government officials at the village level, although such elections have not reached higher levels.

No single person, like Chairman Mao during his lifetime, can control the Chinese population the way Mao did. The Chinese people have become more mature politically after the movements of the Great Leap Forward of 1958–61 and the Cultural Revolution of 1966–76. Since China is now open to the outside world the people can no longer be so easily fooled. Beside the differences in historical circumstances, Mao was a Chinese political genius unique in his century. Mao designated Hua Guofeng to be Chairman of the Party to succeed him, but leadership fell to the hands of Deng Xiaoping instead. Deng was able to assume leadership because he was supported by the top members of the Party. The point is that election within the Party serves as a process to select the able and to limit the power of a potential dictator. Many outside observers had forecasted trouble in the transitions after the deaths of Mao and Deng, only to find that they were wrong. This is a sign of the stability and resilience of the political leadership at the top.

Another occasion when outside observers misjudged the nature of the Chinese leadership is their very pessimistic forecast for the future of Hong Kong after its return to China in 1997. The situation in Hong Kong has turned out to be vastly different from any dire predictions. Yet another example is the devaluation of the Chinese yuan forecasted continuously by foreign commentators for two years during the Asian financial crisis of 1997–9, a subject to be discussed in section 4.4. There was also the prediction during the period of the Asian financial crisis and afterwards of an impending banking crisis, a subject to be discussed in section 4.3. Suffice it to say that positive information about China since 1978 needs to be incorporated into one's thinking in forming a balanced assessment of the country.

Consider the life of an average Chinese citizen. There is much more freedom than before. Are there labor camps? Yes, if the term is defined as prisons in which inmates are required to work. Prisons exist mainly to detain people who have committed crimes. There are not many political prisoners because there are not many people who are strong opponents of the government. By and large, the Chinese people are happy; and they are happy with their government. Students from China who have arrived recently can testify to this point. At Princeton in the late 1990s, one speaker was invited to talk about labor camps in China based on his personal experience in the 1960s. The situation is very different today from what the speaker described. The students from China in the audience felt indignant and jeered him. Part of this freedom is the freedom of any university student to study abroad, even when the government recognizes that many have decided to stay abroad after graduation. People are exposed to TV channels outside the mainland, including in particular those of Hong Kong and Taiwan. The internet and fax machines are available to many people. It is difficult for the government to manipulate news effectively even if it wishes to.

The government requires the support of the population to achieve its program of economic reform and development. For example, in the reform of state enterprises it may be necessary to lay off workers, and the government has to consider the possible effect of discontented workers on political stability. Chinese government leaders, just like political leaders elsewhere, consider maintaining their political power to be more important than almost any other objective. They applied force to disperse students occupying Tiananmen Square because they thought its continued occupation was undermining their authority and threatening the survival of the government. In situations where government power is not threatened, it is reasonable to assume that the government will try to promote the interests of the Chinese people, in addition to their own interests. When the position of a government official or leader is secure, it is his or her desire to serve the country, the possibility of corruption and self-interest notwithstanding. This desire is derived from a Confucian culture that has lasted centuries, and according to which the Chinese were taught to serve their country; and from the ideal of modernizing China generated by humiliation experienced since the defeat in the Opium War of 1840.

The last sentence leads to the third topic of this Introduction, namely, that China's historical and cultural tradition is an important determinant of the country's economic reform process and policies. Several historical cultural characteristics are important in this regard. First, the quality of human capital in the form of skilled and hard-working laborers and entrepreneurs has contributed to economic growth and enabled the reform process to succeed to the extent that market incentives alone cannot. Second, Chinese bureaucracy is at the same time a useful vehicle for guiding economic transformation and a hindrance to economic progress. Third, the traditional way of conducting business through informal social networks and human relations makes it difficult for foreign investors to enter Chinese markets and slows down the introduction of a modern legal system. Fourth, there is an emphasis on the collective welfare of the country as a whole as compared with the freedom of individuals, making the economy more socialistic. Fifth, there is a sense of nationalism. The current Chinese mentality is a combination of pride and the experience of humiliation. They are proud of a civilization that is over 5,000 years old, with distinction in science, mathematics, arts, furniture, china, literature, philosophy, ethics, and politics. After the Opium War of 1840–1 and until 1945, foreign powers one after another carved up parts of China and forced it to sign unequal treaties making concessions. Memories of oppression by Western and Japanese imperialism and the need for national independence are two important components of the Chinese mentality. Nationalism manifests itself whenever the country or any of its components appears to be under attack.

To cite an example of the manifestation of nationalism, consider the controversy in April 2001 over the possible return of the crew of a US spy plane which had landed in Hainan. The Chinese as a nation (including ordinary citizens, and government and military leaders) were very upset by the fact that when a Chinese life was lost, there was no immediate expression of sympathy or regret by the US government. Instead there was only a demand from the spying US side for the Chinese to keep away from the plane and release the crew immediately. In response the Chinese demanded an apology as a condition for the return of the crew. This demand was an expression of the pride and humiliation mentioned above. It was necessary to understand the Chinese mentality in order to resolve the conflict. The final solution took the form of a letter sent from the United States. In this letter the United States did not apologize because the American government and people thought they did nothing wrong. The Chinese felt that they got an apology in the form of two "very sorrys" in the letter, one to the Chinese people and to the family of the deceased pilot for the loss of his life, and a second for landing at a Chinese airport without having first obtained permission. Chinese nationalism and pride were preserved.

In studying the process of economic transformation in China, the roles of the government and of market forces in shaping the changes in economic institutions are important topics. In the course of our study, there are challenging problems that may require the subtle application of existing economic tools or introduction of new concepts and tools. Research on these topics will broaden the scope of modern economics and improve its tools as well, as we discuss in chapter 22. To study changes in economic institutions, one needs to treat some important aspects of the changes as unique events resulting from the efforts of governmental and nongovernmental organizations. The reform process is affected by historical and cultural factors, besides being driven by market forces and incentive considerations.

This book is written in the form of a text for undergraduates, and drafts were used as an undergraduate text at Princeton, but it is written also for the general reader and for graduate students. Graduate students may use supplementary technical material, some included in the references cited in this book. Serious reading is required for an understanding in depth, but a casual reading will be sufficient to get a general picture of China's economy and the process of its transformation. The level of technical difficulty is low. Algebra and elementary calculus are applied in only a couple of places. Simple mathematics is always accompanied by verbal explanations. The remainder of the book is essentially pure text. However, once again, if the general reader still finds the technical material difficult, it can be skipped and the essential meaning will not be lost.

# Part I

# Historical Background and General Survey

# Economic Lessons from History

One event is selected from each major dynasty in China's history to provide important lessons for understanding the present-day Chinese economy. The period of the Republic of China since 1911 is discussed in more detail to provide a historical-institutional setting for the current economic system.

## 1.1 Introduction

Economic globalization is a main feature of the twenty-first century. In the United States the department stores are full of consumer goods produced in China. These include clothing, sports equipment, toys, household tools, and other consumer goods. In China there are more and more American video tapes, CDs and DVDs, books, drugs, and cosmetic products, not to mention Boeing aircraft. The integration of world markets is a major driving force shaping world events. China is playing an increasingly important role in this process. China is well-known for having the largest population – over 1.3 billion people, or over one-fifth of the world total. Ever since the Chinese government introduced economic reform in 1978 from a planned economy toward a market-oriented economy, the country has experienced rapid institutional changes and achieved an economic growth rate of about 9.5 percent per year. The country today is so different from what it was in 1978 that hardly anyone in or outside China in the late 1970s could have expected such dramatic changes.

It is the purpose of this book to study the dynamic process of China's economic transformation and growth. What historical forces drove China to a planned economy in the first place? How did the planned economy work? What were the reasons and driving forces for economic reform? How did such dramatic changes occur after the economic reform? Why was China successful in transforming a planned economy to a market economy? To what extent is the Chinese economy a market economy? How do different economic institutions in China function today? What economic laws are at work to explain the functioning of various aspects of the Chinese economy? What are the current economic problems? What are the prospects for China's future development?

To understand current and possible future development it is important to understand China's historical background. Current economic policies are not decided in a vacuum but are subject to the influence of the cultural and historical traditions of the Chinese people, including the leaders who make the policies and the common citizens whose support is required. Furthermore, history and economics are highly related subjects. Economists draw lessons from history to propose laws of economic behavior and to understand the development of economic institutions. Economic laws enhance our understanding of historical events and help explain the development of economic institutions. History sets the boundaries of current economic thought.

China has the longest living civilization, with a written language that can be traced back to 3000 BC. Throughout Chinese history, we can find examples of economic laws at work, of how people tried to improve their economic well-being or to maximize their satisfaction or profits. We can also find evidence of the market economy at work and of a deep understanding of it on the part of the ancient Chinese. It is the purpose of this chapter to draw several economic lessons from China's history and from some recent historical events that have affected the development of the Chinese economy. In section 1.2 I will select one important event or example from each major dynasty. In section 1.3 a more detailed account will be given for the period between 1911, when the Republic of China was established, and 1949, when the People's Republic of China was founded, because the history of this period is more relevant to the present-day economy. In chapter 2 a historical and institutional account in even greater detail will be provided for the period after 1949, in order to provide a setting for the discussion of economic reform introduced in 1978.

## 1.2   Significant Events in Major Historical Dynasties

China's history went through different dynasties. The people were ruled by an emperor. In theory the emperor was supposed to have received a mandate from heaven to rule. In practice the rule was established by military conquest, but the ruler was guided by a moral principle to be kind to the people, and could remain in power only if he did not deviate too much from this principle. Each emperor was succeeded by his offspring until some successor failed to perform his job adequately and the throne was seized by someone else in a revolution. Then a new dynasty was established. The historians serving in the court of the ruling dynasty wrote about the virtue of its founder, the successful revolutionary, and the vice of the defeated emperor and the previous dynasty. As a familiar Chinese saying goes, "The winner is the emperor; the loser is the bandit."

### 1.2.1   Shang, 1900 BC

Although recorded Chinese history preceded the Shang period, I will start there. Visitors to a museum containing ancient Chinese art objects will find the beautifully and delicately engraved bronze vessels of this period. They will also find tortoise shells on which there are traces of writing. The shells were used for fortune-telling. After the tortoise shells were burned they cracked and formed lines that were interpreted for guidance on what would happen and when one should or should not do certain things. The writing on them is a precursor of the Chinese written language in the form of characters. (The fact that the characters of written Chinese are based on the shapes of objects rather than on the sounds of the spoken words, as in European written languages, may explain partly why the Chinese have a different way of thinking, that emphasizes the concrete, in contrast to the European and American tendency to dwell on the abstract and metaphysical.) Such objects show that Chinese civilization was already fairly advanced 4,000 years ago. It will be pointed out later in our study of the Chinese economy that human capital is a very important element for economic development. Human capital means the knowledge and skill possessed by people. The skill that was used by the Chinese people 4,000 years ago to make bronze vessels has been transferred with further improvements through the centuries to current Chinese laborers who make toys and computers. The abundance of skilled labor in China today is an important factor contributing to its rapid development. So is entrepreneurship, which can be traced back to the training of the mind in ancient Chinese learning and the practices governing human relations in ancient Chinese culture.

### 1.2.2  Zhou, 1100 BC

Chinese civilization was advanced during the Zhou period. Major Chinese classics were written during this period. These classical works are still read by some people in China today, and by most educated Chinese in the first half of the twentieth century. They include the *Book of Changes* (*Yiching*), the *Book of Poems* and the *Book of Li* (etiquette). The *Book of Changes* is available in many Western bookstores. It was designed for fortune-telling, and has been found intriguing by modern mathematicians. The Duke of Zhou, author of the *Book of Li*, was an inspiration to Confucius. At the end of the Zhou dynasty there was the "Spring and Autumn" period, named after a classic of the same title written by Confucius. It was a golden period in the development of Chinese civilization, with diverse schools of thought flourishing. Daoism, for example, advocates inaction, letting nature take its course, and minimum government intervention. Many important ideas about politics, philosophy, and economics can be found in the writings of that period (see Chan 1963).

Confucius's teaching was only one school of thought at that time, but became dominant in the later part of the Han dynasty. Economists debate today whether the Confucian tradition, which is deeply rooted in Chinese culture, is a positive or a negative factor for the country's economic development, although no one can deny that it is an important factor. On the positive side, Confucius's teachings to uphold a high moral standard and to honor one's commitments are helpful in business transactions. They provide a social order under which a market economy can function. They encourage family ties and trustworthiness among friends, which may form the basis for loyalty in a business enterprise.

Confucius valued learning and the acquisition of knowledge, and this may account for the abundance of human capital in China and its neighboring Confucian countries. On the negative side, his thinking is said to promote too much respect for tradition and thus to be a hindrance to progress. The use of personal honor as a safeguard for business commitments might be a poor alternative to a modern legal system – for ethics is considered more important than law under the Confucian tradition. The negative side of respect for social order and family values is the sacrifice of individual freedom and self-interest. Individualism is taken for granted in many Western societies but is not necessarily considered a virtue in China, where social responsibility for the common good is more highly prized.

## 1.2.3    Qin, 200 BC

When the Zhou dynasty became weak, many regional rulers took control of their territories. The period is known as the period of Warring States, which followed the "Spring and Autumn" period. There were seven states competing for the throne. Among them was Qin, which finally succeeded in unifying China. The successful first Qin emperor standardized written Chinese and the units of measurement for weight and length. He directed the completion of a large part of the Great Wall to prevent invasion from the north. He was a strong ruler, in fact a dictator, who hated dissenting intellectuals. He burned many books and killed dissenting scholars. His tomb in the city of Xian is a great tourist attraction. It is over 1.5 kilometers in diameter. It is too large, complicated, and structurally protected for the current Chinese government, even with modern technology, to excavate, except for a small part near its entrance. The excavated soldiers in the entrance, who are supposed to protect the Qin emperor in his grave, are a magnificent example of the arts of the period.

The story of the Qin emperor is significant because 22 centuries later Chairman Mao Zedong of the Chinese Communist Party followed some of his examples. In a famous poem surveying China's history, Mao referred to the Qin emperor with admiration, but was pleased to hint that he would surpass all ancient heroes. Mao succeeded in unifying China in 1949 – a very difficult and important accomplishment in a tumultuous period that we shall describe later in this chapter. In so doing he provided political stability and national pride for the Chinese people. He was a strong ruler. His government simplified written Chinese (over the objections of many Chinese all over the world) and tried to impose one spoken language all over China. China has essentially one written language but many different spoken dialects that cannot be understood by all. He mistreated and sacrificed numerous intellectuals during the periods of "letting one hundred flowers bloom" in 1957 and the Cultural Revolution of 1966–76, sending them to work in the countryside as laborers. He mobilized the masses to build great projects comparable in scale to the building of the Great Wall, such as the commune system in agriculture created in 1958 under the Great Leap Forward movement. To understand present-day China we have to understand Mao's influence, and Mao himself was influenced by his study of Chinese history, including in particular the history of the Qin emperor.

### 1.2.4   Han, 206 BC to 220 AD

The Qin emperor was a strong ruler but his son, who succeeded him, was not able to rule effectively. The dynasty ended soon after his death. The next dynasty, the Han, lasted until 220 AD, including Western Han and Eastern Han. For this dynasty I select a passage written by the great Chinese historian Sima Qian (family name Sima), who wrote a book of Chinese history, *Records of the Historian*. Young (1996: 138) cites and focuses on the following passage from the chapter entitled "The Biographies of the Money Markets."

> There must be farmers to produce food, men to extract the wealth of mountains and marshes, artisans to produce these things, and merchants to circulate them. There is no need to wait for government orders: each man will play his part, doing his best to get what he desires. So cheap goods will go where they will fetch more, while expensive goods will make men search for cheap ones. When all work willingly at their trade, just as water flows ceaselessly downhill day and night, things will appear unsought and people will produce them without being asked. For clearly this accords with the Way and is in keeping with nature.

This quotation shows that in the Han dynasty at least some part of China had a functioning market economy, with farmers, workers, and merchants engaged in production and trade. The market functioned smoothly without government intervention and according to the law of demand and supply. Each person tried to maximize his self-interest, and the invisible hand was at work to coordinate the economic activities of all. The quotation also suggests that Sima had a deep understanding of the workings of the market economy. What he called "the Way" we now call the law of demand and supply. It might be difficult to find a passage in Adam Smith's *Wealth of Nations* that provides a clearer and simpler description of a market economy.

### 1.2.5   Tang, 618–907 AD

Bypassing the dynasties in between, I come to the Tang dynasty. The Chinese have been referred to as the Han people or the Tang people by outsiders. This shows that both were glorious periods of Chinese history. With regard to the Tang dynasty I choose to discuss foreign trade. Although the Han Chinese had traded with foreigners in the north, it was during the Tang dynasty that the Chinese traded with Europeans through the famous Silk Route, which is still traveled today. There was trade between the Chinese and the Romans via this route. There is a memorial site to attract tourists at Dunhuang in Gansu province, where there are cave paintings commissioned by Buddhists as symbols of religious offering. Europeans long ago already desired silk and china from China, but for a long time had to trade through the middlemen in the Middle East. These middlemen also had spice and other goods that the Chinese wanted. The Silk Route reminds us of the importance of foreign trade in economic relations among nations. It marks the beginning of the economic globalization process, though only to a very limited extent by modern standards.

For a long time the Chinese government was not interested in opening China's door widely because it considered the country self-sufficient. There was little that China desired from the West. Only in recent years has China found itself to be behind in technology and become interested in importing foreign technology and encouraging foreign investment.

## 1.2.6   Song, 960–1126

China's market economy was fairly well developed in the Song dynasty. In many ways the economy resembled a capitalist system. People with money set up businesses for profit and there were plenty of rich people. Various productive and commercial activities flourished. One can see such activities in a famous Song painting, *Qingming Festival on the River*, depicting the economic scene of Kaifeng in Henan Province during the Qingming (Sweeping of the Graves) Festival in the spring. In the painting there are people engaged in different forms of production and trade, as well as leisure activities. The people appear well-to-do. Although one may claim that in many respects China had a capitalist economy, in a modern sense, in the Song period, there was a main ingredient lacking: modern technology based on modern science. An interesting question is why China did not develop modern technology earlier than and independently of the West.

The Chinese knew enough mathematics and had scientific knowledge, including astronomy, that could have served as a basis for the development of technology. They also had some fairly sophisticated technology which enabled them to build the Great Wall and many impressive palaces and temples, and to make the explosives and armaments exhibited, for example, in the Xian museum today. The Chinese invented paper, gunpowder, and the compass. One economic explanation advanced for the failure to develop modern technology in the Song dynasty when the knowledge base appeared sufficient is the lack of economic incentives. China had a large amount of inexpensive labor for production in that period. For a technological innovation used in production to pay off, it must be cheaper to use than labor. In the initial stages of introducing a new technology, the cost is high. The payoff is not sufficient until the product can be mass produced by the new technology for a large market. In an economy with a large amount of inexpensive labor a potential innovator might not envisage a sufficient payoff for his innovation, when the process of invention is costly and its success uncertain. In addition to this lack of economic incentive, intellectuals in traditional Chinese society devoted themselves mainly to the study of Chinese classics in order to pass examinations to become government officials who had a higher social and economic status than the rest of the population, and this was considered more important than what money alone could offer. Performing a scientific and technological investigation was a lonely activity, even if it might yield some intellectual satisfaction or economic return. One or two technological innovations in an unsuitable economic environment could not have produced an industrial revolution. A study of the reasons why capitalism based on advanced technology did not develop during the Song period would also need to examine the risk of investment in technological innovation at a time when the population had to migrate to the south following invasion from the north. And there is the question of the possible sources of financing such investment.

### 1.2.7  Yuan, 1279

The Yuan dynasty was founded by the Mongolians. It was the first dynasty not ruled by a Han emperor. Hubilie, the grandson of Genghis Khan, founded the dynasty. The territory of the Mongolian Empire extended to a large part of Europe. The Mongolian rulers assimilated much of Chinese culture and preserved it while they ruled. Through most of Chinese history, Han rulers were not expansionist. A Chinese emperor would welcome tributes from other areas and recognize them as a part of the Chinese sphere of influence, including Vietnam and Korea in the nineteenth century, but very seldom tried to conquer other territories in order to rule them. In keeping with this Chinese historical tradition, the current Chinese government does not appear to have any expansionist intentions. It does consider Taiwan a part of China because the former was historically a part of China. In addition to historical tradition, there are sufficient internal problems, economic and political, to occupy the current government. It has neither the energy, nor the motive, to expand. But if it had the energy and motive, where would it expand? What would the costs and benefits be? As the world's most populous and third largest country, China will gain economic and political influence in the twenty-first century by the natural course of its rapid economic development. It would be self-defeating to rock the boat by engaging in risky military adventures.

### 1.2.8  Ming, 1415

Imperial rule was returned to the Han Chinese in the Ming dynasty. During this period, China began extensive overseas exploration. Chinese ships traveled to southeast and south Asia, and through the Indian Ocean to the Persian Gulf and the coast of east Africa. Menzies (2003) claims that a Chinese fleet led by Zheng He, a eunuch and confidant of the emperor, reached America 70 years before Columbus and circumnavigated the globe a century before Magellan, although such claims are debated by scholars. A large number of Chinese migrated to Taiwan from Fujian province across the Taiwan Strait. Taiwan became a part of China until 1895, when China was defeated in the Sino-Japanese War and surrendered the island to Japan. In 1945, when Japan was defeated at the end of the Second World War, it returned Taiwan to China. Today, there is the possibility of an explosive disagreement between the government of the People's Republic of China and the government of the Republic of China in Taiwan concerning the political status of Taiwan. The PRC government is not interested in the expansion of Chinese territory, but it considers Taiwan a part of China. The situation could be volatile because the PRC government has not given up the possible use of force to settle this disagreement, in addition to which the majority of the people in Taiwan appear not to favor becoming a part of the PRC. The existing stability of their relationship is due to both governments' recognizing that an armed conflict would do neither side any good.

### *1.2.9   Qing, 1760–1911*

The Manchurians took over China and became rulers of the Qing dynasty. After early periods of prosperity and strength, the dynasty became very weak as the rulers in the 1800s were incompetent. The dynasty still considered itself the center of the world, as some Chinese had, while the Western world had advanced a great deal economically, scientifically, technologically, and militarily. The British Empire was expanding. The British were interested in increasing trade with China, mainly to buy Chinese tea and silk. The Chinese were not much interested in what the British had to offer. But one important item offered by the British was opium. To prevent the import of opium, China engaged in the Opium War of 1840 with the British, and was defeated. In the Treaty of Nanking, signed in 1842 after the war, the Chinese agreed to cede Hong Kong to the British, to open other ports, to let British ships enter Chinese rivers, and to allow the British extra-territorial rights on Chinese territory (including the jurisdiction of British consulates over British citizens in China). Since the Treaty of Nanking, many other unequal treaties have been signed, conceding territory and similar rights to other countries, including Germany, France, and Japan. These treaties created great resentment among the Chinese people against their weak and incompetent rulers and the foreign imperial powers that had succeeded in forcing concessions out of them. Nationalism became a strong force in Chinese society. This sentiment persists today in spite of the great progress China has made. An example of this was the mass uproar over the bombing of the Chinese embassy in Serbia in 1999, which the Chinese viewed as reminiscent of mistreatment suffered after the defeat in the Opium War. This sentiment also explains why there was such a great celebration in China before and on July 1, 1997, when Hong Kong was returned by the British to China, for it symbolized the end of foreign domination and the achievement of Chinese independence.

## 1.3   The Republic of China, 1911–

Because space and its relevance are limited I have omitted much of the interesting and exciting Qing period and mentioned only the weak and incompetent Qing government and the Opium War. Historians would find equally interesting material in other dynasties that is missing in our discussion as well. The main point with regard to the Qing period was that the people were unhappy and eager to modernize China, to make it economically and militarily strong and free from foreign domination. Most leaders agreed that China should learn modern science and technology and should improve its political system. There were disagreements as to how to achieve this goal. Some officials in the Qing government proposed drastic reforms under the leadership of a young emperor in 1898, but their attempts at reform were defeated by the Empress Dowager. Others advocated revolution to overthrow the Qing government. For an excellent source on Chinese history from 1869 to 1933, the reader should refer to *The Annals of Mr. Liang Yansun of*

*Sanshui*, volumes 1 and 2 (in Chinese; Hong Kong, private publication, 1939). Parts of its contents are available in English in Au (1999). http://loki.stockton.edu/~gilmorew/consorti/1beasia.htm is a website containing brief descriptions of all the historical dynasties of China as well as details on the Republic of China and the People's Republic of China.

In 1911, the revolutionaries succeeded in overthrowing the Qing dynasty. The Republic of China was established, with Sun Yat-sen serving as its first temporary President. Sun did not have sufficient military power and had to turn over the presidency after only four months to Yuan Shih-kai, a former Qing official who did have military power. Three years later Yuan tried to make himself emperor but failed. The presidency of China changed hands several times between 1916 and 1927, while new premiers and their cabinet members were appointed over a dozen times under an unstable parliamentary system. While political instability was occurring in the government in Beijing there was a separate government in the South. Sun Yat-sen did not support the government in Beijing and tried to be the leader of the government in the South, but managed it only intermittently. The Northern and Southern governments had to share control with different factions, including strong governors of important provinces and warlords who controlled different territories. There were several serious attempts to negotiate a settlement between the Northern and the Southern governments and unify China, but all efforts failed.

In the early 1920s Sun Yat-sen led the Kuomintang (or the Nationalist Party) and solicited the support of members of the Chinese Communist Party to unify China. The well-known Huangpo Military Academy was established with Chiang Kai-shek as its President and Zhou Enlai of the Communist Party serving as director of the political department. In 1925 Sun died. Soon afterwards, Chiang led a northern military expedition, eventually reaching Beijing in 1928. China was nominally unified under Chiang, but his control of China was weak and Japan soon took over Manchuria, the northeastern provinces of China. During the northern expedition Chiang fell out with the Communists and had many of them killed in Shanghai. He accepted the surrender of a number of warlords in exchange for their retaining political and military power in their territories as officials under his government. Chiang's remaining task was to extinguish the Communists. He pursued them through several thousand miles in 1933 until they finally escaped to and settled in the city of Yanan. The escape is known as the Long March. Only 2,000 of the originally over 10,000 Communists survived.

In 1930, Japan began to invade China, starting by taking over Manchuria and establishing Manchukuo under its control. Many Chinese people wanted to fight the Japanese, but Chiang thought that the Communists were the worse enemy. He wanted to annihilate the Communists first before fighting the Japanese. In 1934, one of his generals captured him while he was in Xian and forced him to make peace with the Communists and fight the Japanese together. The Sino-Japanese War officially began in 1937. The Japanese rapidly took over much of the coastal area of China, while the Chiang government was moved to the wartime capital of Chungking, now called Chongqing. The Second World War started in Asia as Japan attacked Pearl Harbor in December 1941, only to be defeated in August 1945. Chiang was the war hero and the Chinese people rejoiced in the victory.

In the first half of the twentieth century, while China was going through revolutions, political instability, and wars, the economy continued to function and develop. It was essentially a market economy as it had been since at least the Han dynasty. Most of the national output consisted of agricultural products produced by family farms, and the majority of the population were peasants. An excellent study of the Chinese farm economy by professor at the University of Nanking, John L. Buck (1930), is based on surveying 2,866 farms in 17 localities of China in the 1920s, including a total farm area of 21,000 acres and a rural population of approximately 17,000 persons. It provides information on the economics of the farm business, including capital investment, receipts, expenses and profits, farm ownership and tenancy, labor cost and efficiency, demographic characteristics of farm families, food consumption and the standard of living. According to Buck, writing in 1930:

> farm land is generally worked by owners, although approximately one-fifth is farmed by tenants and another one-fifth by part owners . . . The production from the farm business in China and in the United States is remarkably equal in quantity per unit of land . . . In the United States the chief means has been the use of capital as well as labor; in China it has been the use of labor, for the most part human labor, and with very little capital . . . The Chinese farmer has by the trial and error method arrived at many sound and practicable conclusions for his situation. His crops are often suited to the soil, and his cropping systems follow the general principle of rotation remarkably well . . . The small size of business and the crowded population led necessarily to a standard of living that is low when compared to the standard of the western farmer . . . Diet, while remarkable in containing many of the elements needed for health and strength, lacks variety mainly in fruits and vegetables, particularly in North China. The direct utilization of grains and to a certain extent of soybeans, however, is probably a more economical procedure than the western way of using so much food largely through animals. (1930: 423–5)

Along with agriculture, handicraft industry and trade were parts of the traditional Chinese market economy. After the Western impact, modern industries and financial institutions began to emerge. Factories producing consumer goods such as textiles, wool and leather products, toys, tobacco and paper products were operating by 1920 if not before, especially in Shanghai, Tianjin, and other coastal cities. The governments in power did succeed in building infrastructure to some extent, including railroads, highways, and seaports. Telephone lines and a telegraph network were built. Electric power supplies became available in major cities. In addition to the old-fashioned banks, new commercial banks were established and functioned as modern banks in taking deposits and extending loans for business working capital and investment. By 1920, the Bank of China and the Bank of Communications were the two largest banks which issued currency, while numerous commercial banks existed in various cities. There was a stock market in Shanghai trading actively in the 1930s. Private life insurance companies were operating. The education system improved, through government effort and private initiative, with help from foreign friends, including missionaries. Private universities coexisted with state universities sponsored by the central government and provincial governments.

A bird's-eye view of the Chinese economy can be found in the estimates of gross domestic product in 1933 and 1952 by industrial origin in table 1.1.

**Table 1.1** Chinese domestic product by origin, in constant 1933 and 1952 prices

| Sector | Net value added in: | | | |
|---|---|---|---|---|
| | (1933 yuan billions) | | (1952 yuan billions) | |
| | 1933 | 1952 | 1933 | 1952 |
| 1. Agriculture | 18.76 | 18.39 | 33.86 | 34.19 |
| 2. Factories | 0.64 | 1.09 | 3.33 | 6.45 |
|    a. Producers goods | 0.16 | 0.46 | 0.84 | 3.15 |
|    b. Consumers goods | 0.47 | 0.63 | 2.48 | 3.30 |
| 3. Handicrafts | 2.04 | 2.14 | 4.41 | 4.72 |
|    a. Identified portion | 1.24 | 0.66 | 2.67 | 1.45 |
|    b. Others | 0.80 | 1.48 | 1.74 | 3.26 |
| 4. Mining | 0.21 | 0.63 | 0.50 | 1.47 |
| 5. Utilities | 0.13 | 0.31 | 0.14 | 0.31 |
| 6. Construction | 0.34 | 0.60 | 1.03 | 1.83 |
| 7. Modern transportation and communications | 0.43 | 0.83 | 1.09 | 2.10 |
| 8. Old-fashioned transportation | 1.20 | 1.20 | 2.61 | 2.65 |
| 9. Trade | 2.71 | 2.88 | 8.19 | 9.66 |
|    a. Trading stores and restaurants | 1.75 | 1.97 | 6.12 | 7.66 |
|    b. Peddlers | 0.96 | 0.91 | 2.07 | 2.00 |
| 10. Government administration | 0.82 | 1.84 | 1.43 | 3.27 |
| 11. Finance | 0.21 | 0.80 | 0.35 | 1.31 |
| 12. Personal services | 0.34 | 0.34 | 0.55 | 0.55 |
| 13. Residential rents | 1.03 | 1.17 | 2.00 | 2.28 |
| 14. Work brigades | | 0.28 | | 0.62 |
| Net domestic product | 28.86 | 32.50 | 59.49 | 71.41 |
| Depreciation | 1.02 | 1.33 | 2.19 | 3.26 |
| Gross domestic product | 29.88 | 33.83 | 61.68 | 74.67 |

**Source**: *T. C. Liu and K. C. Yeh*, The Economy of the Chinese Mainland, *vol. 1. Santa Monica, CA: Rand Corporation, 1963, table 8.*

What lessons can be learned from briefly reviewing the history of the first three decades of the Republic of China? First, in spite of political instability, economic activities carried on and economic development took place between 1911 and 1937. Modern economic institutions evolved naturally in a market economy. The resourcefulness of the Chinese people and their desire and energy to make a better living were sufficient to improve the economy once they were given some freedom and the opportunity to do so. In short, modernization was taking place. China had a market economy which functioned well, although it was still a poor country except for some coastal cities. Economic progress would have been more rapid if there had been internal political stability and no war with Japan. Some observers have remarked that Japan attacked China in 1937 because it was witnessing the progress made in the latter and could not wait any longer. This explains why China was capable of returning to a market economy after economic reform started in 1978, and why, once the Chinese people were given some economic freedom, economic development has been so rapid since 1978. In some respects, including the institutional structure and functioning of the commercial banks and of many industrial enterprises, the current state has not yet reached the high point achieved in the 1930s because it is difficult to abolish the economic institutions and change bureaucratic behavior established under central planning.

A second lesson to learn from studying the events of the first half of the twentieth century in China is the difficulty of establishing democratic institutions there. Sun Yat-sen hoped to establish the Republic of China based on the "three principles of the people," including nationalism, democracy, and the people's welfare. He was inspired by the three "peoples" – of the people, for the people, and by the people – in Lincoln's Gettysburg Address. The Republic of China in those years had a parliamentary system with upper and lower houses, although the representatives were selected by provincial and local governments and not publicly elected. Even such a parliamentary system was not functioning when the presidency changed hands frequently depending on the results of power struggles among political and military leaders. Different parts of China were controlled by different leaders and they did not agree on the person to serve as the president.

Before 1911, China had been ruled by an emperor. The people by tradition respected his authority. They had no idea how to select a leader for the country. Neither had they the desire to do so. If events turned out to be unfavorable, the majority would resign themselves to the situation and merely pray for things to get better. On rare occasions, a small group would rise up to take control and establish a new dynasty. It was under such a tradition that Sun and others wished to establish a democratic republic. Their lack of experience in exercising the responsibilities of a democracy should not be construed to mean that the Chinese people did not treasure freedom, including freedom to choose their work, their residence, their family size, to associate, to express themselves. In fact they largely had such freedoms throughout Chinese history, but having freedoms and having a democratic government are not the same thing. The Chinese were not familiar with modern democratic institutions. Looking back, historians can question whether attempting to establish a democratic republic was the best course for China in 1911. Other alternatives included promoting reform in the Qing dynasty and establishing a new dynasty with a Han emperor and a parliamentary system. Today, China's political structure is expected to change, to keep up with its economic structure. Historical tradition will play an important role in shaping the form that the future government will take.

Third, by examining Chinese history before 1949, we realize how difficult it was for Mao Zedong to unify the country and why he received so much credit in China for having done so. Unification was important for establishing social order and to enable the government to direct the modernization of China – serious mistakes in government policies before 1978 notwithstanding. Unification makes China strong among nations and restores the pride of the Chinese people. Nationalism is a very important force in guiding China's policies for political and economic development at present, and it will remain so in the future.

Soon after the end of the Second World War in 1945, the Chiang Kai-shek government became unpopular. Government officials who were with Chiang in the wartime capital of Chungking (Chongqing) came back to the coastal area to take over the government of these territories. Having suffered through the war, many abused their power and extracted money from the people in the process of regaining control from the Japanese. Chiang failed to discipline them. Civil war with the Communists started and the government financed the war essentially by printing more money, as it did not yet have a sound tax base. That led to inflation, and inflation was unpopular. As the civil war intensified, the government printed even more money. The inflation rate increased accordingly. Hyperinflation occurred in 1948–9. The government introduced a policy to force people to surrender their gold, foreign currency, and precious metal holdings in exchange for paper money that soon became almost worthless. This policy created more resentment. People failing to obey were caught and executed in public in Shanghai. Government popularity hit an all-time low in early 1949. The Chiang government finally fell and moved to Taiwan, and the People's Republic of China was established on October 1st, 1949. Mao declared in Tiananmen Square that the Chinese people had finally risen! In view of the confusion, chaos, and humiliation suffered by the Chinese people since the Opium War of 1840, the majority truly rejoiced with Mao as he declared the establishment of the People's Republic of China. However, many were skeptical of the ideology and tactics of the new government.

## 1.4   Summary of Historical Lessons

In this brief review of very selective historical events I hope to draw the following lessons relevant for understanding the present-day Chinese economy.

First, human capital embedded in the people through cultural tradition is an important factor for the functioning of the economy and for economic development. The Chinese cultural tradition dates back at least to the Shang dynasty some 4,000 years ago. There is evidence of skilled labor in the many Shang dynasty art objects displayed in museums.

Second, the particular characteristics of a culture affect economic behavior, as exemplified by the tradition of Confucianism which originated in the late Zhou period about 2,500 years ago. The ethics of hard work, respect for scholarship, honesty and trustworthiness in human relationships, emphasis on family and social order, and the high value attached to the common good as compared with individual rights, all have effects on the economic behavior of individuals and institutions.

Third, the character and behavior of one political leader can have a great influence on the economic life of the Chinese people, as demonstrated by the great influence of the Emperor of Qin in 200 BC. Recent examples are Mao Zedong and Deng Xiaoping, to whom we shall return later in this book.

Fourth, China has long had a market economy, the operation of which was well understood and well articulated by the great historian Sima Qian in the Han dynasty some 2,000 years ago.

Fifth, foreign trade is an important component of economic activity and was practiced by the Chinese years ago. It flourished in the Tang dynasty, as evidenced by the Silk Route. Its importance to China today will be discussed in chapter 17 below.

Sixth, China had a fairly mature form of capitalism in the Song dynasty some thousand years ago, but did not have advanced technology. Economists can speculate on the reasons for China's not developing economically useful technology when knowledge of mathematics and science was available. The importance of technology for economic development should be emphasized.

Seventh, the Yuan dynasty was ruled by Mongolians and had more territory than any other Chinese dynasty. Whether China has a desire to expand its territory today is an interesting question. In answering this question, an economist will consider not only China's past behavior but also the costs and benefits of expansionism.

Eighth, exploration across the seas was a stimulus for economic development not only in European history but also in the Ming period in China. The migration of Chinese to Taiwan was a result. This is one origin of the PRC government's claim that Taiwan was a part of China, and of its disagreement with the government of the Republic of China in Taiwan on the sovereignty issue. However, economic cooperation has taken place between the two sides of the Taiwan Strait, and investment from Taiwan to the mainland has contributed to the latter's development.

Ninth, the weakness of the Qing dynasty at the crucial time of the expansion of world imperial capitalism explains much of the economic history of China in the last century and a half. Through one military defeat and unequal treaty after another since the Opium War in 1840, the Chinese developed mixed feelings of envy (for the military might) and hostility (because of the aggression) toward foreign imperial powers. This sentiment is still an important factor affecting China's diplomatic and thus political and economic relations with the outside world.

Tenth, the early history of the Republic of China established in 1911 demonstrates at least three points. First, the resourcefulness and energy of the Chinese people were sufficient to develop and maintain the functioning of a market economy even when there was much internal political instability. Second, to establish a democratic republic in China is a difficult task given the cultural tradition of the Chinese people. Like all people, the Chinese treasure freedom, but the majority have not learned how to assume the responsibility of citizenship under a democratic government. Third, national unity was a very important goal and nationalism is an important force behind China's economic and political policies.

# References and Further Reading

*Annals of Mr. Liang Yansun of Sanshui*, vols. 1 and 2 (in Chinese). Hong Kong, private publication, 1939. Reissued as a monograph in the "Modern Chinese Historical Series." Taipei: Wenxing Book Co., 1962.

Au, Steven T. *Beijing Odyssey: A Novel Based on the Life and Times of Liang Shiyi*. Mahomet, IL: Mayhaven Publishing, 1999.

Buck, John L. *Chinese Farm Economy: A Study of 2866 Farms in Seventeen Localities and Seven Provinces in China*. Chicago: University of Chicago Press, 1930.

Chan, Wingsit. *Source Book in Chinese Philosophy*. Princeton: Princeton University Press, 1963.

*China Human Development Report 1999: Transition and the State*, ch. 2, sec. 1. Published for the United Nations Development Program by Oxford University Press, Hong Kong, 2000.

http://loki.stockton.edu/~gilmorew/consorti/1beasia.htm [For information on the dynasties in Chinese history.]

Liu, T. C. and K. C. Yeh. *The Economy of the Chinese Mainland: National Income and Economic Development, 1933–1959*. Santa Monica, CA: The Rand Corporation, 1963.

Menzies, Gavin. *1421: The Year the Chinese Discovered the World*. London: Bantam, 2003.

Smith, Bradley and Wan-go Weng. *China: A History in Art*. New York: Harper & Row, 1973.

Young, Leslie. "The Tao of Markets: Sima Qian and the Invisible Hand." *Pacific Economic Review*, 1 (Sept. 1996), pp. 137–45.

# Questions

1   It is said that human capital is more important than physical capital for economic development. Give a meaningful interpretation of this statement. Provide an illustration with reference to a particular economy.

2   Is Confucianism a positive or negative factor in China's economic development? Explain your answer.

3   It is sometimes said that China is ruled by men and not by law. Give examples of two Chinese rulers to illustrate this statement.

4   Using the language of modern economics, rewrite the paragraph from Sima quoted in section 1.2.4.

5   What was the volume of foreign trade as a percentage of China's gross domestic product in 1978? In the most recent year? The answer can be found in the *China Statistical Yearbook*.

6   China is said to have had a capitalist economy in the Song dynasty. How would you define a capitalist economy? What historical evidence should be found in order to support or refute this statement?

7   What is the level of military expenditure in China as a fraction of GDP? What is the level in the United States? How would an economist determine what the right amount is?

8   What were the economic gains from the overseas exploration occurring in the Ming dynasty?

9   In the later parts of the Qing dynasty China was in need of political changes for the purposes of modernization. Name three alternative courses that China could have taken. Which one was taken? Which one would you prefer, and why?

10   Why was it difficult for China to adopt a democratic form of government in the first half of the twentieth century? Are the difficulties today more or less serious, and why?

11   Describe the Chinese economy in the 1930s briefly, in terms of its various productive sectors and their relative importance. What modern economic institutions existed?

12   What lessons can one learn from studying the history of China from 1911 to 1949 for the purposes of understanding the current economy?

# 2

# Experiments with Planning and Economic Disruptions

The history and economic institutions from the establishment of the People's Republic of China in 1949 to the beginning of economic reform in 1978 are reviewed. The theory and practice of economic planning during this period are studied to provide an understanding of the shortcomings of a planned economy and the need to reform.

## 2.1   The Communist Party Rises to Power

The main purpose of this chapter is to describe how the Chinese economy functioned in the period 1949–78. To do so we need to provide both a historical-institutional account and a theoretical analysis of economic planning as practiced in China during this period. The first two sections of this chapter are historical and institutional. Sections 2.3 to 2.5 are concerned with the theory and practice of economic planning, dealing respectively with a simplified model of a planned economy, the behavior of individual economic units, and the behavior of the planning authority. Section 2.6 describes the government organizations concerned with economic planning.

Before describing the economic institutions and the major economic events from 1949 to 1978, it is useful to review briefly how the Chinese Communist Party came to power. The party was founded in Shanghai in 1921 at a time when China was fractionalized and lacking strong political leadership. There was a political vacuum to fill, and China faced the urgent tasks of improving its political status as a nation and developing its economy. The Soviet Union had just been established under Communism after a successful revolution, and this new country promised to make the former Russia strong and avoid some of the pitfalls of capitalism. Although Communist ideology might sound unreasonable to most people today, it had appeal at that time to some Chinese who wanted to build a better country. In fact, in a prosperous and politically stable country like the United States, many intellectuals joined the Communist Party in the 1930s after the experience of the Great Depression. China was poorer in 1921, did not have a stable government, and had not had a successful experience with modern capitalism. Some people in China associated capitalism with imperialism. They disliked imperialism as it was practiced by the capitalist countries. It did not occur to them that all powerful countries could practice imperialism, whatever form their economic system happens to be. If capitalism and imperialism were evil, a possibly better system could be Communism. Ideologically Communism is the antithesis of capitalism and imperialism.

As we pointed out in section 1.3, Sun Yat-sen cooperated with the Communist Party in the early 1920s in order to unify China under his leadership. Other political and military leaders also wanted to unify China under their leadership. Sun was not in a stronger position than at least three others who occupied the northeast, the north (including Beijing), and central China, while Sun was barely able to lead the south after some military struggles. To succeed, Sun needed the support of the Soviet Union, as no Western nation was willing to support his Nationalist Party or Kuomintang. After Sun's death in 1925, Chiang Kai-shek split with the Communist Party in the course of his northern expedition to unify China. The Communist Party tried to establish influence and control in certain rural areas by working with and helping the farmers. After the Long March of 1933, and being chased by Chiang, the Communists finally settled in Yanan during the Second World War. Their rule was popular among many farmers, although not necessarily among some of the intellectuals who moved to Yanan. Their popularity was witnessed by the American writer Edgar Snow, who was allowed to live there. Snow wrote the well-known book, *Red Star over China*, which depicted the rule of that area as much superior to the Nationalist rule over other areas of China unoccupied by the Japanese. Because of Snow's book, the American media sometimes called the Communists agrarian reformers. Snow's book is probably accurate, and Communist rule in Yanan was by and large popular. This was a factor contributing to the popularity of the Communist Party during the civil war after 1949. The failure of Chiang to control his corrupt officials when they took over the coastal areas from Japanese occupation after the Second World War, and the failure of the economic policies of his government, contributed as much, if not more, to the success of the Communist Party.

The Communist Party excelled in organizational skill and ability to gain support from the masses, even by deception if necessary. Some of this skill was acquired from the Soviet Union. It has been observed that a Communist would try to achieve his goals without regard to means; for a Communist, ends justify the means. During periods of political struggle many Chinese political leaders including Chiang were willing to gain power by harsh means also. For example, to gain support of the Chinese capitalists, the Communist Party deceived them by promising that they could continue the operation of their capitalist enterprises under Communist rule.

## 2.2   Historical Review: 1949–78

### 2.2.1   1949–52: peaceful transition

During the initial three years of the People's Republic of China, the government was quite popular. Many well-to-do people left China before 1949 anticipating the troubles under Communist rule. The majority of those who remained had hopes of better things to come. First a major land reform was introduced, when the government forced the landlords to surrender land to the tenant farmers. This made the farmers happy but the landlords unhappy. To accomplish the desired land redistribution the landlords as a class were brutally extinguished. Mass meetings in the countryside were called and landlords were singled out for criticism. Before each meeting, certain farmers were assigned to tell stories of how the designated landlords had misbehaved and collected unreasonable rents. At the meeting the landlords were denounced and asked to confess their crimes, resulting in their execution. As a result of such meetings many landlords were killed.

In this period, industrialists were allowed to continue the operation of their enterprises. State enterprises belonging to the government of the Republic of China were taken over by the new government. Life in the urban areas remained much as before. Existing educational institutions were allowed to function as before. People had much the same freedom of expression, as long as they did not criticize the Communist Party or the government; they also had freedom to choose their jobs and freedom to travel. The border between Hong Kong and mainland China was open. However, many residents sensed that changes towards a totalitarian regime were soon to come.

### 2.2.2   1953–7: the first Five Year Plan

Things began to change later in 1952. Educational institutions were reorganized. All private universities ceased operation and were incorporated into state universities modeled after the Soviet educational system. The border to Hong Kong was closed. The capitalists were asked to surrender their enterprises step by step, until they became only managers of the enterprise and had to follow government instructions if they were to remain a part of it. The farmers were organized into cooperatives under the pretense that this would improve production and marketing, but they were soon forced to surrender their produce to government procurement agencies. Trade in farm products by private traders soon ceased, and the government became the sole distributor. Many of these changes were made in order that the government could initiate its first Five Year Plan of 1953–7. In addition, political campaigns were initiated during this period to control intellectuals who might be critical of the government. During the campaign "Letting One Hundred Flowers Bloom" of 1957, Mao encouraged intellectuals to criticize the government and speak their minds. Some fell into this trap and were severely punished when they did speak out.

### 2.2.3    1958–61: the Great Leap Forward movement

In 1958 Mao launched the Great Leap Forward movement with the purpose of increasing China's output dramatically and developing its economy rapidly. Mao did not understand economics and was extremely skillful in mobilizing the masses. He thought economic objectives could be achieved in the same way as political objectives and revolutions, simply by rallying mass support. In 1958, he organized the farmers into "communes"; in the previous few years they had been organized successively from family farms, to cooperatives, and more advanced forms of cooperatives. Within less than a year during 1958, almost all farms in China were converted to communes where people worked as a team and ate together in mess halls. Mao also assigned unreasonable output targets for the communes. Industrial output was also to be rapidly increased. People were asked to build furnaces in their backyards to produce iron. To satisfy output targets, finished products were put into the furnace to produce iron and steel. The end result was an economic disaster. Food production was greatly reduced, because of a lack of incentive for farmers working in the communes; because of Mao's misguided policies of growing grain in inappropriate places and of killing birds (causing insects to flourish); and because of bad weather. From 1958 to 1962 it was estimated that over 25 million people died of famine, the most severe in Chinese history.

Besides the reduction of agricultural output, two other causes contributed to the great famine. First, there was a lot of waste in the consumption of food when the farmers and their families ate in the mass dining halls of the communes, as compared with eating at home (see Chang and Wen 1998). In mid-1961, when mass dining was abolished, food shortage became much less serious. Secondly, being eager to achieve the unreasonable output targets set by Party officials following Chairman Mao's slogans, commune officials claimed success in producing a larger amount of output than was actually produced. When the time came for them to deliver the output to procurement agencies, they had to surrender large amounts, at the expense of consumption by members of their own communes, to make the claim of large output credible.

### 2.2.4    1962–5: adjustment after the Great Leap

This was a period of readjustment after the Great Leap. The economy returned to normal. Mao lost political power because of the failure of the Great Leap which he had initiated, although he was still nominally the Chairman of the Communist Party. A more moderate government led by President Liu Shaoqi allowed the farmers to farm on private plots of land, while the commune system still existed nominally. Letting farm families have their own land to farm was a policy later adopted when economic reform took place in 1978. Unreasonable output targets were abolished. In December 1964 Premier Zhou Enlai announced the government's objective to achieve "four modernizations" of China. The four areas were industry, agriculture, defense, and science and technology. The policy was not carried out until after economic reform because of the interruptions of the Cultural Revolution.

## 2.2.5   1966–76: the Cultural Revolution

Mainly to regain his political power Mao initiated the Cultural Revolution in 1966. Mao was a perpetual revolutionary. It was not enough to overthrow the Republic of China on the mainland. He now wanted to overthrow the bureaucracy of the party and government that he had built himself. To do so he appealed directly to Chinese youth, who were organized into the Red Guard. The Chinese government administration and economic system were under attack by millions of Red Guards on the pretext of a cultural revolution. Political power was transferred from the pragmatic economic planners to the radical elements of the Communist Party in the name of destroying an old cultural tradition that was said to hinder social revolution. To be a revolutionary was, and still is, considered good, and a counter-revolutionary considered evil in China. (An outside observer might not understand why in the year 2002, when the country is ruled by the Communist Party, a revolutionary who is supposed to advocate overthrowing the existing regime is considered good and a counter-revolutionary who objects to a revolution or supports the status quo is considered to be bad.) Many elderly people and intellectuals were physically harmed by Red Guards, who invaded private homes and destroyed art treasures and books. Fighting also took place among different factions of the Red Guard, all claiming to be the true followers of Mao. A *Red Book* of quotations from Mao was brandished and treated as a gospel for study and memorization. The education system ceased to function and universities were closed. The ensuing political turmoil, including worker demands for higher wages, led to a resolution to freeze all prices at the end of 1966. The movement lasted for a decade and prevented the proper functioning of the Chinese economy. The economic losses of the Great Leap and the Cultural Revolution were estimated in two papers by Chow and Kwan in the *Journal of Comparative Economics* and *Pacific Economic Review*, 1996; the first of which is discussed in chapter 8.

## 2.2.6   1976–8: Deng Xiaoping assumes leadership

After Chairman Mao died in September 1976, political power was soon transferred from the radical and irrational elements of the Communist Party to more pragmatic planners who wanted to carry out China's fourfold modernization. The Gang of Four who helped engineer the Cultural Revolution were stripped of political power. A political and economic system somewhat resembling the one existing in the early 1960s was restored. Deng Xiaoping became the leader in 1978 because he had the support of the top leadership in the Central Committee of the Communist Party. He took over power from Hua Guofeng, the Chairman designated by Mao to succeed him. As of 2001, Hua remained a member of the Central Committee of the Communist Party. This is one example which illustrates that political succession under Chinese Communist Party rule was peaceful and orderly. Another is the succession after Deng died in 1996. Jiang Zemin succeeded him as the leader smoothly and peacefully. The period of 1976–8 witnessed the re-establishment of political and economic order after the Cultural Revolution. In 1979 the People's Republic of China established formal diplomatic relations with the United States. By that time

China had made a major resolution to initiate economic reform. Before we discuss reform we need to understand how the Chinese planning system worked.

## 2.3   A Model of the Chinese Planned Economy

Any economy, be it a planned economy or a market economy, needs to solve a set of basic economic problems. These problems are production, distribution, and investment or accumulation of capital. What goods should be produced and how to produce them? How are the produced goods to be distributed to the consumers or other producers? How much should be invested to build up the capital stock in order to increase future production?

In a market economy, producers choose what to produce in order to satisfy the needs of the consumers. Consumers express their desire by buying what they want in the market at the lowest price. Under market competition the producers have to produce what the consumers want at the lowest prices. The forces of demand and supply determine what to produce and how much to produce, as well as the market price of each product. Through competition such forces also provide incentives for the producers to innovate in the production of new and better products and in the method of production. Similarly, in the market for factors of production that include labor and services from capital goods, demand and supply determine how much labor to employ and the wage rate of the worker, as well as the amount of capital to employ and the rent of capital goods. Thus the distribution of income generated by production to workers and owners of capital is also determined by demand and supply. Firms determine how much to invest to increase future productive capacity. Consumers decide how much to save from their income. Savings are channeled through banks and other financial institutions to investments. All this is done by an invisible hand. The main task of the government is to provide law and order, and the rules of the game for the market participants. (See chapter 20 below for the role of government.)

By contrast, in a planned economy there is a central planning authority which decides what to produce and how to distribute the goods produced, for both consumer goods and factors of production. It also decides how much to invest and the allocation of investment funds to the producers. All the decisions concerning production, distribution and capital accumulation are centralized and under the control of the planning authority. In a market economy these decisions are decentralized and made freely by the producers and consumers themselves. Hence economic freedom is a main feature of a market economy and is lacking to a large extent in a planned economy. (A planned economy is sometimes called a command economy. I use the former term because it is used by the Chinese government.)

To describe the Chinese planned economy from 1953 to 1978, let us first note that economic planning did not cover the entire Chinese economy because the planning authority could not control all the economic activities of such a large country. Furthermore, planning was interrupted by the political turmoil of the Great Leap Forward movement and the Cultural Revolution. The Chinese planning authority is the Economic Planning

Commission in the State Council. In principle it has control over all physical productive resources, covering land, buildings, machinery, and other capital goods. Directly or indirectly, it controls all enterprises, farms, and factories. It can assign a production target to each farm and each factory to tell it how much of each good to produce. It controls all sources of supply of inputs. In assigning an output quota to a farm or a factory, it also supplies the inputs required for production, such as fertilizer and tractors for farming and materials for industrial production. In addition, it assigns workers to different factories. It can direct a person from a city to work in a particular farm. It can direct a farmer to work on a different farm or to work in the city (although the latter seldom happened in China). Thus, the production of final outputs and the allocation of inputs for production are controlled by the planning authority.

As far as the consumption of final products is concerned, the supplies of all consumer goods are under the control of the planning authority. There are two kinds of consumer goods – rationed and nonrationed. In China, the former included food grains, vegetable oil, meat, sugar, and cotton cloth. These goods are distributed to consumers through a rationing system. Every month each consumer is given a fixed number of ration coupons, which have to be used, in addition to money, to pay for the rationed goods. The nonrationed goods are also sold through stores operated by the authority, but the consumer can decide what and how much to buy, and can pay for these goods by money only.

The income of a factory worker depends on the wage rate that the authority determines. Workers have job security in the sense that they cannot be dismissed; rarely is a worker reassigned to another job. A farmer gets a fraction of the income of the farm on which he or she works. Each farmer accumulates work points throughout the year; at the end of the year the work points of all farm members are added together, and the fraction attributed to each person is calculated. The fraction determines what share of the farm income he or she gets. The total income of the farm is the difference between its revenue and its costs. The revenue is the money value of the products of the farm.

Designated amounts of farm products produced in a commune must be sold to a procurement agency authorized by the planning authority, and the remaining products are left in the commune for distribution to its members. The planning authority decides on the amount and price of each product it will purchase from each farm. By changing the purchase prices and purchase quotas of farm products, the authority controls the incomes of the farmers.

One can compare the functioning of a centrally planned economy with that of a market economy by noting that in each economy there are consumers and producers (including farms and factories). There is a flow of goods or services from one economic unit to another. Consumer goods flow from producers to consumers. Labor services flow from consumers to producers. Material inputs and capital goods flow from producers to producers. The main difference is that in a market economy the flows are determined by the economic units themselves through the market, and in a planned economy the flows are determined centrally by the planning authority. There is a bureau of material supply in the State Council of China which controls the distribution of material from producers to producers. The planning authority orders the producers to produce certain consumer goods and distribute them to the consumers. It assigns laborers to work in various production units. It orders producers to produce material inputs and distribute them to other producers. It also directs the production of capital goods and the construction of investment projects.

When goods and services flow in one direction, money payments for these goods flow in the opposite direction. Consumers pay for the goods they buy. Producers also pay for the inputs and capital goods that they use. In a market economy the buyers and sellers can settle the exchanges directly in a market or through intermediaries who perform the services of commerce and trade. The prices are determined by the forces of demand and supply. In a centrally planned economy the users and the producers have to go through the planning authority or distributors who work under its direction. All prices (including wages for labor services) are determined by the planning authority – in China, through the State Price Commission of the State Council.

In any economy, goods have to be produced for consumption and for capital accumulation. Consumer goods are produced mainly for present consumption, and capital goods are produced in order to expand the future productive capacity of the economy. In a centrally planned economy the planning authority has the responsibility to decide the total amount of each consumer good and capital good to be produced, the specific quantities of each good to be produced by the enterprises under its control, the supplies of each important input to be allotted to these enterprises, and the amounts of capital investment to be allotted to the enterprises. It then decides how the consumer goods are to be distributed to consumers. Work gets done by central command as in an army. The commander of an army directs all the activities of the soldiers and determines their food rations. Great projects were completed by central command all through history, including the Great Wall of China and the pyramids of Egypt. However, only in a planned economy in the twentieth century did a central government authority attempt to direct all the complicated tasks connected with the production of thousands of goods by thousands of enterprises and their distribution to millions of people. In the remainder of this section we examine three difficult tasks of a central planning authority in directing the economic activities of a country.

In a centrally planned economy, the production and distribution decisions are made by the planning authority. In a market economy these decisions are made by millions of individual consumers who try to buy from the cheapest source and thousands of producers who try to sell to maximize gains. No central direction is required, as pointed out by the Chinese historian Sima Qian, whom we quoted in section 1.2.4. Given his or her income and the prices of different products, each consumer decides what to buy from the market. When the price of a commodity goes up, the consumer will consume less of it. Given its production technology and the prices of outputs and inputs, each enterprise decides how much output to produce and how much of each input to use in production. Prices will adjust so that the quantities produced will equal the quantities demanded by the users. Each enterprise only needs to know its own economic conditions, including its technology, the productivity of its workers, the capacity of its capital equipment, the kinds of inputs required, and the demand schedules for its products. It can then determine the kinds and quantities of its outputs to produce and of the inputs to use optimally.

To make such decisions for thousands of state enterprises under central planning, a central authority has three difficult tasks to perform. The first is to obtain a mass of information on the production conditions of all the enterprises under its control and the demand conditions of millions of consumers. Without such a vast amount of information it cannot efficiently choose the thousands of products to produce, assign production quotas to thousands of enterprises, and supply them with appropriate quantities of inputs. In a market economy no single authority needs to have all this information. Each enterprise makes its own output and input decisions knowing only the production and demand conditions facing the enterprise itself. Economic information is decentralized among thousands of enterprises. In a planned economy, the vast amount of economic information has to be centralized in the planning authority, and it is impossible to obtain in practice. Part of the required information is obtained, somewhat inaccurately, by the method of material balancing to be described in section 2.5.

The second difficult task facing the planning authority – even if it could know the economic conditions of each enterprise – is to provide sufficient incentives to each state enterprise manager to produce economically and to expand the productive capacity of the enterprise and introduce new products effectively. In a market economy profit incentives help ensure efficient production, optimal investment, and introduction of new products. In a planned economy, the central authority may allow enterprise managers to share profits, and it may appeal to their sense of patriotism and reward successful ones with honors. The Chinese have accumulated valuable experience concerning the use of nonmaterial incentives. However, it is difficult for the planning authority to judge which enterprise managers should be rewarded when the production targets are set arbitrarily and the economic conditions of the enterprise cannot be ascertained accurately. If each state enterprise is allowed to make production and investment decisions on its own and if prices are determined by market forces and not controlled by the planning authority, the economy is a socialist market economy and no longer a centrally planned economy. China's economic reform (which will be described in the next chapter) to a large extent succeeded in transforming the economy from a planned economy to a socialist market economy.

The incentive problem is particularly difficult to solve in the undertaking of risky investment projects. As compared with the situation in a market economy, the enterprise manager in a planned economy does not receive sufficient reward for taking risks in investing, because the reward for success is limited while the punishment for failure is severe. At the other extreme, the manager may be willing to engage in expensive and wasteful investment projects as long as the result is not recognized to be a failure. For example, without a market test it is difficult to judge whether setting up new plants to produce certain types of cars is economically efficient, since the government monopolizes the production of cars. This applies also to large projects for infrastructure building – perhaps the Three Gorges dams that were built in the late 1990s.

The third task of the planning authority is the setting of prices. In a market economy, prices affect the consumption, production, and distribution of goods. In a centrally planned economy, prices can affect consumption but cannot encourage or discourage production if the enterprises do not operate to make profits. Prices perform an important function in the distribution of consumer goods to consumers and the distribution of producer goods and materials to producers. In the Chinese planned economy, the procurement prices of agricultural products affect the income of farmers; wage rates affect the income of workers.

The prices of consumer goods affect the quantities of these goods that they will purchase. Prices of producer goods and materials affect the revenues of those enterprises producing them and the costs of those enterprises employing them. In setting these prices, the central planning authority has to consider three sets of balances.

First, the total value of all consumer goods produced should be equal to the total value of the quantities that consumers want to buy, given the total value of their incomes. Since the supplies of all consumer goods as well as their prices are set by the planning authority, the total value of all consumer goods is determined. In the meantime, wage rates and purchase prices of farm products help determine the incomes of consumers. Consumers decide how much of their incomes to spend on consumer goods and how much to save. If the total value of the consumer goods that consumers decide to purchase, given their incomes, is larger than the total value of the goods available, there will be hidden inflation, or even open inflation if the prices of some goods are not controlled. In fact, at any price which the planning authority sets for a particular nonrationed good, the supply of that good may not be sufficient to satisfy the demand. In that case there will be shortages, with consumers waiting for more supplies to come. In practice the prices of consumer goods in a planned economy tend to be set too low because of a sense of fairness. Demand therefore tends to exceed supply, and shortage results (as discussed by Kornai 1992).

Second, the planning authority has to set prices so as to balance the total revenue and expenditures of all enterprises under its control. The total revenue of each enterprise is determined by the output quota and the price of the output. Its total expenditure is determined by the quantities and prices of the inputs that it employs and the capital goods that it needs for the targeted expansion. If an enterprise's total revenue exceeds its total expenditure, it has a surplus that belongs to the planning authority. If total revenue is less than total expenditures, the enterprise needs a subsidy from the planning authority to balance its books. If the total revenue from all enterprises is less than their total expenditure, the planning authority has to find ways to subsidize some of the enterprises. In China, during most of the period of planning, state enterprises made profits to be used as government revenues. After economic reform, many state enterprises were operating at a loss and required government subsidies.

Third, the planning authority has to balance the government budget or find ways to finance government deficits. Deficits can be financed in two ways: by issuing new money and by issuing government bonds to be sold at home or abroad. Issuing too much new money will cause inflation, open or hidden. Since prices will affect the balancing of the government's budget, the central authority has to take this factor into account in setting prices.

## 2.4   The Behavior of Economic Units in a Planned Economy

We have described the basic organizational arrangement of a centrally planned economy and the three difficult tasks of the planning authority. How the economy works and how well it works depend on how, and how well, the planning authority performs its functions and how the economy's other units respond to its directions. We will now describe the behavior of the component economic units, including consumers, farmers, workers, farms, and industrial enterprises, leaving the behavior of the central planning authority to the following section.

The behavior of consumers in a centrally planned economy can be explained by the basic theory of consumer behavior presented in economics texts, if the rationing of consumer goods is taken into account. If there is no rationing, the textbook theory is applicable to Chinese consumers. In this theory, a consumer is assumed to rank different bundles of consumer goods according to his or her preferences. Graphically, bundles of goods equally preferred are points on an indifference curve. Given his income and the prices of all goods, the consumer is assumed to choose that bundle on the highest-ranked indifference curve that he or she can afford. The most important implication of this theory is that when the relative price of a commodity goes up, the consumer will buy less of it, given his real income. A demand function for each commodity is derived from the consumer's search for the highest-ranked indifference curve, subject to the constraint of his or her budget. The demand for any commodity is thus a function of consumers' incomes and the prices of all commodities.

When rationing is present, the consumer not only has to pay the price of a rationed good, but also has to surrender a ration coupon for one unit of that commodity. The rationing of a particular commodity is said to be *effective* if all rationed coupons for that commodity are used up. If they are not used up, the ration coupons do not restrict the consumption of that commodity and the demand for it is the same as the demand for a nonrationed commodity. If there are several commodities for which rationing is effective, the theory of consumer behavior can be modified by taking the quantities and prices of these commodities as given. The quantities are equal to the numbers of coupons issued. Subtract the value of these commodities from the consumer's income; the consumer now has a smaller income to spend on the remaining commodities. Given this smaller income (net of the spending on the rationed commodities) and given the prices of the remaining commodities, the consumer now chooses a bundle of the remaining commodities that he or she prefers, subject to budget constraint on purchases of the remaining commodities. The demand for each commodity is a function of the net income and the prices of the remaining commodities. When the relative price of a remaining commodity goes up, its consumption will go down, as usual. In addition we have to allow for the effects of the quantities of effectively rationed commodities on the demand for the nonrationed commodities. If the available quantity of an effectively rationed commodity increases, the demand for a nonrationed substitute will decrease, and the demand for a nonrationed complement will increase. See Neary and Roberts (1980: 25–42) for a theoretical treatment of consumer behavior under rationing which is applicable to China as well.

Secondly, let's consider the behavior of a Chinese farm worker. From 1959 to 1979, the Chinese farms were organized as *communes*, which served as both political-administrative and economic units of the government. Each commune was divided into *brigades*, and each brigade was divided into *work teams*. According to the *Almanac of China's Economy* (1981: 965), the total population of the communes in 1979 was 807.4 million. There were

174.9 million families organized into 53,348 communes, 699,000 brigades, and 5,154,000 teams. On the average, these statistics imply 13.1 brigades per commune, 7.4 teams per brigade, and 157 persons per team. The central planning authority directs each commune to grow particular kinds of crops, assigns production quotas for the products and the amounts to be delivered to a government procurement agency at given prices, and provides the necessary supplies of farm inputs to each commune. The communes also engage in large projects, such as road construction and irrigation, that require the work of an entire brigade, and in sideline nonfarm activities such as the production of light industrial products. Each farmer is paid a fraction of the income of the team to which he belongs. The fraction is the ratio of the number of work points the farmer earns to the total number earned by all team members. An incentive problem arises because the farmer is not paid according to the marginal product of his labor: if he works harder to increase output, he gets very little of the additional output which is shared by all members of the team. Under the commune system, there is indeed little incentive for farmers to work hard.

Third, the behavior of a Chinese industrial worker likewise depends on her working arrangement. In the first place, the worker's job is assigned to her by a labor bureau, which tries to match jobs with workers. As compared with a market system, in which workers find jobs for themselves and enterprises decide for themselves which workers to hire and discharge, this system leads to the mismatching of jobs and workers. Furthermore, the government's labor bureau is less qualified than an enterprise's personnel manager to decide whether a particular worker is suitable for a certain job. The labor bureau staff will often assign the more desirable jobs as compensation for favors. In addition, once assigned a job, the worker cannot be discharged, and she gets the same pay whether she works harder or not. (From 1960 to 1977 the wages of most workers were not changed at all, although some received bonuses or awards of one kind or another. Different wage rates apply to different jobs.) Under these conditions, one can expect to find a lack of incentive and low productivity among the workers, as is in fact the case.

Fourth, consider the behavior of Chinese farms as economic units. A commune is both a political-administrative unit and an economic unit of production formed in the spirit of a planned economy. In such a unit peasants, workers, students, and members of the army engage in farming, fishing, forestry, industrial sidelines, and construction activities. Labor is mobilized to perform the important economic tasks of supplying food and material and of building roads, bridges, irrigation systems, and other construction projects. Each commune is directed by the planning authority to produce particular kinds of products and sometimes to use certain acreage allotments and farming techniques, such as multiple cropping. The lack of expertise on the part of the central planning authority and its staff can lead to, and has led to, the misuse of farmland and low productivity. In reality Chairman Mao emphasized the production of grain at the expense of other crops, even at locations not suitable for grain production. This led to a great loss in agricultural productivity. When the planning authority assigns production targets to each commune, the latter in turn assigns production targets to the brigades and the production teams. The production teams have difficulty getting the farmers to work hard because, as we have pointed out, the farmers do not receive the value of the marginal product of their labor under the payment system. In other words, by commanding farmers to produce as teams and not paying them according to their individual productivity, the commune cannot effectively manage the production of farm products.

Fifth, as in the case of a Chinese factory, inefficiencies can come from three sources. First, with jobs guaranteed and wages independent of productivity, the management has difficulty in motivating workers to work harder, as we have pointed out. Second, a main goal of the management is not to maximize profits, but to meet the production targets set by the planning authority, and there is a lack of incentive for the management to increase outputs beyond the targeted amounts or to introduce new products that satisfy the consumers. Since the management can influence the setting of production targets by providing the planning authority with estimates of the productive capacity of the enterprise, it has an incentive to lower the production targets in order to make them easier to meet. Third, because the management receives materials and other required inputs from the planning authority, it has little incentive to economize on the use of the inputs. Nor does it have much incentive to keep its input estimates low, because the management does not bear the cost of additional inputs but it is penalized if inputs are insufficient to meet the production targets. Waste of material and other inputs will result, leading to the accumulation of large inventories.

## 2.5   Output Planning in Theory and Practice

We will now discuss the behavior of the planning authority in theory and practice. In theory, it is responsible for solving all the economic problems related to the production and distribution of goods and to the accumulation of capital. It has to rely on the above-mentioned individual economic units to carry out all the tasks of production, distribution, and capital accumulation. How and how well the tasks are accomplished depends on the rules set by the planning authority. We have discussed the behavior of each type of economic unit under one set of rules that approximates the actual conditions in China from 1959 to 1978. It is not our task to explain why the planning authority might want to increase the production of one kind of product relative to another kind. Given its objectives, the planning authority has to face the production constraints of the economy: the physical and human resources available, the way productive units are organized, the technology available, and the rules the production units have to follow. When the planning authority attempts to increase the outputs of certain products relative to other products, it will try to increase the production targets of the former products relative to the latter products. How much of one product can be increased when another product is reduced depends on the economy's *production-transformation curve* (also called the *production possibility frontier*). The production transformation curve summarizes the production possibilities in an economy. Given the technology, resources, and organizational arrangements of an economy, the output of one product can be increased only by sacrificing a certain amount of the output of another product. We can conceptualize the planning authority as selecting a point on the production-transformation curve that is most preferred. If the preferences of the planning authority are summarized by a set of indifference curves, the combination of target outputs will be a point at which the production-transformation curve is tangential to an indifference curve.

To understand the shift of output targets along the production-transformation curve of a centrally planned economy, we need to describe how resources are transferred from the production of one commodity to the production of another commodity. When the planning authority desires an increase of one product, it must ensure that sufficient resources will be made available from somewhere else. In other words, if a central planner wishes to produce certain units of good 1, certain units of good 2, and so on, it must make available the inputs required to produce them. The *balancing of inputs* is an essential task for a central planning authority that sets production targets for its production units.

The process of balancing the total requirement in production and total supply of each input is known as *material balancing*, as first practiced in the Soviet Union. It consists of the following steps. First, on the basis of its knowledge of each productive unit (industrial enterprise or farm), including its inputs and outputs of the last period, the central planning authority, through its staff and lower-level administrators, sets preliminary production targets for each enterprise and obtains requests from it concerning the amount of each important input required. Second, the planning authority adds up the quantities of each input required by all production units and compares the total with the total produced by all enterprises. If the two sums are the same, the requirement and the supply of this input are in balance. Otherwise, as a third step, the central planning authority advises some production units to reduce their input requirements, instructs some units to raise their production of the required inputs, and reduces the output targets of enterprises producing less essential products. After some negotiations, the planning authority goes back to the first step by issuing a revised set of production targets for each enterprise and a revised set of inputs to be made available to each enterprise. An annual plan is created based on the output targets so obtained. Details on the misuse of resources in the process of material balancing for one particular state-owned enterprise will be discussed in section 15.2.

Often the balance between the production and the use of each product is achieved only on paper. When actual production takes place, some materials may be in short supply, creating bottlenecks in production, while other materials may be in excess supply, creating large inventories. Excessive inventories held by one enterprise may not be made available to another enterprise that needs them; there is no incentive and no mechanism to transfer the excess material from one enterprise to another. The problem of balancing the demand for and supply of each input is solved in a market economy. When demand exceeds supply, the price of that item will rise to discourage its use and encourage its production. When the consumers as a group decide to have more of product 2 relative to product 1, the relative price of product 2 goes up relative to the price of product 1, and production of product 2 increases while production of product 1 decreases. Producers of product 2 demand more inputs and obtain them from the other producers through the market. All balancing is achieved by the price mechanism, without the interference of a central planning authority.

Li Kaixin describes the management of supplies in China (1982: 613–20). Between 1949 and 1952, supply management was controlled by the Financial and Economic Commission of the Administrative Council. In 1950 eight major materials, including rolled steel, timber, coal, and cement, were allocated directly by the central government or administrative regions, each consisting of several provinces. The number of major materials under state control was increased to 55 in 1952. In the first Five Year Plan of 1953–7, the State Planning Commission increased the number further. Producer goods allocated by government units were classified into three categories: those under unified state allocation, those allocated by different industrial ministries, and those allocated by local authorities. By 1957 the number of products in the first and second categories had increased to 532. These were mainly products of enterprises run by the state at a level not lower than the provincial government or some large-scale state–private joint enterprises, and products of private enterprises entirely purchased and marketed by the state. They were not allowed to be marketed by the enterprises themselves, but were to be supplied by a combination of direct planning through central allocation and indirect planning through the market. They accounted for 70 to 90 percent of all producer goods in the country. The rest was allocated by provincial, municipal, and autonomous regional authorities; they were distributed through market channels.

Li (1982: 613–14) writes:

Between 1958 and 1960, there was a serious shortage of materials, chaotic management and frightening waste, all of which caused great difficulties for major production units and construction projects directly under the control of the central authority. This predicament came about because the production targets of industry – heavy industry in particular – were set so high as to be beyond the capability of the country's economy. To make matters worse, control over allocation and distribution of many kinds of materials in the first and second categories were given over to the local authorities. In 1961, the Party Central Committee and the State Council decided to adopt policies of readjustment, consolidation, expansion and raising standards for the national economy. While reducing the scope of capital construction and readjusting industrial production, the state strengthened its unified control of materials. The number of materials in the first and second categories increased to about 500 . . .

Between 1962 and 1965, the question of controlling the supply of materials was discussed on many occasions by the Party Central Committee and the State Council; decisions for work improvement were made . . .

On controlling the circulation of goods, Comrade Liu Shaoqi's concept of setting up a system of "second commerce" was put into practice. This included establishment of institutions in charge of materials management, i.e., specialized material supply corporations and stations; organizing service teams to keep regular contacts with user enterprises at the grass-roots level; setting up many factories and shops for processing materials according to fixed models . . . As a result, there was a marked improvement in the supply of materials . . .

During the ten years of turmoil between 1966 and 1976, however, the supply of producer goods was seriously disrupted. The ministry in charge of that supply was "smashed." Such state institutions in 24 provinces and autonomous regions were suspended and most of the special goods supply companies, service companies and supply stations were either dissolved or merged . . . Consequently, state control of the allocation and distribution of producer goods was greatly weakened . . .

The institutions in charge of material supply gradually resumed work and some regulations for the management of goods which had proved effective during the 1960s were reinstated. There has been a strengthening of state control for the allocation and distribution of producer goods. Most of the goods in the first category have been placed once again under control of the state organizations in charge of material supplies . . . Meanwhile, local authorities have been enjoying greater power in the control of goods. The goods in the first category under the control of local authorities in 1978 accounted for the following percentages of the national total: coal, 46%, rolled steel, 42%, copper, aluminum, lead and zinc, 36%, timber, 18%, and cement, 71%.

This quotation suggests that the central direction of a planned economy, including the supply and allocation of materials, does not cover all goods and services, but only the most important ones. In China the coverage and the effectiveness of control varied from time to time according to political conditions. This fact has to be borne in mind when discussing the Chinese planned economy up to the late 1970s.

Side by side with the balancing of materials in a centrally planned economy, there is a need to balance the flow of money that accompanies the flow of materials. Each enterprise obtains revenues from the goods that it delivers to the central authority or, at the direction of the central authority, to other enterprises. It incurs expenses for the materials it receives for production. It may have a surplus or a deficit as total revenue exceeds or falls short of total costs. In the event of a deficit, a subsidy from the planning authority is required. In order to have a net transfer of resources to all enterprises for the purpose of capital formation, the planning authority may have to run a deficit in its operation of all enterprises. This deficit can be financed by borrowing from or taxing the public, or by borrowing from abroad. In any case, a government budget has to be prepared in connection with the balancing of the materials to summarize the flows of money. (Accordingly, in September 1980 officials of the State Council of China presented for approval to the National People's Congress the National Economic Plans summarizing the production targets for major products for 1980 and 1981, the Final State Budget for 1979, the Draft State Budget for 1980, and the Projected State Budget for 1981.)

Intimately related to the material and financial flows are the prices of various outputs and inputs controlled by the planning authority. A deficit can become a surplus after certain price changes. Prices in a free market are not controlled, but a central planning authority has many options in setting prices, including the use of market signals. In China the prices of important consumer and producer goods that are distributed through the central planning system are centrally controlled. Prices of products distributed locally are controlled by the local economic administrators. The central planning authority can set prices to control consumption, the distribution of income, the finances of government enterprises, and the rate of inflation. Prices of certain consumer products are set very low to guarantee that each family can afford to purchase some specified quantities. Rent for urban housing is extremely low; prices of food grain are also low, requiring government subsidies. Prices of other consumer goods, such as television sets, are set very high during the period of central planning to discourage consumption. In order to prevent inflation, prices of certain materials are not allowed to change. Prices of certain supplies to farmers are set high as a tax on farmers to support the process of industrial development and national capital formation. At this point in our discussion we only indicate the motivation of the Chinese planning authority for the setting of certain prices, without implying that such practices are either good or bad. We only note that the planning authority regards the setting of prices as a means to control the economy in the process of economic planning.

A description of the behavior of the planning authority would be incomplete without discussing the administrative and political problems of the planning organization itself. First, the leadership of the planning authority may not correctly perceive the economic constraints that limit its economic choices. Grossly unrealistic economic plans that cannot be implemented are not unusual, especially if the person or persons in power do not have the required knowledge of or professional advice on economic matters. The "Great Leap" in China in 1958 and a smaller "leap" in 1978 were illustrations of setting planning targets that could not be achieved. Second, even with a well-trained, professional planning staff, the problems of economic planning and balancing of resources for the entire country are extremely difficult, as we saw in section 2.3 above. One can appreciate the difficult mathematical and informational problems of central economic planning when there are thousands of products and perhaps millions of production units involved, and when the production functions of the production units are not completely known by the economic planners. Third, assuming that a sound and detailed economic plan has been made, the planning authority still faces the problem of supervising its administrative staff who will carry out its orders all the way down to the individual economic units. There are incentive problems associated with the large bureaucracy required for central planning. False reporting and receiving bribes for doing favors for the enterprises are not uncommon practices. Often the appointment of the staff is influenced by political considerations and not by the candidates' professional qualifications. Once on the staff, a person may use his administrative and economic powers to further his own interests, which may differ from the interests of the central planning authority. Fourth, an additional complication on the Chinese scene is that the administrative units of different provinces have their regional economic and political objectives. Local powers have persisted through Chinese history, and the central planning authority has the problem of getting the provincial and local units to work for its national economic goals. The self-interest of lower-level economic administrators often does not coincide with the interest of the national planning authority and creates serious problems in China.

We can briefly summarize the behavior of different economic units in a centrally planned economy. The planning authority has certain objectives, which in theory can be summarized by a set of indifference curves showing which combinations of products are equally preferred. If the planning authority is assumed to function intelligently, it tries to find the most preferred combination subject to the restriction of the production-transformation relations among the different products. In the case of two commodities, the relation is depicted by a production-transformation curve. A planner usually does not know the true production-transformation curve and may seek a point beyond the productive capabilities of the economy. In the process of mobilizing the different economic units to produce and to distribute products for consumption and for capital accumulation, the central planning authority sets production targets, supplies materials necessary for production, balances the supplies of materials with their requirements, balances the financial flows, sets the wage rates and prices, rations the consumption of certain consumer goods, and assigns jobs to the workers. Given the wage system, the employment system, the rationing system, and the setting of prices and production targets by the planning authority, the other economic units – consumers, farmers, workers, farms, and industrial enterprises – respond accordingly, in ways that we have previously analyzed. This is essentially how a centrally planned economy with features abstracted from the Chinese conditions of 1953–78 works.

In reality, the effectiveness of planning and the degree of central control vary according to political conditions. In China the above description is a good approximation of the situation in the period of the first Five Year Plan (1953–7). After 1958 the process of planning was often interrupted, and annual plans were sometimes announced after the fact. Even during the period of the first Five Year Plan, central control of the economy did not cover all economic resources and activities. Provincial and municipal authorities and local markets remained to exert influences on the operation of the economy. Furthermore, the central planning units, instead of giving directions, often relied on the autonomous workings of the bureaux and enterprises under their control to solve the production and distribution problems through barter and other arrangements. As we have pointed out, the control of supply of materials was partial and incomplete, leaving much discretion to local authorities and allowing exchanges by barter between enterprises in certain instances. Concerning the control of prices, before 1966, deviations from the centrally determined prices were permitted within certain ranges in order to meet local demand and supply conditions. After 1966, because of the need to control the political and economic disorder resulting from the Cultural Revolution, the centrally administered prices became more rigid and deviations were not permitted until 1983.

## 2.6 Organization and Administration of Economic Planning

The political power in China resides in the Chinese Communist Party. The Party exercises power partly by placing its members in key positions in the government. The executive branch of the Chinese government is headed by the State Council. The State Council, through its various ministries, directs the economic activities of the country. To appreciate the comprehensiveness of central economic planning, one can examine the organization of the State Council. The State Council is nominally responsible to the National People's Congress, although in practice, at least until the 1990s, the People's Congress exercised little real power. The State Council is headed by the Premier and, as of 1984, two Vice-premiers. A list of the commissions and ministries of the State Council as of April 30, 1981, can be found in the *Almanac of China's Economy* (1981: 57–8). Some consolidations took place in the spring of 1982. The list below applies to the summer of 1982 and contains supplementary material found in Fu (1982: 53–4).

Two commissions were in charge of coordinating the activities of the ministries concerned with economics. The State Planning Commission had overall responsibility for economic planning, including the drafting of five-year and other medium-term economic plans. The Economics Commission reviewed the fulfillment of the annual economic plans and instituted economic reforms. There were 27 ministries dealing with different segments of the economy. They were:

Agriculture and Fisheries
Water Resources and Electric Power
Forestry
Railroads
Chemical Industry
Transportation and Communications
Metallurgical Industry
Posts and Telecommunications
Light Industry
Urban and Rural Construction and
   Environmental Protection
Textile Industry
Machine-building Industry
Finance
Electronics Industry

Coal Industry
State Bureau of Labor
Petroleum Industry
Commerce
Nuclear Energy Industry
Foreign Trade
Aircraft Industry
People's Bank of China
Munitions Industry
Family Planning Office
Space Industry
State Scientific and Technological
   Commission
Geology and Mineral Resources

The following 13 bureaux were also concerned with the management of economic activities:

Bank of China
People's Construction Bank
General Administration of Travel and
   Tourism
Agricultural Bank of China
Bureau of Drug Administration
General Administration of Customs
Bureau of Import–Export Control
   (under Ministry of Foreign Trade)
State Statistics Bureau

State Bureau of Supplies
State Administration of Standards
Industrial and Commercial Administration
   Bureau
State General Administration of Exchange
   Control (under the People's Bank of
   China since 1982)
Administration Bureau for Commodity
   Prices

The ministries and bureaux in charge of economic affairs greatly outnumber the remaining 11 ministries of the State Council:

Foreign Affairs
Culture
National Defense
Education
State Nationalities Affairs Commission
Public Health

State Physical Culture and Sports
Public Security
Cultural Relations with Foreign Countries
Civil Affairs
Justice

The above classification of the Family Planning Office and the State Scientific and Technological Commission as economic and of the ministries of Education and Public Health as noneconomic is arbitrary. I have divided these four ministry-level organizations equally between the two groups for the purpose of counting the ministries and to indicate the importance of economic administration in the affairs of the State Council. Note that among the economic ministries, those concerned with different industries outnumber the two concerned with agriculture and forestry. (As I am describing the organization of the State Council during the period of planning, it is more convenient to use the present tense.) In part, this reflects the complexity of central economic planning for industry as compared with agriculture.

Generally speaking, directions from the central government to the individual economic units go through three intermediate levels of the Chinese government. The first level consisted of 21 provinces, 5 autonomous regions, and 3 municipalities directly under the central government. The 21 provinces are Anhui, Fujian, Ganzu, Qinghai, Guangdong, Guizhou, Hebei, Heilongjiang, Henan, Hubei, Hunan, Jiangsu, Jiangxi, Jilin, Liaoning, Shaanxi, Shandong, Shanxi, Sichuan, Yunnan, and Zhejiang. The 5 autonomous regions are Guangxi, Inner Mongolia, Ningxia, Tibet, and Xinjiang. The 3 municipalities are Beijing (Peking), Shanghai, and Tianjin. In the 1990s Hainan, which was formerly a part of Guangdong, became a province, and Chongqing, which was formerly a part of Sichuan province, became a municipality. On the second level and under each province or autonomous region are large cities and prefectures. On the third level and under each prefecture are counties and small cities. The communes are administrative units under the counties. There are over 2,000 counties and over 50,000 communes (there is a list of counties in the *Almanac of China's Economy* 1981: 59–71). Also on the third level and under each large city are neighborhoods (which are further subdivided into streets and courtyards). Factories are frequently controlled by units of the government at the level of counties and cities, but smaller production and distribution units (like restaurants and retail shops) are frequently controlled at the level of neighborhoods. Some large industrial enterprises are under the direct control of the corresponding industrial ministries or are controlled by corporations directly under the ministries. Some enterprises are under the control of provincial governments.

Through the administrative units at different levels the central government prepares and executes its economic plans. The production and distribution of important consumer and producer goods are centrally planned. These goods include food grains, vegetable oils, pork, beef, lamb, eggs, consumer durable goods, industrial raw materials, and capital goods. To achieve materials balancing in its annual plan, the demand and supplies of the centrally planned commodities from each province are reviewed by the State Planning Commission; deficits from some provinces will be balanced by surpluses from other provinces or by imports. The provincial plans are assembled from economic units within the respective provinces through the administrative units at the county or city level. To execute its plan, the State Planning Commission gives directions through the ministries. In the areas of agriculture–fisheries, forestry, commerce, and light industry which are under the control of the communes, directions from the corresponding ministries pass through the provincial and county administrative units to the communes. In the area of urban industry, directions from the corresponding ministries pass through the provincial and city–county administrative units to the factories or enterprises. The exceptions are large enterprises directly controlled by the ministries and enterprises under the control of provincial governments. Also, very small enterprises like restaurants and retail shops are controlled by units below the level of cities, such as neighborhoods or even streets.

An organization chart or a summary of the organizational structure does not fully describe how much authority the administrators at each level have in the preparation and execution of economic plans. The State Planning Commission might simply assemble the production targets submitted by the individual communes or enterprises through the county–city and provincial levels of the administration. But the State Planning Commission might also use its great powers to order the individual communes and enterprises to change their production targets. The reality is somewhere in between, depending on the particular people in command of the commission and on the particular provinces and/or enterprises involved. Many industrial and commercial enterprises receive directions from two sources, the ministry of the State Council and the administrative unit of the provincial government (see Gao et al. 1980: 47). Interesting questions have arisen concerning the authority of the ministries and of the provincial governments. In general, provincial governments have more authority over the production and distribution of commodities for local consumption, but this general rule does not describe the influence of the provincial government in any particular situation. In any large organization, never mind a country as large as China, it is always difficult to specify precisely how administrators at different levels exercise their authority, but this is not a topic that we need to go into. In China the discussion of political control is complicated by the role of the committees of the Communist Party, which run parallel to the organizations at the different levels of the Chinese government. The Party committees are more powerful than the managers of enterprises and official heads of other state institutions, such as university presidents.

As reform towards a market-oriented economy proceeded, the role of central planning and of the State Planning Commission became less important. In the mid-1980s, compulsory planning was changed to guidance planning. This meant that the targets set by the State Planning Commission were not strict orders but only served as achievement objectives. Even after central planning was gradually abandoned in the 1980s, the convention of setting up Five Year Plans has persisted, up to the tenth Five Year Plan of 2001–5, if only to provide broad targets to guide economic development. When Zhu Rongji took office as Premier in 1998 he tried to begin streamlining the State Council and to reduce government staff by half. By 1999, the State Development Planning Commission, the State Economics and Trade Commission, the Ministry of Finance, and the People's Bank of China were the four organizations in charge of overall economic functions, to be assisted by eight ministries, of Railways, Communications and Transportation, Construction, Agriculture, Water Resources, Foreign Trade and Economic Cooperation, Information Industry, and the Commission of Science, Technology, and Industry for National Defense.

In this chapter we have explained why and how the Chinese Communist Party came to power in 1948 and described how planning worked in China up to 1978. The experience of planning and the economic disruption under Communist rule during this period contributed to the desire for reform in 1978, a subject of the next chapter.

## References and Further Reading

*Almanac of China's Economy, 1981*. Hong Kong: Modern Cultural Company Ltd.

Chang, Gene Hsin and Guanzhong James Wen. "Food Availability versus Consumption Efficiency: Causes of the Chinese Famine." *China Economic Review*, 9 (Fall 1998), pp. 157–66.

*China Human Development Report 1999: Transition and the State*, ch. 2, sec. 2. Published for the United Nations Development Program by Oxford University Press, Hong Kong, 2000.

Chow, Gregory C. *The Chinese Economy*, ch. 2. New York: Harper & Row, 1985. 2nd ed., Singapore: World Scientific, 1987.

Fu, F. C. "The Evolution and Operation of Central Economic Organization in Mainland China." *Economic Papers No. 19*. Taipei: Chung-hua Institution for Economic Research, 1982.

Gao Guangli, Che Li, and Wang Yang. *Zhongguo Shanye Jingji Guanlixue* [*Chinese Business Economic Administration*]. Beijing: People's University Publishing House, 1980.

Kornai, Janos. *The Socialist System: The Political Economy of Communism*. Princeton: Princeton University Press, 1992.

Li Kaixin, "How China Manages its Supplies." *Almanac of China's Economy, 1982*. Hong Kong: Modern Cultural Company Ltd., pp. 613–20.

Lin, Justin Yifu, Fang Cai, and Zhou Li. *The China Miracle: Development Strategy and Economic Reform*, chs. 2 and 3. Hong Kong: Chinese University Press, 1996.

Ma Hong and Sun Shangqing, eds. *Zhongguo Jingji Jiegou Wenti Yanjui* [*Studies of the Problems of China's Economic Structure*], 2 vols. Beijing: People's Publishing Society, 1982.

Neary, J. P. and K. W. S. Roberts, "The Theory of Household Behavior under Rationing." *European Economic Review*, 13 (Jan. 1980), pp. 25–42.

Xue Muqiao. *China's Socialist Economy*. Beijing: Foreign Language Press, 1981.

## Questions

1 Name three groups of people in China who were harmed or deceived in the 1950s by the Communist regime, and the manner in which they were harmed.

2 What are the major differences between a planned economy and a market economy in solving the major economic problems of a society? Start answering by listing the major problems.

3 Name five major ideological beliefs which can serve to characterize Communism.

4 What are the major institutions established under the Chinese planning system? How and how well did they function?

5 Chow and Kwan in two papers in 1996 tried to estimate how large China's economy would have been in 1990 if there had been no Great Leap Forward or no Cultural Revolution. The first paper is discussed in chapter 8. What was the method employed to find an answer? What was the estimate for each of these political events given in chapter 8? (Answer this question only if you do not intend to study chapter 8 carefully but wish to understand the general method and major results by glancing through that chapter.)

6 Imagine that you are the manager of a Chinese state enterprise in 1978. How would you perform your job as compared with the president of a modern corporation?

7   In what way was the fortune of the Chinese consumer in 1978 different from the situation in 1935?

8   Name three difficult tasks that the Chinese planning authority had to perform to organize the productive activities of the country. Explain why these tasks are difficult.

9   Was the behavior of the Chinese consumer in the period of planning different from consumer behavior in a market economy? Explain.

10   Describe the reward system for the Chinese farmer under the commune system. Explain why there was a lack of incentive to work.

11   Describe the working conditions facing the Chinese worker under central planning. Explain why there was a lack of incentive to work.

12   Cite three pieces of evidence to show that the Chinese planned economy was not functioning well. The evidence should show the failure or inefficiency of the economic planning system itself, and cannot include the economic failures of the Great Leap Forward and the Cultural Revolution, which were disruptions of the planning system.

# Economic Reform up to
# the Mid-1990s

Reasons for introducing, major steps in, and explanations for the success of
economic reforms introduced in 1978 are examined. A comparison is made with
Taiwan's experience in transforming its economy. This chapter also discusses whether
the introduction and success of the reform process were inevitable.

## 3.1   Why Economic Reform Started in 1978

Deng Xiaoping took over control of the Communist Party in 1978. He was responsible
for initiating reform of the planned economy towards a more market-oriented economy.
In a sense the change in policy can be interpreted partially as a continuation of the "four
modernizations" (of agriculture, industry, defense and science and technology, as mentioned in section 2.2.4) announced by Premier Zhou Enlai in 1964 but interrupted by the
Cultural Revolution. This explanation was suggested to me by a former Vice-premier of
the PRC. On the other hand, a former Premier once said to me, "the Cultural Revolution
did great harm to China, but it freed us from certain ideological constraints." These
statements indicate that the Cultural Revolution did affect the thinking of top Party
leaders and thus the course of China's economic development. Taking these statements
into account, together with other considerations, I offer the following explanation for the
initiation of economic reform.

There were four reasons why the time was ripe for reform. First, the Cultural
Revolution was very unpopular, and the Party and the government had to distance themselves from the old regime and make changes to get the support of the people. Second,
after years of experience in economic planning, government officials understood the
shortcomings of the planning system and the need for change. Third, successful economic development in other parts of Asia – including Taiwan, Hong Kong, Singapore,
and South Korea, known as the "Four Tigers" – demonstrated to Chinese government

officials and the Chinese people that a market economy works better than a planned economy. This lesson was reinforced by the different rates of economic development between North and South Korea, and between countries in eastern and western Europe. Fourth, for the reasons stated above, the Chinese people were ready for and would support economic reform.

Given these four reasons, was economic reform in 1978 inevitable? My answer is yes. The first two reasons alone were sufficient to motivate the government to initiate reform. The Cultural Revolution made the government so unpopular that both it and the people badly wanted change. The direction of change was clear because economic planning was recognized to be a failure. Given such a situation, there was no other way for China to go. The urgency of the case was such that it had to occur as soon as the political leadership was ready after Chairman Mao's death. The Chinese economic reforms of 1978 are an instance where it is possible to predict major social change by examining the prevailing conditions. Such prediction is easy with hindsight, but more difficult to do before the event.

In this chapter we will survey six major components of economic reform, beginning with agriculture. The purpose of this is to provide the reader with an overall picture of China's reform process up to the middle of the 1990s. That process continues and problems exist today. In chapter 4, some major reform problems and prospects for further reform at the beginning of the twenty-first century will be discussed. The first four chapters aim to present an overall picture of Chinese economic institutions. In later chapters we will return to individual areas in more depth.

As an introduction to our discussion of economic reform, it is useful to point out that the reform process has been spurred by a combination of the effort of central government and the natural desire of the Chinese people and lower-level government units to improve the economic institutions for their own benefit. For example, it was a combination of the efforts of the farmers and the government which changed the commune system. As far as the role of central government is concerned, the process has been a gradual and experimental one and has proceeded in steps. This approach will be discussed in this and the following chapter, and also examined later on in this book with regard to the reform of individual sectors. The discussion will include housing reform, labor mobility in the formation of human capital, the banking and financial sector, state-owned enterprises, the nonstate sectors, foreign trade, foreign investment, legal reform, and education.

Reform of Chinese state-owned enterprises is an example of a gradual approach through experimentation. In this case, the following concepts were accepted and carried out step by step. The first was to give state enterprises some autonomy in production decisions rather than simply forcing them to meet production targets under a system of central planning. The second was to make them financially independent, allowing them to keep profits after paying taxes to the state, rather than treating it all as revenue belonging to the government. The third was to introduce a contract responsibility system, first to selected parts of enterprise under the important reform decision of October 1984, and later to all enterprise in 1987. Under the contract responsibility system, a part or the entirety of an enterprise was allowed to keep all the gain (such as output produced) or profit after surrendering a fixed amount of it to the enterprise controlling the part, or to the government controlling the enterprise. The fourth was a reform of the price system that gradually allowed prices to be determined by market forces. In the meantime a two-tier price system was introduced to allocate scarce resources formerly under the control of central planning, including material inputs to state enterprises and foreign exchange. Under such a system, the government continued to distribute the scarce resource to designated users at an official, below-market price. At the same time a second market was allowed to trade the scarce resource at market prices. The fifth, introduced in 1997, was to restructure state enterprises into shareholding companies. It will be useful to keep this general picture in mind when studying China's reform process in general or in a particular sector.

## 3.2  Agriculture

The inefficiencies of Chinese agriculture under the commune system were generally recognized. Farmers were more knowledgeable about what crops to plant on their land than political leaders and economic planners. Farm workers had no incentive to work hard under the work-point system because they were not rewarded for their labors. There was a brief period after the land reform in the early 1950s when farm households owned land and were able to sell products in the market. Reform of the commune system occurred initially in 1978 and 1979 when commune leaders in some regions discovered through examples initiated by farmers that they could fulfill their output quotas by reorganizing the commune internally. The reorganization followed and improved upon the practices in the 1960s. In essence each farm household was assigned a piece of land and was held responsible for delivering a given quantity of a specified product in order that the commune could satisfy its procurement requirement. After fulfilling the delivery quota, the farm household would be free to keep the remaining output for its own consumption or for sale in the market. This "household responsibility" system has the economic characteristics of private farming in a market economy. It amounted to each farm household leasing a piece of land and paying a fixed rent in the form of the output quota. The economic incentives in this case are the same as those in the case of a Chinese American family renting a space in New York's Chinatown to operate a restaurant.

According to the account of Kate Xiao Zhou in *How the Farmers Changed China* (1996: 4–5), "Farmers attempted unorganized decollectivization, or surreptitious grass-root land reform, in many parts of rural China throughout the 1960s and 1970s. Their efforts finally succeeded in the late 1970s and came above ground when Deng Xiaoping eventually accepted this alternative to Mao's collectivism. He named it 'the household production responsibility system' in order to avoid the term 'decollectivization.'" The household responsibility system was officially adopted by the Fourth Plenum of the Eleventh Central Committee of the Communist Party in September 1979. The rapid increase in agricultural output and in the incomes of the farmers in the years following provided support for this responsibility system.

After 1978, rural markets began to reopen. Farmers were allowed to raise pigs, chickens, and ducks. These activities were banned during the Cultural Revolution as capitalist activities. They also engaged in sideline activities such as handicraft production which were previously the preserve of the communes. China's farm economy in essence returned to the private economy which had existed in the early 1950s before the organization of cooperatives and the establishment of the communes. One difference pertained to the ownership of land. Strictly speaking, ownership of land was and still is collective; it belongs to the commune or the village. The right to use the land belongs to the farmer who is assigned the land. As time went on, the right to use the assigned land came to be guaranteed on a permanent basis and became transferable. Hence the difference between this right to use and ownership is moot. When we measure the extent to which China is a market economy by the percentage of national output produced by financially independent and profit-motivated production units, we can attribute almost all of agricultural output in this percentage. China still has state farms, but they produce less than 1 percent of agricultural output. Thus reform in agriculture succeeded in allowing private farming to return to this sector.

## 3.3   Reform of State-owned Enterprises

Besides the communes the second important production units were the state-owned enterprises. Elements of reform of state enterprises were adopted by the Chinese People's Congress in September 1980. In the opening of that session, Vice-premier Yao Yilin, chairman of the State Planning Commission, announced that experiments with state enterprises with more autonomy and market competition would be greatly expanded in the following two years. Industrial reform had begun in late 1978 with six pilot enterprises in Sichuan Province. By the end of June 1980, 6,600 industrial enterprises that had been allowed to make certain output, marketing, and investment decisions through partial profit retention had produced in value 45 percent of the output of all state-owned industrial enterprises. By the end of 1981 some 80 percent of state-owned industrial enterprises were involved in the reform experiment. The major elements of industrial reform in the early years include, first, some autonomy regarding the use of retained profits, production planning, sales of output, experimentation with new products, and capital investment; second, adoption of features of an "economic responsibility system" by assigning identifiable tasks to low-level units within an enterprise and paying them according to productivity; third, increasing the role of markets; fourth, streamlining the administrative system at local levels for state enterprises under local control; and, fifth, the encouragement of collectively owned enterprises. For the purposes of designing and carrying out economic reform, a Commission for Reconstructing the Economic System was established in the State Council in 1981. The importance of this Commission was signaled by the facts that it was listed first in the organization chart of the State Council, above the State Planning Commission, and that the Premier himself, rather than a Vice-premier, served as its chairman.

The main difference between reform of state-owned industrial enterprises and reform of Chinese agriculture is that privatization was not adopted for state-owned enterprises.

Reform of state-owned enterprises turned out to be more difficult than that for agricultural production. It was much easier to make small farm households behave like private enterprises in a market economy than to make large state enterprises so behave for several reasons. First, ideologically, members of the Communist Party believed in the ownership and control of the major means of production by the state. They were unwilling to surrender control of large state enterprises to nongovernment individuals and allow them to keep substantial profits for themselves, as in the case of small farms. Second, politically, government bureaucrats were unwilling to give up their power and vested interests by allowing the state enterprises to operate independently. Economic ministers wanted to hold on to the state enterprises under their control. The Bureau of Material Supplies wanted to retain its control over the distribution of major materials. Third, economically, unlike small farms that are self-sufficient, large industrial enterprises were dependent on factors outside their control. Given a piece of land, a farm household can produce as it pleases, subject to climatic conditions. A large enterprise needs the supply of equipment and material inputs produced by other enterprises. The entire system of pricing and distribution of industrial products and material inputs had to be changed to enable a state enterprise to produce efficiently once they are allowed to be financially independent. Fourth, administratively, the efficient operation of a large state enterprise is much more difficult than the operation of a family farm which has a long tradition to draw upon. Most state-enterprise managers did not have sufficient knowledge and experience to run a modern enterprise as an independent entity because they had been trained to obey production targets. Even with additional training, managers were reluctant to give up their old habits of dependence on the economic ministries. The mode of operation of a large organization is difficult to change, and this is equally true for a university or large American corporation.

Observing the limited success in the reform of state enterprises and the need to overhaul the entire economic system, the Twelfth Central Committee of the Chinese Communist Party adopted a major decision on October 20, 1984, on economic reform. It consisted of the following seven major elements. First, they resolved to give individual state enterprises autonomy in decisions regarding production, supply, marketing, pricing, investment, and personnel to function as profit-seeking economic units. Second, to reduce the scope of central planning, except in the case of certain major products, and change the method from mandatory to guidance planning. Third, to allow prices of more products to be determined by the forces of demand and supply rather than central control. Fourth, to develop a macroeconomic control mechanism through the use of taxes, interest rates, and monetary policy under an improved banking and financial system. Fifth, to establish various forms of economic responsibility systems within individual enterprises to promote efficiency; and to institute differential wage rates to compensate for different kinds of work and levels of productivity. Sixth, to foster the development of individual and collective enterprises as supplements to state enterprises. Seventh, to expand foreign trade and investment and promote technological exchanges with foreign countries. The slogan was, "Invigorate the microeconomic units and control by macroeconomic levers."

The reform of state enterprises, unlike the privatization of Chinese agriculture, requires an overhaul of the entire Chinese planned economy. The price system has to be made more market determined. Otherwise, the profits of enterprises could not reflect economic efficiency. Yet the notion of the government giving up price control was not acceptable to most economic officials in the early 1980s. The planning apparatus had to be scrapped, or at least greatly modified, which was also an unacceptable notion to many government officials. Hence the steps taken in October 1984 were both revolutionary, given the institutional and ideological tradition up to that point, and limited in scope, because it was not possible to go further – for example, by declaring China's economy to be a market economy, giving up control of prices entirely, and transforming state enterprises to modern corporations.

To return to the further reform of state enterprises, two more major steps were taken after 1984. In 1987 the "contract responsibility system" was introduced to all state enterprises. In that system, each state enterprise signed a contract with the level of government which had control over it. Under the contract, the enterprise committed itself to pay the government a fixed annual tax and could retain all the remaining profits. In practice the profits, if any, were up to the enterprise to distribute to the workers and managers as bonuses, but the managers' compensation was limited by social pressure. The incentive for the management to improve efficiency and take risks was therefore limited. Profits were mainly distributed to workers in order to increase the popularity of and support for the management. A second reason for the limited success of the "contract responsibility system" was that, in practice, when the profit of a state enterprise increased, its supervisory government authority demanded a higher tax than was agreed upon originally. In reality the tax depended on profit and no longer had the desirable incentive effects of a fixed levy. In September 1997, General Secretary Jiang Zemin announced in the Fifteenth Communist Party Congress that state enterprises should be restructured by changing them to shareholding companies. The restructuring has continued and will be discussed in the next chapter.

## 3.4   Price Reform

An important component of the October 1984 decision of the Central Committee of the Communist Party on economic reform is reform of the price system. The main objective was to decontrol the administratively determined prices gradually, and allow prices to be determined by market forces. Without market-determined prices the state enterprises do not receive correct signals to do their economic calculations in the choice of inputs and the planning of outputs. However, the administered prices cannot be decontrolled immediately. First, there is the problem of equity. To allow the prices of basic consumer goods to increase would affect the welfare of consumers, who were subsidized. Second, there would be disruption in the production of state enterprises, which were supplied with low-price inputs under the planning system. A compromise solution was to introduce a two-tier price system. One set of prices remained the same as before. A second set for the same goods could be determined by the market. The state enterprises could still purchase the allotted amounts of inputs and sell given amounts of outputs at the administered prices as before. In addition, each enterprise could purchase additional inputs and sell above-quota outputs at prices determined by the market. The prices in the second tier are determined by the market.

The two-tier price system provides incentives for enterprises to economize on inputs and increase outputs for profit. Under this system, if certain outputs were desired by the market beyond the amounts that could be produced using the centrally allocated inputs, prices would go up and the producers could produce more using more expensive inputs supplied in the market. In producing more outputs the enterprises had to pay for the inputs at market prices and thus had to economize on the use of inputs. Since only the prices of outputs sold at the margin and the prices of inputs purchased at the margin affect the marginal revenue and marginal cost of an enterprise, the enterprise can make optimal economic decisions on the basis of these prices. Receiving given quantities of inputs at below-market prices amounts to receiving a fixed amount of government subsidy. Having to surrender a given quantity of output at below-market price amounts to paying a lump-sum tax. Neither a fixed subsidy nor a lump-sum tax affects the optimal output and input decisions of the firm. Hence the two-tier price system practiced in China in the 1980s was an economically efficient system, given that the existing enterprises had to continue producing. A possible economic inefficiency could result, from the viewpoint of the functioning of a market economy, if certain enterprises were operating at a loss without government subsidies and should discontinue operation. As time went on, the administered prices were gradually changed to coincide with the market prices; and by the 1990s, when the majority of products in China were sold at market prices, the two-tier price system was no longer needed.

Price reform in China was a gradual process beginning in the mid-1980s. After one decade most but not all prices were decontrolled. How rapidly prices should be decontrolled was an important issue discussed at the top level of the Commission for Reconstructing the Economic System. The major concern expressed in allowing rapid deregulation was the adjustments that the producers and consumers had to absorb. Once the government provided subsidies to producers in the form of low input prices and monopolistically protected output prices, and to consumers in the form of low prices of food, clothing, and housing, an attitude of entitlement was formed. It would be politically difficult to change this without social protest. In the case of the producers, the two-tier price system enabled them to keep the entitlement while allowing market incentives to operate at the margin. In the case of consumers, the prices of food items did not increase rapidly after decontrol because of the rapid increase in food supply resulting from the successful reform in agriculture. The extremely low price of housing, in the order of several yuan per month for an apartment, was adjusted upward very gradually until the turn of the century, when most urban housing was privatized. In the meantime there was also a two-tier price system in housing. Public, private, and foreign developers were allowed to build apartments to be sold at market prices for those who could afford them. Urban workers maintained the apartments assigned to them by their employers, or units, at low prices that were gradually increased with increasing wages.

## 3.5   The Banking System

To exercise macroeconomic control as practiced in a market economy in lieu of central planning, a modern banking system had to be established. The People's Bank was a monobank that had branches to accept deposits from the public. Its other functions were to issue currency and to extend loans to state enterprises according to the need specified and approved by the planning authority. It had no authority to decide on these loans. Commercial banks did not exist in the sense of being able to extend credit to enterprises according to the criterion of profitability. In 1983 the People's Bank was nominally transformed into a central bank. Specialized banks, including the Industrial and Commercial Bank of China, Agricultural Bank of China, and the People's Construction Bank of China, were established and given some autonomy in the extension of credit in the early 1980s in the same way that state industrial enterprises were given autonomy in making production decisions. This led to a rapid increase in the supply of currency (since the central bank had to honor the loans extended by the specialized banks) by 50 percent in 1984 and an inflation rate of 8.8 percent in the overall retail price index in 1985.

Reform of the banking system to serve a market economy (the Central Committee of the Chinese Communist Party declared China's economy to be a socialist market economy in October 1992) progressed gradually in the late 1980s and early 1990s. In November 1993, the Third Plenum of the Fourteenth Central Committee of the Communist Party decided to accelerate reform of the financial sector by giving more independence to the People's Bank as a central bank and transforming the specialized banks to commercial banks. Two significant dates are March 18 and May 10, 1995, when the People's Congress passed the Law on the People's Bank of China (effective on the same day) and the Commercial Banking Law (effective July 1, 1995). Although the provisions of these laws were not actually carried out in practice, the laws provide a blueprint for the banking system and serve as a convenient framework for us to understand the working of the system. Banking reform is one important example which demonstrates the rule that institutions cannot be changed by legislation alone. The functioning of and problems facing the banking and financial sector will be discussed in chapter 13.

## 3.6   Foreign Trade and Investment

China's economy was essentially a closed economy before the economic reform. In 1978, the total volume of its foreign trade, or the sum of the values of its exports and imports, amounted to only 7 percent of its national income. Deng's open-door policy encouraged the opening of China to foreign imports and the promotion of exports. By 1987, the volume of foreign trade increased to 25 percent and by 1998 to 37 percent of gross domestic product. Foreign trade is the topic of chapter 17.

Foreign investment, the second component of the open-door policy, was promoted through the opening of different regions of China. First, in 1982 the well-known Shenzhen economic zone bordering Hong Kong was created. Infrastructure was built. Foreign investors could set up factories there to take advantage of the inexpensive and skilled labor and pay them at market-determined wage rates different from the rates prevailing in other parts of China. They also received special tax breaks. In less than a decade Shenzhen developed from a piece of farmland to a modern city. Because of the difference in economic opportunities, citizens of China could enter Shenzhen only with special permission. Soon other economic zones and special areas were created for the convenience of foreign investors. Foreign investment increased from an annual rate of less than US$1 billion in 1978 to nearly US$30 billion in 1998. Foreign investment is the topic of chapter 18.

## 3.7   The Nonstate Sectors

While the reform of state enterprises was not entirely successful, the collective and private sectors were dynamic and expanding. Besides the state enterprises there are three other types of enterprise in China: collective, individual, and overseas-funded, the last having been established under the open-door policy.

Collective enterprises include urban collectives and rural collectives. Some previously state-owned retail stores and small factories in urban areas were transferred to collective ownership. To make the operation of retail stores more efficient they were leased to private or collective owners who operated the store for profit, although the real estate remained state owned. The operation resembled that of a restaurant owned by partners or individuals who rent the space. New collective commercial and industrial enterprises were formed in urban areas.

Township and village enterprises in rural areas were established with the support of local governments that desired to increase revenue. There were opportunities to make money as income increased after the successful reform of agriculture. Unemployed labor could be used for non-agricultural production. Local governments had the land, capital, and human resources to establish these enterprises. They had connections to cut through the red tape required to set up and run such enterprises. As China did not have a sound modern legal system, the personal position of an influential local government official was important to make sure that contracts were honored. The ownership rights of these enterprises were often unclear, and yet they seemed to function well and were profitable. The phenomenon of their success provides a puzzle for economists.

The collective and private sectors grew much more rapidly than the state sector. The *Statistical Yearbook of China, 1997* (p. 413) provides the data in table 3.1 on gross industrial output value by ownership, in billions of yuan. From these data we can see that in 1978 individual and other types of industrial enterprises were nonexistent and state enterprises produced 328.9/423.7, or 77.6 percent of total gross industrial output value. By 1985, the share contributed by state enterprises was reduced to 630.2/971.6, or 65 percent. It was further reduced to only 28 percent in 1996 as compared with 39 percent contributed by collective enterprises. One important conclusion to be drawn from these data is that even if the state enterprises are not increasing their productivity,

**Table 3.1**  China, gross industrial output value by ownership, in billions of current yuan

|      | State-owned | Collective-owned | Individual-owned | Other types | Total |
|------|-------------|------------------|------------------|-------------|-------|
| 1978 | 328.9       | 94.8             |                  |             | 423.7 |
| 1985 | 630.2       | 311.7            | 18.0             | 11.7        | 971.6 |
| 1996 | 2,836.1     | 3,923.2          | 1,542.0          | 1,658.2     | 9,959.5 |

China's economy can continue to grow rapidly if the nonstate sectors remain vibrant, because the state sector accounts for only a small share of the total output. The behavior of the state enterprises will be discussed in chapter 15 and that of the nonstate enterprises in chapter 16.

## 3.8  Institutional Infrastructure

Ever since economic reform began, China's educational system has been improving and gradually been returning to normal. Universities were opened after the interruptions of the Cultural Revolution. Students were given opportunities to take examinations to enter universities and graduate schools. Intellectuals who had been criticized and mistreated were restored to their previous status and given due respect. People were eager to learn. Not only students seized upon the educational opportunities and studied hard. The population as a whole wanted to absorb new ideas and knowledge from the outside world since they had been deprived of such knowledge when China was closed to the outside world. Foreign scholars and professionals of all kinds were invited to China to lecture, in schedules so full that even enthusiastic lecturers became exhausted. The Ministry of Education, or the State Education Commission from 1985 to 1998, sponsored programs to cooperate with foreign educational institutions to improve education in China. At the same time, individual universities were given the freedom to invite foreign scholars to lecture. Students were sent abroad to study, and were permitted to go abroad on their own initiative. Modern textbooks were adopted in university courses. Efforts were made to translate modern texts into and write new texts in Chinese. As time went on, the skill in modern languages and especially English improved rapidly, and texts in English began to be adopted. Privately initiated and funded educational institutions were encouraged in the late 1990s and have flourished since reform began. Schools from the primary level to colleges and professional schools have received support from overseas Chinese. China's education system and education policy are the subject of chapter 21.

   The government has made a serious effort to modernize the Chinese legal system. The effort was motivated by the overarching agenda to modernize China and the need to co-operate and deal with the international business community, especially foreign investors. The Ministry of Education in the early 1980s began to set up programs for legal education.

Many lawyers have been trained. There was also the need to have a modern legal framework for domestic social order. The People's Congress have created many laws governing individual and corporate behavior. A system of courts was set up to enforce the laws. On paper the Chinese laws today are quite comprehensive and modern in content, but (as we will see in chapter 20) the behavior of the Chinese people has not changed greatly simply on account of the enactment of the new laws.


## 3.9   Reform Policies Similar to Those of Taiwan


It is interesting to note that several economic policies adopted by the leadership of mainland China during its reform process were similar to those adopted by the government of Taiwan over two decades earlier.

The first common feature in the growth process of both economies is the reduction of government intervention and the encouragement of private initiative. The role that the government should play in a market economy is addressed in the last two sections of chapter 16. In both economies, to initiate the development process, the government had a set of general policy guidelines. In each case the government reduced its intervention and allowed more private initiatives to assert themselves. In Taiwan in the early 1950s, the idea of a command economy was shared by the leadership of the government of President Chiang Kai-shek, including one of his important economic officials, K. Y. Yin, Vice-chairman of the Taiwan Production Board, 1951–4, and Minister of Economic Affairs, 1955. Partly through the persuasion of the Chinese-American economists T. C. Liu and S. C. Tsiang, Yin began to appreciate the efficient working of the market mechanism. He reduced the scope of government control, initiated policies to liberalize imports, lowered the exchange rate on Taiwanese currency, and encouraged exports (see Scott 1979: 314–45). In the case of the Chinese mainland, the command economy modeled after the Soviet Union was modified in the late 1970s, as we have described. Economic reform began with the privatization of agriculture, the increase in rural markets, and the open-door policy, followed by urban reform to allow more autonomy of state enterprises and the establishment of individual and collective enterprises. Premier Zhao Ziyang deserved much credit for fostering the working of market-oriented economic institutions. Essentially, by giving freedom and economic opportunities, however incomplete, to the people, the governments of both regions succeeded in developing their economies.

Economic liberalization took place in Taiwan through government encouragement of private investment in the form of providing financial services through government banks, the establishment of a stock market, tax exemptions for certain industries, relaxed controls over the establishment of factories, and appropriate adjustments to the prices of government-produced commodities and services (see Li 1976: 9–11). An important step in economic reform on the mainland was the decision of the Central Committee of the Communist Party on October 20, 1984, concerning reform of the economic system. The key elements in this decision include granting individual state enterprises autonomy in decisions regarding production, supply, marketing, pricing, investment, and personnel as independent profit-seeking economic units, reducing the scope of central planning, allow-ing the prices of more products to be determined by the forces of demand and supply rather than by central control, and fostering the development of individual and collective enterprises as supplements to state enterprises, as described earlier in this chapter.

The second element common to the two economies is the importance of the agri-cultural sector in the early stage of the growth process. In both Taiwan and the mainland, the increase in agricultural productivity was achieved mainly by redistributing land to the farmers. In Taiwan, from 1953 to 1957, through the sale of public land to tenant farmers and the redistribution of private tenanted land to the tenant cultivators, the percentage of total farm families which were owner-farmers increased from 36 in 1949 to 60 in 1957. Owner-farmers and part owner-farmers owned more than 83 percent of total farmland in 1957 (see Kuo 1983: 27). On the mainland, through the assignment of the rights of land use to individual farm households under the household responsibility system beginning in 1978, and the abolition of the commune system of collective farming in the early 1980s, almost all the households in China's rural areas had switched to the system of essentially private farming by 1983 (see Lin 1988: S201). I use the term "private farming" because, although the Chinese farmers do not own the land, they have the rights to use the land and, to a large extent, to transfer its use to others. They can sell all the outputs to market for profit, after surrendering a fixed amount of the product to the government procure-ment agent at below-market prices, which amounts to paying a fixed rental for using the land. The incentives are similar to those under private farming. In both economies, agri-cultural productivity increased and there were shifts in output from grain to more profit-able cash crops. See Kuo (1983: ch. 3) for the case of Taiwan, as well as Chow (1993: table XI). The latter reference reports an increase in total agricultural productivity from an index of $\exp(0.01) = 1.01$ in 1980 to $\exp(0.436) = 1.547$ in 1985, which are estimates of the multiplicative factor in a Cobb–Douglas production function for the agriculture sector in the Chinese mainland.

A third common feature is the promotion of exports as an important component of the development strategy. The Taiwan experience is partly contained in the following quota-tion from a speech by K. T. Li in 1968 (see Li 1976: 20–1):

> The growth of many of our industries in Taiwan has been made possible because of the development of overseas markets. Several examples may be cited. In 1966, the cotton textile industry exported 66% of its output; the glass industry, 47%; and the plastics industry, 44%. The ratio for cement was 39% and for steel products, 22%. In such heavily export oriented industries as sugar, canned products and plywood, the ratios were higher than 90%. Thus, without the overseas markets, the present scales of these industries would not have been attainable.

Taiwan's total exports rose from US$169.9 million in 1960 to US$569.4 million in 1966 at an average annual growth rate of 22%. Indeed, the prosperity of the export sector has been a major cause behind the rapid growth of the economy.

The increase in exports accounted for 30 percent of the growth of the gross domestic product (GDP) in 1960. Its contribution rose to 42 percent in 1966. On the mainland, through the encouragement of joint ventures, the decentralization of the control of exports from the central government to provincial and local levels, and the promotion of private and collective enterprises mentioned above, exports as a fraction of national income increased from 5.3 percent in 1977 to 15.1 percent in 1988 and 20.7 percent in 1990 (see *Statistical Yearbook of China, 1991*, pp. 32 and 615).

The fourth element is the government's emphasis on the stability of the general price level. The governments of both regions learned from the bitter experience of hyperinflation in China prior to the establishment of the People's Republic of China in 1949, as inflation was recognized to be an important factor contributing to the collapse of the government of the Republic of China on the mainland. Great efforts were made to restore price stability in Taiwan in the early 1950s. From 1961 to 1972, the consumer price index in Taiwan increased from 42.50 to 58.12, or at an average annual rate of 2.9 percent (see the *Statistical Yearbook of the Republic of China, 1980*, pp. 450–1). From 1977 to 1987, the general retail price index on the mainland increased from 135.0 to 198.0, or at an average annual rate of 3.9 percent (see *Statistical Yearbook of China, 1991*, p. 230). Some inflation took place in Taiwan in 1973 because of the world oil price shock. Double-digit inflation on the mainland took place in 1988 because of the failure of the government to control the supply of money and credit, but price stability was restored by early 1990, mainly by contractionary monetary policy.

The fifth common element is the gradual lifting of restrictions on imports and the setting of an official exchange rate close to the free-market level. The official overvaluation of the New Taiwan (NT) dollar relative to the American dollar was gradually eliminated by increasing the effective exchange rate of NT$15.55 to one US dollar, to somewhere between NT$18.60 and NT$20.43 in 1955, to NT$24.58 buying and NT$24.78 selling in April 1958, and further to an effective rate of about NT$37 by the end of 1958 (see Tsiang et al., 1980: 329–30). Gradual devaluation of the currency of mainland China took place when the official RMB/US dollar (RMB stands for "Renminbi" or "people's currency" in Chinese) exchange rate changed from 1.9 in 1980 to 2.93 in 1985, 4.79 in 1990, and 5.40 in 1992. By 1992, the RMB was nearly convertible, as the official exchange rate and the free-market rate have almost converged, making it easy for people on the mainland to exchange RMB for US and Hong Kong dollars.

There are also differences in the degrees to which market forces are allowed to operate in the two economies of mainland China and Taiwan. I will discuss this in more detail in sections 16.6 and 22.1.1, but for now suffice it to say that the bureaucratic behavior of mainland government economic officials interferes with the working of free enterprise to a larger extent than that of their counterparts in Taiwan. In the 1960s and 1970s foreign investors in Taiwan also experienced corruption, but not to the extent that investors did in the 1980s and 1990s on the Chinese mainland. The reason is that on the mainland there had been a planned economy and a Cultural Revolution, making the bureaucrats very hungry for money. As economic conditions and government administration improve, corruption and disruptive bureaucratic behavior will decrease. Secondly, as we will see in chapter 15 and section 22.1.1, the role of state enterprises is more influential on the mainland, where there is a socialist economy. Nevertheless, there are certain instances in which the mainland government is more open to the outside world. These include permitting foreign investors to participate in the building of economic infrastructure, such as superhighways, and permitting imports of foreign automobiles – both of which were not allowed in Taiwan. One common policy has been restricting foreign commercial banks from entering the domestic market in competition with domestic banks.

As the economy on the mainland experienced rapid growth after 1978, it was being transformed mostly to a market economy in the sense that, by 1990, a large proportion of national output was produced by profit-seeking individuals and enterprises. To estimate this proportion we multiply the percentage of national output produced by each of the five sectors of agriculture, industry, construction, transport and communications, and commerce by the percentage of its output accounted for by profit-oriented producers, and sum the five products. In Chow (1988), I estimated that profit-oriented producers accounted for 97, 20, 51, 8, and 63 percent of the outputs of the above five sectors respectively in 1986, and concluded that about 52.6 percent of the national income in the People's Republic of China in that year was produced by profit-seeking economic units. If we apply the profit-motivated percentages of 97, 40, 51, 8, and 63 respectively to the above five sectors, which contributed 34.65, 45.81, 5.76, 4.89, and 8.95 percent respectively to national income in 1990 (see the *Statistical Yearbook of China, 1991*, p. 35) we would find 60.9 percent of national income being produced by these profit-seeking economic units. The 40 percent figure for industry is based on the fact that state enterprises accounted for only 54.6 percent of output of industry in 1990 (ibid., p. 391). Hence by 1990 China was approximately 61 percent a market economy.

## 3.10   Reasons for the Success of China's Economic Reform

Since economic reform started, China's real output as measured by the gross domestic product in constant prices has grown at an average rate of 9.6 percent per year. This is a remarkable record. Some people have questioned the accuracy of the Chinese official statistics on which the above rate of growth is based. If official statistics tend to overestimate, or underestimate, the level of output, the errors cannot significantly affect the estimate of the rate of growth in a period of over two decades. Official statistics aside, travelers have witnessed the rapid improvement in the standard of living of the Chinese people and the rapid appearance of new buildings in Chinese cities in the 1980s and 1990s. Americans have witnessed a large variety of consumer goods produced in China flooding department stores. There is no question that China has experienced a rapid rate of economic development since reform started. What explains the success of the reform?

First, the Chinese leaders are pragmatic and not subject to ideological restraints. The author was working with the Commission for Restructuring the Economic System of the State Council that had the responsibility to design strategies for reform in the 1980s. At meetings with the top officials of the Commission, any proposals could be discussed. One member made the following remark: "There is nothing of value in the capitalist economic system that we cannot consider and adapt for China." Of course some policies were not proposed because Communist Party members were not ready to accept them at the time. On the subject of pragmatism, Deng Xiaoping said that one should not care whether a cat is black or white as long as it catches mice.

Second, there was no blueprint to model the economic institutions after, and policies were adopted through experimentation. This is a process of learning by doing, or as Deng put it, of "crossing the river while feeling the rocks." The responsibility system was adopted because it had worked well. Reform of state enterprises started by introducing partial autonomy to a small number of them. A larger number and more autonomy were tried later as the experiment proceeded. Another example of experimentation was the policy to allow the Province of Guangdong in 1979 and the special economic zone of Shenzhen in 1982 to adopt more capitalist policies first. The advantages of experiments are two. First, they are used to find out what works. Second, by successful experiments Party members from the old guard could be introduced to the new ways and convinced to give their support to the reform program. As the wise leader Deng advised, "Seek truth from facts." He understood these two points well. In this statement he asked the Party members not to let ideology prevent them from accepting policies that were shown experimentally to be good. Because of the lack of a predetermined blueprint and the use of experimentation, reforms took place gradually and step by step. This process has been characterized as "gradualism," in contrast with the "shock therapy" adopted by some eastern European countries which attempted to change to a market economy almost immediately.

Third, the reform had the support of the Chinese people and of government officials who had experienced the failure of economic planning. They desired a change of course. They also desired a new system after the excesses of the Cultural Revolution. As Premier Zhao Ziyang once remarked to the author, "the Cultural Revolution did great harm to China, but it helped us get rid of many ideological restrictions."

Fourth, there was political stability while the reform took place. The Communist Party remained in power and was able to exercise leadership during the reform process.

Fifth, much credit must be given to the Chinese leaders themselves. Deng in particular should take most of the credit for working behind the scenes to oversee the general direction of the reform. He advocated pragmatism and experimentation. He had to get the support of high-level members of the Communist Party. Some top leaders were not willing to let China deviate from its traditional course, and there was a difficult political balancing act at the top level of the Communist Party. It is difficult to imagine another leader who could have done as well in leading China during the first two decades of reform. Without Deng, the reform would not have been so successful even if it had taken a market-oriented direction in the first place. There were also Zhao Ziyang, a brilliant economic thinker who served as the Premier and later Party General Secretary, and who designed and carried out economic reform, and Hu Yaobang, the humane and highly respected Party Secretary. The subsequent Premier, Zhu Rongji, was also very skillful in managing the economy while General Secretary Jiang Zemin kept the country and the Party in order. There have been numerous able officials in the Chinese government whose contributions cannot be enumerated here. It should be pointed out that the political process practiced in China has been capable of selecting and promoting able and, especially, college-educated people in the government, but the process has not been perfect and the economic system itself has bred corruption.

At the beginning of this chapter we asked whether the initiation of economic reform in 1978 was inevitable. After observing the success of the reform by the early 1990s one can also ask whether success was inevitable. My answer is yes. Given the pragmatic attitude and the ability of the Chinese leaders and government officials, as well as the willingness to experiment and the support of the people, there was no way for the reform *in China* toward a market economy to fail, unless a market economic system does not work better than a planned economy (which no economist believes). Why did almost no one in 1979 forecast the rapid transformation and growth of the Chinese economy that followed? First, very few people at the time understood that these were sufficient conditions for the success of the economic reforms. Perhaps most of the able Chinese leaders themselves did not understand all the conditions. They may have had confidence in their own ability, but may not have known that the market economy could work so well. They may not have known how much support they would get from the people. Second, note the "*in China*" part of the above statement about inevitability. The high degree of success of the reform process was partly due to the accompanying rapid growth of GDP to which able Chinese laborers and entrepreneurs contributed. At a given stage of reform, the human capital of the Chinese people (though this is difficult to measure) made the economy grow fast, and the rapid growth itself pushed the reform forward. The success is judged mainly by the rapid economic growth, and not merely by the extent to which the economy has been transformed to a market economy. Even if institutional changes were limited when judged by the latter criterion, the reform would be considered successful if there were substantial growth. Thus while Chinese laborers and entrepreneurs might not have contributed much to the reform process directly, they contributed to it indirectly through their impact on the rate of economic growth. Not many people in 1979 recognized the quality of China's human capital *and* its role in promoting economic reform indirectly through increasing China's national output. *Without high-quality human capital, economic institutions and market incentives alone cannot produce rapid economic growth.* The important contribution of the Chinese population to the economic performance of Indonesia, Malaysia, Thailand, and Vietnam (before the Vietnam War), and the rapid economic growth of Hong Kong, Singapore, and Taiwan, not to mention the Chinese mainland itself, all attest to this proposition.

The above positive features of China's economic reform process need to be balanced by some qualifications. The political stability and the ability of the government to manage the economy were not perfect. In the late 1980s the banking reforms and monetary policy allowed the rapid increase of the money supply, by 50 percent in 1984 and over 30 percent per year in 1986–8, leading to inflation at an annual rate of 30 percent in the fall of 1988. In the meantime, reform provided opportunities for government officials to extract bribes through control of state assets and the rights to issue permits required to perform economic activities. Corruption became a serious problem. Inflation and corruption in the late 1980s created much discontent among the urban population. Student demonstrations started in April 1989 at the memorial of the death of Party Secretary Hu Yaobang and lasted until June. Tiananmen Square was occupied by thousands of students during the entire two-month period, with new groups of students coming from other parts of China continuously. There seemed to be no end to the student occupation as money was distributed to them from sources in Hong Kong and Taiwan, and perhaps from America as well. The government lost control of the situation and anarchy was likely to result. Failing to end the demonstration by other means, Deng Xiaoping decided to send tanks to disperse the students in Tiananmen Square. Hundreds of people were killed as the tanks approached the square, including citizens of Beijing who tried to stop the tanks and members of the Chinese Red Army. The whole world watched on television as the tanks approached Tiananmen Square, but it was too dark and too far for television cameras to pick up the scene when the tanks arrived at the square. The army and the tanks followed orders to disperse and not to kill the students in the square. By the time the tanks reached the square, about 2 a.m. on June 4, the students were wise enough to withdraw as they saw the tanks approaching.

All over the world, there was an immediate critical reaction to this incident, probably to an extent unexpected by Deng. The government officials and businessmen of many foreign countries refused to go to China. Foreign investment and tourism declined. The government suffered a big shock from internal disagreements on how to handle the demonstrations, which became widespread in several major cities, and from the negative reaction in many parts of the world. However, the policy of reform toward a market economy continued its course, contrary to the expectations of some foreign observers. In February 1992, during his visit to Shenzhen, Deng took the opportunity to reaffirm and in fact to push domestic economic liberalization and the open-door policy further. Later in the year, the Party Congress declared China's economy to be a socialist market economy. By the end of 1992 China had resumed its rapid growth path after the disruption of the Tiananmen incident. The incident served as a test of the stability of China's political system and the able leadership of Deng, who managed to regain support after so much external and internal criticism.

In discussing the reasons for the success of the reform process I have mentioned the contribution of millions of resourceful Chinese entrepreneurs and skillful and hard-working Chinese workers to economic growth. Chinese human capital contributed to growth once the reformed institutions permitted the people to utilize it effectively. Growth itself provides the momentum for more reform. In addition to domestic human capital, both human and financial capital were supplied by thousands of overseas Chinese, in Hong Kong and elsewhere in the world, and by foreign investors. The important contribution of human capital should not be surprising if one recalls that China was experiencing economic development in the 1920s and 1930s, even when there was political turmoil, because of the resourcefulness and energy of its people.

The degree of institutional reform achieved can be measured by the contributions of the market institutions to national output at the beginning of the twenty-first century. The *Statistical Yearbook of China, 1997* (p. 42) provides the following breakdown of the 1996 GDP of 6,859.4 billion yuan: primary industry, 1,388.4; secondary industry, 3,361.3 (0.87 industry and 0.13 construction); tertiary industry, 2,109.7 (0.26 trade, 0.17 transportation and communication). If all primary industry, namely agriculture, 75 percent of industry (since state enterprises account for less than 30 percent of gross industrial output and some of them are profit-oriented), and 50 percent of tertiary industry (since much of retail trade is private) are considered the output of profit-maximizing producers, then 1,388.4 plus 2,521.0 plus 1,054.9, or a total of 4,964.3 of the 6,859.4 billion yuan are so produced. This amounts to 72.4 percent of the Chinese economy being market driven, and is a good index of the stage which market economic reforms have reached. This 72 percent of market-driven gross domestic product happens to coincide with the 28 percent of gross industrial output value produced by state-owned enterprises reported at the end of section 3.7.

# 3.11  Summary

We began this chapter by explaining why China was ready for economic reforms in 1978. We then briefly reviewed the six aspects of economic reform: (1) agriculture, (2) state enterprises, (3) banking, (4) the open-door policy, (5) the nonstate sectors, and (6) institutional infrastructure. Agricultural reform was initiated from the grassroots and succeeded rapidly in returning to private farming. Reform of state-owned enterprises went through different stages and is not completed. Reasons have been provided for the difficulty in reforming state enterprises in contrast with the agricultural sector. Efforts to transform the People's Bank and the specialized banks were outlined briefly, but reform is far from complete. Under the open-door policy, foreign investment and foreign trade rapidly increased, both contributing to China's rapid development. In the meantime the nonstate sectors experienced dynamic growth, with the collective sector surpassing the state sector in industrial output. China's reform policies are similar to those of Taiwan two and a half decades earlier in the promotion of market forces, the reliance on the agricultural sector in the initial stage, the encouragement of exports, the emphasis on price stability, and the gradual decontrolling of foreign exchange. An interesting phenomenon was the blossoming of township and village enterprises operating without clear property rights, and the protection of a functioning modern legal system. The study of this phenomenon provides a challenge to economists accustomed to observing private enterprise in Western market economies. The institutional infrastructure, including the education and legal systems, was also improved in the process of economic reform.

During the two decades of reform, economic growth took place at a phenomenal rate of 9.6 percent per year on average. I have given five reasons for the success of the reform, including (1) the pragmatic approach of the economic reform officials, (2) the use of experimentation, (3) the support of the party and government officials as well as the population, (4) political stability, and (5) the capability of Chinese leaders, especially Deng Xiaoping. The last point illustrates that events in China were often influenced to a large extent by a small number of people. But not all of the phenomenal economic growth can be attributed to economic reform. The high quality and large quantity of human capital in China and the financial and nonfinancial contributions of overseas Chinese and foreign friends have helped greatly once they were given the opportunity to become involved after the reforms.

China's successful reform experience may or may not be relevant for other former Communist economies, depending on the circumstances of each country. I will mention two factors which contributed to the success of China's reform process and were absent from the former Soviet Union. One is the support of numerous overseas Chinese, including those living in Hong Kong and other parts of the world. These people contributed large amounts of financial and human capital to both the reform process and the development of the Chinese economy. The second is the human capital retained by Chinese farmers who still remembered how to operate as private farmers in 1978, whereas it has been suggested that Soviet farmers in the early 1990s were all trained as collective farmers and did not know how to run a private farm. Note also two favorable factors in the Chinese case which Russia could have adopted. These are the maintenance of a stable political system under the Communist Party and the use of gradualism and experimentation rather than rapid privatization in the reform of state enterprises. Economists and historians can debate whether Russia's economic reform would have been much more successful if this alternative course had been taken.

The subject matter of chapters 3 and 4, and several later chapters on particular economic institutions, is the dynamic process of transforming economic institutions. The economics of transition, dealing with this process, has become an important topic in economics because of the reforms in China and in other formerly Socialist countries. The field differs from much of traditional economics in not taking economic institutions as a given. The economics of transition deals with problems facing economies in the process of institutional changes. In the study of the transformation of economic institutions, two important issues are of particular interest. One is the choice between gradual change and rapid change – this is the issue of gradualism versus "shock therapy." For example, under the latter policy, prices are decontrolled almost immediately and state-owned enterprises are privatized quickly. The second is the relative roles of the central government action and the nongovernment sectors, and the interaction of the two, in the economic reform process: how much action the government should take and where and when institutional changes should be allowed to evolve naturally by market forces. China's reform has followed the course of gradualism. Some institutions, including the household responsibility system in agriculture and the growth of township and village enterprises, resulted from natural market forces once the government allowed them to evolve.

As an appendix to this chapter I provide a brief description of China's geography together with a map of China. In the next chapter I will discuss the problems and prospects of reform at the beginning of the twenty-first century.

# Appendix: China's Geography

China is situated in the eastern and southeastern part of Asia, with its coast bordering the Pacific Ocean. It is the third largest country in the world, after Russia and Canada, having 9.6 million square kilometers in land area. It occupies one-quarter of the area of Asia and one-fifteenth of the area of the globe. There are many climatic zones, varying from tropical and equatorial in the south to frigid-temperate in the north. There are mountains and plateaus in the west and plains and hilly areas in the coastal regions along the Pacific ocean. Two great rivers, the Yellow River and the Yangtze, flow from the west to the east. High rainfall is concentrated in the coastal areas. The country's farmland covers about one-tenth of total land area. It is found mainly in the northeastern provinces, the north, areas around the Yangtze, and the Pearl River Delta in Guangdong Province. There are rich mineral deposits.

Administratively China is divided into 27 provinces or autonomous regions and 4 municipalities directly under the supervision of the central government. The former include (1) Hebei, (2) Shanxi, (3) Inner Mogolia [in the central north], (4) Liaoning, (5) Jilin, (6) Heilongjiang [in the northeast], (7) Jiangsu, (8) Zhejiang, (9) Anhui, (10) Fujian, (11) Jiangxi, (12) Shandong [along or close to the east coast], (13) Henan, (14)

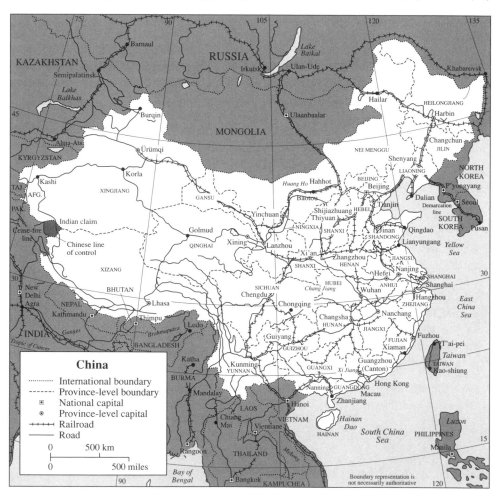

**Figure 3.1**   Contemporary China

Hubei, (15) Hunan, (16) Guangdong, (17) Guangxi, (18) Hainan [in the middle and south], (19) Sichuan, (20) Guizhou, (21) Yunnan, (22) Tibet [in the west and southwest], (23) Shanxi, (24) Gansu, (25) Qinghai, (26) Ningxia, and (27) Xinjiang [in the north-west]. The last 9 listed provinces in the western region are relatively poor, and targeted for more rapid economic development in a national effort to equalize the incomes of different regions. Western development will be discussed in chapter 10. The municipalities include Beijing, and Tianjin in the north, Shanghai at the delta of the Yangtze River, and Chongqing, formerly the capital of Sichuan province and designated in 1999 as a municipality in order to serve as the administrative center for developing the west.

See figure 3.1 for a map of China including these administrative divisions.

# References and Further Reading

*China 2020*, ch. 1. Washington, DC: World Bank, 1997.

Chow, Gregory C. "Market Socialism and Economic Development in China." Research Memorandum 340. Princeton: Princeton University Econometric Research Program, 1988.

Chow, Gregory C. "Capital Formation and Economic Growth in China." *Quarterly Journal of Economics*, 108 (Aug. 1993), pp. 809–42.

Chow, Gregory C. *Understanding China's Economy*, part I. Singapore: World Scientific Publishing Company, 1994.

Ishihara, Kyoichi. *China's Conversion to a Market Economy*. Tokyo: Institute of Development Economies, 1993.

Kuo, Shirley W. Y. *The Taiwan Economy in Transition*. Boulder, CO: Westview Press, 1983.

Li, K. T. *The Experience of Dynamic Economic Growth in Taiwan*. New York: Mei Ya Publications, 1976.

Lin, Justin Yifu. "The Household Responsibility System in China's Agricultural Reform: A Theoretical and Empirical Study." *Economic Development and Cultural Change*, 37 (April 1988), S199–S224.

Lin, Justin Yifu, Fang Cai, and Zhou Li. *The China Miracle: Development Strategy and Economic Reform*. Hong Kong: Chinese University Press, 1996.

Perkins, Dwight. "Reforming China's Economic System." *Journal of Economic Literature*, 26 (June 1988), pp. 601–45.

Reynolds, Bruce L. *Chinese Economic Reform: How Far, How Fast?* San Diego, CA: Academic Press, 1988.

Scott, Maurice. "Foreign Trade." In Walter Galenson, ed., *Economic Growth and Structural Change in Taiwan*. Ithaca, NY: Cornell University Press, 1979.

*Statistical Yearbook of China*. Beijing: State Statistical Bureau, various years.

*Statistical Yearbook of the Republic of China*. Taipei: Directorate General of Budget, Accounting and Statistics, various years.

Tsiang, S. C., Klein, L. R., and Nerlove, M. "Exchange Rate, Interest Rate, and Economic Development." *Quantitative Economics and Development*. New York: Academic Press, 1980, pp. 309–46.

Vogel, Ezra. *One Step Ahead in China: Guangdong Under Reform*. Cambridge, MA: Harvard University Press, 1989.

Zhou, Kate Xiao. *How the Farmers Changed China: Power of the People*. Boulder, CO: Westview Press, 1996.

# Questions

1 Name four major economic institutions that needed to be reformed in 1978 for China to become a market economy. Describe each institution briefly.

2 Ezra Vogel, in his book *One Step Ahead in China* (1989), gives examples of reform policies first allowed in the province of Guangdong. What are some of these policies?

3 Dwight Perkins (1988) discusses China's reform processes in the 1980s. What topics does he raise which are omitted in the discussion in this chapter?

4 The "household responsibility system" in Chinese agriculture amounts to having the farmers pay a fixed rent to lease the land for farming. Using a diagram, with output measured along the horizontal axis and revenue and cost along the vertical axis, as in standard economic texts, explain why the introduction of a fixed cost does not affect the output of a profit-maximizing farm.

5 When the "contract responsibility system" was introduced in 1987, under which a state enterprise paid a fixed tax to the government and retained the remaining profits for itself, was the economic incentive for the management of a state enterprise the same as for a farm household under the responsibility system? Why or why not? Were the conditions affecting economic efficiency the same? Why or why not?

6 China has had several episodes of inflation between 1978 and the present. Plot the inflation rate $y$ in percent per year against the percentage rate of increase $x$ in the supply of currency circulation of the same year, and against the rate $x$ of the preceding year in a second diagram. What are the slopes of these two regression lines of $y$ on $x$?

7 In this chapter, what is the proposed measure of the increase in foreign trade in China? Can you suggest an alternative measure?

8 Similarly, what is the proposed measure of the increase in foreign investment? Can you suggest an alternative?

9 It has been suggested that the productive efficiency of state-owned enterprises has grown more slowly than that of collectively owned enterprises from 1985 to 1997. How would you measure the rate of growth of productive efficiency? What data would be needed to compute this measure?

10 Discuss the important steps taken in reforming China's education system.

11 Discuss the important characteristics of the Chinese legal system.

12 Cite three conditions favorable to the success of China's economic reform which were absent in the Soviet Union in the 1990s.

# 4

# Further Reform:
# Problems and Prospects

This chapter discusses major problems facing the Chinese economy and the prospects for its continued successful transformation and rapid growth. The sectors covered include state-owned enterprises, the banking sector, foreign trade and investment, and agriculture. The impact of China's entry into the WTO on its economic, legal, and political institutions is also examined.

## 4.1   Introduction

China's economic transformation is a continuing process. The economic institutions of all countries change continuously, but those in transition from a planned economy like China's are experiencing more institutional changes by design. We have described the most important changes from 1978 to the mid-1990s in the previous chapter. The state-enterprise system, the banking and financial system, the system for foreign trade and investment, and the agricultural sector were facing unresolved problems in the 2000s, which we will presently describe. We will also include in this chapter an evaluation of the impacts of China's joining the World Trade Organization and an examination of the factors affecting the prospects for future development of the economy. This chapter is a survey of the economic institutions and problems. Specific sectors will be discussed in more detail and depth in later chapters.

## 4.2   Enterprise Reform

In his report to the Fifteenth Congress of the Chinese Communist Party in September 1997, General Secretary Jiang Zemin devoted section V to "Economic Restructuring and Economic Development Strategy," stating:

The state-owned sector must take up a dominant position in major industries and key areas . . . but in other areas, efforts should be made to reorganize assets. We should support, encourage and help diverse forms of collective economy . . . in their development . . . Public ownership can and should take multiple forms . . . Now there have appeared a large number of diverse forms of joint stock cooperative ventures in the urban and rural areas . . . Properly manage large enterprises while relaxing control over small ones . . . We should encourage mergers, standardize bankruptcy procedure, divert laid-off workers, increase efficiency by downsizing staff, and encourage reemployment projects . . . The Party and the government . . . will help them with their welfare, organize job training, open up new avenues of employment . . . We shall build a social security system, introducing an old-age pension and medical insurance system . . . , and improve the unemployment insurance and social relief systems. Establish public accumulation of funds for urban housing and accelerate the reform of the housing system.

From this statement several important points should be observed. First, the government still intends to maintain ownership and control of certain major industries. Second, the development of the nonstate sectors is being encouraged. Third, the development of state-owned enterprises can take multiple forms. The large state enterprises will be better managed and control will be relaxed over the small ones. Fourth, in the process of reforming and downsizing the state enterprises, the government has the responsibility of providing job training and a social security system to protect the welfare of workers.

There are four types of enterprises in China: state-owned, collective, individual-owned, and overseas-funded. The state-owned sector has declined in importance steadily since the early 1980s. It accounts for less than 30 percent of total industrial output at the turn of the century. Inefficiency of state enterprises has been said to be a major problem in the Chinese economy. But the seriousness of this problem is exaggerated on two counts. First, the productivity of state enterprises has been steadily increasing in the last two decades, although at a slower rate than that of the collective and private sectors. Second, the relative importance of the state enterprises has been declining and the effect of the performance of the state sector on the growth of the entire economy is less important than before. To the government and to the economy, however, state enterprises are still a big burden. They require government subsidies; the entitlement of staff and workers is a drain on the government budget and economic resources. And the entitlement includes more than their wages: the entire support system, including schools for their children, healthcare for their families, and retirement benefits, is very costly. Reducing the size of the enterprises creates an unemployment problem.

Several factors affect the economic efficiency of the state enterprises. There is a shortage of competent and well-trained managers and staff to operate a modern enterprise, alongside which there is a tendency to make management decisions based on personal relations and for personal gain at the expense of the enterprise. This is part of the bureaucratic tradition, magnified under the institution of central planning. An enterprise manager, like a bureaucrat, has control over economic assets which can be used for personal benefit, as we will discuss in chapters 15 and 19. The system does not provide the management with appropriate incentives to work for the benefit of the enterprise – they are on a much lower pay-scale than managers in similar collective enterprises. Nor is there a suitable governance system. Many staff and workers still have the habit of the "iron rice bowl," i.e. relying on the state to guarantee their job security. In addition, the equipment and technology of some state enterprises need to be updated. One important condition more favorable to the reform of state enterprises than the reform of the banking sector is the high degree of competition from collective and foreign enterprises in both the domestic and foreign markets. Competition has forced the state enterprises to be more efficient, but has not been allowed to enter the banking sector to the same extent.

The main avenue of continued reform of state enterprises, as stated in the report of General Secretary Jiang Zemin, is to change them to shareholding companies. For the small and medium-sized enterprises, restructuring has taken place whereby managers and workers purchased shares according to their wages, and members of a board of directors were elected by the shareholders. For example, if the monthly wage of a worker is 600 yuan, he or she may pay 2,000 yuan for the shares, while the high-level managers may pay 5,000 to 10,000 yuan for the shares. The shares can be traded among shareholders but are not sold to the public. For large state enterprises, restructuring takes a variety of forms, but mostly the form of a shareholding corporation. Shares can be purchased by outsiders. The shares of a minority of state enterprises which are qualified according to their financial performance can be traded in the Shanghai, Shenzhen, Hong Kong, and even the New York stock exchanges according to the regulations of the exchanges. Various levels of government retained controlling shares for the very large and important state enterprises, following the principle enunciated by General Secretary Jiang in September 1997. Others were sold to overseas Chinese and other foreign owners.

The State Economic and Trade Commission and its branches at provincial, city, and county levels are responsible for restructuring the state enterprises under their jurisdiction. Directions on restructuring are given centrally in Beijing at meetings involving Party and government leaders of all provinces. These officials in turn transmit the directions to lower levels in all parts of China. As economic adviser to the Shandong Provincial Government, I met with officials of the Economic and Trade Commission in Shandong on issues of enterprise reform and visited a number of state enterprises which had recently been transformed to shareholding companies in 1997–8. The level of competence of these officials was high.

To appraise the prospects of success of the effort to restructure state enterprises in China, the following observations can be made. First, restructuring efforts in the early 2000s are a continuation of a series of attempts beginning in 1979 to reform the state enterprises to make them financially independent, efficient, and profitable. It is an evolutionary process, and dramatic results should not be expected in a short time. Second, there is a tendency for the managers of state enterprises to hold onto their power and resist changes. Third, the success of an enterprise depends on many factors, of which its ownership and governance structure are only two. Other important factors are the ability and resourcefulness of its managers and workers, the particular industry it is in, the degree of competition, etc. No matter how the corporations of a country are organized, some will make profits while others will lose money. Restructuring cannot make all, or almost all, Chinese state enterprises profitable, as they are subject to competition from collective and foreign companies. Fourth, on the positive side, the problems with state enterprises are not so urgent that they require immediate solutions. The government is proceeding at a deliberate speed. It is making sure that not too many workers are laid off in any period, that the laid-off workers are given some compensation, usually equal to about one-third of their monthly wage, and are provided training to reenter the job market. Fifth, also on the positive side, by allowing foreign capital, management, and technology to come in through joint ventures and even buyouts of failing state enterprises, many have been and will be improved in performance. The topic of state enterprise behavior will be discussed in more depth in chapter 15.

In the latter part of 1998, when the Asian financial crisis was affecting the Chinese economy, the privatization of state enterprises was slowed down for fear that the selling prices of the enterprises might become too low and corrupt officials might benefit from the sales when there was insufficient government supervision. In March 1998, Premier Zhu Rongji announced that the state-enterprise restructuring should be completed in three years. His main objectives were to make profitable the majority of the 50 largest state enterprises, which were operating at a loss, and to restructure most small and medium-sized state enterprises into shareholding companies. The announcement of these objectives served to rally government officials to speed up the reform. By January 2001, the government reported that two-thirds of the 6,600 largest state-owned enterprises had surrendered to the state net profits in the year 2000 totaling 230 billion yuan, although some might have falsified their accounts under pressure, as the government acknowledged.

Two serious consequences of failing state enterprises are the bad debts they owe the state banks and the unemployment of laid-off workers due to restructuring. The former is unlikely to lead to a banking crisis; we will look at this more closely in the next section. Besides the unemployment problem, some workers had their wages reduced, possibly by 50 percent or more. Some did not receive their regular salaries. These problems are concentrated in provinces with a large number of state enterprises, including the provinces in the northeast. But the unemployment problem in China should remain under control for three reasons. First, as just pointed out, the pace of enterprise restructuring in terms of laying off workers is being monitored and will not be so rapid that it creates excessive unemployment. Second, the Chinese people are resourceful and the market economy is working, and thus many laid-off workers have found other jobs in the market, especially in the service sector. Third, the government is stimulating the economy by building infrastructure at a higher rate than was previously planned. This will create employment.

## 4.3   Banking Reform

Before banking reform started in the early 1980s the People's Bank of China served mainly to issue currency, to accept savings deposits from the public, and to provide credit to state enterprises under the guidance of central planning. In 1983 the People's Bank was officially changed to a central bank, but it did not function as one because commercial banks did not exist. Rather, there were four specialized banks: the Industrial and Commercial Bank, the Agricultural Bank, the People's Construction Bank, and the Bank of China (which dealt with foreign transactions). The first three were given some autonomy to extend credit to state enterprises, but were also subject to central government direction. They were under local political pressures to extend credits for regional economic development. As a result, excessive expansion of credit led to inflation in 1985, 1988, and 1993. The chief tool to stop credit expansion was the imposition of credit quotas. In March and May 1995 the People's Congress passed the Law on the People's Bank of China and the Commercial Bank Law, respectively. Both are modern in content, making the People's Bank a modern central bank and the specialized banks modern commercial banks – *in principle*, though not in practice, as economic institutions do not change by legislation alone.

To relieve the four state banks of political pressure to extend credit, three "policy banks" were created in 1994 to provide loans to state enterprises for the purpose of carrying out particular economic development policies. These are the State Development Bank, the Agricultural Development Bank, and the Import and Export Bank. By early 1998 these policy banks accounted for only about 6 percent of the loans of the big four banks. Since the early 1990s, new commercial banks have also appeared on the scene, taking the form of corporations with shareholders and boards of directors. However, the largest, the Bank of Communication, has only government organizations at different levels as shareholders, while the others have private enterprises but not individuals as shareholders. In the late 1990s these banks accounted for about 15 to 20 percent of loans and 8 to 10 percent of deposits. These new banks have more flexibility in decision-making and function slightly more like modern commercial banks. Their ownership structure has prevented them from operating more efficiently.

Modernization of the Chinese banking system will take time. Bank managers still behave like bureaucrats holding onto their economic power. There is still political pressure and economic temptation to extend credit at higher risk than benefit–cost calculations justify. The management and staff need more training and experience before they can operate as modern commercial bankers.

Furthermore, of their loan totals, the four state banks are coping with 20 to 25 percent nonperforming loans, some US$200 billion out of a total of nearly US$1 trillion, as a result of past obligations to finance state enterprises. About 80 percent of all the loans of the four state banks consist of loans to state enterprises. To solve these problems a number of measures were taken in the late 1990s. Thereafter, local bank managers were appointed by the bank's headquarters, not subject to approval of the local government, and the four state banks were free from local-government interference in their credit policy. The loan quota system has been abolished but the state banks are still required to make loans to finance government investment. The central bank issued a directive in 1997 requiring the state banks to reduce the percentage of nonperforming loans by 2 to 3 percent per year in each of the following 7 years. An RMB270 billion (RMB = "the people's currency") bond issue was planned to increase the capital–loan ratios of the state banks. The People's Bank was required to behave like the US Federal Reserve system, providing closer supervision of the behavior of the commercial banks.

Is the Chinese banking system in a crisis situation? The answer appears to be no, in spite of the problems and shortcomings of the system just mentioned. In a market economy with a modern banking system a banking crisis occurs when many loans become nonperforming. As a consequence, banks do not have liquidity to pay depositors, and the depositors withdraw their deposits, further aggravating the liquidity problem. Numerous bad loans usually result from unprofitable investment in real estate, construction, infrastructure-building, or other major productive activities in an overheated economy. This was an essential characteristic of the finance sectors of the countries which experienced the 1997–9 financial crisis in Asia. The Chinese situation is different. Speculative investments, though they exist in the real estate markets and in the production of consumer goods, are less serious and subject to government supervision. More importantly, people have confidence in the value of their deposits in the banks because they believe that the government owns the banks and implicitly guarantees their deposits. The fact that 20 to 25 percent of total bank loans are bad has not affected this confidence and is not likely to lead to large withdrawals of deposits. Given the high savings rate of the Chinese people and the limited alternatives for their savings, in the decade of the 1990s the ratio of savings deposits to GDP in China was rising: personal bank deposits increased by 23 percent in 1997, though at the lowest rate in a decade, partly because other forms of liquid assets have become available. Improvement in liquidity in the banking sector was further evidenced by the reduction of its loans-to-deposits ratio from 200 percent in 1991 to 140 percent in 1998.

The large amount of nonperforming loans in the banking system was a symptom rather than a major cause of the Asian financial crisis of 1997–9. The crisis started in Thailand in July 1997, when the Thai baht was suddenly devalued and a large amount of foreign capital was instantly withdrawn. Three major conditions were responsible. First is the development of modern financial institutions which make international capital flows extremely rapid. Second is a speculative bubble associated with overinvestment in real estate and industry in Thailand in conditions of rapid economic growth. The third is the failure of the Thai government to devalue its currency. It tried to support the exchange rate by selling dollar futures so that the loss of foreign reserves was not recognized until the date of payment. Once this was recognized, the foreign investors and the public in general lost confidence in the baht, causing a rapid devaluation and more outflow of foreign capital. Without the support of foreign short-term capital, the banking system became illiquid and unable to provide working capital to the manufacturing sector. Lack of confidence in investment prospects in Thailand led international investors to withdraw their short-term capital from other Asian countries, including Indonesia, Malaysia, and South Korea. This is the phenomenon of contagion in a financial crisis.

Conditions similar to those causing a financial crisis in Thailand could lead to a financial crisis in other countries. Speculative bubbles from overinvestment and the sudden withdrawal of foreign capital in today's financial institutions could and did occur in other countries. Soon after the Asian crisis there were financial crises in Russia and Brazil in 1998. Financial crisis has been a feature of capitalist economies for at least a century, now amplified by the free flow of financial capital across national borders. There is no need to appeal to a notion of Asian "crony capitalism" as the cause of the Asian financial crisis of 1997–9. Financial institutions in Asian countries certainly have their shortcomings; but these did not prevent the Asian countries from growing rapidly before 1997 and recovering after 1999.

Conditions in China during this period were different. First, much larger percentages of foreign investment in countries like Thailand, Malaysia, and Indonesia were portfolio or financial in nature. Foreign investors could, and did, withdraw their money quickly when investment opportunities appeared unfavorable. Most foreign investments in China, on the other hand, were in the form of direct investment that could not be withdrawn at short notice. Moreover, capital flows in and out of China are restricted. Second, the governments in Thailand and Indonesia maintained exchange rates which overvalued their own currencies before the crisis occurred. The central bank of Thailand covered up the loss of a large amount of foreign reserve to support the Thai currency by selling dollars in the futures market. Once the loss of foreign reserves and the overvaluation of the Thai baht were recognized by investors, the risk to their investments became apparent and they withdrew their money swiftly, leading to a sharp devaluation of the baht. The Chinese currency was not overvalued. Third, as mentioned above, the Chinese banking system is different in the sense that the people consider it to be a government institution that protects their deposits, making a bank-run unlikely.

In order to deal with the large amounts of bad debt in the balance sheets of the four large state-owned commercial banks, the Chinese government in 1999 set up four asset-management companies, each serving to restructure the bad debts of one large bank. The method of restructuring is for the asset management company to take over the bad debts of the bank it serves in exchange for its own debt. The purpose is to strengthen the structure of the balance sheet of the commercial banks. The asset-management company in turn tries to collect from the state enterprises part or the whole of the debts in its possession. It has the power to supervise and monitor the financial position of the state enterprises, being their creditor. It can also sell the debts in the market, possibly at a price below book value.

Whether the asset-management companies (AMCs) will succeed or not depends on their ability to fight the bureaucracy in both the state banks and the state-owned enterprises. The AMCs have to convince the state banks to reduce the book values of their assets and to collect money from the state enterprises in debt. Besides the ability of the managers of AMCs to perform these required tasks, there may also be a lack of incentive on their part. The AMCs themselves are state-owned enterprises and are subject to the shortcomings of the enterprises they are attempting to reform. Lack of power, lack of incentive, and possible lack of able personnel will affect the prospects for successful restructuring of the bad debts in China's commercial banks. As long as the bad debts do not increase rapidly and the Chinese people keep on making deposits, the commercial banks will continue to function.

Banking reform is only one aspect of the reform process and shares some of the characteristics of reform in other state sectors. First, it has been a gradual process, allowing the institutions to evolve so that the reformers can learn which options are best for China, and permitting experimentation to test the effectiveness of the options and to prepare the people to adjust to the new institutions. Second, to the extent that the People's

Bank was a part of the central planning apparatus and the commercial banks are mostly state-owned, the reform is slow because of bureaucratic resistance. Third, reform of the commercial banks should draw from experience in the partially successful reform of the state enterprises (the responsibility system, use of joint ventures, and encouraging competition from the private sector) and in the successful development of the nonstate sector (including the rural and urban credit cooperatives, and the entry of foreign banks and banks from Hong Kong and Taiwan). In spite of its present shortcomings, the Chinese banking system appears to be serving some basic functions of financial intermediation, although not efficiently. The banking system can be expected to improve in time, but only slowly. China's banking and financial system will be more thoroughly discussed in chapter 13.

## 4.4   Foreign Trade and Investment during the Asian Financial Crisis

After the introduction of the open-door policy in China, foreign trade and investment have continued to increase. In 1997, when the Asian financial crisis occurred, total exports amounted to US$182.7 billion, about 20 percent of GDP. This figure represents an increase of 21 percent from 1996, compared with a growth rate of only 1.5 percent from 1995 to 1996. Imports to China totaled $142.4 billion in 1997, resulting in a trade surplus of $40.3 billion. Total trade volume was $325.6 billion in 1997, about 36 percent of GDP. In March 1998, foreign trade volume was 7.9 percent higher than a year before, with exports increasing 9.24 percent and imports increasing 6.23 percent. However, in May 1998 exports fell by 1.5 percent, falling for the first time in 22 months, and the January–May export growth rate was reduced to only 8.6 percent. By September 1998, exports were down 6.7 percent compared with the previous year, although the trade surplus was maintained by the reduction of imports.

As a component of aggregate demand, exports were weakened as a result of the currency devaluations in, and the reduced demand from, several Asian countries including Japan during the Asian financial crisis of 1997–9. While some of the state-owned companies engaged in foreign trade were not doing well, private and foreign-invested companies were taking an active role in promoting Chinese exports in a variety of consumer goods to the world market. In the first four months of 1998, foreign-invested companies exported some 42 percent of the national total. Even when the rate of increase in the volume of exports was smaller in 1998, the rate of growth in GDP was affected only moderately because exports account for only 20 percent of GDP. (Note that in 1996 China's GDP grew by 9.6 percent while its exports grew by only 1.5 percent.) In the meantime the government adopted a variety of measures to stimulate exports, including the lowering of export duties and the refund of taxes on raw materials used to produce exports.

In 1997 the flow of foreign direct investment (FDI) continued to be strong, 10.1 percent higher than 1996. In the first five months of 1998, FDI fell by 1.49 percent compared with the same period in 1997. The trade surplus and the surplus in the capital account helped increase the amount of foreign reserves in China from $2.3 billion in 1977 to $142.8 billion by the end of 1997. Since China continued to have a trade surplus during the first few months of 1998, and foreign investment continued to flow in (though at a slower rate), foreign-exchange reserves should have been accumulating accordingly, but in fact increased much more slowly in the first few months of 1998 for reasons to be discussed below.

Besides the inflow of foreign reserves from a trade surplus and from foreign investment, the value of Chinese currency was supported by a large amount of foreign reserves and by its strong purchasing power. China's currency was strong compared with the US dollar, at an exchange rate of 8.3 yuan per dollar, because China had a lower inflation rate than the United States. Retail prices in China in March 1998 were 1.2 percent lower than in the same period in 1997 and remained nearly constant in the middle of 1998. These factors provided strong fundamentals for the value of the Chinese currency and made a devaluation unnecessary. Even if the trade surplus were to fall because of competition in the world markets from Asian countries which had devalued their currencies, the economic fundamentals and the political will of the Chinese leadership were strong enough to prevent a devaluation of Chinese currency. Earlier in 1998, when both President Jiang Zemin and Premier Zhu Rongji pronounced that there would not be a devaluation, they intended the Chinese economy to serve as a stabilizing force in the financial crisis. The Chinese economy was strong enough to play such a role.

Nevertheless, in spite of strong fundamentals supporting the value of the Chinese currency, many people inside and outside of China were still expecting the RMB to devalue against the dollar. The lack of confidence in the future value of the RMB, partly caused by misconceptions of the Western press, led people to put some of their money in US dollars rather than in RMB and Chinese exporters to retain their foreign-currency earnings abroad. As a result, China's foreign reserve increased by only $1 billion in 1998 from $140 billion, even when there was a trade surplus of $30 billion and an inflow of foreign investment of $27 billion. The black (free) market rate on the RMB in Hong Kong was about 10 percent lower than the official rate in October 1998. Thus there was a devaluation of Chinese currency in terms of the market rate, although not in the official rate.

Observing the weakening of the RMB, the government decided to impose restrictions on the flow of foreign currency out of China. The restrictions made it more difficult to obtain approval for legal applications for foreign exchange. Chinese officials claimed that such restrictions only meant enforcing existing laws, but in practice, delays and the inconvenience of obtaining foreign currency made the yuan less convertible and the stable official exchange rate economically less meaningful. The risk of outflow of foreign capital evident during the financial crisis also slowed down the opening of the Chinese capital account, which would usually follow the opening of foreign-trade transactions in the process of economic development.

Fundamentally the yuan was a strong currency because of the slow inflation rate, the large stock of China's foreign reserves, and the continued increase in foreign reserves from a trade surplus and the flow of foreign investment. If neighboring countries had retaliated by further devaluing their currencies, it would have diminished any possible gain from China's devaluation. From a political perspective, the government tried to maintain the value of the RMB because it was attempting to play a positive role in contributing to the stability of Asian financial markets. At the end of 2000, the general and unjustified skepticism about the stable value of the RMB had already yielded to the economic fundamentals. The free-market exchange rate of the yuan in Hong Kong and in mainland China returned to or even slightly exceeded its official exchange rate. As the same economic fundamentals continue to operate at present, in the longer run the yuan may have a tendency to appreciate against the dollar, just as the Japanese yen did during the 1960s to 1980s, a period of rapid Japanese economic growth and export expansion.

## 4.5    The Impact of WTO Membership

At the turn of the twenty-first century, China was in the process of joining the World Trade Organization (WTO). Members of the organization receive the benefits of having access to the markets of fellow members and bear the costs of opening their own domestic markets to foreign competitors. The conditions for China to enter WTO include: (1) the lowering of tariffs on imports, (2) permitting foreign firms to sell directly in Chinese domestic markets, and (3) the opening of the telecommunication and finance sectors to more foreign competition. China agreed to lower its tariffs on agricultural products from 31.5 percent to 14.5 percent overall by January 2004. Tariffs on industrial products would be lowered from 35 to 17 percent in a period of five years. Foreign manufacturers, including automobile companies, would be able to sell their products directly to domestic consumers without having to go through Chinese trade organizations. China also agreed to open its service industries. Foreign investors would be able to own up to 40 percent of the shares in commercial banks in China, and up to 48 percent of telecommunications and insurance companies, to increase to 50 percent two years after joining the WTO. Foreign banks would be able to offer services in local currencies to Chinese corporations. Foreign firms would be able to hold minority shares in securities fund management joint ventures, at 33 percent initially and increasing to 49 percent three years after joining. Foreign firms would also be able to provide accounting, management consulting, architecture, and engineering services.

   The lowering of tariffs would lead to an increase in the imports of both agricultural and industrial products for consumers. The prices of these products are expected to decline and the quality of the products would improve, both to the benefit of Chinese consumers. Competition will force Chinese producers to lower their prices and improve the quality of their products. Those firms that cannot compete will have to adjust, some possibly going bankrupt. Foreign manufacturers operating in China will also provide competition, with effects similar to those of lowering tariffs on imports. Local foreign producers have the advantages over importers of being able to use the low-cost labor in China and saving the cost of transporting the final products to China. Financial and telecommunication firms in China will have to upgrade their products to survive foreign competition.

**Table 4.1**  China's gross domestic product and its major components (yuan 100 millions)

| Year | GDP | Primary industry | Industry | Construction | Tertiary industry |
|------|-----|------------------|----------|--------------|-------------------|
| 1978 | 3,624.1 | 1,018.4 (0.281) | 1,607.0 (0.443) | 138.2 (0.038) | 860.5 (0.237) |
| 1988 | 14,928.3 | 3,831.0 (0.257) | 5,777.2 (0.387) | 810.0 (0.054) | 4,510.1 (0.302) |
| 1998 | 79,395.7 | 14,599.6 (0.184) | 33,429.8 (0.421) | 5,262.0 (0.066) | 26,104.3 (0.329) |

**Source**: China Statistical Yearbook, 1999.

WTO membership will also affect China's economic structure. Since WTO membership requires China to lower tariffs on agricultural and manufactured products and allows foreign firms to enter China's manufacturing and selected service sectors, there will be structural changes in China's economy. Structural changes include changes in the relative importance of different industrial sectors and of state versus nonstate sectors. In the former category, one expects the relative decline of the agricultural sectors and the relative increase in importance of certain service sectors dealing with financial services and telecommunications. In the latter category, one can expect the relative decline of the state sector compared with the nonstate sectors and a possible increase in the efficiency of Chinese enterprises as tariffs are lowered, foreign firms enter the Chinese market, and they are subjected to more foreign competition. These general observations can be made more specific by observing the historical trends in the relative growths of the major sectors.

Table 4.1 provides the statistics on China's gross domestic product and its major components. As is common in the process of economic development, the share of primary industry consisting of agriculture and forestry continued to decline from 0.281 (the figure in parentheses after the output value) in 1978 to 0.184 in 1998, while the fraction of tertiary industry continued to increase from 0.237 to 0.329. The 10 percentage-point decline in the share of primary industry from 1978 to 1998 was made up of a 9 percentage-point increase in the share of tertiary industry and a 1 percentage-point increase in industry and construction combined. The 6 percentage-point increase in the tertiary industry during the first decade was from trade, transportation, and communication, as these sectors had been neglected during the period of central planning. The slower increase in the relative share of tertiary industry in the second decade was made up of activities such as banking, finance, and telecommunications.

Tertiary industry is expected to increase its share of GDP partly as a result of China's entry into the WTO. The stimulus to the domestic service industry provided by foreign competition and expected foreign investment in this industry will lead to more rapid growth than otherwise. The high-technology component of the manufacturing sector will increase in importance partly because of the expected increase in foreign investment. The domestic manufacture of consumer durables – especially automobiles – will suffer from the increase in imports, while increased foreign investment in the automobile industry will help increase domestic production of automobiles. The net effect is likely to be a slower growth in the domestic automobile industry because domestic producers will not be able to produce automobiles of the same quality as cheaply as the competing imports. The expected growth in both the service and the manufacturing sectors will lead to a further decline in the share of agriculture, but this will take place even without entry into the WTO. The relative decline in the agriculture sector will be hastened by foreign competition from the lowering of tariffs on agricultural products. The total effect of WTO entry on China's industrial composition is limited, however, as I will suggest presently, after we discuss the impact on the nature of China's economic institutions.

Premier Zhu Rongji's main motivation for promoting China's entry into the WTO was to use foreign competition to speed up economic reform in both the industrial and service sectors. In the late 1990s reform in both sectors was slow because of the vested interests of a group of managers appointed under a previous administration and holding onto their positions. Simply formally changing the state enterprises to shareholding companies does not lead to the replacement of incumbent managers or to the adoption of new ways of doing things. The same inertia applies to the banking sector. Foreign competition provides a more powerful force to combat such inertia. Firms that fail to compete will have to find ways to downsize, to reorganize, or to adopt new technology and new ways of management to survive. But how successful such outside pressure will be depends on how strong the inertia is. In addition, for fear of creating too much social instability the government cannot and will not allow the competition to come in too rapidly. The slow speed of entry to China's market is codified in a schedule which lowers tariffs gradually and permits foreign firms to enter China's financial and telecommunications industries by steps. Informally, there is red tape and other means to delay foreign competition which can be exercised by central, provincial, and local government officials. These officials have the power to approve foreign economic activities in China, and they can use it with or without the direction of the central government in Beijing which signs the agreement to enter the WTO.

Such possible delays are recognized by Western observers. For example, in an article published on a business website, Heidi Brzybyla of *Bloomberg News* wrote:

> Hundreds of companies, from Boeing and Microsoft to Caterpillar and Ford, joined in a high-powered alliance to get the United States to back China's admission to the World Trade Organization. Now many executives acknowledge that it could be years before they see any real dividends.
>
> Automotive companies like Ford and Germany's Daimler Chrysler AG say sales will be limited because China will only gradually lift tariffs, distribution restrictions and other barriers. Some banks say China's offer of concession is vague. And US agricultural sales to China are expected to rise to $3 billion during the next five years – double the present level, but still less than 1 percent of projected farm exports in 2000.
>
> "We're looking on down the road," said Gina Capalbo, international government affairs manager at Ford. That is because China's limit on foreign ownership of automobile plants wasn't even addressed in the agreement, and tariff cuts won't be completed for another five years, Capalbo said. As a result, vehicle sales in China during the next five years will be "modest," she said. Ford, which owns a 30 percent stake in an assembly plant in China and has five joint-venture component factories, has no plans to build new facilities there because of the agreement, she said. (Brzybyla 1999)

This article quoted less-than-enthusiastic remarks from executives of Boeing, Motorola (the largest US investor in China), and Daimler Chrysler. Bankers say that their prospects of increasing business in China are unclear. The only concrete gain is expected from the reduction of agricultural tariffs from 31.5 to 14.5 percent overall by January 2004, and the termination of subsidies to Chinese exports. US farm exports to China are expected to increase.

Li et al. (1999) applied a dynamic computational general equilibrium model of the Chinese economy consisting of 41 sectors and 10 types of households to study the impact of WTO membership. Four aspects of WTO membership are discussed: (1) tariff reduction; (2) abolition of nontariff barriers to industrial products in steps; (3) increased import quotas on agricultural products and abolition of all import quotas eventually; (4) phasing out of quotas on China's exports of textiles and clothing to developed economies. The impact of WTO membership on economic growth comes from two sources. The first is the gain from specialization through international trade. This gain is achieved by a change in the composition of outputs. With lower tariffs and more foreign goods made available in domestic markets, total products for consumption will increase. Increased exports will also stimulate the growth of GDP. The second is the gain from increase in efficiency within each industrial sector. Competition from imports and from foreign-owned enterprises in China will force domestic firms to become more efficient.

The study estimated that China's real GDP in 2005 would be 1.5 percent higher from the first source due to the above policies. This increase is derived from increased specialization from trade according to China's comparative advantage, as WTO entry will allow more agricultural imports and textiles and clothing exports, in particular. If the gain in total factor productivity is incorporated, the average annual growth rate in GDP from 1997 to 2010 will be 1 percent higher after entry into the WTO. Bear in mind that the annual growth rate projected for this period is approximately 7.5 percent. I believe that it might serve as an upper bound on the effect of WTO entry. There will be inertia to inhibit the forces that promote both sources of output growth. In fact these forces were already operating in the 1990s, and are expected to operate even without WTO membership.

One should also consider the impact of WTO membership in hastening the modernization of China's legal system as it is forced to deal with more and more foreign firms. The impact on legal institutions will include changes in formal institutions and laws, and to some extent in the legal behavior of the Chinese people. Concerning the former, in the last two decades many new commercial laws governing corporate behavior, bankruptcy, the behavior of banks and other financial institutions have been enacted by the Chinese People's Congress. Furthermore, the Chinese judicial system for law enforcement has been modernized and improved. The practice of litigation is now more widespread and the number of lawyers has increased dramatically. We will discuss the modernization of the Chinese legal system in chapter 20. However, the people's lack of understanding of commercial law may be strong enough to make the change in their legal behavior slow. One example is the lack of respect for intellectual property. On October 5, 2000, the *New York Times* financial section reports that there was widespread pirating of a popular film produced by the central government itself, and the pirated copies were being shown in theaters all over the country, but the government could not stop it. This suggests that some Chinese people do not always follow the laws regarding matters related to money and business, although they appear to respect criminal codes to a larger extent. There are also signs at the beginning of the 2000s that as the country gets richer and the government makes greater efforts to enforce laws, Chinese citizens tend to be more law abiding. One important role of the WTO is to settle disputes on matters related to world trade between countries; this will help promote order in international business activities.

WTO membership will have an effect on China's political system also. From the description of the historical background of Communist Party rule in chapters 1 and 2, we can conclude that historical conditions in China were once not favorable to the development of democratic institutions. Beginning with imperial rule, there was no period of political stability between 1911 and 1949 for democratic institutions to develop, as a result of different political factions in China struggling for power and the pressures of Japanese imperialism. Communist Party rule since 1949 is both a positive and a negative factor in the development of democratic institutions. On the positive side, the Party has provided China with political stability and a unified government, and has led China through successful economic reform of the inefficient economic institutions of 1978. The Party has thus provided economic conditions favorable to the development of democratic institutions. On the negative side, the strict one-party rule has destroyed some of the initial growth of democratic institutions developed under the Republic of China, and has turned the clock backward on movement toward democracy.

The balance of the two sets of forces just mentioned has been positive since economic reform started in 1978, as the following evidence suggests. Progress towards democracy has already taken place to some extent in China, although perhaps to a lesser degree than the progress in economic development. First, the representatives to the People's Congress have always been elected, though indirectly: the representatives at the lowest level in villages or city blocks were publicly elected. Representatives at a higher level were elected from and by representatives of the level immediately below. However, before the early 1980s the representatives at the National People's Congress automatically passed the legislation proposed to them by the executive branch as decided by the Central Committee of the Chinese Communist Party. Since the 1980s representatives in the People's Congress have increasingly exercised their own power by casting negative votes to proposed legislation. Part of their autonomy is derived from the need to legislate new laws for a market economy. The new legislation has required experts in the Congress to form committees of specialists to draft the law.

A second noticeable change is the widespread village elections for government officials in thousands of villages all over China. After the commune system was abolished in the 1980s, many public services formerly administered by the communes were neglected, including public security, protection of public land and other resources, and so forth. People in villages decided to elect their government officials publicly to make sure that such services are provided. The election is open and fair. Many observers believe that these directly elected village governments can serve as the foundation for the establishment of democratic governments at higher levels. The position of the central government at the turn of the twentieth century was to protect and even encourage these village elections, for they serve a useful social function, but to limit them to the village level.

Concerning the future development of democratic institutions, one can expect that as the Chinese people become richer and more educated, they will be more interested in and more able to participate in democratic activities. Thus the demand for democratic institutions has increased and will continue to increase. On the supply side, institutional change can come from government initiatives and/or from political upheavals. The latter possibility appears unlikely since the Chinese people by and large appear to be happy with their economic conditions, and the minority of dissatisfied people do not seem to have the will or the power to overthrow the present government and establish their own government. Corruption, unemployment, and economic disparity are three important potential causes of dissatisfaction, but the number of people affected and the degree of dissatisfaction are not sufficient to generate political disruption on a national scale. Assuming no large-scale political disruption, the question is whether and how the current government will be willing to institute democratic reform.

In answering this question, one can reasonably assume that the Chinese Communist Party, like any political party in the world, is most concerned with maintaining its political power; and that democratic institutions will only be initiated or accepted if they do not threaten the Party's power. Nonetheless, there are forces in the Party structure which push the institution of democracy forward. I will only point out such forces at work, but cannot speculate on the specific mechanism for the establishment of democracy. Neither will I specify what Chinese democracy ought to be. For the purposes of the present discussion, I use the term "democratic institutions" to mean, broadly, institutions that guarantee citizens certain basic rights and allow them to participate in the election of representatives to the legislature and executive branch of government.

The positive forces for the development of democratic institutions include (1) the changing worldview of political leaders in China and (2) the changing environment in which the leaders exercise their political power. All top political leaders in China have traveled abroad and learned to some extent how modern democratic institutions function. New leaders have studied world affairs more recently, and some have been trained abroad and will assume greater political power in the future. The changing environment includes the inefficacy of old-fashioned political control by manipulating the news, when the news media have improved technologically to include radio and TV reception from Hong Kong and Taiwan, and, especially, information via the internet. Not only will the population demand more democratic institutions, but the willingness of the government to promote such institutions will also increase, provided that they are consistent with one-party rule. Working against these positive forces is the desire of bureaucrats to hold on to their power under existing rule. It is difficult to predict how political changes will take place to accommodate the social changes resulting from economic modernization initiated by the Communist Party. Without losing political control, the Party may be willing to share power and responsibility with a wider segment of Chinese society. In June 2001, capitalists were allowed to join the Party. Other means to increase democratic participation would be to support non-Party candidates in elections at higher than village levels, and to appoint non-Party officials in important government positions.

Membership in the WTO could increase both the demand for and the supply of democratic government. On the demand side, the further economic development and economic modernization made possible under the WTO will increase the people's interest in a democratic government and their ability to participate in it. On the supply side, the view of government leaders will become more global and modern-oriented: for example, speeding up the growth of the telecommunication industry will help to promote the development of a more open society. Such effects on the political institutions in China are positive, but one cannot expect them to change very rapidly. There are inhibitions derived from the historical, social, and bureaucratic traditions of China.

It is difficult to predict how political changes will take place to accommodate the social changes resulting from the economic modernization initiated by the Communist Party. However, to maintain political stability, the Party needs to make adjustments in response to the reality which its economic reform policies have created. If it wishes to do this without losing its political control, one solution is to share some of its political power and responsibility with wider segments of Chinese society. One example is the announcement on July 1, 2001 (the eightieth anniversary of the founding of the Party), by General Secretary Jiang Zemin, that capitalists will be allowed to join the Party. Other means to increase democratic participation are to encourage or support non-Party candidates in elections for offices at higher than village levels, and to nominate or appoint non-Party members for important government positions. Meanwhile, the old ideology of the revolutionary period has to be modified to include principles required to lead and govern a modern society, such as more freedom of expression.

In summary, I have suggested reasons the WTO membership could have positive impacts on China's institutions. The impacts are small, because the provisions of the membership are limited in scope. The effects are expected to be gradual, not only because the terms of membership are introduced in steps, but because economic, legal, and political institutions are difficult to change. There is inertia in all three sets of institutions. Besides the formal provisions to open China's economy gradually, the central government is monitoring the speed of changes to avoid social instability. At the same time, the local governments and bureaucrats will slow the changes with red tape if they find them too threatening to local economic institutions.

Slow changes in China's institutions may be desirable. Sudden changes in economic institutions may involve a level of unemployment which is politically disruptive. Additional unemployment could be caused by the failure of domestic manufacturers, such as those in the automobile industry, to compete with foreign imports. Rapid changes in legal institutions may involve breaking down the social fabric of China as it abandons its former ways of settling disputes and gets accustomed to the new legal system. As political stability is important in promoting progress toward democratic institutions, rapid changes in political institutions may be counterproductive. Some observers consider the social changes which have taken place in China since 1978 to have been as rapid as the Chinese people could absorb.

Besides the substantive provisions for entry, WTO membership has a symbolic significance. Symbolically, China's position in the world economic community is recognized. The conditions for entry to the WTO will serve as a blueprint for China's institutional changes for at least a decade, even if the agreed-upon provisions do not take effect as early as the formal statements claim. In the meantime, helping the Chinese leaders project a better image of themselves in the world community will improve their own confidence to govern and the confidence of the Chinese people in their leaders. The psychological effects of the status of membership may make the leaders more willing to adopt democratic reforms and make the Chinese citizens more willing and patient in following their leaders as they guide the gradual political change in China toward a more democratic government. (The fact that in July 2001 Beijing was awarded the 2008 Olympics may have similar effects.) I make this positive concluding statement under two assumptions. First, the most important objective of all political leaders, including the Chinese, is to make their political power secure. Second, if their political power is assured, and notwithstanding the bureaucratic inertia underlying the one-party rule in China, the Chinese political leaders are likely to try their best to modernize China and fulfill the dream of generations of Chinese since the Opium War of 1840.

## 4.6   Agriculture and Rural Poverty

China's economic reform began with the introduction of the household responsibility system in agriculture, which assigned a piece of land to each farm household and allowed it to retain all the products after paying a fixed amount to the government procurement agent. This led to rapid increase in agricultural productivity. However, in the late 1980s and the 1990s, agricultural productivity and the incomes of farmers did not increase as rapidly because of economic and noneconomic problems. As of 2006 we can usefully discuss the problem of rural poverty in terms of the following three components.

The first is the income gap between the urban and rural residents. The problem of rural poverty is not due to the low income *level* of the rural population. The per capita income of rural residents has increased fairly rapidly, in the order of 5.5 percent per year since 1989, and the percentage of rural residents with income below the poverty line has declined rapidly (see Chow 2000). It is true that the gap in per capita income between urban and rural residents has widened, but the rate of increase in the latter has been so rapid that the rural population, on average or as judged by the poorest among them, is much better off economically than before. If one insists on using income as the chief measure of rural poverty the problem has to be viewed either as (1) the deterioration of the *relative* income of the rural residents in spite of the rapid increase in absolute income, or (2) as discontent among the rural population actually created by the improvement in income itself (i.e. increasing expectations). Since neither of these two interpretations of the problem of rural poverty appears to be sufficient to explain the seriousness of the current problem, one has to seek other explanations. Two are given below.

The second component is central government's unfavorable treatment of rural residents as compared with urban residents. First, it has spent less on infrastructure investment in rural areas than in urban areas. It invested only a limited amount to improve agricultural productivity. Second, it provided fewer welfare benefits, including healthcare and education subsidies, to rural residents. Although much labor mobility was allowed so that farmers could move to urban areas to find work, those working in the urban areas are subject to discrimination. The migrating workers do not have residence permits in the cities and cannot receive services such as healthcare and schooling for their children. Third, although the commune system was abolished, procurement of farm products by government agencies has continued, and the procurement prices were often set below market prices. In the meantime farmers were not allowed to sell their products to private traders, as private trading and transportation of grain were prohibited. Thus the market economy does not function in the distribution and pricing of grain for the benefit of the farmers.

The neglect of central government in dealing with the rural problems is probably not by design but a result of the historical development of economic reform. The initial success of the privatization of farming in the early 1980s, which improved the economic conditions of the farmers, did not require further government intervention. The strategy of "letting some people get rich first" resulted in the income gap between the urban and rural population. The urban population's historical entitlement to housing and welfare benefits excluded the rural population – this was inherited from the period of economic planning and not a new policy favoring the urban population while the collapse of the commune system took away welfare benefits to the rural population. Finally, the need to deal with other important reform problems concerned with the state enterprises, the banking and financial system, and the open-door policy, together with the human and financial resources required to accomplish them (including resources for the building of infrastructure for the special economic zones as a part of the open-door policy) have also contributed to the neglect of the rural population. When the Chinese government finally recognized the seriousness of the farmers' problems, perhaps valuable time had been lost.

The third, and perhaps most important, component of the rural poverty problem is that the farmers' rights can be violated by the illegal activities of local government officials. The most disconcerting example is the confiscation of land from farmers for urban development, while the farmers receive a compensation that is arbitrary and well below market price. Second, many farmers and other rural residents are not paid what they are entitled, such as wages for public work and for teaching in public schools; sometimes wages are not paid on time or not paid at all. Third, farmers are subject to illegal levies. This violates the principle of allowing the farmers to retain all the output after paying a fixed rent for the use of land under the household responsibility system. The levies include land taxes on acreage that is not actually used, a special tax for growing commercial crops rather than grain and livestock, and fees for schools, road construction and other services provided by the local government. One reason for the extra levies is the tax reform of 1994 which increased the proportion of government revenue paid to the central government (from 22.0 percent in 1993 to 55.7 percent in 2004), at the expense of provincial and local governments. Another reason is the central government's policy of assigning to local governments the responsibility for providing a "compulsory education" of 9 years to rural residents.

Chen and Wu (2005: 108–9) provide an illustration of the extortion of illegal levies in a village. The village Party secretary led a troop of several armed tax collectors to each house to collect a "school construction fee" of 6 yuan when all school buildings were in good condition. When one housewife did not have money to pay, the collectors took away a television set. After returning home and finding out about this incident, the husband was brave enough to visit the county Party secretary to file a complaint, but was ignored. When the village secretary learned of the visit, he went back to the house for a second time to take away a bicycle. This story illustrates the lawlessness and abuse of power of local officials. At least in this case, the problem is not one of poverty, since the farm household has a television set and a bicycle, but of the violation of the farmers' rights.

Through much of Chinese history local government officials have considered themselves privileged and as having the authority to rule over the peasants. The abuse of power under the PRC is worse because the officials are given even more power. More well-publicized stories of the abuse of power by local Party and government officials are documented in Chen and Wu (2005), which also describes the multilevel bureaucracy in village–township–county governments that protect each other's interests and positions and fail to carry out central government policies that are intended to benefit farmers. Chapter 1 of the book tells the story of citizens of a village wishing to report to the county officials the illegal levies and false financial accounting by village officials, but receiving mistreatment by the latter, who sent policemen to jail one accuser; later he was beaten to death.

The abuse of power by local officials is known to be fairly widespread, as evidenced partly by the large number of demonstrations and protests by the farmers reported in the news media. Some 200 to 300 protests or demonstrations per day were reported in 2004. Zhang (2006: 19–20) quoted statistics provided by Han (2003) that some 34 million farmers have lost their land to local government land grabs, and statistics provided by the Ministry of Construction show that, between January and June 2004, 4,026 groups and 18,620 individuals had lodged petitions over allegedly illicit land confiscations, compared to 3,929 groups and 18,071 individuals for the entire year of 2003.

Rural poverty became China's number one economic and social problem in 2006. We will discuss the government's solution to this problem in section 10.2.4.

## 4.7   Prospects for Reform

There are three sets of forces affecting the Chinese reform process in the early twenty-first century. First is the role of the government, which is by and large positive in initiating reform in state enterprises and the banking system, and in promoting foreign trade and investment. It also allows privatization to take place in agriculture, and township and village enterprises to develop. For economists who believe in limiting the role of government in a market economy, the experience in China confirms the important role of the government in carrying out institutional reform and implementing economic policies to deal with crisis situations, the latter in developed economies as well. To the extent that government actions are required, the competence of government officials is an extremely important factor determining the success of economic reform and economic policies. China has selected some very competent people to serve as government officials, the prevalence of corruption notwithstanding. And the Chinese government has the will to modernize the Chinese economy, as evidenced by its efforts at reform since 1978.

Second, there are market forces pushing the reform forward. Private enterprise and foreign investment are important components of such forces. Joining the WTO will add impetus in that direction. But third, there is also institutional inertia to slow down the process, including government bureaucracy and vested interests in state enterprises and the banking system. Although explicit government policies are exercising a positive force toward reform, the bureaucratic behavior of government officials and managers of state enterprises and state-owned commercial banks is inhibiting the process. People in general are slow in changing their habits and old ways of doing things, especially when a change would damage their own interests. There is a lack of trained and competent personnel to run modern enterprises and commercial banks, and the development of human capital is a time-consuming process.

These three sets of forces should be kept in mind when we examine the prospects for future evolution of China's economic institutions.

For almost two decades, continued economic growth and reform have been the two most important characteristics of the Chinese economy. These characteristics persisted during the Asian financial crisis and are likely to continue in the first decade of the twenty-first century. Reform of the banking system and of state enterprise remain two of the most important tasks facing the Chinese government. The Asian financial crisis of 1997–9 did have both positive and negative impacts on economic reform. On the negative side, the speed of reform was somewhat reduced, as evidenced by the introduction of restrictive policies on foreign-exchange transactions and on the privatization of state enterprises. On the positive side, the crisis provided new experience for policy-makers, and new observations for economists, on the nature of desirable institutional changes. Examples are the need to have transparency in financial institutions and more effective supervision of commercial banks by the central bank. The appropriate degree to which to restrict international capital flows and the appropriate speed and sequencing of trade and investment liberation have to be studied carefully. In any case the Asian financial crisis of 1997–9 led to a re-examination of existing economic institutions and will benefit the outcome of reform in the long run. When the crisis receded, economic reform resumed its speed in China as it had after the political shock of Tiananmen Square in 1989. The Chinese government seems determined.

The main purpose of the first four chapters of this book has been to provide a broad picture of the Chinese economy from a historical-institutional perspective. Such a picture will help us understand the Chinese economy in the twenty-first century. I hope to have conveyed to the reader the following major characteristics of the Chinese economy, leaving further details on individual sectors or topics to remaining chapters.

First, although China was at one time a planned economy, by the turn of the century it has become essentially a market economy. As a first approximation one should treat China's economy as a market economy.

Second, and related to the first, is that the economic ideology of traditional Communism has almost completely disappeared. To anticipate and assess the future economic policies of Chinese government officials, one should understand them as pragmatic and by and large intelligent decision-makers whose objective is to improve the market economy of China. Such an understanding would avoid the mistakes of many Western observers in predicting a return to central planning after the Tiananmen incident and in predicting a devaluation of the yuan, a banking crisis, and a serious unemployment problem during the Asian financial crisis of 1997–9.

Third, as a qualification of the first, the Chinese market economy has many short-comings and economic reforms are not completed. In spite of shortcomings, the economy has grown and will continue to grow rapidly in the next decade or two because of the resourcefulness of the Chinese people, and because it is not necessary to have a perfect economic system to sustain a fairly high rate of growth.

Fourth, further reform of China's economic institutions will be a slow process because the institutional changes that could be made easily *were* made in the first two decades of reform, leaving the difficult ones ahead. The characteristics of the Chinese economy as described in this book should remain essentially valid for the first one or two decades of the twenty-first century.

Fifth, to understand the nature of the inertia preventing further reform, one must examine the Chinese historical traditions up to the PRC period. For example, a bureau-cratic tradition, made more authoritarian during the PRC period, has led and will lead to bureaucratic behavior in the management of state enterprises, and will restrict the free-dom of private enterprise to enter the market and function as effectively as in an open market economy. Reform of formal legal institutions alone cannot easily change the legal and bureaucratic behavior of the Chinese population.

Sixth, one can expect both the nationalism aroused after China's defeat in the Opium War of 1840 and the strong urge for modernization and economic development to affect China's stance in dealing with other nations in economic and diplomatic relations.

In summary, one might call the Chinese economy a "bureaucratic market economy" (its official designation is "socialist market economy"). It is bureaucratic in two senses. First, the state-owned institutions, including the commercial banks and the state enter-prises, are controlled and run by bureaucrats. Second, the nonstate enterprises, both domestic and foreign, have to deal with bureaucrats in the government, and sometimes also bureaucrats in the state sector, to conduct their business. Both institutional character-istics hamper the growth of the Chinese economy and are unlikely to change in the near future. The problem of corruption will be further discussed in chapter 19.

# References and Further Reading

Brzybyla, Heidi. "Companies Could Wait Years for China Benefits." wgsiwyg//241/http:// seatlepoi.nwsource.com/business, accessed Nov. 18, 1999.

Chen, Guidi and Chuntao Wu. *Chinese Farmers Survey* [*Zhongguo Nongmin Diaochai*]. Taipei: Ta-Ti Publishing, 2005.

Chow, Gregory C. "China's Economic Policy in the Context of the Asian Financial Crisis." *Pacific Economic Review*, 5 (Feb. 2000), pp. 97–108.

Han, Jun. "Chinese Collective Land Ownership into Shareholder Ownership" [Jiang Tudi Nongmin Jiti Suyou Dingjie Wei An Gufen Gongyouzhi]. *China Economic Times* (*Zhongguo Jingji Shibao*), Nov. 11, 2003.

Lau, Chung-ming and Jianfa Shen. *China Review 2000*, chs. 8, 9, and 10. Hong Kong: Chinese University Press, 2000.

Li, Shantong, Zhi Wang, Fan Huo, and Lin Xu. *WTO: China and the World.* Beijing: China Development Publishing Co., 1999 (in Chinese).

Woo, Wing Thye, Jeffrey Sachs, and Klaus Schwab. *The Asian Financial Crisis: Lessons for a Resilient Asia*, chs. 2 and 7. Cambridge, MA: MIT Press, 2000.

Zhang, Xiabo. "Asymmetric Property Rights in China's Economic Growth." Washington, DC: International Food Research Institute, Development Strategy and Government Division, DSGD Discussion Paper no. 28, Jan. 2006.

# Questions

1   When state enterprises were transformed in the late 1990s to shareholding companies, what prevented them from increasing efficiency in the same manner as modern corporations?

2   What are the prospects for reform of state enterprises in the first decade of the twenty-first century?

3   What are the main differences between the management in a Chinese shareholding company and in a modern US corporation?

4   What are the problems facing the Chinese state enterprises?

5   What major factors contributed to the Asian financial crisis of 1997–9 but were absent in China?

6   What was the major signal of a possible banking crisis in China during the period of the Asian financial crisis? Why was China able to avoid such a crisis?

7   By what means did the Chinese government attempt to solve the problem of large amounts of nonperforming loans in the commercial banks? What are the prospects of success?

8   What were the economic fundamentals which supported the value of the Chinese currency and made it unnecessary for China to devalue its currency in 1997–9?

9   What are the main provisions for China's entry into the WTO? How are these provisions supposed to help China's economic development?

10   When China enters the WTO, what are the likely impacts on the relative shares of the three major productive sectors of the Chinese economy? Explain.

11   What are the possible disadvantages of China's joining the WTO? Are the disadvantages serious?

12   Name six important institutional characteristics of China's economy which affect its functioning and future development.

# Part II

# Analysis of the Macroeconomy

# 5

# Economic Growth

In this chapter, we estimate a neoclassical model of economic growth based on an aggregate production function of the Chinese economy, and use it to assess the importance of different factors in their contribution to the rate of growth and to forecast the Chinese gross domestic product. The last section looks at the question of whether China's real GNP will catch up with US real GNP by 2020, and answers in the affirmative.

## 5.1 The Neoclassical Model of Economic Growth

The study of China's economy requires both a historical-institutional approach and a theoretical-quantitative approach. We have applied the former in the first four chapters and will apply the latter in chapters 5, 6, 8, and others. Some economic models, such as those used in chapters 5, 6, and 8, have general applicability in many countries. However, in applying them we have to be aware of the historical-institutional conditions. Making a mistake in understanding the broad picture can lead to errors in specifying the models, in estimating the parameters of the models, and in using them for prediction.

In this chapter we will first provide a model of economic growth and then apply it to study the growth of real GDP in the Chinese economy. The model employed is based on the neoclassical model studied by Robert Solow (1956). It consists of four equations. The first is a production function explaining aggregate output by capital and labor inputs. The second is a definition of investment as the rate of change in capital stock. The third explains investment as a fraction of aggregate output. The fourth explains the growth of the labor force. These four equations explain the four variables: aggregate output, investment, capital stock, and labor.

Let real output or GDP in constant prices be denoted by $Y$, investment by $I$, capital stock at the end of period $t$ by $K_t$ and labor force by $L$. The production function to be employed is the Cobb–Douglas production function.

$$Y_t = Ae^{\alpha t}K_t^{\beta}L_t^{\gamma} \tag{5.1}$$

In equation (5.1), $\beta$ and $\gamma$ are respectively the proportional rate of change of output with respect to capital and labor, or the effects of a unit change in $\ln K$ and $\ln L$ on $\ln Y$. If $\beta + \gamma = 1$ the production function is said to satisfy constant returns to scale. This means that if $K$ and $L$ both increase by a constant proportion, output will increase by the same proportion. This can be shown by changing $K$ and $L$ to $cK$ and $cL$ respectively, where $c$ is a positive constant; output $Y$ will be changed to $c^{\beta+\gamma}Y$.

The parameter $\alpha$ measures the exponential rate of change in output through time, even if both capital and labor inputs remain constant. This is the change in $\ln Y$ per unit of time which may result from technological or institutional change due to economic reform. If $\alpha = 0$, such change in total factor productivity is non-existent. If $\alpha = 0.03$, $e^{\alpha} = 1.0305$ and $e^{\alpha t} = 1.0305^t$, total factor productivity increases by 3.05 percent per year. In this example, 0.03 is the exponential rate of growth and 0.0305 is the annual rate of growth. The former is slightly smaller because it is the annual rate used for continuous compounding, leading to a slightly larger growth rate in one year. These two growth rates will be used in future analysis, depending on convenience.

The second equation in the growth model describes the growth of capital by investment, i.e.,

$$K_t = K_{t-1} + I_t \tag{5.2}$$

where $I$ stands for net investment. Equation (5.2) can be considered a definition of net investment $I$, the change in capital stock from the beginning to the end of period $t$. If $I$ denotes gross investment from which depreciation of capital stock has not been subtracted, $K_{t-1}$ on the righthand side of (5.2) has to be replaced by $(1 - d)K_{t-1}$, $d$ being the rate of depreciation, to account for the depreciation of existing capital stock. To explain investment $I$, a simple assumption is that it is a fraction of output $Y$ which the model already explains. This makes up the third equation. The fourth equation explains the growth of labor input $L$. This equation may specify a given rate of growth for $L$. Given these four equations we can explain the four variables and thus the growth of the Chinese economy. The most important and difficult equation to ascertain empirically is the production function. Once the production function (5.1) is known, equation (5.2) is given as a definition. The remaining two equations for investment and labor can easily be specified, but we have to make sure that the simple assumptions underlying these equations agree with the historical conditions of the Chinese economy.

## 5.2    Data on Output, Capital, and Labor

In the study of the relation between aggregate output and inputs in this chapter and of other econometric relations in the remainder of this book, we will rely on official Chinese data. A reader may ask how reliable these data are, and whether the Chinese State

Statistics Bureau responsible for collecting and publishing the data might falsify some data for political purposes. In Chow (1985) I tried to address these questions. Like statistical data in other countries, some data are more reliable than others. For example, data on the wage rate, employment in state enterprises, and consumption expenditures of urban residents during the period of central planning are probably reliable because the government needed these data to set production targets and to issue ration coupons. Data on population are moderately reliable and have been improved since the early 1980s, when China received technical help from the United Nations to improve its population census. The extent of data falsification is probably limited. During the Great Leap Forward of 1958–9, Chairman Mao wanted the communes to achieve unreasonably high output targets, and some communes did falsify their output data. However, when the local offices of the State Statistics Bureau received these inflated output data they adjusted them downward, for it is the duty of an official of the Bureau to report data accurately and honestly. Some officials may not succeed in this mission, but they all have a responsibility to do so. Pressure on the communes to achieve high output targets does not apply to them. The reliability of the data is also affected by the competence of these officials. They may not be as well trained as those in economically more developed countries.

Reliability should be judged also by the purpose of the user. For example, national income data may not be very accurate in the levels but accurate enough to measure the average rate of change during a long period. In general, Chinese official statistics are accurate enough for econometric analysis. Even if there is doubt about their accuracy for a particular study, we should use them to see what the result turns out to be. If the result is consistent with our prior knowledge, there is a degree of mutual confirmation. If the result is not consistent, we should investigate whether it is the data or the prior knowledge that is incorrect, and try to make an appropriate correction. My own experience in using Chinese official data to study the Chinese economy has led me to believe that they are accurate enough to be useful if they are applied properly. Studies reported in chapters 5, 6, and 8 show reasonable results when judged by economic theory and related empirical studies.

There are Chinese official data on national income and labor force. National income data were revised in 1994 because of a change in the national accounting system. Before 1994, China adopted the Soviet concept of estimating national income as the total output of five major sectors – agriculture, industry, construction, transportation, and commerce. Some service items, such as imputed rents from housing and educational services, are excluded. National income plus imports minus exports equals "national income available," which is decomposed into consumption and "accumulation." "Accumulation" means net investment. Beginning with the *Statistical Yearbook of China, 1994*, national income data consistent with international standards have been published. The data include gross domestic product, its industrial origins in terms of primary (agriculture), secondary (industry and construction), and tertiary industry. GDP is also decomposed into its final uses: consumption, capital accumulation (gross investment before depreciation is deducted), and exports minus imports. Thus the new data on GDP differ from the previous data on national income because of the inclusion of certain service items and depreciation of capital stock.

In the latter part of 2005 official GDP data were revised upward by over 16 percent in order to include service items which were omitted in previously published GDP data. When the Chinese National Statistical Bureau changed its GDP data in 1994, not all service items were included in the revision. Some additional items were found by sample surveys and noticed by officials of the Statistics Bureau, who decided to include them by adjusting the level of GDP upward substantially in 2005. Our study of the production function reported in this chapter uses GDP data before the 2005 revision. It would be of interest to find out whether the conclusions would change by using the new data. In section 5.4 below we will report the results from estimating aggregate production using GDP data as revised in 1994, and find the results to agree with those obtained in Chow (1993) using official national income data before the 1994 revision. The reliability of Chinese official statistics is discussed further in Chow (2006).

Data on capital stock have been constructed in Chow (1993), where production functions for the aggregate economy and for the five industrial sectors are reported. These production functions were estimated using annual data from 1952 to 1980. Data for the years 1958–69 were excluded from the estimation of the functions because the level of output during these years (encompassing the Great Leap Forward and the Cultural Revolution) was well below the capacity output specified by the production functions. Here historical-institutional information enters our treatment of a theoretical model. If we take the natural logarithm of both sides of the Cobb–Douglas production function, assuming $\alpha = 0$ and $\gamma = 1 - \beta$, and subtract $\ln L$ on both sides, we obtain a linear equation explaining $\ln(Y/L)$ by $\ln(K/L)$. Using Chinese data from 1952 to 1980 to plot $\ln(Y/L)$ against $\ln(K/L)$, Chow (1993) found that the points are close to a straight line as this production function suggests, except for the points from 1958 to 1969, which fall below the straight line. This plot supports the historical-institutional evidence that the two political movements affected production adversely, and accordingly our decision to omit data for these years in the estimation of an aggregate production function for the normal years. The statistical analysis of this chapter is based on the work of Chow and Lin (2002), which has updated Chow (1993).

The *China Statistical Yearbook, 1999* (CSY99) provides data on nominal GDP 1952–98 (p. 55), real GDP 1978–88 (p. 58), labor force 1952–98 (p. 134), nominal gross capital formation 1978–88 (p. 68). Since this section is an extension of Chow (1993), data on national income, labor, and capital are taken from Chow (1993) up to 1980 and then constructed for the years thereafter based on the sources cited above. Strictly speaking we wish to use net domestic product as the output variable as in Chow (1993). Since gross domestic product is available from official sources after 1978, we use GDP as the output variable under the assumption that the two variables are proportional to each other. This assumption is justified if depreciation is a constant fraction of GDP. This is the case if the ratio of $K_{t-1}$ to GDP is constant, as we have confirmed by examining the data from 1978 onward as given in table 5.1.

From 1952 to 1978, our output series is proportional to the national income series used in Chow (1993), with the 1978 value set equal to the GDP value of 3,624.1 given in table 5.1. The capital stock series is also taken from Chow (1993), which provides $K = 2,213$ hundred million yuan as the initial capital at the end of 1952 (including

**Table 5.1**  Data on GDP, labor, and capital

| Year | GDP | L | K | t |
|------|------|--------|--------|----|
| 1952 | 799 | 20,729 | 2,213 | 0 |
| 1953 | 911 | 21,364 | 2,381 | 0 |
| 1954 | 964 | 21,832 | 2,576 | 0 |
| 1955 | 1,026 | 22,328 | 2,761 | 0 |
| 1956 | 1,170 | 23,018 | 2,978 | 0 |
| 1957 | 1,223 | 23,771 | 3,211 | 0 |
| 1958 | 1,492 | 26,600 | 3,590 | 0 |
| 1959 | 1,615 | 26,173 | 4,148 | 0 |
| 1960 | 1,591 | 25,880 | 4,649 | 0 |
| 1961 | 1,119 | 25,590 | 4,844 | 0 |
| 1962 | 1,046 | 25,910 | 4,943 | 0 |
| 1963 | 1,158 | 26,640 | 5,126 | 0 |
| 1964 | 1,349 | 27,736 | 5,389 | 0 |
| 1965 | 1,578 | 28,670 | 5,754 | 0 |
| 1966 | 1,846 | 29,805 | 6,224 | 0 |
| 1967 | 1,713 | 30,814 | 6,528 | 0 |
| 1968 | 1,601 | 31,915 | 6,826 | 0 |
| 1969 | 1,910 | 33,225 | 7,183 | 0 |
| 1970 | 2,355 | 34,432 | 7,801 | 0 |
| 1971 | 2,520 | 35,620 | 8,485 | 0 |
| 1972 | 2,592 | 35,854 | 9,133 | 0 |
| 1973 | 2,807 | 36,652 | 9,874 | 0 |
| 1974 | 2,839 | 37,369 | 10,615 | 0 |
| 1975 | 3,075 | 38,168 | 11,445 | 0 |
| 1976 | 2,993 | 38,834 | 12,193 | 0 |
| 1977 | 3,227 | 39,377 | 13,025 | 0 |
| 1978 | 3,624 | 40,152 | 14,112 | 0 |
| 1979 | 3,900 | 41,024 | 15,273 | 1 |
| 1980 | 4,204 | 42,361 | 16,438 | 2 |
| 1981 | 4,425 | 43,725 | 17,268 | 3 |
| 1982 | 4,824 | 45,295 | 18,297 | 4 |
| 1983 | 5,349 | 46,436 | 19,515 | 5 |
| 1984 | 6,161 | 48,197 | 20,928 | 6 |
| 1985 | 6,991 | 49,873 | 22,755 | 7 |
| 1986 | 7,611 | 51,282 | 24,822 | 8 |
| 1987 | 8,491 | 52,783 | 27,123 | 9 |
| 1988 | 9,448 | 54,334 | 30,085 | 10 |
| 1989 | 9,832 | 55,329 | 33,445 | 11 |
| 1990 | 10,209 | 63,909 | 36,565 | 12 |

**Table 5.1**   (*cont'd*)

| Year | GDP | L | K | t |
|------|------|------|------|------|
| 1991 | 11,148 | 64,799 | 39,776 | 13 |
| 1992 | 12,735 | 65,554 | 43,589 | 14 |
| 1993 | 14,453 | 66,373 | 48,994 | 15 |
| 1994 | 16,283 | 67,199 | 55,006 | 16 |
| 1995 | 17,994 | 67,947 | 61,856 | 17 |
| 1996 | 19,719 | 68,850 | 69,304 | 18 |
| 1997 | 21,455 | 69,600 | 77,218 | 19 |
| 1998 | 23,129 | 69,957 | 85,692 | 20 |
| | Average exponential rate of growth | | | |
| 1952–98 | 0.07316 | 0.02644 | 0.07949 | |
| 1952–78 | 0.05815 | 0.02543 | 0.07126 | |
| 1978–98 | 0.09268 | 0.02776 | 0.09019 | |

**Notes**: *GDP = real GDP in 1978 prices*; L = *labor in 10,000 persons*; K = *capital in 1978 prices*; t = *time.*

nonland fixed capital plus inventory = 1,493 and land = 720, table VI, p. 822). To update Chow (1993) we keep land at 720 (which is a constant included in capital stock) and accumulate nonland net capital formation using equation (5.2). From 1953 to 1980, net investment *I* is the same as "accumulation" in official statistics (presented in Chow 1993: 815, table III). It includes net fixed investment and inventory changes. These "accumulation" data can be treated as being in constant 1952 prices or 1978 prices, because during the period of planning, the prices of investment goods did not change materially.

After 1980 we adopt the following method to convert nominal into real gross capital formation in order to construct a capital stock series. First, the ratio of nominal to real GDP provides a GDP price deflator which is used to deflate the sum of nominal consumption and gross capital formation to obtain real domestic final expenditures in 1978 prices. Second, we convert nominal consumption to real consumption by using the general consumer price index (CSY99, p. 294), which is linked with the general retail price index (p. 294) for the period 1981–5. Third, we subtract real consumption from real domestic final expenditures to obtain real gross investment *I* (including inventory investment). We then construct our capital series *K* for the period 1981–98 based on the equation: $K(t) = (1 - d)[K(t) - 720] + I(t) + 720$. The depreciation rate *d* equals 0.04, which is slightly lower than the average depreciation rate of nonland fixed capital, 0.045, found in *China Report: Social and Economic Development 1949–1989*, published by the China Statistical Information and Consultancy Service Center, 1990. We use a slightly lower depreciation rate because our *K* includes inventory. We have thus obtained a capital stock series to update the production function of Chow (1993).

The data on real GDP in 1978 prices, labor input in units of 10,000 persons, and capital stock in 1978 prices are presented in table 5.1 for the period 1952–98. The average exponential rates of growth for each variable are summarized at the bottom of the table for three periods: 1952–98, 1952–78, and 1978–98. The two subperiods are the periods before and after the economic reform. As can be seen from the table, the GDP growth rates are much higher in the second period, whose average exponential growth rate is 0.09268 or 9.7 percent per year compared with the 0.05815 exponential growth rate or 6.0 percent per year in the first period, yielding an average exponential growth rate of 0.07316 or 7.6 percent per year for the entire period. The average exponential growth rates of labor and capital are 0.02776 (2.8 percent) and 0.09019 (9.4 percent), respectively, for the second period, compared with the rates of 0.02543 (2.6 percent) and 0.07126 (7.4 percent) for the first period. Thus the growth rates of labor and capital are also higher in the second period, but only moderately, supplementing the significant contribution of increasing total factor productivity to the GDP growth during this period. Note that there is a substantial increase in the official estimate of labor force in 1990 which was the result of a new census, but we chose not to smooth the data since we are studying long-term trends which are hardly affected by this census result.

## 5.3   A Review of Regression Analysis

The production function (5.1) contains 3 parameters to be estimated: $\alpha$ to measure the exponential rate of growth of total factor productivity (TFP), $\beta$ to measure the elasticity of output with respect to capital stock, and $\gamma$ to measure the elasticity of output with respect to labor. If we take the natural logarithm of (5.1) we have a linear equation explaining $y = \ln Y$ by $x_1 = \ln K$, $x_2 = \ln L$ and time $t$ as follows:

$$y_t = \ln A + \beta x_{1t} + \gamma x_{2t} + \alpha t + \varepsilon_t \tag{5.3}$$

where $\varepsilon_t$ is a random residual added to allow for the fact that the dependent variable $y_t$ does not satisfy the linear regression equation on the righthand side exactly. The random residual represents the combined effect of many factors, such as weather conditions, morale of the workers, etc., which affect output but are not included in the measured inputs. Often the random residual is assumed to have a normal or Gaussian distribution, given by the density function $f(\varepsilon) = (2\pi)^{-1/2}\sigma^{-1}\exp[(\varepsilon/\sigma)^2/2]$. This normal distribution has a mean of zero and standard deviation of $\sigma$. The standard deviation $\sigma$ in the context of the residual in the regression equation (5.3) measures how well the equation can explain the dependent variable $y$ and is called the standard error of the regression.

Once we have available data on $y$, $x_1$, $x_2$, and $t$ ($t = 1$ for a designated year and increases by 1 for each following year), we estimate the unknown parameters $\ln A$, $\beta$, $\gamma$, and $\alpha$ by choosing their values which minimize the sum of squared deviations of $y$ from the linear function of these variables given on the righthand side of (5.3). This procedure is called the least-squares method. To explain this method of least squares when there is only one explanatory variable, consider the model (5.1) when $\alpha = 0$ and $\gamma = 1 - \beta$. In this special case, we can take the logarithm of (5.1) and subtract $\ln L$ from both sides to yield the regression equation $\ln(Y/L) = \ln A + \beta\ln(K/L)$. The intercept $\ln A$ and the slope $\beta$ are estimated by the least-squares method, which minimizes the sum of $[\ln(Y/L) - \ln A - \beta\ln(K/L)]^2$ over all sample observations.

It is extremely important to recognize, by the logic of statistical inference, that the least-squares estimates of the parameters are different from the true values of the parameters. The true values cannot be known for certain unless we have an infinite number of observations. Statisticians distinguish between an assumed population, or a probabilistic model which generates the data, and a sample, which consists of only a finite set of data drawn from the assumed data-generating process. Equation (5.3) is the population, the data-generating process. The data for the years 1952 to 1988, excluding 1958–69, are a sample drawn from this generating process. The true values of $\ln A$, $\beta$, $\gamma$, and $\alpha$ cannot be estimated precisely unless we have an infinite number of observations. Our least-squares estimates change from sample to sample if we can imagine sampling from the data-generating process repeatedly. The random residual $\varepsilon$, representing weather, worker morale, etc. for the period 1952 to 1988, would be different for different draws from the same specified normal distribution. To perform this thought experiment, imagine adding more years of observations when they become available in the future. If the least-squares estimates are recomputed using these additional observations, they will be different.

Capturing the idea that the least-squares estimates can change from sample to sample by imagining different draws for the random residual in equation (5.3), we can understand a sampling distribution of the estimates as they might be generated from different samples. In a particular sample the least-squares estimate of $\beta$ may turn out to be 0.61. Since the estimates vary from sample to sample, it is extremely unlikely that the true value of $\beta$ is also 0.61. In fact, even if the true value of $\beta$ is 0.20, it is still possible for the estimate obtained by using one sample of 20 observations to be as large as 0.61. The important question is how likely it is that this will occur. Statistics provides us with ways to calculate a "standard error" for the estimate 0.61. This standard error is the standard deviation of the sampling distribution of the estimates. It is often reported below the point estimate in parentheses. If the standard error is 0.12, for example, and if the sample consists of 18 or more observations, then we can be about 95 percent sure that the interval 0.61 plus or minus 2 (in fact 1.96 for normal $\varepsilon$) times 0.12 will include the true value of the parameters. Since the low end of this interval is $0.61 - 0.24$, or 0.37, the value 0.20 is excluded. One can conclude with 95 percent confidence that the elasticity of output with respect to capital stock is between 0.37 and 0.85. The important application of the standard error of an estimated regression coefficient is that if the confidence interval includes zero, the coefficient is said to be statistically insignificant. In this case the data do not provide sufficient evidence to reject the hypothesis that the variable has no effect on the dependent variable. Usually there are two statistics reported for a regression. One is $R^2$, which is the ratio of the variance of the estimates of $Y$ given by the regression equation to the variance of the actually observed $Y$. This ratio can vary from 0 to 1. A value near 1 shows that a high fraction of the variance of $Y$ is explained by the regression equation, and signals a good regression equation. Another useful statistic is the standard error of the regression, denoted by $s$. It is an estimate of the standard error $\sigma$ of the distribution of the population regression $\varepsilon$.

When time-series data are used to estimate a regression equation, often we find serial correlation in the residuals. We estimate the residual $\varepsilon$ by its sample counterpart $e$, which is the difference between $y$ and the estimated regression equation, whereas $\varepsilon$ is the difference between $y$ and the true, but unknown, regression equation. Given data on $e_t$, we can estimate a regression

$$e_t = \rho e_{t-1} + u_t \qquad\qquad\qquad (5.4)$$

If we find $u_t$ to be serially uncorrelated, we can re-estimate equation (5.3) by subtracting $\rho$ times the values of its variables in period $t - 1$ from the values at period $t$, and observing that the regression of $y_t - \rho y_{t-1}$ on $x_{1t} - \rho x_{1t-1}$, etc. will have residual $u_t$, which no longer has a serial correlation. This two-step procedure, of estimating a regression equation with serially correlated residuals, is known as the Cochran–Orcutt procedure and will be applied to estimating Cobb–Douglas production functions for China.


## 5.4   Estimating Production Functions for China


Chow (1993) found no increase in total factor productivity (TFP) before 1980 because the estimate of $\alpha$ in equation (5.1) is not significantly different from zero. Given this fact, we estimate Cobb–Douglas production functions by introducing a trend beginning with $t = 1$ in 1979, the year after economic reform started (see the positive deviations after 1979 of log output from the estimates by the production functions in table VIII of Chow 1993: 825). As pointed out above, the years 1958–69 are considered to be abnormal years and excluded in all regressions. Table 5.2 presents three estimated equations for the period 1952–98.

Equation (1) does not impose the restriction $\beta + \gamma = 1$ and is estimated by regressing $\ln(GDP)$ on $\ln(L)$, $\ln(K)$ and $t$. If we consider the three economic variables as being generated by a system of autoregression equations or a VAR (see section 6.5 for an explanation of VAR) including a trend, this regression can be interpreted as a long-run equilibrium relation or a cointegration relation (see Engle and Granger 1987). Since the restriction $\beta + \gamma = 1$ is easily accepted, equation (2) imposes this restriction and is a regression of $\ln(GDP/L)$ on $\ln(K/L)$, whereas equation (3) allows for first-order serial correlations in the residuals by applying the Cochran–Orcutt transformation using observations beginning in 1953.

In equation (1) the coefficient of $\ln(K)$ is 0.6158 and the coefficient of $\ln(L)$ is 0.4162, both with reasonably small standard errors. These values agree with the estimates 0.6353 and 0.3584, respectively, obtained by Chow (1993: 882) for the period 1952–80. Since the hypothesis that their sum equals one is easily accepted, we impose this restriction in equation (2) and obtain a capital exponent of 0.6342 and a trend coefficient of 0.0281. The first coefficient is in agreement with the result given in table VII of Chow (1993: 823) based on old official national income data (revised in 1994, as presented in table 5.1) for output and the sample period 1952–80, excluding 1958–69. Equation (3) allows for first-order serial correlation in the residuals. The estimated correlation coefficient is 0.797; the Durbin–Watson statistic was originally 0.6638 and is raised to 1.5211 after adjustment of serial correlation. The estimates of both the capital elasticity of output and the trend coefficient in equation (3) are almost the same as in equation (2).

To examine whether the output elasticity of capital has remained unchanged throughout the entire sample period 1952–98, we add a product $dd \ln(K/L)$ to equation (3), where $dd$ is a dummy variable taking the value one for the period 1979–98 and zero before. This variable measures the incremental coefficient of $\ln(K/L)$ for the period 1979–98. The estimated coefficient is $-0.00378$ with a standard error of 0.0045 and is therefore statistically insignificant. The coefficients of $\ln(K/L)$ and $t$ are 0.6286 and 0.0273, respectively, remaining almost the same as in the absence of the added dummy variable. The data are thus consistent with a constant output elasticity of capital throughout the entire sample period 1952–98. A similar analysis applied to equation (2) yields a coefficient of $-0.0063$ for the variable $dd* \ln(K/L)$, with a standard error of 0.0029 making the coefficient significantly different from zero, but the numerical value is very small. Hence the value of this parameter is found to be quite stable for China in the period 1952–88. However, in the long run it is likely to decrease gradually when capital becomes more abundant relative to labor, or the labor exponent will increase, as the results from introducing the variable $dd* \ln(K/L)$ in equations (2) and (3) above suggest, and as Chow and Lin (2002, table 2) have found for the decrease in the share of capital in total output in Taiwan from 0.53 in 1951 to 0.41 in 1999. The share of labor in total output for the United States is about 0.7, as labor is scarce relative to capital.

Table 5.3 presents the decomposition of the rate of GDP growth into its factor components based on the estimates given by the second equation in table 5.2. This decomposition is derived by taking derivatives of all variables in equation (5.3) with respect to time. The derivative of the log of each variable gives the exponential rate of change of the variable through time. Thus the exponential rate of growth of real output equals the exponential rate of growth of capital times its coefficient, plus the exponential rate of growth of labor times its coefficient, plus the coefficient of $t$, which measures the

**Table 5.2**  Regression estimates of production functions, 1952–98

| Equation | Intercept | ln(K) | ln(L) | ln(K/L) | t | $R^2$/s |
|---|---|---|---|---|---|---|
| (1) | 2.1104 | 0.6158 | 0.4162 | | 0.0282 | 0.9975/ |
|     | (1.5130) | (.0812) | (.2130) | | (.0025) | .04915 |
| (2) | −1.7504 | | | 0.6342 | 0.0281 | 0.9940/ |
|     | (.0396) | | | (.0254) | (.0025) | .04842 |
| (3) | −1.7336 | | | 0.6385 | 0.0264 | 0.9931/ |
|     | (.0823) | | | (.0504) | (.0051) | .03393 |

Notes: *Dependent variable is ln(GDP) or ln(GDP/L). Figures in parentheses are standard errors of estimates. L = labor, K = capital stock, sample period = 1952–98, sample size = 35 (1958–69 omitted), $R^2$ = adjusted $R^2$, s = standard error of the regression.*

exponential rate of growth of TFP. The larger an input's growth rate and the larger its coefficient, the larger its contribution to the growth rate of output.

In the period 1952 to 1978, when there was no increase in TFP, the exponential growth rate of GDP 0.058 is contributed by two inputs, capital and labor. Capital contributed 0.045 and labor 0.009 to the rate 0.058 of exponential growth of GDP. 0.045 is the product of the exponential rate of growth of capital, 0.07126 (from table 5.1), times the capital coefficient 0.6342 from table 5.2. The contribution of labor, 0.0093 equals the exponential growth rate of labor, 0.02543, times the labor coefficient (1 − 0.6342). The sum of the contributions is 0.0545. It is slightly smaller than the actual growth rate, 0.05815, from 1952 to 1978 because our production function does not fit the data perfectly. In the period 1978–98, capital contributed 0.058, labor 0.010, and the increase in TFP 0.028 to the rate of exponential growth of GDP, 0.093. For the entire period 1952 to 1998 capital contributed 0.050, labor 0.010, and the increase in TFP 0.012 (which is 20/46 of 0.028), to the rate of 0.073 of exponential growth of GDP. The sum of the estimated contributions for each period is not far from the actual GDP growth rate as shown by the S/A ratios in table 5.3. In percentage terms, the contributions of capital, labor, and increase of productivity to GDP growth are 69, 13, and 17 percent respectively for the period from 1952 to 1998. The corresponding percentages for Taiwan from 1951 to 1999 reported in Chow and Lin (2002) are approximately 39, 21, and 40. One reason for the difference is that mainland China is relatively labor abundant, leading to a smaller labor coefficient and a smaller contribution from labor relative to capital, as explained below. A second reason is that an increase in the TFP of mainland China occurred only after 1979, resulting in a slower overall rate of increase in TFP for the entire period from the early 1950s to the late 1990s.

A very important difference between the two economies is the smaller exponent of labor in the production function for the mainland as compared with that for Taiwan. The accuracy of this small estimate was carefully examined in Chow (1993), where factor shares observed during the market economies of 1953 and the 1920s were cited to support such a low estimate. In those periods, China's economy was a market economy to a significant extent. For the case of a competitive market economy, capital and labor are paid by their marginal product, and the shares of total output distributed to these two factors of production equal the coefficients $\beta$ and $1 - \beta$ respectively, under the assumption of constant returns to scale. To demonstrate this proposition, simply find the marginal

**Table 5.3**  Sources of and contributions to GDP growth for various sample periods

| Equation under | Sample period | Sources of growth | | | | | | Contributions to growth (%) | | | |
|---|---|---|---|---|---|---|---|---|---|---|---|
| | | K | L | t | S | A | S/A | K | L | t | R |
| K/L | 1952–78 | 0.04519 | 0.00930 | 0.00000 | 0.05449 | 0.05815 | 0.93706 | 77.7 | 16.0 | 0.0 | 6.3 |
| | 1978–98 | 0.05765 | 0.01015 | 0.02818 | 0.09598 | 0.09268 | 1.03559 | 62.2 | 11.0 | 30.4 | −3.6 |
| | 1952–98 | 0.05041 | 0.00967 | 0.01225 | 0.07233 | 0.07316 | 0.98866 | 68.9 | 13.2 | 16.7 | 1.2 |

**Notes:** K = *capital*, L = *labor*, t = *time*, S = *sum of estimates*, A = *actual GDP exponential growth rate*, R = *100 − contributions of* K, L, *and* t.

product of labor by taking the partial derivative of output produced by the Cobb–Douglas production function (5.1) with respect to $L$. The resulting derivative or marginal product of labor equals $(1 - \beta)Y/L$. If wage $w$ equals marginal product, $w = (1 - \beta)Y/L$. Multiplying both sides of this equation by $L$, we get $wL = (1 - \beta)Y$. In other words, the total payment to labor equals a fraction $(1 - \beta)$ of output $Y$. Hence the share of labor in total output can be used to estimate the elasticity of output with respect to labor $(1 - \beta)$.

An estimate of the labor share in Chinese agriculture for the period 1921–4 was obtained in Chow (1993: 827) based on data provided in Buck's classic study (1930), which surveyed 2,866 farms in 17 localities in 7 provinces of China. Total farm receipts averaged 376.24 yuan (Buck 1930: 86). Value added per farm is obtained by subtracting nonlabor cash expenditures of 40.11 yuan to yield 336.13 yuan. Expenditures on hired labor and imputed value of family labor equaled 89.09 (ibid.: 86). Since there was one additional labor operator per family of 2.29 working persons, the labor cost of 89.90 is multiplied by 3.29/2.29 to yield 127.99 yuan. Labor share is therefore 127.99/336.13 or 0.38, very close to the estimate of $0.37 = 1 - 0.63$, 0.63 being the capital exponent estimated in equations (2) and (3) in table 3.2 (Buck 1930). This is an instance of using an estimate from another source to check the accuracy of an estimate obtained by using official Chinese data. The agreement between the two confirms the accuracy of the current estimate as well as the usefulness of the official data. (See the estimate 0.6 for $\beta$ in Mankiw et al. (1992), based on data for many developing countries.) Low labor exponents were also found in table XII of Chow (1993: 833) for the production functions of the industry, construction, and transportation sectors.

The main reason for the low elasticity of output with respect to labor is that labor is abundant in China. In the extreme, such surplus labor may yield almost zero marginal output. Since the Cobb–Douglas production function is an approximation to the input–output relation with constant elasticities, the small marginal output of labor is reflected in its small exponent. As the economy grows, the ratio of capital to labor will increase and labor will not be in such relative abundance; the labor exponent will increase. Our examination of Chinese data indicates that the abundance of labor has persisted even after the two decades of rapid growth since 1978. This finding is consistent with the existence of very poor regions in western China and the low wage rates of workers in those regions.

## 5.5   Use of the Neoclassical Growth Model to Forecast GDP

We can summarize the neoclassical model of growth in the following equations.

$$L_t = aL_{t-1}$$
$$I_t = bY_{t-1}$$
$$K_t = (1 - d)K_{t-1} + I_t$$
$$Y_t = Ae^{0.0281t}K_t^{0.6342}L_t^{0.3658}$$
$$t \text{ (year 1979)} = 1$$

$$(5.5)$$

The growth rate $a$ for the labor force from 1978 to 1998 is 1.0281, but it was smaller in the late 1990s and is expected to be small from 1999 onward because of the introduction of the one-child-family policy in 1980. One could use a labor growth rate of 1.011, the approximate growth rate in 1995–7 before the Asian financial crisis. Since the labor coefficient is only 0.3658, the decrease in the labor growth rate from 1.028 to 1.011 reduces the exponential rate of GDP by only 0.3658 × 0.017, or 0.006. The coefficient $b$ can be estimated by the ratio of the sum of investments to the sum of real GDP in the period 1978–98, which equals 0.3373. Starting with actual data in 1998 as given in table 5.1, and setting the constant A in the production function in equations (5.5) at a value which makes the righthand side of the function equal to the actual value of real GDP in 1998, we can use the equations in (5.5) to forecast real GDP from 1999 to 2010. This is left as an exercise for the reader.

Without actually carrying out this numerical exercise, we can make an approximate estimate of the average annual rate of growth of Chinese GDP in the first decade of the twenty-first century. This estimate can be made by decomposing the exponential rate of growth of real GDP into its three components. The contribution of labor will be reduced by 0.006, as we have just discussed. The contribution of capital will be slightly smaller than it was in the last decade of the twentieth century because, although the capital coefficient is the same and the ratio of saving or investment to GDP is the same, the rate of growth of capital stock itself would be slightly smaller. The slightly smaller growth in capital stock comes from a slightly smaller growth in GDP, due to the reduction of labor's contribution by 0.006, since investment is proportional to GDP. However, this effect is extremely small because a 0.006 reduction in the growth rate of investment (proportional to GDP) translates to a mere 0.0006 reduction in the growth rate of capital stock if investment is one-tenth of capital stock. There is a third-round effect, as the smaller capital stock growth itself affects GDP growth by the capital coefficient 0.63 × 0.0006. A generous estimate of the reduction in the exponential rate of growth of capital stock would thus be 0.0015. Since the contribution of capital to the exponential growth rate of GDP is reduced by this rate times the capital coefficient of about 0.63, the end result is about 0.001. Combining the two reductions in capital and labor contributions, the total reduction in the exponential rate of GDP growth is about 0.007. One may consider a possible reduction in the growth of TFP by as much as 0.010 from 0.028 to make the total reduction as large as 0.017; the rate of growth will still be about 0.093 − 0.017, or 0.076. But a large reduction in TFP growth is unlikely, since there is still plenty of new technology in the developed world that the Chinese can adopt. There are also further institutional improvements that China can make, although such improvements are expected to be slow.

The above assessment of future growth of real GDP in China is based on the values of only four parameters. The first two parameters are the elasticity $\beta$ of output with respect to capital and the exponential rate of growth $\alpha$ of TFP in the production function, if we are willing to assume constant returns to scale, an assumption supported by the data. The estimate of $\beta$ is fairly accurate for two reasons. First, it is based on large variations in the data in a sample of observations from 1952 to 1998 and is found to be unchanged in the two subperiods before and after 1978. Second, the corresponding labor elasticity $(1 - \beta)$

is confirmed by the labor share of income in the 1920s and in 1953, when the market economy was functioning. Given the accuracy of β and the assumption of constant returns to scale, a regression of $\ln(Y/L)$ on only two variables, $\ln(K/L)$ and $t$, that uses wide-ranging observations from 1952 to 1998, can provide an accurate estimate of the remaining coefficient of $t$, which measures the exponential rate of increase in TFP. The remaining two parameters are the rate of increase in $L$ and the rate of increase in $K$, which is determined by the fraction of national output going to investment. Some inaccuracy in estimating the former is not important for an accurate forecast of GDP, because its value is small and the value of labor elasticity in the production function is also small. The fraction of national output going to investment appears to be a stable parameter if one observes the data for mainland China in the 1980s and 1990s and that for Taiwan and other east Asian countries in the process of development. If the values of the four parameters used in the neoclassical growth model are all fairly accurate, our assessment of future GDP growth in China will be reasonably accurate.

This discussion of economic forecasting based on the values of parameters in an econometric model shows why a model is useful. We came out with a forecast of above 7.5 percent per year on average for China's GDP growth in the first decade of the twenty-first century. One might say that such a forecast could have been obtained without using an econometric model: it is simply based on a moderate reduction of the growth rate prevailing in the last decade of the twentieth century. But without a model we would not know how much the moderate deduction ought to be, or whether the forecast should be a moderate increase. The parameters of a model summarize the quantitative characteristics of an economy, as illustrated by the four parameters of the model in this chapter. If there is any reason for the value of any parameter to change we can incorporate the change in our forecast. A case in point is the parameter measuring the rate of increase in the labor force; another parameter is the rate of increase in total factor productivity. For example, if China's membership in the WTO will raise this rate, as we discussed in section 4.5, the adjustment in this parameter can also be incorporated in our forecast. Government policy, such as economic reform and membership in the WTO, could lead to changes in parameters, including the rate of investment as a percentage of GDP, the population growth rate, and the rate of increase in TFP. Without a model the effects of these changes, and of government policy, cannot be taken into account in a forecast.

Where has historical-institutional information been utilized in the above analysis? First, the exclusion from our sample of data from the years 1958–69 is based partly on this information. Second, the specification of an increase in total factor productivity beginning in 1979 is also based on such information. Third, we are willing to accept that the percentage increase in total factor productivity has been fairly constant from 1979 on, and will not decline by more than one percentage point for the purposes of forecasting real output one decade ahead. This judgment is consistent with the smooth and gradual process of economic reform in the past, a trend which one can expect to continue in the future. Fourth, the constancy of the ratio of investment to GDP is based on the institutional assumption that the investment behavior of both the state and nonstate sectors remains the same. Fifth, the reduction in the growth rate of the labor force reflects the effects of the one-child-family policy and market forces (to be discussed in chapter 11).

If institutional changes occur to invalidate any of these assumptions, our model has to be modified to take them into account.

Having constructed capital stock data for mainland China and estimated Cobb–Douglas production functions, we can draw the following conclusions.

First, one production function with constant returns, constant capital and labor exponents, and a constant exponential rate of increase in TFP can explain the data on GDP growth in China from 1952 to 1998, except that TFP remains constant in 1952–78 and begins to increase at a constant rate after 1979.

Second, the capital exponent is about 0.6 and the annual increase in TFP beginning 1979 is about 0.03.

Third, for the period 1978–98, capital contributes about 62 percent, labor 11 percent and TFP 30 percent to the 0.093 exponential rate of GDP growth in China.

Fourth, in the last years of the sample period, the rate of labor force growth started to decline as a result of the one-child policy introduced in 1980, and market forces. This is expected to slow down future growth in GDP by about 0.6 percent.

Fifth, a significant finding is the small exponent of about 0.4 for labor in China. This can be interpreted as a result of the very large supply of labor relative to capital stock. Approximating the input–output relation by a function with a constant elasticity with respect to labor yields a low estimate of this elasticity. The elasticity is expected to increase as the economy accumulates more capital, but there is no evidence up to this point of its increase, suggesting that labor is still in abundance in China.

Sixth, capital accumulation has been the most important factor for increasing output in China, contributing above 70 percent to the growth in 1952–98. This is the result of a large rate of gross investment relative to GDP which amounts to over 30 percent in the last decade.

Seventh, the exponential growth rate of GDP in the first decade of the twenty-first century is expected to be above 0.075, because the only factors contributing to the decline from the historical 0.093 rate appear to be moderate reductions in the rate of growth of the labor force and possibly in the rate of growth of TFP.

## 5.6   How Large will the Chinese Economy be in 2020?

If we project the growth of Chinese GNP to 2020 using two alternative rates of growth of 7.5 and 6.0 percent, how large will the Chinese economy be? Admittedly, positing an annual growth rate of 7.5 percent up to 2010 might be reasonable, but projecting it to 2020 may serve only as the upper bound of a reasonable forecast. Compounding an annual growth rate at a factor of 1.075, or an exponential growth rate of 0.07232, for 22 years, gives an increase in lnGDP of 1.59105, or a multiple of 4.91. For the purpose of comparison with US GNP, we use an initial value of US$3,983.6 billion as China's "GNP measured at PPP [purchasing power parity]" in 1998. This figure is given in the World Bank report, *Entering the 21st Century* (2000: table 1, p. 230). Multiplying the 1998 GDP of $3,983.6 by 4.91 gives 19.56 or about 20 trillion 1998 US dollars in 2020. Note that the *China Statistical Yearbook, 1999* (table 3.1) gives China's GNP in 1998 as 7,801.78 billion yuan. The ratio 7,801.78/3,983.6 is 1.958 for conversion from Chinese yuan to US dollars by purchasing power parity (PPP), very different from the 1998 exchange rate of 8.3. PPP conversion is based on the amount of yuan which could be used to buy the same bundle of goods in China as one dollar could buy in the United States in 1998. The 1.958 conversion rate in the World Bank report could be challenged, although I, for one, would not challenge it, based on my casual observations of relative prices in China and the United States.

It may be of interest to compare China' GNP with US GNP in 1998 and in 2020 using the PPP criterion. US GNP in 1998 was 7.923 trillion (again, see table 1 of *Entering the 21st Century*). This is about twice as big as the Chinese figure of 3.9836 trillion cited in the last paragraph. Will China have caught up with the United States by 2020 in terms of the level of GNP? That depends on the rate of growth of US GNP from 1998 to 2020. One way to answer this question is to find out what rate of growth of US GNP would make the GNPs of the two countries equal in PPP 1998 US dollars. Beginning from 7.923 trillion in 1998, for US GNP to grow to 20 trillion (or by a factor of 20/7.923, or 2.524) in 22 years, the exponential rate is ln(2.524)/22 or 0.042. It seems unlikely that the US economy will grow at an average exponential rate of 0.042, or an annual rate of 0.043, from 1998 to 2020. Therefore, it is reasonable to suppose that the Chinese economy will overtake the US economy in terms of the size of its real GDP or GNP by 2020, on the assumption that the Chinese growth rate will average 7.5 percent per year up to 2020.

To use a lower and perhaps more reasonable rate, let China's exponential growth rate be reduced to 0.06. This figure is slightly lower than the rates given in the World Bank's *China: 2020*, which projected the following growth rates: 1996–2000: 8.4 percent; 2001–10: 6.9 percent; 2010–20: 5.5 percent; 1996–2020: 6.6 percent. Compounding an exponential rate of 0.06 for 22 years gives a factor of 3.75. This makes China's GNP in 2020 equal to 3.9836 trillion × 3.75, or 14.94 trillion. The growth factor for the US to reach this figure is 14.94/7.923, or 1.885, in 22 years. Dividing ln(1.885) by 22 gives 0.0288 as the US exponential growth rate required just to keep up with China in 2020. An exponential growth rate of 0.0288, or an annual growth rate of 2.92 percent, is about the median of the growth rates projected by American economists in 2001. Hence the Chinese economy can be expected to generate about the same real GDP as the US economy in 1998 PPP terms in 2020, under the assumption of only a 6 percent annual growth for China.

## References and Further Reading

Buck, John L. *Chinese Farm Economy*. Chicago, IL: University of Chicago Press, 1930.

Chow, Gregory C. "Chinese Statistics." *The American Statistician*, 40 (Aug. 1985), pp. 191–6.

Chow, Gregory C. "Capital Formation and Economic Growth in China." *Quarterly Journal of Economics*, 108 (Aug. 1993), pp. 809–42.

Chow, Gregory. "Are Chinese Official Statistics Reliable?" *CESifo Economic Studies*, 52(2) (2006), pp. 396–414.

Chow, Gregory and Anloh Lin. "Accounting for Economic Growth for Taiwan and Mainland China: A Comparative Analysis." *Journal of Comparative Economics*, 30 (2002), pp. 507–30.

Engle, Robert and C. W. J. Granger. "Co-integration and Error Correction: Representation, Estimation and Testing." *Econometrica*, 55(2) (1987), pp. 251–76.

Mankiw, N. Gregory, David Romer, and David N. Weil. "A Contribution to the Empirics of Economic
Growth." *Quarterly Journal of Economics*, 108 (1992), pp. 407–38.

Solow, Robert M. "A Contribution to the Theory of Economic Growth." *Quarterly Journal of
Economics*, 70 (Feb. 1956), pp. 65–94.

Young, Alwyn. "The Tyranny of Numbers: Confronting the Statistical Realities of the East Asian
Growth Experience." *Quarterly Journal of Economics*, 110(3) (1995), pp. 642–80.

World Bank. *China: 2020*. New York: Oxford University Press, 1997.

World Bank. *Entering the 21st Century: World Development Report 1999/2000*. New York: Oxford
University Press, 2000.

# Questions

1   Using the data in table 5.1, estimate by least-squares a Cobb–Douglas production
    function without a trend for the sample period 1952–80, excluding 1959–69, under
    the assumption of constant returns to scale.

2   Add a trend term to the regression in question 1 and test the statistical significance of
    its coefficient. What can one conclude about the presence of an increase in total factor
    productivity in China during this period?

3   What are the four parameters in the neoclassical model of economic growth? What
    numerical values of these parameters for China can you justify? Give your justification
    of each. About which do you have most doubt concerning their accuracy when used
    to forecast China's future GDP, and why? Change them to new values and justify
    your change. How does the change affect the estimate of exponential rate of growth
    of GDP in the first decade of the twenty-first century? Explain.

4   Using the model summarized by equations (5.5), project real GDP for China annually
    from 1999 to 2010.

# 6

# Economic Fluctuations

The multiplier-accelerator model is introduced to explain economic fluctuations in general and national income in China in particular. In connection with the estimation of such a model for China, the important econometric concept of a system of simultaneous equations is set forth, including endogenous and predetermined variables, structural and reduced-form equations, and the two-stage least-squares method for estimating the parameters of structural equations. Further, the econometrics of a vector autoregression (VAR) system is discussed, and an important application to China's economy is provided.

## 6.1 The Multiplier-Accelerator Model of Economic Fluctuations

Supply and demand are two key concepts in economics. In the neoclassical model of economic growth discussed in chapter 5, output is assumed to be determined by factors on the supply side. The quantities of aggregate capital and labor inputs are assumed to determine aggregate output through the production function. In the multiplier-accelerator model discussed in this chapter, output is determined by aggregate demand. Both models are simplifications of the reality. One can combine the equations explaining both the supply and demand sides of the economy to build a model, but it is interesting to see how well each of these two simplified models performs in explaining economic data. The purposes of the two models are different. The model in chapter 5 was used to explain growth trends, ignoring year-to-year fluctuations. The model in this chapter is used to explain year-to-year fluctuations.

The neoclassical economic growth model in the last chapter is built upon the aggregate production function. The function shows how much output the economy can produce given the quantities of the two inputs and the state of technology as summarized by the total factor productivity (TFP). TFP may be assumed to be a constant or to follow an exponential trend. The aggregate production function shows capacity output, disregarding the fact that actual output may fall short of capacity output. It is an equation describing the supply or production side of the economy. Given the production function, we need to determine the amounts of the two inputs through time to explain GDP growth. Labor input is assumed to be given exogenously, or to grow at a given constant rate. Capital stock grows according to the identity equating capital stock at the end of period $t$ to depreciated capital stock at the end of period $(t - 1)$ plus gross investment. Gross investment is assumed to be a fraction of GDP. The idea behind this assumption is that the higher the output or national income, the more the economy can afford to invest. In this growth model, the larger the fraction of GDP devoted to investment at the expense of consumption, the higher the rate of capital formation and hence the higher the rate of GDP growth.

In this section, the model of economic fluctuations, or of national income determination in the short run, is based on the forces of aggregate demand. In the early 1930s, when the United States experienced the Great Depression, Keynes wrote the *General Theory of Employment, Interest and Money* (1936). The theory suggests that aggregate output in the short run cannot be explained by assuming full employment or the full utilization of resources – like the growth model in chapter 5. In the thirties, over 20 percent of the American labor force was unemployed. If actual output deviates substantially from the capacity output specified by the production function, what determines it? Keynes' answer is aggregate demand. By way of the national income identity, national output can be decomposed into outputs from different industries. National output can also be decomposed into expenditure by consumers $C$, on investment $I$, by government $G$, and on net exports $X$ (exports minus imports). The familiar national income identity is

$$Y = C + I + G + X \tag{6.1}$$

If the four components on the righthand side of equation (6.1) can be explained, national income $Y$ can be explained.

Keynes (1936) proposed the simple hypothesis that $C$ is a linear function of $Y$, with a slope (called the marginal propensity to consume) of less than 1 and a positive intercept. The shortcomings of this Keynesian consumption function were pointed out by Friedman (1957), who proposed that $C$ is proportional to permanent income under the permanent income hypothesis. Permanent income, as distinguished from current income $Y$ used by Keynes, measures the long-run income of the individual during his lifetime. The relation of consumption to current income implies that individuals with higher incomes tend to consume proportionally less. Individuals with different levels of permanent income consume the same proportion of their permanent income. One approximation of the consumption function based on permanent income is

$$\begin{aligned} C_t &= a_0 Y_t + a_1 C_{t-1} = a_0 Y_t + a_1(a_0 Y_{t-1} + a_1 C_{t-2}) \\ &= a_0(Y_t + a_1 Y_{t-1} + a_1^2 Y_{t-2} + \dots) \end{aligned} \tag{6.2}$$

The first equality sign introduces lagged consumption $C_{t-1}$ as an explanatory variable affecting current consumption. If we use this consumption function to substitute for $C_{t-1}$

and continue the process to eliminate past consumption, we obtain consumption as a weighted average of past incomes with geometrically declining weights. This weighted average is given by the term in parentheses on the second line of equation (6.2). It is used to measure permanent income in Friedman (1957). Thus (6.2) states that consumption is proportional to permanent income.

The difference between the Keynesian consumption function and Friedman's consumption function has an important implication for the fate of capitalism. If consumption is a decreasing fraction of income, it does not generate sufficient aggregate demand for consumption when income increases. As an economy grows, the demand for consumable goods generated by the consumption function becomes proportionally less. Unless another component of aggregate demand, such as government expenditure, increases sufficiently to compensate for the deficiency generated by the demand for consumption goods, the economy will cease to grow. A capitalist economy is doomed to be stagnant as it grows richer. This does not happen if consumption is proportional to permanent income. As income increases, the same fraction of income will be generated by the demand for consumption expenditures.

To explain investment expenditures $I$ by the acceleration principle, we assume that the desired capital stock $K_t^*$ at the end of period $t$ is a function $a + bY_t$ of current output, and that the change in capital stock $K_t - K_{t-1}$ is a fraction $\beta$ of the difference $K_t^* - K_{t-1}$. These two assumptions imply

$$K_t = \beta(a + bY_t) + (1 - \beta)K_{t-1}$$

This equation, which explains capital stock $K_t$, has the same form as consumption function (6.2) explaining $C_t$. By definition, net investment is the rate of change of capital stock, or $I_t = K_t - K_{t-1}$. To obtain an equation for net investment we subtract an analogous equation for $K_{t-1}$ from the above equation for $K_t$ to yield

$$I_t = K_t - K_{t-1} = \beta b(Y_t - Y_{t-1}) + (1 - \beta)I_{t-1} \tag{6.3}$$

According to equation (6.3), net investment is determined by the rate of change in national income and not by the level of income. Income is a flow, or output per unit of time, as speed is distance traveled per unit time. The rate of change in income corresponds to rate of change in speed, or acceleration. Hence (6.3) is said to satisfy the acceleration principle, as investment is explained by the rate of change in income.

The acceleration principle can explain why investment fluctuates more than consumption. Let income be 100, 105, and 106 in periods 1, 2, and 3 respectively. If consumption is proportional to income, it will be proportional to 100, 105, and 106, or will increase by 5 percent and by about 1 percent in periods 2 and 3 respectively. On the other hand the first component of investment according to equation (6.3) is proportional to 5 and 1 for periods 2 and 3 respectively, implying a drastic reduction from period 2 to period 3, instead of a small increase, as in the case of consumption. This drastic reduction is moderated by the effect of lagged investment, which enters as a second explanatory variable in equation (6.3). If we wish to explain gross investment $I_t^G = K_t - (1 - d)K_{t-1}$, where $d$ is the rate of depreciation of capital stock, we subtract $(1 - d)K_{t-1}$ from $K_t$ and use the same equation for $K_t$ to obtain an equation similar to (6.3), except that the rate of change of income is replaced by $Y_t - (1 - d)Y_{t-1}$ and the lagged value of net investment is replaced by the lagged value of gross investment on the righthand side. To test the acceleration principle statistically, one can estimate a regression of investment on $Y_t$, $Y_{t-1}$, and $I_{t-1}$. The acceleration principle is considered confirmed if the coefficient of $Y_{t-1}$ equals the negative of the coefficient of $Y_t$ when net investment is the dependent variable, or equals $-(1 - d)$ times the coefficient of $Y_t$ when gross investment is the dependent variable. Such statistical evidence has been found by numerous studies of investment expenditure in the US and in China as reported in Chow (1957, 1960, 1967, 1985a, 1985b).

Equations (6.1), (6.2), and (6.3) provide three equations to explain the three endogenous variables $Y$, $C$, and $I$. The model for national income determination is complete if we assume that government expenditure $G$ and net exports $X$ are exogenous, namely determined outside the system. Alternatively we can apply the model to explain Chinese national income data if we define $C$ to include both private and government consumption and if we exclude net exports $X$ from our definition of national income. This is indeed what the Chinese official statistic on "national income available" before 1994 measures. National income available equals national income minus net exports. It is the sum of consumption $C$ (which includes government consumption) and "accumulation" (which equals net investment).

## 6.2  Dynamic Properties of the Multiplier-Accelerator Model

Let us study the characteristics of the time path of "national income available" generated by the above version of the multiplier-accelerator model. In this model, $Y$ denotes "national income available," which excludes net exports $X$, and $C$ includes government consumption. Hence the variables $G$ and $X$ in equation (6.1) can be omitted. Equations (6.1), (6.2), and (6.3) determine the three endogenous variables $Y_t$, $C_t$, and $I_t$ in each period $t$, given the values of the predetermined variables $C_{t-1}$ and $I_{t-1}$. As a matter of terminology, variables are called endogenous variables if their values are determined by solving the system of equations used to describe the economy. Variables are called predetermined variables if their values are taken as given when the equations are solved for the values of the endogenous variables. Predetermined variables are either exogenous or are variables whose values are dated before the current period. The exogenous variables are assumed to be determined by factors outside the system which can affect the system but cannot be affected by it.

If we use equation (6.1) to eliminate the variable $Y$ and solve equations (6.2) and (6.3) algebraically we can express $C$ and $I$ as linear functions of the predetermined variables as follows.

$$C_t = \pi_{11}C_{t-1} + \pi_{12}I_{t-1} + \pi_{10}$$
$$I_t = \pi_{21}C_{t-1} + \pi_{22}I_{t-1} + \pi_{20} \tag{6.4}$$

These equations are known as "reduced-form" equations. Each reduced-form equation expresses an endogenous variable as a function of the predetermined variables. The original system of simultaneous equations (6.1), (6.2), and (6.3) are known as "structural" equations. Each structural equation can have more than one endogenous variable. The reduced-form equations are obtained by solving the structural equations algebraically for the endogenous variables. To appreciate how reduced-form equations can be obtained by solving the structural equations the reader should refer to question 2 at the end of this chapter.

As a numerical example of the reduced-form equations (6.4), consider the following parameter values, written in vector form, with each parameter on the lefthand side equal to the numerical value in the corresponding position on the righthand side.

$$(\pi_{11} \ \pi_{12} \ \pi_{10}) = (-0.2 \ \ 2.25 \ \ 15)$$
$$(\pi_{21} \ \pi_{22} \ \pi_{20}) = (-0.8 \ \ 2.25 \ \ 15) \tag{6.5}$$

If the initial values $C_0 = 45.9$ and $I_0 = 13.0$ are given, we can use equations (6.4) to compute $C_1$ and $I_1$ for period 1, and given these, to compute the values of $C_2$ and $I_2$ for period 2, and so forth. Thus the time paths of $C$ and $I$, and therefore of $Y$, can be generated by the model comprised of (6.1) to (6.3), after they are solved to obtain the reduced-form equation (6.4). The reader will find it instructive to trace out the time paths of $C$ and $I$ in this model as suggested in question 1 at the end of this chapter.

The above numerical exercise illustrates that the interaction of a consumption function specified by equation (6.2), and an investment equation (6.3) based on the acceleration principle, can generate oscillations in national income and its components. This important point was first discussed in Samuelson (1939) for deterministic models with no random residuals added to equations (6.2) and (6.3). On the importance of introducing random elements into economic models, Frisch (1933: 197, 202–3) writes:

> The examples we have discussed . . . show that when [a deterministic] economic system gives rise to oscillations, these will most frequently be damped. But in reality the cycles . . . are generally not damped. How can the maintenance of the swings be explained? . . . One way which I believe is particularly fruitful and promising is to study what would become of the solution of a deterministic dynamic system if it were exposed to a stream of erratic shocks . . . Thus, by connecting the two ideas: (1) the continuous solution of a determinate dynamic system and (2) the discontinuous shocks intervening and supplying the energy that may maintain the swings – we get a theoretical setup which seems to furnish a rational interpretation of those movements which we have been accustomed to see in our statistical time data.

Ragner Frisch was the first Nobel Prize winner in economic sciences (in 1969, shared with Jan Tinbergen), and these remarks were very perceptive and influential. A deterministic model can be converted into a stochastic model by adding random residuals to the structural equations (6.2) and (6.3). This would result in random residuals in the reduced-form equations (6.4), which are derived from (6.2) and (6.3) algebraically, using the identity (6.1). We can solve the reduced-form equations (6.4) forward in time by incorporating random draws of these residuals. The time path for each dependent variable is a stochastic time series.

The study of dynamic characteristics of stochastic time series generated by a system of simultaneous equations like (6.1) to (6.3), with random residuals added to (6.2) and (6.3), advanced rapidly in the late 1960s and 1970s. Some results are reported in Chow (1968, 1975). In Chow (1968) it was shown that a system of equations, which consists only of equations like (6.2) to describe different components of $Y$ but does not include equations like (6.3) based on the acceleration principle, cannot generate oscillations. In other words, Samuelson (1939) shows that a combination of (6.2) and (6.3) can, but does not necessarily, generate oscillations, whereas Chow (1968) shows that the inclusion of acceleration-type investment equations is necessary. Chow (1968) and Chow (1975) discuss the meaning of business cycles for time series generated by a system of stochastic equations, while Chow (1975) also uses the tools to study the cyclical properties generated by a particular econometric model reported in Chow (1967).

## 6.3  An Econometric Method for Estimating Parameters of Linear Stochastic Equations

Since the parameters of the structural equations (6.2) and (6.3) and of the reduced-form equations (6.4) are unknown, an economist needs to estimate them from data on $Y$, $C$, and $I$. Prior to estimation we need to add random residuals $u_{1t}$ and $u_{2t}$ to equations (6.2) and (6.3) respectively. Such residuals are required because the equations cannot fit the data exactly without them. It is often assumed that these random residuals satisfy a multivariate normal distribution with zero means and some covariance matrix. The two residuals are correlated in general because some factors other than the predetermined variables included in the system may affect both consumption and investment. Once $u_{1t}$ and $u_{2t}$ are added to equations (6.2) and (6.3), some linear functions of them, denoted by $v_{1t}$ and $v_{2t}$, will appear respectively in the reduced-form equations (6.4) for $C_t$ and $I_t$ as a result of the algebra in solving (6.2) and (6.3) for (6.4). If in doubt, the reader should solve (6.2) and (6.3) with residuals $u_{1t}$ and $u_{2t}$ added to obtain the reduced-form equations and examine the relation between the residuals $v_{1t}$ and $v_{2t}$ in (6.4) and the former residuals. Since the $u$'s affect the values of the endogenous variables through affecting the values of the $v$'s in the reduced-form equations, all endogenous variables are correlated with the residuals of the structural equations. For example, $Y_t$ is an endogenous variable and is correlated with $u_{1t}$ in the consumption equation (6.2) and also with $u_{2t}$ in the investment equation (6.3).

A basic assumption justifying the use of the least-squares method for estimating the coefficients of a regression equation is that the residual will be uncorrelated with each of the explanatory variables. Without this assumption, the least-squares estimates will not equal the true values of the regression coefficients even if the sample size is infinitely large. This assumption is not satisfied if we apply the least-squares method to estimate the structural equations (6.2) and (6.3), because the explanatory variable $Y_t$ on the righthand side is correlated with the residual in each equation. To overcome this problem, one can apply the two-stage least-squares method. In the first stage we estimate that part of $Y_t$, which is uncorrelated with the residuals $u_{1t}$ and $u_{2t}$. In the second stage we apply least-squares to estimate (6.2) and (6.3) with $Y_t$ replaced by the part estimated in stage 1. To estimate that part of $Y$ which is uncorrelated with the $u$'s, one can regress $Y_t$ on the predetermined variables $C_{t-1}$ and $I_{t-1}$. By assumption, a predetermined variable is uncorrelated with all $u$'s and all $v$'s. This is the first-stage regression in the two-stage least-squares method 2SLS for estimating the structural parameters in a system of linear stochastic equations. From this stage we compute the estimated value of $Y_t$ using the linear regression function on $C_{t-1}$ and $I_{t-1}$. In the second stage we use the estimated $Y_t$ in lieu of the actual $Y_t$ to estimate the structural equations (6.2) and (6.3) by the least-squares method. For example, to estimate consumption equation (6.2) we regress the variable $C_t$ on the estimated $Y_t$ and $C_{t-1}$. The estimated $Y_t$ is uncorrelated with the residual $u_{1t}$ because it is a linear function of the predetermined variables and the predetermined variables are assumed to be uncorrelated with the $u_{1t}$.

## 6.4   Estimating a Multiplier-Accelerator Model of the Chinese Economy

Chow (1985b) uses Chinese official data from 1952 to 1982 on national income available and its two components $C$ (including government consumption) and $I$ (called accumulation) to estimate equations (6.2) and (6.3) by the two-stage least-squares method. The estimated structural equations are

$$C_t = -5.0456 - 0.0935\,Y_t + 1.2502\,C_{t-1} \qquad R^2 = 0.9933$$
$$\quad\;\;(2.7645)\;\;(0.1358)\quad\;\;(0.2251) \qquad\qquad s^2 = 18.489$$

$$I_t = 1.5643 + 0.6656\,(Y_t - Y_{t-1}) + 0.8920\,I_{t-1} \quad R^2 = 0.8787$$
$$\quad(3.7992)\;\;(0.2729)\qquad\qquad\quad\;(0.0722)\quad\; s^2 = 103.027 \tag{6.6}$$

In the second stage of applying the 2SLS method, the variable $Y$ on the righthand side of each equation is replaced by its estimate obtained from the first-stage regression. In the consumption function the coefficient of income is statistically insignificant. This result is a piece of evidence leading one to reject equation (6.2) as an appropriate consumption equation, but it supports a different version of the permanent income hypothesis as formulated by Hall (1978).

In equation (6.2), permanent income is defined as a weighted average of current and past incomes with geometrically declining weights. This definition is consistent with the adaptive expectations hypothesis. According to this hypothesis, expected or permanent income $Y^e_t$ is formed by a partial adjustment process. By a partial adjustment process in the formation of expectation, we mean that the change in expectation, in our case the change in expected income $Y^e_t - Y^e_{t-1}$, equals a fraction $a$ of the forecasting error

$Y_t - Y_{t-1}^e$, so that expectation $Y_t^e$ is only partially adjusted to equal the actual $Y_t$. By using this equation to eliminate past expected incomes as in equation (6.2), we find expected income to be a weighted average of current and past incomes with geometrically declining weights, namely $a[Y_t + (1 - a)Y_{t-1} + (1 - a)^2 Y_{t-2} + \ldots]$, as specified in equation (6.2).

Another definition of permanent income is based on the rational expectation hypothesis. According to this hypothesis, the consumer chooses the consumption path which maximizes his lifetime expected utility. In the last period $t - 1$ his consumption was proportional to his permanent income of that period. Since $C_{t-1}$ already contains all information on permanent income in $t - 1$ which is relevant in estimating permanent income in period $t$, no other variables observed at $t - 1$ will have any effect on $C_t$. In the second-stage regression the estimated income variable is a linear function of $C_{t-1}$ and $Y_{t-1}$. Given $C_{t-1}$, therefore, this income estimate will have no effect on $C_t$. In other words $C_{t-1}$ is the only variable observed in period $t - 1$ that affects $C_t$. This version of the permanent income hypothesis, as advanced by Hall (1978), is consistent with Chinese data, as the above estimated consumption function shows.

We have just reviewed two versions of the permanent income hypothesis for the explanation of consumption. The first version is based on the formation of permanent income by the adaptive expectation hypothesis. The second is based on the formation of permanent income by the rational expectation hypothesis. Which hypothesis is better for the study of which economic phenomena is an interesting question not yet resolved. The reader may wonder why either hypothesis is applicable to the explanation of aggregate consumption in China, where the economic institutions are different. In chapter 2, when we studied the Chinese economy during the period of planning, we pointed out that the behavior of Chinese consumers is not different. This point is empirically confirmed in chapter 9. The existence of rationed commodities should not affect total consumption expenditure, the variable which we wish to explain. It only limits the quantities of rationed commodities that can be purchased. In this discussion we do assume that total consumption expenditure is determined by the demand of consumers. One might argue that it is determined instead by the supply made available by Chinese economic planners. Such an issue cannot be settled by general arguments; an economist can only pursue his research by choosing hypotheses which he deems appropriate. If the results are consistent with the hypotheses, he will keep them in future research. Other researchers might choose different hypotheses to explain the same phenomena and proceed likewise. In the present case, the reader is welcome to start with a hypothesis based on the notion that aggregate consumption is determined by the supply side and formulate her model accordingly. The results can be compared.

The investment equation is consistent with the acceleration principle, showing the importance of the rate of change in income in explaining investment. This principle is applicable not only to the demand for investment expenditures but to the demand for the purchase of consumer durable goods. We can go through the same derivation to arrive at a demand function for the purchase of durable goods by first assuming that the desired stock of consumer durables, like the desired capital stock $K^*$, is a function of income or output. Second, we assume as before that the change in the stock of durable goods is a fraction of the difference between the desired stock and the actual stock at the end of the preceding period. The resulting equation explaining the purchase of durable goods is the same as the one explaining gross investment following the acceleration principle. This principle may help explain the slowdown in the purchase of consumer durables in China in 1998 after the Asian financial crisis had started in July 1997. Although real GDP continued to increase in 1998, it was increasing at a slower rate. Recall our numerical example with $Y$ equalling 100, 105, and 106 in three consecutive periods. In period 3, $Y$ continues to increase but at a slower rate than in period 2, leading to a decline of investment, as its first component in equation (6.3) is proportional to 5 in period 2 and to 1 in period 3. The rate of growth of real GDP in China in 1998 did not decrease as much as this numerical example, but it might be sufficient to explain the observed reduction in the purchase of consumer durables in China in 1998. To the extent that the acceleration principle can account for the reduction, it indicates that the phenomenon of weak demand is only temporary. Once the economy recovers, the demand for consumer durables will increase again.

After the structural equations (6.6) are estimated, we can solve them to obtain reduced-form equations (6.4). A second method of obtaining the reduced-form equations is simply to apply least squares to estimate them directly. To understand the possible difference between the results obtained by these two methods, note that the first method obtains the parameters of the reduced-form equations by solving the structural equations algebraically. This means that the reduced-form parameters are functions of the structural parameters. As an example, let there be only one structural parameter $\beta$ and two reduced-form parameters $\pi_1$ and $\pi_2$. If the latter two parameters can be calculated from the value of $\beta$ this means that $\pi_1 = f_1(\beta)$ and $\pi_2 = f_2(\beta)$ for some functions $f_1$ and $f_2$. This also means that $\pi_1$ and $\pi_2$ are algebraically related. To see that, use the first equation to solve $\beta$ as a function of $\pi_1$ and substitute this for $\beta$ in the second equation for $\pi_2$, making $\pi_2$ a function of $\pi_1$. We can see from this example that in general if there are fewer parameters in the structural equations than in the reduced-form equations, the parameters of the reduced-form equations are subject to algebraic restrictions. In this case, solving for the reduced-form parameters gives a different result from estimating them directly by the least-squares method, as the latter imposes no such algebraic restrictions. When there are the same number of parameters in both the structural equations and reduced-form equations, the two methods give identical results. In our example, there are 6 parameters in both. (There cannot be more structural coefficients than reduced-form coefficients. If the model specifies more structural coefficients, some of them cannot be estimated even with a sample of infinite size, and these parameters are said to be unidentified.) The econometrics of simultaneous equations is discussed in Chow (1983).

Applying least squares to estimate the reduced-form equations directly gives

$$C_t = -4.2852 + 1.1225C_{t-1} - 0.0495I_{t-1} \quad R^2 = 0.9933$$
$$\quad (2.1247) \ (0.0424) \quad\quad (0.0719) \quad s^2 = 18.489$$

$$I_t = -3.8511 + 0.2439C_{t-1} + 0.5787I_{t-1} \quad R^2 = 0.8787$$
$$\quad (5.0154) \ (0.1000) \quad\quad (0.1696) \quad s^2 = 103.027 \quad\quad (6.7)$$

By examining the residuals from these reduced-form equations, one can measure the impacts of political shocks on consumption and investment (see Chow 1985b, table 2). The standard errors of the reduced-form consumption and investment equations are respectively 4.3 and 10. Observed residuals of the regression equation twice as large as its standard error can be considered abnormal. For example, in the year 1961 when the economic collapse from the Great Leap was most severe, the residuals of the consumption and investment equations were respectively −7.98 and 25.9. In the years 1967–8 of the Cultural Revolution, the residuals of the consumption equation were −0.87 and −8.86, and of the investment equation were −15.96 and −9.49. For a study of the macroeconomic effects of these two political movements, see chapter 8.

The reader may have noticed that in estimating the model in this chapter, in contrast with the estimation of the model in chapter 5, data for the years 1958–69 are not excluded. The decision to include observations for these years is based on the judgment that, while these observations deviate too much from the production function which specifies the relation between capacity output and available inputs, they do not deviate from the short-run relations specified in equations (6.2) and (6.3), in which the dependent variable of the preceding period is included as an explanatory variable. The inclusion of a residual in each of these equations suffices to incorporate the effect of the Great Leap or the Cultural Revolution on period $t$, given that the effect on the variable in period $t − 1$ is already included in the righthand side of the equation. Thus the estimated residual measures the effect of a political movement on the dependent variable of a period $t$, in addition to its effect on the same variable in the preceding period $t − 1$. For a study of the long-run economic effects of the Great Leap Forward and the Cultural Revolution, the reader is referred to chapter 8.

More recent data are now available, in the light of which it would be interesting to re-estimate the consumption and investment equations. This is left as an exercise for the interested reader. (See questions 3 and 5 below.) The reduced-form equations can be used for forecasting, as $C_t$ and $I_t$ can be calculated from their values in the preceding period. (See question 6.)

## 6.5   A Vector Autoregression (VAR) System

An alternative model to the model of simultaneous equations for the study of economic fluctuations is the model of vector autoregression, abbreviated VAR. It is a system of econometric equations each explaining one variable by its own lagged values and the lagged values of all other variables in the system. As an example let $p$, $y$ and $m$ denote the natural logarithms of a price index $P$, real output $Y$ and the stock of money $M$ respectively. A VAR for these three variables (considered as a vector, hence the name) may be the following:

$$p_t = a_0 + a_1 p_{t-1} + a_2 y_{t-1} + a_3 m_{t-1} + a_4 p_{t-2} + a_5 y_{t-2} + a_6 m_{t-2} + u_{1t}$$
$$y_t = b_0 + b_1 p_{t-1} + b_2 y_{t-1} + b_3 m_{t-1} + b_4 p_{t-2} + b_5 y_{t-2} + b_6 m_{t-2} + u_{2t}$$
$$m_t = c_0 + c_1 p_{t-1} + c_2 y_{t-1} + c_3 m_{t-1} + c_4 p_{t-2} + c_5 y_{t-2} + c_6 m_{t-2} + u_{3t} \qquad (6.8)$$

The main difference between a VAR and a simultaneous equation system is that it does not distinguish between endogenous variables and predetermined variables. Each variable is treated as an endogenous variable and explained by its own lagged values and the lagged values of all other variables in the system. Such a VAR was estimated for China by Chow and Shen (2005) using Chinese data given in table 7.1, except for the variable $M$, which is $M_1$ or $M_2$ in the paper, instead of currency in circulation, as in the table 7.1.

To study the effect of monetary policy using such a model one cannot simply use the coefficients $a_3$ and $b_3$ in equation (6.8), which show the effects of $m_{t-1}$ on log price $p$ and log output $y$ respectively. The reason is that $m$ itself is determined by its own lagged values and the lagged values of $p$ and $y$. If the government is to exercise any monetary policy affecting $m$ it has to be other than what the lagged variables on the righthand side of the equation for $m$ in (6.8) would determine, that is, it has to show up in the residual $u_{3t}$. Therefore, to study the effect of "monetary shocks" (those factors other than the lagged variables already included in the righthand side of (6.8) as represented by $u_{3t}$), we have to trace the effects of $u_{3t}$ on each variable at $t$, $t + 1, \ldots, t + k$, by solving the equations (6.8) forward given the initial values of $p_{t-1}$, $y_{t-1}$, $m_{t-1}$, $p_{t-2}$, $y_{t-2}$, and $m_{t-2}$. There is a technical problem in attributing the effects of $u_{3t}$ on $p_t$ and $y_t$, since it does not appear in the first two equations of (6.8), but $u_{1t}$ and $u_{2t}$ in these equations may be correlated with it. Leaving this technical problem aside, we can solve equations (6.8) for $t$, $t + 1$, and so forth. The effect of $u_{3t}$ on $p_{t+k}$ is the "impulse response" of $p_{t+k}$ to a shock (impulse) in $m$. Sims (1980) advocated the use of VAR in economics, including the calculation of impulse responses.

Chow and Shen (2005) found the impulse responses of log price and log output to a monetary shock, which can be plotted as in figure 6.1. The vertical axis measures the impulse response of log price or log real GDP in units of its own standard deviation to a money shock of one standard deviation. The horizontal axis measures the future year in which the effect will occur. This figure confirms the proposition of Milton Friedman (1994) on the effects of monetary policy on aggregate output and prices: the effect on output takes place within a few months, but it disappears quickly (if there were a long-lasting effect one could promote economic growth simply by printing money); the effect on prices comes later, but it is longer lasting. Similar impulse responses are found using Chinese $M_2$ data and using US data as reported in Chow and Shen (2005). This VAR model will provide empirical support for our discussion of monetary policy in chapter 7.

## 6.6   Econometric Models of the Chinese Economy

In this chapter we have provided two simple models of the Chinese macroeconomy. The first is a system of simultaneous equations and the second is a VAR system. Each model is constructed with its own objective. Chapter 8 will provide another model constructed by a different method and for a different purpose. Econometric model-building in China

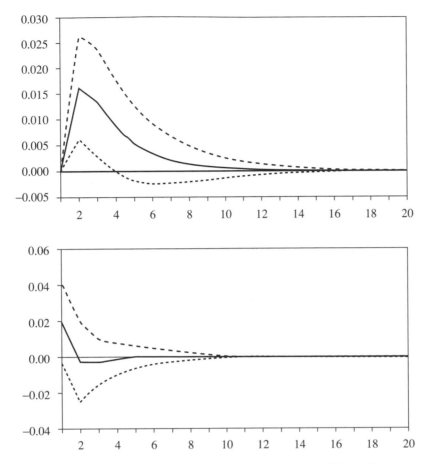

**Figure 6.1**   Impulse responses of price (top panel) and real output to Chinese $M_1$ shocks

started in the summer of 1980 when a group of seven American economists and statisticians, including the author, led by Professor Lawrence Klein of the University of Penn-
sylvania, went to Beijing to give a summer workshop on econometrics at the invitation
of Vice-president Xu Dixin of the Chinese Academy of Social Science. Since then, econometric modeling has advanced and become an important activity in China. Foreign
scholars have constructed econometric models of China, some in collaboration with
Chinese colleagues.

   Interested readers could refer to Klein and Ichimura (2000). The econometric models
reported by them consist of a system of equations. There are more equations than in the
models reported in chapters 5 and 6. For example, to explain the macroeconomy, equations for both the supply side (production functions) and the demand side (consumption
and investment) are included. There are equations explaining not only price level (as in

the second model in this chapter), but also interest rates, exchange rates, exports, imports, and balance of payments, etc. There is also a Computable General Equilibrium Model that explains the outputs of different sectors by the demand and supply equations of each sector – hence the term "general equilibrium." Such a model was referred to in section 4.5, in our discussion of the economic impact of China's entry into the WTO on the rate of growth of GDP. There is yet another kind of model: it is constructed under the assumption that economic decision-makers continuously optimize a multiperiod objective function over time in making their economic decisions. An example will be given in chapter 8 below.

# References and Further Reading

Chow, Gregory C. *Demand for Automobiles in the United States: A Study in Consumer Durables.* Amsterdam: North-Holland Publishing Company, 1957.

Chow, Gregory C. "Statistical Demand Functions for Automobiles and Their Use for Forecasting." In A. C. Harberger: *Demand for Durable Goods.* Chicago: University of Chicago Press, 1960.

Chow, Gregory C. "Multiplier, Accelerator, and Liquidity Preferences in the Determination of National Income in the United States." *Review of Economics and Statistics*, 44 (Feb. 1967), pp. 1–15.

Chow, Gregory C. "The Acceleration Principle and the Nature of Business Cycles." *Quarterly Journal of Economics*, 82 (Aug. 1968), pp. 403–18.

Chow, Gregory C. *Analysis and Control of Dynamic Economic Systems.* New York: John Wiley, 1975.

Chow, Gregory C. *Econometrics.* New York: McGraw-Hill, 1983.

Chow, Gregory C. *The Chinese Economy.* New York: Harper and Row, 1985a.

Chow, Gregory C. "A Model of Chinese National Income Determination." *Journal of Political Economy*, 93 (Aug. 1985b), pp. 782–92.

Chow, Gregory C. and Yan Shen. "Money, Price Level and Output in the Chinese Macro Economy." *Asia-Pacific Journal of Accounting and Economics*, 12(2) (Dec. 2005), pp. 91–111.

Friedman, Milton. *A Theory of the Consumption Function.* Princeton: Princeton University Press, 1957.

Friedman, M. *Money Mischief.* New York: Harcourt Brace & Co., 1994.

Frisch, R. "Propagation Problems and Impulse Problems in Dynamic Economics." In *Economic Essays in Honour of Gustav Cassel.* London: Macmillan, 1933.

Hall, Robert E. "Stochastic Implications of the Life Cycle–Permanent Income Hypothesis," *Journal of Political Economy*, 86 (Dec. 1978), pp. 971–87.

Keynes, John Maynard. *General Theory of Employment, Interest and Money.* New York: Harcourt, Brace and Co., 1936.

Klein, Lawrence R. and Shinichi Ichimura. *Econometric Modeling of China.* Singapore: World Scientific Publishing Co., 2000.

Samuelson, Paul A. "Interactions Between the Multiplier Analysis and the Principle of Acceleration." *The Review of Economics and Statistics*, 21 (1939), pp. 75–8.

Sims, C. A. "Macroeconomics and Reality." *Econometrica*, 48 (1980), pp. 1–48.

# Questions

1  Using the reduced-form equations (6.4), the numerical parameters given in (6.5), and the initial values $C_0 = 45.9$ and $I_0 = 13.0$ of $C$ and $I$, compute the paths of $C$ and $I$ up to period 11. Comment on the nature of these time paths. Does the variable $I$ tend to fluctuate more than $C$? If so, why?

2  Solve structural equations (6.6) to obtain reduced-form equations for $C_t$ and $I_t$. First eliminate $Y_t$ and $Y_{t-1}$ in the structural equations by using equation (6.1).

3  Using the data given in table 5.1 of chapter 5, construct $Y$ = net domestic product, $C$ = consumption, and $I$ = net investment, all in constant 1978 prices. Estimate reduced-form equations (6.4), and compare the results with equation (6.7). Net investment in 1952 equals 130. Capital stock $K_{1952}$ at the end of 1952 equals 2,213 as reported in table 5.1, implying that capital stock at the end of 1951 is 2,083. Net investment $I_t$ is the difference between capital stocks at the end of year $t$ and capital stock at the end of year $t-1$. Net domestic product $Y$ = gross domestic product minus depreciation. Depreciation in year $t$ equals 0.04 ($K_{t-1} - 720$), where 720 is land value, which does not depreciate. Consumption $C_t$ can be approximated by the difference between net domestic product $Y$ and net investment $I$; approximated because net domestic product also includes net exports.

4  Examine the residuals of the reduced-form equations in question 3 for 1989, 1990, and 1991. What can you conclude about the economic impact of the tragic Tiananmen event of 1989?

5  Using the data obtained in question 3, estimate structural equations (6.2) and (6.3). How do the results compare with those reported in Chow (1985b) and in equations (6.6), based on pre-1994 or prerevised official data up to 1982?

6  Using the regressions obtained for question 3, forecast national output in China up to 2010. Compare the forecasts with those obtained, or at least discussed in the text, by using the neoclassical growth model of chapter 5. Even if you have not done a numerical projection of real GDP up to 2010 using the growth model of chapter 5, comment on the exponential rate of growth of real GDP from 1999 to 2010, computed from forecasts based on the reduced-form equations estimated in question 3.

# Macroeconomic Policies

Monetary and fiscal policies are discussed in general and in the institutional setting of the Chinese economy. Monetary policy is discussed in terms of the supply of money rather than the control of the interest rate. Section 7.3 contains a statistical model to explain the rate of inflation in China.

## 7.1 Introduction

There are three sets of forces driving the macroeconomy. The first set affects economic growth, including the state of technology as summarized by the production function, the savings rate, and the rate of population growth, as we saw in chapter 5. The second set affects short-run changes, such as the acceleration principle and people's expectations. These two are sometimes considered separately as a way of organizing our thoughts about macroeconomic changes. There are some factors affecting both the long and the short run, such as the demand conditions for a country's exports and political movements like the Great Leap and the Cultural Revolution. The third set is government policies. We have studied economic forces affecting growth and fluctuations, and will study the effects of political movements in the next chapter. We turn to government policies in this chapter.

Chinese economic institutions have been evolving. The evolutionary process is considered gradual by those who advocate shock therapy as a means of institutional reform, but is in fact very rapid judged by the great adjustments which the Chinese people and institutions have had to make. The study of the Chinese economy has emphasized institutional reform more than economic policy. As the institutional changes have slowed down, the study of economic policy in China is receiving more attention. From the viewpoints of the Chinese government and observers of China's long-term development, economic reform is still an important topic and affects the formulation of economic policies.

During the period of planning in the late 1970s, economic policy was embedded in the Five Year Plans. The plans covered output targets for different sectors and industries. The targets were then allocated to individual state enterprises. In the mid-1980s, the concept of compulsory planning was changed to guidance planning. Macroeconomic control mechanisms began to be used to control aggregate economic activities. Today, we can understand China's macroeconomic policy in terms of monetary policy and fiscal policy. The former has taken the form mainly of controlling the supply of currency and bank credits, but also of controlling the banks' deposit and lending interest rates. The latter takes the form of the level of government expenditures. We will study these policies in turn.

Before we begin, perhaps it is useful to review the development of the roles of fiscal and monetary policy in economics. Keynes' *General Theory*, which I referred to in section 6.1, provided the economic justification for fiscal policies. According to Keynes' formulation of the consumption function, aggregate consumption expenditure as a fraction of national output decreases as aggregate output increases. This relationship leads to a declining rate of growth as the economy grows. It was used to explain the US depression in the early 1930s. If this hypothesis is valid, an economy requires additional sources of aggregate demand, other than aggregate consumption expenditures, to sustain its growth. Government expenditure was considered such an additional source. The expenditures of the New Deal under President Franklin Roosevelt were justified by the Keynesian theory of aggregate demand. The US economy did not recover substantially from the depression until the Second World War, when expenditure on the war provided a stimulus to the economy. At the end of the war, there was serious concern that, when the high level of government expenditure was reduced, the US economy was heading towards another depression. This concern led to the enactment of the Full Employment Act of 1945. The Act gave responsibility to the President to maintain full employment in the economy and created the Council of Economic Advisers to provide him with advice.

A depression did not occur right after the war. In fact, postwar economic development was rapid. In the early 1950s, Milton Friedman, at the University of Chicago, began to challenge two basic ideas underlying the Keynesian theory of national income determination. One idea is the consumption function, which we looked at in section 6.1. The second is the notion that aggregate "autonomous expenditure" $A$, defined by $Y = C + A$, is a good predictor of national income $Y$. This notion is related to the stability of the Keynesian consumption function explaining $C$ by $Y$. If $C$ can be explained by $Y$ very closely, then we can solve for $C$ using this consumption function to express $Y$ as a function of $A$. Since Friedman challenged the Keynesian consumption function, he also challenged the relation between $Y$ and $A$ by proposing an alternative theory to explain $Y$. The alternative theory is the quantity theory of money, based on the quantity equation $Mv = PY$. $M$ is the quantity of money; $P$ is the price index for real output $Y$, so the product $PY$ is nominal output. The symbol $v$ denotes velocity of circulation. If $PY = 100$ billion and $M = 20$ billion, $v = 5$, meaning that on average the 20 billion of money is being circulated 5 times in one year to pay for the annual output of \$100 billion. By comparing the correlation between $Y$ and $A$ and the correlation between $Y$ and $M$, Milton Friedman and David Meiselman (1963) found that the latter correlation was higher for most of the historical episodes that they examined. This was the beginning of the rise of monetarism, the notion that monetary policy is important, in the 1960s and 1970s.

Policy-makers in China since 1949 have always believed in the quantity theory. The quantity equation $Mv = PY$ can be found in economics textbooks in the period of economic planning before 1978 because it can be found in the writing of Karl Marx. By the quantity theory, which assumes that $v$ is approximately constant, if $M$ increases proportionally more than real output $Y$, the price level $P$ will increase. Although empirically the price level $P$ is not always proportional to the ratio $M/Y$, as the quantity theory implies, it does tend to move in the same direction as this ratio. But a greater influence than Marx on the economic officials of the PRC was the high level of inflation in China during the period 1946–9, which they attributed correctly to the rapid increase in money supply under the Nationalist government. They did not forget that inflation experience, which is a testimony to the quantity theory of money. Current Chinese economic officials also believe in the use of government expenditure as a stimulus to real GDP, as we will see later in this chapter.

## 7.2   Monetary Policy

Ever since the founding of the People's Republic of China in 1949, the Chinese government has paid attention to the supply of money. Government officials in 1949 realized that printing too much money, like the previous government of the Republic of China, led to serious inflation and was a major cause of their predecessors' unpopularity and downfall. Within months after the new government took power, it was able to set up a stable monetary system. It issued a new currency, the renminbi (RMB), or "People's currency," in exchange for the old currency at rates fairly favorable to the population holding the old currency. Since the supply of the new currency was limited and the quantity was not increasing rapidly, the price level soon stabilized. The government succeeded in maintaining price stability, in the sense of having an inflation rate of less than 3 percent for most years, until the early 1980s. The only exception was in 1961–2, when the supply of goods decreased by some 30 percent as a result of the Great Leap, leading to higher prices.

By monetary policy I mean the use of money supply or the rate of interest to influence the level of macroeconomic activities. To understand the effects of money supply on the macroeconomy we rely on the Friedman (1994) propisition that when money supply increases, whatever the cause (but independently of the known influences of other variables as captured in a VAR), prices and real output will both increase, but real output will first increase before prices and the effect on output will die down more rapidly than the effect on prices. This proposition is supported by the VAR model for China we examined in section 6.5. We will use this proposition to interpret the history of inflation and output changes in China when government policy has led to changes in money supply. In much of the discussion below, money supply is measured by the amount of currency in circulation $M_0$. The discussion will remain valid if we use a broader measure of money such as

$M_1$ or $M_2$, since these measures tend to move together even though the broader measures have increased through time relative to $M_0$. $M_1$ is defined as $M_0$ plus demand deposits and $M_2$ equals $M_1$ plus saving deposits. Data on currency in circulation is given in the last column of table 7.1. In 1990 when $M_0$ equals 2,644.4, $M_1$ and $M_2$ are respectively 6,950.7 and 15,293.4. In 2002 when $M_0$ equals 17,278.0, $M_1$ and $M_2$ are respectively 70,881.8 and 185,007.0 (see the *China Statistical Yearbook, 2003*, table 19-4).

To review the history of inflation in China, we provide in table 7.1 four sets of data: the general retail price index (column 1), the ratio of the price index in the current year to the index in the preceding year as a measure of inflation (column 2), an index of real GDP (column 3), which is proportional to the real GDP in constant prices (given in table 5.1 of chapter 5), and the amount of currency in circulation (column 4). The most important variable that can explain the inflation rate is the ratio of currency in circulation to real GDP. If GDP is constant, a larger amount of currency in circulation will result in higher prices. Given the amount of currency in circulation, prices will be higher the smaller the quantity of real output. Table 7.1 shows an inflation rate of 16.2 percent in 1961. During this year of the Great Leap there was a large increase in money supply from RMB96.1 (100 million yuan) to 125.67. More importantly, the real output index was concurrently reduced from 43.9 in the previous year to 30.9. Thus the ratio of money supply to real output increased a great deal in 1961, causing a high level of inflation.

In the era of economic reform there have been several episodes of inflation, all associated with a rapid increase in money supply, as we can see in table 7.1. Money supply can

**Table 7.1**   Data on inflation and its determinants

| Year | General retail price index | Price index preceding year = 100 | GDP index 1978 = 100 | Currency in circulation (100 millions), year end |
|------|------|------|------|------|
| 1952 | 0.8227 | 99.6 | 22.0 | 38.55 |
| 1953 | 0.8506 | 103.4 | 25.1 | 39.60 |
| 1954 | 0.8705 | 102.3 | 26.6 | 41.19 |
| 1955 | 0.8793 | 101.0 | 28.3 | 40.13 |
| 1956 | 0.8793 | 100.0 | 32.3 | 57.03 |
| 1957 | 0.8926 | 101.5 | 33.7 | 52.80 |
| 1958 | 0.8947 | 100.2 | 41.2 | 67.59 |
| 1959 | 0.9028 | 100.9 | 44.6 | 74.98 |
| 1960 | 0.9308 | 103.1 | 43.9 | 96.10 |
| 1961 | 1.0820 | 116.2 | 30.9 | 125.67 |
| 1962 | 1.1229 | 103.8 | 28.9 | 106.66 |
| 1963 | 1.0567 | 94.1 | 32.0 | 89.76 |
| 1964 | 1.0177 | 96.3 | 37.2 | 80.26 |
| 1965 | 0.9904 | 97.3 | 43.5 | 90.82 |
| 1966 | 0.9875 | 99.7 | 50.9 | 108.25 |
| 1967 | 0.9801 | 99.3 | 44.5 | 121.97 |

**Table 7.1**   (cont'd)

| Year | General retail price index | Price index preceding year = 100 | GDP index 1978 = 100 | Currency in circulation (100 millions), year end |
|------|------|------|------|------|
| 1968 | 0.9809 | 100.1 | 44.2 | 134.12 |
| 1969 | 0.9698 | 98.9 | 52.7 | 137.29 |
| 1970 | 0.9676 | 99.8 | 65.0 | 123.56 |
| 1971 | 0.9603 | 99.2 | 69.5 | 136.23 |
| 1972 | 0.9581 | 99.8 | 71.5 | 151.02 |
| 1973 | 0.9639 | 100.6 | 77.5 | 166.33 |
| 1974 | 0.9691 | 100.5 | 78.3 | 176.36 |
| 1975 | 0.9706 | 100.2 | 84.9 | 182.70 |
| 1976 | 0.9735 | 100.3 | 82.6 | 203.82 |
| 1977 | 0.9934 | 102.0 | 89.0 | 195.37 |
| 1978 | 1.000 | 100.7 | 100.0 | 212.27 |
| 1979 | 1.020 | 102.0 | 107.6 | 267.71 |
| 1980 | 1.081 | 106.0 | 116.0 | 346.20 |
| 1981 | 1.107 | 102.4 | 122.1 | 396.34 |
| 1982 | 1.128 | 101.9 | 133.1 | 439.12 |
| 1983 | 1.145 | 101.5 | 147.6 | 529.78 |
| 1984 | 1.177 | 102.8 | 170.0 | 792.11 |
| 1985 | 1,281 | 108.8 | 192.9 | 987.83 |
| 1986 | 1.358 | 106.0 | 210.0 | 1,218.36 |
| 1987 | 1.457 | 107.3 | 234.3 | 1,454.48 |
| 1988 | 1.727 | 118.5 | 260.7 | 2,134.03 |
| 1989 | 2.034 | 117.8 | 271.3 | 2,344.02 |
| 1990 | 2.077 | 102.1 | 281.7 | 2,644.37 |
| 1991 | 2.137 | 102.9 | 307.6 | 3,177.80 |
| 1992 | 2.252 | 105.4 | 351.4 | 4,336.00 |
| 1993 | 2.549 | 113.2 | 398.8 | 5,864.70 |
| 1994 | 3.102 | 121.7 | 449.3 | 7,288.60 |
| 1995 | 3.561 | 114.8 | 496.5 | 7,885.30 |
| 1996 | 3.778 | 106.1 | 544.1 | 8,802.00 |
| 1997 | 3.808 | 100.8 | 592.0 | 10,177.60 |
| 1998 | 3.709 | 97.4 | 638.2 | 11,204.20 |
| 1999 | 3.598 | 97.0 | 684.1 | 13,455.50 |
| 2000 | 3.544 | 98.5 | 738.8 | 14,652.70 |
| 2001 | 3.516 | 99.2 | 794.2 | 15,688.80 |
| 2002 | 3.470 | 98.7 | 857.4 | 17,278.00 |
| 2003 | 3.467 | 99.9 | 940.1 | 19,745.99 |
| 2004 | 3.564 | 102.8 | 1031.3 | 21,468.30 |

be measured by the amount of currency in circulation. The episodes include 1985, 1988, and 1993. In all three cases there was a rapid increase in money supply at an annual rate of about 50 percent, compared with some 20 to 25 percent in other years. The increase in money supply can be said to be a government policy, but its effect was not necessarily intended. In 1984, when enterprise autonomy was introduced for state enterprise reform, state enterprises went directly to the banks for credit. There was insufficient control of the extension of credit. In fact the banks were mistakenly given autonomy in much the same way as the state industrial enterprises. Credit was extended as a result of political pressure and willingness on the part of bank managers to extend loans to enterprises in their home province for the purpose of promoting local economic development or expansion of economic activities. When credit was extended by the local banks, which were branches of the People's Bank, the enterprises receiving the credit could convert it to cash for wage payment and other expenses. The People's Bank had to issue currency to honor the credit of its branch banks. The end result was an increase in currency in circulation of about 50 percent from January 1984 to January 1985. Inflation in 1985 was 8.8 percent: high compared with the low inflation rate achieved up to 1984.

The increase in money supply in 1988 was also unintentional and resulted from the reform process. Reform gave enterprises and consumers much freedom in the latter part of the 1980s. Aggregate demand and national output were expanding at a high rate. Unless the government made a serious effort to control the supply of credit, inflation would occur. The government failed to make such an effort. In 1988, the money supply again expanded by 48 percent. Furthermore, the government announced a policy to fix the prices of some important consumer goods at the level prevailing at the end of 1998. In response to the announcement, producers hastened to increase prices before the deadline. In the fall of 1988 the price index was increasing at an annual rate of over 30 percent, although the annual rate of inflation was 18.5 percent. This rate was much higher than the 8.8 percent rate in 1985 because of the delayed effects of the substantial increases in money supply in the years before 1988, which had not occurred before 1985. Inflation, together with corruption, contributed to discontent and student demonstrations in the spring of 1989.

In response to the serious inflation in the fall of 1988, the government tried to restrict the increase in money and credit creation by assigning credit quotas to the banks of different regions and provinces. In addition, interest rates on bank deposits were raised to attract deposits and to reduce the quantity of money in circulation, thus making the price level lower. Because of the absence of a properly functioning modern banking system, the government mainly applied administrative means to control the money supply, namely the assignment of credit quotas to banks in different regions. A second instrument of monetary policy was to increase the interest rates on saving deposits in order to induce people to put their money in the banks rather than spending it. Deposit rates were increased to over 11 percent per year to make the real rate of interest positive and attractive enough to depositors to increase their deposits. The policy worked, and inflation stopped in 1990.

After Deng announced the policy of speeding up reform, rapid development, and further opening of China's door, during his "Southern Expedition" to Shenzhen in

February 1992, people began to invest more and the economy started booming. Banks received the green light to expand credit for investment projects. From the end of 1991 to the end of 1996 money stock increased from 3,177.8 to 8,802.0, or at an average annual rate of 22.5 percent per year. The inflation rates in 1993, 1994, and 1995 were 13.2, 21.7, and 14.8 percent respectively.

We now turn briefly to the effects on output associated with the large increases in money supply in the above episodes. Since the average rate of annual growth of real output was about 9.5 percent from 1979 to 1998, any increase much above that average can be considered large. Output increased by 170/147.6, or 15.2 percent in 1984, and by 192.9/170, or 13.5 percent in 1985, when money supply increased very rapidly in 1983–4. It increased by 260.7/234.3, or 11.3 percent, in 1988, and by 449.3/398.8, or 12.7 percent, in 1994. This is a part of the history of China's economic fluctuations as measured by changes in total output.

To slow down inflation in the mid-1990s, the government again turned to administrative and economic means: issuing credit quotas to regional banks and raising interest rates on deposits. A strong and well-respected administrator in the person of Zhu Rongji was appointed to head the People's Bank and solve the inflation problem. Zhu was determined and was feared by the heads of the bank's provincial branches. He told them that they would lose their jobs if the credit quotas were exceeded. The expansion of credit was put under control. Inflation was slowed to 15 percent in 1995, 6 percent in 1996, 1 percent in 1997, and −2.5 percent in 1998. The rates in 1998 and 1999 were affected by the reduction in aggregate demand due to the Asian financial crisis which started in July 1997. The money supply in these years increased slowly also. Zhu Rongji became Prime Minister in March 1998, partly on account of his successful performance in controlling inflation and maintaining economic stability in the mid-1990s.

When he took office in 1998, Premier Zhu announced two macroeconomic policy objectives, fully recognizing the "formidable challenges due to the financial crisis in southeast Asia." The objectives were to maintain a real growth rate at 8 percent or more in 1998 and an inflation rate of not more than 3 percent. As President of the People's Bank and later Vice-premier, Zhu Rongji deserved much credit for reducing the rate of inflation in China from 22 percent in 1994 to a negative figure in 1998 by reducing the rate of growth in the money supply. Realizing the need to stimulate the economy, he was prepared to raise the inflation rate target to 3 percent by adopting a more expansionary monetary policy. By September 1998, currency in circulation in China reached RMB10 trillion, an increase of only 16 percent from the previous year. Total credit also increased by 17 percent in the same period. Since inflation had slowed down, nominal interest rates also came down. In March 1998, the one-year deposit rate went down to 5.2 percent and the one-year official lending rate to 7.9 percent. Commercial banks were allowed to set their lending rates within a fairly narrow range, between 10 percent below and 20 percent above the official lending rate.

In the years 1998 and 1999, China was affected by the Asian financial crisis, although only to a moderate extent. Economic growth was slower. Perhaps at the time it would have been better for the People's Bank to exercise a more expansionary monetary policy by increasing credit and the money supply more rapidly. Some economists think that it is possible to restrict the expansion of credit, but not possible to increase money and credit when there is no demand for them. The impossibility of extending credit during times of slow growth because of lack of demand is known as a liquidity trap. In the Chinese case the government was trying to raise aggregate demand following the Asian financial crisis by increasing expenditure on the building of infrastructure. Instead of financing expenditure by issuing bonds, the government could and should have financed some of the projects by issuing more money, or non-interest-bearing government debt. It would have solved the problem of the liquidity trap, if such a phenomenon did indeed exist.

To summarize the effects of monetary policy, the increase in money supply from 8,802 at the end of 1996 to 17,278 in 2002 amounted only to an average annual increase of 11.8 percent as compared with 22.5 in the 5 years before. There was price stability, and in fact a slight deflation, during this period, as the data in table 7.1 shows.

In the 1980s and 1990s, monetary policy in China was exercised mainly by the administrative means of assigning credit quotas and the economic means of setting interest rates. Credit creation and contraction through the commercial banks, by changing reserve requirements and by open-market operations, was not possible because commercial banks were not operating effectively. The use of more modern means of macroeconomic policy-making will require some time to develop in China, as there are problems in reforming the banking system (which will be discussed fully in chapter 13). One problem in monetary policy that has not yet been resolved is the practice of simultaneous control of interest rates on loans and on deposits, often leading to insufficient profit margins for the commercial banks. These rates should be market determined to a larger extent than at present in China. This problem is recognized by the People's Bank, and the deregulation of interest rates is taking place gradually. As new commercial banks appear to compete with the four large state commercial banks at the turn of the century, there is a need for the People's Bank to monitor all commercial banks in order to prevent them from being financially irresponsible. In 2003, a commission was established to take over the function of the People's Bank in supervising the commercial banks.

Macroeconomic developments up to 2004 are also consistent with the Friedman proposition that increase in money supply first leads to increase in output and then to increase in prices. Money supply increased rapidly in 2002–3, mainly as a result of the large inflow of foreign exchange acquired through a large trade surplus and large inflow of foreign investment. The acquired foreign exchange was converted into Chinese currency or reserves in the banks. This led to rapid expansion of money and credit, and to increases in investment and output in 2003. The annual rate of increase in $M_2$ was about 13 percent in January 2002, rose to over 18 percent at the end of 2002 and to over 21 percent in mid-2003, and was reduced to about 18 percent at the beginning of 2004. China's real GDP increased at a rate of 9.1 percent in 2003 and 9.8 percent in the first quarter of 2004, as compared with 8.0 percent in 2002 (see table 7.1). Signs of inflation began to show in the last quarter of 2003, with the rate of inflation rising to over 5 percent annually in July 2004 (the highest rate in 7 years). From January to October 2004 the overall level of domestic consumer prices increased by 4.1 percent, while that of capital goods in circulation grew by 14 percent, a year-on-year increase of 3.3 percentage points and 6.5 percentage points respectively.

During the period 2002–4 the central government again relied on administrative means to restrict the credit extended by provincial banks, and to limit the amount of provincial investment projects. The People's Bank also raised the interest rate. These policies were only partially successful, as economic forces are often difficult to control by administrative means. If the Chinese government had revalued the RMB, raising its value in relation to the US dollar, China's trade surplus would have been reduced, and there would have been less inflow of foreign exchange. The money supply would not have increased as much. If the banks had had less money to lend there would have been no need for the government to restrict their credit, which was used to finance construction projects. The alleged "overheating" of the economy during this period would not have taken place.

We have discussed monetary policy mainly in terms of controlling the quantity of money. Historically, economists have found a relation between the quantity of money and the rate of inflation. Inflation can be measured by the ratio $P_t/P_{t-1}$ of a general price index for period $t$ to the index for period $t - 1$, less one, as we have done using data in column 2 of table 7.1. Alternatively, it can be measured by the natural logarithm of this ratio $\ln(P_t/P_{t-1}) = \ln P_t - \ln P_{t-1}$. For such a large proportional change in the price index, as from 0.9308 in 1960 to 1.0820 in 1961, the first measure of inflation gives 0.162, and the second measure gives 0.151, not very different from the first. For smaller proportional changes in the price index, the two measures are closer. To examine the relation between money supply and inflation, we use the data in table 7.1 on (1) the retail price index $P$, (2) China's gross domestic product in real terms $Y$, (3) the amount of currency in circulation as a measure of money supply $M$, (4) the ratio of money supply to real GDP $M/Y$, (5) the inflation rate as measured by $\ln P_t - \ln P_{t-1}$. The rate of increase in money supply, which can be measured by $\ln M_t - \ln M_{t-1}$, forms the basis of much of our discussion of monetary policy and its effect on the inflation rate. Note the three inflation episodes of 1985, 1988, and 1993–5.

It is a useful exercise to estimate a regression of the inflation rate $\ln P_t - \ln P_{t-1}$, on the rate of increase in money supply $\ln M_t - \ln M_{t-1}$ of the same year and/or of the preceding year.

As we have pointed out, a better explanation of inflation is to use the rate of change of the ratio $M/Y$ instead of the rate of change of the money supply itself. This formulation is based on the quantity theory of money. The quantity theory states $Mv = PY$, or $P = v(M/Y)$, where $v$ is the income velocity of circulation of money, measuring the ratio of money income $PY$ to the stock of money $M$. Second, we need to specify the possible delayed effects on the inflation rate of the change in the ratio $M/Y$ of the same year and of the preceding year, and of the inflation rate of the preceding year. Thus $(M/Y)_t$, $(M/Y)_{t-1}$ and $\ln(P_{t-1}/P_{t-2})$ are three variables that can affect the current inflation rate. Change in the ratio $M/Y$ in the preceding year enters as an explanatory variable because of its delayed effect. The inflation rate of the preceding years enters because it can capture the effects of the changes in $M/Y$ further back in time, as the dependent variable of the preceding year always captures the delayed effects of changes in $M/Y$ of the previous years. Thus we have two more variables to explain the inflation rate in addition to the ratio $M/Y$. Both are used to capture the delayed effects of $M/Y$. These delayed effects are embedded in the formulation of a dynamic equation to be discussed in the next section. Chow (1987) estimated such an equation using data up to 1993. This equation is useful not only for our understanding of the effect of monetary policy on inflation, but also for the formulation of monetary policy. We can determine the right credit quotas to impose, once its effect on inflation is quantitatively ascertained.

## 7.3   An Econometric Analysis of Inflation and of Monetary Policy in China

Consider a general method for estimating the delayed effects of a variable $x$ on a variable $y$. (Note the distinction between this lower-case $y$ and real GDP, denoted by $Y$.) In the example of the explanation of the price level, $y$ is the natural log of the price level $P$ and $x$ is the natural log of the ratio $M/Y$ of money supply to real output. The relation between these two log variables can be justified by taking the logarithm of both sides of the equation $P = v\,(M/Y)$ without considering the delayed effects of $x = M/Y$. The natural logarithm is used also because a linear relation between $\log P$ and $\log(M/Y)$ is a better approximation to the data than a linear relation between $P$ and $M/Y$. In the dynamic equation, $y_t$ is affected not only by $x_t$ but possibly by past values of both variables. In the long run, let us assume that there is an equilibrium relation between the two variables given by $y - \alpha_0 - \alpha_1 x = 0$. The dynamic equation has an error correction mechanism built into it. The correction mechanism specifies that a positive deviation $u_{t-1} = y_{t-1} - \alpha_0 - \alpha_1 x_{t-1}$ from equilibrium in the last period will assert a negative effect on the change $\Delta y_t = y_t - y_{t-1}$ of the dependent variable in the current period. Thus the coefficient $\gamma$ of this deviation $u_{t-1}$ in the regression of $\Delta y_t$ is negative. The dynamic equation proposed attempts to explain $\Delta y_t$ by $\Delta x_t$, past changes of both $x$ and $y$, and by this error-correction term, i.e.,

$$\Delta y_t = \beta_0 + \beta_1 \Delta x_t + \beta_2 \Delta x_{t-1} + \beta_3 \Delta y_{t-1} + \gamma u_{t-1} + \varepsilon_t \tag{7.1}$$

where $u_{t-1} = y_{t-1} - \alpha_0 - \alpha_1 x_{t-1}$ and $\varepsilon_t$ is a random residual.

Let $\ln P$ be the dependent variable $y$ and $\ln(M/Y)$ be the explanatory variable $x$. Using $M_2$ for $M$, Chow and Shen (2005) plotted $\ln P$ against $\ln(M_2/Y)$ for the period 1952 to 2002, as shown in figure 7.1.

The points in figure 7.1 fall approximately along a straight line. The exceptions are the years after 1998, when prices increased less than the fitted line would predict, probably because of low aggregate demand after the Asian financial crisis of 1997–9 – in such a period, increase in money supply may have a smaller effect on prices.

If we fit a linear regression using the data of figure 7.1, we obtain

$$\log(P) = -0.7127 + 0.3738\log(M_2/Y), \qquad \text{Adjusted } R^2 = 0.9639$$
$$\quad\;\;(0.031)\quad\;(0.0102)$$

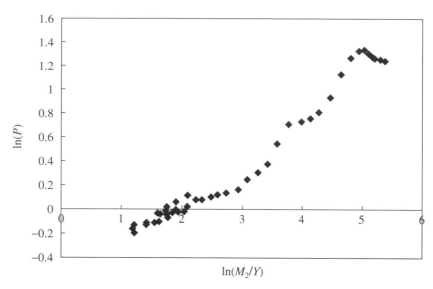

**Figure 7.1**   Plotting $\log(P)$ against $\log(M_2/Y)$

The test of the hypothesis that the coefficients of $\log(M_2)$ and $\log(Y)$ are equal in magnitude but opposite in sign gives an $F$ statistic of 7.88, rejecting the null hypothesis at the 1 percent significance level. By using $\log(M_2)$ and $\log(Y)$ separately, we get

$$\log(P) = -0.417 + 0.4637\log(M_2) - 0.5768\log(Y), \quad \text{Adjusted } R^2 = 0.9646$$
$$\quad (0.109) \ (0.033) \qquad\qquad (0.0729)$$

We will treat the last equation as a co-integration equation, or a long-run equilibrium relation among these three variables (see Engle and Granger 1987). The residual $u_t$ of this regression measures the degree to which the dependent variable is out of equilibrium. A positive value of this residual for the previous period will have a depressing effect on the dependent variable in the current period, and a negative value will have a positive effect.

To explain the inflation rate $\Delta\log P$ we use its own lagged value, the current and lagged values of $\Delta\log Y$ ($Y$ being real GDP) and $\Delta\log M_2$, as well as the lagged value of the residual of the co-integration equation $u_{t-1}$:

$$\Delta\log(P) = -0.007 + 0.106\Delta\log M_2 - 0.182\Delta\log Y \quad \text{Adjusted } R^2 = 0.661$$
$$\quad (0.009) \ (0.058) \qquad\qquad (0.06)$$
$$+ \ 0.55\Delta\log(P_{-1}) - 0.036\Delta\log(M_{2,-1}) + 0.16\Delta\log(Y_{-1}) - 0.2u_{-1},$$
$$\quad (0.108) \qquad\qquad (0.58) \qquad\qquad (0.07) \qquad\qquad (0.058)$$

The above is known as an error correction equation because of the last term. As $\Delta\log(M_2)_{-1}$ is not significant, it is omitted in the following regression:

$$\Delta \log(P) = -0.006 + 0.12\Delta \log M_2 - 0.19\Delta \log Y \quad \text{Adjusted } R^2 = 0.666$$
$$(0.008) \quad (0.051) \qquad\qquad (0.058)$$
$$+ 0.57\Delta \log(P_{-1}) + 0.17\Delta \log(Y_{-1}) - 0.21u_{-1},$$
$$(0.093) \qquad\qquad (0.07) \qquad\qquad (0.055)$$

This error correction equation, with the lagged change in $\log(M_2)$ omitted, explains the data well. The coefficient of the error correction term has the correct negative sign. It also passes the Chow test of parameter stability when the data are divided by using 1978 as the beginning year of the second period. This result suggests that although economic reform after 1978 may have affected many aspects of the Chinese economy, the relation between price level, output, and money supply has remained essentially the same. However, we have found the above error correction equation to have very large residuals in the years 1961, 1988, and 1993–4. The 1961 residual was associated with the failure of the Great Leap, the 1988 residual with the rapid inflation preceding the Tiananmen incident, and the 1993–4 with the economic expansion following Deng's policy announced during his Southern Expedition of 1992.

Chow (1987) estimated an error correction equation to explain the inflation rate $\Delta \ln P$ in China for the period 1952 to 1985 using currency in circulation to measure $M$, as reported in the first edition of this book:

$$\Delta \ln P = 0.00422 + 0.1430\Delta \ln(M/Y) + 0.2176\Delta \ln P_{-1} - 0.3771u_{-1} \quad R^2 = 0.7174$$
$$(0.00376) \quad (0.0201) \qquad\qquad (0.1098) \qquad\quad (0.1209) \qquad\qquad\qquad (7.2)$$

Note that $\Delta \ln(M/Y)_{-1}$ was omitted because its coefficient was found to be statistically insignificant. The deviation $u$ from the long-run relation was the residual of a regression of $\ln P$ on $\ln(M/Y)$ which was first estimated. Since lagged values of the explanatory variables are not used as explanatory variables and the equilibrium relation is estimated using the levels of the variables and not their differences, there are two more observations for 1952 and 1953 available to estimate this regression. The equilibrium relation is estimated to be:

$$\ln P = 0.9445 + 0.2687\ln(M/Y)$$

The lagged value of the residual $u_{t-1}$ of this regression equation was used as an independent variable representing the error correction term in the estimation of equation (7.2). The above long-run equilibrium relation between $\ln P$ and $\ln(M/Y)$ is called a "co-integration" relation, as suggested by Engle and Granger (1987).

Given equation (7.2) and given a model to forecast real output $Y$, government policymakers can assess the effects of increasing the money supply $M$ on inflation one or two years in advance. In fact I estimated an early version of equation (7.2) in response to a request from the office of Premier Zhao Ziyang in June 1985 to project the inflation rate in 1985, as he was concerned about the effect of the rapid increase in the money supply in 1984 by nearly 50 percent in one year.

Chow and Shen (2005) also estimated a VAR for $\ln P$, $\ln Y$, and $\ln M$ (where $M$ may be $M_2$ or $M_1$) using the lagged values for two preceding periods (described in section 6.5), and obtained the impulse responses of ln$P$ and ln$Y$ to monetary shocks which were plotted in figure 6.1. The econometric analysis described in this section justifies the verbal description of the effects of monetary policy in the last section.

## 7.4   Basic Facts about Government Revenue and Expenditure

In 1978 total government budgetary revenue was 31.2 percent of GDP (see table 7.2), with 57.2 billion, or 50.5 percent of the total, being revenue from state enterprises. By 1985, most of government revenue came from taxes collected from large state enterprises. Because of this small tax base, by 1989 government revenue accounted for only 15.8 percent of GDP and by 1994 for only 11.2 percent. In 1994 a major change in the tax system was enacted to widen the tax base (see Gordon and Li 2005). The tax rate on enterprise income was lowered from 55 percent to 33 percent. A new value-added tax (VAT) at 17 percent was levied on most goods and services, with a lower rate of 13 percent on agricultural products and inputs, energy and minerals. The national government collects VAT, excise tax, and income tax from enterprises under its control. Local governments were given responsibility for collecting business taxes, income taxes from local firms and individuals, agricultural taxes, and property taxes. As a result of the tax reform, the central government in 1994 collected 55.7 percent of the total budgetary revenue, a large jump from 22.0 percent in 2003. The percentage of government revenue to GDP has increased from 10.7 in 1995 to 18.0 percent in 2002.

In 1978 total government budgetary expenditure was smaller than total revenue, leaving a surplus. Since 1979 there has been a government deficit every year, except for 1985 (see table 7.3). In 2002 the deficit of 315 billion amounted to 16.7 percent of total revenue but only 3 percent of GDP. China has maintained a conservative stand on managing its budget by not allowing government deficits to increase beyond its ability to finance them. Table 7.3 shows the main items of government expenditure. In 2002, economic construction constituted 30.3 percent of total expenditure; social, cultural, and educational development 26.9 percent; and national defense 7.74 percent (or 1.63 percent of GDP). Even after being corrected for possible underestimation, China's defense expenditure is a small fraction of GDP. Economic construction made up 6.37 percent of GDP. It is an item which can be expanded to increase aggregate demand when the economic conditions call for such an increase. We will turn to government expenditure as an instrument of fiscal policy in the next section.

## 7.5   Fiscal Policy

Fiscal policy consists mainly of setting the amount of government expenditure given the level of government revenue, which is determined by the tax structure and the economic

**Table 7.2** Budgetary revenue and its sources

| Year | Total revenue (yuan 100 millions) | Percentage of budgetary revenue to GDP | Total taxes revenue | Industrial & commercial tax | Tariffs | Agricultural & related tax | Income tax from state-owned enterprises | Income tax from collectively owned enterprises | Percentage collected by central government |
|---|---|---|---|---|---|---|---|---|---|
| 1978 | 1,132.26 | 31.2 | 519.28 | 462.12 | 28.76 | 28.40 | | | 15.5 |
| 1980 | 1,159.93 | 25.7 | 571.70 | 510.50 | 33.53 | 27.67 | | | 24.5 |
| 1985 | 2,004.82 | 22.4 | 2,040.79 | 1,097.47 | 205.21 | 42.05 | 595.84 | 100.22 | 38.4 |
| 1989 | 2,664.90 | 15.8 | 2,727.40 | 1,760.49 | 181.54 | 84.94 | 583.59 | 116.84 | 30.9 |
| 1990 | 2,937.10 | 15.8 | 2,821.86 | 1,858.99 | 159.01 | 87.86 | 604.12 | 111.88 | 33.8 |
| 1991 | 3,149.48 | 14.6 | 2,990.17 | 1,981.11 | 187.28 | 90.65 | 627.59 | 103.54 | 29.8 |
| 1992 | 3,483.37 | 13.1 | 3,296.91 | 2,244.21 | 212.75 | 119.17 | 624.77 | 96.01 | 28.1 |
| 1993 | 4,348.95 | 12.6 | 4,255.30 | 3,194.49 | 256.47 | 125.74 | 582.91 | 95.69 | 22.0 |
| 1994 | 5,218.10 | 11.2 | 5,126.88 | 3,914.22 | 272.68 | 231.49 | 609.75 | 98.74 | 55.7 |
| 1995 | 6,242.20 | 10.7 | 6,038.04 | 4,589.68 | 291.83 | 278.09 | 759.38 | 119.06 | 52.2 |
| 1996 | 7,407.99 | 10.9 | 6,909.82 | 5,270.04 | 301.84 | 369.46 | 822.33 | 146.15 | 49.4 |
| 1997 | 8,651.14 | 11.6 | 8,234.04 | 6,553.89 | 319.49 | 397.48 | 794.43 | 168.75 | 48.9 |
| 1998 | 9,875.95 | 12.6 | 9,262.80 | 7,625.42 | 313.04 | 398.80 | 743.93 | 181.61 | 49.5 |
| 1999 | 11,444.08 | 13.9 | 10,682.58 | 8,885.44 | 562.23 | 423.50 | 639.00 | 172.41 | 51.1 |
| 2000 | 13,395.23 | 15.0 | 12,581.51 | 10,366.09 | 750.48 | 465.31 | 827.41 | 172.22 | 52.2 |
| 2001 | 16,386.04 | 16.8 | 15,301.38 | | 840.52 | 481.70 | | | 52.4 |
| 2002 | 18,903.64 | 18.0 | 17,636.45 | | 704.27 | 717.85 | | | 55.0 |
| 2003 | 21,715.25 | 18.5 | 20,017.31 | | 923.13 | 871.77 | | | 54.6 |
| 2004 | 26,396.47 | 19.3 | 24,165.68 | | 1,043.77 | 902.19 | | | 54.9 |

**Source:** *China Statistical Yearbook, 2003*, tables 8-1, 8-2, and 8-4.

**Table 7.3** Budgetary expenditure by function

| Year | Total expenditure | Economic construction | Social, cultural, & educational development | National defense | Government administration | Other | Budget surplus |
|------|-------------------|-----------------------|---------------------------------------------|------------------|---------------------------|-------|----------------|
| 1978 | 1,122.09 | 718.98 | 146.96 | 167.84 | 52.90 | 35.41 | 10.17 |
| 1980 | 1,228.83 | 715.46 | 199.01 | 193.84 | 75.53 | 44.99 | −68.90 |
| 1985 | 2,004.25 | 1,127.55 | 408.43 | 191.53 | 171.06 | 105.68 | 0.57 |
| 1989 | 2,823.78 | 1,291.19 | 668.44 | 251.47 | 386.26 | 226.42 | −158.88 |
| 1990 | 3,083.59 | 1,368.01 | 737.61 | 290.31 | 414.56 | 273.10 | −146.49 |
| 1991 | 3,386.62 | 1,428.47 | 849.65 | 330.31 | 414.01 | 364.18 | −237.14 |
| 1992 | 3,742.20 | 1,612.81 | 970.12 | 377.86 | 463.41 | 318.00 | −258.83 |
| 1993 | 4,642.30 | 1,834.79 | 1,178.27 | 425.80 | 634.26 | 569.18 | −293.35 |
| 1994 | 5,792.62 | 2,393.69 | 1,501.53 | 550.71 | 847.68 | 499.01 | −574.52 |
| 1995 | 6,823.72 | 2,855.78 | 1,756.72 | 636.72 | 996.54 | 577.96 | −581.52 |
| 1996 | 7,937.55 | 3,233.78 | 2,080.56 | 720.06 | 1,185.28 | 717.87 | −529.56 |
| 1997 | 9,233.56 | 3,647.33 | 2,469.38 | 812.57 | 1,358.85 | 945.43 | −582.42 |
| 1998 | 10,798.18 | 4,179.51 | 2,930.78 | 934.70 | 1,600.27 | 1,152.92 | −922.23 |
| 1999 | 13,187.67 | 5,061.46 | 3,638.74 | 1,076.40 | 2,020.60 | 1,390.47 | −1,743.59 |
| 2000 | 15,886.50 | 5,748.36 | 4,384.51 | 1,207.54 | 2,768.22 | 1,777.87 | −2,491.27 |
| 2001 | 18,902.58 | 6,472.56 | 5,213.23 | 1,442.04 | 3,512.49 | 2,262.26 | −2,516.54 |
| 2002 | 22,053.15 | 6,673.70 | 5,924.58 | 1,707.78 | 4,101.32 | 3,645.77 | −3,149.51 |
| 2003 | 24,649.95 | 7,410.87 | 6,469.37 | 1,907.87 | 4,691.26 | 4,170.58 | −2,934.70 |

**Source:** *Statistical Yearbook of China, 2004*, tables 8-1 and 8-8.

conditions. During the period of planning, aggregate output could be controlled by the government through the setting of output targets for state enterprises. There was no need for fiscal policy to stimulate aggregate demand. Such a need has arisen since economic planning became less important and market forces were allowed to determine aggregate output. Chinese government economic officials believe in the use of fiscal stimuli when aggregate demand is insufficient, as advocated by Keynes.

A notable example occurred in 1998 during the Asian financial crisis and a period of slower growth in China. Premier Zhu Rongji stated at a press conference on March 19, 1998, that to achieve an 8 percent growth rate in 1998, the main policy would be to increase domestic demand. He said, "To stimulate domestic demand, we will increase investment in construction of infrastructure, such as railways, highways, agricultural land and water conservancy facilities, municipal facilities, and environmental protection facilities. We will also increase investment in high-tech industries and in the technical renovation of existing enterprises." A figure quoted in the Western press is a total of US$1.2 trillion of investment in the three years 1998 to 2000. If the figure were converted to Chinese RMB by an 8 to 1 ratio, the average of $400 billion per year would become 3,200 billion yuan of investment each year from 1998 to 2000. In 1997, investment in fixed assets increased by 9 percent in real terms to reach 2,350 billion yuan. If one allowed for an inflation rate of 3 percent and projected the 2,350 figure forward using an annual growth rate of 13 percent in money terms for three years, the amounts of fixed investment in 1998, 1999, and 2000 would be 2,656, 3,000, and 3,391 billion yuan respectively. Therefore, the average of 3,200 billion yuan represented an achievable stimulation program.

Economic trends at the time suggested that China's economy continued to grow in 1997, but the rate of growth slowed down in 1998. Industrial output grew by 11.2 percent in real terms in 1997, with the state sector growing at only 5.5 percent but the collective and privately-owned sectors growing at 11 and 14 percent respectively. In the first three months of 1998, industrial output in constant prices still increased by 9.7 percent over the same period in 1997, whereas the growth of real GDP during these three months was 7.2 percent, smaller than the target rate of 8 percent for 1998. In the third quarter of 1998, real GDP grew at 7.6 percent, compared with 6.8 percent in the second quarter. Many infrastructure projects were underway, including the introduction of state-of-the-art technology to agriculture, and a new railway linking the northeastern and southern regions as a part of a planned 245-billion-yuan railway construction project over five years, among others.

Thus China adopted the Keynesian way of stimulating aggregate demand by increasing government expenditure, especially in infrastructure-building. Another component of the increase in government expenditure was caused by severe floods in the summer of 1998 in the central and northeastern regions, in response to which the government took decisive action. Retail sales as a component of aggregate demand grew at an annual rate of 7 percent in the third quarter of 1998. As of early November the government was still expecting to achieve the target growth rate of 8 percent, or something close to it. The growth of over 7 percent during the first three quarters was already a remarkable achievement. The actual growth in real GDP in 1998 turned out to be 7.8 percent. Some observers believe that the high figure in 1998, when other Asian countries suffered a negative growth rate, was partly the consequence of false statistical reporting. Overestimation might have resulted from over-reporting by provincial government sources which were under pressure to achieve the output targets assigned to them by central government. To what extent such over-reporting existed and was not corrected by the State Statistics Bureau is an open question.

To study the quantitative effect of government expenditure, one can use a simple Keynesian model consisting of the following equations, with $Y$ denoting real net domestic product, $C$ denoting real consumption expenditure, $I$ denoting real net investment expenditure, $G$ denoting real government expenditure, and $X$ denoting net exports (exports minus imports).

$$Y = C + I + G + X$$
$$C = a_0 + a_1 Y + a_2 C_{-1}$$
$$I = b_0 + b_1 (Y - Y_{-1}) + b_2 I_{-1}$$

If $Y$ denotes gross domestic product instead of net domestic product, $I$ will be gross investment and the coefficient of $Y_{-1}$ in the investment equation will be $-(1 - d)$ instead of $-1$. We can treat government expenditure $G$ and net exports $X$ as exogenous variables. Then the above three equations can be used to determine the three endogenous variables $Y$, $C$, and $I$. Each of these three variables can be explained by a reduced-form equation, obtained by solving the above three structural equations for the endogenous variables. Each reduced-form equation has $C_{t-1}$, $I_{t-1}$, $G_t$, $G_{t-1}$, $X_t$, and $X_{t-1}$ as explanatory variables. The lagged values of $G$ and $X$ enter because lagged $Y$ in the equation for $I$ is a function of these variables. Thus the effects of fiscal policy, of the manipulation of government expenditure $G$, on the macroeconomy can be evaluated by the use of these reduced-form equations. (See question 4 at the end of this chapter.)

In section 6.4 we estimated a model with one variable, "accumulation," replacing the sum $I + G + X$ in the above model. One can also use the method presented in that section to estimate the coefficients of the consumption and investment equations in the above model. Once these coefficients are estimated, we can solve the structural equations to obtain the reduced-form equations. As an exercise, the reader might wish to estimate this model using Chinese data. Such a model has shortcomings, but it may suffice to provide a first approximation to evaluate the effects of government expenditure on real GDP.

# References and Further Reading

Chow, Gregory C. "Money and Price Level Determination in China." *Journal of Comparative Economics*, 11(3) (Sept. 1987), pp. 319–33.

Chow, Gregory C. and Yan Shen. "Money, Price Level Output in the Chinese Macro Economy." *Asia-Pacific Journal of Accounting & Economics*, 12(2) (Dec. 2005), pp. 91–111.

Engle, Robert and C. W. J. Granger. "Co-integration and Error Correction: Representation, Estimation and Testing." *Econometrica*, 55(2) (March 1987), pp. 251–76.

Friedman, Milton. *Money Mischief*. New York: Harcourt Brace & Co., 1994.

Friedman, Milton and David Meiselman. "The Relative Stability of Monetary Velocity and the Investment Multiplier in the United States, 1897–1958." In *Stabilization Policies*. Englewood Cliffs, NJ: Prentice-Hall for the Commission on Money and Credit, 1963, pp. 165–268.

Gordon, Roger and Wei Li. "Taxation and Economic Growth in China," ch. 2 of Yum K. Kwan and Eden S. H. Yu (eds.), *Critical Issues in China's Growth and Development*. Singapore: Ashgate, 2005.

Keynes, J. M. *The General Theory of Employment, Interest and Money*. New York: Harcourt, Brace and Co., 1936.

# Questions

1   Using the data in table 7.1, estimate a regression of the change in the log of the price index on the change in the log of the ratio of money supply to real GDP.

2   Using the data in table 7.1, estimate equation (7.1) to explain the rate of inflation in China. Comment on the difference between your estimated equation and equation (7.2).

3   Estimate the model suggested at the end of section 7.5. Comment on the effect of government expenditure on real GDP in China. What is the value of the coefficient of government expenditure $G$ in the reduced-form equation explaining real GDP? The coefficient is termed the "government expenditure multiplier."

4   Assume that the structural equations (6.6) of chapter 6 remain valid, and $Y = C + I + G$, where $G$ stands for government expenditure. Solve these equations to obtain the reduced-form equations for $Y$ by substituting out $C$, $C_{t+1}$, $I$, and $I_{t+1}$. By how much will $Y_t$ and $Y_{t+1}$ change when $G_t$ increases by 1 billion yuan?

5   Estimate the model given in the last section using up-to-date data from the *China Statistical Yearbook*. Using this model answer question 4.

6   Estimate a VAR for $\ln P$, $\ln Y$, and $\ln M$ using data provided in table 7.1. Plot the impulse responses of $\ln P$ and $\ln Y$ to monetary shocks.

# 8

# The Effects of Political Movements on the Macroeconomy

This chapter attempts to measure the economic damage that the Great Leap Forward and the Cultural Revolution did to the Chinese macroeconomy. To do so, an econometric model is employed which enables one to isolate the effects of these political movements as abnormal deviations of the actual values of two economic variables from two equations of the model during the years of the movements. By removing these deviations and solving the model through time, we find the paths of the economic variables if the movements had not occurred. The differences between these counterfactual paths and the actual paths are the losses due to the movements. Some mathematical sophistication is required to understand the model.

## 8.1  Specification of a Dynamic Optimization Model of the Chinese Economy

In this chapter we propose to measure the economic effects on the Chinese macroeconomy of two major political movements. The two movements are the Great Leap Forward of 1958–61 and the Cultural Revolution of 1966–76. To do so we need to have a model of the evolution of the Chinese economy. In this model the effects of the two political movements show up in much larger residuals (the parts of the data which the model cannot explain) than the residuals in normal times. If we replace these abnormally large residuals, which are attributed to the effects of political movements, by ordinary residuals and solve the model to obtain the time path of the economy, the difference between the historical time path and the simulated time path (net of the effects of the movements) can be attributed to the political movements. The idea is simple, but it requires some technical discussion to explain how the study is actually carried out.

So far, I have presented four models as useful tools to understand the Chinese economy: the economic growth model in chapter 5, the Samuelson multiplier-accelerator model and the VAR model in chapter 6, and the model of equation (7.1) in chapter 7, explaining inflation. In this section I add a fifth model. It differs from the previous models in being derived explicitly from the assumption that the economic decision-makers act as if they continuously tried to maximize some objective function over time. To assume that economic agents maximize an objective, such as utility or profit, is a fundamental tool of economic theorizing. However, Keynes' *General Theory* and the previous three economic models are constructed by using assumptions about behavioral relations directly, without necessarily explicitly deriving the rule governing behavior from maximizing principles. Examples are the equations explaining the growth of the labor force and the amount of investment in the model in chapter 5, and the relation of desired capital stock to output which is used to derive the acceleration principle.

The model in this chapter explains both growth and fluctuations. It is derived explicitly from optimization and has only one sector. It includes aggregate output, consumption, investment, physical capital stock, and total labor force as major variables. Aggregate output is produced by physical capital and labor according to a Cobb–Douglas production function, as in the model in chapter 5. Output is divided into consumption and net investment (measured by "accumulation" in Chinese official statistics), as in the model in chapter 6. Capital stock increases with the flow of investment, an equation already explained in chapter 5. The novelty is that, to determine investment, we assume that actual investment equals planned investment plus an error. Planned investment is determined by the assumption that a central planner in China maximizes a multiperiod objective function with consumption per laborer as the argument. The error may be affected by political events.

The second novelty is the assumption that the logarithm of total factor productivity (TFP) follows a "random walk with drift" in normal years. The term in quotes will be explained later. In abnormal years, such as during the Great Leap and the Cultural Revolution, the residual of the random-walk process can also be affected. This assumption concerning TFP differs from that adopted in chapter 5, where the log of TFP is assumed to follow a linear trend.

Thus the effects of political events are modeled by two elements in the model: deviation of actual from planned investment, and the residual of the random-walk process for productivity. Having estimated such a model, one can remove the abnormal deviations and residuals in order to measure the economic effects of the two political events. In this section we specify the model and the data. Section 8.2 discusses the concept of a solution to the optimization model, in the same sense that the reduced-form equations are a solution to the simultaneous equations model in chapter 6. Section 8.3 explains the method of estimation and the parameter estimates. The discussion will be nontechnical. (For technical details the reader can refer to Kwan and Chow 1996.) Section 8.4 reports on the time paths of major variables obtained by simulating the model by removing the shocks from the two political events. It provides measures of economic losses attributable to these events. Section 8.5 concludes this chapter.

The econometric model consists of four equations. A Cobb–Douglas production function determines aggregate real output $Q$ by physical capital stock $K$ and labor $L$ with constant returns to scale. Denoting $Q/L$ and $K/L$ by $q$ and $k$ respectively and net investment per laborer by $i$, we can write the production function, the output identity, the capital accumulation equation, and the equation explaining total factor productivity $A$ as follows:

$$q_t = A_t k_t^{1-\alpha} \tag{8.1}$$
$$q_t = c_t + i_t \tag{8.2}$$
$$k_{t+1} = k_t + i_t \tag{8.3}$$
$$\ln A_{t+1} = \gamma + \ln A_t + \eta_{t+1} \tag{8.4}$$

where $\eta$ is a random shock to the logarithm of total factor productivity $A$. The first three equations are familiar from the growth model of chapter 5. Note, however, that the capital accumulation equation is obtained by dividing the original identity in aggregate variables by labor $L$ in two adjacent periods, and is therefore only an approximation.

Equation (8.4) specifies a "random-walk" process for the time series $\ln A$. The process simply means that the change in $\ln A$ in each period $t$ is random, given by a constant $\gamma$ plus the random variable $\eta$. The constant $\gamma$ is the "drift." Since we are tracking $\ln A$ continuously through time using equation (8.4), we can include data in the abnormal years which are excluded in estimating the model of chapter 5. If $\ln A$ is assumed to be a constant or to follow a linear trend, its values will be much below normal during the abnormal years affected by the political movements and cannot be included in the estimation of the model. In chapter 5 we assumed that total factor productivity has the form $Ae^{\gamma t}$, which implies that the log of total factor productivity equals $\ln A + \gamma t$ or follows a linear trend. The first difference of logTFP in this formulation is $(\ln A + \gamma t) - (\ln A - \gamma[t-1])$, or simply $\gamma$. By contrast, in this chapter we assume that the first difference of logTFP equals $\gamma$ plus a random variable $\eta$. No wonder in the literature, the first formulation is called a "deterministic trend," and the latter a "stochastic trend."

The data for aggregate output $Q$ are national income used (*Statistical Yearbook of China, 1994* [hereafter *SYB*], p. 40) divided by the implicit price deflator of national income. The price deflator is the ratio of national income in current prices (*SYB*, p. 33; measured in 100 million yuan) to national income in 1952 prices; the latter equals 589 (national income in 1952 in 100 million yuan) times the index of real national income (*SYB*, p. 34; = 100 in 1952) divided by 100. In Chinese official statistics, national income used equals consumption plus accumulation (net investment) in current prices. In our model this identity is assumed to hold in constant prices. We have estimated real national income used $Q$, real consumption $C$, and real net investment $I$ by dividing their current values (*SYB*, p. 40) by the above price deflator. Labor $L$ is the total labor force (*SYB* p. 88). Given $K = 2{,}213$ (100 million yuan) in 1952 (an estimate from Chow 1993b: 821), we estimate $k$ in 1952 by $K/L$ and $k$ in later years by equation (8.3).

Since the model so far has five variables ($q$, $k$, $c$, $I$, and $\ln A$) and only four equations, we need to find an extra equation or a way to determine one of the first four variables. To do so we assume that the Chinese economy evolves as if there were a central planner who, knowing the parameters of the model we have specified, tries to determine investment $i$ by maximizing the following objective function at the beginning of each period $t$:

$$E_t \sum_{i=1}^{\infty} \beta^{t+i} \log c_{t+i} \tag{8.5}$$

subject to the constraints in (8.1) to (8.4). The symbol $E_t$ in equation (8.5) denotes mathematical expectation given information at period $t$ which will be available when the value of the control variable is set. $\beta$ is the discount factor. In chapter 5 we assumed that investment is a constant fraction of GDP of the previous year. Here we assume that it is determined by the result of planning. Planning is done by solving the above optimization problem.

## 8.2   The Solution of the Dynamic Optimization Problem

To appreciate the optimization problem specified in the last section, let us review a basic approach to economic theorizing. It is to assume that an economic agent tries to maximize some objective function. A simple example is the theory of consumer demand. The objective function in this case is the utility function $u(x_1, x_2)$, where the two arguments are the quantities of two consumption goods such as food and clothing. In order to derive the demand functions for these two goods, the consumer is assumed to maximize the above utility function subject to the budget constraint $p_1x_1 + p_2x_2 = I$, where the $p$'s denote the prices of the two goods and $I$ denotes the consumer's income. This problem is static, dealing with only one period. The problem becomes dynamic when more than one period is involved.

An example of a maximization problem for two periods might have an objective function $\beta \log c_1 + \beta^2 \log c_2$ where the amounts of consumption in periods 1 and 2 are arguments. The discount factor $\beta$ makes consumption in period 2 less desirable than the same amount of consumption in period 1. The problem of section 8.1 extends the number of periods to infinity. In addition, it introduces uncertainty because of the stochastic element in equation (8.4). Given uncertainty in future TFP, future consumption becomes uncertain no matter how investment is planned. Hence it is necessary to take mathematical expectation or some form of average of future utility paths in order to define the objective function to be maximized. Since equation (8.4) explaining total factor productivity has a stochastic element $\eta$, future output, consumption, investment, and capital all become stochastic and uncertain. The problem becomes a stochastic dynamic optimization problem, in contrast with a deterministic static optimization problem of the textbook consumer stated in the last paragraph. This is a maximization problem subject to the constraints given by equations (8.1) to (8.4).

In a stochastic dynamic optimization problem there are control or decision variables and state variables. The values of the control variables are chosen to maximize the objective function. The evolution of the state variables is specified by dynamic equations. One state variable is $\ln A_t$. Its evolution is specified by equation (8.4). A second state variable is capital stock $k_t$. The dynamic optimization problem can be solved by defining the control variable as investment per laborer $i$, or alternatively by the next-period capital stock $k_{t+1}$, since these two variables are related by equation (8.3). Determining one implies determining the other. By the optimal path of the control variable is meant that path which makes the value of the objective function (8.5) the highest. We will find it more convenient to choose $k_{t+1}$ as our control variable.

Since the paths of future TFP, output, consumption, and capital stock are all uncertain, it cannot be optimal today to specify a path for the control variable for all future periods. As an example, it would not be optimal for the Open Market Committee of the US Federal Reserve to announce the path of the optimal federal fund rate for all future periods. The rate has to depend on the most recent economic information at the time of the decision. Hence, the solution to this optimization problem takes the form of an equation for the control variable as a function of the state variables which contain the important information at the time. That is, in each period, when the values of the state variables $\ln A_t$ and $k_t$ are given, the policy-maker can use this equation to compute the value of $k_{t+1}$, which enables him to achieve the maximum value of the objective function (8.5), if he applies this procedure every period in the future. In particular we will approximate this optimal decision rule by an equation of the form

$$\ln k_{t+1} = g + G_1 \ln A_t + G_2 \ln k_t \tag{8.6}$$

Kwan and Chow (1996, Appendix) shows how such an optimal decision rule can be mathematically derived, in case some readers are interested.

The maximization assumption underlying the above model of the Chinese economy might be questioned. A critic might claim that economic planners in China are not so rational as to have a specific objective function. She might say, just look at what happened to rational economic planning during the Great Leap and the Cultural Revolution. Our response is that during these abnormal periods there were exogenous shocks to the production and investment processes in China (caused to a large extent by the behavior of Chairman Mao). These large shocks were outside the control of the economic planners. However, in spite of the existence of such shocks, the planners still attempted in each period to maximize the above objective function from that period forward. This setup is no different from the assumption that a consumer tries to maximize a utility function subject to a budget constraint in deriving a demand function. An actual consumer is as unlikely to be able to solve the mathematical problems presented in an economics textbook, as a Chinese economic planner was to be able to solve the mathematical problem of this chapter. Economic theorizing based on the assumption that economic agents act as if they tried to maximize some objective function is a powerful tool to derive implications on economic behavior. It does not require that the actual economic agents can solve the mathematical problems involved. If my memory is correct, Robert Solow once explained this by saying that the path of a billiard ball may satisfy certain differential equations, but that does not mean that the billiard ball knows how to solve the differential equations.

In the framework of the dynamic optimization model, the observed Chinese time-series data on output, consumption, and capital are interpreted as the outcome of a dynamic optimization process. The solution to the dynamic optimization problem gives the time paths of these economic variables. In contrast to the approach of chapter 6, where a system of structural equations serves to explain the time paths of economic variables, here we use the solution of a dynamic optimization problem to determine the time paths of economic variables. This is a very important statement about the method of economics. Economists build models to explain economic phenomena. A quantitative model requires numerical parameters and can be used to explain statistical data. The model presented in chapter 6 of a system of simultaneous structural equations explains the data $C_t$ and $I_t$ on consumption and investment. To do so, the structural equations are solved algebraically to obtain the reduced-form equations. The reduced-form equation for $C_t$ explains $C_t$ by $C_{t-1}$ and $I_{t-1}$ and likewise for the reduced-form equation explaining investment $I_t$. The model of this chapter uses dynamic optimization to explain investment. Investment, or equivalently $k_{t+1}$, is determined not by solving algebraic equations but by solving a mathematical optimization problem. Once $k_{t+1}$ is determined, the remaining equations in the model are used to determine the other economic variables. The path of consumption can be used to evaluate the value of the objective function (8.5).

Let us examine carefully how the model can explain or generate economic data through time. Given the values of the parameters, we solve a dynamic optimization problem to determine investment $i_t$, or alternatively to determine $k_{t+1} = k_t + i_t$, since $k_t$ is known. The solution expresses $\ln k_{t+1}$ as a linear function of $\ln k_t$ and $\ln A_t$ as given by equation (8.6). The last two variables are the state variables. Given their values at time $t$, we can determine their future values as follows. Determine $\ln A_{t+1}$ by equation (8.4). Determine $\ln k_{t+1}$ by the optimal control equation (8.6). These two state variables can thus be solved forward recursively through time. Given the future path of $k$, the future paths of $q$, $I$, and $c$ are determined by equations (8.1), (8.3), and (8.2) respectively. Equation (8.4) for $\ln A_{t+1}$ and the optimal control equation (8.6) for $\ln k_{t+1}$ are the "reduced-form" equations of this model that are used to explain the time paths of the relevant economic variable. Equation (8.4) is subject to a random shock $\eta$. The optimal control equation for $\ln k_{t+1}$ explains only planned investment, or equivalently planned capital stock for the next period. The actual investment or actual capital stock in the next period may deviate from the planned value. The deviation is due partly to errors in carrying out the plan, but more importantly, during the periods of the two political movements studied in this chapter, to the effects of these movements. We thus have a random shock $\eta$ affecting total factor productivity, and a random element in carrying out the investment plan. Both are assumed to be affected by the disruptive force of political events. The historical values of these two shocks are plotted in figures 8.1 and 8.2 respectively. Since the shocks can be measured, the effects of the political movements can be quantitatively assessed – this will be done in the next section.

Among the possible shortcomings of this model are its treatment of technology, population, and the labor force as exogenous, and its failure to incorporate the possible effects of political movements on human capital formation, a subject discussed in section 12.3. In spite of these possible weaknesses, a study based on the above model can provide a first approximation in measuring the economic effects of the two major political events, and can serve as a benchmark for incorporating other important effects in future research.

## 8.3   Statistical Estimation

The parameters of our model include $(\alpha, \beta, \gamma)$ and the variance of the residual $\eta$ in the process (8.4) governing the evolution of total factor productivity. How are the numerical

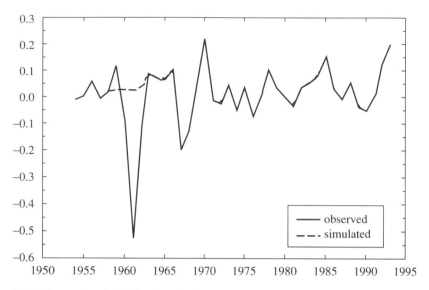

**Figure 8.1**   Observed and simulated residual 1

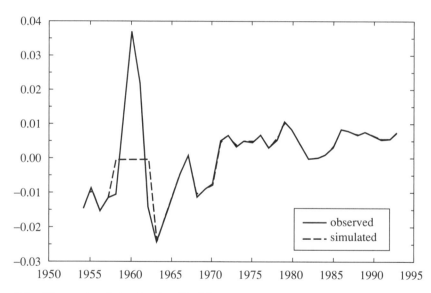

**Figure 8.2**   Observed and simulated residual 2

values of these parameters determined? They are determined by the same principle that the values of the coefficients of a linear regression are determined by the least-squares method. In the latter case, we first choose a criterion of best fit. If we choose the smallest sum of the squared deviations of the values computed by the regression function from the actual values of the dependent variable, we have the least-squares method. We can imagine trying out different values of the regression coefficients to make this sum of squared deviations the smallest, but there are mathematical methods to get the results for sure and more quickly. Similarly, in the present case we first choose a criterion for good fit, which is known as the value of the likelihood function. The bigger the value of the likelihood function, the better the fit. If we apply this principle to the case of fitting a linear regression function, under the assumption that the residual is normally distributed, the principle of maximizing the likelihood function is the same as the principle of least squares. The principle of maximum likelihood can be applied to models other than linear regressions like the one used in this chapter.

To understand the maximum likelihood method, we first observe that different values of the parameters $(\alpha, \beta, \gamma)$ will lead to different time paths of the variables to be generated by the economic model. As we have pointed out, equations (8.4) and (8.6) are used to generate the paths of the state variables $\ln k$ and $\ln A$. Given the paths of these two state variables, the paths of the remaining economic variables $q$, $I$, and $c$ can be determined by using equations (8.1) to (8.3). Note that to generate these paths we need to solve a dynamic optimization problem to determine the optimal decision function (8.6). The important point is that the time paths of the economic variables are dependent upon the values of the three parameters, after a mathematical optimization problem is solved. Secondly, the value of the likelihood function depends on how far the time paths of the economic variables generated by the model described above are from the historically observed values. The closer the two sets of paths, the higher the value of the likelihood function. When we estimate the numerical values of the parameters, we choose the values in such a way that, if these values are used, the time paths of the economic variables determined by solving the model (using the steps described above) will be as close to the actual economic data as possible, as judged by the value of the likelihood function. The technical details of estimating the numerical values of the parameters by the "maximum likelihood" method are elaborated in Kwan and Chow (1996).

The "maximum likelihood" estimates of $(\alpha, \beta, \gamma)$, with standard errors given in parentheses, are:

$$(\hat{\alpha}, \hat{\beta}, \hat{\gamma}) = [.7495 \ (.0108), .9999 \ (.0001), .0218 \ (.0025)] \tag{8.7}$$
$$\text{mean log likelihood} = 6.6120, \text{ sample size} = 40.$$

The estimate of 0.7495 for labor elasticity of production appears high, but may still be useful for our purpose of obtaining deviations caused by political events. It is higher than the estimate of about 0.4 reported in Chow (1993b, esp. table VII) and above in chapter 5, but these studies use a deterministic trend for log total factor productivity, whereas the current estimate is based on a "stochastic trend" as specified by equation (8.4). The reasons for the difference in the results obtained by using different specifications of the trend in total factor productivity require further investigation. Suffice to note here that the period 1958–69 was excluded when the deterministic trend was used, and that two different deterministic trends were specified for the periods before and after 1978. Using equation (8.4) with the same $\gamma$ for the entire sample period forces a positive $\gamma$ for the period 1952 to 1978, when $\gamma$ should be zero. This provides a partial explanation for the

**Table 8.1**   Some sensitivity analysis parameters

| $\hat{\alpha}$ | $\hat{\beta}$ | $\hat{\gamma}$ | *Mean log likelihood* |
|---|---|---|---|
| 0.4 | 0.9627 (0.0050) | 0.0046 (0.0011) | 5.9754 |
| 0.5 | 0.9715 (0.0037) | 0.0083 (0.0017) | 6.2012 |
| 0.6 | 0.9817 (0.0024) | 0.0132 (0.0024) | 6.3869 |
| 0.7 | 0.9940 (0.0015) | 0.0194 (0.0033) | 6.5456 |

observed growth in per capita GDP in 1952–78, which otherwise would have to be explained by the growth of the capital/labor ratio, thus reducing the estimate of $1 - \alpha$. The value of the estimate of $\alpha$ is thus biased upward. Perhaps the analysis of this chapter could be improved by assuming that $\alpha$ is zero, or takes a different value, before 1978.

The estimate of 0.9999 for the annual discount factor is also reasonable in view of the high value which Chinese planners are supposed to place on future consumption, or current investment at the expense of current consumption. This parameter is considered difficult to estimate statistically and is often imposed *a priori* in empirical studies of real business cycles in the United States. The positive drift of the log total factor productivity of 0.0218 is also reasonable, as the sample includes the postreform years 1978–93. It is consistent with Chow (1993b), which found no positive deterministic trend in total factor productivity during the sample period from 1952 to 1980, but a positive trend from 1979 on. Unlike Chow (1993b), the present study extends the sample period to 1993 and, in estimating model parameters, does not exclude any observations which are considered abnormal. This extension is possible partly because a stochastic trend specified by equation (8.4) is used for log total productivity rather than a linear deterministic trend as in Chow (1993b).

Because the exponent $\alpha$ of labor in the Cobb–Douglas production appears to be high, we use a smaller value of $\alpha$ to observe the effects on the estimates of the other two parameters. For this sensitivity analysis we present in table 8.1 estimates for the remaining two parameters, when the labor elasticity parameter is fixed *a priori* at other values sometimes chosen in growth accounting exercises (see e.g. Li, Gong, and Zheng 1995).

## 8.4   Measuring the Effects of Two Political Events

To estimate the economic effects of the Great Leap Forward alone, we change the estimated residuals of the two reduced-form equations (8.4) and the optimal control equation (8.6) for $\ln k_{t+1}$ in the years 1958–62, to the mean values of the corresponding residuals in the remaining years; see figures 8.1 and 8.2. Columns 2 and 3 of table 8.2 present actual output per laborer $q_t$ (which can be generated by our model if the estimated residuals are used in the two equations), and simulated output $q_t^*$, which is generated by our model if the estimated residuals in the years 1958–62 are changed to the mean values

**Table 8.2** Effects of the Great Leap Forward

| Year | Output | | Consumption | | Capital stock | | Log productivity | |
|------|--------|--------|-------------|--------|---------------|--------|------------------|--------|
| | Observed | Simulated | Observed | Simulated | Observed | Simulated | Observed | Simulated |
| 1952 | 2.9283 | 2.9283 | 2.3011 | 2.3011 | 10.676 | 10.676 | 0.48132 | 0.48132 |
| 1953 | 3.2227 | 3.2227 | 2.4780 | 2.4780 | 11.303 | 11.303 | 0.56285 | 0.56285 |
| 1954 | 3.3276 | 3.3276 | 2.4794 | 2.4794 | 12.048 | 12.048 | 0.57888 | 0.57888 |
| 1955 | 3.4661 | 3.4661 | 2.6715 | 2.6715 | 12.896 | 12.896 | 0.60262 | 0.60262 |
| 1956 | 3.7717 | 3.7717 | 2.8500 | 2.8500 | 13.691 | 13.691 | 0.67214 | 0.67214 |
| 1957 | 3.9038 | 3.9038 | 2.9310 | 2.7747 | 14.612 | 14.612 | 0.69025 | 0.69025 |
| 1958 | 4.1304 | 4.1525 | 2.7289 | 2.9482 | 15.585 | 15.741 | 0.73053 | 0.73336 |
| 1959 | 4.7393 | 4.4162 | 2.6635 | 3.1322 | 16.986 | 16.946 | 0.84648 | 0.77647 |
| 1960 | 4.6947 | 4.6959 | 2.8339 | 3.3274 | 19.062 | 18.230 | 0.80816 | 0.81959 |
| 1961 | 3.2774 | 4.9924 | 2.6465 | 3.5344 | 20.923 | 19.598 | 0.42542 | 0.86270 |
| 1962 | 3.0530 | 5.3069 | 2.7342 | 4.2926 | 21.554 | 21.056 | 0.37407 | 0.90581 |
| 1963 | 3.3543 | 5.8781 | 2.7680 | 4.5729 | 21.873 | 22.070 | 0.43750 | 0.99625 |
| 1964 | 3.6400 | 6.4285 | 2.8314 | 4.8570 | 22.459 | 23.376 | 0.51262 | 1.0714 |
| 1965 | 3.9385 | 7.0076 | 2.8712 | 5.1104 | 23.268 | 24.947 | 0.58258 | 1.1413 |
| 1966 | 4.4182 | 7.9173 | 3.0654 | 5.6422 | 24.335 | 26.844 | 0.62628 | 1.2450 |
| 1967 | 3.9337 | 7.0975 | 3.0963 | 5.3530 | 25.688 | 29.119 | 0.55660 | 1.1153 |
| 1968 | 3.6809 | 6.6849 | 2.9024 | 4.9747 | 26.525 | 30.864 | 0.48213 | 1.0409 |
| 1969 | 4.0273 | 7.3599 | 3.0919 | 5.4272 | 27.303 | 32.574 | 0.56482 | 1.1236 |
| 1970 | 4.9087 | 9.0246 | 3.2916 | 6.2019 | 28.239 | 34.507 | 0.75429 | 1.3130 |
| 1971 | 5.0405 | 9.3203 | 3.3235 | 6.2964 | 29.856 | 37.329 | 0.76684 | 1.3256 |
| 1972 | 5.1180 | 9.5159 | 3.5018 | 6.5478 | 31.573 | 40.353 | 0.76810 | 1.3268 |
| 1973 | 5.4831 | 10.249 | 3.6789 | 6.9632 | 33.189 | 43.321 | 0.82451 | 1.3833 |
| 1974 | 5.4627 | 10.262 | 3.6958 | 6.9540 | 34.993 | 46.607 | 0.80751 | 1.3663 |

**Table 8.2** (cont'd)

| Year | Output | | Consumption | | Capital stock | | Log productivity | |
|---|---|---|---|---|---|---|---|---|
| | Observed | Simulated | Observed | Simulated | Observed | Simulated | Observed | Simulated |
| 1975 | 5.8133 | 10.974 | 3.8447 | 7.3186 | 36.760 | 49.915 | 0.85738 | 1.4161 |
| 1976 | 5.6731 | 10.759 | 3.9225 | 7.3361 | 38.729 | 53.570 | 0.81990 | 1.3786 |
| 1977 | 5.8764 | 11.194 | 3.9762 | 7.4969 | 40.479 | 56.993 | 0.84404 | 1.4028 |
| 1978 | 6.5737 | 12.576 | 4.1718 | 8.0845 | 42.379 | 60.690 | 0.94469 | 1.5034 |
| 1979 | 6.9773 | 13.402 | 4.5635 | 8.8103 | 44.781 | 65.181 | 0.99046 | 1.5492 |
| 1980 | 7.1944 | 13.873 | 4.9267 | 9.4212 | 47.195 | 69.773 | 1.0080 | 1.5667 |
| 1981 | 7.2277 | 13.990 | 5.1806 | 9.8049 | 49.463 | 74.225 | 1.0008 | 1.5596 |
| 1982 | 7.6748 | 14.908 | 5.4636 | 10.415 | 51.510 | 78.410 | 1.0507 | 1.6094 |
| 1983 | 8.2453 | 16.072 | 5.7936 | 11.144 | 53.721 | 82.903 | 1.1119 | 1.6706 |
| 1984 | 9.0219 | 17.643 | 6.1797 | 12.032 | 56.173 | 87.831 | 1.1907 | 1.7494 |
| 1985 | 10.490 | 20.579 | 6.8177 | 13.562 | 59.015 | 93.442 | 1.3291 | 1.8878 |
| 1986 | 11.107 | 21.854 | 7.2579 | 14.450 | 62.687 | 100.46 | 1.3711 | 1.9298 |
| 1987 | 11.438 | 22.570 | 7.5423 | 14.988 | 66.536 | 107.86 | 1.3855 | 1.9443 |
| 1988 | 12.408 | 24.554 | 8.1293 | 16.238 | 70.431 | 115.44 | 1.4528 | 2.0115 |
| 1989 | 12.492 | 24.785 | 8.2737 | 16.466 | 74.710 | 123.76 | 1.4447 | 2.0034 |
| 1990 | 12.409 | 24.684 | 8.3370 | 16.514 | 78.928 | 132.08 | 1.4243 | 1.9830 |
| 1991 | 12.806 | 25.536 | 8.6106 | 17.069 | 83.000 | 140.25 | 1.4432 | 2.0019 |
| 1992 | 14.512 | 29.005 | 9.5145 | 19.074 | 87.196 | 148.72 | 1.5559 | 2.1147 |
| 1993 | 17.491 | 35.036 | | | 92.194 | 158.65 | 1.7286 | 2.2874 |
| | | | | | | | | |
| mean | 6.7323 | 12.244 | 4.4410 | 7.9904 | 39.606 | 57.273 | 0.90151 | 1.3469 |
| std dev | 3.6746 | 8.1727 | 2.0767 | 4.7878 | 22.816 | 42.633 | 0.35652 | 0.47905 |

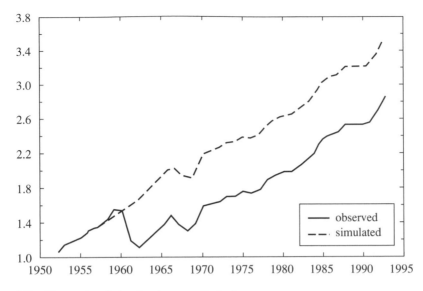

**Figure 8.3**  Observed and simulated output (in log)

of the remaining years. The remaining columns of table 8.2 are the corresponding actual and simulated series for consumption, capital stock, and log productivity.

From table 8.2 and figure 8.3 we observe that simulated output (which would have occurred absent the Great Leap) is about twice actual output in 1993. This result is derived from two sources. First, simulated total factor productivity in 1993 is about 0.56 higher than the actual value in logarithm, or about 1.74 times the actual value. Second, simulated capital stock per laborer in 1993 is 1.72 times the actual value, as can be readily computed from the relevant entries in table 8.2. According to our model, and commonly used models of real business cycles for the US economy, shifts in productivity due to shocks are permanent. Observe in table 8.2 and figure 8.4 that simulated log productivity in 1962 is 0.9058, or 0.5587 higher than actual log productivity. The last figure equals (2.2874 − 1.7286), the difference between simulated and actual log productivity in 1993. Such a parallel shift in log productivity due to the Great Leap is clearly shown in figure 8.6. This is a characteristic of our model, as equation (8.4) has a unit root which implies a permanent shift in total factor productivity when its residual changes. The permanent shift in productivity in turn implies that output, consumption, and capital (see figure 8.5) will all undergo a permanent level shift. There is no effect on the steady-state growth rate of each variable.

To see the extent of the permanent level shift, we generate 500 residuals for equations (8.4) and (8.6) from a bivariate distribution estimated by the maximum likelihood method above, and use them to extend the series of the observed residuals as well as our modified residuals that end in 1993. Output, consumption, and capital are calculated according to these two extended residuals series. Examining the last 100 entries reveals that the steady state has been attained, as evidenced by the balanced growth of the three variables.

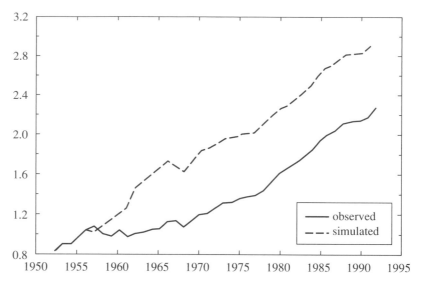

**Figure 8.4**   Observed and simulated consumption (in log)

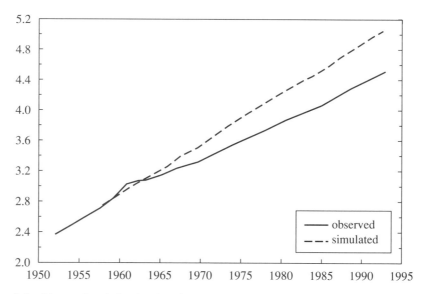

**Figure 8.5**   Observed and simulated capital (in log)

Taking the ratio of the two output series gives the permanent level effect which we report in table 8.3 (the row labeled "Steady state") .

To assess the effect of the Cultural Revolution and the combined effect of the two movements, we have performed a simulation exercise similar to that described above by removing the residuals of the turbulent years. Table 8.3 provides a short summary for

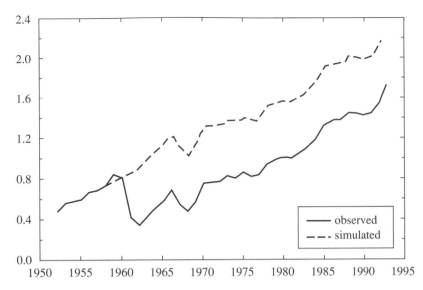

**Figure 8.6**   Observed and simulated Solow residual (in log)

**Table 8.3**   Simulation/observed level in 1992

|  | *Great Leap* | *Cultural Revolution* | *Both* |
| --- | --- | --- | --- |
| Output | 2.0031 | 1.2033 | 2.7130 |
| Consumption | 2.0047 | 1.2022 | 2.7261 |
| Capital | 1.7208 | 1.1537 | 2.1687 |
| Steady state | 2.1074 | 1.2204 | 2.9238 |

**Notes**: $(\hat{\alpha}, \hat{\beta}, \hat{\gamma}) = (0.7495, 0.9999, 0.0218)$.

comparison with the Great Leap case; tables similar to table 8.2 are available on request. For example, the output level by 1992 would have been 2.7 times higher than otherwise if both political movements had never occurred. To show the degree of sensitivity of our results, tables 8.4 and 8.5 give similar comparisons when the other parameter values reported in section 8.3 are used.

Absent the Cultural Revolution, output in China in 1992 would have been 1.20 times as large as the actual figure. This estimate might be considered too small. The possibility of underestimation is mainly due to the omission of the effect on human capital formation in our model. Given that human capital is not considered, and within the confines of our model, the measured effect appears reasonable. The disruption of the Cultural Revolution in the production of physical output in China is recognized to be much smaller than the disruption of the Great Leap. The relative magnitudes of 1.2 and 2.0 seem quite plausible.

**Table 8.4**   Simulation/observed level in 1992

|              | Great Leap | Cultural Revolution | Both   |
|--------------|------------|---------------------|--------|
| Output       | 2.5446     | 1.2355              | 3.6549 |
| Consumption  | 2.5680     | 1.2349              | 3.7277 |
| Capital      | 1.9708     | 1.1643              | 2.5461 |
| Steady state | 3.2856     | 1.3111              | 5.2465 |

Notes: $\hat{\alpha}$ *fixed at 0.5*, $\hat{\beta} = 0.9715$, $\hat{\gamma} = 0.0083$.

**Table 8.5**   Simulation/observed level in 1992

|              | Great Leap | Cultural Revolution | Both   |
|--------------|------------|---------------------|--------|
| Output       | 2.2907     | 1.2217              | 2.2082 |
| Consumption  | 2.3008     | 1.2207              | 3.2459 |
| Capital      | 1.8614     | 1.1597              | 2.3796 |
| Steady state | 2.6306     | 1.2648              | 3.9152 |

Notes: $\hat{\alpha}$ *fixed at 0.6*, $\hat{\beta} = 0.9817$, $\hat{\gamma} = 0.0132$.

The Cultural Revolution had a significant effect on the production of human capital when many schools and universities were closed or ceased to function properly. The estimate of 1.2 can thus serve as a benchmark for studying the effects of the Cultural Revolution through its effect on the accumulation of human capital.

# 8.5   Conclusions

We have presented in this chapter a very simple econometric model to measure the effects of two major political events in China. The model is based on a dynamic optimization framework. It assumes that an economic planner in China tries to maximize a multiperiod object function in making consumption and investment decisions. The values of the parameters of the optimization model as estimated by maximum likelihood are reasonable. The dynamic optimization framework is useful for studying economic behavior and the effects of political events in China, as in other countries.

Concerning the effects of the Great Leap and the Cultural Revolution, our results indicate that absent the former, output and consumption per laborer in 1992 would have been 2.0 times as large as that observed; that absent the latter, output and consumption would have been 1.2 times as large; and that if neither had occurred, output and consumption would have been 2.7 times the actual amounts. These estimates are based on a coefficient of unity (or a unit root) in the first-order autoregression equation (8.4) determining the logarithm of total factor productivity. If we allow this coefficient to be less than unity, the effects of productivity shocks resulting from political events and other factors will not be permanent and become smaller as time goes on. Chow and Kwan (1996) have dropped the unit root assumption in equation (8.4) and applied the same method to estimate the economic effects of the two political events in China. These more conservative estimates show that without the Great Leap output, the per capita figure in China in 1993 would have been 1.2 to 1.7 times as great as the actual. Without the Cultural Revolution, the corresponding figure would have been 1.08 to 1.12 times as great.

## References and Further Reading

Chow, Gregory C. *Econometrics*. New York: McGraw-Hill, 1983.

Chow, Gregory C. "Dynamic Optimization without Dynamic Programming." *Economic Modeling*, 9 (1992), pp. 3–9.

Chow, Gregory C. "Optimal Control without Solving the Bellman Equation." *Journal of Economic Dynamics and Control*, 17 (1993a), pp. 621–30.

Chow, Gregory C. "Capital Formation and Economic Growth in China." *Quarterly Journal of Economics*, 108 (1993b), pp. 809–42.

Chow, Gregory C. *Dynamic Economics: Optimization by the Lagrange Method*. New York: Oxford University Press, 1997.

Chow, Gregory C. and Y. K. Kwan. "Economic Effects of Political Movements in China: Lower Bound Estimates." *Pacific Economic Review*, 1 (1996).

Goffe, William L., Gary Ferrier, and John Rogers. "Global Optimization of Statistical Function." In Hans M. Amman, D. A. Belsley, and Louis F. Pau, eds., *Computational Economics and Econometrics*. Dordrecht: Kluwer, 1992, p. 1.

Kwan, Y. K. and Gregory C. Chow. "Estimating Economic Effects of Political Movements in China." *Journal of Comparative Economics*, 23 (1996), pp. 192–208.

Kwan, Y. K. and Gregory C. Chow. "Chow's Method of Optimal Control: A Numerical Solution." *Journal of Economic Dynamic and Control*, 21(4–5) (1997), pp. 739–52.

Li, Jingwen, Feihong Gong, and Yisheng Zheng. "Productivity and China's Economic Growth, 1953–1990." In K. Tsui, T. Hsueh, and T. Rawski, eds., *Productivity, Efficiency and Reform in China's Economy*. Hong Kong: Chinese University Press, 1995.

Lin, Justin Y. "Collectivization and China's Agricultural Crisis in 1959–1961." *Journal of Political Economy*, 98 (1990), pp. 1228–52.

*Statistical Yearbook of China, 1994*. Beijing: State Statistical Bureau, 1994.

## Questions

1  Compare the model consisting of equations (8.1) to (8.5) of this chapter with the model given by equation (5.5) of chapter 5. What three equations are common to both models? What equations are distinctive to each?

2  Explain why you might or might not prefer the model in this chapter to the model of equation (5.5) in chapter 5, and for what purposes.

3   The approach taken in this chapter assumes that to measure the effect of any historical
    event on an economy, one needs to construct a model of the evolution of the economy
    which incorporates the impact of the historical event. By removing the impact, one
    can use the model to determine the evolutionary path of the economic variables
    absent the event. What equations are used to measure the shocks of political events?
    Write out these equations and explain how the political shocks are measured.
4   What are the state variables in the model in this chapter? Given the values of the state
    variables at time $t$, explain how one can compute the future values of all the variables
    in the model.
5   Name the parameter common to the models in this chapter and chapter 5 which has
    been estimated to have fairly different values. Can you explain the difference? Hint:
    The trends are differently modeled. No observations in 1958–69 are omitted here.
    Given the above two differences, would the model in this chapter, compared with the
    model of chapter 5, attribute relatively more of the variation of $q = Y/L$ to the trend
    specified than to $k = K/L$, thus reducing the coefficient of $k$? If so, why?

# Part III

# Topics in Economic Development

# 9

# Consumption

Trends in per capita consumption show that before 1978 the annual exponential rate of increase from 1957 to 1978 was 0.0142 for peasants, 0.0248 for nonpeasants, and 0.0174 for all households, and that after 1978 it was 0.0695 for peasants and 0.0624 for nonpeasants. Before 1978 the increase for nonpeasants was due mainly to an increase in the participation of women in the labor force, without an increase in real wage. Cross-provincial data are used to study the relations between total per capita household expenditure and expenditures on food, clothing, housing, and miscellaneous for peasants in 1981 and 1998 as linear functions in the logarithms of the variables. The coefficients or elasticities are compared with those of other countries and of Shanghai and Beijing in the 1930s. Commercialization of urban housing and forecasting the demand for personal computers are discussed in the last two sections.

## 9.1   Trends in Per Capita Consumption

Before economic reform began in 1978, the emphasis of economic policy had been on the speeding up of industrialization through physical capital formation at the expense of consumption. After reform began, economists in China agreed that the main objective of all socialist economic activities is to satisfy the people's consumption needs. (See Ma and Sun 1982: 10, and Yang 1982: 543.) They recognized that among the major causes of the distortions in the economic structure existing in China at that time were the overemphasis on developing heavy industry at the expense of agriculture and light industry and the excessively high rate of accumulation at the expense of consumption (see Ma and Sun 1982: 7). While heavy industry greatly expanded from 1952 to 1978, per capita consumption in China advanced only slowly. Since 1978, consumption has increased more rapidly. I will elaborate on these two statements in this section.

**Table 9.1**   Per capita consumption and urban wage rate

|      | Per capita consumption index | | | Average annual wage of state-owned units |
|------|----------------|----------|-------------|--------------------------|
|      | All households | Peasants | Nonpeasants |                          |
| 1957 | 122.9 | 117.0 | 126.3 | 637 |
| 1967 | 142.9 | 136.2 | 145.3 | 630 |
| 1977 | 168.5 | 151.0 | 201.3 | 602 |
| 1978 | 177.0 | 157.6 | 212.6 | 644 |
| 1978 | 100.0 | 100.0 | 100.0 | |
| 1985 | 181.3 | 194.4 | 147.5 | 1,213 |
| 1988 | 214.9 | 220.4 | 187.3 | 1,853 |
| 1992 | 270.3 | 257.2 | 249.9 | 2,878 |
| 1995 | 338.8 | 318.6 | 300.0 | 4,625 |
| 1996 | 362.2 | 349.5 | 307.5 | 6,280 |

To examine the trends in per capita consumption in China, it will be informative to examine the data for all households and for peasants and nonpeasants separately. The *Statistical Yearbook of China, 1990* (p. 291) provides an index of the per capita consumption of each group from 1952 to 1989 with 1952 = 100. These data are recorded in the top half of table 9.1. The *China Statistical Yearbook, 1997* (p. 292) provides the same from 1978 to 1996 with 1978 = 100. These data are recorded in the bottom half of table 9.1.

From the data in the top half of table 9.1, the annual exponential rate of increase in the index of per capita consumption of all households (from 122.9 to 177.0) from 1957 to 1978 amounts to 0.0174. The rate was 0.0142 for peasants and 0.0248 for nonpeasants. These rates were very small as compared with the rates of growth for the period 1978–96, 0.0695 and 0.0624 for peasants and nonpeasants respectively. Three conclusions can be drawn from these data. First, for both peasants and nonpeasants, per capita consumption grew much more slowly in the two decades before economic reform than after economic reform, in the order of 1.4 and 2.5 percent annually for the two groups before, and 7.0 and 6.2 percent after reform. Second, in the prereform period, consumption per capita increased more for nonpeasants as a result of government policies to tax the peasants heavily and to encourage more participation of women in the urban labor force; the rate of increase was slightly higher for the peasants after reform partly because the household responsibility system was brought in early to benefit the peasants. Third, a discrepancy between per capita real income growth (close to 4 percent annually) and per capita consumption growth occurred in the prereform period when the policy was to achieve growth at the expense of consumption, but the discrepancy disappeared during the postreform period when increasing consumer welfare was considered an important objective of economic development.

The data presented in table 9.1 show that for the period 1978–96 the average annual rate of increase in per capita consumption for all households is larger than both components. There is no inconsistency in these data. When per capita consumption of the nonfarm population was about three times that of the farm population, an increase in the fraction of nonfarm population would raise per capita consumption of the entire population even if per capita consumption of either group remained constant. Hence the 1996 index of 362.2 for all residents can be used to compute an average annual rate of growth of 0.0715 between 1978 and 1996. This result supports our main conclusion concerning the much higher rate of growth in per capita consumption after economic reform than before.

To examine more recent trends using slightly different data I have found in the *China Statistical Yearbook, 2003*, table 10-1, the annual consumption expenditure of city households in 1989, 1997, 2001, and 2002 to be respectively 1,211, 4,186, 5,309, and 6,030 yuan. For rural households the per capita living expenditures are 535, 1,617, 1,741 and 1,834 respectively. To find appropriate price indices to deflate these nominal figures one can use table 9-2 of the same yearbook for the consumer price index for urban areas and for rural areas in these four yours. The former (with 1978 = 100) are 219.2, 481.9, 479.9, and 475.1. The latter (with 1985 = 100) are 157.9, 322.3, 316.5, and 315.2. Using these price indices to convert nominal consumption per capita into real consumption per capita in 1989 prices, we have, for 1997, 2001, and 2002 respectively, 1,904, 2,415, and 2,782 for city households. The corresponding real expenditures are respectively 792, 869, and 919 for rural residents. The above real consumption figures imply an average exponential rate of growth between 1989 and 2002 of 0.0640 for urban households and 0.0416 for rural households. Using the above data from the 2003 yearbook one concludes that for city households the exponential rate of growth of per capita consumption for the period 1989–2002 was 0.064, slightly higher than the rate 0.0624 for the period 1978–96. For the rural households the rate of growth 0.0416 of per capita consumption appeared to have declined in the later period, as compared with 0.0695 in 1978–96, a fact consistent with the slower increase in agricultural productivity in the 1990s as compared with the 1980s.

The last column of table 9.1 (taken from the *Statistical Yearbook of China, 1981*, pp. 435–6 and the *China Statistical Yearbook, 1999*, table 5-18) shows that average annual wage in all state-owned enterprises in China was about the same in 1978 as in 1957. Deflated by the cost of living index of staff and workers (126.6 and 144.7 with 1950 = 100), the real wage in 1950 yuan was 503.2 in 1957 and 445.1 in 1978, a reduction of 11.5 percent. The wage rate was held low for more than two decades up to 1978 and was allowed to increase after 1978 when economic policy was changed to expand the production of consumer goods. How can the reduction in real wage be reconciled with the increase in per capita consumption of nonfarmers from 126.3 to 212.6, or by 68 percent, during the same period? The main explanation for the increase in the index of per capita consumption expenditure while the average real wage declined is the increase in the ratio of the number of employed persons to the total urban population.

The *Statistical Yearbook of China, 1999*, table 4-1, shows an increase of urban population from 99.49 million in 1957 to 172.45 million in 1978, while the number of employed persons in urban areas (table 5-4) increased from 32.05 million in 1957 to 95.14 million in 1978. In other words, the labor participation rate increased from

32.2 percent in 1957 to 55.2 percent in 1978. This increase in the labor participation rate was due to the government's policy to encourage women to participate in the labor force. The combined effect on per capita income of the increase in labor force participation 55.2/32.2 and real wage reduction 445.1/503.2 is a factor of 1.52, nearly sufficient to explain the 68 percent increase in real consumption per capita from 1957 to 1978 for nonagricultural residents given in table 9.1. We can conclude that the increase in per capita consumption of the nonagricultural residents between 1957 and 1978 is due mainly to a large increase in the ratio of employed to total urban population, combined with a moderate reduction in the real wage rate. To the extent that an increase in per capita consumption is due to an increase in labor participation, increase in consumer welfare is less because there is less leisure time and less time to produce nonmarket consumer goods and services at home (such as home-cooked meals, laundry, and childcare).

The data in table 9.1 indicate a widening of the gap between the consumption levels of peasants and nonpeasants from the 1950s to 1978 and a narrowing of the gap from 1978 to 1996, but a slight widening again in 1985–98. The per capita real consumption of peasants increased by only 29 percent between 1957 and 1978. Even after the gap was narrowed after 1978, we still find the annual per capita consumption of agricultural residents in 1998 to be only 1,892 yuan compared with 6,201 yuan for non-agricultural residents. To what extent there was a higher fraction of consumption in the form of nonmarket goods for the agricultural residents which was not reported in the official statistics is not known. Furthermore the purchasing power of a yuan might be higher for the agricultural residents than for nonagricultural residents.

Was the slow increase in per capita consumption of all farm families between 1957 and 1978 also affected by an increase in the ratio of the number of farm laborers to total farm population? The answer is no. The *China Statistical Yearbook, 1999*, table 4-1, gives a total rural population of 547.04 and 790.14 for these two years; table 5-4 gives the number of rural employed persons to be 205.66 and 306.38 million respectively. The ratios are respectively 0.376 and 0.387, not much different from each other.

One important component of per capita consumption should be noted. Average housing space for the population in cities and towns decreased from 4.5 square meters in 1952 to 3.6 square meters in 1977 (see Yang 1982: 548). Very few new houses were built in urban areas during this period. Housing space was redistributed and rationed to urban residents at extremely low cost. Housing expenditure had a very small weight in the statistics on consumption expenditures. Since economic reform, urban housing construction has been very rapid, and construction activities in the cities can be witnessed even by tourists. The *China Statistical Yearbook, 1999*, table 10-26, reports per capita living space in urban areas of 3.6 square meters in 1978, 6.0 square meters in 1986, and 9.3 square meters in 1998. The same table gives per capita living space in rural areas to be 8.1 square meters in 1978, 15.3 square meters in 1986, and 23.7 square meters in 1998. The ratio of rural to urban housing space per capita increased slightly from 2.25 to 2.55 from 1978 to 1986 and has remained at 2.55 in 1998. These statistics can easily be checked by sampling the housing space available in urban and rural areas. This remark is made especially for readers who are skeptical of the high rate of growth of the Chinese economy reported in official statistics. Anyone who has traveled to China several times between

1979 and 1998 will agree that the very high rate of growth of about 9.5 percent per year on average is consistent with casual observations. The traveler would have witnessed all the construction activity and new buildings in the urban and rural areas, and the improvement in the food, clothing, and consumer durable goods available to ordinary citizens.

To give an idea of the consumption levels on different items, the *China Statistical Yearbook*, 2003, table 10-11, shows a list of consumer durables and the number of each owned per 100 urban households at the end of each year from 1999 to 2002. The numbers of refrigerators are respectively 77.74, 80.10, 81.90, and 87.38. The numbers of color TV sets are respectively 111.57, 116.60, 120.50, and 126.38. The numbers of video disc players are 24.71, 37.50, 42.60, and 52.57. The numbers of computers are 5.91, 9.70, 13.30, and 20.63. The numbers of cell phones are 7.14, 19.50, 34.00, and 62.89. The numbers of automobiles are 0.34, 0.50, 0.60, and 0.88. The growth of ownership of cell phones by a factor of 9 during the 4 years from 1999 to 2002 was phenomenal. The growth of computers by a factor of 3.5 and the growth of automobiles by a factor of 2.6 were impressive. There appears to be a lot of room for further increase in the consumption of automobiles, computers, and mobile telephones. Domestic and foreign investors have been keeping their eyes on the Chinese markets for these products and are actively participating in development of them.

## 9.2 Household Expenditure Patterns

In the preceding section we discussed the changes in total consumption per capita through time. A study using such data is a *time-series analysis*. In this section we study the composition of family consumption expenditures at one point in time among different groups of consumers. This exemplifies a *cross-section analysis*. It is of interest to examine how households increase their expenditures on different kinds of consumption goods as their total consumption expenditure increases. Such studies of consumer expenditure patterns originated more than 100 years ago. As Houthakker (1957: 532) wrote:

> Few dates in the history of econometrics are more significant than 1857. In that year Ernst Engel (1821–96) published a study on the conditions of production and consumption in the Kingdom of Saxony, in which he formulated an empirical law concerning the relation between income and expenditure on food. Engel's law, as it has since become known, states that the proportion of income spent on food declines as income rises. Its original statement was mainly based on an examination of about two hundred budgets of Belgian laborers collected by Ducpetiaux. Since that date the law has been found to hold in many other budget surveys; similar laws have also been formulated for other items of expenditure.
>
> With the formulation of Engel's law an important branch of econometrics took its start, though it was not until our days that consumption research was placed on a sound theoretical and statistical basis ... His successful attempt to derive meaningful regularities from seemingly arbitrary observations will always be an inspiring example to the profession, the more so because in his day economic theory and statistical techniques were of little assistance in such an attempt ...

*Econometrics* is the art and science of using statistical methods for the measurement of economic relations. Our present task is to study the relations between total consumption expenditures of Chinese households, and expenditures on food and other major consumption categories. We will use data for Chinese peasants in 1981 and in 1998.

For 1981 data on the per capita consumption expenditure of Chinese peasants and its four major components – food, clothing, housing and fuel, and all other items – for 28 provinces and municipalities (with the exception of Tibet) see table 9.2. The data are based on a sample survey of 18,529 farm households conducted in 1981 and are reported in the *Statistical Yearbook of China, 1981* (pp. 441, 445–6). Observations for the 28 provinces permit us to examine how per capita expenditures on the four categories of consumption change as total consumption expenditure changes.

The four types of expenditures are plotted against total expenditure in figures 5.1, 5.2, 5.3, and 5.4, respectively, of Chow (1985), where the axes are measured on a logarithmic scale. Each data point is marked by a number corresponding to the province or municipality shown in table 9.2: 1 for Beijing, 2 for Tianjin, and so on. These figures indicate that the relations between the logarithms of the four categories of expenditures and the logarithm of total expenditure are approximately linear. Therefore, for each category $j$ ($j = 1, 2, 3, 4$) we can postulate a regression relation

$$\log y_{ij} = \alpha_j + \beta_j \log x_i + e_{ij} \quad (i = 1, \ldots, 28) \tag{9.1}$$

where $y_{ij}$ denotes per capita consumption expenditure in the $i$th province for the $j$th consumption category, $x_i$ denotes per capita total consumption expenditure in the $i$th province and $\beta_j$ is the elasticity of demand for the $j$th consumption category with respect to total expenditure. $e_{ij}$ is the residual pertaining to the $i$th province in the regression for the $j$th consumption category; it is assumed to be a random drawing from a normal frequency distribution with mean zero and standard deviation $\sigma_j$.

Using the 28 observations provided in table 9.2, four regression equations can be estimated by the least-squares method, yielding the results for food:

$$\log y_{i1} = 0.587 + 0.790 \log x_i \quad R^2 = .872$$
$$\phantom{\log y_{i1} = }(.313) \quad (.059) \quad\quad s^2 = .00650 \tag{9.2a}$$

Clothing:

$$\log y_{i2} = -0.962 + 0.789 \log x_i \quad R^2 = .535$$
$$\phantom{\log y_{i2} = }(.760) \quad (.144) \quad\quad s^2 = .0383 \tag{9.3a}$$

Housing and fuel:

$$\log y_{i3} = -6.073 + 1.783 \log x_i \quad R^2 = .843$$
$$\phantom{\log y_{i3} = }(.794) \quad (.151) \quad\quad s^2 = .0418 \tag{9.4a}$$

Miscellaneous:

**Table 9.2**  Rural consumption expenditure per capita and its components by province, 1981 (yuan)

| Province | | 1<br>Total<br>expenditure | 2<br>Food | 3<br>Clothes | 4<br>Housing<br>and fuel | 5<br>All other<br>items |
|---|---|---|---|---|---|---|
| Total | | 190.81 | 113.83 | 23.57 | 29.26 | 24.15 |
| 1 | Beijing | 312.99 | 163.11 | 36.00 | 58.43 | 55.45 |
| 2 | Tianjin | 249.17 | 126.42 | 37.49 | 51.50 | 33.76 |
| 3 | Hebei | 164.66 | 85.93 | 23.48 | 28.07 | 27.18 |
| 4 | Shanxi | 147.78 | 85.86 | 23.88 | 17.70 | 20.34 |
| 5 | Inner Mongolia | 177.12 | 110.74 | 24.77 | 16.08 | 25.53 |
| 6 | Liaoning | 258.50 | 139.06 | 35.88 | 41.60 | 41.96 |
| 7 | Jilin | 246.07 | 152.39 | 34.04 | 28.94 | 30.70 |
| 8 | Heilongjiang | 175.23 | 101.98 | 29.27 | 19.08 | 24.20 |
| 9 | Shanghai | 389.85 | 198.10 | 43.25 | 95.86 | 52.64 |
| 10 | Jiangsu | 225.54 | 128.22 | 25.80 | 42.64 | 28.88 |
| 11 | Zhejiang | 226.46 | 147.01 | 31.75 | 54.96 | 32.74 |
| 12 | Anhui | 193.26 | 117.90 | 21.49 | 30.79 | 23.08 |
| 13 | Fujian | 199.25 | 123.50 | 19.98 | 31.34 | 24.43 |
| 14 | Jiangxi | 194.17 | 117.99 | 20.52 | 36.35 | 19.31 |
| 15 | Shandong | 178.95 | 89.56 | 27.03 | 31.69 | 30.67 |
| 16 | Henan | 165.57 | 89.08 | 24.51 | 28.64 | 23.34 |
| 17 | Hubei | 183.78 | 114.75 | 22.58 | 25.90 | 20.55 |
| 18 | Hunan | 207.59 | 135.98 | 23.06 | 27.87 | 20.68 |
| 19 | Guangdong | 266.05 | 157.72 | 21.32 | 50.26 | 36.75 |
| 20 | Guangxi | 171.45 | 115.93 | 14.93 | 20.22 | 20.37 |
| 21 | Sichuan | 184.07 | 121.21 | 20.65 | 22.51 | 19.70 |
| 22 | Guizhou | 162.51 | 105.16 | 18.93 | 23.48 | 14.94 |
| 23 | Yunnan | 137.75 | 91.83 | 15.90 | 16.75 | 13.27 |
| 24 | Shaanxi | 148.46 | 92.10 | 18.82 | 18.88 | 18.01 |
| 25 | Gansu | 135.23 | 92.99 | 16.37 | 12.28 | 13.59 |
| 26 | Qinghai | 153.48 | 103.43 | 18.90 | 14.91 | 16.24 |
| 27 | Ningxia | 141.68 | 89.06 | 20.11 | 13.22 | 19.29 |
| 28 | Xinjiang | 168.58 | 98.98 | 35.08 | 15.21 | 19.31 |

**Source**: Statistical Yearbook of China, 1981, *pp. 445–6*.

$$\log y_{i4} = -3.378 + 1.248 \log x_i \quad R^2 = .797$$
$$\quad\quad (.650) \quad (.123) \quad\quad s^2 = .028 \tag{9.5a}$$

where the numbers in parentheses are the standard errors of the corresponding regression coefficients. Thus, the total-expenditure elasticities of demand for food, clothing, housing

**Table 9.3**  Per capita consumption expenditure of peasant households surveyed in 1978–81

|                                         | 1978   | 1979   | 1980   | 1981   |
|-----------------------------------------|--------|--------|--------|--------|
| Number of farm households surveyed      | 6,095  | 10,282 | 15,914 | 18,529 |
| Per capita total expenditure (yuan)     | 116.06 | 134.51 | 162.21 | 190.81 |
| Food                                    | 78.59  | 86.03  | 100.19 | 113.83 |
| Clothing                                | 17.74  | 17.64  | 19.19  | 23.57  |
| Housing and fuel                        | 11.95  | 16.00  | 22.46  | 29.26  |
| Other items                             | 10.78  | 14.84  | 19.57  | 24.15  |

Source: Statistical Yearbook of China, 1981, *pp. 441 and 443.*

(including fuel), and all other items, based on a sample survey of Chinese peasants in 1981, are estimated to be 0.79, 0.79, 1.78, and 1.25, respectively.

These estimates, based on cross-section data, are close to the estimates obtained from the time-series data on per capita consumption expenditures by all peasant households surveyed in 1978, 1979, 1980, and 1981 given in table 9.3. Per capita expenditures on the four consumption categories in the years 1978–81 are plotted against per capita total expenditure also in figures 5.1 to 5.4, respectively, of Chow (1985). The regression line fitted to the four time-series observations for the years 1978–81 in each figure has almost the same slope as the corresponding regression line fitted to the 28 cross-section observations for the year 1981 (see question 1 below). Unfortunately, the *Statistical Yearbook of China, 1981*, does not contain similar data on urban families that we could analyze in the same manner.

The estimate 0.79 for total expenditure elasticity of demand for food confirms Engel's law, which states that the proportion of income spent on food declines as income rises. Note that we have used total expenditure instead of income. The estimate of income elasticity would be slightly smaller than the estimate of total-expenditure elasticity; it is the product of the latter elasticity and the elasticity of total expenditure with respect to income that is not more than 1. According to our estimate, when total expenditure increases by 1 percent, the expenditure on food increases by 0.79 of 1 percent, with a standard error of 0.06. Engel's law states that the income elasticity of demand for food is less than 1.

It is interesting to compare our estimates of the four elasticities with the estimates of Houthakker (1957), who has made an international comparison of household expenditures on the same four categories for 33 countries using household budget surveys for different periods ranging mainly from the 1920s to the 1950s. Houthakker has found that regression functions that are linear in the logarithms of the variables fit the data well. The data used by Houthakker are mainly expenditures for different families, whereas the data available to us are per capita expenditures for different provinces. Since families with different total expenditures may be different in size, Houthakker has tried to isolate the effect of family size on expenditures by introducing family size as a separate explanatory variable, besides total family consumption expenditure, in the regression of family expenditure for each consumption category. In other words, he has estimated linear regressions of log expenditures for the four categories on log total expenditure and log family size when data on family size are available. When data on family size are not available, he has attempted to adjust the estimates of the elasticities of demand for food. For example, a regression of log food expenditure on log total expenditure based on a survey of families in Shanghai in 1929–30 has yielded an (unadjusted) estimate of 0.769 for the total expenditure elasticity of demand (see table 9.4). Insofar as families with large total expenditures tend to be larger in size, and as family size has a positive effect on food expenditure, this estimate is too large. The figure 0.769 is adjusted downward to 0.617 using a formula given by Houthakker (1957: 545). No adjustments for the other three elasticities are made, because the estimates of the effects of family size on these consumption goods are less uniform among countries. Our estimates given in equations (9.2) to (9.5) are based on per capita (and not per family) data, so the effect of family size is already accounted for (see question 2 below).

Houthakker's estimates of the elasticities for the four expenditure categories with respect to total expenditure are given in table 9.4. The author concludes his multicountry study (p. 551) as follows:

> Some final comments are in order. What has been shown is mainly that the elasticities of the four main items of expenditure with respect to total expenditure are similar but not equal, and that the elasticities with respect to family size are rather similar (but also unequal) for food and miscellaneous items, and irregular for clothing and housing. To return to the problem of development planning mentioned in the beginning of the paper: if no data on the expenditure patterns of a country are available at all, one would not be very far astray by putting the partial elasticity with respect to total expenditure at .6 for food, 1.2 for clothing, .8 for housing, and 1.6 for all other items combined, and the partial elasticity with respect to family size at .3 for food, zero for housing and clothing, and 1.4 for miscellaneous expenditures. But it would be prudent not to use those guesses for wide extrapolations, and more prudent still to organize a survey and cross-classify the results.

The total expenditure elasticity of demand for food estimated from the survey of Chinese peasants is somewhat higher than the 0.6 figure proposed by Houthakker. This difference may be explained by his suggestion (p. 547) that "the elasticity for food with respect to total expenditure might be higher for the countries and time periods with lower total expenditure, though the evidence is equivocal." The estimate of elasticity for clothing is somewhat lower, and for housing somewhat higher in the case of the Chinese peasants surveyed in 1981, than the corresponding average figures used by Houthakker. Two related explanations for the differences can be offered. First, the surveys used by Houthakker are mainly for urban families, and it is reasonable to suppose that urban people tend to spend more on clothing than peasants do as their incomes increase. To the extent that people spend less on clothing, they will spend more on other things, including housing. Second, the demand for housing by Chinese farmers is perhaps subject to fewer restrictions than the demand for clothing. Chinese peasants are relatively free to build their own houses, while the supply of clothing may be more limited. Observe that the elasticities for clothing and housing estimated from urban families in Peiping (in 1927) and in Shanghai (in 1929–30) as given in table 9.4 are much closer to the international

**Table 9.4**  Elasticities *b* for four expenditure groups with respect to total expenditure, and adjusted elasticities for food

| Country | Food | | Clothing unadjusted b | Housing unadjusted b | Miscellaneous unadjusted b |
|---|---|---|---|---|---|
| | Unadjusted b | Adjusted b | | | |
| Australia, Queensland | .390 (.037) | a | 1.025 (.043) | 1.180 (.076) | 1.323 (.087) |
| Austria | .732 (.041) | .590 | 1.589 (.063) | .634 (.042) | 1.422 (.046) |
| Belgium | .849 (.010) | .849 | 1.338 (.087) | .794 (.014) | 1.992 (.066) |
| Brazil | .802 (.028) | .795 | 1.332 (.105) | 1.227 (.136) | 1.174 (.120) |
| Burma, Rangoon, Hindustani | .826 (.024) | .826 | .775 (.069) | .947 (.037) | 1.465 (.073) |
| Burma, Rangoon, Tamils, Telegus, Uriyas | .847 (.036) | .847 | .658 (.049) | 1.316 (.113) | 1.430 (.042) |
| Burma, Rangoon, Chittagonians | .703 (.024) | .703 | 1.448 (.101) | 1.031 (.103) | 1.630 (.096) |
| Canada | .867 (.051) | .712 | 1.250 (.069) | .777 (.079) | 1.085 (.028) |
| Ceylon | .856 (.037) | .810 | 1.108 (.063) | 1.118 (.168) | 1.290 (.053) |
| China, Peiping | .651 (.011) | .591 | 1.328 (.054) | .940 (.032) | 1.489 (.041) |
| China, Shanghai | .769 (.065) | .617 | 1.609 (.045) | .714 (.046) | 1.440 (.100) |
| Cuba | .704 (.020) | a | 1.104 (.034) | 1.160 (.061) | 1.292 (.033) |
| France | .581 (.035) | a | 1.404 (.062) | .781 (.059) | 1.621 (.033) |
| Germany 1928 (combined) | .532 (.058) | .383 | 1.070 (.050) | .946 (.133) | 1.454 (.082) |
| Germany 1951 | .579 (.034) | .526 | .436 (.086) | .681 (.024) | 1.552 (.042) |
| Ghana, Accra | .952 (.024) | .840 | .967 (.098) | .635 (.062) | 1.365 (.029) |
| Ghana, Kumasi | .954 (.032) | .818 | 1.042 (.091) | .618 (.044) | 1.495 (.084) |
| Ghana, Sekondi-Takoradi | .823 (.037) | .654 | 1.289 (.065) | .725 (.065) | 1.600 (.064) |
| Ghana, Akuse | .873 (.037) | .791 | .865 (.086) | 1.142 (.099) | 1.503 (.059) |

**Table 9.4**   (*cont'd*)

| Country | Food | | Clothing unadjusted b | Housing unadjusted b | Miscellaneous unadjusted b |
|---|---|---|---|---|---|
| | *Unadjusted* b | *Adjusted* b | | | |
| Guatemala, | .750 | .508 | 1.308 | 1.029 | 1.548 |
| Guatemala City | (.036) | | (.091) | (.087) | (.012) |
| India, Bombay, | .709 | .709 | .486 | 1.475 | 1.538 |
| single workers | (.049) | | (.050) | (.099) | (.103) |
| India, Bombay, | .837 | .837 | .775 | .733 | 1.801 |
| workers, families | (.015) | | (.141) | (.068) | (.407) |
| India, Bhopal City | 1.004 | .821 | .900 | .730 | 1.223 |
| | (.013) | | (.045) | (.042) | (.060) |
| India, Punjab | .943 | .811 | 1.161 | .764 | 1.391 |
| | (.027) | | (.252) | (.037) | (.024) |
| Ireland | .775 | .621 | 1.224 | .583 | 1.358 |
| | (.052) | | (.194) | (.038) | (.039) |
| Italy | .615 | a | 1.219 | | |
| | (.026) | | (.034) | | |
| Japan 1953 | .648 | .563 | 1.398 | .906 | 1.387 |
| | (.017) | | (.149) | (.031) | (.011) |
| Libya | .895 | .805 | 1.830 | .900 | 1.403 |
| | (.073) | | (.165) | (.165) | (.329) |
| Northern Rhodesia | .514 | .393 | 1.081 | .229 | 1.308 |
| | (.109) | | (.093) | (.131) | (.040) |
| Panama, Panama | .790 | .717 | 1.226 | .932 | 1.232 |
| City | (.055) | | (.064) | (.072) | (.030) |
| Philippines, Manila | .810 | .757 | 1.141 | .874 | 1.312 |
| | (.028) | | (.037) | (.047) | (.026) |
| Portugal, Porto | .779 | .623 | 1.296 | .564 | 1.246 |
| | (.047) | | (.445) | (.301) | (.122) |
| Puerto Rico, | .699 | .692 | .957 | 1.049 | 1.177 |
| San Juan | (.040) | | (.026) | .083 | (.076) |
| Puerto Rico, | .812 | a | 1.147 | .963 | 1.315 |
| whole territory | (.031) | | (.055) | (.108) | (.019) |
| Sweden | .843 | .652 | 1.139 | .749 | 1.261 |
| | (.092) | | (.077) | (.061) | (.087) |
| United States 1950 | .816 | .642 | 1.336 | .731 | 1.222 |
| | (.025) | | (.048) | (.273) | (.037) |

[a] *Adjustment not possible.*
**Source**: *table III of Houthakker, 1957: 546–7.*

averages. The higher elasticity for clothing in Shanghai than in Peiping is noteworthy because the residents of the cultural city of Peiping in the late 1920s were known to dress more modestly than the residents of the cosmopolitan Shanghai. There is no reason to believe, and no evidence to suggest, that the consumption behavior of the Chinese people is very different from that of the other people in the world. In fact, the regularities documented in table 9.4 and in equations (9.2) to (9.5), with the differences reasonably explained, are encouraging to students in their search for universal laws in economics.

## 9.3   Rural Per Capita Consumption Expenditures in 1998 by Province

It would be interesting to see whether the total expenditure elasticities of demand for food, clothing, and housing for rural households which were estimated in equations (9.2) to (9.4) using data obtained in 1981 have changed. Table 9.5, taken from table 10-19 of the *Statistical Yearbook of China, 1999*, presents similar data for 1998 as table 9.2 does for 1981. Using the data in table 9.5, we have estimated equations (9.2b) to (9.4b) to find out whether the elasticities have changed.

Based on the data in table 9.5, the results are as follows.

Food:   $\log y_{i1} = 1.288 + 0.742 \log x_i \quad R^2 = .919$
$$\phantom{\log y_{i1} = 1.288}(.301)\quad(.041)\qquad s^2 = .00668 \tag{9.2b}$$

Clothing:

$$\log y_{i2} = -1.134 + 0.779 \log x_i \quad R^2 = .462$$
$$\phantom{\log y_{i2} = -1.134}(1.148)\quad(.156)\qquad s^2 = .0970 \tag{9.3b}$$

Housing and fuel:

$$\log y_{i3} = -5.472 + 1.475 \log x_i \quad R^2 = .903$$
$$\phantom{\log y_{i3} = -5.472}(.660)\quad(.090)\qquad s^2 = .0320 \tag{9.4b}$$

Comparing with the corresponding estimates given in (9.2a) to (9.4a) one finds that the total-expenditure elasticities of food, clothing, and housing are close to the estimates 0.790, 0.789, and 1.783 estimated using data for 1981. This shows the stability of economic parameters. Secondly, to the extent that the two sets of estimates differ, there is a reasonable economic explanation. Between 1981 and 1998, per capita income grew by a large amount. As income increases, food expenditures account for a smaller fraction of total expenditures. Total expenditure elasticity of demand for food is expected to decrease, as can be observed by comparing the elasticities for the rich and poor countries given in table 9.4. As housing becomes more generally available and is less of a luxury item, total expenditure elasticity of demand for housing decreases, as can be seen also by

**Table 9.5** Rural consumption expenditure per capita and its components by province, 1998

| Region | Living expenditure | Food | Clothing | Residence |
|---|---|---|---|---|
| Nation | 1,590.33 | 849.64 | 98.06 | 239.62 |
| Beijing | 2,873.20 | 1,215.08 | 231.51 | 439.63 |
| Tianjin | 1,976.70 | 911.39 | 172.62 | 333.52 |
| Hebei | 1,298.54 | 616.90 | 111.72 | 212.10 |
| Shanxi | 1,056.45 | 592.19 | 114.35 | 96.38 |
| Inner Mongolia | 1,577.12 | 867.38 | 112.17 | 197.16 |
| Liaoning | 1,702.68 | 898.87 | 157.63 | 230.42 |
| Jilin | 1,471.46 | 799.69 | 114.00 | 233.28 |
| Heilongjiang | 1,464.64 | 805.33 | 120.58 | 225.75 |
| Shanghai | 4,206.89 | 1,775.04 | 238.58 | 876.39 |
| Jiangsu | 2,336.78 | 1,117.01 | 135.09 | 399.23 |
| Zhejiang | 2,890.65 | 1,361.80 | 164.07 | 532.51 |
| Anhui | 1,333.05 | 732.14 | 72.30 | 205.63 |
| Fujian | 2,025.09 | 1,101.64 | 111.42 | 265.25 |
| Jiangxi | 1,538.24 | 899.37 | 67.08 | 221.48 |
| Shandong | 1,595.09 | 804.64 | 116.37 | 241.08 |
| Henan | 1,240.30 | 700.78 | 85.03 | 177.59 |
| Hubei | 1,699.43 | 918.95 | 88.88 | 274.61 |
| Hunan | 1,889.17 | 1,107.23 | 91.45 | 251.73 |
| Guangdong | 2,683.18 | 1,370.70 | 100.97 | 423.33 |
| Guangxi | 1,414.76 | 808.82 | 51.84 | 202.17 |
| Hainan | 1,246.12 | 767.42 | 51.23 | 110.56 |
| Chongqing | 1,343.35 | 831.08 | 63.07 | 178.00 |
| Sichuan | 1,440.77 | 871.83 | 78.22 | 182.27 |
| Guizhou | 1,094.39 | 757.55 | 51.00 | 104.95 |
| Yunnan | 1,312.31 | 801.99 | 60.23 | 191.78 |
| Tibet | 710.26 | 497.41 | 85.68 | 40.30 |
| Shaanxi | 1,181.38 | 590.90 | 79.29 | 179.56 |
| Gansu | 939.55 | 556.85 | 53.42 | 116.45 |
| Qinghai | 1,117.79 | 694.62 | 93.06 | 146.97 |
| Ningxia | 1,327.63 | 706.56 | 104.39 | 203.65 |
| Xinjiang | 1,450.29 | 713.34 | 148.06 | 200.13 |

comparing the estimates for the rich and poor countries given in table 9.4. Since two of the three elasticities reported above have been reduced as compared with the corresponding elasticities estimated using 1981 data, the remaining one for clothing being about the same, would one expect the total expenditure elasticity of demand for the remaining miscellaneous items to have risen in 1998? To find out the answer the reader should answer question 3 below.

## 9.4   Consumption of Housing in Rural and Urban Areas

Ever since the household responsibility system enabled the farmers in China to increase their income from 1978 on, total consumption expenditures of farm families have increased accordingly. Since the construction of farm housing was not controlled by the government, farmers used their income to improve their existing housing and to build new houses on the land assigned to them. The construction of new housing increased according to the increase in demand. Travelers to the rural areas of China in the 1980s could witness the increase in quantity and the improvement of quality of the houses of farm families. Rural housing has been private ever since economic reform started. The per capita floor space of rural households was 8.1 square meters in 1978, 9.4 in 1980, 14.70 in 1985, 17.83 in 1990, 21.01 in 1995, and 22.45 in 1997 (see table 10-1 of the *Statistical Yearbook of China, 1999*). Thus the freedom to build private houses in the rural areas enabled the supply of housing to increase rapidly between 1978 to 1985.

When economic reform started in 1978, urban housing in China was essentially provided by the working unit for its staff and workers and their families. The monthly rent per housing unit was very low. It was only 3 or 4 yuan per month, while the average monthly wage of a worker was about 54 yuan. Top leaders in the Commission for Reconstructing the Economic System in the early 1980s realized the need to privatize urban housing and to increase rents as a part of price reform toward market-determined prices. There were more important tasks listed in the Decision of the Central Committee of the Chinese Communist Party in October 1984, on economic reform, which we discussed in chapter 3. The existing entitlement of the staff and workers prevented the government from increasing rent rapidly. Members of the Commission for Reconstructing the Economic System recognized that housing should eventually be "commercialized." This means making housing a commodity subject to the laws of demand and supply. One important consideration in housing reform was how to compensate the residents if rents were allowed to increase. An obvious proposal was to increase urban wages to compensate for the increased rent, but this would lead to increases in the prices of outputs. There was a concern about possible inflation resulting from the increases in rents, wages, and prices.

In 1986 I suggested to Premier Zhao Ziyang and other members of the Commission that staff and workers should be given the right to purchase the apartment units which they occupied. The purchase price could be determined by the working unit that owned the apartments. The working unit would have an incentive to sell the apartments at low prices because the apartments required costs to maintain and did not generate much income. Each unit could decide the prices of its apartments, and the prices should not be regulated by government policy. The tenants had the option of continuing as tenants in the apartments which they occupied or of buying them. This proposal was based on the principle of Pareto optimality in economics. The principle states that economic welfare in a society is increased if no one is worse off but someone is better off. Under this plan no staff or worker could be worse off because there was the option of keeping the existing apartment. No working unit could be worse off because it could determine the prices of the apartments. Since the rental incomes under the existing system were so low, the working units would be willing to sell the apartments at low prices. The prices would be low enough that some staff and workers would decide to buy. Even if only a small fraction of the staff and workers decided to buy when the proposed policy was first introduced, the economy would still be better off because any transaction benefits both the buyer and seller. As time went on the wages of the staff and workers would increase and more apartment units could be sold.

When I visited Guangzhou on July 10, 1993, Mr. Yi Zhenqiu, Director of the Guangdong Provincial Office for Reconstructing the Economic System, told me that about 65 percent of the urban housing in Guangdong province had been sold to occupants at much below market prices along the lines suggested in the above proposal. By 2000, over 90 percent of urban housing in China had been sold to the residents under a government subsidy plan which included selling the apartments at lower than market prices and providing subsidized mortgaged payments at low interest rates. In the late 1980s and 1990s new private housing was built on a large scale in many cities in China. Some was financed by foreign investment. Therefore a private housing market was being developed continuously. Many well-to-do Chinese citizens and foreigners were able to buy or rent these housing units at market prices which were higher, adjusted for quality difference, than the prices at which the urban staff and workers purchased or rented the units occupied by them.

This policy of housing reform allowed a two-tier price system. One is determined by market forces. The second is the state sector. The prices in the state sector were allowed to adjust gradually towards the prices of the market sector. Once a private sector was allowed to develop, efficiency gain was achieved. In the meantime the state sector was improving through the application of Pareto's principle of optimality. Any sales transaction between a state employer and its staff or workers improved the welfare of both. This statement would be true under my original proposal for urban housing commercialization, but it has to be qualified because the tenants were forced to acquire their units within a specified time period, even though at below market prices. The actual policy was better than my proposal based on free choice because it enabled the government to eliminate the housing subsidy as an entitlement. Under my proposal a Pareto improvement could be achieved even if the government were unable or unwilling to eliminate the urban housing subsidy. Although urban housing reform took almost two decades, it could be considered successful judged by the increase in housing space per capita in urban areas. Per capita floor space in urban areas increased from 3.6 square meters in 1978, 3.9 in 1980, 5.2 in 1985, 6.7 in 1990, 8.1 in 1995, to 9.3 in 1998 (see table 10-1 of the *China Statistical Yearbook, 1999*), with the increase from 1995 to 1998 being larger than for rural housing as reported in the first paragraph of this section. The availability of private housing in rural areas beginning in 1978 enabled the supply of housing in the rural sector to catch up with demand more rapidly than in the urban areas.

## References and Further Reading

Chow, Gregory C. "Technological Change and the Demand for Computers." *American Economic Review,* 57 (Dec. 1967), pp. 1117–30.

Chow, Gregory C. *The Chinese Economy.* New York: Harper & Row, 1985; 2nd ed., Singapore: World Scientific Publishing Co., 1987.

Houthakker, H. S. "An International Comparison of Household Expenditure Patterns, Commemorating the Centenary of Engel's Law." *Econometrics,* 1957, 25, pp. 532–51.

Ma Hong and Sun Shangqing. *Zhongguo Jingji Jiegou Wenti Yanjiu* [*Studies of the Problems of China's Economic Structure*]. Beijing: People's Publishing Society, 1982, 2 vols.

Platten, Miriam. *Forecasting Computer Demand in China.* AB thesis, Department of Economics, Princeton University, 2001.

World Bank. *China 2020: Development Challenges in the New Century.* Washington, DC: World Bank, 1997.

Yang Janming, "Renmin Shenghuo Xiaofei Jiegou" [Structure of People's Consumption]. Ch. 18, *Zhongguo Jingji Jiegou Wenti Yanjiu* [*Studies of the Problems of China's Economic Structure*]. Beijing: People's Publishing Society, 1982, vol. 2, pp. 543–61.

## Questions

1  Using the time-series data in table 9.3 of the years 1978 to 1981, estimate the regression equation of per capita consumption of each of the four categories on per capita total expenditure. Compare the elasticities of these equations with the corresponding elasticities in equations (9.2a) to (9.5a).

2  Let $Y_i$, $X_i$ and $N_i$ be respectively the expenditure on a certain commodity, total consumption expenditure, and the size of family $i$ in a sample. Let letters $y$ and $x$ denote per capita expenditure on the same commodity and per capita total expenditure respectively. Explain the assumptions underlying the following two equations:

$$\log y = \alpha + \beta \log x + \varepsilon$$

and

$$\log Y = \alpha + \beta \log X + \gamma \log N + \varepsilon$$

Which equation would you prefer to use for studying consumer behavior in China and why?

3  Using the data in table 9.5, estimate the total expenditure elasticity of demand for miscellaneous items in 1998 (obtained by subtracting the expenditures on food, clothing, and housing from total expenditure) and compare the result with the estimate for 1981. Comment on the difference.

4  Referring to table 9.4, can you tell whether there are systematic differences between the total expenditure elasticities of demand for food, clothing, housing, and the remaining expenditures of developed and developing countries? If so, what are the differences? Can you explain the differences?

5  Describe two main characteristics in the process of "commercialization" or privatization of urban housing in China. Could China have solved the problem using a different strategy?

# 10

# Western Development and Environmental Policies

Beginning with Premier Zhu Rongji's statement in 2001 on eight important tasks for China's economic development, which includes the development of the poor region of western China, the chapter reviews the justification of this project in a market economy and its main features. The government policy on development of the agriculture sector and of the rural areas in general will be discussed. One related topic is the protection and improvement of the environment, which will be considered in the second part of this chapter. A study on the factors affecting industrial pollution of air and water is reported which shows how economic reform helps reduce pollution.

Developing the poor western region and improving the environment are two important tasks of the Chinese government in the twenty-first century. To appreciate the importance of these tasks in the overall planning strategy of the Chinese government, one can refer to Premier Zhu Rongji's "Report on National Economic and Social Development during the Tenth Five Year Plan," delivered to the People's Congress on March 5, 2001 (see the *People's Daily Overseas Edition* for that day, where it is summarized on p. 2).

The report stated the following eight most important tasks to be achieved during the tenth Five Year Plan period of 2001–5. These tasks are, in the order listed in sections 3 to 10 of the Report, (1) increasing the productivity and income of the agricultural sector, (2) changing the structure of industry towards more high-technology industry, (3) developing the western region in a strategy of regionally balanced economic development, (4) investing in human capital in a strategy of promoting science, technology, and education for the betterment of the nation, (5) deepening reform and the open-door policy, (6) raising the living standard of the people and completing a social welfare system, (7) maintaining a sustainable economic development strategy, and (8) building a democratic society with the rule of law and spiritual culture and a national defense system. Tasks (1) and (3) is the subject of the first half of this chapter, task (4) the subject of chapters 12 and 21, task (5) the subject of chapters 4, 13, 15–18, task (6) the subject of chapters 9 and 12, task (7) the subject of the second half of this chapter and chapter 7, task (8) the subject of chapter 20, and task (2) the subject of section 20.4.

By the end of the meeting of the Central Committee of the Communist Party of China in October 2005, which treated the problem of regional income inequality as a major issue, the government had abolished agricultural tax on a large scale, instituted tuition-free compulsory education among the poverty-stricken, intensified efforts to carry out the transfer of payments, and adjusted the cut-off point of personal income tax in order to achieve a higher degree of social harmony. However, much of the problem of eliminating poverty remained.

## 10.1    Inequality in Per Capita Consumption and East–West Disparity

An important reason for adopting a strategy for western development is the inequality of income or consumption per capita among residents of the west and the east in China. Table 9.5 provides information on the distribution of per capita consumption by province. To measure the degree of inequality of consumption across provinces, one can take natural logarithms of per capita consumption expenditure, to be denoted by $z$, and compute the standard deviation of $z$ using provincial observations. The standard deviation measures the degree of variation of per capita consumption in proportional terms. Comparing the standard deviation estimated from the 1998 data with the estimate from the 1981 data tells us whether consumption inequality among provinces has changed during this period. The standard deviation of the natural logarithm of rural consumption expenditure per capita in 1981, computed for the 28 provinces listed in table 9.2, is 0.2612, compared with 0.3475 in 1998 for the same 28 provinces based on the data in table 9.5. Thus consumption inequality among provinces increased between these two years, at the average rate of $(0.3475 - 0.2612)/17 = 0.00508$, or about half of a percentage point per year. To see whether the increase in consumption disparity has slowed down I have computed the same standard deviation for 1993, using data on page 281 of the *Statistical Yearbook of China, 1994*, and obtained 0.3370. The average rate of increase in the standard deviation in the five years from 1993 to 1998 is $(0.3475 - 0.3370)/5 = 0.0021$, much slower than 0.00508. Thus the rate of increase in disparity slowed down in the late 1990s but was still in the range of two-tenths of one per cent per year.

A related question is whether rural per capita consumption increased in the poorest provinces and at what rate. From table 9.2, the three provinces with lowest consumption in 1981 were Gansu, Yunnan, and Ningxia, with per capita rural consumption of 135.23, 137.75, and 141.68 respectively. From table 9.5, in 1998 these three provinces had per capita rural consumption of 939.55, 1,312.31, and 1,327.63 yuan. The general retail price index given in table 9-2 of the *Statistical Yearbook of China, 1999* is 110.7 in 1981, 128.1 in 1985, and 370.9 in 1998; the general consumer price index for rural areas is 100.0 in 1985 and 319.1 in 1998. To approximate the increase in consumer prices for rural areas we assume the same proportional increase in these two indices between 1981 and 1985 to obtain a value of 86.4 for the latter index in 1981. The increase in rural consumer prices from 86.4 to 319.1 is a factor of 3.69. The increase in the nominal value of per capita consumption is $939.55/135.23 = 6.95$ for Gansu, 9.81 for Yunnan, and 7.89 for Qinghai. If we consider the two other poorest provinces as of 1998 among the original 28, namely Shanxi and Guizhou, with consumption per capita of 1,056.45 and 1,094.39, and consider their improvement from the 1981 values of 147.78 and 162.51 in table 9.2, we find factors of 7.15 and 6.73. Thus Guizhou is the province which improved the least between 1981 and 1998. The improvement in real consumption during this period is only a factor of 6.73/3.69 or 1.82. In terms of exponential rate of increase per year, Guizhou experienced a rate of 0.035.

To summarize our discussion on disparity as measured by the dispersion in rural consumption per capita among provinces, the disparity has increased at the rate of about half a percentage point per year between 1981 and 1998, but the rate of increase has slowed down to 0.2 of a percentage point in the last 5 years of this period. There have been significant increases in the level of real consumption per capita in all provinces in the meantime. Even Guizhou, the province with the slowest rate of increase among the original 28 provinces, experienced an average exponential rate of increase of 0.035 per year.

What policy implications, if any, can be drawn from these facts? To the extent that the poor provinces have not caught up with the rest, it is morally desirable and politically necessary for the government and the rich provinces to assist them in improving their productivity and standard of living. This is a motivation for the government's policy of western development, a subject to be treated in the next section. While attention is paid to western development, one should not lose sight of the need to continue the development of the rich provinces along the coast. These provinces are still very poor compared with some other regions in Asia and the rest of the world. If China is to compete in the global economy it needs to have institutions and people that can do the job. In order to do this it is necessary to have communities that have per capita incomes not much below world standards. Here comes the paradox of increasing disparity. The communities made up of the high-quality institutions and people who can compete in the world market are bound to be rich communities like Hong Kong and Shanghai. Their presence will increase our measure of income disparity among regions.

## 10.2    Developing the Western Part of China

### 10.2.1    The government's reasons for western development

As shown in table 9.5, there is much income disparity among the regions of China, with the western region being the poorest. The Chinese divide the 27 provinces (some administratively called autonomous regions) on the mainland into four regions. The northeast consists of Liaoning, Jilin, and Heilongjiang. The middle region consists of the 8 provinces of Shanxi, Hebei, Henan, Hubei, Hunan, Guangdong, Guangxi, and Hainan. The eastern region consists of 6 provinces, Jiangsu, Zhejiang, Anhui, Fujian, Jiangxi, and

Shandong. The western region consists of 10 provinces, Sichuan, Guizhou, Yunan, Tibet, Shaanxi, Gansu, Qinghai, Ningxia, Inner Mongolia, and Xinjiang, and the Chongqing municipality. Please refer to the map in the appendix to chapter 3.

The land of the western region covers an area of about 5.4 million square kilometers, accounting for 66 percent of the national territory. The general population in the region is 285,000,000, or 23 percent of the national population. The western regions are rich in energy resources. The 60 minerals which have been discovered in the nation can be found in the region, among which minerals such as titanium, copper, mercury, lead, and zinc are numbered first in national reserves. The reserves of coal account for 38.6 percent of those of the whole nation, with oil 41 percent, steel 46.8 percent, potassium 96.7 percent, and water energy 82.3 percent. The reserves per capita are much higher than the average level in the nation. The western regions will become a resource warehouse for future industrialization and modernization in China. The region has advantages in agricultural and livestock husbandry. It is an important area for growing commodity grain as well as for transferring cottons. There is great potential for developing utilizable land resources for agriculture in general. In addition, the western regions also enjoy the advantages of bordering on several neighboring countries. This is beneficial for developing trade along the borders, and economic as well as technological cooperation.

From the political point of view, the development of the west is important. It was a part of the development strategy announced by Deng Xiaoping in the early 1980s and pursued by Premier Zhao Ziyang in the mid-1980s. To achieve rapid national development Zhao told the people that the eastern coastal provinces should be allowed to develop first, but after the eastern provinces become rich they should help promote western development. Such a strategy was accepted by the people and was carried out. At the end of the 1990s, it was time for the government to carry out the second part of its strategy and to fulfill its promise to the people in the western region.

Finally, from the economic development point of view, there are plenty of land and natural resources in the western region. Mineral deposits are plentiful. Oil and gas can be explored and extracted. Water resources can be utilized for agriculture and for electricity generation. Land can be used to lower the population density of the coastal regions. The development of these resources will be good for increasing output and will improve consumption standards for the entire economy.

## 10.2.2  Economic justifications for western development

We have pointed out the reasons for China's government to develop the west. Are these reasons justified from the economic viewpoint?

First, income inequality by itself is not necessarily a sign of poor economic performance. If rewards are given for talent and effort, differences in income among individuals in a society will naturally result. Of course, having talent and good working habits may themselves be the outcome of an individual's luck, including inherited intellectual and physical traits, family wealth, and family education. Similarly, if talents and efforts differ among the residents of different regions, there will be differences in regional incomes.

Here also good fortune may play a role. Some regions have better resources just as some individuals have better inherited traits than others. Some regions are better located just as some individuals are better positioned socially because of family connections. While income inequality among people and regions is not necessarily bad, and is in fact necessary to promote talents and to encourage hard work, it is generally agreed that helping the disadvantaged is socially desirable. Helping the disadvantaged is not the same as preventing those who are able from becoming rich. Helping the development of the western regions of China is not the same as stifling the development of the coastal regions. I believe that this point is well understood by the leaders of China. We should regard the policy of western development as a strategy to help the disadvantaged and to improve their productivity, and not just to equalize China's regional income distribution, because there is no effort to make the coastal provinces develop more slowly.

In fact, maintaining the rapid growth of the eastern region is necessary for China's rapid development, but the result may be to perpetuate or even widen the income disparity between the east and the west. China still needs a rich coastal region to help develop the poor western region. This main tenet of the development strategy in the 1980s to encourage the east to get rich is still true in the twenty-first century. The difference is that the government can pay attention to western development because the country is now in a better position to pay for it. Because of its geographical and cultural advantages the eastern region has been able to develop very rapidly. The government is trying to develop the west partly to help the disadvantaged and partly because it is complementary to the development of the east.

Given the importance of western development, the government recognizes that the east needs to be further developed because a richer eastern region can help develop the west. China needs very talented people and world-class institutions to develop the entire country. These institutions are mostly located in highly developed regions where salaries are high and facilities are modern. The eastern region is not up to world standards yet.

For China's economic and educational institutions to be world class it may not need a very high per capita income, but only a sizable sector consisting of very talented people and very good economic and educational institutions. In the early years of the People's Republic of China, the Party and government leaders failed to recognize this point. The best factories, commercial banks, and stock markets were destroyed in the 1950s. The best universities were closed. The most learned people and able entrepreneurs were mistreated and not allowed to use and develop their talents. The Chinese government has learned an expensive lesson and now allows the most talented to flourish to a considerable extent. The main exceptions are the limitations to private entrepreneurship (discussed at the end of chapter 16) and to intellectual freedom (discussed in chapter 21). Both limitations are derived from the basic notion that the government needs to control all aspects of life.

Building infrastructure is generally accepted as a government responsibility because the amount of capital and the risk involved may be too large for private investment, especially in the Chinese context at the turn of this century. The Chinese government has allowed and in fact encouraged foreign private capital to come to build infrastructure, including superhighways. Private capital did come. The first and best-known privately funded superhighway is the toll road connecting Hong Kong and Guangzhou built by the

Hong Kong entrepreneur Gordon Wu. The risk from the viewpoint of an outside investor is higher than for the government, who can go through red tape and guide the project to completion more easily than a foreign investor. A government engaged in national development planning may also have more information than the private investor concerning the total development strategy, and this affects the profitability of each investment project. The Yangtze River dams might be too large and difficult a project for foreign investors, requiring tens of billions of US dollars and the resettling of millions of people in the area. Perhaps not enough foreign capital would be forthcoming to build all the infrastructure that the government wishes to build, including infrastructure for the western region.

Granted the need for infrastructure-building, what is the economic justification for the government to develop the west by moving people and physical resources to the region? As far as migration is concerned, people have moved from the poor provinces to the richer provinces in the coastal areas to earn a better living. This migration is economically efficient because the wage or marginal productivity of a laborer in the richer provinces is higher. A laborer working one month to receive 200 yuan in the west now gets 350 yuan in the east. His movement raises national income by 150 yuan per month. Then why move the high-productivity people from the east to the west? The same question can be asked for the movement of physical and financial capital. People in a market economy invest their capital in the east because their rate of return is higher. They invest to build a factory in the east to get a return of 15 percent per year. They would build the factory in the west if the rate of return were higher. The same is true for government capital. One justification for the government to move human, physical, and financial capital to the west is economy of scale. When sufficient numbers of people and amounts of capital move, the rates of return can be higher.

Infrastructure-building also requires and justifies moving human and physical resources to the west. These resources are needed to build not only physical infrastructure like railroads and highways, but also soft infrastructure like legal and educational institutions. From the viewpoint of China's western development strategy, some of its current economic disadvantages, including geographical location, lack of convenient transportation, and lack of talented people, will become less relevant in the age of cyberspace of the twenty-first century. With modern technology, people can do research, communicate for business management, and trade without regard to location. However, economy of scale enters here as well, even in the age of cyberspace. Silicon Valley in California is successful because many talented people in related fields are located in one place. Furthermore, these people require good transportation facilities when they take business trips or travel just for pleasure. The government hopes that when the west becomes more developed, the east and in fact the whole economy will get more resources for development, and the people in both the west and the east will be better off.

## 10.2.3   Government strategy

Western development was made a top priority government policy in 1999. A Leading Group for Western China Development was formed in the State Council with Premier

Zhu Rongji as its chairman. The city of Chongqing in Sichuan province was made a municipality in 1999 and given a leadership role to promote western development.

To provide research support for the formulation of appropriate strategies, the Municipal Government of Chongqing, the Chinese Academy of Social Science, the Ministry of Foreign Trade and Economic Cooperation, and the Representative Office of UNDP to China jointly initiated a research project on "The Development of the Western Part of China and Chongqing in the 21st Century." In June 2000 these organizations jointly sponsored the Chongqing International Symposium for the Development of the Western Part of China to discuss the strategies required. Several hundred government officials from Beijing and from related provinces, Chinese and foreign scholars, and interested international officials participated in this symposium. The invitation to participants stated:

> The implementation of the western China development strategy and the acceleration of western China's development are important components of the modernization strategy of China. In the middle 1980s and early 1990s China's leader Mr. Deng Xiaoping advanced the idea of "two big situations." One refers to fully developing the advantages of the eastern coastal areas, accelerating reform and opening to the outside world. The second situation refers to achieving a comfortable living for the entire Chinese population and helping the western part to expedite its development.
>
> The goals, steps, and measures of western China development have already been listed in the medium- and long-term plans for national economic and social development. The Chinese government plans to accelerate infrastructure construction, to enhance ecological environment protection and improvement, to emphasize the readjustment of the industrial structure of the west, to promote the development of science, technology and education and training, and to take the deepening of reform and opening up as the great impetus behind the western development.

We thus note that there are five major components in the official western development strategy. First is infrastructure construction. Second is environmental protection and improvement. Third is adjustment of the industrial structure in the west. The existing structure of industry is the result of past attempts to build in the west heavy and defense industries under central planning. More emphasis on consumer goods industry is contemplated. Fourth is the promotion of science, technology, and education. Fifth is carrying out further economic reform and the open-door policy.

The last two components are policies that apply to the development of the nation as a whole. The second is also a national policy, which we will discuss in the second half of this chapter. Infrastructure-building and industrial structure readjustment involve the direct allocation and reallocation of resources by the government.

Infrastructure-building includes land, air, and water transportation facilities, power generation plants, and water conservation projects (with the large dams along the Yangtze River being most notable and subject to scrutiny in the foreign media). Improving transportation facilities, especially the building of railroads and highways, is necessary for the development of the west. It would permit the shipment of natural resources and products from the west to the coastal areas and indirectly to the rest of the world. It would allow modern technology and equipment to be transported to the west. Science and education

are the soft components of infrastructure broadly defined. Their importance is fully recognized by Chinese government leaders. The hard and soft components complement
one another. Transportation facilities are required, for example, to build good universities
and sustain their staff. Educated personnel with knowledge of science and technology
are required for the construction of modern transportation facilities and power plants.
However, it is difficult to evaluate how successful an infrastructure-building project
will be. The government is devoting a large amount of resources to infrastructure. Even
if the end result is good, the cost might be higher than it is worth. A careful study
is needed to reach valid conclusions concerning the Chinese government's efforts to
develop the west.

In summary, the Chinese government conceives of western development as a part of
the overall development strategy. In this strategy the continuation of the development
of the east is also considered a priority. The east has to be further developed in order for
China to be competitive in the world economy. High-technology industry should be
developed in the coastal areas. Western development not only serves to raise the standard
of living for the population in the west, but to provide resources and markets for the
products of the east. The entire economy is expected to benefit from the increase in
aggregate demand resulting from the western development strategy. First, there will
be an increase in investment demand in the form of infrastructure-building, a subject
discussed in section 7.5. Second, as the western regions get richer, demand for consumer goods will also increase. The government emphasizes the use of market forces
to achieve western development. The building of physical infrastructure and of human
capital will make the economic environment in the west more attractive for domestic and
foreign investment. A larger and more integrated domestic market is good for the national
economy.

## 10.2.4   Development of the agricultural sector and rural areas

Since the Chinese government's policy for the development of the agricultural sector is
closely related to its western development strategy, this is the proper place to discuss it.
Readers interested in the reform of Chinese agriculture should consult Johnson (1996,
1998). In section 4.6 we discussed three important problems facing Chinese farmers.
Here we describe recent policies announced by the government under the "three-farm
policy" for farming, rural areas, and farmers. In 1993, the "three-farm policy" was introduced to improve productivity in farming, promote economic development of rural areas,
and increase the income of farmers. It includes increasing capital investment in rural
areas, helping farmers to use better technology and better methods of farming, reducing
the corruption and misbehavior of local government officials, and providing economic
assistance to farmers. The development of the agricultural sector was the first important
task mentioned in Premier Zhu Rongji's work report of March 2001 to the National
People's Congress.

In February 2004, the State Council announced a set of policies to improve the living
conditions of farmers. These included the following:

1. Support the development of agricultural production in grain-producing areas to increase farmers' income. This includes providing incentives to farmers, improving methods of production and for preserving quality of land, and increasing government investment in agriculture.
2. Change the structure of agricultural production by improving output mix, management, and technology.
3. Develop industrial and service industries in rural areas, including the encouragement of township and village, as well as private, enterprises. (Township and village enterprises, perhaps involving less capital than those that flourished in the 1980s, and of more primitive nature (tied to agricultural production), did not develop in the very poor regions probably because of a lack of human capital among the residents and a lack of incentives on the part local government officials to promote them.)
4. Assist the farmers in moving to urban areas to find work by reducing various levies collected from them by city governments and by giving responsibility to the latter for the training of the incoming farmers and for the education of their children.
5. Establish a market mechanism for the distribution and marketing of grain by allowing more distribution channels, including collectives, and by the promotion of farm products.
6. Build infrastructure for rural areas, including water supplies, roads, and electricity in poor areas.
7. Carry out reform in rural areas including reform of the tax system.
8. Continue to improve programs to reduce poverty by subsidies and other means.
9. Strengthen the leadership of the Communist Party in putting the above policies into practice.

An important step was taken in 2005 when the central government decided to abolish all taxes on farmers. This policy seemed to be a good move if one compares the costs and benefits of taxing the farmers. The benefits are small, since such taxes accounted for only about just over one percent of total government revenue. The costs of taxing farmers are much larger, including an increase in their discontent, which might lead to social instability, and the provision of an excuse for local government officials to impose illegal levies. Although some local officials might continue to impose such levies, the policy of allowing no taxes on farmers makes it more difficult for them to do so.

On February 21, 2006, and for three consecutive years (according to *People's Daily Online* of February 23, 2006), the Central Committee of the Chinese Communist Party and the State Council issued their most important "Number 1 Document" on the subject of agriculture, farmers, and countryside development. This document is more comprehensive and systematic than the previous two. Agriculture and rural areas are to receive higher fractions of national fiscal spending, budgetary investment on fixed assets, and credit. In 2005, over 300 billion yuan (37.5 billion US dollars) from the budget of the central government was allocated to support rural development, a 50 percent increase from the 2002 figure. In addition to direct financial support, the government announced the abolition of agricultural tax as of January 1, 2006, which totals 22 billion yuan (2.75 billion dollars) in the previous year. Higher tax will be levied on use of arable land, and the newly added taxes will be used on rural development.

The document covers:

a) Infrastructure building that will include the provision of safe drinking water and clean energy supplies (by the use of methane, straw gasification technology, small hydropower, solar energy, and wind farms, and by the upgrading of power grids) and the construction of country roads.

b) A national support system for agriculture and the farmers consisting of:

1) direct subsidies to grain production (to be raised to 50 percent of the grain risk fund used to stabilize market price) and to grain farmers for the purchase of high-quality seeds and farm machinery,

2) improvement of agricultural production and marketing,

3) facilitating the migration of rural labor by removing discriminatory restrictions on migrant workers in urban job markets and providing them with a social security system gradually, possibly with a guarantee of subsistence allowances in rural areas (insurance for occupational injuries to cover all migrant workers),

4) increase in funding for the rural compulsory education system, and reduction or exemption of tuition for students included in the system in western areas, to be extended to all rural areas,

5) the training of farmers to make them well-educated and technologically literate with basic knowledge in management, with 100 million to be trained by 2010, including 50 million in agricultural technology and another 50 million in other sectors,

6) a social assistance program covering 50 million people and four areas (regular social assistance providing minimum living subsidies to poor urban and rural residents, emergency assistance for people suffering in disasters, temporary assistance to low-income migrants to urban areas, and social assistance from donations), with the total of assistance amounting to only 0.02 percent of GDP,

7) more financial support for the new rural cooperative healthcare system (since rural residents, who account for some 60 percent of the nation's total population, only have access to 20 percent of the country's medical resources) from both the central and local fiscal systems in 2006, to cover almost all the rural areas in 2008. The plan is to cover 40 percent of China's counties in a new government-backed medicare cooperative program for farmers in 2006, and to promote the program to all the rural areas in the next few years. Under the plan the government will allocate 40 yuan per farmer, while the farmers will pay 10 yuan each, towards setting up a clinic in every village in the near future,

8) rural financial reform for community financial institutions in order to provide agricultural insurance and easily accessible loans to rural households and small and medium enterprises.

c) Streamlining the functions of the multilevel government system (central, provincial, county, township, and village) by elimination of the operational functions of township governments within five years, and in the interim changing their functions from engaging in investment and operation of their own projects and production of grain to creating a favorable environment for the farmers; the finances of counties will be placed under the direct control of the provincial governments or of the villages themselves.

d) Village planning that is environmentally friendly, by remodeling existing houses rather than constructing new ones, efficient use of land, energy, and materials for the construction of farm housing, and the preservation of ancient villages and residences.

The "three-farm" policies announced above were incorporated in the Eleventh Five Year Plan passed by the National People's Congress on March 14, 2006, under the heading of "building a new socialist countryside" and "according to the requirement of advanced production, improved livelihood, a civilized social atmosphere, clean and tidy villages, and democratic administration." The budget allocated for these policies amounted to 339.7 billion yuan from the central government in 2006, while 297.5 billion yuan from the central government budget was spent on agriculture, rural areas, and farmers in 2005 – an increase of 34.9 billion yuan from 2004.

In summary the policies of the central government aim mainly at redirecting economic resources to the rural areas (items (a) and (b) listed above) and also at streamlining the administration of different levels of local governments (item (c)).

One may raise two questions concerning the Chinese government's solutions above, one on the incentive problem for local Party officials and the other on the possibility of enforcing a policy to solve the third component of the three-farm problem mentioned in section 4.6. In item (c) above, streamlining the multilevel local government structure, one wonders why the township government and Party officials will not be allowed to take part in the establishment and operation of enterprises that may benefit rural development, as the officials in the 1980s and 1990s were able to develop township and village enterprises for the benefit of China's economic development. Without the opportunities to benefit from rural development, township officials may resort to corruption or the obstruction of development projects. Secondly, one wonders why there is no explicit mention of the abuse of power by local Party officials and of specific disciplinary actions for their offenses. A more detailed discussion of these questions is beyond the scope of this section. It will be interesting to follow future development based on this policy document to find out how well its provisions are being put into practice.

## 10.3   Environmental Policies

The government of the People's Republic of China neglected and practically ruined much of the physical environment of the country for three decades from the 1950s to the 1970s. According to documentation by Judith Shapiro (2001), Chairman Mao was responsible for a lot of this damage. The government began to pay some attention in the 1980s, and has been paying serious attention to protecting and improving the environment since the mid-1990s.

Parts of China's physical environment were ruined unintentionally, by neglect or ignorance. For example, there is Kunming Lake near the city of Kunming in Yunnan

Province. The government decided to fill a part of the lake to increase land for agricultural production. Not only was the beauty of the lake affected, but the ecology of the area around it was changed, with the result that insufficient rainfall is available for the growing of some crops. Forests in many parts were cut down to provide lumber and firewood, and there was soil erosion affecting the amount of sand and mud flowing into the rivers and increasing the likelihood of flood. It is said that the very serious flood in 1998 was the result of the lack of environmental protection in the years preceding it. Reduction of green areas has allowed deserts to form. For example, Beijing is now getting more blowing sand from its northwest. Pollution has also become a serious problem in many cities. Since 1987, because of government efforts, water pollution has decreased in China, but air pollution has not.

The air and water in China, especially in the urban areas, are among the most polluted in the world. Of the world's 10 most polluted cities in the year 1999, 9 are reported to be in China. Air pollution comes from industrial waste and from the burning of coal for cooking and heating in many cities. The extensive use of coal for energy is one reason for air pollution. As the country becomes industrialized, pollution from both industrial and consumer sources will increase because of higher levels of output and consumption, the latter from increase in the use of automobiles, unless pollution per unit of output or consumption can be reduced.

The Chinese government became aware of the environmental problems and has made serious attempts to protect and improve China's environment. In 1979, China passed the Environmental Protection Law for Trial Implementation. The 1982 Constitution included important environmental protection provisions. Article 26 of the Constitution requires that "the state protects and improves the environment in which people live and the ecological environment. It prevents and controls pollution and other public hazards." There are also provisions on the state's duty to conserve natural resources and wildlife.

Based on these provisions a number of special laws have been enacted. These include the Water Pollution Prevention and Control Law of 1984, the Air Pollution Prevention and Control Law of 1987, the Water and Soil Conservation Law of 1991, the Solid Waste Law of 1995, the Energy Conservation Law of 1997, and several important international agreements, including the Kyoto and Montreal Protocols.

Like many other laws in China, these laws are poorly enforced. The main reasons are the lack of a modern legal enforcement system, the lax attitude of the Chinese people towards such laws, and the economic costs of obeying them. The same reasons apply to the poor enforcement of the laws to protect intellectual property rights. These reasons will continue to hinder the enforcement of environmental laws for some time to come.

However, environmental conditions will improve in China for three reasons. One is the government's strong resolve. The second is that in many circumstances, unlike the case of the enforcement of laws to protect intellectual properties, the government has the power to enforce the law because the operation of an industrial enterprise requires the approval of and often economic assistance from the government. The government not only punishes offenders but provides economic incentives for people to act according to the economic welfare of society. There are a number of incentive schemes adopted by the Chinese government for industrial producers. For a particular industry, a limited amount of rights to pollute are auctioned to the highest bidders among industrial enterprises which find it necessary to produce waste material. Levies to polluters, restrictions on the quantity of pollution permitted, and the sales of tradable permits are economic means to control pollution in China. Wheeler, Dasgupta, and Wang (1999) have provided econometric evidence that a pollution levy does have a negative effect on the quantity of water and air pollution per unit of output, as we will discuss in the next section. Third is that as the economy gets richer the demand for cleaner water and air will increase, and so will the ability to pay for the cost to achieve it.

Because of the above-mentioned government policies, state and nonstate enterprises have tried to find cleaner technology to produce and to generate power from coal. Governments of cities like Shanghai have tried to adopt urban planning strategies that are friendly to the environment. Space within a city is reserved for planting trees in order to improve air quality. Travelers to Beijing, Shanghai, and Guangzhou in 1998 to 2000 would have noticed that these cities became cleaner and the air quality improved during this period.

In evaluating China's environmental protection policies, observers residing in developed economies should bear in mind that China is still a fairly poor country in the process of economic development. Such a poor country is eager to get rich quickly. In so doing its people may be willing to inhale some slightly polluted air and drink some slightly polluted water to enable industrial output to increase. The cost of producing the same output with less pollution will be higher. In other words, allowing some pollution will enable gross domestic product to be higher, even when we allow for the cost of pollution (which has been estimated to be 3–8 percent of GDP: *China 2020*, p. 71). In terms of announced policy, the Chinese government appears to be taking the protection and improvement of the environment seriously. It is unwilling to sacrifice the quality of the environment to increase current output. It appears to be aware of the possible effects of damaging the environment on future output and future economic welfare in general. Yet the standard of environmental protection may still be more lenient than that in a more developed economy.

## 10.4   A Study of Industrial Pollution

This section summarizes the main findings of a study on industrial pollution in China reported in Wheeler, Dasgupta, and Wang (1999). The main purposes of this study were to assess the effects of different factors on industrial pollution, to look at the impact of economic reforms and of pollution regulation, and to examine whether China can improve its environment and achieve economic growth at the same time.

First let's begin with some facts. Industrial pollution accounts for over 70 percent of total pollution, including 70 percent for waste water, 72 percent for $SO_2$ emissions, 75 percent for flue dust, and 87 percent for solid wastes, according to estimates of China's State Environment Protection Agency (SEPA). The remaining sources are non-industrial productive sectors and consumers. Since 1987, water pollution has improved but air pollution has not for the country as a whole. Approximately 4,000 people suffer premature death from air pollution related illness each year in Chongqing, 4,000 in Beijing, and 1,000 in Shanghai and Shenyang. Industrial pollution tends to be less serious, not more, in the more developed provinces. For example, the rich areas of Shanghai, Beijing, and Guangdong have less air pollution than the poor areas of Sichuan, Chongqing, and Liaoning, for reasons that will be discussed presently.

To study the factors contributing to pollution, an econometric analysis is performed. Both air and water pollution are studied. Pollution by industrial enterprises is measured by pollution density, which is the amount of air pollution or organic water pollution (chemical oxygen demand, or COD) in waste water discharged per unit of industrial output. The analysis is based on the following hypotheses. First, regulation is an important factor. It is measured by "effective levies," the amounts of levies actually collected (effective) per unit of above-standard discharge of air pollutants or waste water. Richer regions demand better environmental quality and tend to have better enforcement of environmental regulations. Second is industrial composition. If coal mining is highly polluting, then having a larger fraction of industrial output in this industry increases pollution intensity. Third is the size of the plant. There are economies of scale in the sense that a larger plant can produce the same output with less emission of pollutants. Fourth, state-owned enterprises tend to have higher pollution density partly because of their lower productive efficiency.

Using cross-section data for 29 provinces in the period 1987–93, an equation was estimated to explain the log of air or water pollution intensity in province $j$ ($j = 1, 2, \ldots,$ 29) by the above explanatory variables. The first is the log of effective levy in province $j$. The second is a set of variables $s_{kj}$, for the share of industrial output in province $j$ contributed by industry $k$, where different $k$'s represent coal mining, transportation equipment, chemical fibers, etc. The third is the share of industrial output in province $j$ produced by large plants. The fourth is the share of industrial output in province $j$ produced by state enterprises. The coefficients of log effective levy in the three air pollution intensity (separated into $SO_2$ intensity, smoke intensity, and dust intensity) equations and the water pollution intensity equation are respectively −0.321, −0.796, −0.434, and −0.835 (tables A.2 and A.1 of Wheeler, Dasgupta, and Wang, 1999). All coefficients are statistically significant, showing that increasing effective levies will lead to reduction in pollution intensity. The coefficients of shares of industrial output are reasonable. The coefficients of the share of output produced by large plants in the above four equations are negative and significant. The coefficients of the share of output produced by state enterprises are all positive and significant.

The results of the above statistical analysis show that economic reform will lead to less air and water pollution by increasing the average size of industrial plants and by reducing the share of output produced by state enterprises. Economic reform also will lead to better regulation in the form of increased effective levy. To measure this effect, a second equation is estimated to explain the log of effective levy by relevant economic variables. The variables include log pollution density, log population density, log income per capita, log industry share. Higher pollution density requires larger effective levy. The fact that its coefficient is positive (table A.1 (b)) for the levy on water (COD) implies that government regulation is effective in the sense of charging more in the provinces where pollution intensity is high. The positive coefficients of log population density and of log income per capita would imply that economic reform will lead to increase in effective levy through increasing these two explanatory variables. The second coefficient also explains why richer communities in China tend to have less pollution.

However, higher levy and even lower pollution intensity do not imply cleaner air or water. The latter is measured by the amount of pollutant per unit of air or water. Pollution intensity measures only the amount of pollutant per unit of industrial output. As the economy grows, the amount of industrial output also grows, leading to lower-quality air or water if pollution intensity remains the same. The quantitative analysis of the paper cited suggests that, by choosing appropriate policies on pollution levies, China can indeed reduce pollution intensity at a faster rate than the rate of growth of industrial output, and thus improve its environment as the economy grows.

# References and Further Reading

*China 2020*, ch. 6. Washington, DC: World Bank, 1997.

Dong, Xiao-Yuan, Shunfeng Song, and Xiaobo Zhang. *China's Agricultural Development: Challenges and Prospects*. Hampshire: Ashgate, 2006.

Johnson, D. Gale. "China's Rural and Agricultural Reforms: Successes and Failures." University of Chicago, Office of Agricultural Economics Research, no. 96-03, Aug. 15, 1996. Reprinted by Chinese Economy Research Unit, University of Adelaide, Working Paper no. 96/12, Feb. 1996.

Johnson, D. Gale. "China's Rural and Agricultural Reforms in Perspective." University of Chicago, Office of Agricultural Economics Research, Paper no. 98.02. Presented at the Land Tenure, Land Market, and Productivity in Rural China Workshop, Beijing, May 15–16, 1998.

Shapiro, Judith. *Mao's War Against Nature*. New York: Cambridge University Press, 2001.

Wheeler, David, Susmita Dasgupta, and Hua Wang. "Can China Grow and Safeguard Its Environment? The Case of Industrial Pollution." Paper presented before the Conference on Policy Reform in China, Center for Research on Economic Development and Policy Reform, Stanford University, Nov. 18–20, 1999.

# Questions

1   In the first section of this chapter we measure disparity among provinces using rural consumption per capita. Would you prefer using rural income per capita instead? Explain your answer. Table 10-16 of the *Statistical Yearbook of China, 1999* provides data on the per capita net income of rural households for all provinces for selected years from 1978 to 1995 and annually from 1995 to 1998. Would you expect our results to change much if income data are used instead of consumption data?

2   What are the reasons for the Chinese government to adopt the western development strategy? Are these reasons sound?

3   What are the main components of China's western development strategy?

4  In what respects does the western development strategy adopted by the Chinese government follow the rules of the market economy? Are there any respects in which the rules of a market economy are violated?

5  In what ways did the Chinese government neglect the protection of the environment from the 1950s to the 1970s?

6  Describe the major components of the environmental policy of China.

7  Explain why rich communities tend to have less pollution.

8  Name four of the most important factors that can explain pollution density in a province, pollution density being defined as the quantity of pollutant (air or water) emitted per unit of output. How is each factor measured? Explain why the coefficient of each factor should be positive or negative.

9  What are the channels through which economic reform will lead to less pollution?

# 11

# Population

After discussing the role of population and human capital in economic development, this chapter studies the growth trends in China's population and the government's population policy. It includes a critical evaluation of China's population policy. It also presents economic explanations of the rate of growth of population, in particular the birth rate.

## 11.1   The Role of Population and Human Capital in Economic Development

Among economists known for their pessimistic predictions for the world, one of the best-known is the English economist and clergyman Thomas R. Malthus (1766–1834). In *An Essay on the Principle of Population* (1798), Malthus argued that if left unchecked, population would grow faster than the food supply, leading to starvation and economic stagnation. His prediction failed to materialize, however, partly because technological progress increased the supply of food and other consumer goods and partly because population growth slowed down when people's incomes increased. Although Malthus's theory turned out to be wrong, it contains partial truths for some countries that had difficulty in achieving economic development for fairly long periods. For these countries, population growth was as fast as, if not faster than, the growth in food supply. An increase in per capita national income or output in these countries would require a reduction in the rate of population growth, or an increase in the rate of output growth, or both.

Chairman Mao Zedong made a statement in 1949 that encouraged the growth of China's population in the late 1950s and the 1960s:

A large population in China is a very good thing. With a population increase of several fold we still have an adequate solution. The solution lies in production. The fallacy of the

Western capitalist economists like Malthus that the increase of food lags behind the increase
of population was long ago refuted in theoretical reasoning by the Marxists; it has also been
disproved by the facts existing after the revolution of the Soviet Union and in the liberated
region of China.

In 1958 Mao's statement was used as a basis for criticizing Professor Ma Yin-Chu for
advocating family planning and population control. In 1975 Ma was rehabilitated, and
the earlier criticism of him was recognized to be a mistake. Most economists in China
believe, correctly or incorrectly, that if not for the mistaken population policy, the Chinese
population would have been smaller and per capita income in China would be much
higher in the 1980s. Since the early 1970s, Chinese leaders have tried to curtail the
growth of population, hoping to undo the harm of the population policy in the 1960s. We
will say more on this reversal in policy later in this chapter.

How is it possible for output per person to increase when population increases?
Why does a larger population imply a smaller output per capita? In the United States,
some would argue that the increase in population from immigration during the first half
of the twentieth century actually helped increase national output to the extent that per
capita output became higher than otherwise. Although such a conjecture might be mistaken, it makes one think twice before jumping to the conclusion that an increase in
population necessarily means a reduction in national output per capita. This conclusion is
likely to be valid for countries with very limited resources in comparison to the size of
their populations. Imagine many people farming on a small piece of land. The marginal
product of labor declines as the number of farmers increases. The marginal product
of labor is the partial derivative of output with respect to labor, holding the quantity of
land and capital fixed. Using a Cobb–Douglas production function with labor, land, and
capital as three factors, and under the assumption of constant returns to scale, one can
easily see that the marginal product of each factor declines as the quantity of that factor
increases, holding the remaining two factors constant. When the marginal product of
labor declines, the increase in output by adding the fifteenth farmer is smaller than the
increase in output by adding the fourteenth farmer. As we pointed out in chapter 5, the
marginal product of Chinese labor is low because of the very large population. Lewis
(1955) makes the strong assumption that for some less-developed countries with a large
population relative to land, the marginal product of agricultural labor is practically zero.
If more people mean only more mouths to feed and very little extra output, output per
person will decrease as the number of people increases.

How is it possible for output per person to increase when population increases?
Economic development has been observed in many countries, including China, where
national income per capita increased while total population also increased. Again using a
Cobb–Douglas production function with constant returns to scale, one can easily show
that output per person can increase even when the number of persons engaged in production increases, provided the quantities of other inputs become larger relative to the
quantity of labor. Given the ratio of the quantity of other inputs to labor, output per
person can also increase when there is technological change or when the quality of labor
improves. Improvement in the quality of labor occurs through education, on-the-job
training, and better healthcare. These are different forms of investment in human capital.

While population measures the quantity of labor without adjustment for quality, the amount of human capital measures the quantity of labor after adjustment for quality. Holding the quality of labor fixed, one finds that an increase in the quantity of labor or population leads to a reduction in output per person unless it is matched by increases in other inputs or by the improvement of technology. Holding population fixed, one finds that investment in human capital leads to an increase in output per person in the short run. In the long run it can lead to improvement in technology. The productivity of a given population is likened to the productivity of a given piece of land: it can be increased greatly by investment. Just as fertilizer, irrigation, and crop-rotation increase the productivity of land, so do education, on-the-job training, and better healthcare increase the productivity of people. However, the question remains whether, with fewer people, increase in capital, technological change, and investment in human capital would lead to a greater increase in per capita output.

In section 11.2 we present and analyze data on China's population and its growth rates. Section 11.3 is concerned with population policy in China and its possible effect on population growth. In section 11.4 we present an evaluation of this policy. Section 11.5 discusses economic explanations of the birth rate.

## 11.2   The Chinese Population and its Rate of Growth

In the early 1980s China received aid from the United Nations to improve its population census and population studies. As early as 1979, a team of scholars from China came to Princeton University and other centers of population studies in the United States to learn about recent developments in demography.

Official data on the Chinese population were fragmentary at that time, but have since improved in quality and have been published. The *China Statistical Yearbook 1999*, table 4-1, gives data for 1952, 1957, 1962, 1965, 1970, 1975, 1980, and annually from 1985 to 1998 on total population, and population by sex and by residence in urban and rural areas. The *Statistical Yearbook of China, 2003*, table 4-1, gives the same data for 1978, 1980, 1985, and annually from 1989 to 2002. Total population increased from 574.8 million in 1952 to 987.0 million in 1980 and 1,284.5 million in 2002. The exponential rate of increase before 1980 was 0.0193, and since 1980 has been 0.0120. The proportion of rural population was 87.54 percent in 1952, 82.08 percent in 1978, and 60.91 percent in 2002, showing the high degree of urbanization since 1978.

The rate of population growth, usually expressed as the increase per 1,000 persons per year, is the difference between the birth rate and the death rate, provided that there is no net migration to or from the country concerned. According to table 11.1 (based on table 4-2 of the *Statistical Yearbook of China, 2000*, with data in the first three columns from 1998 to 2002 taken from table 14-2 of the *Statistical Yearbook of China, 2003*), the death rate in China decreased steadily from the 1950s to the 1970s, reaching to 6.25 per 1,000 in 1978. This is an indication of the great improvement in healthcare in China during this period. Other contributing factors include the availability of cleaner water and the more

**Table 11.1**   Annual birth rate, death rate, and natural growth rate of the Chinese population, 1952–2004

| Year | National | | | City | | | Country | | |
|------|------------|------------|-------------------------|------------|------------|-------------------------|------------|------------|-------------------------|
|      | Birth rate | Death rate | Natural growth rate | Birth rate | Death rate | Natural growth rate | Birth rate | Death rate | Natural growth rate |
| 1952 | 37.00 | 17.00 | 20.00 |       |      |       |       |       |       |
| 1957 | 34.03 | 10.80 | 23.23 | 44.48 | 8.47 | 36.01 | 32.81 | 11.07 | 21.74 |
| 1962 | 37.01 | 10.02 | 26.99 | 35.46 | 8.28 | 27.18 | 37.27 | 10.32 | 26.95 |
| 1965 | 37.88 | 9.50  | 23.38 | 26.59 | 5.69 | 20.90 | 39.53 | 10.06 | 29.47 |
| 1971 | 30.65 | 7.32  | 23.33 | 21.30 | 5.35 | 15.95 | 31.86 | 7.57  | 24.29 |
| 1975 | 23.01 | 7.32  | 15.69 | 14.71 | 5.39 | 9.32  | 24.17 | 7.59  | 16.58 |
| 1978 | 18.25 | 6.25  | 12.00 | 13.56 | 5.12 | 8.44  | 18.91 | 6.42  | 12.49 |
| 1980 | 18.21 | 6.34  | 11.87 | 14.17 | 5.48 | 8.69  | 18.82 | 6.47  | 12.35 |
| 1985 | 21.04 | 6.78  | 14.26 |       |      |       |       |       |       |
| 1986 | 22.43 | 6.86  | 15.57 |       |      |       |       |       |       |
| 1987 | 23.33 | 6.72  | 16.61 |       |      |       |       |       |       |
| 1988 | 22.37 | 6.64  | 15.73 |       |      |       |       |       |       |
| 1989 | 21.58 | 6.54  | 15.04 | 16.73 | 5.78 | 10.95 | 23.27 | 6.81  | 16.46 |
| 1990 | 21.06 | 6.67  | 14.39 | 16.14 | 5.71 | 10.43 | 22.80 | 7.01  | 15.79 |
| 1991 | 19.68 | 6.70  | 12.98 | 15.49 | 5.50 | 9.99  | 21.17 | 7.13  | 14.04 |
| 1992 | 18.24 | 6.64  | 11.60 | 15.47 | 5.77 | 9.70  | 19.09 | 6.91  | 12.18 |
| 1993 | 18.09 | 6.64  | 11.45 | 15.37 | 5.99 | 9.38  | 19.06 | 6.89  | 12.17 |
| 1994 | 17.70 | 6.49  | 11.21 | 15.13 | 5.53 | 9.60  | 18.84 | 6.80  | 12.04 |
| 1995 | 17.12 | 6.57  | 10.55 | 14.76 | 5.53 | 9.23  | 18.08 | 6.99  | 11.09 |
| 1996 | 16.98 | 6.56  | 10.42 | 14.47 | 5.65 | 8.82  | 18.02 | 6.94  | 11.08 |
| 1997 | 16.57 | 6.51  | 10.06 | 14.52 | 5.58 | 8.94  | 17.43 | 6.90  | 10.53 |
| 1998 | 15.64 | 6.50  | 9.14  | 13.67 | 5.31 | 8.36  | 17.05 | 7.01  | 10.04 |
| 1999 | 14.64 | 6.46  | 8.18  | 13.18 | 5.51 | 7.67  | 16.13 | 6.88  | 9.25  |
| 2000 | 14.03 | 6.45  | 7.58  |       |      |       |       |       |       |
| 2001 | 13.38 | 6.43  | 6.95  |       |      |       |       |       |       |
| 2002 | 12.86 | 6.41  | 6.45  |       |      |       |       |       |       |
| 2003 | 12.41 | 6.40  | 6.01  |       |      |       |       |       |       |
| 2004 | 12.29 | 6.42  | 5.87  |       |      |       |       |       |       |

frequent use of boiled water. In many countries, as the economy developed, the death rate declined. In Taiwan, for example, the death rate decreased from 9.9 per 1,000 in 1952 to 4.7 in 1979, while the infant death rate decreased from 37.2 per 1,000 to 9.8 during the same period (see the *Statistical Yearbook of China, 1982*, p. 3).

A most important result of economic development is that while the death rate declines, the birth rate will eventually decline by even more, so that the natural rate of population growth ("natural" meaning not counting net migration) will decrease significantly. This has happened in country after country in western Europe, as well as in the United States and Japan. In Taiwan, the birth rate decreased from 46.6 per 1,000 in 1952 to 24.4 in 1979, resulting in a natural rate of increase of 46.6 – 9.9, or 36.7, in 1952, as compared with a natural rate of increase of 24.4 – 4.7, or 19.7, in 1979 (see the *Statistical Yearbook of China, 1982*, p. 3). In recent years economists have devoted much attention to explaining why the birth rate declines during economic development.

It may be pointed out that in some countries government policy concerning family planning has contributed to the decline in the birth rate. However, in most Western countries where the decline occurred, there was no government intervention in family planning. What made the potential parents voluntarily limit the number of children in the family is an interesting economic question that will be discussed in section 11.5.

For China, column 2 of table 11.1 shows that the birth rate declined from 37.00 per 1,000 in 1952 to 34.03 in 1957, 30.65 in 1971, 23.01 in 1975, and then to 18.21 in 1980; rose to 23.33 in 1987; and declined steadily to 12.86 in 2002.

What explains the moderate decline in the Chinese birth rate from 1952 to 1957? These were years of fairly rapid industrialization and very little government intervention in family planning. According to the survey article on family planning by the Policy Research Section of the Family Planning Office of the State Council published in the *Almanac of China's Economy, 1981* (p. 761), although the Chinese government advocated family planning as early as the 1950s, not much in the way of a concrete program and economic policy was implemented until the 1970s: "Although we advocated family planning work, we did not devise specific measures to implement it" (p. 762). Therefore, it is difficult to attribute the decline in birth rate between 1952 and 1957 to the government policy on family planning. More noticeable is the rapid decline in city birth rate from 44.48 per 1,000 in 1957 to 21.3 in 1971 (shown in column 5), which cannot be attributed to government birth control policy.

The *Statistical Yearbook of China, 1990*, p. 90, reports the birth rates from 1958 to 1961 as 29.22, 24.78, 20.86, and 18.02, and the death rates to be 11.98. 14.59, 25.43, and 14.24. The abnormally low birth rates and the abnormally high death rates during these four years, as compared with the more normal rates in 1957 and 1962, are the consequences of the great economic disaster of the Great Leap Forward, which began in 1958, and of the economic recovery after 1961. Note that the birth rate declined year after year from 1958 to 1961, while the death rate increased to an extremely high level of 25.43 per 1,000 in 1960. (See question 1 below.)

The same source as in the last paragraph also reports the birth rates in 1963 and 1964 to be 43.37 and 39.14, higher than in the neighboring years 1962 and 1965. These high rates might be attributed to the economic recovery from the Great Leap and to efforts to make up for the children lost during the famine years. Rapid increase in real GDP was accompanied by more agricultural market institutions, including rural markets and private plots assigned to the farm households still under the commune system. Why did the birth rate continue to decline after 1987? To what extent is this the result of government policy? Although the government advocated family planning from the early 1970s on, strong measures were not taken until the late 1970s. Yet there was already a continued drop in the birth rate from 37.88 in 1965 to 18.25 in 1978. This shows that economic forces rather than government population policy can cause a significant drop in the birth rate. In the urban areas the large increase in the participation of women in the labor force might have contributed to this decline. The increase in birth rate between 1980 and 1987, in spite of the one-child-family policy (to be discussed in the next section), is another piece of evidence suggesting that economic forces in these years of prosperity were more important in shaping the growth of population than government restriction.

A general summary of the data in table 11.1 is that as China reduced its death rate from 17 per thousand in 1952 to only 6.41 per thousand in 2002, close to the standard of developed economies (5.7 for Taiwan in 1997 and 5.8 for the United States in 1999), the birth rate has been reduced even more from 37 per thousand to 12.86 per thousand in 2002. As a result, the natural rate of population increase was reduced from 20.00 per thousand in 1952 to only 6.45 in 2002. This natural growth rate is already lower than the 9.5 rate for Taiwan in 1997 and the 8.5 rate for the United States in 1999. It is a very low growth rate if China is considered a developing country.

# 11.3   Population Policy

Family planning was introduced by the Chinese government in 1971. Policy consisted of encouraging later marriage, longer intervals between births, and a smaller number of children per family. According to a survey article on family planning published by the Family Planning Office in the *Almanac of China's Economy, 1981* (pp. 762–3), the guidelines and policies of the Communist Party and the Chinese government related to family planning have become more explicit since 1978. In 1980 the government called for stricter controls on population growth with the slogan "one couple, one child." Practical measures were devised to reward couples who agreed to have only one child. This article states (pp. 763–4):

> On September 25, 1980, the Central Committee of the CPC [Chinese Communist Party] issued an open letter calling on Communist Party and Youth League members to take the lead in limiting population growth to one child per couple. This letter spelled out the general target and the policies of population control in China. Each province, municipality, autonomous region, prefecture, county and commune appointed one leading comrade – sometimes even the top leader – to take responsibility for family planning work. The work was to be put often on the agenda for discussion and review, so that problems in connection with the implementation of family planning could be solved promptly . . .
>
> The effective control of the birth rate in 1980 was ensured by the following measures:
>
> 1) We launched a popular educational campaign via mass media to provide information about family planning and to encourage couples of childbearing age to volunteer to practice birth control . . .

2) We practiced family planning by implementing economic measures. In 1980, economic rewards and penalties were introduced. Rewards were given to those units and individuals who had done good work on family planning. Those couples who volunteered to have only one child received regular child care allowances. Economic penalties were levied on the few who, after patient ideological education, still paid no attention to family planning and the very few individuals who undermined this work were punished . . .

3) We used models in family planning. Cadres at all levels and the broad masses of party and Youth League members conscientiously took the lead in having only one child. Parents who had passed childbearing age persuaded their married children to have only one child . . .

4) We stressed knowledge about eugenics . . .

5) We paid attention to the study of new trends and to the solution of new problems . . .

6) We have intensified our cooperation with other countries in family planning work . . .

In summary, family planning work achieved good results in 1980, mainly through renewed ideological education supplemented by appropriate and necessary economic measures. However, there are still problems to be tackled, such as: the uneven development of the work; relatively more multiple births in remote and mountainous regions; the shortage of technical personnel; bad management and primitive, coercive working methods; the shortage of contraceptives and their poor quality; and inadequate implementation of the "one couple, one child" policy . . .

The Constitution adopted at the Fifth National People's Congress in 1978 stipulates in Article 53: The State advocates and encourages family planning. Article 12 of the marriage law adopted at the Third Session of the Fifth National People's Congress in 1980 stipulates: Husband and wife are duty bound to practice family planning. It is the legal obligation of every Chinese citizen to abide by the law and practice family planning, including the practice of late marriage and birth control.

How much effect the policy spelled out here has had on population growth in China is difficult to ascertain. There are reports that the Chinese people were strongly affected by the strict measures of population control. For example, *People's Daily*, April 7, 1983, carried an article with the headline, "Anhui Provincial Women's Association Survey Reports: Drowning of Female Infants in Rural Areas Serious, Affecting the Balance of Sex Ratio Among Infants." The article reports that, according to a survey of Suixi and Huaiyuan counties conducted by the Anhui Provincial Women's Association, in some areas the number of reported male births far exceeded the number of female births, by a ratio of as much as 5 to 1 in some cases. The article attributes this situation to the traditional preference for male children, which led to the infanticide by drowning of many female infants. In one production brigade in Huaiyuan County, more than 40 female infants were drowned in 1980 and 1981. In the Meizhuang brigade of Lunwang Commune, 8 children were born in the first quarter of 1982; while 3 males survived, 3 of the 5 females were drowned, and the other 2 females were abandoned. In view of the above, the Anhui Provincial Women's Association proposed to strengthen socialist education, making the people realize that the drowning of infants is a crime. At the same time, the association declared that people should be taught that males and females are equal and the traditional prejudices against females should be criticized. (The numbers of male and female births in the two counties and selected communes are recorded in tables 11.2a and 11.2b.) This news report is just one example, albeit a very dramatic one,

**Table 11.2a** Comparison of male and female births in Suixi and Huaiyuan counties

| County | Year | Total | Male | % Male | Female | % Female | Difference |
|--------|------|-------|------|--------|--------|----------|------------|
| Suixi | 1979 | 11,522 | 5,950 | 51.6 | 5,572 | 48.4 | 3.2 |
| | 1980 | 11,554 | 6,115 | 52.9 | 5,439 | 47.1 | 5.8 |
| Huaiyuan | 1980 | 13,487 | 7,593 | 56.3 | 5,894 | 43.7 | 12.6 |
| | 1981 | 10,768 | 6,266 | 58.2 | 4,502 | 41.8 | 16.4 |

**Table 11.2b** Comparison of male and female births in selected communes in Huaiyuan County, 1981

| Location | Total | Male | % Male | Female | % Female | Difference |
|----------|-------|------|--------|--------|----------|------------|
| Commune S | 133 | 83 | 62.4 | 50 | 37.6 | 24.8 |
| Commune L1 | 104 | 66 | 63.5 | 38 | 36.5 | 27.0 |
| Commune L2 | 231 | 145 | 62.8 | 86 | 37.6 | 25.6 |
| Commune H | 285 | 164 | 57.5 | 121 | 42.5 | 15.0 |
| Brigade Z | 9 | 7 | 77.8 | 2 | 22.2 | 55.6 |
| Brigade N | 8 | 7 | 87.5 | 1 | 12.5 | 75.0 |
| Brigade Q | 10 | 9 | 90.0 | 1 | 10.0 | 80.0 |

Source: People's Daily, *April 7, 1983.*

of the reactions of the Chinese rural people to the family planning measures of the government.

There appears to be sufficient evidence to indicate that as a result of the one-child-family policy and the strong preference for males, the ratio of male to female population was increased. In the *China Population Statistics Yearbook 2000*, published by the China Statistics Press, one can find data on the sex ratio (female = 100) as of 1999 by age group (see table 1–2 therein). The ratio was 119.54 for ages 0–4, 114.45 for ages 5–9, 107.99 for ages 10–14, 109.94 for ages 15–19, 98.08 for ages 20–4, and 98.76 for ages 25–9. The population of ages 19 or below in 1999 was born in 1980, the year when the one-child-family policy was introduced. The older population was not affected by the policy and hence had a more normal ratio of about 98. Note that the ratio was 108.01 for the 19-year-olds, 104.00 for the 20-year-olds, and 97.71 or below for the 21-, 22-, 23-, and 24-year-olds. I thank D. Gale Johnson of the University of Chicago for calling my attention to these data.

To what extent the one-child-family policy has affected the total birth rate (excluding infanticide) is difficult to ascertain. The *Statistical Yearbook of China, 1990* (p. 90) shows that in spite of the stricter measures introduced in 1980, the birth rates in 1981 and

1982 were higher than they had been in 1978 and 1979. One possible explanation for the increase in the birth rate is the agricultural reforms, which permitted farm families to operate as private farm households, thus increasing the value of children in terms of their marginal product accrued to the family. It is possible that economic forces are at work that may have stronger effects on the birth rate than the political and economic measures of the government family planning program. The net effect of these dramatic stories about abnormally low rates of female births in particular locations has not been noticeable in the statistics on total population by sex. Table 4–1 of the *Statistical Yearbook of China, 1999*, reports the proportion of males in the total population to be 51.90 in 1952, 51.45 in 1980, 51.52 in 1990, and 50.98 in 1998.

Another aspect of the government program is to encourage people to marry at later ages. Since 1971 the government had advocated a marriage age of 28 or above for males and 25 or above for females. In 1981 a new marriage law went into effect raising the legal minimum marriage age, but there was reportedly a reduction in local pressure on people to marry even later than the legal minimum age, partly to compensate for the continued strong pressure toward the one-child family. Ansley Coale, in a letter (made available to the author for publication) dated January 1983 to Song Jian, Vice-president of the Chinese Demographic Association, comments on the effects on the birth rate of the new policy regarding marriage.

I suspect that the effect of changing mean age of childbearing is not fully appreciated in China, and that there may have been some errors in policy that come from this lack of full understanding. The point is as follows: Suppose over a long period of time that each cohort of women (those born in the same year) bears an average of 3/10 of a child annually as each cohort passes from age 23 to age 28. The women in these cohorts would bear, on average, a total of 1.5 children, more or less in line with the childbearing targets of Chinese policy. Now suppose that in a given year (say 1981), because of a sudden decline in age at marriage, the women reaching age 22 in this year begin childbearing at that age, and then continue for five years (to age 27) at the rate of 3/10 of a child annually. Each cohort of women continues to bear an average total of 1.5 children. But in the calendar year of 1981, childbearing begins at age 22 (the younger women start earlier) and extends to age 27 (the older women are still following the old regime). Thus the total fertility rate for 1981 is not 1.5 but 20 percent higher, at 1.8. This increase in total fertility rate during each calendar year lasts for five years, until the cohorts following the old regime have finished their childbearing. Moreover, the extra births occurring during this time would not be offset by any subsequent reduction, unless there were a subsequent increase in the mean age of childbearing. The extra births would be a permanent addition to the population of China, and would in turn contribute to more births in the future.

Thus, a relaxation in the efforts to maintain a high age at marriage leads to a temporary increase in the birth rate, even if the efforts to restrict the number of children born per family to a level of 1.5 remain fully successful. I have heard, although I am not sure that my information is correct, that Chinese authorities have felt that the efforts to restrict childbearing to one or at most two children, is so successful that there was no need any longer to maintain the pressure towards late marriage. For the reasons outlined above, a relaxation in pressure to keep marriage late in fact produces a temporary increase in the birth rate of possibly substantial magnitude.

According to an article in *People's Daily*, March 14, 1982, the new marriage law had the effect of increasing the number of marriages in 1981 as compared with 1980. This increase, however, probably could partly explain the time pattern of the birth rates 18.21, 20.91, 21.09, 18.62, and 17.50 respectively in the five years from 1980 to 1984 as reported in the *Statistical Yearbook of China, 1990*, p. 90.

In 1983, the one-child policy was liberalized somewhat by allowing two children in rural areas if the first child was a girl. Penalties for having the second child in urban families amount to 10 to 20 percent of the combined wages of both parents for 3 to 14 years and also to a loss of job in many cases. Sometimes a large lump-sum fine is imposed which goes as high as 40 percent of the annual earnings of one adult. In the late 1990s the enforcement of the one-child policy became less strict and more families could afford the economic penalties of having more than one child, but the central government as of 2004 has not given up its one-child policy. However, city governments are given some flexibility in formulating their own policies. Governments of several cities including Shanghai have relaxed the conditions for having a second child. As of 2003 the conditions required to have a second child in Beijing were that both parents had to be single children and that they must prove the first child to have some kind of disability; to apply for having a second child a family had to wait at least 4 years after the birth of the first child, or the mother had to be no less than 28 years of age. Shanghai did not have the 4-year waiting period.

## 11.4  Evaluation of China's Population Policy

Let us consider the pros and cons of China's one-child-family policy by first citing the reasons given to justify this policy. First, it is said that China is overpopulated. Second, as an elaboration of the first point, China is too poor to feed its large population. Third, as a special case of the second, having a lower population growth rate will help increase economic growth per capita. Let us consider these arguments in turn.

It is true that China is the most populous country in the world, with almost 1.3 billion persons at the turn of the twentieth century. However it is geographically a large country, being the third largest in the world ranking below only Russia and Canada. One needs to have some criterion to judge how many people are too many. In terms of population density, or the number of persons per unit of land, China is less densely populated than almost all countries in western Europe, Japan, and Taiwan. It has more cultivated cropland per capita than Taiwan, 0.27 acres compared with 0.12 acres as of 1980, although the average quality of the land in Taiwan, allowing for rainfall, is probably better. In addition, a high population density or a small amount of land per person does not set a severe limitation even on agricultural output, which depends on the choice of crop, fertilizer, and technology. If China were not treated as one country but its individual provinces considered separately, the population densities of most provinces would not be large compared with European countries. Also, in the most densely populated provinces the per capita incomes are highest. Therefore it does not make sense to say that China is overpopulated in the sense of population density.

Second, one may judge the size of the population in terms of China's output. China is self-sufficient in food supply; it exports more food than it imports. It would be economically advantageous to import some agricultural products in exchange for some Chinese exports. By 1999 China's per capita income was not very low. It was about US$750 if one converts the income figure in yuan to US dollars using the official exchange rate of 8.3 yuan per dollar, but it was 4 times this amount or US$3,000 if we allow for the higher purchasing power of the yuan than that indicated by the official exchange rate (see section 5.6 for the conversion rate of 2 yuan per dollar according to purchasing power parity; see also Ren and Chen 1995). Third, a higher birth rate resulting from relaxing the one-child policy will not slow down the growth rate of real GDP substantially. In the last two decades of the twentieth century the average annual rate of growth has been about 9.5 percent. Not only is this growth rate large enough to absorb a population growth rate of less than 1 percent in 1998 as shown in table 9.1, but the population policy is unlikely to affect the natural growth rate by more than 0.5 percent, as we have not uncovered a substantial effect of the policy from the data in table 11.1. Thus there is no economic need for this policy and its effect on the per capita GDP growth rate is so small as to make it unnecessary.

Having dispelled the common justifications for the policy, we turn to its possible harmful effects. First, from the long-run economic point of view, human capital will be needed in the future for China's continued development, and human capital starts with human beings. Today a child might be costly, but 18 years from now (if not sooner, as in the countryside) the adult will be productive. Without giving birth to children today how can we have sufficient human capital in the future? In particular, the one-child policy will lead to an unreasonably high ratio of old people to the working population, making it difficult for the working population to support the senior population. Second, the family structure of China will be distorted by the policy as the relationships between brothers and sisters, nieces and nephews, aunts and uncles, will disappear. The single child is often spoiled by the parents and two sets of grandparents. Third, the policy is an infringement on the freedom of the Chinese people. In no other country in the world does, and in no other time throughout Chinese history did, the government decide arbitrarily on the number of children each family is allowed to have. It would not be an infringement of freedom to use economic incentives, such as charging a higher cost for public education for the second and third child, or to provide information, such as knowledge of contraceptives and family planning, to help reduce the national birth rate. Let anyone who favors the current policy be subject to it and she would likely become more critical. If we do not like it for ourselves why should we wish it for the people living in China? Besides being an infringement on the rights of citizens, the policy has negative effects on the economic development of China. For one thing it makes the quality of life worse for Chinese families, possibly affecting the willingness of educated Chinese living overseas to return home.

In summary, the arguments in favor of the one-child-family policy are not well supported. The possible harmful effects of the policy can be serious. There is even an argument that a larger population is beneficial to a country's economic growth. According to this argument, economic growth depends on new knowledge being applied to an economy, as new knowledge is an important factor for increasing total factor productivity. If there are more people there will be more new knowledge created for two reasons. First, more people provide a larger market and make it more profitable to produce and adopt new knowledge. Second, having more people increases the probability of having a sufficiently large group of talented people to do the research for technological innovations. Certainly it is much easier to select a thousand very talented people from 1 billion than from 200 million. It is the top of the research team that does the most innovative work in acquiring or applying new knowledge for the benefit of economic growth. China has benefited from a large population from which very talented people have been selected. Some of them have appeared in top graduate schools around the world.

## 11.5   Economic Explanation of the Birth Rate

Why did increasing per capita income in many developed countries lead to a decrease in the birth rate?

An answer can be provided by performing a cost and benefit analysis of having children. On the benefit side, children are productive for farm families, but become less so when the farmers use more technology to replace human labor in production and many farmers transfer out of agriculture to nonfarm activities. As urbanization takes place, the benefits of having children for production decrease while the costs of having children increase. The costs include higher rental for a larger family, or, until recently in China, more congestion in urban housing, high education costs in urban areas, and the high cost of taking away valuable time from the mother who can work. In addition, rich urban families demand high-quality education for their children. All these economic forces are at work on the Chinese mainland, as they have been in Taiwan and in other more developed areas. It is understood that people do not produce children entirely for economic reasons. However, to the extent that economic considerations are important, an analysis based on economic calculations can yield a fruitful explanation and prediction of the birth rate.

Becker (1981: 95–102) applies the traditional theory of demand to explain the number of children that a family decides to have. Let the utility function of a family be written as

$$u = u(n, Z)$$

where $n$ denotes the number of children and $Z$ denotes the quantity of consumption goods. The budget constraint is

$$pn + \pi Z = I$$

where $p$ denotes the cost per child, $\pi$ denotes the price per unit of consumption goods, and $I$ denotes full income, which includes nonlabor income plus the maximum labor income that can be earned by using all the time available to the adult family members.

The cost of having a child includes the market goods the child consumes and the cost of time spent by the parents in rearing the child. As in traditional theory, the consumer unit is assumed to maximize the above utility function subject to the stated budget constraint. The demand for children derived from this maximization process is a function of the relative price of a child and full income. An increase in the relative price of children, or in the ratio of $p$ to $\pi$, will reduce the demand for children relative to consumption goods if real income is held constant. This is the substitution effect of a change in $p$. Under normal circumstances, an increase in income will increase the demand for children.

Becker (1981: 86–7) cites evidence that over the last several hundred years farm families have been larger than urban families. Part of the explanation is the low cost of rearing children on farms, including the costs of food and housing. Furthermore, the net cost of rearing children is reduced if they contribute to family income by working. Insofar as children have been more productive on farms than in the cities, the net cost of having children is lower for farm families. As an economy develops and agriculture becomes more mechanized, the cost advantage of raising children on farms is reduced. This may explain why urban–rural fertility differentials have narrowed in developed countries during the twentieth century, and even disappeared in the United States. The increase in earning power of women in the past 100 years in developed countries is a major cause of both the increase in the participation of married women in the labor force and the decline in fertility rates, the latter due to the increase in opportunity cost of rearing children. The increase in the earning power of women in China has probably had the same effects since the 1960s.

Besides economic calculations, the availability of birth control methods also affects the fertility rate. Becker (1981: 99–102) believes that the effect is small for three reasons. First, the simple birth control methods of increasing the marriage age, reducing the frequency of coition, and prolonging breast feeding that were known and practiced for centuries are already quite effective in reducing the fertility rate. Second, some evidence, including the high birth rate of poor Indian families that were informed of and encouraged to use birth control methods, suggests that the methods may not be very effective. Third, the methods are not necessary to reduce fertility because we have observed large reductions in fertility in many societies before these methods are developed. The relevance of the third point to the Chinese situation is the reduction in the birth rate in China from 35.05 per thousand in 1966 to 18.21 in 1980, without much government intervention.

Concerning the income effect on the demand for children, Becker (1981: 102) cites cross-section evidence of the positive relation between family income and the number of children. However, there are also instances of negative relations between income and fertility. One possible explanation is that the cost of having children increases with income because the wives of men with higher incomes tend to have higher potential or actual earnings also. The observed relation between the number of children and family income is a combination of the income effect and the price effect, and not a pure income effect, holding the price of rearing children fixed. One important lesson from this economic analysis of the fertility rate is that economic considerations may be more effective in influencing the birth rate than coercion, and that a government wishing to reduce the birth rate may find economic means to achieve its objective preferable to coercion.

The above analysis of the economic factors which lead naturally to a reduction in the birth rate as an economy becomes more urbanized and as more women participate in the urban labor force, applies to China. The reduction of the birth rate in China from 23.33 in 1987 to 16.03 in 1998 might be explained, partly at least, by these factors. As casual evidence, one hears more and more urban families in China expressing a desire to have a small family. If these forces are at work, the coercive one-child-family policy becomes unnecessary even for those who think that China's population should grow slowly. One additional factor that may further reduce the birth rate in China is the provision of social insurance for old age to a wider group of people than the staff and workers in state-owned enterprises, which the government has been instituting since the September 1997 report of General Secretary Jiang Zemin quoted in section 4.1. Chinese families desire children partly to provide security for old age. Social insurance will reduce the need for children as providers in old age and thus lead to a reduction in the birth rate.

## References and Further Reading

*Almanac of China's Economy, 1981*. Hong Kong: Modern Cultural Co. Ltd., 1982.
Becker, Gary S. *A Treatise on the Family*. Cambridge, MA: Harvard University Press, 1981.
Lewis, W. Arthur. *The Theory of Economic Growth*. Homewood, IL: Irwin, 1955.
Ren, Ruoen and Kai Chen. "China's GDP in US Dollars Based on Purchasing Power Parity." Working paper. Washington, DC: World Bank, Jan. 1995.

## Questions

1   Using the data provided in the text for the years 1958 to 1961 while discussing the death and birth rates of table 11.1, (a) estimate the extra deaths during these four years in China in millions of persons, assuming the normal death rate to be 10.80 per thousand, the rate in 1957; (b) estimate the number of babies which would have been added to the population in these four years assuming the normal birth rate to be 34.03 per thousand as in 1957.

2   What are the economic explanations of the changes in the birth rate? Try to explain the Chinese birth rates in the last half century using the relevant explanations.

3   Are you in favor of or against the one-child policy in China? Give the reasons for your answer.

4   Do you believe that the one-child policy in China has been effective in reducing the birth rate? Cite some evidence for your answer.

# 12

# Human Capital

After discussing the importance of human capital and a method to measure its quantity, this chapter reviews the theories of supply of and demand for labor given the quantity of human capital. It then presents a theory on investment in human capital, a major factor being the rate of return to investment. A study on the rates of return to schooling, a very important form of investment in human capital, for both urban and rural workers in China is reported. The chapter ends with a discussion of health services and the welfare system in China.

## 12.1 The Importance of Human Capital and its Measurement

Before the 1960s, economists considered physical capital (including land) and labor to be the two main factors of production. The accumulation of physical capital was considered the most important means to achieve economic development. This viewpoint follows from the observation that poor countries had a lot of labor, and it is the quantity of capital available for each laborer that determines the output per laborer and hence the per capita income of a country. The proposition that output per laborer increases as capital per laborer increases can be observed from the Cobb–Douglas production function. When both sides of the function are divided by the quantity of labor $L$, the resulting equation explains $Y/L$ as an increasing function of $K/L$ where $Y$ denotes output and $K$ denotes physical capital stock. To achieve economic development in terms of increasing per capita output, therefore, the country should increase capital more rapidly than the increase in population.

At the beginning of the 1960s economic thinking began to change, partly as a result of the important work of T. W. Schultz (1961) and of Gary S. Becker (1964). Available macro- and microeconomic data indicated that knowledge, training, and skill possessed by humans might be as important as, if not more important than, physical capital in the determination of output. On the macro level, the rapid recovery of the European countries and Japan after the destruction of a sizable fraction of these countries' physical capital seemed to suggest that it was the knowledge and skill of the people that helped promote the post-Second World War recovery and rapid development. From the growth experience of the United States, Solow (1957) already observed that his neoclassical model (1956) using only physical capital and labor in the production function failed to explain entirely the aggregate growth in the United States. The observed growth rate was higher than what the contributions of capital and labor could explain using the neoclassical production function. Recall that we found the same for the aggregate growth of China after 1979 as discussed in chapter 5. The part of the log of output not explained by a production function using capital and labor is termed the Solow residual, and we have found a positive trend for the Solow residual in China. The importance of human capital relative to physical capital in the economic development of a country is partly due to the immobility of human capital across national borders. While the need for more physical capital could be met by foreign investment, it is difficult to increase human capital in a country because receiving education and on-the-job training is a very slow process and the success of that process depends on existing human capital inherited from tradition.

On the micro level, it was found in a number of studies that the wage and therefore the implied marginal productivity of labor were higher as the education level increased. This fact is considered a piece of evidence to suggest that human capital contributes to output. A well-known study by Mincer (1969) explains log wage by age, age squared, and the log of the number of years $S$ of schooling using cross-section data. The regression coefficient of $S$ is used to measure the rate of return to schooling. Why this regression coefficient measures the rate of return will be explained in section 12.4. This regression function has become known as the Mincer equation, and we will see an application of it to China later in this chapter. Both macro and micro data have confirmed the importance of human capital in increasing productivity. An interesting question studied by economists is whether the rate of return on investment in human capital is higher than in physical capital. Some evidence cited in Becker (1964) suggests that it is higher in the United States. The reason is that there is underinvestment in human capital because potential investors cannot legally be guaranteed its return in the future. It is difficult if not impossible for a private investor to enforce a contract that requires a college student to pay a part of his future earnings as interest for a loan extended to him. The uncertainty of future payments requires a high rate of interest and thus leads to less capital being invested to finance the formation of human capital than otherwise.

The productivity of human capital on the aggregate level can be measured in the framework of a production function. We need some measure of the quantity of human capital to be used in an aggregate production function. One such measure is to replace the number of employed persons in an aggregate production function by a weighted sum of the numbers of employed persons with different education levels. The weights depend on the education levels. For example, there may be three educational levels: primary school completed, high school completed, college or professional school completed. If the numbers of employed persons in these three categories are $n_1$, $n_2$, and $n_3$ and their average wages are $w_1$, $w_2$, and $w_3$, the number of laborers adjusted for the quality of human capital will be $H = [n_1w_1 + n_2w_2 + n_3w_3]/w_1$. If we use $H$ to measure the quantity of human capital we count a person having only primary education as one person, a person having a high school education as $w_2/w_1$ persons, etc. A quality index $Q$ of human capital (measured by education levels above the primary level in the above example) imbedded in the entire body of employed persons can be defined as the ratio of the above weighted sum $H$ to the sheer number of persons employed $L$ (all assumed to have at least primary school education). In other words, $H = LQ$. An aggregate Cobb–Douglas production function that allows for the quality of human capital can be written as $Y = AK^{\alpha}L^{\beta}Q^{\gamma}$. In the production function which does not introduce an index $Q$ of the quality of the labor force, $AQ^{\gamma}$ is absorbed in the measurement of total factor productivity or the Solow residual. Thus introducing a measure of human capital can help explain a part of TFP or the Solow residual in the production function specified in chapter 5.

In the remainder of this chapter we will first discuss in section 12.2 the utilization of existing human capital, which is determined by the supply of and the demand for labor. We will then discuss the increase of human capital through investment, a subject of section 12.3. Investment in human capital, like the utilization of existing human capital, is also determined by demand and supply. The demand for investment is dependent on the rate of return. Investment in human capital can take the forms of schooling, on-the-job training, health improvement, migration to improve the payment to the services from human capital, etc. In section 12.4 a study to measure the rate of return to schooling in China in the late 1980s will be reported. Section 12.5 deals with healthcare in China.

## 12.2   Labor Supply and Demand

Given a country's population what determines its labor force? The size and age distribution of a country's population determine to a large extent its labor force. The potential supply of labor is limited by the number of persons of working age. However, the actual supply of labor depends on many economic factors that affect the willingness of the people of working age to work. In a society where people freely choose whether to work, where to work, and how much to work, the supply of labor depends on the monetary and nonmonetary returns of the job opportunities as compared with the returns from alternative uses of a person's time, mainly recreation, education, work in the household, and childbearing. The effects on choice of occupation of monetary and nonmonetary (or pecuniary and nonpecuniary) advantages and disadvantages of different occupations were aptly discussed in chapter X of book I of Adam Smith's *Wealth of Nations* (1776). People respond to economic incentives regarding not only how many hours to work but also whether to work. The latter decision affects a person's decisions to start working and to retire (so that the working age is itself a variable to be determined by economic forces) as well as whether he or she will seek employment during working age. By not working, a person can enjoy her leisure, go to school to improve her skills, engage in investment in human capital, or spend time in childbearing. In the United States, for example, during periods of economic depression or recession some people return to school or remain in school longer than otherwise. As the United States economy slows down, graduate and professional schools find an increase in the number of applicants.

In a society such as China in the 1980s, people also responded to the pecuniary and nonpecuniary rewards in supplying their labor, but the choices open to them were more limited. Starting from the educational stage, the small fraction of people fortunate enough to enter college could not and to some extent still cannot freely choose their major field of study. The number of students majoring in each field in each college or university is under the direction of the Ministry of Education. Once a major is chosen, it is very difficult, if not impossible, to change it. After a student graduated from college or from middle school, he or she was assigned a job by the Labor Bureau of their city or county of residence. Once assigned to a job, the person would have difficulty changing to another job. Even under this rigid system, however, people try their best to choose the occupation of their own liking and to get assigned to a better or more suitable job by influencing the personnel in the Labor Bureau through the back door. If a person does not like his job, he will try to take sick leave more often and put in fewer hours actually working. In short, the actual supply of labor in each occupation in China, as elsewhere, is affected by economic incentives, given the age distribution of the population.

Table 12.1 presents data on the total size of the labor force, its composition, and its ratio to total population in selected years. It is interesting to observe the rapid increase in the number of individually employed urban laborers since 1979, after economic policy was changed to allow greater freedom in establishing individual businesses. The last column of table 12.1 shows a continually rising ratio of employed persons to total population. In section 9.1 we pointed out that the increasing percentage of persons employed in urban areas was the major factor responsible for the increase in consumption per capita between 1957 and 1978, when the real wage rate showed no increase. This increase in

**Table 12.1**   Number of employed persons in China (10,000s)

| Year | Total | Workers and staff | Individual urban laborers | Rural laborers | Ratio of employed to total population |
|------|-------|-------------------|---------------------------|----------------|---------------------------------------|
| 1949 | 18,082 | 809   | 724 | 16,549 | 0.3338 |
| 1952 | 20,729 | 1,603 | 883 | 18,243 | 0.3606 |
| 1957 | 23,771 | 3,101 | 104 | 20,566 | 0.3677 |
| 1965 | 28,670 | 4,965 | 171 | 23,534 | 0.3952 |
| 1978 | 39,856 | 9,499 | 15  | 30,342 | 0.4140 |
| 1979 | 40,581 | 9,967 | 32  | 30,582 | 0.4160 |
| 1980 | 41,896 | 10,444 | 81 | 31,371 | 0.4245 |
| 1981 | 43,280 | 10,940 | 113 | 32,227 | 0.4325 |
| 1982 | 44,706 | 11,281 | 147 | 33,278 | 0.4403 |

**Source**: Chinese Statistical Abstract, 1983, *p. 18; the last column is the ratio of the first column to total population*.

labor participation is harder to explain. The age distribution of the population does not appear to be the answer, because the fraction of the population of working age was not continuously increasing. Why has a higher percentage of the Chinese people, and women in particular, become employed in more recent years?

What economic conditions might have caused this increase? While a thorough study of this question remains to be undertaken, we can set forth the approach that an economist would take to answer it, besides attempting to attribute the increase entirely to government policy.

Like any other commodity or service, the quantity of labor employed depends on the demand for and the supply of labor. We will first present a theory of the supply of labor and then discuss the demand for labor, which in China is influenced to a large extent by government policy, especially during the period of central planning. The simplest theory of the supply of labor is based on the individual laborer's choice between working hours and leisure hours, given the total number of hours available to the individual, net of the hours required to sleep and perform other necessary tasks for survival. Using indifference curve analysis, one can study a consumer's choice between the consumption of leisure time and of market goods, just like the choice between any two consumer goods. The reader is urged to follow this discussion by drawing a diagram. The horizontal axis measures the consumption of leisure time. Assume that the worker has a maximum of 100 hours (per week) to sell. The difference between 100 and the individual's leisure time is the number of working hours, which is measured along the horizontal axis from the point (100,0). The vertical axis measures the quantity of other consumption goods. By a theorem of Hicks (1946) on group demand, provided that the relative prices of a group of commodities remain unchanged, the group can be treated as a single commodity from the viewpoint of demand theory. This theorem justifies the measurement of the consumption of all commodities other than leisure time along the vertical axis.

Denote the quantities of leisure time and of the group of other consumption goods respectively by $x_1$ and $x_2$. Let the wage rate be $0.40 per hour and the price per unit of the other commodities be $2.00. By giving up all leisure time, or by working 100 hours, the worker can earn $40, which is sufficient to purchase 20 units of consumption goods. By not working at all, the individual consumes 100 hours of leisure time but has no income to buy any consumption goods. His budget constraint is

$$\$0.40x_1 + \$2.00x_2 = \$40 \tag{12.1}$$

which can be depicted by a budget line to be designated AB. The wage rate of $0.40 per hour can be interpreted as the price of consuming one hour of leisure time. The cost of this consumption is the forgone earnings. The equilibrium point, given the budget line AB, is a point designated $b$ at which the budget line is tangential to an indifference curve. This point shows the purchase of 50 hours of leisure time, or $100 - 50 = 50$ working hours, and the consumption of 10 units of other commodities.

The theory of consumer demand is entirely applicable here for the choice between leisure time (and thus working time) and other consumption goods. The indifference curve in this context is identical with the indifference curve for any two commodities except for the labeling of the axes. If the wage rate decreases from \$0.40 to \$0.32 per hour, the budget constraint will be changed to

$$\$0.32x_1 + \$2.00x_2 = \$32 \tag{12.2}$$

and the budget line changed from AB to AC. By working 100 hours, or having no leisure time, the worker-consumer will have an income of \$32, which permits him to buy 16 units of the other commodities. His new equilibrium point will be a point designated $c$ in your diagram.

As before, the change from point $b$ to point $c$ can be broken down into a substitution effect and an income effect. The substitution effect is the change from point $b$ to point $d$. It indicates that the worker will choose to consume more leisure, or to work less, when the wage rate is reduced relative to the price of the other commodities, or when the relative price of consuming leisure is reduced, provided that his real income is held fixed. Holding real income fixed, by Slutsky's definition, means having the new budget line pass the old equilibrium point $b$ but changing its slope to that of the budget line AC. Holding real income fixed, according to Hicks's text (1946), means making the new budget line parallel to AC but tangential to the same indifference curve as before. The difference between the two definitions is minor when the change in price is small. For both definitions the substitution effect is always negative, according to standard demand theory. In the case of labor supply, this means that reducing the wage rate will always increase the consumption of leisure or decrease the supply of labor if real income is held fixed.

The income effect is the change from point $d$ to point $c$. A reduction in the wage rate means a reduction in income if the price index of the other commodities is unchanged. This will ordinarily reduce the consumption of leisure or increase the supply of working hours, provided that leisure is not an inferior good. The income effect of a reduction in the wage rate under normal circumstances is to reduce the consumption of leisure or to increase the supply of labor hours. Conversely, the income effect of an increase in the wage rate is ordinarily to reduce the supply of labor hours. The substitution effect of an increase in the wage rate is always to increase the number of working hours. When wages increase, the combined income and substitution effect is ordinarily an increase in the supply of working hours, because the substitution effect ordinarily dominates the income effect. However, it is possible that in certain ranges of the wage rate, especially when the wages are high, the income effect may dominate the substitution effect. In this case an increase in wage will call forth fewer working hours. Such a possibility can give rise to a backward-bending supply curve. This supply curve shows that when the wage rate increases from a low level, the supply of labor increases, but when the wage rate increases much further, the supply of labor is eventually reduced. In spite of this possibility, the response to a wage increase is ordinarily an increase in the supply of labor hours.

This theory of labor supply is confined to the decision of a single individual making his or her decision independently. While it is useful, it fails to account for the interdependence of the decisions of different members of the same family. A richer theory to explain the consumption, labor supply, and in fact the number of births of a family can be formulated by considering the joint decisions of a family as an economic unit. A family is assumed to maximize a utility function that may have as its arguments the consumption of physical commodities and services, the leisure times (and thus working hours) of its adult members, and perhaps the number of children. The number of children was introduced in the utility function presented in section 11.5. Here we briefly indicate how a theory based on family decisions can explain such phenomena as the decisions of housewives to work as well as the number of working hours each family member is willing to supply.

The potential income of the household includes its nonlabor income plus the hours available to the adult family members for work, times their wage rates. By "work" is meant both market work (as part of the labor force) and work in the household. Married women not in the labor force spend most of their working hours doing household work. Albert Rees (1979: 4) explains the behavior of such a household as follows.

> Decisions about the allocation of time will reflect the total resources of the household, of which the most important are the time of household members of working age and the household's income from sources other than work. These decisions also reflect the opportunities for market work available to members of the household, including their potential market wage, their comparative advantages in nonmarket activities, and the amount and nature of household work that needs to be performed. An increase in the family's resources, unaccompanied by any other change in opportunities – such as an inheritance that substantially increases nonlabor income – should reduce total labor supply. Thus it might lead the family to decide that a teenage son should stay in school longer, that the elderly grandfather should retire earlier, or that the working wife should become a full-time homemaker . . .
>
> A rise in the wage for the market work open to some members of the household may induce more participation by these members. Thus a rise in the salaries of schoolteachers (relative to other wages and prices) should induce some women who have left work to care for their families to return to teaching. They could use some combination of hired domestic help, purchased services, and the reallocation of household duties to other members of the family to make up for the loss of some of their time in the home, or the family could consume somewhat less of the "goods" produced by work in the home, such as a tidy kitchen, home cooking, or a well-kept garden, and instead could consume more market goods.

This discussion merely sketches some essential features of a theory of labor supply based on family decision-making and is far from being a presentation of the theory itself. For a more thorough discussion, the reader may refer to Rees (1979, chs. 1 and 2) and Becker (1964, chs. 1 and 2). A more formal theory, using the approach in the context of explaining the number of children in a family as given in section 11.5, can be derived by introducing leisure or hours of work as an additional variable in the utility function.

Turning to the demand for labor, we will first comment on the marginal productivity theory of demand in the case of competitive markets and then discuss the demand for labor in China. Recall the theory of demand for labor by a competitive firm that tries to maximize profits. Labor will be hired by the firm until the value of its marginal product equals its cost or the wage rate. If the firm has monopoly power, so that its demand curve is not infinitely elastic (or horizontal) but is negatively sloping, it will hire labor until its marginal revenue product equals its cost. Marginal revenue product is the extra revenue that the firm receives by selling the extra output produced by the additional unit of labor. If the demand curve is horizontal, or the price of the product remains the same when more is sold, marginal revenue product equals the value of the marginal product, which is equal to the marginal product times the price of the product. When the firm is facing a negatively sloping demand curve, the extra revenue from selling the marginal product will be somewhat less because the price of the product has to be reduced. The extra revenue equals the marginal product times the marginal revenue obtained by selling the extra product, and is called the marginal revenue product. This refinement aside, the essence of the marginal productivity theory of demand for labor is that labor will be hired if it produces more than or at least as much as its cost or the wage rate, implying that when its price is reduced, more will be hired.

As an illustration, assume a Cobb–Douglas production function $Y = AK^{\alpha}L^{\beta}$ for the firm. Here we hold as fixed the quality $Q$ in the amount of human capital $H$ (which equals $LQ$ in the discussion near the end of section 12.1), and leave the subject of investment in human capital to section 12.3. The marginal product of labor, or the partial derivative of the quantity of output $Y$ with respect to the quantity of labor $L$, is $\beta AK^{\alpha}L^{\beta-1}$. When we set this marginal product equal to the wage rate $w$ and solve the resulting equation for $L$ we obtain a demand function for labor which takes the form $L = (\beta A)^{1/(1-\beta)}K^{\alpha/(1-\beta)}w^{-1/(1-\beta)}$. This demand function for labor $L$ shows that when wage rate $w$ increases the demand for labor decreases. When the quantity of capital stock $K$ increases the demand for labor $L$ increases. The reason is that as capital stock increases the marginal product of labor increases.

Does the marginal productivity theory of demand for labor have relevance in China, where government policy affects the demand for labor in a significant way? The answer is yes if the government plans efficiently. Government policy affects the demand for labor at two levels. First, to the extent that government economic planning affects the development of agriculture and industry in China, it affects the demand for labor. Just as in a market economy, technology and the stock of capital in China affect the demand for labor through the production function. Government policy influences the stock of capital and technology, and therefore indirectly influences the demand for labor. Second, given the capital stock and technology, government labor policy may affect the number of laborers hired in various activities.

If the government guarantees a job to every person of working age and if the labor bureaus assign jobs to all physically able adults, one might think that this will affect the demand for labor and assure full employment of the labor force. The Chinese experience, however, has shown otherwise. In the late 1970s and early 1980s, the government labor bureaus could not find jobs for many youths in urban areas. These people were in the state of "waiting for job assignment" or, in other words, in the state of unemployment. In addition, many people holding a job were not fully employed. Just assigning a job to a person is not equivalent to creating a demand for the person's labor services. Just keeping a laborer working in some job does not imply that she or he is productive if the products are of little economic value as a result of mistakes in economic planning. Many organizations were overstaffed and people on the payroll had very little to do. Chinese universities, for example, often had more teachers, administrators, and maintenance workers than students. Each Chinese worker was guaranteed job security – the "iron rice bowl" that could not be broken – no matter whether his or her work contributed to the productivity of the employing organization. Thus, government labor policy affects the number of jobs assigned more than the demand for labor.

Since economic reforms were initiated in 1978, market forces have been allowed to influence the demand for labor and the marginal productivity theory of demand has become more relevant. First, agricultural reforms have permitted many individual farm households to operate as independent economic units. Such profit-maximizing units will hire additional laborers according to the value of their marginal product compared with the cost of hiring. Farm families will also engage in nonfarm activities according to profit-maximizing principles. Second, unemployed youths and other people in urban areas have been encouraged to start small individually or collectively operated businesses. If these businesses are profit maximizing, the marginal productivity theory becomes relevant. Third, government industrial enterprises have had some autonomy in their production, pricing, and hiring decisions and were encouraged to operate as independent economic units. The tendency to use profit-maximizing calculations makes the hiring decisions of these firms, to the extent that they have authority, dependent on marginal productivity considerations. Fourth, the township and village enterprises, or TVEs, have complete autonomy in their hiring decisions. Finally, even an enterprise operating under the direction and for the interest of the central government should be instructed to hire laborers up to the point where the value of the marginal product just covers the wage, for this is simply a principle of economic efficiency. How can an enterprise be operating efficiently if it has to take care of extra laborers who are not productive, in the sense that their marginal product has less value than the wage cost? Yet the Chinese government in the early 1980s did not extend to the state-owned enterprises complete freedom to hire and discharge workers for the purpose of achieving economic efficiency. To that extent, the marginal productivity theory fails to explain the actual hiring behavior of these enterprises. Enterprise reform in the late 1990s was introduced to remedy this deficiency by laying off some excess workers.

By encouraging private individuals to establish their own businesses and find their own employment in the early 1980s, the Chinese government was recognizing the insufficiency of the employment opportunities that it could provide and the need to supplement them with opportunities provided by individual or collective businesses. Some economists point to the increase in employment during the three decades after 1949 as evidence of the success of the Chinese government's employment program. However, this view overlooks the fact that by being a monopoly in the supply of jobs until the economic reforms, the government probably prevented millions of useful jobs from being created by individual initiatives and thus deprived millions of Chinese people of job opportunities. The government might deserve some credit in creating certain jobs if the work involved is economically productive, but one has to consider what jobs could have been created by private individuals using the resources controlled by the government. In any case, even if government job creation is economically beneficial in many instances, government monopoly of the job market cannot be optimal, for optimality would require that no individuals outside the government could have the ability to employ human resources as efficiently.

The development of a free labor market proceeded at a rapid pace in the late 1990s and the beginning of the twenty-first century. An article in *People's Daily* of January 3, 2005, reports that 40 percent of China's urban employees work as freelancers, including both white- and blue-collar jobs such as lawyers, writers, journalists, translators, maids, labor contractors, and laborers selling their services on temporary terms. There are more than 100 million such freelancers who sell their services to employers and yet do not have a long-term commitment to any of them, according to Wang Donglin, Vice-minister of Labor and Social Security. This is in sharp contrast with the situation during the prereform period, when almost all urban workers had one employer for their entire lives and could not change their jobs.

In this section we have described certain important elements in the theory of the supply of and the demand for labor. The theoretical framework is useful for empirical studies of the demand for and supply of labor in China.

## 12.3   Investment in Human Capital

The productivity of a human being may be likened to the productivity of a piece of barren land. It can be increased by investment through education, training, and healthcare. The value of human resources far exceeds that of physical resources in the form of capital goods. In the United States, for example, the total payment to labor has accounted for approximately 75 percent of national income, the remaining 25 percent being derived from payments to capital in the form of rent, profit, and interest (even profit is sometimes attributed to the return to entrepreneurship, a form of earning from human management skills). Investment in human capital is therefore very important in economic develop-ment. It has been suggested that the reason why the United States is rich is that it has an abundance of human capital, relatively more so than physical capital which is plentiful in absolute terms when compared with that of many other countries. We noted in section 12.1 that Germany and Japan recovered rapidly after the Second World War because both were heavily endowed with human capital.

The Chinese government has placed a strong emphasis on improving the educational level of the Chinese people since 1949, especially in spreading secondary education to the masses. Table 12.2 shows official data on Chinese student enrollment by level of school from 1949 to 1981. Total school enrollment increased from 54.4 million in 1952 to 194.75 million in 1981, or by somewhat less than fourfold, while population increased by less than twofold. During the same period, enrollment in institutions of higher learning increased more than sixfold; enrollment in secondary schools increased more than sixteenfold; and enrollment in primary schools increased somewhat less than threefold. The number of students per 1,000 population increased from 109.4 (71,805/656.63) in 1957 to 191.8 (194,753/1,015.41) in 1981. An important element of education in China is political indoctrination. In the early 1950s, Communist Party and Youth League organiza-tions were founded in schools to carry out political and ideological work among Chinese youth. For a description of the educational system and educational policy in China up to

**Table 12.2**  Student enrollment by level of school, 1949 to 1981 (10,000 persons)[a]

| Year | Total | Institutions of higher learning | Secondary schools[b] | | Primary schools |
|------|-------|------|------|------|------|
| | | | Secondary specialized schools | Regular secondary schools | |
| 1949 | 2,577.6 | 11.7 | 22.9 | 103.9 | 2,439.1 |
| 1950 | 3,062.7 | 13.7 | 25.7 | 130.5 | 2,892.4 |
| 1951 | 4,527.1 | 15.3 | 38.3 | 156.8 | 4,315.4 |
| 1952 | 5,443.6 | 19.1 | 63.6 | 249.0 | 5,110.0 |
| 1953 | 5,550.5 | 21.2 | 66.8 | 293.3 | 5,166.4 |
| 1954 | 5,571.7 | 25.3 | 60.8 | 358.7 | 5,121.8 |
| 1955 | 5,788.7 | 28.8 | 53.7 | 390.0 | 5,312.6 |
| 1956 | 6,987.8 | 40.3 | 81.2 | 516.5 | 6,346.6 |
| 1957 | 7,180.5 | 44.1 | 77.8 | 628.1 | 6.428.3 |
| 1958 | 9,906.1 | 66.0 | 147.0 | 852.0 | 8,640.3 |
| 1959 | 10,489.4 | 81.2 | 149.5 | 917.8 | 9,117.9 |
| 1960 | 10,962.6 | 96.2 | 221.6 | 1,026.0 | 9,379.1 |
| 1961 | 8,707.7 | 94.7 | 120.3 | 851.8 | 7,578.6 |
| 1962 | 7,840.4 | 83.0 | 53.5 | 752.8 | 6,923.9 |
| 1963 | 8,070.1 | 75.0 | 45.2 | 761.6 | 7,157.5 |
| 1964 | 10,382.5 | 68.5 | 53.1 | 854.1 | 9,294.5 |
| 1965 | 13,120.1 | 67.4 | 54.7 | 933.8 | 11,620.9 |
| 1966 | 11,691.9 | 53.4 | 47.0 | 1,249.8 | 10,341.7 |
| 1967 | 11,539.7 | 40.9 | 30.8 | 1,223.7 | 10,244.3 |
| 1968 | 11,467.3 | 25.9 | 12.8 | 1,392.3 | 10,036.3 |
| 1969 | 12,103.0 | 10.9 | 3.8 | 2,021.5 | 10,066.8 |
| 1970 | 13,181.1 | 4.8 | 6.4 | 2,641.9 | 10,528.0 |
| 1971 | 14,368.9 | 8.3 | 21.8 | 3,127.6 | 11,211.2 |
| 1972 | 16,185.3 | 19.4 | 34.2 | 3,582.5 | 12,549.2 |
| 1973 | 17,096.5 | 31.4 | 48.2 | 3,446.5 | 13,570.4 |
| 1974 | 18,238.1 | 43.0 | 63.4 | 3,650.3 | 14,481.4 |
| 1975 | 19,681.0 | 50.1 | 70.7 | 4,466.1 | 15,094.1 |
| 1976 | 20,967.5 | 56.5 | 69.0 | 5,836.5 | 15,005.5 |
| 1977 | 21,528.9 | 62.5 | 68.9 | 6,779.9 | 14,617.6 |
| 1978 | 21,346.8 | 85.6 | 88.9 | 6,548.3 | 14,624.0 |
| 1979 | 20,789.8 | 102.0 | 119.9 | 5,905.0 | 14,662.9 |
| 1980 | 20,419.2 | 114.4 | 124.3 | 5,508.1 | 14,627.0 |
| 1981 | 19,475.3 | 127.9 | 106.9 | 4,859.6 | 14,332.8 |

[a] Excludes spare-time schools.
[b] Excludes workers' training schools.
**Source**: Statistical Yearbook of China, 1981, *p. 451.*

the early 1980s, see the report by Ji Hua (1982). Chapter 21 will discuss more recent developments in China's education system and policy.

It is noteworthy from table 12.2 that during the economic collapse in 1961–2 following the Great Leap Forward, total student enrollment declined, the secondary specialized schools being most seriously affected. Also noteworthy is the reduction in enrollment in institutions of higher learning during the Cultural Revolution from 1966 to 1976, with enrollment dropping from 674,000 in 1965 to a low of 48,000 in 1970. The Cultural Revolution, as people in China know, was engineered by Mao Zedong, who had lost political power in the early 1960s as a result of the failure of the Great Leap Forward. To regain political power from the more pragmatic leadership of the Communist Party, including President Liu Shaoqi, Mao rallied Chinese youth in the name of a cultural revolution. The youths attacked local party administrative personnel and organizations and interrupted the functioning of colleges and universities. Besides the party leadership that had taken over political control of China from Mao in the early 1960s, a main target was the Chinese intellectuals, whom Mao also distrusted. Many intellectuals were sympathetic to Mao's revolutionary cause during a period of war and political disorder in the 1940s, and Mao had no hesitation in using them, because without their support the Communist movement might not have succeeded.

In 1957 Mao advocated the free expression of diverse ideas and opinions, saying "Let 100 flowers bloom"; but when some intellectuals expressed opinions highly critical of Mao's regime, they were imprisoned, sent into internal exile, removed from their jobs, or otherwise silenced. The Cultural Revolution was another occasion in which the intellectuals were victimized. Certain elements in society, including those having capitalist or feudal ideas, were identified as targets for attack. Each unit, or organization, was required to identify a certain number of these undesirable elements, and the required number were usually found. Professors and other individuals so identified were paraded on the streets carrying signs of their classification. They also had to confess their guilt in public. Such humiliations drove a large number of intellectuals to commit suicide.

From September 1966 to February 1972, all universities were closed in China. From February 1972 to the autumn of 1976, universities were open again, but admission was decided by political considerations rather than by scholastic qualifications. Youths from workers' and peasants' families having insufficient academic qualifications were assigned by their units to go to universities. The quality of instruction was below standard, and the preparation of the students was generally inadequate. Therefore, for 10 years from September 1966 to September 1976, college education in China practically stopped. The disruptive effect on the formation of human capital was tremendous. From table 12.2 we can estimate roughly that at least 700,000 to 800,000 students of college age did not receive a college education for 10 years, and note that the enrollment in institutions of higher learning was as high as 947,000 in 1961, a figure regained only after 1979. In the meantime, most of the teaching staff in colleges and universities could not continue their research and learning. In addition, more than 100 million primary and middle-school students were receiving low-quality education, as the Cultural Revolution interrupted education at the lower levels as well.

To get a rough estimate of the economic loss caused by this interruption of the educational process, note that the value of one year of education would include not only the direct cost of providing the education (tuition, subsidies to the school, and the like) but also the forgone earnings of one year's work by the individual, for these are the costs of education. For example, in choosing to spend one year in college rather than working, an individual must figure that the present value of that year's education, in terms of the increase in future earnings, should at least equal the wage that he or she could earn plus the tuition and other direct costs of education during that year. From the social point of view, the Chinese government, by putting a person through college for one year rather than assigning him or her to work, must figure that the present value of that year's education as measured by the increase in the individual's future productivity should at least equal his or her forgone product plus the direct cost of education during that year. In fact, the value of education often turns out to be larger than given by the above calculation, because investment in education has been found to yield higher returns than investment in physical assets. Estimates of the rate of return to college and high school education in the United States can be found in Becker (1964, chs. 4 and 6). Using this calculation, we can conclude that the economic loss to China is at least equal to that of putting some 700,000 to 800,000 persons with college education and a large fraction of 100 million persons with primary or secondary education out of work for 10 years, plus the waste in teachers' time and the physical and other human resources tied up with the educational institutions for 10 years. China will not recover from this loss for many decades to come.

After 1977 the Chinese educational system returned fairly rapidly to a normal state, granted the loss of qualified teachers due to the Cultural Revolution. How efficient is the Chinese system in promoting investment in human capital? Let us consider both the demand for and the supply of educational services. In a market economy individuals choose to get educated because the monetary and psychic returns to education at least cover the costs of education, including the forgone earnings and the direct costs paid while in school. As Becker (1964: 1) writes:

> Some activities primarily affect future well-being; the main impact of others is in the present. Some affect money income and others psychic income, that is, consumption. Sailing primarily affects consumption, on-the-job training primarily affects money income, and a college education could affect both. These effects may operate either through physical resources or through human resources. This study is concerned with activities that influence future monetary and psychic income by increasing the resources in people. These activities are called investments in human capital.
>
> The many forms of such investments include schooling, on-the-job training, medical care, migration, and searching for information about prices and incomes. They differ in their effects on earnings and consumption, in the amounts typically invested, in the size of returns, and in the extent to which the connection between investment and return is perceived. But all these investments improve skills, knowledge, or health, and thereby raise money or psychic incomes.
>
> Recent years have witnessed intensive concern with and research on investment in human capital, much of it contributed or stimulated by T. W. Schultz. The main motivating factor

has probably been a realization that the growth of physical capital, at least as conventionally measured, explains a relatively small part of the growth of income in most countries. The search for better explanations has led to improved measures of physical capital and to an interest in less tangible entities, such as technological change and human capital . . .

From the economic point of view, an individual decides to invest in himself or herself according to the same principle that he or she uses to invest in physical assets. In investing in physical assets, an individual estimates the extra future revenues to be derived from this asset and discounts them by the rate of interest to calculate their present value. If the present value is larger than the present cost of the investment, the investment will be undertaken. Equivalently, the rate of return to the investment is the rate of interest that would make the present value of the extra income stream equal to the present cost of the investment. When the rate of return so calculated is higher than the market rate of interest used to compute the present value, it means that the present value is larger than the cost of the investment. In the case of investment in human capital through education and training, the individual also compares the present value of the extra future monetary and psychic incomes to be derived from the education with the cost of education. The total cost of education includes the direct costs (tuition, fees, and so on) and the earnings forgone by not working while receiving the education, which is the opportunity cost of the individual's time. Again, the rate of return to education is that rate of discount that would equate the cost of education with the present value of the extra monetary and psychic income resulting from education. When the future returns are raised, people will invest more in education, just as in the case of investing in physical assets. An interesting topic is the social return to education. In our rough estimate of the value of the loss of human capital during the Cultural Revolution earlier in this section, we assumed that the increase in the value of human capital to society due to education is at least equal to its total cost. To estimate the social value of education empirically is not an easy task. However, the study of the private return to education is important because the return affects the demand for education by private citizens.

In China the incentive to invest in human capital – that is, the demand for education – has been affected by the limited opportunities available to individuals after receiving the education. As discussed previously, the choice of one's major field of concentration, employment opportunities (including the nature of the work and the location of the job), and the possibilities of advancement and of receiving a high income are all limited by government policy, which attempts to restrict, control, and direct individual actions. Such restrictive policies and practices dampen the individual's incentives to get an education. As a farmer is unwilling to invest in physical capital for his farm unless he can earn a healthy return by such an investment, a young person is unwilling to expend energy to get educated unless the education will enable him or her to earn additional monetary and psychic incomes in the future. By limiting the individual's economic opportunities, the government in effect discourages him or her from getting educated. This partly explains why so many young people in China had low morale and drifted aimlessly. On the positive side, since 1979 some Chinese students and scholars have been allowed to study or to receive additional training abroad. Some 8,000 of them were in the United States in the early 1980s and the number has increased steadily. By and large, they were well motivated, and their performance has been extremely impressive. One explanation is that these people were carefully selected for their past achievements and high motivation. Another explanation is that these people realized that future opportunities would be open to them at home and abroad to utilize the additional education and training received abroad. Large investments in human capital are crucial for rapid economic development. The demand for such investments will be limited if people are not given the opportunities to benefit freely from such investments.

To turn now to the supply of educational services: The Chinese government has succeeded in expanding educational facilities at all levels, as evidenced by the large increases in student enrollment shown in table 12.2 and commented on earlier. Ji Hua (1982: 743–4), of the Chinese Ministry of Education, reports that soon after the Communist government gained control over China in 1949, it took over all public and private schools and merged them with missionary schools that had been financed by foreign subsidies, and established control over all schools.

> After 1952, the institutes of higher learning and their departments were reorganized, teaching reforms were introduced and the unified college enrollment system and system of assigning college graduates were adopted. In this way, higher education was brought under the control of state planning . . . Chinese schools at all levels formulated for each subject matter a set of teaching plans, a syllabus and textbooks – all of them geared basically to actual conditions in China. In 1961, . . . we worked out three sets of basic rules for schools: the "Draft Provisional Regulations Concerning the Work in Institutes of Higher Learning Directly under the Ministry of Education" (which became "Sixty Regulations for Institutes of Higher Learning"); the "Draft Provisional Regulations Concerning the Work in Full-time Middle Schools" (which became the "Fifty Regulations for Middle Schools"); and the "Draft Provisional Regulations Concerning the Work in Full-time Primary Schools" (which became the "Fifty Regulations for Primary Schools") . . .

The most important characteristic of the supply of education in China is that practically all educational services (outside the family) are provided and controlled by the government. Before 1949 many primary and middle schools were private, as were some of the best colleges and universities. It is difficult for an educator associated with a successful private university to appreciate a government's policy of monopolizing the supply of education. To say the least, the failure to allow the establishment of private universities and educational institutions at lower levels must have deprived the Chinese of a large supply of educational services that would have been forthcoming from private resources. In 1980 a Hong Kong alumnus of Lingnan University previously located in Canton (now Guangzhou) offered a contribution of US$10 million if that university could be reopened. This gift was not accepted. On an encouraging note, by 1982, private individuals had already begun to establish vocational schools on a limited scale in some cities in China. The private Tianjin United University was founded by a group of alumni of United, Beijing, Qinghua, Zhejiang, and Yenjing universities and opened in September 1983 with an enrollment of approximately 1,200 part-time students, who were staff and workers in Chinese enterprises. It offered 14 concentrations in the humanities, natural sciences, law, engineering, medicine, and economics. Government monopoly of education may be gradually abandoned in the future for the sake of economic development.

Since the establishment of formal diplomatic relations with the United States in January 1979, the government of the People's Republic of China has sent students and visiting scholars to the United States and other Western countries to study and to receive additional training. Even allowing for the possibility that some students might not return to China, this investment will contribute significantly to increasing the stock of human capital in China. Perhaps the increase will eventually outweigh the tremendous loss of human capital that occurred when the large majority of Chinese students and scholars visiting the United States and other Western countries in 1949, when the new regime was established, decided not to return home. We will devote chapter 21 to a discussion of China's education system and policy. Much of the material of this section was written in 1984 and helps to highlight the problems facing the formation of human capital at the time. Chapter 21 incorporates developments up to the year 2000 so that the reader can appreciate the difference in perspectives and the progress made.

Emigration, like the lack of incentive to get educated, contributes to a loss in human capital for a society. Both can result from restrictive government policies. In spite of strong measures to prevent emigration, millions of Chinese did escape to Hong Kong, where the Chinese population increased from about 1 million in 1948 to over 5 million in the late 1970s. Many emigrants to Hong Kong continue to migrate to the rest of the world. Before 1949, when movement of the Chinese population between Hong Kong and mainland China was completely free, there had been no large influx of population to Hong Kong. Migration is considered by economists as a form of investment in human capital on the part of the individual doing the migrating, because it increases the present value of the future earnings of individuals involved. Emigration from China helps raise the personal earnings of the emigrants. Migration within China by individuals seeking better job opportunities would raise both the earnings of the individuals and Chinese national income. When a laborer receiving a monthly wage of 50 yuan in the countryside (measuring the value of his marginal product there) moves to a city to earn a monthly wage of 90 yuan, not only his monthly income increases by 40 yuan, but the monthly national income of China increases by 40 yuan as well. The value of his human capital as the discounted present value of his future earnings will increase accordingly. Thus the restriction of labor mobility within China could be considered an obstruction to investment in human capital.

If educated Chinese people migrate abroad to seek a better life, it is described as a "brain drain." Brain drain is considered a loss to the "country" from which these people migrate. The "loss" needs to be qualified in three senses. The first comes from the definition of the word "country." If the country is defined as a collection of nationals and the emigrants are among the nationals, then the improvement in the welfare of these nationals is beneficial to the country. The validity of this point depends on one's concept of a "country." In the United States, where individualism is considered a virtue and the country is no more than what the citizens wish it to be for their self-interest, the above proposition is valid. If the country is viewed as a collective unit having a life of its own and the citizens are supposed to serve the country more than themselves, then this proposition has less validity. Second, to regard the emigration of educated people as a loss is short sighted. When the conditions of the country improve many of these people will return with the knowledge and experience acquired abroad and will benefit the home country. This has happened to many people from Taiwan who have returned home from the United States since the 1990s. Third, even when the Chinese-educated emigrants are staying abroad many of them are helping China in various ways. As professors in American universities they visit China during their holidays to teach and promote research and work on projects useful for China in their spare time. Other professionals are equally helpful. In the 1980s I established programs with the Chinese State Education Commission to help hundreds of graduate students from China to go to graduate schools to study economics in the United States and Canada (see section 21.4.1). Many have their doctoral degrees, but only a small number have returned to China as of 2001.

Besides schooling and migration, another form of investment in human capital is on-the-job training. In a market economy such as that of the United States, on-the-job training is provided by private enterprises. General training improves the skills that are useful to many other firms, besides the employer-firm providing it, and its cost is mostly borne by the employee-trainees. Specific training improves the skills that are useful only to the firm providing it, and its cost is mostly borne by the employer. Becker (1964, ch. 2) provides a theoretical discussion of both types of on-the-job training and other forms of investment in human capital. In China, on-the-job training is provided in many state-owned enterprises. The Chinese government has an extensive program to improve the skills of workers, as reported in an article by Zheng Ji (1982) of the Policy Research Department of the State Bureau of Labor.

According to Zheng (1982: 699–700), the labor departments and some large factories and mines have set up many vocational training schools. Between 1949 and 1980 some 1.43 million students were trained in these schools. The government also established a new apprenticeship system, which was a modification of the old system under which the majority of China's skilled workers were trained. The system of vocational training was interrupted during the Cultural Revolution of 1966–76. Vocational schools were restored afterward, with enrollment rising to 680,000 in 1980.

The students spend half of their time in school workshops or in productive enterprises to receive on-the-job training, and the other half in classes for general and technical education ... In recent years, more than one million apprentices have been enrolled each year in industrial enterprises owned by the state. The duration varies from trade to trade and from profession to profession. In general, it lasts three years; at a minimum, no less than two years.

Vocational training of on-the-job workers is mainly provided by the enterprises, which will draw up plans and train workers systematically in accordance with their own production needs and with the workers' technical competence. Enterprises generally set up a special office to deal with this matter. On-the-job training is provided in various forms. Different forms are used for different trades and workers, and training may be full-time, part-time or spare-time. Workers are paid basic wages during the period of training, and receive rewards for exemplary results. (p. 700)

# 12.4    Measuring the Rates of Return to Schooling in China

Given that investment in human capital is important for economic development, what motivates people to invest in human capital, to receive more education and training, or to acquire more knowledge and skills? People try to get educated for various reasons, some financial and some nonfinancial. The latter includes the enjoyment of being able to read Tang poetry or Shakespeare or to appreciate classical music. The economic reason is to be able to earn a higher income. To the extent that the economic reason is operating, it is important to find out how much more income one can earn by additional education, that is, to measure the rate of return to education. The rate of return to an asset, such as a bank deposit or a stock, is the percentage increase in its value during a given period. If you put $100 in the bank and find your deposit increased to $105, then the rate of return to your investment is 5 percent per year. In a similar manner consider yourself as possessing human assets (human capital). Assume that your human capital is worth $1 million now. $1 million is the present value of your lifetime earnings from your human capital and excludes the earnings from the physical assets that you own. If by going to school for one year you find your human capital worth $1.05 million one year later, then the rate of return to human capital in your case is 5 percent in a year. Here we assume that without the additional year of education your wage next year would be the same as this year, and in fact that the future wage profile of your whole life would be the same as if it started a year later, so that your human capital next year would be worth $1 million instead of 1.05 million. In this calculation of the rate of return, we include in the cost of investment only the time you lose by getting your wage profile one year later and ignore the cost of tuition.

Having clarified the meaning of the rate of return to investment in human capital by schooling, we can measure the percentage change in wage (assumed to be proportional to the discounted present value of human capital) resulting from one additional year of schooling. Using regression analysis, the dependent variable is log wage since the change in log measures percentage change. The independent variables are the number of years $S$ of schooling and other relevant variables. Mincer (1969) used years of experience $E$ and its square as two other additional variables. This regression equation was found to be a good approximation to the data in numerous studies and is known as the Mincer equation. Johnson and Chow (1997) used the Mincer equation as the basic model to fit wage data taken from the 1988 Chinese Household Income Project conducted by Keith Griffin and Zhao Renwei (1993) in cooperation with the Chinese State Statistical Bureau. There were data on individuals belonging to 10,258 urban households and 9,009 rural households. Only individuals earning the basic monthly wage are included in the study. The basic equation to be estimated is

$$\ln \text{wage} = \beta_1 + \beta_2 S + \beta_3 E + \beta_4 E^2 + \beta_5 \text{Fem} + \beta_6 \text{Com} + \beta_7 \text{Min} + u$$

where $S$ is years of schooling (6 for primary school, 12 for upper middle school, 14 for community college or professional school, and 16 for college or above), $E$ is experience

**Table 12.3**  Estimates of wage equations

|        | $\beta_1$ | $\beta_2$ | $\beta_3$ | $\beta_4$ | $\beta_5$ | $\beta_6$ | $\beta_7$ |
|--------|-----------|-----------|-----------|-----------|-----------|-----------|-----------|
| Rural  | 3.990     | 0.0402    | 0.0195    | −0.0002   | −0.0748   | −0.0454   | −0.1937   |
|        | (.0732)   | (.0059)   | (.0040)   | (.0001)   | (.0345)   | (.0427)   | (.0856)   |
| Urban  | 3.695     | 0.0329    | 0.0449    | −0.0006   | −0.0902   | 0.0680    | −0.0445   |
|        | (.0173)   | (.0010)   | (.0010)   | (.0000)   | (.0060)   | (.0066)   | (.0130)   |
| Pooled | 3.744     | 0.0320    | 0.0419    | −0.0005   | −0.0850   | 0.0629    | −0.1183   |
|        | (.0175)   | (.0011)   | (.0010)   | (.0000)   | (.0062)   | (.0070)   | (.0495)   |

($age - S - 6$), and Fem, Com, and Min are respectively dummy variables taking the value 1 if the person is a female, a Communist Party member, and/or a member of an ethnic minority (other than Han). There are 17,261 individuals from urban and 1,677 individuals from rural households in the sample. The estimates are given in table 12.3.

From estimating the rural and urban regressions separately, the rates of return per year to investment in schooling are estimated to be 4.02 percent for the rural sample and 3.29 percent for the urban sample. Both rates of return are very low as compared with estimates for other developing economies which are in the order of 10 percent or higher. One explanation is that in the year 1988 the wage scales of China were determined to a large extent by nonmarket forces and influenced by the wage structure which had been set under central planning. Another possible explanation is that for urban workers other benefits than wage, such as the amount of subsidized housing, are not included in the dependent variables. If these explanations are ruled out and wages in 1988 were determined by marginal products as in other market economies, then the results would mean that an additional year of schooling contributed only little to the productivity of the individual. The accuracy of the estimates for the rural sample as indicated by their standard errors in parentheses is much lower than for the urban sample mainly because of its relatively smaller sample size.

Among other noteworthy results recorded above, the coefficient of experience squared is negative as expected, since as a person gets older than the most productive age his wage declines. Being a female reduces one's wage by about 7.5 percent (with a large standard error) for a rural worker and by 9.0 percent (with a standard error of 0.6 percent) for an urban worker. Being a member of the Communist Party increases the wage of an urban worker by 6.8 percent (with a standard error of 0.66 percent) but its effect on the wage of a rural worker cannot be accurately estimated. Being a minority (other than Han) reduces a rural worker's wage by 19.4 percent (with a standard error of 8.5 percent) and an urban worker's wage by 4.5 percent (with a standard error of 1.3 percent).

The study also pooled the rural and urban data to run two pooled regressions. In a pooled regression all rural and urban data are used to estimate the coefficients of all other independent variables under the assumption that these coefficients are identical for both rural and urban individuals. The first pooled regression assumes the coefficient of $S$ is also identical for both groups. It gives 0.0334 (.0011) as the estimate of the rate of return for both samples. The second pooled regression allows for two different rates of return for rural and urban workers while assuming all other coefficients in the regression to be the same. To allow for the two different rates one uses a simple algebraic device by adding the product of $S$ and a rural dummy as an additional independent variable. The product is zero for urban workers since the dummy variable is zero. The coefficient of $S$ thus measures the rate of return for the urban sample. For the rural sample the rate of return is the coefficient of $S$ plus the coefficient of this product.

This second pooled regression is reported above, which omitted the coefficient 0.0162 (0.0054) of this product variable. The coefficient of $S$ in this regression is 0.0320 (.0011). The estimate 0.0320 is the rate of return to schooling for urban workers, and the sum 0.0320 + 0.0162 is the rate of return to schooling for rural workers, the difference in the rates of return being 0.0162. One possible explanation of this difference is that the wage structure in rural areas in 1988 was closer to being market determined than in urban areas. In rural areas, there were township and village enterprises which might be paying wages closer to market wages. The interpretations of the other coefficients are as given for the two separate regressions. There is another coefficient (not reported above) for the rural dummy variable equal to −0.1183 (.0495), showing that rural wages are about 12 percent lower than urban wages. This might reflect the difference in the cost of living in the rural and urban areas. As the Chinese economy and its wage structure become more nearly market determined, one can expect that similar regressions will yield a high rate of return to schooling.

## 12.5   Health Services

Another form of investment in human capital is the improvement of health. Since 1949 the Chinese government has had an extensive program to improve the health of the Chinese people. One indicator of the improvement achieved is the decline in the annual death rate from 17 per 1,000 in 1952 to 6.34 per 1,000 in 1980, as shown in table 11.1. Wei Zhi (1982), of the Ministry of Public Health, reports that such infectious diseases as plague, smallpox, venereal diseases, kalazar, recurrent fever, and typhus have been successively eradicated or brought under control. While schistosomiasis was once prevalent in 347 counties of 12 provinces and more than 10 million people suffered from this disease in an area of 13,000 square miles infested with snails, in the past 31 years snails have been wiped out in two-thirds of the affected areas and two-thirds of the sufferers have been cured. The incidence of malaria has been greatly reduced. Keshan disease, Kaschin-Beck disease, and endemic fluorosis have been partly controlled. The incidence of acute infectious diseases such as poliomyelitis, measles, diphtheria, pertussis, and tetanus in newborn infants has decreased considerably. Mortality caused by respiratory diseases, digestive diseases, and acute infectious diseases has dropped, and chronic, noninfectious conditions – heart and cerebrovascular diseases and malignant tumors – have become the leading causes of death. Wei writes:

Much has been done with regard to environmental, industrial, food, and school hygiene, as well as health protection from radiation. Since 1971, systematic tests and surveys have been carried out on the water quality of five big water systems, including 177 rivers, five lakes and six bays, and on the air quality in 75 cities, producing 730,000 items of scientific data. We have organized several nationwide campaigns for screening and treating occupational diseases . . .

In the past 31 years, 406,000 students have graduated from higher medical colleges . . . From 1949 to 1980, the number of medical and health institutions rose from 3,600 to 181,000, an increase of 49.2 times; hospital beds from 80,000 to 1,982,000, an increase of 24.8 times; and professional medical and health workers from 541,000 to 3,535,000, an increase of 6.5 times. Among the latter, health technicians increased from 505,000 to 2,798,000, an increase of 5.5 times; and physicians from 360,000 to 1,153,000, an increase of 3.2 times. From 1949 to 1980, based on the average number for every thousand persons, hospital beds increased from 0.15 to 2.02, health technicians from 0.93 to 2.85, and physicians from 0.67 to 1.17. (pp. 753–4)

The *Statistical Yearbook of China, 1981* (p. 477), shows that of the 3.535 million health workers in health institutions in 1980, 2.798 million were classified as medical personnel, among whom 1.153 million were physicians, 0.466 million were nurses, and 1.179 million were other medical personnel. The medical personnel here listed excluded part-time health workers in urban and rural areas. Among the physicians, 262,000 were doctors of traditional Chinese medicine, 447,000 were senior doctors of Western medicine, and 444,000 were junior doctors of Western medicine who had received two to three years of training after high school. In 1980 there were also 1.463 million rural "barefoot doctors" among the part-time health workers in rural areas. The main difference between medical services in China and in the United States is the low cost and the associated lower quality of medical services in China. Concerning the training of physicians and other health workers, China is willing to use a large number of physicians, some with much less training than physicians in the United States receive. As a result, many people in China are able to obtain fairly inexpensive medical service. In the United States, doctors are often too well trained for the common illnesses they treat, as there are restrictions which prevent less-trained physicians from practicing. The quality of other medical services, including services provided in hospitals, is also much higher in the United States. Much of the new equipment for health examinations and health care is very expensive. It is very costly to provide the best care with a minimum risk to all patients. The cost of medical care can be reduced tremendously by lowering the quality and increasing the risk to the patients slightly, as is done in China.

William Hsiao (1983) points out that China provides healthcare through a three-tier system that is managed and financed locally. In the first tier, the part-time bare-foot doctors provide preventive and primary care. For more serious illnesses, they refer patients to the second tier: commune health centers, which may have 10 to 30 beds and an outpatient clinic serving a population of 10,000 to 25,000, and which are staffed by junior doctors. The most seriously ill patients are referred by the commune health centers to the third tier: county hospitals staffed with senior doctors. The cooperative medical system that organizes the barefoot doctors and provides other medical services to the rural population is part of the commune system and is financed by the communes' welfare funds.

Thus the CMS served the dual role of a supplier and a collector of insurance funds for the farmers to pay for the services. Healthcare can be adequately supplied in a planned economy if the planning authority, as represented by the Commune leaders in the present case, controls all resources to produce healthcare, including capital facilities, personnel, and medical supplies.

After economic reforms in agriculture the above healthcare system collapsed as the system of Communes collapsed. Publicly provided healthcare became the responsibility of the local governments which, in poor regions, did not have the financial resources from taxation to supply adequate healthcare. The facilities and services deteriorated. Barefoot doctors found it more profitable to work full-time in farming or to set up private practices outside the system. As the incomes of farmers increased the demand for better-quality medical care increased. With limited supply, prices went up. The low-income farmers cannot afford to pay for healthcare of the same quality as was previously supplied under the collectively financed CMS.

In the words of the World Bank (1997, p. 3): "The shift away from a communal system deprived the rural cooperative medical system of its sources of community-based financing. As communes gradually disappeared, so did the cooperative medical system. Only about 10 percent of the rural population is now covered by some form of community-financed healthcare, down from a peak of 85 percent in 1975. (There is much variation in coverage among provinces, however, because of differences in interpretation of national policy.) As a result, some 700 million rural Chinese must pay out of pocket for virtually all health services. Without insurance, medical expenses can lead to deferral of care, untreated illness, financial catastrophe, and poverty."

For the urban population, before economic reform, health centers and hospitals associated with state-owned enterprises and other government institutions cared for the employees and their family members. With urban economic reform in the 1990s, state-owned enterprises were made financially independent and downsized. State enterprises and other government organizations had difficulty in financing the healthcare of their employees. During this period, along with the restructuring of the state enterprises to become share-holding companies that are to be relieved from their burden to provide welfare support to their employees and their families, the Chinese government was in the process of establishing a medical insurance system to replace the previous system. Under the new insurance system introduced in 1998, in addition to a government contribution, the employer contributes 6 percent and the employee contributes 2 percent of his wage. The large number of nonstate enterprises can also participate in this insurance system or can afford to pay wages to their employees that are sufficient for them to be self-insured. In other words, the government has instituted a new insurance system to pay for healthcare for the urban population after the gradual reform of the state enterprises, but has not provided a similar insurance system for the rural population after the rapid privatization of farming.

Besides government neglect, the second reason for the rural population to receive much less adequate healthcare is their low income, since between 50 to 60 percent of health expenditure is individual (see Chow, 2007). In 2002, the per capita consumption expenditure of the middle income group among urban households was 5,452.94 yuan, about 3.3 times the corresponding figure of 1,645.04 yuan for rural households. The ratio of the mean net urban income per capita of 7,730.3 yuan to rural income per capita of 2,476 yuan in 2002 is 3.11 (see the *China Statistical Yearbook 2004*, table 10-1). Table 3 of Chow (2007) also shows how much more the urban residents spent on medicine and medical services in 2002 than the urban population. As a result of government neglect and income disparity the rural population receives much less healthcare than the urban population in China. This is one of the most important social-economic problems in the country. For a discussion of the problem of rural poverty in general see Chow (2006).

When the demand for and supply of healthcare in China is studied in Chow (2007), it is found that income elasticity of demand is about unity for both the urban and rural populations, and price elasticity is about 0.63; and that the supply of healthcare as measured by per capita expenditure in constant prices, by the number of hospital beds or the number of doctors and other hospital personnel per 1,000 population, remained about constant between 1989 and 2004. Given a rapid increase in demand generated by an increase in income and a constant supply, the price of healthcare in China has increased rapidly since the late 1980s. The failure to increase supply can be traced to the public supply of healthcare. An experiment to privatize healthcare in Suqian City, Jiangsu, between 2000 and 2005 demonstrated conclusively that allowing a private supply can lead to rapid increase in the supply and to lower prices. It is hoped that the Chinese government will give up its conception that healthcare should be publicly supplied and adopt economic reforms similar to that of Suqian by allowing or even encouraging the establishment of private hospitals. The public supply of healthcare is the most striking example in China's reform toward a market economy of a traditional idea from the period of economic planning surviving into the present.

## 12.6   The Social Welfare System

Since the mid-1990s, the Chinese government has attempted to set up step by step a nationally unified social security system for the urban population, under the central management of the labor and social security administration departments, and with social insurance funds partly contributed by central government. Labor and social security departments at all levels are responsible for the collection, management, and payment of the social insurance funds. Besides contributions from employers and employees, central government allocated 98.2 billion yuan in 2001 for social security payments, 5.18 times the amount in 1998, as it was expanding the system to cover larger segments of the population in steps. (All statistics on the development of the social security system can be found in the website of *The People's Daily*, http://english.peopledaily.com.cn/, under "White Paper on Labor and Social Security in China" in the section "White Papers of the Chinese Government.")

In 1997, a uniform, basic old-age insurance system for enterprise employees was established, financed by 20 percent of the enterprise wage bill and 8 percent of the employee's wage. A part of the premiums from enterprise goes to mutual assistance funds and the rest to personal accounts, while the premiums from the employees go entirely to personal accounts that belong to the employees themselves and can be inherited. Employees participating in this program increased from 86.71 million in late 1997 to 108.02 million at the end of 2001, while the number receiving pensions increased from 25.33 million to 33.81 million, with the average monthly basic pension per person increasing from 430 yuan to 556 yuan. The rural population pay their own insurance premiums and withdraw funds from personal accounts with subsidies from the government.

In 1999, an unemployment insurance system was introduced, financed by 2 percent of the wage bill paid by employers and 1 percent paid by employees. Unemployment insurance benefits are lower than the minimum wage but higher than the minimum living allowance guaranteed for all laid-off workers. The period of drawing insurance depends on the length of the period in which insurance payments have been paid, with 24 months as the maximum. The number of persons insured increased from 79.28 million in 1998 to 103.55 million in 2001.

On healthcare, important policies were announced on January 15, 1997, in the "Decision on Health Reform and Development by the Central Party Committee and State Council." The basic objective of the Decision is to ensure that every Chinese will have access to basic health protection. For the rural population the strategy is to develop and improve the Cooperative Medical System (CMS) through education, by mobilizing more farmers to participate and gradually expanding its coverage. For urban employees a basic medical insurance system was established in 1998, financed by 6 percent of the wage bill of employing units and 2 percent of the personal wages. By the end of 2001, 76.29 million employees had participated in basic insurance programs. In addition, free medical services and other forms of healthcare systems covered over 100 million of the urban population. The establishment of a health insurance system is concerned with the demand side of health services. On the supply side, in 2004 the government is in the process of allowing a few hospitals in urban and rural areas to be run privately to reduce the burden on the government. But the stated government policy is still public supply of healthcare.

In terms of saving for old age, the urban population have their own personal accounts with amounts depending on their own contributions. Their old age insurance system has features similar to the pension system in American universities, with both the employer and the employee contributing to the fund, and with each employee having his personal account. The rural population in China have more freedom to choose their work but are not guaranteed unemployment benefits like urban workers. Many of them are not provided with adequate healthcare, although it is the stated policy of the Chinese government to provide basic healthcare for the entire population.

# References and Further Reading

Becker, Gary S. *Human Capital*. New York: National Bureau of Economic Research, 1964.
Chow, Gregory C. "Rural Poverty in China: Problem and Policy." Princeton University Center for Economic Policy Discussion Paper No. 134, Sept. 2006.
Chow, Gregory C. "An Institutional and Economic Analysis of Health Care in China." *World Development*, forthcoming 2007.

Chow, Gregory C. and Anloh Lin. "Accounting for Economic Growth in Taiwan and Mainland China: A Comparative Analysis." *Journal of Comparative Economics*, forthcoming.

Griffin, K. and Renwei Zhao. *The Distribution of Income in China*. New York: St. Martin's Press, 1993.

Hicks, J. R. *Value and Capital*, 2nd ed. London: Oxford University Press, 1946.

Hsiao, W. "Transformation of Health Care to 800 Millions." Mimeo. Boston: School of Public Health, Harvard University, 1983.

Ji Hua. "Education in China." In *Almanac of China's Economy, 1981*. Hong Kong: Modern Cultural Company Ltd., 1982.

Johnson, Emily and Gregory Chow. "Rates of Return to Schooling in China." *Pacific Economic Review*, 2 (June 1997), pp. 101–13.

Mincer, Jacob. "Schooling, Age, and Earnings." *Human Capital and Personal Income Distribution*. New York: National Bureau of Economic Research, 1969.

Rees, A. *The Economics of Work and Play*. New York: Harper and Row, 1979.

Schultz, T. W. "Investment in Human Capital." *American Economic Review*, 51 (March 1961), pp. 1–17.

Solow, Robert M. "A Contribution to the Theory of Economic Growth." *Quarterly Journal of Economics*, 70 (1956), pp. 65–94.

Solow, Robert M. "Technological Progress and the Aggregate Production Function." *Review of Economics and Statistics*, 39 (1957), pp. 312–20.

Wei Zhi. "China's Health Services." In *Almanac of China's Economy, 1981*. Hong Kong: Modern Cultural Company Ltd., 1982.

Zheng Ji. "Employment, Wages, Workers' Welfare and Labor Protection in China." In *Almanac of China's Economy, 1981*. Hong Kong: Modern Cultural Company Ltd., 1982.

# Questions

1   Write down an aggregate production function that incorporates human capital. How would you measure human capital in this function? What data are needed to estimate this measure of human capital?

2   Explain how the supply of labor is determined. Does this theory of labor supply apply to China? Explain your answer.

3   Explain how the demand for labor is determined. Does this theory of labor demand apply to China? Explain your answer.

4   What factors affect the aggregate level of investment in human capital in China?

5   What is the Mincer equation for determining the wage of a person? How is this equation used to determine the rate of return to schooling?

6   What were the rates of return to schooling in China for rural and urban workers in 1988? How do these rates compare with those for developing countries in general? What might explain the difference?

7   To estimate the rates of return to schooling for rural and urban workers a researcher can perform two regressions using the rural and urban data separately, or perform one regression by pooling both sets of data. Explain the meaning of pooled regression. Which method would you prefer? Why?

# Part IV
## Analysis of Individual Sectors

# 13

# The Banking and Financial System

Commercial banks will be discussed first in section 13.1, to be followed by a discussion of the People's Bank in section 13.2. Factors affecting the functioning of the banking system will be examined in section 13.3. Possible weaknesses of the banking system and possible directions for reform are subjects of sections 13.4 and 13.5 respectively. Section 13.6 discusses some of the financial problems facing the banking system including the large amount of bad loans. Other financial institutions are the subject of section 13.7. We end this chapter by discussing the role of the Chinese government in reforming the financial system.

## 13.1  Commercial Banks

As pointed out in section 3.5, before economic reform began in 1978, China's banking was performed by the People's Bank and its branch banks. The main function of the People's Bank was to supply currency in circulation and funds (credits) to state enterprises and other government units under the direction of central planning, and to accept savings deposits from the public, with the assistance of its branch banks in various locations. While receiving savings deposits, the branch banks did not exercise discretion in extending loans to public enterprises. Total deposits and currency were easily controlled by the People's Bank. State enterprises received investment funds and working capital according to central planning, and not through the market with commercial banks acting as a financial intermediary.

Following economic reform towards a more market-oriented economy, the People's Bank was changed to a central bank in 1983. Three specialized banks, namely, the Industrial and Commercial Bank of China, Agricultural Bank of China, and the People's Construction Bank of China were established, in addition to the Bank of China dealing with international transactions. These banks were given some autonomy in the extension of credits in the early 1980s, in the same manner that state industrial enterprises were given autonomy to make production decisions. The autonomy given led to a rapid increase in the supply of currency (since the central bank had to honor the loans extended by the specialized banks) in 1984 by 50 percent and an inflation rate of 8.8 percent of the overall retail price index in 1985. Reforms of the banking system to serve a market economy (as the Central Committee of the Chinese Communist Party declared China's economy to be a socialist market economy in October 1992) progressed gradually in the late 1980s and early 1990s. In November 1993, the Third Plenum of the Fourteenth Central Committee of the Communist Party decided to accelerate reform of the financial sector by giving more independence to the People's Bank as a central bank and transforming the specialized banks to commercial banks. Two significant dates are March 18 and May 10, 1995, when the People's Congress passed respectively the Law on the People's Bank of China (effective on the same day) and the Commercial Banking Law (effective July 1, 1995). Although there is some distance between the provisions of these laws and current practice, the laws provide a blueprint for the banking system and serve as a convenient framework for us to understand the working of the system.

Commercial banks are mainly the three previously mentioned specialized banks and the Bank of China (specializing in international transactions), owned by the state, but there are other, much smaller commercial banks. According to the Commercial Banking Law (chapter 1, article 3), the functions of the commercial banks in China are similar to those of modern commercial banks in other countries. These include accepting deposits from the public, extending credit, settling accounts in domestic and foreign currencies, discounting commercial papers, issuing own bonds, selling and trading government bonds, engaging in interbank transactions, buying and selling foreign exchange, providing credit guarantee, collecting and making payments for customers, providing insurance, safety deposit boxes, and other services which the People's Bank approves. The banks are responsible for their own profit and loss (article 4). In extending credit, they should strictly examine the creditworthiness of the borrowers and insure the payment of their debt on schedule (article 7). They should not engage in "improper" competition (article 9), although the term "improper" is not clearly defined. Banks are established by the approval of the People's Bank. Without such approval, no person or unit is allowed to accept deposits or engage in activities similar to those of the commercial banks (chapter 2, article 11). The minimum capital for a commercial bank is 1 billion RMB. It is 100,000 RMB for an urban collective commercial bank (article 13; 1 US dollar is worth about 8.3 RMB).

How well the commercial banks function depends on several factors. First is the level of competence of the managers and staff in performing the above-stated functions. Former managers of the branches of the People's Bank under central planning are not equipped to manage a modern commercial bank. Former staff of the same banks are ill-equipped to examine the creditworthiness of potential borrowers and evaluate the risks of their proposed projects. Much education and training are required to improve the quality of the personnel of the commercial banks. The leadership in the People's Bank has been fully aware of this need and attempted to provide training for its staff and the staff of the commercial banks. Related to competence is the mentality of the staff. In the period of central planning, good service to customers was not practiced, and perhaps considered a nuisance to the provider. Incentives are needed to change the attitude of the staff.

Second is the internal structure of incentives provided for the commercial bank managers and staff. Some managers were appointed through the influence of local party leaders and might be obliged to approve loans to serve the interest of these leaders, either for personal gain or for the development of the local economy at the expense of the national interest. The system of rewards may not be conducive to good management. Marginal financial and nonfinancial reward to management and staff may not be sufficient to cover the marginal cost of hard work, honesty, abstaining from favoritism, and risk-taking.

Third is the external structure of incentives and rewards to the managers and staff. By external I mean factors coming outside of the internal organization and wage structure of the commercial bank itself. These include policies and stipulations by the central bank and morals and customs of the Chinese bureaucracy and society in general. For example, by placing a low ceiling on the interest rate that a commercial bank can charge on its loans and requiring it to pay high interest rates on deposits of different maturities, the People's Bank may force commercial bank managers to seek risky investment opportunities or to restrict the quantity of certain types of deposits. The degree of corruption, in the form of receiving side payments for extending loans for example, is influenced by social sanction and the severity of punishment, in addition to the economic power granted to the banking bureaucrats.

I have mentioned three factors which affect the functioning of a commercial bank in China. There is room for improvement in all three. To get a picture of how well the commercial banks have worked from a macroeconomic perspective, we note that the amount of demand deposits as a percentage of Gross Domestic Product has increased from 30.7 percent in 1985, to 33.2 percent in 1990, and to 35.7 percent in 1995. (For GDP figures, see World Bank, 1996, table 1, p. 72; for demand deposits, see ibid., p. 85, table 14.) The ratio of quasi-money (M2 − M1, consisting mainly of savings deposits) to GDP increased from 16.3 percent in 1985, to 35.1 percent in 1990, and to 76.1 percent in 1995 (see ibid., p. 85). Thus the commercial banks have been providing an outlet for savings during these years in increasing ratios to national income, in spite of their institutional weaknesses. On the credit side of the banks' balance sheet, the ratios of loans to enterprises and individuals to GDP in 1985, 1990, and 1995 were respectively 0.702, 0.893, and 1.082 (see ibid., table 14, p. 85). The commercial banks have been serving as financial intermediaries, although in 1995 many were operating at a loss because of the regulated high interest on time deposits and low interest on loans.

## 13.2  The People's Bank

The objectives of the People's Bank are to formulate and carry out monetary policy, improve macroeconomic regulation, and exercise control over financial enterprises and markets (chapter 1, article 1 of the Law on the People's Bank). The People's Bank is a central bank under the direction of the Executive Council (article 2). It is therefore a part of the executive branch of the Chinese government and does not have the independent authority exercised by the Federal Reserve Bank of the United States. The objectives of monetary policy are to stabilize the value of the currency and in doing so to promote economic growth (article 3). By article 4, the Bank's responsibilities are to (1) formulate and carry out monetary policy, (2) issue the People's currency and manage its circulation, (3) approve, manage, and supervise monetary institutions, (4) supervise and manage the financial markets, (5) issue rules and orders for the regulation of monetary institutions, (6) manage the reserves of foreign exchange and gold for the government, (7) manage government financial accounts, (8) ensure the normal functioning of the payment and clearance system, (9) provide statistical data, surveys, analysis, and forecasts of the financial sector, (10) serve as the country's central bank, and engage in international financial activities; and perform other duties as decided upon by the State Council. Note that there is no mention of deposit insurance for commercial banks, perhaps because the Chinese people have confidence that their deposits in the state-owned commercial banks are implicitly insured by the state. In 2003 the China Banking Regulatory Commission was formed to take over supervisory functions (3) to (5) listed above, perhaps because in the Chinese institutional context banks and other financial bodies require a separate organization in the State Council to supervise.

The People's Bank is to determine the quantity of money supply, the rates of interest, the exchange rate and related matters subject to the approval of the State Council, but can execute other decisions under its jurisdiction independently before reporting to the State Council (article 5). It provides reports of the states of monetary policy and of financial supervision to the People's Congress (article 6). It is independent of the interference of provincial and local governments and their administrative units and of any social organizations and individuals (article 7). Its capital is entirely supplied by the state and is owned by the state (article 8). The President of the People's Bank is nominated by the Prime Minister, approved by the People's Congress, and appointed by the President of the People's Republic of China. Its Vice-presidents are appointed by the Prime Minister (article 9). A monetary policy committee is established by the People's Bank at its discretion for the conduct of monetary policy (article 11).

The instruments for the conduct of monetary policy (article 22) include: (1) setting reserve requirements for financial institutions, (2) setting the central bank's base interest rate, (3) rediscounting for financial institutions which have established accounts in the People's Bank, (4) providing loans to the commercial banks, (5) buying and selling government bonds, bonds issued by government units, and foreign exchange, and (6) other instruments as determined by the State Council. The purchase and sale of government bonds and bonds of government units are conducted through financial institutions (article 24). The central bank establishes accounts for commercial banks and other financial institutions but cannot incur net debt in the accounts (article 25). It cannot incur net debt in the account of the government and cannot directly issue or purchase government bonds (article 28). This means that the central government cannot obtain financing by issuing bonds directly to the People's Bank, although the commercial banks can hold government bonds. The People's Bank has authority to examine and supervise the accounts of the financial institutions. Items (1) through (5) allow the central bank to regulate the amount of base money (currency and deposits in the central bank) and the amount of deposits in commercial banks (part of money supply) in relation to the base money, as in the case of other central banks. Under item (6), the People's Bank can and does continue its past practice of allocating credit quotas to the commercial banks, by provinces and sometimes by categories of loans.

## 13.3 Factors Affecting the Functioning of the Banking System

How well the People's Bank conducts its monetary policy can be discussed at three levels. The first is the institutional design of the central banking system. The second is the competence of and the incentives provided to the staff in the People's Bank. The third is the implementation of the policies determined by the central bank through the commercial banks in practice. Concerning the reality and design of the institution of the central bank, one should note that banking reform is a part of the institutional reform from a planned economy to a market economy. The People's Bank was a part of the central planning apparatus under the Ministry of Finance. When the planning apparatus was changed to regulate a market economy, the design and functioning of the People's Bank changed with it, now serving as an organization of the State Council. In China today, economic planning still plays an important role in the market economy, especially macroeconomic planning. The objective of the People's Bank as a central bank is not only to maintain price stability but also to promote economic growth. It participates in carrying out an industrial policy by extending credits to some sectors at the expense of others, for example, to agriculture and to certain large and medium-size state enterprises in 1995. It sets targets for money supply, and the interest rates for bank loans and for bank deposits simultaneously. These targets may be inconsistent with the rates of interest as determined by market forces, given the supply of money. In brief, the degree of planning exercised by the central bank might be inconsistent with market allocation of resources.

Second, assuming that the planning activities assigned to the central bank cannot be left to market forces alone, one has to rely on the ability and competence of the central planners and the incentive structure for these planners. Regarding incentives, one difference between the central bankers in China and in the United States is due to the fact that the latter has a two-party system. Prior to a Presidential election, the incumbent administration tends to pressure the Federal Reserve Bank to adopt an expansionary monetary policy to increase aggregate demand. In China, political pressure could come from the desire of a political leader to seek more rapid growth, as in November 1992, or to stop inflation rapidly for fear of public discontent, as might be the case in 1994 and 1995. Even when central bankers can resist political pressure, their planning staff might be incompetent in economic forecasting. Overestimating the future inflation rate can lead to a monetary policy that is too restrictive for price stability and growth. The existence of political pressures and human error has led some economists to advocate the reliance on rules rather than discretion in the formulation of monetary policy.

Third, having formulated its monetary policy does the People's Bank have the ability to carry it out satisfactorily? The effects of monetary policy have to work through the commercial banks. Monetary policy can take the form of targeting the quantity of money, the rate of inflation, or the regulation of the rate of interest. In the case of monetary targeting, let the monetary target be defined either as the quantity of M1, which equals currency M0 plus demand deposits in commercial banks, or the quantity of M2 which equals M1 plus time deposits. The central bank can control only base money (currency and reserves of commercial banks in the People's Bank). The ratio of money supply to the quantity of base money, or the monetary multiplier, can vary according to the actions of the commercial banks, subject to the reserve requirement set by the central bank. Technical difficulties in controlling the base money may occur. For example, the People's Bank may be forced to buy foreign exchange earned by exporters unless it sets limits to such purchases. The commercial banks can exercise discretion in changing the monetary multiplier, and sometimes even violate reserve requirements set by the central bank.

To obtain a macroeconomic picture of the end results of the People's Bank's action in controlling money supply, note first that since the economic reform in 1978, China's inflation has been mild compared with the inflation rates of many eastern European countries and Russia under economic reform. The average annual rate of increase in the overall retail price index from 1979 to 1995 is 8.1 percent (see World Bank 1996, table 32, p. 102). There were several episodes of inflation, in 1985 (8.8 percent), 1988 (18.5 percent), 1993 and 1994 (13.2 percent and 21.7 percent), all associated with an annual increase in the supply of money by close to 50 percent (see table 7.1 in chapter 7 above, and table 13.1 in the present chapter). These are recognized as mistakes in the conduct of monetary policy, but it is harder to attribute the mistakes to ill-management that could have been avoided, or to the banking institution itself.

From table 13.1, one finds that in 1990, following the tragic events at Tiananmen, the supply of money, as measured by M0, M1, or M2, increased moderately from the first quarter of 1990 to the first quarter of 1991. The same can be said for the year ending in the first quarter of 1992. In February 1992, Deng Xiaoping had his famous Southern Expedition and called for more reform, openness to the outside world, and a more rapid rate of economic growth. A more expansionary monetary policy followed, as evidenced by the large increase in all three measures of money supply from the first quarter of 1992 to the first quarter of 1993 by about 50 percent. When inflation became noticeable in the second quarter of 1993, there was an attempt by the central bank under the direction of Zhu Rongji to slow down the expansion of money supply. This resulted in a slower rate of increase from the first quarter of 1993 to the first quarter of 1994.

As inflation continued in 1994, by 21.7 percent according to the retail price index, further attempts were made to slow down the increase in money in 1995. The targeted increase in M2 for 1995 was 23 to 25 percent. (See Survey and Statistics Bureau of the People's Bank, 1996, p. 17.) The actual increase in M2 turned out to be 29.5 percent, somewhat higher than targeted. The rates of increase in both M1 and M2 were smaller in 1995 than in 1994, being 29.5 percent and 34.5 percent respectively for M2, and 16.8 percent and 26.2 percent respectively for M1. (See Survey and Statistics Bureau of the People's Bank, 1996, p. 18.) Annual increase in the retail price index was reduced to 8.3 percent in December 1995, relative to December 1994 (ibid., p. 104). The events in 1994 and 1995 demonstrated that the People's Bank did succeed in controlling money

**Table 13.1** Monetary aggregates: major financial indicators (yuan 100 millions)

|  | M2 | M1 | M0 | Demand deposits | Savings deposits | M2 – M1 quasi-money |
|---|---|---|---|---|---|---|
| 1990.03 | 12,480.3 | 5,672.2 | 2,154.6 | 3,517.6 | 5,765.9 | 6,808.1 |
| 1990.06 | 13,187.3 | 5,805.1 | 2,096.2 | 3,708.9 | 6,218.4 | 7,382.2 |
| 1990.09 | 14,228.0 | 6,327.2 | 2,300.4 | 4,026.8 | 6,646.9 | 7,900.8 |
| 1990.12 | 15,293.4 | 7,011.9 | 2,644.4 | 4,367.5 | 7,034.2 | 8,281.5 |
| 1991.03 | 16,249.7 | 7,069.1 | 2,585.6 | 4,483.5 | 7,812.8 | 9,180.6 |
| 1991.06 | 17,051.1 | 7,280.8 | 2,517.3 | 4,763.5 | 8,257.1 | 9,770.3 |
| 1991.09 | 18,245.7 | 7,972.2 | 2,730.0 | 5,242.2 | 8,654.1 | 10,273.5 |
| 1991.12 | 19,349.9 | 8,635.2 | 3,177.8 | 5,457.4 | 9,107.0 | 10,714.7 |
| 1992.03 | 20,608.3 | 8,877.6 | 3,117.2 | 5,760.4 | 9,956.0 | 11,730.7 |
| 1992.06 | 22,118.3 | 9,666.6 | 3,155.9 | 6,510.7 | 10,441.0 | 12,451.7 |
| 1992.09 | 23,563.9 | 10,556.4 | 3,559.4 | 6,997.0 | 10,852.3 | 13,007.5 |
| 1992.12 | 25,102.2 | 11,720.2 | 4,336.0 | 7,384.2 | 11,545.4 | 13,682.0 |
| 1993.03 | 29,460.2 | 14,032.5 | 4,557.9 | 9,474.6 | 12,526.3 | 15,427.7 |
| 1993.06 | 30,860.2 | 14,701.1 | 4,863.6 | 9,837.5 | 13,100.9 | 16,159.1 |
| 1993.09 | 31,795.6 | 14,422.9 | 5,074.8 | 9,348.1 | 14,323.5 | 17,371.7 |
| 1993.12 | 34,879.8 | 16,280.4 | 5,864.7 | 10,415.7 | 15,023.5 | 18,599.4 |
| 1994.03 | 37,010.3 | 16,437.0 | 5,834.6 | 10,602.4 | 17,157.3 | 20,573.3 |
| 1994.06 | 40,039.5 | 17,676.4 | 5,781.5 | 11,894.9 | 18,349.9 | 22,363.1 |
| 1994.09 | 42,513.5 | 19,009.5 | 6,412.9 | 12,596.6 | 19,970.2 | 24,504.0 |
| 1994.12 | 46,923.5 | 20,540.7 | 7,288.6 | 13,252.1 | 21,518.4 | 26,382.8 |
| 1995.03 | 50,297.1 | 21,026.2 | 7,271.0 | 13,755.2 | 23,762.7 | 29,270.9 |
| 1995.06 | 53,150.3 | 21,420.4 | 7,003.9 | 14,416.5 | 25,572.1 | 31,729.9 |
| 1995.09 | 56,813.2 | 22,493.0 | 7,368.9 | 15,124.1 | 27,569.7 | 34,320.2 |
| 1995.12 | 60,750.5 | 23,987.1 | 7,885.3 | 16,101.8 | 29,662.2 | 36,763.4 |

**Note**: *the statistics before 1992 covered those of banks and credit cooperatives.*
**Source**: *the People's Bank of China* Quarterly Statistical Bulletin, *1996.*

supply to a considerable extent, although the outcome was not strictly according to target. Also, the assignment of credit quotas continued to be used as an instrument for control, in addition to the first five instruments set forth in article 22 of the Law for the People's Bank cited above. Under the reign of Zhu Rongji, who became Prime Minister in 1998 but still had an important influence on the action of the People's Bank, monetary policy continued to be very restrictive after 1996, leading to a reduction in the price level in 1998 (as we discussed in chapter 7).

## 13.4   Possible Weaknesses of the System

In section 13.1, I mentioned the degree of competence of the banking staff, the organization and incentive system in the banks, and external influences as three sets of factors affecting the functioning of the commercial banks. Nothing more will be said about the first. Regarding the second, as the largest four commercial banks are state-owned and state-managed organizations, they are subject to some of the inefficiencies of state enterprises. Incentive problems for the management and the staff, inability to discharge workers, and bureaucratic behavior among the staff are all present. Attempts to reform state enterprises have had only limited success. The reasons include the difficulty of designing a reward system suitable for the managers of large enterprises (the responsibility system, leasing the enterprise to the management works better for small enterprises), inertia in changing the bureaucratic behavior of the staff, including the privileged loan officers and even the bank officials receiving deposits, and the unwillingness to discharge inefficient workers, as job security was a part of the social welfare system. Bureaucratic behavior includes not only poor service to customers, but corruption and misuse of bank funds for illegitimate purposes. However, as state industrial enterprises have improved their efficiency (see Jefferson and Rawski 1994: 56), presumably the commercial banks in China have also. More evidence on this subject is needed. The influence of the policies of the People's Bank on commercial bank behavior will be discussed in the next subsection.

### The People's Bank

A major weakness of the Chinese central banking system is alleged to be its lack of independence from the executive branch of the government. In fact the Law on the People's Bank explicitly stipulates that the People's Bank is under the direction of the State Council. This institutional arrangement can be contrasted with the independence of the US Federal Reserve Bank from the executive branch of the United States government. From the Chinese point of view, if macroeconomic planning (for a market economy) is an important responsibility of the State Council, why should the conduct of monetary policy not be a part of its responsibility? Placing the central bank under the control of the Executive Council enables the Council to coordinate monetary and fiscal policies. Political influence may be bad for economic planning sometimes, but it may be necessary at other times if political influence means the influence of political factors, including the need for political stability. Giving the executive branch of the government more authority, including the control of the central bank, is useful because it enables the government to do good things. It can be harmful because it permits the government to do bad things. Some mistakes, as in the inflation episodes cited, are not sufficient evidence to condemn the system itself. For example, the mistake of involving the United States in the Vietnam War is not sufficient to discredit the institution of the American presidency.

Space does not allow a long discussion here on the possible merits of the independence of the central bank from the executive branch in China. A case for an independent central bank as an institution to achieve a low inflation rate has been presented by Eijffinger and De Haan (1996). Whatever one's opinion on this subject, the institutional arrangement for the central bank appears to be settled in China, at least in the foreseeable future, as it is clearly stated in the Law on the People's Bank enacted on March 18, 1995.

In the conduct of monetary policy, however, the People's Bank might improve its performance by drawing some lessons from experience accumulated since the early 1980s. First, it should avoid mistaken policies of excessive increase in money supply, as in 1984, 1988 and 1992. It should prevent its branches from creating excessive credit, which led to inflation in the 1980s. This could be done even under the direction of the Executive Council. The People's Bank can argue for this case, as the economic planning authority in the State Council has become aware of the danger of a rapid increase in money supply. Second, it should be more consistent in formulating its policies regarding money supply and the interest rates on the loans and deposits of the commercial banks. High rates on certain time deposits and low rates on loans have forced commercial banks to find risky and possibly illegal outlets for their funds. Third, it can impose severe penalties, financial and otherwise, on commercial banks and their officials for diverting funds for illegitimate use.

## 13.5   Possible Directions of Reform

Chinese government officials and economists are aware of the possible weaknesses of the current banking system and are trying to improve its performance. They have made serious efforts to invite outside experts to come to China to train the staff of the Central Bank and commercial banks. The following is a list of possible directions for institutional reform.

### *Directions for commercial banks*

1) Consider variations of the contract responsibility system for the commercial banks, drawing from the partially successful experience from similar reform for state enterprises. Branches of the commercial banks and smaller units under them can be made financially independent in order to create incentives for the management of each unit to make profits by improving its operations.

2) Allow branches of the commercial banks to issue their own stocks to be sold to the public, thus increasing the share of private ownership and eventually the influence of private shareholders on the management.

3) Encourage joint ventures with foreign commercial banks. Provisions of China's entry into the WTO as discussed in section 4.5 can facilitate such developments.

4) Increase labor productivity by discharging incompetent workers and paying them a pension equal to a fraction of current salaries. Provide on-the-job training and schooling for workers.

5) Encourage competition from foreign and Hong Kong banks by allowing a limited number of them to register as commercial banks, an experiment now underway in special areas. These foreign competitors can serve as examples to show how a bank should operate, provide training for domestic banking personnel, and stimulate better performance by domestic banks. As China joins the WTO, foreign competition will increase as foreign banks can offer services in local currencies to Chinese corporations.

6) Facilitate nonbank institutions such as rural and urban credit cooperatives to function in absorbing savings and providing funds for investment and other legitimate economic activities. Informal financial institutions have contributed to financing the economic development in Taiwan when the commercial banks there were not operating efficiently. Why not allow the legal credit cooperatives in mainland China to serve as useful financial intermediaries? These cooperatives cannot cause excess increase in money supply if they do not have the power of the commercial banks in making loans without deposits of an equal amount.

## Directions for the People's Bank

7) Try to maintain a stable and moderate rate of increase in money supply. The rate can be somewhat higher than the rate of increase in real gross domestic product, as the ratio of money demand to money income tends to increase gradually during economic development. Avoid too much fine-tuning when there is insufficient knowledge about future trends in real output and the price level.

8) Given its authority to control money supply and the rates of interest simultaneously, the central bank may target a moderate growth in money supply and regulate the rates of interest only mildly by allowing the bank loan rate and deposit rates to be determined mainly by the forces of demand and supply. Avoid setting an arbitrary low interest rate for loans. If funds are scarce, the users of funds should pay a high rate to ensure efficient allocation of capital. In 1998 and 1999, as inflation slowed down, the nominal interest rates on deposits were reduced in steps, since the rates no longer had to cover the loss which the depositor incurred to cover the cost of inflation. In reality then, interest rates have been set close to the rates determined by market forces.

9) With the consent of the Executive Council, try to do less in the form of allocating credit quotas for special industries and enterprises. The responsibility to finance special industrial development projects was formally assigned to three policy banks, the State Development Bank, the Export/Import Bank, and the Agricultural Development Bank established in 1994. These banks are to relieve the People's Bank of its responsibility in allocating credit for special economic sectors. To carry out industrial policies (i.e., policies that promote the development of special industrial sectors) it might be better to use fiscal policies of providing subsidies to the targeted enterprises for a finite period rather than to use monetary policy. Providing targeted industries or enterprises a fixed sum for development in a finite period enables the government to know the exact cost for developing a particular industry or a particular kind of enterprise. It also limits the dependence of the receiver and forces it to become economically viable. Extended periods of

subsidy would allow mistakes to persist in choosing the types of enterprises for support and lead to misuse of resources. Before a sound fiscal system is instituted, the government may be forced to use bank credits to some extent in financing industrial development.

10) Increase the reserve requirement for commercial banks (at the same time compensate them by providing more reserves), so that the commercial banks will have less power to create money (including deposits) and the People's Bank can have a tighter control of the money supply. This would also reduce the risk of bank failures and the need for deposit insurance.

## 13.6    The Financial Condition of Commercial Banks and the Bad-loan Problem

In an article in the *Asian Wall Street Journal* of October 12, 2000, John Langlois discussed the high taxes on China's banks. The Chinese Ministry of Finance and the State Bureau of Taxation imposed three kinds of taxes or write-offs on the banks: (1) an 8 percent turnover tax on accrued gross income, only partially adjusted for nonreceipts, (2) a write-off on nonperforming loans to be restricted to less than 1 percent of total loans per year, and (3) a 33 percent tax on net income. For example, the Bank of China in Beijing in 1999 reported 15 percent of its loans as nonperforming and posted only 0.6 percent of total loans as a write-off for tax purposes. This bank paid $837 million in taxes that year. In a public lecture given at Princeton University and hosted by Professor Langlois on May 2, 2001, Chinese Vice-minister of Finance Liqun Jin justified the taxes by saying that as a stockholder of the commercial banks the Chinese government was entitled to the pay-ment of dividends which the banks did not issue. Furthermore, if the government did not extract payments from the banks' gross income, they would spend the money extravagantly in the form of high wages to the employees. This is another illustration of the corporate governance problem of how to ensure that the management and staff of a government-owned institution will perform in the best interest of the stockholders. It also shows that the commercial banks were operating at a profit in spite of the large amounts of bad loans.

As reported at the end of section 13.1, the ratio of bank loans to GDP in 1995 was about 1.1, a ratio remaining roughly constant in the 1995–2000 period. The four large commercial banks have about 70 percent of the country's banking assets. If the bad loans are 20 percent of their assets they amount to 14 percent of GDP. Fourteen percent of the 1998 GDP of 7,970 billion yuan is about 1,116 billion. The four asset management corporations (AMCs) established to help restructure the assets of the four state commer-cial banks, as discussed in section 4.3, operate by buying the bad loans from the banks at par value in exchange for their own notes. The AMC notes alone are not risky, as the AMCs may not be able to collect from the state enterprises. Langlois points out that by getting a note from an AMC a commercial bank can no longer write off its bad loans for tax purposes. In the meantime the bank pays a 33 percent income tax on profit and an 8 percent turnover tax on gross revenue, both including the interest paid by the AMC on the note. A serious problem in the reform of the banking system and the restructuring of bank assets is having one kind of bureaucrat to deal with another kind of bureaucrat, as we pointed out in section 4.2. The bad loans are owed by state enterprises. The notes of an AMC are claims on a state organization. By June 2000 the AMCs had issued notes totaling 1,300 billion to the state-owned commercial banks, but had difficulty selling the bad loans acquired.

Although one may be skeptical of the ability of the AMCs to solve the problem of the nonperforming loans, are there other solutions? One possible solution is for the People's Bank simply to issue more currency to cover the bad loans. A drawback of this solution is that it may set a bad precedent and encourage the commercial banks to become irresponsible in their lending behavior in the future if they expect to be bailed out again, but this drawback applies to the AMCs bailing them out as well. One should find out how much inflation the required increase in money supply would create. If the income elasticity of demand for currency is 1.2, that means that when real output or real income in China is increased by 10 percent, the demand for currency in real terms will increase by 12 percent. The government can increase supply of currency by 12 percent without causing inflation because all the extra money will be absorbed by the economy at a constant price level. If the increase in money supply is 15 percent starting from 100, and the desired real value of money balance is only 112, the price level $P$ has to adjust to make the actual real value of money balance $115/P$ equal to the desired balance 112. In other words, $P = 115/112 = 1.027$, or $P$ has to increase by about 3 percent. The quantity of currency in circulation in China at the end of 1998 is 1,120 billion yuan, as shown in table 7.1 of chapter 7. The income elasticity of demand for money is about 1.16 (see Chow 1994: 237). Without inflation, China's money stock could be increased by an exponential rate of 1.16 times the exponential rate of increase in income, the latter being about 0.08. This exponential rate of increase of 0.093 from 1,120 billion allows an increase in money supply of 109 billion yuan. If a 2 percent inflation is allowed, the exponential rate of increase in money stock can be about 0.113, yielding an increase in money supply of 125 billion. This amount compares with the 1,116 billion yuan of bad loans of the four commercial banks. In 5 years, allowing for the growth of the Chinese economy, if all the newly printed money is used to solve the bad loan problem, about 70 percent of the bad loans will be eliminated. Some of the remaining 30 percent could be collected from the state enterprises. This calculation shows that the Chinese government has the financial ability to solve the bad loan problem, but using the newly printed money for this purpose would entail a sacrifice of its possible use for other important government expenditures.

According to the *People's Daily* of October 29, 2004, the nonperforming loan ratio remained as high as 14.65 percent. There were three other banking problems, as stated by Li Wei, Vice-chairman of the China Banking Regulatory Commission, at the Chinese Business Summit on Monday October 25, 2004. First, "Business financing relies too much on bank loans, with highly concentrated risks." In the first half of 2004, bank loans accounted for 83 percent of the investment in nonfinancial sectors. "In recent years, the negative impact of blind investment and low-level duplicated construction emerged," he said. "There are also increased risks for bank loans." Second, the major banks do not have effective management and the role of a board of directors has not been fulfilled. Third, state-owned banks focused on long-term loans to large cities and enterprises, while short-term loans and loans to small and medium-sized companies and small counties and villages were neglected in recent years. He said that reform was being carried out to address the above problems, and that a new banking system was being established in China, combining the state-owned commercial banks with banks of other forms.

At the end of August 2004, the total assets of various banks in China were 2.97 billion yuan (357.8 million US dollars), making up 90 percent of capital of all financial sectors in China. More than 62 foreign financial groups from 19 countries have established 199 financial branches in 21 cities and 152 foreign banks from 38 countries and regions have set up 216 offices in 22 cities, according to government figures.

## 13.7   Other Financial Institutions

Banks are the most important of all financial intermediaries. All financial institutions perform an important economic function by channeling the savings of individuals and enterprises or other institutions to suitable investments. The Chinese banks accept deposits from Chinese consumers and extend loans to enterprises. Unfortunately, bank loans were not and, to a large extent, are still not extended according to the credibility of the borrower and the profitability of his project. Other financial institutions include state and provincial trust and investment corporations, stock markets, mutual funds, pension funds, and insurance companies. China had stock markets and insurance companies before the establishment of the PRC. These institutions were destroyed by the government of the PRC. The government has reestablished stock markets and insurance companies and is in the process of promoting the formation of other financial institutions.

### 13.7.1   Trust and investment corporations

In 1981 the PRC government decided to establish the China International Trust and Investment Corporation (CITIC) to attract foreign capital for economic development. Mr. Rong Yiren, a former capitalist in Shanghai during the period of the Republic of China, was named its president. The appointment signaled the government's interest in doing things in a capitalist way, as far as the attraction of foreign capital was concerned. Foreign investors were indeed attracted to put money in this Corporation, partly because some believed that their investments were backed by the Chinese government.

Through the years, provincial governments have promoted the establishment of international trust and investment corporations in their provinces. One notable example is the Guangdong International Trust and Investment Corporation (GITIC). It attracted a lot of attention because it was on the verge of bankruptcy in late 1998 at the height of the Asian financial crisis. Foreign banks had invested in GITIC partly because they believed that their investments were backed by the Provincial Government of Guangdong Province. When GITIC suffered substantial losses (some said because the bureaucrats administering it had channeled money to unproductive uses or speculative investments), the foreign investors demanded compensation from the Guangdong Provincial Government. The government responded by saying that GITIC was legally an independent financial entity, not a part of the government; foreign investors should realize that they had invested at their own risk. The government as an investor to GITIC was in the same position as other investors and lost money itself.

It was the decision of Premier Zhu Rongji to allow GITIC to go bankrupt and not to bail it out using resources from the central government. This decision was made as a warning to provincial governments and other government organizations which try to set up investment trusts that they should be responsible for their losses; the Premier also wanted to let international investors know that they too cannot depend on the central government to bail them out. In this particular instance, the foreign investors did recoup part of their losses because they were given priority claim to the remaining assets of GITIC.

## 13.7.2   Stock markets

We pointed out in chapter 3 that in the early 1990s the Shenzhen and Shanghai stock markets were established. Since the opening of the stock markets there have been some 250 laws and regulations promulgated on the stock markets. These include the Company Law of the PRC, Interim Regulations on the Management of Issuance and Transaction of Stocks, Regulations on Stocks of Foreign Investment of Joint Stock Limited Companies Listed Abroad, Interim Measures Prohibiting Cheating Activities in Securities, Administrative Measures on Stock Exchange, Temporary Regulations on Control of Qualification of Stock Exchange Personnel, Detailed Measures of Implementation on the Publication of Information by Public Stock-issuing Companies, etc. The large number of such laws and regulations enacted partly reflects the government's view that the development of stock markets has to be heavily regulated by the government.

By the end of 1998, the number of listed companies in the two stock exchanges increased to 851 from 745 in 1997. The market value of the listed shares amounted to almost 2 trillion yuan, equal to about 25 percent of China's national output. In 1998, US$770 million of foreign capital was raised by issuing B and H shares outside China, while A shares of the same companies could only be purchased by Chinese citizens. By 1997 there were 98 firms in China serving as securities dealers. Some 2,440 securities offices were scattered in the cities above county level. There were about 100,000 persons working in the sector. In January 1998 I visited a securities trading room in the city of Jinan, capital of Shandong Province, and saw over 150 people, mostly women dressed in traditional country-style clothing, staring intensely at a board with changing stock price quotes and seemingly getting ready to make a transaction at any moment. All the people in the trading room had to have an account with a sufficient balance before they could trade.

Some institutional details of the Shanghai stock market will be given in chapter 14 as background material for our discussion of a model to explain the prices of stocks traded in that market from 1993 to 1998. It is worthwhile pointing out that in China there are two kinds of stock traded. "A" shares are reserved for Chinese citizens who buy them in Chinese currency; "B" shares are reserved for foreign investors and are traded in US dollars. Such a system insulates the Chinese investors from speculation by foreign investors, since such speculation affects mainly the prices of B shares. On February 28, 2001, the government decided to allow Chinese citizens to use foreign currency to buy B shares traded in both the Shanghai and Shenzhen stock markets. There was a rush to buy; investors formed long lines to wait for the markets to open. The prices of B shares increased rapidly to hit the daily 10 percent limits set by the State Security Commission on price changes in one day. Trading was closed on March 1 because the price limits were reached and there were no more B shares offered for sale. A large number of Chinese investors ready to pay US dollars for the stocks were greatly disappointed.

The growth of the stock markets, the relative importance of the Shanghai and Shenzhen markets and of A, B, and H shares (H shares being traded in Hong Kong) can be measured partly by the number of listed companies in table 13.2 (derived from table 19-11 of the *China Statistical Yearbook, 1999*). The total value of the stocks of the 851 companies traded in both markets in 1998 amounted to 1,951 billion yuan, while the issue of B and H shares provided foreign capital of US$770 million.

In only 14 years, China's stock market has developed into Asia's third biggest market, with more than 1,300 listed companies, 4 trillion yuan (US$483 billion) of market capitalization, and more than 70 million stock traders. It has been estimated that the market might even become the world's second biggest, after the United States, in the next decade. For over a decade, listed companies have been the biggest beneficiaries from the fast expansion of the bourses, raising altogether more than 800 billion yuan (US$96.6 billion) of funds. But the overall dividends the companies have paid their investors total only about 72.2 billion yuan (US$8.7 billion). The Shanghai composite index fell below the psychologically important 1,300 level and touched a 5-year low on September 9, 2004.

**Table 13.2**  The number of companies listed in Chinese stock markets

| Year | National | Shanghai Stock Exchange | Shenzhen Stock Exchange | A shares only | A&H shares | A&B shares | B shares only |
|------|----------|-------------------------|-------------------------|---------------|------------|------------|----------------|
| 1990 | 10  | 8   | 2   | 10  | 10  |    |    |
| 1991 | 14  | 8   | 6   | 14  | 14  |    |    |
| 1992 | 53  | 29  | 24  | 53  | 35  |    | 18 |
| 1993 | 183 | 106 | 77  | 183 | 140 | 3  | 34 |
| 1994 | 291 | 171 | 120 | 291 | 227 | 6  | 54 |
| 1995 | 323 | 188 | 135 | 323 | 242 | 11 | 58 |
| 1996 | 530 | 293 | 237 | 530 | 431 | 14 | 69 |
| 1997 | 745 | 383 | 362 | 745 | 627 | 17 | 76 |
| 1998 | 851 | 438 | 413 | 851 | 727 | 18 | 80 |

*Foreign investors*

Since China formally introduced the Qualified Foreign Institutional Investors (QFII) scheme in December 2002, 20 foreign institutions have acquired QFII licenses, which enable them to invest in yuan-traded A shares, bonds, and mutual funds within authorized investment quotas. QFII has also created a new channel of foreign investment in China. To foreign investors, the Chinese market is attractive largely because of the rosy economic outlook, the strong renminbi and the vast growing potential of the capital market, though presently, compared to the overseas markets, the A share market is still overpriced, while the quality of the listed firms and market fundamentals is still lagging behind. But even with price gaps and flaws in the market system, a growing number of foreign investors are still heading on with capital market expansion plans in China.

The American International Group (AIG), which launched the first foreign insurance company in China in 1992, is now developing into the country's asset management business. Its fund management joint venture with China's Huatai Securities, AIG-Huatai Fund Management Co., is expected to open for business soon, with each of the two sides holding 33 percent. AIG intends to increase the ratio of stakes in the fund venture to 49 percent next year, also the maximum ratio China allows a foreign company to hold in such ventures, according to Joel Epstein, AIG Country Manager in China. In only 2 years after China's entry to the World Trade Organization, the country already has more than a dozen fund management joint ventures in operation or preparation. When asked if the timing of entering the securities business is appropriate as the stock market is weak, Epstein said the strategy was based on confidence in the Chinese economy and long-term prospects. Similar expectations of good investment returns over the long term have also pushed QFIIs to apply for investment quotas including UBS, which quickly used up an initial US$600 million quota, the biggest granted by the Chinese authorities to a QFII. As A share companies see their prices getting closer to that of H shares, they may find themselves more attractive to overseas investors. Apart from equity funds, more new products such as bond funds, index funds, guarantee funds, and monetary market funds have entered the market.

One problem with the pricing of many stocks traded in the Chinese stock markets is the high proportion of "nontraded" shares held by the government or by the management of the corporation itself. This is the result of the government policy to retain the ownership of the largest state-owned enterprises. In the period 2003–5 the government introduced a policy to privatize some of these enterprises by asking the management to sell shares in the stock exchanges. Since the state-owned shares accounted for more than 95 percent of the total shares in many instances, such sales increased the supply of the traded shares significantly and depressed their prices. The government had to stop such selling several times and design schemes to prevent its significant depressing effect on the prices of traded shares. One scheme being discussed in 2005 was to compensate the owners of the traded shares by a fraction, such as 1 to 5, of the state-owned shares to be offered for sale in the market. In the Fall of 2005 price indices of the Shanghai and Shenzhen stock markets were at a 4-year low, while the Chinese economy had been growing rapidly. One explanation is that the fraction of wealth in China that is held in the form of the traded stocks is extremely low, and China's rapid growth did not derive from the profits of the enterprises which had shares traded. The second explanation is the policy for privatization noted above. The third reason is the allegedly unconventional pricing of stocks in initial offers. Many listed companies relied on government support for being listed. The pricing of initial offers, and the trading and supervision systems, did not follow a regular set of rules. Disclosure of financial statements was limited and inaccurate. Finally, price trends in stock markets are not always explainable by economic fundamentals.

### 13.7.3   Insurance companies and other financial institutions

As the People's Bank Law and the Commercial Bank Law were enacted, so were the Insurance Law and other laws for the regulation of the financial sector. The domestic insurance business, after being suspended for over 20 years, has been reopened. Foreign insurance companies have been allowed to operate in China. The *China Statistical Year-Book, 1997* (p. 621) reports that at the end of 1996 there were 126,130 persons employed in the various branches and the headquarters of the People's Insurance Company of China, out of a total of 2.1 million persons employed in the entire state banking and insurance system, which includes the People's Bank, the four state commercial banks, the two policy banks, and the Bank of Communications. The total amount insured by the People's Insurance Company of China (ibid., p. 629) increased from 6,895 (yuan 100 millions) in 1985, to 19,366 in 1990, 66,039 in 1995, and to 98,179 in 1996. The average annual exponential rate of growth from 1990 to 1996 is a phenomenal 0.271. From 1995 to 1996 the exponential rate of growth went up to 0.397, or up 48.7 percent. One can expect the insurance business in China to grow at a rate much higher than the GDP growth rate in the next decade or two.

Chinese citizens have begun to own stocks. Most of the investors own individual stocks. It may take time for mutual funds to become popular, as these funds took years to become a major financial institution in the United States. Pensions will be provided by a social security scheme to be administered by the government at different levels. Pension funds will become an important source of savings and investment. The Chinese government had issued 389.1 billion yuan of treasury bonds by the end of 1998. In addition, 270 billion yuan worth of special treasury bonds were issued by the Ministry of Finance to the four state-owned commercial banks.

## 13.8   The Role of the Chinese Government in Reforming the Financial System

It is useful to summarize the view of the Chinese government on financial reform and then to comment on the appropriate role of the government. In March 1999, Premier Zhu Rongji stated in his government report:

We should do a better job in implementing the guiding principles and plans formulated at the National Conference on Financial Work which was held by the Central Committee of the Communist Party in 1997.

First, we should work to improve the system separating the operation and administration of the banking, securities, insurance and trust sectors, and implement the responsibility system for financial supervision and control to intensify the supervision and control of all types of financial institutions.

Second, we should accelerate the reform of state-owned commercial banks, ensure autonomy in the operation of the banks, continue to make progress in the efforts to establish bank branches and sub-branches based on the economic divisions and workloads, streamline institutions, cut the size of their staffs and tighten internal control. We should practice the five-category assets classification for bank loans and gradually set up financial assets management companies to handle the nonperforming loans now held by banks. We should implement a strict responsibility system for the quality of new bank loans.

Third, we should do a good job of operating noncommercial banks, carry out the state industrial policies and raise the efficiency of the utilization of funds.

Fourth, we should standardize and safeguard the financial order in accordance with law. We should inspect and rectify nonbank and local financial institutions, reduce the risks of financial institutions and maintain financial stability. We should promote the steady development of other commercial banks and credit cooperatives in both urban and rural areas in the process of reform. We should earnestly implement the "Securities Law" to standardize and develop the securities market. In addition, we should rectify and standardize the insurance market to promote the sound development of the insurance industry. We must deal severely with actions of financial institutions in violation of regula-tions of codes of conduct and relentlessly punish financial criminal activities in accordance with the law.

It is interesting to note that points 1, 2, and 4 (in part) of Premier Zhu's statement advocate respectively the use of the responsibility system for financial supervision, establishment of state-owned commercial bank branches and the downsizing of their staffs, and the promotion of other commercial banks and credit cooperatives. These points are similar to points 1, 2, 4, and 6 stated above in section 13.5. The material of section 13.5 was contained in a paper, "How Well does the Chinese Banking System Function?," which I presented at an international conference "China: Toward a Modern Financial System," sponsored partly by the Chinese Finance Association and held in Beijing on 23–4 August 1996. At the end of that conference I met Zhu Rongji, then Vice-premier, for over an hour, as reported in *The China Daily* of August 24. (See my website, www.princeton.edu/~gchow, for a copy of the article.) I was pleased to find that Premier Zhu shared similar views when I read the above-quoted statement on a CD-rom distributed to participants invited to attend the Fiftieth Anniversary Celebration of the founding of the PRC on October 1, 1999. Point 3 of the above statement simply restates the function of the policy banks, which we have already discussed.

One interesting issue is the extent to which the government should regulate its financial institutions. It is necessary and desirable for the government to set up ground rules for the conduct of financial institutions. The government should ensure that the banks report their financial conditions in a transparent set of accounts, preferably following an internationally accepted accounting standard. The People's Bank has the responsibility of supervising the operations of commercial banks, as stipulated by the People's Bank Law; making sure, for example, that they do not hold an excessive amount of risky assets and their outstanding loans satisfy a reserve ratio requirement. For an international investment trust, the experience of the failure of GITIC in 1998 suggests that its balance sheet needs to satisfy similar requirements. Companies issuing stocks to be traded in a stock market should also have a transparent and economically sound balance sheet. Such responsibilities of the Chinese government were emphasized in the fourth point of Premier Zhu's statement quoted above. However, besides setting basic rules of conduct, to what extent should the government interfere with the market?

One area which the Chinese government has attempted to influence is the price of stocks. When stock prices were low in 1999, the government tried to give signals that the prices would become higher and tried to encourage citizens to buy. The reason for this policy was to increase the value of the stock so that consumers would buy more in a depressed market for consumer durables. The government also suggested that it would support the stock market and not let the prices fall below a certain level. A shortcoming of such a policy is that when investors lose money in the stock market they will hold the government responsible.

A second reason for limiting government intervention is the observation that natural evolution of economic institutions by market forces can, though does not always, lead to economically efficient and well-designed institutions. The natural evolution of stock markets, mutual funds, insurance companies, and other financial institutions in other countries in the world and in pre-1949 China testifies to this point. So does the natural evolution of the successful township and village enterprises in China, a topic to be discussed in chapter 16. One recognizes the important role of the Chinese government in actively establishing or reestablishing financial and other economic institutions. In the process of doing so, the government in Beijing also needs to give opportunities to other institutions, including private, collective, and lower-level government organizations, to develop economic institutions to suit their needs.

Providing freedom for these other individuals or organizations to play their role in institutional development can only add to what the central government alone can accomplish. Besides the successful experience of township and village enterprises in the 1980s, the flourishing of commercial banks financed by private capital in China in the 1920s is another testimony. This view conforms to the principle of allowing decentralized decision-making and unleashing market forces rather than centralizing decision-making under government planning – a subject which we discussed in chapter 2. In the present application of this principle, decision-making refers to decisions to establish economic institutions and not decisions on the allocation of resources given a set of economic institutions. The record of the last two decades of the twentieth century suggests that the Chinese government has been slow in allowing nonstate financial institutions to flourish. At the beginning of the twenty-first century it is more difficult to start a nonstate commercial bank than it was during the 1920s. The flourishing of private commercial banking in that period is well documented in the *Annals of Mr. Liang Yansun of Sanshui*, which we looked at in chapter 1.

# References and Further Reading

*Annals of Mr. Liang Yansun of Sanshui*, vols. 1 and 2 (in Chinese). Hong Kong, private publication, 1939. Reissued as a Monograph in the "Modern Chinese Historical Series," Taipei: Wenxing Book Co., 1962.

Chow, Gregory C. *Understanding China's Economy*. Singapore: World Scientific Publishing Co., 1994.

Chow, Gregory C. "How Well does the Chinese Banking System Function?" Paper presented before the International Conference, "China: Toward a Modern Financial System," Beijing, Aug. 23–4, 1996.

Chow, Gregory C. "China's Economic Policy in the Context of the Asian Financial Crisis." *Pacific Economic Review*, 6 (Feb. 2000), pp. 97–108.

Eijffinger, Sylvester C. and Jacob De Haan. "The Political Economy of Central-Bank Independence." *Special Papers in International Economics*, no. 19. Princeton University: International Finance Section, 1996.

Jefferson, Gary H. and T. Rawski. "Enterprise Reform in Chinese Industry." *Journal of Economic Perspectives*, 8 (1994), pp. 47–70.

Langlois, John D. "Taxing China's Banks Into Oblivion." *The Asian Wall Street Journal*, Oct. 12, 2000.

World Bank, *The Chinese Economy: Fighting Inflation, Deepening Reforms*. Washington, DC: World Bank, 1996.

Yi, Gang, *Money, Banking and Financial Markets in China*. Boulder, CO: Westview Press, 1994.

# Questions

1 In what way is the law for China's commercial banks different from that of the US?

2 In what way do you expect the Chinese Commercial banks to behave differently from those in the US?

3 Name three important institutional differences between the People's Bank and the Federal Reserve Bank of the US.

4 What are the weaknesses of the Chinese banking system?

5 What are some possible ways to improve the Chinese banking system?

6 What were the alleged reasons that China had a banking crisis during the Asian financial crisis of 1997–9? Why was China able to withstand a banking crisis?

7 Assume that the income elasticity of demand for real money balances (currency in circulation) is 1.2 and that real GDP was increasing at 8 percent per year in 1998: how much additional money could the People's Bank print in 1998 without causing inflation? How does this amount of money compare with the amount (in RMB billions) which was injected into the Chinese commercial banks to help solve the problem of bad loans? How does this amount compare with one-fifth of the total value of nonperforming loans (one-fifth is used with the goal of solving the problem of bad loans in five years)?

8 Summarize the three major elements of banking reform introduced in 1988 to solve the problem of nonperforming loans.

9 Cite and discuss briefly two possible reasons for expecting failure of the asset management companies to restructure the commercial banks' assets in China.

10 Cite and discuss briefly three factors that affect how well the commercial banks function.

# 14

# Shanghai Stock Price Determination

This chapter provides a simple model to explain the prices of the shares or stocks of different enterprises listed in the Shanghai Stock Market. The prices are found to be determined by the same theory that applies to more mature markets like the New York Stock Exchange and the Hong Kong Stock Exchange. The purposes of presenting the analysis and the results are three. First, it is to convey the idea that Chinese investors behave in the same rational way as investors in more developed economies. Second, it illustrates a useful method to study financial markets. Third, it shows that when the three stock markets have different behavioral patterns, the differences can be explained by the differences in economic environment which affect investors' expectations. The chapter ends with some comments on the role that the government plays in regulating the stock market.

## 14.1   Introduction

Whether prices of stocks traded on the Shanghai Stock Market can be explained by the same theory as prices in mature markets such as the New York Stock Exchange and the Hong Kong Stock Exchange is an interesting question. Soon after the establishment of the People's Republic of China in 1949, trading of stocks ceased to exist. Stocks were first traded on the Shanghai Stock Exchange in 1992. From 1978 on, China was in the process of transformation from a planned economy to a market economy, and 1992 was also the year in which the Central Committee of the Chinese Communist Party declared China's economy to be a socialist market economy. At the beginning of 1998, when the research reported in this chapter began, there were only five full years from 1993 to 1997 to observe the behavior of stock prices in the Shanghai Stock Exchange. During this period, the market participants in China presumably were learning about the market. Skeptics of this research might suggest that the Chinese investors were not well informed because they were not well educated, or that the financial market data were insufficient or even inaccurate. However, one cannot object to the application of a particular economic stock price model to Shanghai stock market data on such *a priori* grounds alone. Whether or not a hypothesis is correct should be determined by statistical evidence and not by presumption. Hence, it is interesting to investigate whether prices in Shanghai follow the same patterns observed in mature markets by econometric analysis.

The model of stock price determination adopted in this chapter was first used in Chow (1958). It is based on the present-value model that states that the price of a stock at the beginning of time period $t$ is the sum of the expected discounted values of all of its future dividends. Since future dividends are uncertain, Chow (1958) proposes to summarize them by only two parameters, namely the expected level $E_t d_t$ and the expected growth rate $E_t g_t$, where $E_t$ denotes the psychological expectation conditional on information available at the beginning of year $t$, $d_t$ denotes the natural logarithm of dividend $D_t$ distributed during year $t$, and $g_t$ denotes the rate of growth of dividends as measured by the change in the logarithms of dividends $d_t - d_{t-1}$ from period $t - 1$ to period $t$. These expectations are assumed to be formed adaptively using past data, as specified in section 14.2, where the model of stock prices is formulated. Section 14.3 presents the empirical results for 47 stocks in the Shanghai Stock Exchange, most of which entered the market after 1992. Section 14.4 compares the results with those observed from the Hong Kong Stock Exchange as reported in Chow and Kwan (1997), and the New York Stock Exchange as reported in Lin (1998). Section 14.5 concludes.

## 14.2   A Model of Stock Price Determination

Our model of stock price determination is based on the present-value model. Given a constant discount rate $r$, the present-value model is

$$P_t = E_t \sum_{s=0}^{\infty} D_{t+s}/(1 + r)^{s+1}$$

where $P_t$ is the price of a stock at the beginning of period $t$, $D_t$ is the forthcoming dividend during period $t$, and $E_t$ is the psychological expectation conditioned on information at the beginning of period $t$. Thus $P_t$ is a function of the expectations of $D_{t+1}$, $D_{t+2}$, $D_{t+3}$, and so forth. If the patterns of future growth of dividends in logarithmic or percentage terms are expected to be the same for two stocks, their prices would be proportional to their dividends. If the dividends of one stock are expected to grow faster, its price should be higher. The price of a stock for one company depends on how many shares the company decides to issue. It would be half as much when the company decides to split one share into two. To eliminate the effect of the arbitrary number of shares issued on our model, we decide to formulate a model to explain the logarithm of stock price rather than stock price itself. In the model we assume that $\ln P_t = p_t$ is a linear function of only two parameters, namely, the expectation $E_t d_t$ of $\ln D_t$ and the expectation $E_t(d_t - d_{t-1}) = E_t g_t$ of the rate of growth $g$ of dividends.

To complete the theory we need to specify how these two expectations are formed. We assume that they are formed by adaptive expectations as follows

$$E_t d_t = E_{t-1} d_{t-1} + c(d_{t-1} - E_{t-1} d_{t-1}) = c[1 - (1 - c)L]^{-1} d_{t-1}$$
$$E_t g_t = E_{t-1} g_{t-1} + b(g_{t-1} - E_{t-1} g_{t-1}) = b[1 - (1 - b)L]^{-1} g_{t-1} \qquad (14.1)$$

The first half of each equation simply states that the change in the psychological expectation of each variable, be it $d$ or $g$, is a fraction of the difference between its actual value and its expected value in the last period $t - 1$. Thus expectation is changed adaptively by such an adjustment. In the second half of each equation $L$ denotes the lag operator, which operates on a variable $d_t$ by the definition $L d_t = d_{t-1}$, $L^2 d_t = d_{t-2}$, etc.

Note that one can manipulate the operator $L$ using the rules of algebra. For example, if we follow the equation

$$d_{t-1} + 3 d_{t-2} = L d_t + 3 L^2 d_t = (L + 3 L^2) d_t$$

we find from the second equality sign that we can factor out $d_t$ on the righthand side. Here $(L + 3 L^2)$ becomes an operator itself to be applied to the variable on its righthand side. In equation (14.1) we have applied the identity

$$1 + x + x^2 + x^3 + \ldots = [1 - x]^{-1}$$

which is valid provided that the infinite series has a finite sum. We let $x = (1 - c)L$, to yield

$$[1 - (1 - c)L]^{-1} = 1 + (1 - c)L + (1 - c)^2 L^2 + \ldots$$

Then this infinite series can be multiplied by $d_{t-1}$ on its righthand side term by term to yield

$$[1 - (1 - c)L]^{-1} d_{t-1} = [1 + (1 - c)L + (1 - c)^2 L^2 + \ldots] d_{t-1} = d_{t-1} + (1 - c) d_{t-2} + (1 - c)^2 d_{t-3} + \ldots$$

This result should agree with the result obtained by repeatedly substituting out the expectations of past periods using the first half of each equation in (14.1). Using the lag operator $L$ and manipulating it algebraically provides a convenient method to derive results involving lagged variables, as we have just demonstrated. Using the lag operator saves a lot of algebraic substitutions.

Under our assumptions, the present-value model for the logarithm of stock price $p$ at the beginning of period $t$ can be written as

$$p_t - \delta \cdot E_t d_t + \alpha \cdot E_t g_t + \gamma^* \qquad (14.2)$$

The coefficient $\alpha$ in equation (14.2) is expected to be smaller than the coefficient $\delta$ because $E_t g_t$ is the expected growth rate for only one year ahead based on the past history of dividends and $E_t d_t$ is the expected value of log price for only one year ahead based on the same history. If growth had no effect one would expect the stock price to be roughly double when the level of dividend doubles. In this case the coefficient of $E_t d_t$ would be one. We can expect it to be somewhat less than one because the adaptive expectation hypothesis based on past history of dividends is not a perfect theory. Concerning the expected rate of growth, the present-value model of stock price requires the whole pattern of growth of all future dividends. $E_t g_t$ is not a very accurate indicator of the entire pattern of future growth. A poor measure results in a smaller coefficient.

We will use the last parts of equation (14.1) to replace $E_t d_t$ and $E_t g_t$ in equation (14.2) to derive an equation for $p_t$ that can be estimated using data on past $p$'s and $d$'s. The derivation takes the following steps. First, substitute the last parts of equation (14.1) for the expectation variables in equation (14.2). Second, multiply the resulting equation by the operator $[1 - (1 - b)L][1 - (1 - c)L]$ on the lefthand side. Third, multiply out the product of the two terms in square brackets to get $1 - (2 - c - b)L + (1 - c)(1 - b)L^2$. Fourth, convert all products of the lag operator $L$ and the variables into appropriate lagged variables without involving the lag operator. The result is

$$p_t = \beta_1 p_{t-1} + \beta_2 p_{t-2} + \beta_3 d_{t-1} + \beta_4 d_{t-2} + \beta_5 d_{t-3} + \gamma \tag{14.3}$$

where $\gamma = \gamma^* bc$, $\beta_1 = (2 - c - b)$, $\beta_2 = -(1 - c)(1 - b)$, $\beta_3 = c\delta + b\alpha$, $\beta_4 = -c\delta(1 - b) - b\alpha(2 - c)$, and $\beta_5 = b\alpha(1 - c)$. The reader is advised to work through the above four steps in the derivation of (14.3). See question 5 below.

Investors are assumed to think in real values rather than in nominal values, so that all data on stock prices and dividends should be in constant prices. We obtain these data by dividing data in current prices by an appropriate general price index. Since the five coefficients ($\beta_1, \beta_2, \ldots, \beta_5$) in (14.3) are derived from four structural parameters, $b$, $c$, $\delta$, and $\alpha$, there is one nonlinear restriction on the coefficients ($\beta_1, \ldots, \beta_5$). Equation (14.3) is a linear function of the five coefficients ($\beta_1, \ldots, \beta_5$), but a nonlinear function of only the four parameters ($b$, $c$, $\delta$, $\alpha$). It will be estimated by the method of nonlinear least squares. The method minimizes the sum of squared residuals of equation (14.3) with respect to the four parameters. By choosing numerical values for the four basic parameters, the values of the five coefficients of equation (14.3) can be computed. Given the values of the five coefficients and data on the variables on the righthand side of (14.3), a predicted value of $p$ corresponding to the righthand side variables is computed. The difference between the actual value of $p$ and the above predicted value forms a residual. The numerical values of the four parameters which make the sum of squares of these residuals over all the sample data the smallest are chosen to be the least-squares estimates. These estimates can be computed using a standard computer program for statistical analysis.

The literature on the present-value model relevant to the above formulation includes, among others, Chow (1958), Gordon (1962), Campbell and Shiller (1987), Chow (1989), Barsky and DeLong (1993), and Donaldson and Kamstra (1996). Chow (1958) proposes and estimates equation (14.2). Gordon (1962) studies an equation $P_t = D_t/(r - g_t)$ where $D$ is current dividend, whereas our formula is based on expected log dividend $E_t d_t$. The remaining four references all combine the present-value model with a particular model for the time series of dividends under rational expectations. While both Campbell and Shiller (1987) and Chow (1989) find strong statistical evidence for rejecting such a model, Chow (1989) also finds strong statistical evidence in support of the present-value model combined with adaptive expectations. This chapter reports additional evidence on the present-value model combined with adaptive expectations. Note that the time series on dividends for Shanghai stocks are very short, making it difficult to estimate time-series models for dividends under rational expectations.

## 14.3 Empirical Findings from the Shanghai Stock Exchange

For a Chinese enterprise to issue stocks to be traded on the Shanghai or the Shenzhen Stock Exchange, an application has to be submitted to the Stock Exchange Regulation Commission in Beijing for approval. The application contains important financial data about the enterprise, including balance sheet data and profit and loss statements to the extent they are available. The application must first be approved by a provincial or local authority before submission to the Commission. The main criteria for approving the application are the company's performance, the clarity and reliability of its financial reporting, and the need for its financing according to the objectives of China's economic development program. Hence, the opening of the Shanghai Stock Exchange is part of the Chinese economic reform and development process. One important aspect of enterprise reform has been to restructure the state enterprises into modern corporations. The large and well-managed ones have shares that are traded publicly. Many medium-size state enterprises have become shareholding companies, but their shares are traded only internally among staff and workers of the enterprises. Most state enterprises are not qualified to be traded on the Shanghai Stock Exchange, because the criteria for admission to the Exchange are very strict. According to my conversations with several enterprise managers, many more enterprises wish to raise capital by issuing stocks than are approved by the authorities. The criteria for admission were determined in order to promote China's economic reform and development.

In applying the criteria for admission in practice, however, there could be political influence or even corruption, as in other situations requiring approval of government officials. There could also be falsification of financial data. Yet the strict admission standard has the effect of making the information on the enterprise's performance available to the public and thus enabling the investors to make decisions according to the present-value model proposed.

There is a Shanghai Index of 30 representative stocks, similar to the Hang Seng Index of the Hong Kong Stock Exchange and the Dow Jones Index for industrial stocks of the New York Stock Exchange. All three indices consist of blue-chip stocks. We decided to include in our sample only the stocks listed in the Shanghai Index, for the purpose of comparing the results of our study with similar studies using the stocks included in the other two indices. In the first stage of this study, two colleagues at Shandong University

**Table 14.1**  List of companies and observation numbers

| Companies | '96 | '97 | '98 | Companies | '96 | '97 | '98 |
|---|---|---|---|---|---|---|---|
| 1. Tsingtao Brewery | 3 | 2 | 1 | 25. Shanghai Hero | | 39 | |
| 2. Shanghai Pechem | | 5 | 4 | 26. Guangzhou Ship | | 41 | 40 |
| 3. Qingdao Haier | | 7 | 6 | 27. Yuyuan Tourist | 44 | 43 | 42 |
| 4. Fujian Cement | | 9 | 8 | 28. Huallian Corp | | 46 | 45 |
| 5. N. China Pharm | | 11 | 10 | 29. Pudong Da Taxi | | 48 | 47 |
| 6. Changhong Elec | | 12 | | 30. Jinqiao Export | | 50 | 49 |
| 7. Jiangsu Chunlan | | | 13 | 31. Wai Gao Qiao | | | 51 |
| 8. Tonghua Dongbao | | 14 | | 32. Harbin Pharm | | | 52 |
| 9. Yizhen Chem | | 15 | | 33. Jinan Qinqi | | | 53 |
| 10. Guomai Ind Co | | 17 | 16 | 34. Tianjin Global | | | 54 |
| 11. Shen Ergy Co | | 19 | 18 | 35. Dongfang Elec | | | 55 |
| 12. AJ Co | | 21 | 20 | 36. Tibet Pearl | | | 56 |
| 13. Eastern Comms | | | 22 | 37. Star Lake | | | 57 |
| 14. Mei Yan | | 24 | 23 | 38. Meng Dian | | | 58 |
| 15. Xinjiang Tebian | | | 25 | 39. Shanghai Haixin | | 60 | 59 |
| 16. Guangzhou Steel | | | 26 | 40. Urban & Rural | | | 61 |
| 17. First Provision | | 28 | 27 | 41. P&T Equip Co | | | 62 |
| 18. Hangzhou Jiefang | | 30 | 29 | 42. Xiamen Eng Mach | | | 63 |
| 19. Lansheng Corp | | | 31 | 43. Kunming Machine | | | 64 |
| 20. Wangfujing Group | | | 32 | 44. Maanshan Iron | | 66 | 65 |
| 21. Lujiazui Develop | | | 33 | 45. Chlor Al Kali | 69 | 68 | 67 |
| 22. Dazhong Taxi | 36 | 35 | 34 | 46. Shanghai 3F | | 70 | |
| 23. E. Ch. Computer | | 37 | | 47. Tian Qiao Dept | | 72 | 71 |
| 24. Shanghai Tongji | | 38 | | | | | |

in China and I were able to obtain data for only 22 of the 30 companies included in the Shanghai Index. These are the first 22 companies listed in table 14.1, which provided data for at least three years prior to the beginning of 1998 as required by equation (14.3), with three lagged dependent variables. The first row of table 14.1 shows that data required to explain stock price in the years 1998, 1997, and 1996, numbered 1, 2, and 3 respectively, are available for the company Tsingtao Brewery (which produces the well-known beer), and so on for the other entries in the table. According to equation (14.3), dividend data for at least the years 1995, 1996, and 1997 are needed to explain the price of a stock at the beginning of 1998. Only two of these 22 companies have data from 1993 on, which provides three observations for each. Two observations are available for each of 10 companies and one observation only is available for the remaining 10. Hence, the total number of observations from the first stage of our study is 36. The results obtained using these 36 observations were similar to those reported in column 1 of table 14.2 and supported the present-value model as formulated here, but the standard errors of the estimates were larger because of the small sample size. Therefore, in the second stage, we decided to obtain more data. Many companies are excluded from our sample because they did not declare any dividends for three consecutive years in the period we studied, as required in the estimation of equation (14.3). We succeeded in obtaining data for 25 additional companies, i.e., those listed in table 14.1 after number 22, consisting of 36 observations. Hence, the total number of observations is 72. All data are divided by the retail price index for conversion to constant price figures.

Many companies in the sample did not issue dividends in cash but in stock dividend. When dividends were issued in the form of stocks, we treat as dividend the market value of the stock dividend issued. The price of the stock itself was adjusted to reflect the larger number of shares. For example, if there were one million shares selling at $10 per share before the issue of stock dividend, and two shares were given for 100 old shares, the price after the issue would be close to $10/1.02 and the dividend per share was treated as 0.02 ($10/1.02). The price per old share was converted to (10/1.02), or whatever the market price of the post-dividend share was, times 102/100. In the above example, if the same stock dividend were conditioned on the share owner paying $0.01 for each share issued, the value of dividend per share would be 0.02 ($10/1.02) − 0.01. Many such calculations were made in the data. After the dividend data are divided by the retail price index, many companies show decreasing dividends in constant prices, because the retail price index from the end of 1993 to 1997 was respectively 1.132, 1.378, 1.582, 1.687, and 1.695, showing an increasing trend. However, this does not affect the testing of our hypothesis that the logarithm of stock price is positively correlated with the expected growth in log dividend.

Using the 72 observations on the prices of stocks of 47 companies at the beginning of 1996, 1997, or 1998, we estimate 7 parameters, i.e., $b$, $c$, $\delta$, $\alpha$, and three year dummies, and the residual variance of the nonlinear regression function (14.3), where $\gamma$ was changed to $\gamma(96)$, $\gamma(97)$, and $\gamma(98)$ to capture the separate economic effects of the years 1996, 1997, and 1998 respectively. The nonlinear regression routine minimizes the sum of squared residuals of the regression function (14.3) including three time dummy variables with respect to the parameters ($b$, $c$, $\delta$, $\alpha$, $\gamma(96)$, $\gamma(97)$, $\gamma(98)$). The coefficients ($\beta_1, \ldots, \beta_5$) are found by the relations given below equation (14.3).

Table 14.2 summarizes the results from estimating the nonlinear regression function (14.3) using the 72 observations on stocks traded on the Shanghai Stock Exchange. It also presents the results of Chow and Kwan (1997) from estimating the same regression function using data on 17 companies for the years 1982 to 1993 traded on the Hong Kong Stock Exchange and included in the Hang Seng Stock Price Index, with a total of 204 observations and including additional company dummy variables, for 16 of the 17 companies. Table 14.2 also includes the results of Lin (1998) from estimating the same regression using data on 30 companies included in the Dow Jones Industrial Average in January 1998 for the years 1953–98 with a total of 1,380 observations, and including both time and company dummy variables. In the Shanghai sample, there are simply not sufficient observations to introduce company dummy variables. The standard deviation of regression residuals, $s$, is slightly lower for Hong Kong partly because there are company dummy variables.

**Table 14.2**   Estimates of parameters of equation (14.3) explaining log stock price

| Shanghai 1996–8 (47 firms; 72 observations) | Hong Kong 1982–93[a] (17 firms; 204 observations) | United States 1953–98[b] (30 firms; 1,380 observations) |
|---|---|---|
| $b = 0.9321$ (.1221) | $b = 0.8695$ (.1281) | $b = 0.8690$ (.0352) |
| $c = 0.2993$ (.0845) | $c = 0.5708$ (.1081) | $c = 0.1520$ (.0352) |
| $\alpha = 0.0569$ (.0495) | $\alpha = -0.0115$ (.0532) | $\alpha = 0.1809$ (.0367) |
| $\delta = 0.5722$ (.1687) | $\delta = 0.5668$ (.0696) | $\delta = 0.7323$ (.0675) |
| $\beta_1 = 0.7636$ | $\beta_1 = 0.5597$ | $\beta_1 = 0.9332$ |
| $\beta_2 = 0.0731$ | $\beta_2 = -0.0560$ | $\beta_2 = -0.0723$ |
| $\beta_3 = 0.1847$ | $\beta_3 = 0.3135$ | $\beta_3 = 0.3192$ |
| $\beta_4 = 0.0702$ | $\beta_4 = -0.0279$ | $\beta_4 = -0.2957$ |
| $\beta_5 = 0.0977$ | $\beta_5 = -0.0043$ | $\beta_5 = 0.0696$ |
| $R^2 = 0.7848$ $s = .2635$ | $R^2 = 0.7011$ $s = .2177$ | $R^2 = 0.9112$ |

[a] Chow and Kwan (1997, tables 1 and 2).
[b] Lin (1998, tables 3-3 and 3-4).

From the first column of table 14.2, one observes that both adjustment coefficients $b$ and $c$ in the adaptive formation of expected rate of growth and expected level of log dividend, respectively, are between zero and one. Both expected variables have a positive effect on log stock price, as our model predicts. The standard errors of the parameter estimates are given in parentheses. The relative weights of expected growth and expected level of dividends in the determination of log stock price are as given by $\alpha$ and $\delta$. The estimate of $\alpha$ is much smaller than the estimate of $\delta$, for reasons given below equation (14.2). The point estimates of the $\beta$ coefficients are unconstrained least-squares estimates provided for reference. Although our sample is small compared with the samples in the other two studies, table 14.2 shows that the parameters are fairly precisely estimated as judged by the standard errors. Our results show that the present-value model, as formulated in this chapter, explains the data well.

One can test the hypothesis that our model of stock price determination is correct by testing that the set of nonlinear restrictions on the coefficients of regression function (14.3) is correct. If the restriction imposed by the model through the specified relations between the five regression coefficients $\beta_i$ and the four basic parameters is incorrect, the regression equation obtained by estimating equation (14.3) directly without going through the specified relations as we did would improve the fit significantly. This means that the sum of squares of the residuals from the nonlinear regression we fitted would be much larger than the sum of squares of the residuals of equation (14.3), with all coefficients estimated freely without being restricted by the specified relations with the four parameters. The sum of squared residuals of the unrestricted linear regression with $\beta_1, \ldots, \beta_5$ $\gamma(96), \gamma(97), \gamma(98)$ as coefficients, denoted $B$, equals 4.3893 with $72 - 5 - 3 = 64$ degrees of freedom. The number of degrees of freedom is the number of data points minus the number of estimated parameters. The sum of squared residuals of the restricted nonlinear regression (14.3) with the same three year dummies, denoted $A$, equals 4.5128 with

$72 - 4 - 3 = 65$ degrees of freedom. The sum of squared residuals $A$ from the restricted regression is always larger than the sum of squared residuals $B$ from the unrestricted regression in the sample. The important question is whether the means of the squared residuals from the two regressions in the population are the same. If so, the restricted regression is as good as the unrestricted regression, and the theory is correct.

Assuming the means of the squared residuals to be the same for the two regressions in the population, we ask how likely it is to obtain a difference $(A - B)$ as large as $(4.5128 - 4.3893)$. If it is highly unlikely, our conclusion is to reject the assumption that the theory is correct. To find the probability that the difference $(A - B)$ can be as large as the one observed in our sample, we compute the statistic $(A - B)/s^2$ where $s^2$ is the residual variance of the unrestricted regression, which equals $B/64$. Assuming normally distributed residuals, the above statistic has an $F(1, 64)$ distribution where 1 stands for testing only one restriction and 64 for the number of degrees of freedom in the denominator. The probability distribution of these statistics depends on these two parameters. It was first derived mathematically by R. A. Fisher, considered the father of modern statistics, and hence was given the name F-distribution. The probability that this statistic takes values as large as the value observed can be looked up in statistical tables included in common computer software. The observed value is $(4.5128 - 4.3893)/(4.3893/64)$ or $1.801$. From the table for the $F(1, 64)$ distribution, the probability of obtaining a value as large as this value is 18 percent, not small enough for us to reject the assumption that the theory is correct. This is a piece of statistical evidence supporting our model of stock price formation. The year dummies $\gamma(t)$ for the beginning of 1996, 1997, and 1998 are, respectively, $0.852$, $1.229$, and $0.524$. These are the time effects on the prices of Shanghai stocks net of the dividend effects. They reflect the optimism at the beginning of 1997 compared with 1998, and the pessimism of 1998 compared with even 1996.

# 14.4   Comparison with Findings for Hong Kong and New York Stocks

As pointed out, table 14.2 also presents estimates of equation (14.3) using the data on stocks traded on the Hong Kong Stock Exchange and on the New York Stock Exchange. First, we note the remarkable similarity in the three sets of estimates of the unrestricted $\beta$ coefficients and the four structural parameters. The behaviors of these markets are strikingly similar according to our model, in spite of their institutional differences. The adjustment coefficient $b$ in forming expectation for the growth rate $g$ is high in all three cases, reflecting the importance of the most recent growth rate. The smaller adjustment coefficient $c$ in forming expectations for the level of log dividend in all three cases reflects the importance of past levels. The coefficient $\delta$ of $E_t d_t$ is in all cases larger than the coefficient $\alpha$ of $E_t g_t$ as expected, because the latter is not an accurate measure of the long-term growth of dividends far into the future on which stock price depends. It appears that the estimate of $\alpha$, which measures the importance of the projected rate of growth of dividends, is slightly lower for Hong Kong than for Shanghai, although not significantly so. This may reflect the fear on the part of investors that past growth in dividends of a Hong Kong company, which contributes to a positive expected growth variable in our model, could not be projected into the future as the transfer of sovereignty of Hong Kong to the Chinese government in 1997 approached. The estimate of $\alpha$ for Shanghai is low compared with the estimate for the US, possibly reflecting the uncertainty on the part of investors in projecting a short history of growth rates for the newly listed companies in Shanghai into the future, whereas in a mature and stable economy like the US, the dividend behavior of the companies included in the Dow Jones Industrial Average has been observed for a long time and can serve as a more reliable indicator of future dividend growth.

# 14.5   Concluding Comments

The main purpose of this chapter is to provide an explanation of prices of stocks traded in the Shanghai Stock Exchange. From table 14.2, our results are remarkably consistent with the present-value model of stock prices as implemented by choosing $E_t \log D_t$ and $E_t \Delta \log D_t$ as the two most important parameters and assuming that these expectations are formed adaptively. The results are encouraging because the Shanghai Stock Exchange is new, having started only in 1992, and because Chinese investors have been allowed to buy stocks only since the early 1990s. This same model, which explains the prices of stocks traded in mature stock markets in Hong Kong in the 1980s and 1990s as reported in Chow and Kwan (1997) and in the United States as reported in Chow (1958) and in Lin (1998), is found to be applicable to prices of stocks traded in a developing economy where investors are just beginning to learn how to buy stocks and the economic institutions are otherwise very different. For future research, it would be interesting to find out whether the prices of the B shares of the same companies traded in Shanghai, insofar as these B shares exist, and of the shares traded in the Shenzhen Stock Exchange reveal similar behavior.

Concerning the role that the Chinese government plays in regulating the stock exchanges, we have mentioned in section 14.3 that the Stock Exchange Regulation Commission exercises control over the applications of enterprises to have their stocks traded in the exchanges. In addition, government economic officials watch the stock market price indices closely. If there are signs of overinvesting that appears to have led to abnormally high prices, the government discourages people from investing by raising margins. The signals are stronger than the well-known remarks by Federal Reserve Chairman Allan Greenspan on the "irrational exuberance" of investors. When the stock prices are considered too low, the government wages a campaign to get people to invest. This is not as strong a measure as that taken by the Central Bank of Taiwan, which directly intervened in the stock market in 1998 by purchasing a substantial amount of stock to raise the price index during the Asian financial crisis.

Government intervention in the stock market in China is more direct than in the United States but probably less than in some other Asian economies. Government intervention faces at least two problems. First, to the extent that market forces are powerful, government intervention may not be effective. For example, when foreign investors participate in buying the stocks of different countries to balance their investment portfolios, the prices of the stocks of all countries are determined by the economic and psychological forces of the entire world and are beyond the financial resources and control of a single government. Statistical correlations of the movements of stock price indices of different markets around the world testify to this point. The influence of the domestic government is somewhat larger if the market is isolated, but is still limited because it has to compete with market forces within the entire country. Second, if the government takes an active role in influencing the prices of stocks, the public will hold it responsible if the prices move in an unfavorable direction. There is no need for the government to put itself in such a position.

## References and Further Reading

Barsky, Robert and J. Bradford DeLong. "Why Does the Stock Market Fluctuate?" *Quarterly Journal of Economics*, 108 (May 1993), 2: 291–311.

Campbell, John and Robert Shiller. "Cointegration and Tests of Present Value Models." *Journal of Portfolio Economics*, 95 (Oct. 1987), 5: 1062–88.

Chow, Gregory C. "The Formation of Stock Prices." *Econometrica*, 26 (Oct. 1958), 4: 604–5.

Chow, Gregory C. "Rational Versus Adaptive Expectations in Present Value Models." *Review of Economics Statistics*, 71 (Aug. 1989), 3: 376–84.

Chow, Gregory C. and Yum K. Kwan. "Rational Expectations is not Necessarily Valid to Econometric Models: Evidence from Stock Market Data." *Pacific Economic Review*, 2 (Oct. 1997), 3: 149–63.

Chow, Gregory C., Zhao-zhi Fan, and Jin-yan Hu. "Shanghai Stock Prices as Determined by the Present-Value Model." *Journal of Comparative Economics*, 27 (1999), pp. 553–61.

Donaldson, R. Glen and Mark Kamstra. "A New Dividend Forecasting Procedure that Rejects Bubbles in Asset Prices: The Case of 1929's Stock Crash." *Review of Financial Studies*, 9 (Summer 1996), 2: 333–83.

Gordon, Myron, J. *The Investment, Financing and Valuation of the Corporation.* Homewood, IL: R. D. Irwin, 1962.

Lin, Jonathan. *The Present Value Model of Stock Prices Under Rational and Adaptive Expectations: Evidence from the US Stock Market.* Princeton, NJ: AB thesis, Dept. of Economics, Princeton University, 1998.

## Questions

1. Define the lag operator $L$. Write out $[1 - (1 - c)L]^{-1}d_t$ explicitly.
2. State the present-value model of stock price verbally and mathematically. What are the four parameters determining the price of the stock according to the theoretical model specified in this chapter?
3. List the major assumptions made to specify the present value of stock price used in this chapter.

4  Explain the adaptive expectations hypothesis. Give one economic example of this hypothesis unrelated to the present-value model.

5  Derive equation (14.3) from equations (14.1) and (14.2) algebraically using the lag operator $L$, and check the relations between the five coefficient $\beta$'s and the four basic parameters $c$, $b$, $\delta$, and $\alpha$ given below equation (14.3).

6  Explain the meaning of the parameters $c$ and $b$ and of the coefficients $\delta$ and $\alpha$ in equation (14.2). Which of these four parameters have values for the Hong Kong and New York Stock Exchanges that are very different from the values for the Shanghai Stock Exchange? What economic conditions can explain the differences and how?

7  Question 5 refers to only four parameters in the model, and yet there are five coefficients in the regression equation (14.3). What is the basic principle used in estimating only four parameters when the regression has five coefficients?

8  The year dummy variables have coefficients 0.852, 1.229, and 0.524 for the years 1996, 1997, and 1998 respectively. Explain the meaning of these numbers. What do they have to say about these three years?

9  One way to compare the behavior of Chinese stock-market investors with that of investors in other markets is to formulate a hypothesis on the relation between the price of a stock and its dividends, and compare the parameters of this relation estimated with Chinese data and the parameter values estimated with data from other markets. The hypothesis adopted in this chapter consists of two parts, one concerning the factors determining the logarithm of stock price, and the second on the determination of these two factors. State both parts clearly.

# 15

# The Behavior of State Enterprises

To discuss the behavior of Chinese state enterprises, sections 15.1 and 15.2 describe respectively the organization and the operation of a state enterprise under central planning using the case of the First Lathe Factory of Beijing in 1960. Sections 15.3 and 15.4 provide two simple models to describe the behavior of Chinese state enterprises under planning and in the early stage of enterprise reform. These two simple models serve to illustrate the effects of changing institutional environment on management behavior. As pointed out in section 4.3, state enterprises have been transformed to shareholding companies resembling modern corporations in form. In behavior, however, these Chinese state enterprises may be different from modern corporations in Western market economies. Section 15.5 explains the differences in behavior by pointing out some of the unresolved problems of enterprise reform.

## 15.1 Organization of a State Enterprise under Central Planning

Before describing the organization and operations of Chinese industrial enterprises during the period of economic planning, let me mention briefly the process by which Chinese industry was placed under government control after 1949. A description of this process can be found in Cheng (1982, ch. 5). In 1949 the PRC government took over those state corporations which it identified as bureaucratic capital and confiscated 2,858 industrial enterprises employing more than 750,000 workers. The new regime's state industrial enterprises accounted for 41.3 percent of the gross output value of China's large, modern industries and 34.7 percent of all industrial output. During 1951 and 1952 the government took over all foreign enterprises (see Cheng 1982: 138–40). In 1952–3 private enterprises were placed under government control, while the number of state corporations and stores increased. In 1954–7 private enterprises were transformed into joint ventures and absorbed into the state sector, with the former owners receiving a nominal interest payment on their capital. In the meantime, handicraftsmen and peddlers were organized into cooperatives, first in the form of supply and marketing cooperatives as an aid to individual handicraftsmen, and later in the form of producers' cooperatives under the direction of the government. By 1957 practically all industrial enterprises were either state owned or collectively owned. In 1957 there were 170,000 industrial enterprises, of which 58,000 were state owned and 112,000 were collectively owned. The state-owned enterprises, though smaller in number, accounted for a much larger fraction of gross industrial output value. In 1981 there were 84,200 state-owned enterprises, 296,800 collectively owned enterprises, and 185,500 commune-run enterprises, accounting for 78.30, 14.80, and 6.24 percent of gross industrial output value, respectively, leaving only 0.66 percent accounted for by "others" (*Statistical Yearbook of China, 1981*, pp. 207 and 212).

To study Chinese industry at a microeconomic level, let us examine the operation of an individual enterprise, as reported in *Survey of the First Lathe Factory of Beijing*. Although published in 1980, this report was actually written in 1961, by a team headed by Ma Hong, the president of the Chinese Academy of Social Sciences in the early 1980s. The government of the Municipality of Beijing appointed the team to study the operations and problems of the First Lathe Factory under its jurisdiction. The report that resulted was internally circulated among government officials and was finally published in 1980. To my knowledge it is the first work concerning the Chinese economy published in China in two decades. When I visited China in the summer of 1980 to give lectures in econometrics in Beijing as a guest of the Chinese Academy of Social Sciences, I tried to find written material on the Chinese economy. Upon inquiring among friends and colleagues from several universities and research institutions in China, and searching in bookstores, I found books on economic philosophy, but not a single published empirical study of any aspect of the Chinese economy. In the fall of 1980 I received a copy of the above *Survey* from Mr. Ma Hong. In 1961 the factory surveyed was the largest factory of the machine-building industry in Beijing, having more than 6,000 staff and workers. It was very well run, receiving the great honor of being designated the "Red Flag Factory" in 1959. In 1949 this enterprise was established by combining three companies, one having been established in 1921 by American capital, the second having been founded in 1911 by Chinese capital, and the third having been operated by the government of the Republic of China. The enterprise was transformed in the period of the first Five Year Plan with Soviet technical assistance and expanded a great deal between 1957 and 1960, when the number of skilled workers increased from 838 to 4,227. Its history is illustrative of the development of large state-owned industrial enterprises during the period 1949–61.

Administratively speaking, the First Lathe Factory was under the First Ministry of Machine Building, which later transferred its control to the government of the Municipality of Beijing. Its organization chart as of 1957 is presented in figure 15.1. When the Chinese government took over industrial enterprises in the early 1950s, it generally left the organization and administration of the enterprises unchanged. Figure 15.1 shows no difference from the organization chart of a privately operated enterprise, except perhaps for the nonprofessional school under the education department.

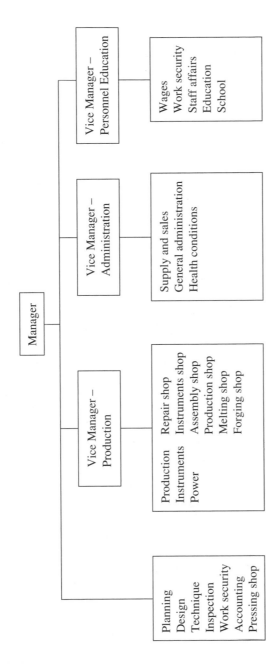

**Figure 15.1** Organization of the First Lathe Factory, 1957

In the late 1950s, when the government began to exercise tighter control over the lives of industrial workers and staff, a large factory or state-administered institution had to provide housing, medical services, and schools for its employees. During the Great Leap Forward of 1958–60, industrial enterprises and communes were asked to increase production at unreasonable rates. The First Lathe Factory was greatly expanded, and its organization was changed several times. New products were introduced, so that it became a large factory producing lathes, milling machines, and other machine tools, some being produced in quantity while others were individually ordered. The committee that prepared the survey recommended reorganization of production according to the specialized nature of the production processes.

Concerning the administration of this lathe factory, questions arose as to how much and what kind of responsibility should be assigned to the shops and lower-level units. The survey contains an interesting discussion of these questions. A more important administrative problem is the appropriate division of authority between the factory manager and the secretary of the Communist Party committee authorized to supervise this factory. As we pointed out in section 2.6, central economic planning in China is controlled not only by government officials, from the various ministries of the State Council down, but by the Communist Party through its committees at the various levels parallel to the government economic administration. Each factory has a Party committee headed by a secretary. Each shop in a factory also has a Party committee headed by a secretary. The division of authority between the management of the factory at various levels and the corresponding Party secretary creates administrative problems which have to be resolved.

The basic principle is that the Communist Party should exercise leadership in all aspects of Chinese economic life. In a factory the Party secretary is given a leadership role which, in practice, varies from place to place and from time to time. For example, since 1979, with modernization the main concern of the Chinese government, managers in general have more authority than before. The manager is supposed to manage "under the leadership of the Party committee." According to the experience of the First Lathe Factory up to 1961, the leadership role assumed by the Party secretary has created two main problems (*Survey*, 1980: 82–6). First, the Party secretary in certain situations became the factory administrator. When the Party committee met, it became an executive meeting of the factory management. Second, and related to the first, no one would take responsibility for certain important administrative matters. The factory manager and other administrators depended on the Party secretary to make decisions and take responsibility for them. Frequently, for matters large and small, people waited for decisions to be made by the Party committee, acting as if only that committee had the authority to decide. In practice, it was not easy to determine what should fall under the authority of the committee. The Party secretary could and did become involved in administrative details. On average, the Party secretary had to attend more than one committee meeting a day, and some lower-level Party secretaries had to attend two or more meetings a day, "taking some five to six hours per day" (p. 84).

Supervision by the Communist Party extended to several administrative levels below that of the factory manager. The lathe factory's Party committee had 13 members, among whom four were assigned management responsibilities. The Party committees at the shop level also had members who held regular administrative positions, varying from 20 to 40 percent of total committee membership. This illustrates the Party's method of maintaining control by placing its members in administrative positions of government units at various levels, as discussed in section 2.6. An additional problem in the lathe factory, created by the multilevel Party supervision, was that the lower-level Party secretaries sometimes disobeyed or even changed the orders of the factory manager and deputy managers. The lower-level administrators sometimes hesitated to execute orders from the managers, wanting to consult with the Party secretary. Interference by Party members in administrative matters is a serious problem in Chinese industry, especially when the members do not have the required educational background or administrative experience to play a leadership role.

## 15.2   Planning and Operations of a Large-scale State Enterprise

This section describes the planning process of the First Lathe Factory and its operations, including the supply of materials, the distribution of its products, and the composition of costs and profits. Under the direction of central planning, the production plan of a state-owned enterprise has to be approved by a bureau under the appropriate ministry of the State Council. The evolution of industrial planning in China is well documented by the history of the First Lathe Factory of Beijing (*Survey*, 1980: 30–4). In the period 1949–52, central planning was beginning to take shape, and the Chinese planners did not have much experience. A production plan of 1950 for the lathe factory was drafted, which included three sections on output, labor, and materials. In 1951 the administrative bureau of the machine industry issued planning targets for each factory, including quantity of output, value of output, total wage, and other items, but no financial or cost targets. Output estimates were based on the required labor and material inputs. In 1952 the planned targets became more comprehensive, including output quantity, output value, wages, material supplies, and cost of production, as well as their relationships. These targets were issued to the factory. The factory did not issue targets to its various shops, beyond directing them to produce specified quantities of outputs.

During the period of the first Five Year Plan (1953–7), the method of planning became crystallized and plans became more comprehensive. Rather than simply using total labor and material inputs to estimate total cost, the lathe factory gathered more detailed data on the labor hours and materials actually used in the production of different products. The factory was placed under the supervision of the Second Bureau of the First Ministry of Machine Building. It received planning targets for output quantity, output value, number of employees, total wage bill, output per unit of labor (or labor productivity), amount and rate of cost reduction, amount of working capital, amount of material inventory, and total profit. These targets were issued annually, except for the output target, which was quarterly. A quarterly plan was drafted by the factory and submitted to the Second Bureau for approval before execution; it also served as the basis of evaluation by the Second Bureau at the end of the period.

The industrial ministries and their affiliated bureaux made up more than 40 forms to be filled out by the factories concerning their production and related activities. A planning department in the lathe factory had the responsibility for making up the production plan and making sure that its various output, input, cost, and profit elements were consistent. Other departments were responsible for the planning of material supplies, repair of machinery, wage rates, cost accounting, and technical coordination (see figure 15.1). These plans were coordinated by the planning department, resulting in an overall plan consisting of its "output, technical, and financial" components. This overall plan was submitted to the Second Bureau, and through the bureau to the First Ministry of Machine Building for approval. Given this plan, the factory began to issue targets to the various shops concerning output, total labor hours, use of materials, machinery, tools, and energy, and other cost items. The survey committee of the lathe factory pointed to two defects of this planning system (*Survey*, 1980: 31). First, individual initiatives were not properly considered in the planning process, which emphasized the calculation of various numbers concerning outputs and inputs. Second, the procedure of filling out the many forms was unduly complicated and time-consuming.

In the period between 1958 and 1961, as the Great Leap Forward was launched, the plans of the factory became unrealistically optimistic. The idea was that the higher the output targets the better. "It was better to overestimate than to underestimate outputs." "The people could accomplish anything, however high the targets were." There was no realistic basis for the plans. For example, in 1960 the factory issued targets to the shops demanding an increase in output of more than 5 percent per *month*. As a result, from January to July, the cumulative production fell short by 600 milling machines, which amounted to one-quarter of the targeted output for this period. In the meantime, the targets issued to the factory by its supervising Machinery and Electric Bureau of Beijing were incomplete and inconsistent in regard to output and material supplies. For example, in 1960 the factory was directed to produce 2,296 general-purpose milling machines, which required 5,754 tons of steel, but only 2,604 tons were allotted, and of the quantity allotted, only 76 percent was actually delivered. There were similar shortages of electrical machinery and other required equipment. Planning in the factory was in a state of confusion. There was insufficient statistical information on labor hours and materials required for individual products. It was impossible to provide a consistent overall plan in its "output, technical, and financial" components. In 1961, when the survey was conducted, the output targets were still unrealistic in terms of the supplies allotted. For example, the targeted output of milling machines in the first quarter would require 310 tons of steel, but the Machinery and Electric Bureau could provide only 173 tons. The bureau directed an increase of 20 percent in output per unit of labor, a reduction of 10 to 15 percent in production costs, and a planned profit not lower than in the preceding year. Some detailed calculations by the survey team showed that these targets were mutually inconsistent.

In terms of timely completion of the several stages of the planning process, more delays occurred after 1958. Before that year, the production plan was completed fairly early and few changes were made after the plan was approved. The Second Bureau of the

First Ministry of Machine Building issued production targets to the enterprise in August or September. The enterprise studied the targets, had discussions with the Second Bureau, prepared and completed the forms for the plan on the required supply of materials, and reported back to the Second Bureau in October or November. On the basis of the total supplies at its disposal, the bureau approved the targets of material supplies for the first quarter and the planned supplies for the entire year. After 1958, however, the plans in the several stages were often delayed and subject to large upward revisions of production targets. The lathe factory had to keep three sets of books for the different plans with increasing output targets. When production targets were raised, the needed supplies of materials were not increased accordingly, creating shortages and leading to underfulfillment of targets. The survey team recommended more careful collection and analysis of data and the preparation of a well-coordinated plan, which should be followed seriously.

In the operation of an industrial enterprise under central planning, a most difficult problem is to supply the right quantities and qualities of tools and materials. In the lathe factory some of the tools were supplied from outside, and some were produced by the factory itself. Supplying tools from outside presented serious problems (*Survey*, 1980: 44). Before 1958, the factory could obtain these tools directly from suppliers in the market. From 1958 on, orders for these tools had to be placed through a First Supply Station of Beijing before a sales agreement could be obtained from the supplier. Only about 20 percent of the required supplies were obtained this way. Supplies from the market became limited. Additional supplies were obtained "through the back door" from suppliers with whom the factory had established personal connections. After 1960, some of the supplies previously available in the market were no longer available in the Beijing area, though they were still available in the northeastern provinces. However, these provinces controlled their supplies and made them available only to local factories. The lathe factory tried to contact those local factories to purchase the supplies, but could not get them shipped out because such a shipment would have constituted smuggling. Finally, the factory sent staff members to bring the tools back in person. Concerning the mostly specialized tools produced by the factory itself, a census taken on the rate of their utilization revealed that of 450 tools produced, as many as 120, or 25 percent, were placed in storage and never utilized because of duplicate ordering, mistakes in design, mistakes in production, or lack of parts. The survey team summarizes the tools situation with the words "short in supply, slow in production, poor in administration, and wasteful in utilization" (p. 49).

Serious problems also arose in the supply of materials. Of steel alone, 545 kinds were needed. The allotment of supplies according to specifications under the production plan was often insufficient. Sources of supply were often not reliable. Furthermore, when a change was made in the production plan, the supplies could not be changed accordingly, as we noted earlier in this section. When the shortage in quantity and the mismatch in specifications were considered together, the actual shortage of suitable materials became even greater. For example, in the production of lathes, three different types of steel in 17 different forms were used. In the first quarter of 1961 the plan called for 130 tons of steel with these specifications, but the bureau approved only 9 tons consisting of two types and three forms, meeting only 7 percent of the plan. When the supplies did not fit specifications,

**Table 15.1**   Cost and profits of First Lathe Factory of Beijing

| Year | Output (number of machine tools) | Total cost (10,000 yuan) | Profits (10,000 yuan) | Profits remitted to government (10,000 yuan) | % | Profits remitted to Machine-Electric Bureau, Beijing (10,000 yuan) | % | Profits retained by factory (10,000 yuan) | % |
|------|------|------|------|------|------|------|------|------|------|
| 1957 | 615   | 718   | 426   | 393   | 92.3 | 6   | 1.4  | 27  | 6.3  |
| 1958 | 1,159 | 1,156 | 1,139 | 901   | 79.1 | 35  | 3.1  | 2   | 17.7 |
| 1959 | 1,461 | 1,523 | 1,321 | 1,047 | 79.1 | 158 | 11.9 | 116 | 8.8  |
| 1960 | 2,131 | 2,001 | 2,414 | 1,911 | 79.1 | 302 | 12.5 | 201 | 8.3  |

Source: Survey of the First Lathe Factory of Beijing, *1961, pp. 63–5.*

large pieces of steel would be cut into small pieces, a round piece would be cut into a square piece, and so on, leading to waste in labor and materials.

Part of the problem in the supply of materials was due to the change in distribution policy after 1958. Before that year, after approving the plan for material supplies, the Second Bureau ordered the factories to negotiate contracts for materials directly with the suppliers. The two parties settled any differences between themselves. The materials were shipped directly from the suppliers to the factories. After 1958, however, the Machinery and Electric Bureau of Beijing centralized all purchases of material supplies, had them shipped from the suppliers to a warehouse, and distributed them from the warehouse to the factories under its own supervision. It became difficult for the factories to obtain materials according to the required specifications. The factories had to get whatever was available, trying to get ahead of the line as soon as a delivery arrived at the warehouse, and often sending three or four persons to the bureau to negotiate for the supplies. When the supplies were undependable, production became slow and inefficient.

The products of the lathe factory itself were sold to the government and distributed over China through the centralized distribution process. Data on output, total cost, profit, and the distribution of profit for the four years 1957 to 1960 are shown in table 15.1. Note that profit was large as compared with total cost, because appropriate returns to capital or interest costs were not included as a part of cost. In the calculation of cost, a low depreciation rate on capital is applied, and no forgone interest charge is included. Most of the profits were submitted to the central government. After supervision of the factory was transferred to the Machinery and Electric Bureau of Beijing, some profits also went to that Bureau. Small portions of profits were retained by the factory to be used for technical coordination, experimentation with new products, a work safety program, expenditures on small capital items, and workers' welfare and wage bonuses. Profits from state-owned enterprises provided a large fraction of the total revenues of the Chinese government, about 43 percent in 1980.

As far as cost is concerned, the data shown in table 15.2 apply to No. 2 General-Purpose Lathes, which accounted for about 50 percent of the factory's total costs. The

**Table 15.2**   Cost breakdown for No. 2 General-Purpose Lathes

| Year | Average cost (yuan per unit) | Materials as % of cost | Administrative expenses as % of cost | Wages as % of cost |
|------|------------------------------|------------------------|--------------------------------------|--------------------|
| 1957 | 9,819 | 49.1 | 44.6 | 6.3 |
| 1958 | 6,919 | 56.1 | 37.6 | 6.3 |
| 1959 | 7,171 | 53.2 | 42.3 | 4.5 |
| 1960 | 6,164 | 56.4 | 38.9 | 5.7 |

**Source**: Survey of the First Lathe Factory of Beijing, 1961, p. 65.

most striking fact from these data is the low labor cost as a percentage of total cost. It would not be easy to find another country in which labor cost accounts for only 5 or 6 percent of the cost of manufacturing lathes. One reason is that the wage rates were low. A highly paid worker of this lathe factory, named Wang, earned 80 yuan a month in 1957 and 74.5 yuan a month in 1960; a lower-paid worker, Lin, earned 35.2 yuan a month in 1957 and 50.4 yuan in 1960; an even lower-paid worker, Zhang, earned 18.4 yuan per month in 1958 and 26.7 in 1960 (*Survey* 1961: 247–9).

## 15.3   A Simple Model of a State Enterprise under Central Planning

In this section I present a simple model to explain management behavior in a Chinese state enterprise under central planning. This model is intended to capture certain important features of the institutional environment facing a state enterprise, while leaving out other less important features. Whether such a modeling exercise is useful for the purpose at hand depends on whether the included institutional features capture some of the most important aspects of reality. We call the model in this section model A, to be distinguished from model B of the next section, which is applicable to the institutional environment at an early stage of enterprise reform. The fact that these two models are different, and that both are different from a model suitable for a private enterprise in a developed market economy, demonstrates two important points in the application of economics to the study of the Chinese economy. First, institutional knowledge is required and should be taken into account in economic modeling. Second, the method of economic theorizing is applicable to different societies provided that the special institutional features are properly incorporated. The second point suggests the possibility and the hope that as we attempt to apply economic tools to study different economies, the tools themselves will be improved and the field of economics will be broadened and advanced.

In model A for a state enterprise under central planning in China, I assume that in the short run the enterprise is assigned given quantities $k$ and $n$ of capital and labor respectively. Thus, in this model, and model B in the next section, I abstract from the long-run investment decision for the accumulation of capital. In reality, the enterprise was assigned a production target and sometimes targets for value of output and total wage, but no financial or cost targets, as pointed out in the previous section. Since the main criterion for enterprise performance is output quantity, I assume for simplicity that the objective function of the manager is

$$u = u(y, \ 1 - m_1 - m_2) \tag{15.1}$$

where y denotes the quantity of output of the enterprise, $m_1$ denotes management effort for coordinating production, and $m_2$ denotes management effort for negotiating with planning authorities or ministries supervising the enterprise. The argument $1 - m_1 - m_2$ measures the manager's leisure time. The derivatives of the utility function $u$ with respect to both arguments are positive. The production function is

$$y = f[k, \ n, \ x(m_2), \ m_1] \tag{15.2}$$

where $x$ denotes the quantity of material inputs, the supply of which can be increased by management effort $m_2$. The explicit use of management effort $m_1$ in the production function captures one aspect of what Leibenstein (1966) termed X-efficiency. Management effort undoubtedly affects output, given the quantities of other inputs. The efficiency of labor input $n$ is also affected by the institution of the Chinese remuneration system for workers, which does not reward additional effort and hence discourages the workers from working hard. In the production function we choose to define $n$ and other inputs as the quantities actually used and as recorded by statistics of the enterprises. Alternatively, one can choose to measure inputs by efficiency units, being the above quantities each multiplied by an efficiency factor that depends on institutional arrangements. I have subsumed the effects of such efficiency factors under total factor productivity in the production function. In the framework of the production function (15.2), given the quantities of other inputs, a larger quantity of labor input $n$ is required to produce a given output $y$ than in the case of an institution with better labor incentives. The efficiencies of capital, labor, and material inputs are all affected by management effort $m_1$ as this is allowed for in the production function (15.2).

The manager is assumed to maximize $u$ subject to the constraint of this production function. This formulation also captures the idea of Kornai (1979, 1980) concerning a soft-budget constraint. By a soft-budget constraint is meant that the management is not financially constrained, or that its budget can be expanded by negotiating with the planners. First, profit is not included in the objective function, so that there is no reason to economize on the cost of inputs. Second, insofar as an increase of output is desirable and can be achieved by an increase of the use of inputs, there is an incentive for the manager to negotiate for more material and other inputs. This captures the behavior under the institution of a soft-budget constraint. Much has been written on the subject. A notable example is the work of Goldfeld and Quandt (1988), which employs a stochastic rather than a deterministic model and uses profit rather than output in the objective function.

Our formulation is deterministic and simple. Yet it captures some of the most important characteristics of the soft-budget constraint.

For illustration and for possible econometric implementation, I will employ the following special form for the objective function:

$$u = y(1 - m_1 - m_2)^\theta \qquad (15.3)$$

where 1 is the quantity of maximum possible effort, and $1 - m_1 - m_2$ measures "leisure." I use the following special form for the production function:

$$y = b(k, n)m_1^\alpha x^\beta = a(k, n)m_1^\alpha m_2^\gamma \qquad (15.4)$$

where $b$ is a function of capital $k$ and labor $n$, which are treated as fixed, and where by assuming $x = cm_2^\delta$ I have substituted this expression for $x$ on the righthand side, defined the function $a(k, n)$ accordingly, and defined $\gamma = \beta\delta$. Substituting the righthand side of (15.4) for $y$ in (15.3) I obtain

$$u = am_1^\alpha m_2^\gamma (1 - m_1 - m_2)^\theta \qquad (15.5)$$

Having eliminating the constraint (15.4) by substituting it into the objective function (15.3) to obtain (15.5), I can solve the original constrained maximization problem by maximizing (15.5) with respect to the decision variables $m_1$ and $m_2$.

The first-order conditions for maximization are

$$\frac{\partial u}{\partial m_1} = \alpha m_1^{-1} y(1 - m_1 - m_2)^\theta - \theta y(1 - m_1 - m_2)^{\theta-1} = 0$$

$$\frac{\partial u}{\partial m_2} = \gamma m_2^{-1} y(1 - m_1 - m_2)^\theta - \theta y(1 - m_1 - m_2)^{\theta-1} = 0 \qquad (15.6)$$

For an interior solution with $1 - m_1 - m_2$ being positive these conditions become

$$\alpha m_1^{-1} - \theta(1 - m_1 - m_2)^{-1} = 0 \quad \text{or} \quad (\alpha + \theta)m_1 + \alpha m_2 = \alpha$$
$$\gamma m_2^{-1} - \theta(1 - m_1 - m_2)^{-1} = 0 \quad \text{or} \quad (\gamma + \theta)m_2 + \gamma m_1 = \gamma \qquad (15.7)$$

The two equations in (15.7) can be solved for management efforts $m_1$ and $m_2$. To illustrate, if $\theta = .5$, $\alpha = .7$, and $\gamma = .4$, the solution is $m_1 = .4375$ and $m_2 = .25$. Thus about 44 percent of management effort would be spent for management and 25 percent for negotiations with authorities for inputs, leaving about 31 percent for leisure. Reducing $\gamma$ from .4 to .2 would produce a solution $m_1 = .5$ and $m_2 = 1/7$, increasing the effort for management and the leisure time, while reducing the effort for negotiation, as one would expect.

The above model captures three important aspects of the functioning of Chinese state enterprises under central planning. First, the laborers are inefficient as depicted by the functions $b(k, n)$ and $a(k, n)$ in (15.4). Second, management effort $m_1$ is limited by the desire to balance the possibly small benefits from increasing output with the disutility of applying additional effort. Third, the use of material and other inputs may be inefficient because of the lack of cost consideration in the objective function and of the desire to bargain for more inputs in order to achieve a higher output. This implication of the model is consistent with the observed delays in delivery of materials and the large quantities of physically defective or unsuitable items under China's planning system. Given the poor quality of material delivery, the managers would need to order more materials to produce a given quantity of output. Such inefficiency in the use of material inputs can be incorporated in the specification of the production function (15.4). The production function (15.4) and the utility function (15.3) form the basis for the manager's decision to apply effort $m_2$ to increase the supply of inputs. One characteristic of China's industrial production is the large stock of inventory in relation to output. This phenomenon can be explained by using model A if one introduces the stock of inventory as an additional argument in the production function, or simply reinterprets the symbol $x$ to mean the stock rather than the flow of materials. Alternatively one can assume a constant ratio between the stock and the flow of material inputs as a characteristic of the production function.

For the analysis of production in the longer run, we can apply the above modeling of the manager's effort $m_2$ for increasing material supply $x$ to the increase of capital stock $k$ through negotiation with the supervising authorities. This is another aspect of the soft-budget constraint which existed in China under central planning.

## 15.4   A Simple Model of a State Enterprise after Initial Reform

The main distinction between the assigned objective of a state enterprise before and after the initial state enterprise reforms is that management in the latter case is asked to maximize profits rather than to achieve output targets, and thus to include cost calculations in production decisions. A discussion of the nature of the initial reform of state enterprises has been provided in chapter 3. The purpose of the government in changing the objective function is to increase economic efficiency. The limited success of enterprise reform at that stage is due to the loose connection between enterprise profits and additional benefits to the manager. This loose connection will be incorporated in model B. To analyze management behavior after the initial reforms, I assume the objective function of the manager in model B to be

$$v = v(py - qx, m_1) \tag{15.8}$$

where $p$ and $q$ are the prices for delivering marginal output and buying marginal inputs, respectively. Although profit $py - qx$ is an argument in the utility function, it may have a small effect on management's utility. The production function is assumed to be

$$y = f(k, n, x, m_1) \tag{15.9}$$

The argument $m_2$ is omitted from both the utility and the production functions because material inputs are assumed to be available for purchase at price $q$ and not through bargaining. One could study a more complicated model by assuming a part of the material input to be obtained by bargaining with authorities at below-market prices under China's dual price system at the time. The reader may wish to pursue this as an exercise. (See question 1 below.)

Again, to simplify exposition and for possible econometric implementation, I employ the following special form for the utility function

$$v = (py - qx)(1 - m_1)^\theta \tag{15.10}$$

and the production function (15.4). Substitution of (15.4) into (15.10) yields the function

$$v = (pbm_1^\alpha x^\beta - qx)(1 - m_1)^\theta \tag{15.11}$$

which is to be maximized with respect to $m_1$ and $x$. The first-order conditions are

$$\frac{\partial v}{\partial m_1} = \alpha pym_1^{-1}(1 - m_1)^\theta - \theta(py - qx)(1 - m_1)^{\theta-1} = 0$$

$$\frac{\partial v}{\partial x} = (\beta pyx^{-1} - q)(1 - m_1)^\theta = 0 \tag{15.12}$$

For an interior solution with $1 - m_1 > 0$, these conditions yield

$$\begin{aligned} m_1 &= \alpha py/[\alpha py + \theta(py - qx)] = \alpha/[\alpha + \theta(1 - \beta)] \\ x &= \beta py/q \end{aligned} \tag{15.13}$$

Note that the equation for $x$ in (15.13) has been used to simplify the equation for $m_1$ above. According to the equation for management effort $m_1$, the larger the $\theta$ (or elasticity of the management's utility with respect to leisure) compared with the normalized elasticity 1 with respect to profit, the smaller will be the management effort. In other words, the smaller the weight given to profit as compared with the disutility of management effort, the smaller will be the management effort. The larger the elasticity $\alpha$ of output with respect to management effort $m_1$, the larger will be the management effort. The larger the elasticity $\beta$ of output with respect to input $x$, the larger will be the management effort because a larger $\beta$ implies a larger marginal product of $m_1$. To illustrate, if $\theta = .5$, $\alpha = .7$, and $\beta = .3$ (which corresponds to $\delta = 2/3$ and $\gamma = \delta\beta = .2$ in model A), $m_1$ would be 2/3. Compared with model A having the above coefficients (for $\delta = 2/3$ and $\gamma = .2$), this solution for $m_1$ in model B is larger than the sum $m_1 + m_2 = 4.5/7$ for model A. This comparison implies that under model B managerial effort is larger than the combined managerial and negotiation efforts of the less productive model A under central planning.

The second equation of (15.13) for the demand for input $x$ is the familiar equation for a competitive firm in a market economy. The competitive firm in a market economy is assumed to maximize profits subject to the constraint of a Cobb–Douglas production function. Its demand equation for input $x$ is the same as the second equation of (15.13). Demand for input $x$ is set to equate its price $q$ to the value of its marginal product, which is $p$ times the marginal product $\beta y/x$.

We note the following differences in behavior between model A (under central planning) and model B (prevailing after initial urban economic reforms in the 1980s). In model B there is: (1) a tendency to maximize profits by increasing management effort, and (2) a tendency to economize on the use of material inputs because profits enter the objective function of the manager. Note, however, that these tendencies are weak if the relative elasticity parameter $\theta$ is large, reflecting the unimportance of marginal profits in the manager's utility function. This is the case for large and medium-size state enterprises, compared with small state enterprises. In large state enterprises, marginal profits yield only small benefits to the manager, after an allowable amount of profit has been used for distribution as bonuses to management, staff, and workers, both in cash and in the form of consumer durables. By contrast, the high profit incentive for the owner-manager of a private enterprise in a market economy, and for some small state enterprises in China, is captured in model B, with $\theta$ set equal to zero. The appropriate link between marginal profits and the manager's marginal benefits remains a serious problem in enterprise reform in China. Even after the restructuring of state enterprises to become shareholding companies, the managers are still appointed by the board of directors consisting of the same people. The compensation system did not improve significantly and there remains the problem of the board having to monitor the behavior of the managers. The board members themselves often are bureaucrats who lack incentives to do a good monitoring job.

If the stated differences between models A and B correctly depict the realities of China, one should observe higher efficiency in Chinese state industry and lower ratios of material inventories to output after urban economic reforms. In Chow (1993), I presented the increases in total productivity of Chinese industry from 1981 to 1985 as percentage deviations of actual industrial output from the output computed from an aggregate Cobb–Douglas industrial production function. The parameters of this production function were estimated using annual data from the period 1952 to 1980 (excluding the years 1958–69). The fractional deviations from 1981 to 1985 are respectively −.006, .001, .042, .104, and .202. The corresponding increases in agricultural productivities are .077, .181, .269, .422, and .436 (see ibid., table XI). Increases in industrial productivity occurred later (as industrial reforms also occurred later than agricultural reforms) and were smaller in magnitude (as the incentive system in terms of the rights to asset management was more problematic in industry). Concerning the ratio of material inventory to output, I present below the ratio of the value of circulating assets to net output (in 1980 prices) in Chinese industry using data from Chow (1993: tables I and V). For the years 1970, 1975, 1980–5 respectively, the ratios are .956, .950, .805, .851, .844, .821, .809, and .829, which show some decline after economic reforms. Concerning the ratio of capital stock to output I cite Chow (1993: tables I and V), which shows the ratio of capital stock in industry to national income produced by industry (in 1980 prices) to be 4.13 in 1975, 3.95 in 1980, and to be 4.14, 4.14, 4.03, 3.83, and 3.58, respectively from 1981 to 1985. The decline in the ratio from 1980 or 1981 to 1985 may reflect an increase in efficiency. Thus the decreases in the ratios of circulating assets to industrial output and of total capital stock to industrial output are manifestations of the increase in total factor productivity cited above.

Further industrial reforms after 1985 had to deal with the problems of (1) labor efficiency, (2) efficiency in the use of material and other inputs, (3) managerial incentives, all of which can be discussed in the framework of the two models of this and the previous section, as well as (4) the more market-oriented pricing of outputs and material inputs for which the present discussion provides only a part of its microeconomic foundation. Our discussion has incorporated two important reasons explaining the relative efficiencies of large and small state enterprises. First, for small enterprises, the weights given to profits in the utility function are larger in terms of the parameter $\theta$. Second, for small enterprises, the prices $p$ and $q$ of outputs and inputs are more likely to reflect the market conditions of demand and supply under existing Chinese institutional arrangements. For large state enterprises, how to provide sufficient incentives to management in the form of an appropriate system for distributing marginal profits, and to prevent bureaucratic managers from extracting rents from the enterprise without increasing output (carrots and sticks), remain two important problems to be resolved in enterprise reform. These and other problems of corporate governance are important. The Chinese government does not have an ideal solution for them, but has experimented with feasible and quite satisfactory solutions, as evidenced by the continued improvement in the performance of state enterprises. Feasible solutions include the contract responsibility system introduced in 1987 (as previously discussed), and restructuring to form shareholding companies (to be discussed in the next section). A foreign observer should be cautious in attempting to find an "optimum" governance system for Chinese state enterprises, for the latter require very special assumptions.

## 15.5   State Enterprise Restructuring in the Late 1990s and its Effects on Enterprise Behavior

Reform of Chinese state enterprises continued through the last two decades of the twentieth century, as we pointed out in chapters 3 and 4. In the late 1990s, to carry out further reform there were the following problems to be resolved.

a) Who should be given responsibility to carry out the reform, and what kinds of incentives can be provided for carrying out the transformation? Consider the government official in charge of the enterprise at the central or provincial level. What kind of responsibility, if any, should be given to him in carrying out the restructuring of his enterprise? Can he be trusted to improve an existing enterprise by reorganization or restructuring, or to sell the enterprise through auction? Would he be willing to give up his power by making the enterprise independent? Can corruption be avoided during the transformation? He should be provided incentives to do a good job and be prevented from extracting bribes when money changes hands as the enterprise is reorganized or being sold. If the enterprise manager is not to be trusted with carrying out the necessary restructuring, who should be trusted?

b) Management incentives. Under reorganization, what will make the new management work hard in order to make the enterprise profitable? Can we use the management compensation experience from the township and village enterprises to design a good compensation system? It is recognized that having a good management is extremely important for an enterprise. It can lead to improvement in the use of labor, capital, and technology. It can change a loss-making enterprise to a profit-making one.

c) Corporate governance. Who should control the management and how? What are the incentives for the governing board?

d) Labor welfare. How to prevent an undue amount of labor discontent is a very serious problem in state enterprise reform. According to a survey of 205 managers of state enterprises reported by Reuters in September 1997, about 50 percent of respondents believed fears of unemployment would be the biggest brake on the reforms. China's official urban unemployment rate was about 3 percent at the end of 1996. The low unemployment rate is partly due to the fact that laid-off workers receiving partial compensation are not counted as unemployed. The People's Bank has estimated the urban jobless rate including millions of surplus workers from the countryside to be about 8 percent. The government has to determine a politically acceptable amount of compensation for each dismissed worker. This may vary according to location and circumstances. In the case of a sell-off, the net sale price of the enterprise plus government subsidy has to cover the total amount of labor compensation. Even if the sales price does cover this amount, what prevents the management or the government bureaucrat from taking the money from the sale before paying the laid-off workers? Such situations have been reported.

In the reform policy adopted to restructure the state enterprises to become shareholding companies the following solutions were carried out.

a) The State Economics and Trade Commission was given responsibility to oversee the transformation of state enterprises. Since state enterprises are under the control of government ministries and bureaux at different national, provincial, and city levels, the commission of the corresponding level will be responsible for the possible transformation of all state enterprises under its jurisdiction. As restructuring requires compensation to the dislocated employees, the speed of restructuring is governed partly by the budget available to the Commission at each level. The speed should not be so fast as to create too much social instability. It is the responsibility of the officials at the appropriate level of the State Economics and Trade Commission to direct the restructuring of each state enterprise under its jurisdiction. The manager follows its instructions.

b) For many small and medium-size enterprises, management compensation appeared to be sufficient. Since shares of these enterprises are owned by staff and workers in proportion to their initial payment for the shares, the management personnel having more shares will automatically receive a larger fraction of the profits. In addition, the salaries they receive are higher. Management compensation for very large state enterprises did not appear adequate. In the late 1990s an able manager in a township and village enterprise could earn about three times as much as a comparable manager of a state enterprise, up to 300,000 to 400,000 RMB per year, compared with about 100,000.

c) Many small and medium-size state enterprises, but not the large ones, became separate entities owned by nongovernment shareholders. Staff and workers were asked to buy shares approximately proportional to their earning power. Share owners would help elect the manager. The shares could be transferred among the staff and workers but not to outsiders. If an enterprise makes a large loss it may go bankrupt. The State Ministry or Provincial Department will no longer subsidize it since it is financially independent. In practice, because of the undesirable social consequences of allowing a large state enterprise to go bankrupt, loss-making large state enterprises are still subsidized and cases of bankruptcy are few.

d) Workers can be discharged with severance pay for two years, about equal to one-third of their existing wage. In a state enterprise in Shanghai, for example, the average monthly wage might be 500 RMB and severance pay may be 150 to 200. Furthermore, when an enterprise is operating at a loss, it can and does reduce the wages of the workers, possibly to less than 50 percent. In the province of Heilongjiang, it was reported in the *People's Daily*, September 27, 1998, that over 20 percent of the province's entire workforce could not receive their regular salaries. These facts suggested that China was reluctantly accepting the market solution of reducing wages and increasing unemployment to increase enterprise profitability, although the solution was being monitored carefully to avoid political instability.

After the restructuring process, many small and medium-size enterprises appeared to behave more like enterprises of similar size in a less-developed capitalist market economy. The reason is that the systems of management, worker compensation, and other incentives are similar. The incentive system for the management of large state enterprises was not yet resolved. The managers were still underpaid. They were bureaucrats appointed by a board of directors which consisted of the same government and Party officials as before. The government board had neither incentives nor ability to monitor the behavior of the enterprise managers. It is alleged that political considerations entered heavily in the appointments to large state enterprises, and that foreign competition from China's membership in the World Trade Organization was brought in to force the inefficient state enterprises to improve their performance.

The difference in economic efficiency observed for many small and medium-sized state enterprises and for large state enterprises can be characterized by the following propositions. First, many small and medium-sized state enterprises have been privatized in the sense that most shares are in private hands and that the enterprise is truly financially independent and cannot rely on government subsidies. Second, many large state enterprises are still government owned, are managed by government bureaucrats, and can depend on government subsidies. Third, the mere restructuring of almost all state enterprises to become shareholding companies does not guarantee efficiency if the government owns a majority of the shares, and if the bureaucrats in the governing board and in the management of the enterprises have sufficient monopoly power to collect economic rents to benefit themselves without having to earn profits for the enterprise. Fourth, an entirely state-owned enterprise can be efficient, without being a shareholding company, if the bureaucrats involved can derive economic benefits not by collecting economic rents but by earning profits for the enterprise, subject to competition from other state and nonstate enterprises.

A crucial point about enterprise efficiency is that the legal form of ownership is not necessarily the most important determining factor, as some economists have assumed. A shareholding company is not necessarily efficient. A state-owned enterprise can be efficient if it is subject to competition and there is no way for the bureaucrats managing the enterprise to make money except by making profit for the enterprise. The last condition is necessary but not sufficient for efficiency. The bureaucrats should be allowed to share a part of the profit. Therefore, to determine whether an enterprise manager will perform his or her best for the benefit of the enterprise, the crucial question is not the legal form of ownership. Rather there are two crucial questions. First, can the manager benefit substantially from his position without having to increase profit for the enterprise? If the answer is yes, one cannot expect him to work hard for the enterprise, although there are exceptional cases of managers with patriotic or other high moral principles. If the answer is no, the second question is whether he can benefit substantially from the profits that he helps make for the enterprise. If the answer is no, one cannot expect him to work for the benefit of the enterprise. If the answer is yes, one can expect so. In summary, not allowing a manager to acquire economic gains without working, and allowing him to acquire such gains by working for the benefit of the enterprise, are two necessary and sufficient conditions for him to devote his energy to managing the enterprise well.

Considering the development of the Chinese economy, we should take into account both the inefficiency of many large state enterprises in China and the already small and continually declining role of state enterprises in the nation's economy. In chapter 5, we provided a model which implies a substantial rate of economic growth for the Chinese economy at the beginning of the twenty-first century. A substantial rate of growth is possible because growth depends on the nonstate sectors which have accounted for over 70 percent of China's GDP and will account for an even larger share in the future. We will turn to the nonstate sectors in the next chapter.

# References and Further Reading

Cheng, C. Y. *China's Economic Development, Growth and Structural Change*. Boulder, CO: Westview Press, 1982.

Chow, Gregory C. *The Chinese Economy*, ch. 4. New York: Harper & Row, 1985.

Chow, Gregory C. "Capital Formation and Economic Growth in China." *Quarterly Journal of Economics*, 108 (1993), pp. 809–42.

Chow, Gregory C. *Understanding China's Economy*, sec. 14.4. Singapore: World Scientific Publishing Co., 1994.

Goldfield, Stephen M. and Richard E. Quandt. "Budget Constraints, Bailouts, and the Firm Under Central Planning." *Journal of Comparative Economics*, 12 (1988), pp. 502–20.

Granick, David. *Chinese State Enterprises: A Regional Property Rights Analysis*. Chicago: University of Chicago Press, 1990.

Kornai, Janos. "Resource-Constrained Versus Demand-Constrained Systems." *Econometrica*, 47 (1979), pp. 801–20.

Kornai, Janos. *Economics of Shortage*. Amsterdam: North-Holland, 1980.

Lau, Chung-ming and Jianfa Shen, eds. *China Review 2000*, ch. 9. Hong Kong: Chinese University Press, 2000.

Leibenstein, Harvey. "Allocative Efficiency vs. 'X-efficiency.'" *American Economic Review*, 56 (1966), pp. 392–415.

*Statistical Yearbook of China, 1981.* Beijing: State Statistical Bureau.

*Survey of the First Lathe Factory* of *Beijing* (In Chinese). Prepared by the Survey Team of Beijing's First Lathe Factory. Beijing: Chinese Social Science Publishing Co., 1961.

Wen, G. J. and D. Xu, eds. *The Reformability of China's State Sector.* Singapore: World Scientific Publishing Co., 1996.

# Questions

1　Modify model B in section 15.4 to allow for the fact that some inputs of state enterprises are supplied by government suppliers and the remainder can be purchased in open markets at a higher price under the dual-price system. What changes need to be made to the model? What new conclusions will emerge?

2　How did the policies introduced in the reform of state enterprises in the 1980s affect the behavior of these enterprises? Answer verbally and in terms of the parameters of model B in section 15.4.

3　How did the policies introduced in the reform of state enterprises in the late 1990s affect the behavior of medium-size and large state enterprises? Answer verbally and in terms of the parameters of model B, or another model of your own.

4　What data are required and how can you use them to measure whether there was an improvement in the productive efficiency of Chinese state enterprises in the 1980s and 1990s?

5　In what ways did a manager of a large Chinese state enterprise in the planning period behave differently from a manager of a large private enterprise in the US today?

6　Why was it that when many state enterprises were transformed in the late twentieth century to shareholding companies like modern corporations, efficiency did not seem to increase?

7　What are the prospects of reform of state enterprises in the first decade of the twenty-first century?

8　In what way do you expect a Chinese shareholding company to behave differently from a modern corporation in the United States?

9　What are the problems facing the Chinese state enterprises?

10　Name the three industries in which state enterprises accounted for the largest shares of Chinese gross output value, and their approximate shares. Do the same for the smallest shares of gross output value.

11　In model B, which represents management behavior of state enterprises after economic reform, and was described in section 15.4, what is the meaning of the parameter $\theta$? Do you expect the value of this parameter to be larger or smaller for a large state enterprise than for a small state enterprise? Explain.

12　What are the main differences between model B of section 15.4 and the model for the short-run theory of the firm presented in economics textbooks? What is the objective function which management is assumed to maximize in the latter model, with capital stock assumed to be fixed? Compare this objective function with function (15.10) after making similar assumptions about special functional forms.

# 16

# The Nonstate Sectors

Section 16.1 presents data to show that the Chinese nonstate sectors have grown more rapidly than the state sector. Sections 16.2 and 16.3 discuss respectively the private sector and the collective sector consisting of the dynamic township and village enterprises. Section 16.4 presents a statistical method to measure the relative efficiency at one point in time and the relative growth of efficiency through time between the state and nonstate enterprises. The nature of a free-market economy is discussed in section 16.5, which includes a brief discussion of the economy of Hong Kong. Section 16.6 deals with the special characteristics of the Chinese market economy.

## 16.1   Relative Growth of Nonstate Sectors

China's economy is a market economy to a considerable extent. How well it functions therefore depends more on the functioning of the nonstate sectors than on the state enterprises. Since China introduced economic reform in 1978, the importance of the state sector has continued to decline, while the nonstate sectors have gained in importance. China has four types of enterprises in terms of ownership. These are state, collective, individual, and other enterprises. The fourth type includes joint ventures and foreign-owned enterprises as well as individuals. In 1980, the first two types of enterprises contributed respectively 76.0 and 23.5 percent of the country's gross industrial output value. State enterprises played a dominant role. Collective enterprises in the communes played a secondary role, while private and foreign enterprises were insignificant. In 1996, the corresponding percentages changed to 28.5, 39.4, 15.5, and 16.6 respectively. State enterprises accounted for less than 30 percent of gross industrial output and collective enterprises almost 40 percent. Both private and other enterprises accounted for about 16 percent. The collective enterprises consisted mainly of township and village enterprises that had grown rapidly.

Private enterprises are guaranteed equal economic rights to those of state enterprises by a new constitution in 1998. Foreign enterprises and joint ventures grew as a result of the encouragement of foreign investment, a subject discussed in chapter 18.

It may be more relevant to consider the relative importance of the four types of enterprises in terms of their contribution to gross national product rather than gross industrial output value only. The agricultural sector accounted for 1,384.42 of the 6,685.05 billion yuan of China's GDP in 1996. This amounts to 20.7 percent of gross output. As a rough estimate of the fraction of GDP in 1996 produced by the state sector, one may treat this 20.7 percent as nonstate. Of the remaining 79.3 percent one may apply the industrial sector percentage of 28.5 to conclude that the state sector accounted for about 0.285 of 0.793 or 22.6 percent of China's GNP. This estimate of the relative share of the state sector is based on the assumption that the nonagricultural and the remaining nonindustrial sectors that consist of construction, transportation, and trade have the same relative share of 0.285 from the state enterprises as the industrial sector. The assumption appears reasonable in view of the growth of nonstate activities in construction, transportation, and trade. As measured by the contribution to GNP, the state sector accounts for about 22.6 percent. Its contribution to nonagricultural output is approximately 28.5 percent, the reported share of industrial output.

An alternative measure of the economic importance of the state enterprises is by number of employees. In 1996 there were 688.5 million employed persons, with 198.2 million residing in urban areas and 490.3 in rural areas (*China Statistical Yearbook, 1997*, pp. 96–7). Of the urban 198.2 million, 112.4 or 56.7 percent were listed as employed by state-owned enterprises. Thus while the state enterprises produced only 28.5 percent of the gross industrial output value they employed about 56.7 percent of the labor force in urban areas. As measured by the number of employees, the state enterprises are more important in Chinese industry than they are by share of output. This also means that the state enterprises have lower average productivity of labor. However, the productivity of *workers* in state enterprises is not as low as the comparison of the above shares of output and of *labor force* would suggest. Many of the staff and workers counted in the labor force of the state sectors are supporting personnel working in schools and clinics that serve the employees of the state enterprises; they also include government employees. These people should not be included in measuring worker productivity. One important problem in the reform of state enterprises at the turn of the century from the viewpoint of productive efficiency is the reduction of the labor force which they employ. The associated unemployment problem and the program to retrain workers and to provide the unemployed with adequate compensation were discussed in chapter 4.

In section 16.2 we provide some historical material on private enterprises in China before 1949. In section 16.3, we discuss the township and village enterprises. In section 16.4 we explain how regression methods can be applied to measure the relative productive efficiency of township and village enterprises compared with state enterprises. Section 16.5 is devoted to an examination of the nature of a free-market economy. Understanding the working of a free-market economy provides a perspective for the understanding of China's market economy. The characteristics of the latter are the subject of section 16.6.

## 16.2    Private Enterprises Prior to 1949

The relative growth of the nonstate enterprises mentioned in the last paragraph occurred not by government design but by the natural evolution of economic institutions. The only role that the government needs to play is to provide political stability, law, and order, and not to intervene negatively in this evolutionary process. It is the ingenuity of the people and the opportunities available to improve their economic well-being that prompted them to set up new enterprises. As we pointed out in section 1.3, even with much political instability, the Chinese market economy continued to develop in the 1920s and 1930s.

Of the private enterprises that had naturally evolved, one should mention handicraft industries in the rural areas and the more modern textile, paper, tobacco, toys, and machine tool factories. The relative importance of the industrial sector was reported in table 1.1 of section 1.3. By the 1920s China had a number of smoothly functioning commercial banks. Private citizens could form commercial banks according to the law prevailing. The bank staff were able to provide loans according to the principles of risk and expected rates of return. Interest rates were determined by market forces. There was a smoothly functioning stock market in Shanghai. These facts are cited here to show that private enterprises evolve by themselves once opportunities are available. This point applies to the growth of the township and village enterprises (TVEs) in the 1980s. However, the characteristics of the TVEs are different from the Chinese private enterprises existing before 1949. It is the explanation of these characteristics that we turn to in the next section.

## 16.3    Economic Conditions for the Growth of Township and Village Enterprises

During the early years of economic reform, private enterprises could not be expected to occupy an important place in the national economy. Ordinary Chinese citizens simply did not have sufficient capital to start a business of any scale. The farmers were poor. So were the urban wage earners. Township and village governments had financial resources to form new enterprises. They had money, land, and buildings. They were also creditworthy in borrowing money from the state banks. They could even apply political pressure to obtain credit from the banks. When there were no adequate modern commercial laws to protect private enterprises, the TVEs were protected by the political power of the government units that sponsored them. Most importantly, these enterprises had the best human capital. The township or village government officials who took the initiative to set up these enterprises were by and large able people, because under the Chinese political system a large fraction of able people (not necessarily having high moral standards) were concentrated in the Communist Party and the government at all levels. These were economic conditions that made possible the establishment and operation of the TVEs. The motivations for their existence were the need and desire to increase revenue for township and village government and to provide employment to their citizens. Once agricultural productivity was increased by the return to private farming under the household responsibility system, there was excess labor in the rural areas. Providing employment for the laborers was an important task of local government. Essentially local government seized the economic opportunities to start enterprises and hire managers to run them.

The establishment of enterprises in China through government initiatives is not new to the PRC regime in the 1980s. It has a long historical tradition. The enterprises themselves might not be government owned either entirely or essentially. Yet it was often the government or a certain important government official that helped start such an enterprise. A case in point was the establishment of the famous Bank of Communications in 1907 through the initiative of Mr. Liang Shiyi, a government official in the Qing dynasty. Liang had the idea of raising private capital through the bank in order to buy back certain railroads owned by foreigners as well as to build new railroads for China. The bank was financed by both government funds and private capital. (See the *Annals of Mr. Liang Shiyi*, vol. 1, page 65.) The Bank of Communications still exists today in mainland China and Taiwan. The Bank of China, now a government bank engaged in foreign transactions, was established about the same time. Then as now, many able people in China were government officials who considered it their duty to serve the country under the ideal of the Confucian tradition. The same ideal persisted in the regime of the Republic of China and the PRC. Of course, besides Confucian ideals, pragmatism and self-interest also entered into the decisions of township and village government officials to establish enterprises in their localities. Government initiative in such ventures might be economically desirable, but government bureaucrats are also capable of interfering with, and even of establishing government enterprises to compete with, private enterprises in areas that the latter handle well under a free-market system. Later in this chapter we will have more to say about such behavior, and China's "bureaucratic market economy."

In many ways, the TVEs did not have the economic disadvantages which made the state enterprises inefficient. They had to be financially accountable, as they were set up to make money in the first place. In other words, they had to face a hard budget constraint. As we discussed in chapter 2, under central planning, money and credit were allocated to state enterprises. The state enterprises are said to face a soft budget constraint. A budget constraint is a mathematical relation between revenue and expenditure. It is soft if revenues are not earned in a hard way but can come from an appeal to the planning authority, a relation we have modeled in section 15.3. Second, the TVEs had no burden of excess workers who could not be easily laid off as in the case of state enterprises. These recently established enterprises could select the workers they liked and hire as many as needed. They paid the workers as much as they were worth. Third, competition among the TVEs was keen, since many township and village governments could set up such enterprises. They were set up only if there was sufficient demand in the market to ensure the profitability of the enterprises. There was free entry of new TVEs to generate competition in the market.

In 1996 the rural TVEs employed about 130 million workers and accounted for about one-third of the GDP produced in rural areas. The urban collectives (including about half the state-owned units under the control of local governments) employed 115 million workers and accounted for about one-third of the GDP also. Thus the total number of persons, 245 million, employed by TVEs and urban collectives was 245/688.5 or 35.6 percent of China's labor force. The growth of the TVEs and urban collectives was entirely unexpected by Deng Xiaoping, the leader behind China's economic reform, as he openly admitted in 1991. This shows that simply by allowing the Chinese people and lower-level government units to exercise their economic freedom, new economic institutions will naturally develop.

As will be discussed in chapter 22, the emergence of the TVEs provides challenges to the traditional thinking of some economists accustomed only to the functioning of the market economies of Western developed countries. One common belief is that private ownership is required for the efficient operation of an enterprise. This belief appears to be contradicted by seemingly efficient TVEs in China which are collectively owned or publicly owned. In this example, public ownership confers the advantages mentioned above. Second, the property rights of different parties are not clearly defined in a legal contract establishing the enterprises. The parties include the local government units, the managers, and other investors. Principal-agent theories have been applied to study the relationships between the venture capitalists and the entrepreneurs in a modern market economy. Under what contractual arrangements would an entrepreneur have more financial control of the enterprise, paying only a fixed amount of interest to the venture capitalist, etc.? Similarly, under what contractual arrangements in a Chinese TVE would the manager reap more of the profits of a TVE while paying the local government essentially a fixed rate of return on its capital, etc.? The point here is that such contracts are not clearly written down in the Chinese case. Third, and related to the second point, it is often said that a modern legal system is required for the proper functioning of economic units in a market economy. China does not have such a legal system, and yet the TVEs appear to function effectively. These points are further discussed in chapter 22.

What are the reasons for the success of the TVEs? Besides the economic advantages over the state enterprises mentioned above, there are different answers. One appeals to the allegedly cooperative nature of the Chinese people, who have been influenced by traditional Chinese culture. The Chinese are supposed to work in a TVE or an urban collective in a cooperative spirit. Cooperation refers to the internal relationships among staff and workers of the same enterprise. A second explanation appeals to the existence of competition among enterprises. Enterprises are subject to competition in selling their products and in the employment of labor and other inputs which are priced in competitive factor markets. There is freedom of entry of potential TVEs and urban collectives. Competition also exists among provincial and local governments interested in promoting TVEs within their own jurisdiction to increase revenue. These governments try to provide a favorable environment for the TVEs and collectives. The favorable environment includes better infrastructure and a better system to settle disputes.

In the 1990s the economic growth of the TVEs appeared to slow down. There are several explanations. First, the markets for their products are said to be saturated. Any growth starting from zero cannot continue at the same rate, as in the early period, for long. Second, once the TVEs and collectives became successful, the sponsoring governments began to tax them more heavily and asked them to absorb more workers. Third, corruption among local government officials serving a supervisory role is said to have increased, and with it the extraction of economic rents from the TVEs. Statistics show declining profit rates and increasing debt/equity ratios for many of these enterprises.

To ensure the survival of the TVEs reforms were instituted in 1992. Some of these enterprises were reorganized into joint stock cooperatives. Under this system managers and workers became part owners. More capital got injected into the enterprises. The managers and workers were expected to have better incentives as part owners. The reform was successful for some TVEs. This system was later introduced for state enterprises, as we saw in chapters 4 and 15. It is a system of partial privatization, as the local government units in many instances still control shares of the new joint stock cooperatives.

# 16.4    Econometric Measurement of the Relative Efficiency of State Enterprises and TVEs

We mentioned in the last section reasons for the TVEs to be economically more efficient than state enterprises, and cited some statistics to indicate the low labor productivity of state enterprises. It would be of interest to measure the relative efficiency and the relative change in efficiency for state enterprises and TVEs or collectives. Jefferson, Rawski, and Zheng (1992) provided statistical analyses of the productive efficiency of state and nonstate enterprises. Here we discuss the econometric method which can be employed to measure relative efficiency and relative growth in efficiency between state and collective enterprises.

First, efficiency needs to be defined. A useful definition of efficiency is total factor productivity (TFP) in the Cobb–Douglas production function introduced in chapter 5. Let $Y_i$ denote output of the $i$th enterprise, $K_i$ its capital stock, and $L_i$ its labor force. Assuming that all enterprises have the same capital and labor exponents and that these exponents sum to unity, we can write the production function of the $i$th enterprise as

$$\ln (Y_i/L_i) = \ln A_{\mathrm{I}} + \beta \ln (K_i/L_i) \tag{16.1}$$

We denote by $A_{\mathrm{I}}$ the total factor productivity of the enterprises belonging to group I, say the state enterprises. If $A_{\mathrm{II}}$ denotes the total factor productivity of the enterprises belonging to group II, the TVEs, then the difference $\ln A_{\mathrm{II}} - \ln A_{\mathrm{I}} = \ln (A_{\mathrm{II}}/A_{\mathrm{I}}) = d$ shows the total factor productivity of enterprises in group II relative to group I. The justification for using TFP to measure productive efficiency is that it measures output while holding the quantities of the two inputs constant. If one enterprise can produce more than another, it may be using more inputs and cannot be considered more efficient. Only by accounting for the contributions of the two inputs using a production function can we measure productive efficiency by TFP. The higher the TFP the more efficient is the enterprise, because it can produce more by using the same amounts of the two inputs.

The above measurement of productive efficiency is valid under the assumption that the capital and labor exponents are the same for firms in groups I and II. This assumption makes it possible to isolate the effects of both inputs on the quantity of output. If the two exponents cannot be assumed to be identical for the two groups of enterprises, the comparison of productive efficiency will be more complicated (that will not be discussed here). A second assumption in our method of measuring productivity is the assumption that the two exponents sum to unity. This assumption is made for convenience. It is not a necessary assumption. Without using the second assumption but maintaining the first, we would write the production function as a linear function of two variables $\ln K_i$ and $\ln L_i$ and not of just one variable as in equation (16.1). These two assumptions can and should be tested statistically using the relevant data, as we did for the aggregate production function in chapter 5.

To proceed to statistical analysis, we need sample data for $n_1$ state enterprises and $n_2$ TVEs for a given year, say 1996. We introduce a dummy variable $d$ which is given a value 1 if the data belong to a TVE and a value 0 if the data belong to a state enterprise. We use all $n_1 + n_2$ observations to estimate a regression of the form (16.1), noting that for the TVEs an additional variable which takes the value of 1 for all observations is introduced. Since $d$ is an estimate of $\ln A_{II} - \ln A_I$, if the estimated value is positive and larger than twice its standard error we conclude that the TVEs are productively more efficient than the state enterprises. This test starts with no prior conception that the TVEs should or should not be more efficient. If we start with a preconception, based on the reasoning stated earlier in this section, that the TVEs should be more efficient than the state enterprises, we would need weaker evidence to support our preconception. If the estimated value of $d$ is only 1.6 times its standard or larger, we can conclude that the TVEs are more productive. The former test is known as a two-tail test. Both a positive and a negative $d$, provided it is large enough in absolute value, can justify rejecting the null hypothesis that the productivity of the two groups of enterprises is equal. The latter test is a one-tail test of the null hypothesis that a predesignated group II is supposed to be more productive than the other group. Only a positive, but smaller, value of $d$ can justify the conclusion that group II is more productive.

The above analysis is concerned with the relative productivity of state enterprises and TVEs in one year. A second question is whether one group increases its efficiency faster than the other. To measure the change in productivity we can introduce $\ln A_I + \alpha_I t$ as the natural log of the total factor productivity for group I, and $\ln A_{II} + \alpha_{II} t$ for group II. $\alpha_I$ and $\alpha_{II}$ respectively measure the exponential rates of change in total factor productivity of state enterprises and TVEs. We combine all $n_1 + n_2$ observations for one year and need to acquire similar data for several consecutive years to estimate regression (16.1), with the dummy variable $d$ defined as before and with two separate coefficients for the trend variable $t$. If the estimate of $\alpha_I$ turns out to be significantly larger than that of $\alpha_{II}$, we can conclude that the productivity of state enterprises improved more than that of the TVEs.

The term "significantly larger" is explained in standard statistics texts. If we do not have observations for several consecutive years but only for two years, can we apply the above method? If yes, exactly how? If not, why not? This question is left for the reader to ponder.

# 16.5   Characteristics of a Free-market Economy

Before discussing the characteristics of the Chinese market economy, it is useful to summarize the important characteristics of a free-market economy. How does a free-market economy function? By answering this question we can better understand the Chinese market economy by comparing it with a free-market system, without necessarily implying that China should adopt such a system.

Hong Kong's economy has been ranked at the top among all economies in the world in terms of its being closest to a free-market economy. There is much that the mainland can learn from Hong Kong on how a market economy functions. Much learning has already taken place through trade, investment, cultural exchanges, and personal travel. In this section I discuss some conditions for the proper functioning of a free-market economy.

The free-market system is one of the most ingenious of human inventions. It was not invented by a single or a few persons and not by a government. It has evolved as an economic institution to satisfy the needs of society in different parts of the world. For example, in China not only were important institutions of industry and trade flourishing in the Sung dynasty but the great historian Sima Qian of the Han dynasty had already written about the law of the markets through the invisible hand in a language as clear as that in Adam Smith's *Wealth of Nations* (Sima Qian was quoted in section 1.2.4).

Why does the free-market system function so well? It provides freedom and opportunities for individuals and families to better themselves by hard work and ingenuity. Through competition the market selects the best to produce for individual profits and at the same time for the needs of the society. Thus there is harmony between the self-interest of the individual and the common good. This generalization is valid only under three conditions. First, the rules of the game in market competition have to be clear, effectively enforced, and fair. To ensure that competition works for the common good, it has to be well-defined and enforced effectively. This means that a properly functioning legal system has to be in place. It is not enough for a set of laws governing economic conduct to be enacted; the citizens should be law abiding. Second, the domain of the market economy has to be spelled out and the role of the government in the economy has to be clarified. Third, a suitable political institution is needed for the government to exercise its roles. These three topics will be discussed in sections 20.3, 20.4, and 20.5 respectively.

For the present purpose, we single out for comment certain important characteristics of a free-market economy that can be observed in the Hong Kong economy. Regarding the rule of law, Hong Kong has a sound legal system and people are by and large law abiding. People can start new enterprises and manage existing enterprises under the law with little interference from a bureaucracy. Economic exchanges are free in the sense that imports and exports are not regulated and import tariffs are low except for a small number of items like automobiles. The taxing of automobile imports can be justified by the cost to society in the form of emissions and traffic congestion created by the use of automobiles. Taxes on wages are low, with a constant marginal rate of about 17 percent above a certain amount, below which no tax needs to be paid. It is a flat tax. There is no capital gains tax that can interfere with the mobility of capital.

Regarding the economic role of the government, at least during the colonial time up to 1997, the government tried not to interfere with the market by engaging in acts such as selling low-priced real estate to affect the supply of housing and thus housing prices, or buying and selling stocks in the Hong Kong Stock Exchange. The government did engage in infrastructure-building quite successfully. This includes good roads, much better than in most urban areas of mainland China, the maintenance of a seaport, and the support of several universities. Public and private education exist side by side to offer free choice to the parents and students. There was a good public health service which provided affordable healthcare to the poor. There was no social insurance. Since 1997, however, the public healthcare system has been changed and a new pension and social insurance system has been instituted. To pay for a pension fund the employers and employees each contribute 5 percent of the employee's wage or salary. As of 2001, observers in Hong Kong thought that this new pension plan institution reduced profit margins for the employers and reduced disposable income for the employees. Both contributed to slowing down the rate of economic growth in Hong Kong, at least for the short run.

In terms of the way the economic decisions of the Hong Kong government were made, the process was not democratic because the government itself was not democratic. The Governor was appointed from London. In the executive branch the Chief Secretary (just below the Governor and serving as the head of all secretaries) and all other secretaries were also appointed. Since the 1980s there has been a gradual process of allowing a proportion of the members of the Legislative Council to be elected and the Council itself to have more power. After 1997, the Chief Executive was elected by a group of some 400 members of an election committee appointed by the mainland government. The members are by and large prominent citizens of Hong Kong. During the colonial period, the economy was a free-market economy while there was no democracy. After 1997, the economy is still mainly a free-market economy, although some observers consider the interference in the real estate market and in the stock exchange (with the declared intention of punishing speculators during the Asian financial crisis) as violations of the free-market principles practiced before 1997. Furthermore, the introduction of a compulsory social insurance system could also be viewed by some as interference in the free choice of the people in the use of their savings.

Since the introduction of the social security system in the United States in the 1930s many people consider such a system desirable and even essential for a market economy. There are reasons to think otherwise. From the viewpoint of allowing people to make their own choice on how much to save and in what form to save their income for old age, a social pension system is an infringement of freedom of choice. It forces people to save a designated amount and put it in a special form of investment decided by the government, in the form of US government security in the United States. The former restriction reduces the consumer's utility. The latter restriction affects the allocation of capital resources and reduces the efficiency in the use of capital. The justification of a social pension is that unless the government enforces such a system people do not know how to save for their old age. This judgment may be valid for some people but is not valid for a majority of US citizens, who have both the means and the intelligence to plan for their life after retirement. Government should not interfere with their allocation of consumption over their own lifetime as it should not interfere with their choice between Chinese food and Italian food. Once a person's income or savings is above some minimum amount there is no justification for the government to impose a social insurance system on them. It is justified for the government to assist elderly people when they are needy by some form of negative income tax. If a person's retirement income is below a certain level, the government may use general tax revenue to subsidize them without administering a vast social security program for the entire population. Hong Kong did not have a social security system until the turn of the twenty-first century.

The discussion of the last paragraph has relevance for China. However, in discussing the merits of a social insurance system for China, as for the United States, one has to take into account the historical tradition and political reality. Just as in the United States, the objections to social security presented above might be valid, but there is no possibility of changing the system substantially. Any social entitlement, once established, is difficult to eliminate. This includes the entitlement of very inexpensive housing for Chinese workers which we discussed at the end of chapter 9. Chinese workers also are entitled to a set of retirement benefits from the state-owned enterprises. It is a challenging problem to design a scheme that preserves the incentives for and freedom of Chinese citizens to save for themselves and their family members, and at the same time takes into account the responsibility of the government as well as the tradition of social entitlement. This is one of many similar problems facing the government and society in transforming a planned economy with many social entitlements to a market economy.

## 16.6   Characteristics of the Chinese Market Ecomomy

The future of the Chinese economy is dependent on the performance of the nonstate sectors. Can we expect the TVEs and private enterprises to continue to improve their performance? Can we expect new nonstate enterprises to enter the market? What can we expect of the foreign and jointly owned enterprises? It is difficult to answer these questions precisely, but some hints can be derived by examining the characteristics of the Chinese market economy.

As previously pointed out, the characteristics of the Chinese market economy have evolved, and will continue to evolve, through time. Economic fundamentals and the nature of Chinese society have as much to do with the evolution as government design. In the mid-1980s, the Chinese leaders were talking about "building socialism with Chinese characteristics." This means that whatever the Chinese economic institutions become, the results will satisfy this slogan. The slogan was created to allow the pragmatic leaders to develop whatever they liked without being confined to a strict ideology. Any violation of Communist ideology as understood in the prereform period can be explained away by the phrase "Chinese characteristics." In 1992, when the Central Committee of the Chinese Communist Party declared that China's economy is a socialist market economy, the word "market" was emphasized, although the word "socialist" was kept to indicate that China is still a socialist country. What will become of the socialist market economy in China remains to be seen.

At the turn of the century there is one important element in China's socialist market economy which appears difficult to change. It is the Party and government bureaucracy which limits the extent to which free enterprises can flourish in China. The political system is not expected to change rapidly short of a great political disturbance. Such a political disturbance, although possible, is not likely because the government has been doing well both in terms of domestic economic policy and foreign policy. The economy has continued to improve. The international status of China has continued to move upward. The government is quite popular among a large number of Chinese citizens. If the political structure does not change, it is unlikely that the bureaucratic behavior of government officials will greatly improve. Bureaucratic behavior includes corruption and other means of extracting economic rents from citizens and foreign investors. Such behavior is based on the economic power of the bureaucrats in granting the necessary licenses or permission to conduct business. The economic benefits of such bureaucratic behavior are so tempting that orders and threats of punishment cannot stop it. The difficulty of stopping corruption is shown by the continued attempts of the Party leaders to do so from the 1980s on. Executing a few offenders is helpful but not sufficient to ensure the success of the anticorruption effort.

The political system and bureaucratic behavior in China affect the way nonstate enterprises can function. First, to start an enterprise, whether domestic, or partly or entirely foreign, an entrepreneur has to go through the bureaucracy. This can involve approval by bureaucrats of many government units that have or claim to have jurisdiction over the activities of the enterprises. Money and inconvenience follow. Second, the nature of the enterprise can be restricted as a result of negotiations with the bureaucrats at the initial and later stages when they still have the authority. Third, the size of Chinese nonstate enterprises can be limited not only by bureaucratic behavior but by the official political view to limit them. The Chinese political and bureaucratic system favors state enterprises. The large state enterprises play a central role, as acknowledged and stated in the important report of General Secretary Jiang Zemin to the Central Committee of the Chinese Communist Party in September 1997. They are treated more favorably than nonstate enterprises. As I mentioned earlier, one can characterize the Chinese market economy as a "bureaucratic market economy."

Under the Chinese political and bureaucratic system it is difficult for large private enterprises to function. The system allows township and village enterprises to flourish because the owners and managers are themselves bureaucrats. The degree of bureaucracy at the beginning of the twenty-first century is worse than it was in the 1920s, because the bureaucrats were given much more power under the rule of a strong Communist Party. Under the Chinese bureaucratic market system, it is extremely difficult, if at all possible, for nonstate entrepreneurs to establish large, multinational corporations such as Microsoft in the United States or, on a smaller scale, the very successful enterprises in Taiwan and Hong Kong. Thousands of potential world-class entrepreneurs in China have their hands tied by the political and bureaucratic environment when they wish to use their talents for self-fulfillment and for the modernization of the Chinese economy. Some of these people have to channel their energy through the government political and economic organizations, but working under such organizations is more restricted than being an entrepreneur in a free market. This is the major limitation on the nonstate enterprises in China and on the Chinese market economy in general. There is some hope that this bureaucratic system will change slightly through time. Gradual improvement of the legal system will likely take place following China's entry into the World Trade Organization. WTO membership may help reduce bureaucracy and promote the rule of law, creating a slightly more level playing field. In the process, the conflict between state bureaucracy and nonstate enterprises may be partly resolved to benefit the Chinese market economy.

Under the heading of China's bureaucratic market economy we can include one more institutional characteristic. It is government interference in free trade. The respect for free exchange is a basic principle underlying a market economy. The Chinese government follows this principle only to a limited extent. Examples of violation are heavy government involvement, to the extent of being a monopoly, in the distribution of grains and other basic agricultural products, and government participation in international trade, a subject of the next chapter.

## References and Further Reading

Friedman, Milton. *Capitalism and Freedom*. Chicago: University of Chicago Press, 1962.

Jefferson, Gary H., T. Rawski, and Y. X. Zheng. "Growth, Efficiency and Convergence in China's State and Collective Industry." *Economic Development and Cultural Change*, 40, no. 2 (Jan. 1992), pp. 239–66.

Lau, Chung-ming and Jianfa Shen, eds. *China Review 2000*, chs. 14 and 23. Hong Kong: Chinese University Press, 2000.

Wong, John, Rong Ma, and Mu Yang, eds. *China's Rural Enterprises: Ten Case Studies*. Singapore: Times Academic Press, 1995.

## Questions

1  Give the main reasons why township and village enterprises produce more efficiently than state-owned enterprises.
    (Hint: Use production functions and dummy variables for questions 2, 3 and 4.)

2  To perform an econometric study to find out whether township and village enterprises did produce more efficiently than state enterprises in a certain industry in 1988, what data can a researcher use? How can these data be used for a suitable regression analysis? How do you determine whether the productive efficiency of the township and village enterprises is higher or lower than that of the state-owned enterprises?

3  To find out whether the productive efficiency of state enterprises improved from 1988 to 1996, what regression equation should the researcher estimate? Under what circumstances would one conclude that there was a statistically significant improvement between these two years?

4 To find out whether the efficiency of township and village enterprises had increased more than the efficiency of state enterprises, what regression equation would the researcher estimate? How would one decide that the increase in efficiency for township and village enterprises was more?

5 What are the important institutional arrangements of a market economy which make an enterprise efficient but which were absent in the 1980s for the Chinese township and village enterprises? In the absence of these institutional factors, how do you explain the efficiency and growth of the TVEs in China?

6 What makes private enterprises flourish in China? What limits the operation of private enterprises in China?

7 How would you measure the relative importance of the nonstate sector in China compared with that of the state sector?

8 What makes Hong Kong a free-market economy, more so than other market economies? In what respects, if any, has Hong Kong's market economy changed since 1997?

9 In what way is China's market economy different from other market economies?

10 In what ways is "bureaucratic market economy" a description of China's economy? Specify its characteristics.

11 Give two examples of problems with previous entitlement programs that the Chinese government is facing in transforming the planned economy to a market economy.

12 Should Hong Kong have introduced its present social pension system? Why or why not?

# 17

# Foreign Trade

This chapter begins in section 17.1 with some facts about China's foreign trade, and then provides in section 17.2 some basic theory to understand trade patterns. Section 17.3 discusses the determination of exchange rates and section 17.4 China's trade policy. Section 17.5 is an evaluation of China's foreign trade policy, beginning in the 1980s, in terms of the possible advantages and limitations of a free-trade policy. Section 17.6 looks at the pros and cons of protectionism in the US and at China's expanding trade surplus with America.

## 17.1  Some Statistics of China's Foreign Trade

Table 17.1 (see the *China Statistical Yearbook, 1999*, table 17-3, and *Yearbook 2005*) shows that in US dollars, the volume of foreign trade (total imports plus exports) increased from 1.94 billion in 1952, to 4.59 in 1970, 20.64 in 1978, 38.14 in 1980, 115.44 in 1990, and 323.5 in 1998. The volume was very small up to 1978 and has increased very rapidly since then as a result of the open-door policy. In Chinese yuan the volume in 1998 was 2,684.97 billion as converted by the official exchange rate of 8.29 yuan per dollar, with the official exchange rate very close to the market rate that people can use in free markets like Hong Kong. This amounts to 33.8 percent of China's GDP of 7,939.57 billion.

China's exports grew from 16.76 billion yuan in 1978 to 15,223.6 billion in 1998. Its imports grew from 18.74 billion yuan in 1978 to 1,162.61 billion in 1998. As percentage of GDP, the former was 19.2 percent and the latter was 14.6 percent in 1998. China went from an import surplus country in the late 1970s and 1980s to an export surplus country in the 1990s. Since the volume of trade reached 33.8 percent of its GDP, China is an open economy. In the four years from 1998 to 2002, the volume of foreign trade almost doubled (see table 17.1). By 2003 the volume of foreign trade increased to 65 percent of

**Table 17.1** Total Chinese imports and exports

| Year | Yuan 100 millions | | Total imports | Balance | US$ 100 millions |
| | Total imports & exports | Total exports | | | Total imports & exports |
| --- | --- | --- | --- | --- | --- |
| 1952 | 64.6 | 27.1 | 37.5 | −10.4 | 19.4 |
| 1957 | 104.5 | 54.5 | 50.0 | 4.5 | 31.0 |
| 1962 | 80.9 | 47.1 | 33.8 | 13.3 | 26.6 |
| 1965 | 118.4 | 63.1 | 55.3 | 7.8 | 42.5 |
| 1970 | 112.9 | 56.8 | 56.1 | 0.7 | 45.9 |
| 1975 | 290.4 | 143.0 | 147.4 | −4.4 | 147.5 |
| 1978 | 355.0 | 167.6 | 187.4 | −19.8 | 206.4 |
| 1980 | 570.0 | 271.2 | 298.8 | −27.6 | 381.4 |
| 1985 | 2,066.7 | 808.9 | 1,257.8 | −448.9 | 696.0 |
| 1986 | 2,580.4 | 1,082.1 | 1,498.3 | −416.2 | 738.5 |
| 1987 | 3,084.2 | 1,470.0 | 1,614.2 | −144.2 | 826.5 |
| 1988 | 3,821.8 | 1,766.7 | 2,055.1 | −288.4 | 1,027.9 |
| 1989 | 4,155.9 | 1,956.0 | 2,199.9 | −243.9 | 1,116.8 |
| 1990 | 5,560.1 | 2,985.8 | 2,574.3 | 411.5 | 1,154.4 |
| 1991 | 7,225.8 | 3,827.1 | 3,398.7 | 428.4 | 1,356.3 |
| 1992 | 9,119.6 | 4,676.3 | 4,443.3 | 233.0 | 1,655.3 |
| 1993 | 11,271.0 | 5,284.8 | 5,986.2 | −701.4 | 1,957.0 |
| 1994 | 20,381.9 | 10,421.8 | 9,960.1 | 461.7 | 2,366.2 |
| 1995 | 23,499.9 | 12,451.8 | 11,048.1 | 1,403.7 | 2,808.6 |
| 1996 | 24,133.8 | 12,576.4 | 11,557.4 | 1,019.0 | 2,898.8 |
| 1997 | 26,967.2 | 15,160.7 | 11,806.5 | 3,354.2 | 3,251.6 |
| 1998 | 26,849.7 | 15,223.6 | 11,626.1 | 3,597.5 | 3,239.5 |
| 1999 | 29,896.2 | 16,159.8 | 13,736.4 | 2,423.4 | 3,606.3 |
| 2000 | 39,373.2 | 20,634.4 | 18,638.8 | 1,995.6 | 4,742.9 |
| 2001 | 42,183.6 | 22,924.4 | 20,159.2 | 1,865.2 | 5,096.5 |
| 2002 | 51,378.2 | 26,947.9 | 24,430.3 | 2,517.6 | 6,207.7 |
| 2003 | 70,483.5 | 36,287.9 | 34,195.6 | 2,092.3 | 8,509.9 |
| 2004 | 95,539.1 | 49,103.3 | 46,435.8 | 2,667.5 | 11,545.5 |

GDP and grew at the rate of 35 percent per year. In 2004, the trade volume reached 1.1 trillion US dollars, as compared with 620.8 billion in 2002, and had a growth rate of 30 percent. China became the third largest trading country in the world, next to the United States and Germany.

To account for the total volume of trade of 323.9 billion US dollars in 1998 [620.8 billion in 2002], China's main trading partners were Japan (57.9 billion) [101.9 billion], the United States (54.9 billion) [97.2 billion], Hong Kong (45.4 billion) [69.2 billion], Republic of Korea (21.3 billion) [44.1 billion], Taiwan (20.5 billion) [44.6 billion], Germany (14.3 billion) [27.8 billion], and Europe (58.7 billion) [112.6 billion] (reported in the *China Statistical Yearbook 1999*, Table 17-7 [*Yearbook 2003*, table 17-7]). As a category of commodity for exports, manufactured goods accounted for 163.2 billion of the 183.8 billion of total exports in 1998 (table 17-8). These are manufactured products such as textiles, clothing, shoes, toys, sporting goods, and tools that are found in stores in the United States. In the first 9 months of 2004, China's traditional export commodities, such as textiles, apparel, furniture, cases, and boxes, grew respectively by 26.4 percent (from year to year), 19.4 percent, 40 percent, and 23.2 percent. Exports of machinery and electronic products, and of high-tech products, increased by 44.0 and 54.3 percent respectively. Among them, notebook computers, mobile phones, and liquid crystal displays grew more than 100 percent.

## 17.2  Explanation of Trading Patterns under Free Trade

A basic principle in a market economy is free exchange or free trade. If you exchange two cans of tennis balls for my box of golf balls and the exchange takes place voluntarily, it must mean that both persons benefit. Otherwise one of us would not have traded. The same applies if I give you five dollars instead of one box of golf balls, if you happen to be a merchant, a store owner, or an importer of tennis balls. When both persons benefit and no other person in the economy is worse off, the economy is said to achieve a Pareto improvement, or economic welfare of the economy is improved. Therefore, trade should not be prohibited. This basic idea of free trade should be kept in mind when we examine China's foreign trade policy. We should always ask on what economic principle the Chinese government is justified in preventing free trade from occurring.

In this chapter we wish to explain why China exports and imports the kinds of goods it does, and why one US dollar is worth 8.3 Chinese yuan in the free market in Hong Kong and other places. We offer explanations of the observed trade pattern and the exchange rate under the assumption that free trade exists. This assumption is not entirely true because there are restrictions to trade and on foreign exchange transactions. Yet provided that the restrictions are not too severe, the trade pattern and the foreign-exchange rate observed will not be too far from what the theory based on free trade implies. Applying the theory also enables us to measure the distortion introduced by trade restrictions and to predict what will happen, at least in qualitative terms, when the restrictions are lifted. The following theoretical discussion in this section may require slow and careful reading if the reader wishes to master the subject. It is written much like an economics text. However, if the reader wishes to get a general idea only, the principles are stated in words after some possibly tedious explanations. Grasping the principles will be sufficient for understanding foreign trade in China.

### 17.2.1   David Ricardo's theory of comparative advantage

When trade is allowed to occur freely, what determines the commodities that a country will export and those that it will import? The Ricardian theory states that a country will export goods which it can produce relatively cheaply and import goods that it can produce relatively expensively. The word "relatively" refers to the price of the export good and the import good at home compared with the relative price in the world market, or in a foreign country. For example, assume that in China shoes are cheap relative to computers, as one computer in China can be traded for 20 pairs of shoes. In the United States shoes are relatively more expensive in the sense that one computer can be traded for only 10 pair of shoes. The relative price of shoes is low in China and it pays for China to export shoes to the United States and import computers. Likewise the relative price of computers is low in the United States and it pays the United States to export computers to China. China is said to have a comparative advantage in the production of shoes and the United States is said to have a comparative advantage in producing computers. In the domestic market without foreign trade, it costs China 20 pairs of shoes to get one computer. If China could sell 20 pairs of shoes to the United States for two computers it would definitely gain from such a trade. Let China trade 15 pairs of shoes for one computer with the United States, both countries gain. This discussion does not involve the exchange rate between the Chinese yuan and the US dollar. We can imagine trading to take place by barter without having to consider the exchange rate at this point.

Comparative advantage is measured by relative price, which equals the slope of the production possibility curve or production transformation curve in a market economy. In the United States in the above example it means that giving up one computer would release resources to be used to produce 10 more pairs of shoes. We can use a diagram with its $x$ and $y$ axis measuring respectively the quantity of shoes and computers which a country can produce. The combinations of the quantities of these two goods that the country can produce form a production transformation curve. The slope of this curve is negative because to increase the output of shoes measured along the $x$ axis, the quantity of computers measured along the $y$ axis has to decrease. As long as the slopes of the production possibility curves of two countries at the current levels of production are different, it will be advantageous for both countries to trade at a ratio between the two rates indicated by the slopes of their production possibility curves. We have just answered the question concerning what commodities to trade by using the concept of comparative advantage, or the relative slopes of the production possibility curves of two countries.

## 17.2.2   The Heckscher–Ohlin theory of trade

A natural second question is what determines the slopes of the production transformation
curves of different countries. The answer can be found in possible differences in technology
and in the amounts of inputs available. By definition the technology of a country is partly
summarized by its production transformation curve. In the theory of Heckscher (1919)
and Ohlin (1933), technology as defined below is assumed to be identical in different
countries, so that differences in transformation curves are attributed to differences in the
quantities of basic resources available. Furthermore, in contrast with the Cobb–Douglas
production function, the production function employed assumes that each production
process, or each productive "activity" in the words of Koopmans (1951), requires fixed
amounts of different inputs for the production of one unit of output. To illustrate, assume
that there are two production processes or activities, one for producing shoes and the other
for producing computers. In general, there could be two or more production processes for
producing shoes or computers, but we simplify our discussion in this illustration. Process
1 requires 2 units of labor and 0.5 units of capital to produce 1 unit of shoes. Process 2
requires 5 units of labor and 5 units of capital to produce 1 unit of computers. The
technology is summarized by the coefficients in table 17.2, which are the input requirements per unit of output in each of the two "activities" or production processes.

Let there be 100 units of labor and 50 units of capital available in an economy. Let $x_1$
and $x_2$ denote the outputs of shoes and computers, respectively. To produce the output
quantities $(x_1, x_2)$, $2x_1 + 5x_2$ units of labor and $0.5x_1 + 5x_2$ units of capital are required,
according to the input coefficients of table 17.2. Since these input requirements cannot
exceed the inputs available, we have the following two inequality restrictions on the outputs:

$$2x_1 + 5x_2 \leq 100 \qquad (17.1)$$
$$0.5x_1 + 5x_2 \leq 50 \qquad (17.2)$$

Consider a diagram with $x_1$ and $x_2$ measured along the horizontal and vertical axes
respectively. Geometrically, the output combinations $(x_1, x_2)$ that satisfy the inequality
constraint (17.1) are points on or below a certain line, to be denoted by $B$. The output
combinations $(x_1, x_2)$ that satisfy the inequality constraint (17.2) are the points on or
below a certain line, to be denoted by $A$. Readers wishing to follow this example in depth
need to use paper and pencil to draw the relevant lines $B$ and $A$ and follow the discussion

**Table 17.2**   Illustrative input coefficients for two production processes

| Input | Process 1: Shoe production | Process 2: Computer production | Quantity of input available |
|---|---|---|---|
| Labor | 2 | 5 | 100 |
| Capital | 0.5 | 5 | 50 |

using the diagram. Such inequalities are used in a linear programming problem where the objective is to maximize a linear function of the variables, although no such objective function is specified here. The economy's production transformation curve is given by two line segments. The first segment is taken from the left portion of line A before it intersects with line B. The second segment is taken from the right portion of line B after it intersects with line A. For the points $(x_1, x_2)$ on the first segment, all 50 units of capital are used up and there are units of labor unused (since these points are below the restriction B specified by the inequality (17.1)). For the points on the second segment, all 100 units of labor are used up and there are units of capital unused (since these points are below the restriction A specified by the inequality 17.2). Thus, we have derived the production transformation curve for an economy from its technology, as summarized by the input coefficients of each production process and its supply of inputs (see question 3 below).

Assume that the same technology is available in countries A and B. However, let country A have only 50 units of capital but more than 200 units of labor. Its production transformation curve will be simply line A specified in the last paragraph because the constraint (17.1) is not binding. Let country B have only 100 units of labor but more than 100 units of capital. Its production transformation curve will be simply line B referred to in the last paragraph because the constraint (17.2) is not binding. Thus, we have derived the linear production transformation curves A and B for the two countries A and B from the technology of table 17.2 by assuming different supplies of the two inputs for the two countries. Country A is assumed to have plenty of labor and country B plenty of capital. According to table 17.2, the production of shoes requires relatively more labor and less capital compared with the production of computers. In the production of shoes the ratio of labor requirement to capital requirement is 2/0.5, or 4. In the production of computers the ratio is 5/5, or 1. In other words, the production of shoes is relatively labor-intensive while the production of computers is relatively capital-intensive. Since country A has more labor than country B (200 units as compared with 100 units) and country B has more capital than country A (100 units as compared with 50 units), country A will specialize in the production of the labor-intensive commodity (shoes) and country B will specialize in the production of the capital-intensive commodity (computers). Such a specialization was discussed in terms of comparative advantage earlier in this section, but in terms of the Heckscher–Ohlin theory we are able to trace the source of the specialization to the relative supplies of inputs or factors of production.

This example illustrates a basic Heckscher–Ohlin theorem in international trade. A country with plenty of labor (or capital) will tend to specialize in producing labor-intensive (or capital-intensive) commodities and will export these commodities in exchange for the capital-intensive (or labor-intensive) commodities. This theorem holds true when the production transformation curves of the countries concerned are nonlinear. To illustrate, let us modify the above example by assuming country A to have 180 units of labor and 50 units of capital and country B to have 100 units of labor and 80 units of capital. The production transformation curve of each country will consist of two line segments, but the main part of country A's is given by line A and country B's by line B. Country A will still produce shoes for export and country B will still produce computers for export. The demonstration of this result is left as an exercise (see question 1 below).

By completing this exercise, the reader will find that the theory of Ricardo is useful in determining the quantities of exports and imports of each country and the relative prices of the commodities traded. What the Heckscher–Ohlin theory adds to the Ricardian theory of comparative advantage is the relation between the production transformation curve, which defines comparative advantage, and the relative supplies of the factors. By the Ricardian theory we say that country A exports shoes because it has a comparative advantage in producing shoes as revealed by a comparison of the slope of its production transformation curve with the slope of the production transformation curve of country B. By the Heckscher–Ohlin theory we say that country A exports shoes because the production of shoes is labor-intensive and country A has plenty of labor compared with country B. Although the above illustrative example is artificial for the purpose of explaining a theory, the theory is relevant for the explanation of the kinds of exports from China. China exports shoes, clothing, sports equipment, toys, and other goods that require inexpensive labor, which is plentiful in China. It needs to import computers, automobiles, and other capital-intensive products in exchange. China will soon export computers. Why?

Using the production transformation curve we can point out that if country A exports "shoes" (which stands for any labor-intensive product in this artificial example), it means that in country A the marginal rate of substitution of shoes for computers (which stands for any capital-intensive product) is large compared with country B, or the price of shoes relative to computers is low (if a competitive market is allowed to function) compared with country B or the world market. After country A exports shoes and imports computers, the price of shoes relative to computers will increase in country A because its domestic supply of shoes decreases and the supply of computers increases. The relative price of shoes to computers will continue to increase until it equals the relative price in the world market and there is no further gain by an additional export of shoes, if we can make the unrealistic assumption of zero transportation and distribution costs for imports and exports. In the meantime, after the opening of the world market and the increases in the demand for domestic shoes and in the price of shoes in country A, the demand for labor also increases, since labor is used intensively in the production of shoes. Similarly, the import of computers lowers the demand for domestically produced computers as well as the price of computers. The demand for capital also decreases, since capital is used intensively in the production of computers. With the increase in demand for labor and the decrease in demand for capital, the price of labor will go up and the price of capital goods will go down. An exposition of the effects of international trade on the prices of resources or inputs based on the Heckscher–Ohlin theory can be found in Kenen (1984, ch. 4).

To make the above artificial example relevant for China, we think of the labor-intensive commodity "shoes" as clothing, sports equipment, toys that the Chinese export, and think of the capital-intensive commodity "computers" in the example as high-technology products such as computers and automobiles that the Chinese would import. The theory says that if free trade is allowed the prices of capital-intensive products relative to labor-intensive products will decrease. Furthermore the price of labor itself will increase compared with the price of capital. In the process of economic development with free trade, the wage rate of a developing economy such as China goes up because China is able to sell labor-intensive products like clothing, toys, etc. to a world market that commands high prices.

This is almost like having the Chinese laborers producing shoes to be sold in the United States at the prices of the United States. The Chinese laborers still cannot command the same wage as a US worker making shoes because there is a high transportation and distribution cost (including profits for the Chinese exporters, the American importers, and the American distributors) to make the price received by the Chinese shoe producers much lower than (perhaps equal to only 10 to 15 percent of) the price of shoes that American consumers pay. Yet the ability to export shoes to the United States still raises the wage of Chinese workers in a shoe factory.

It might be suggested that the Heckscher–Ohlin theory as presented here has limited applicability because of its assumption that the same technology is available to each country. We know that developing economics lack some advanced technology which is available in more developed economies. To allow for this under the framework of the Heckscher–Ohlin theory, we can define a new technology as the possession of some special resources required to apply the technology. For example, if China does not have certain advanced technology to produce high-quality computers or automobiles, we can treat this as China having no or a limited supply of certain engineers who can supervise the production of these products. To illustrate this point in the framework of the Heckscher–Ohlin theory, let country A have the technology given by table 17.2. Let country C have a better process for producing shoes, one that requires only 1 unit of labor and 0.5 units of capital. The technology of country C can be summarized by the input coefficients of two processes, the first (called process 3) having coefficients 1 and 0.5 for labor and capital respectively, and the second having coefficients 5 and 5 as in table 17.2. One may say that country C has a different technology from that of country A. However, on closer examination it might turn out that the reason process 3 uses less labor than process 1 in the production of shoes is that it employs a special machine that is not available to country A. This particular machine, let us say, cannot simply be imported because it has to be developed locally together with the training of the labor to use it. There are two ways to model the technologies of countries A and C. One is to use two different tables of input coefficients, as suggested above. The alternative is to use the same table for both countries, as given in table 17.2. This table consists of input coefficients for three processes, each employing up to three inputs. The technology of table 17.2 is assumed to be available to both countries A and C, but country A has no supply of the third input.

The use of a special input in the last paragraph to get around the difference in technology between two countries might appear to be artificial. To make the specification of technology more appealing, let us change the third factor from a "machine" to scientific and technical personnel who are capable of developing or using the technology in country A. Instead of saying that country A lacks the technology incorporated in process 3, which requires 1 and 0.5 units of labor and capital respectively to produce one unit of shoes, one can say that country A has all the technology given by table 17.3 but lacks scientific and technical personnel (which replaces "machine" as the third input). Proponents of the Heckscher–Ohlin theory would claim that most of the modern technology used in production in the developed countries is public knowledge available to all countries in the world. Any country can use it, provided that technical and managerial personnel are available. One can claim that the same, or almost the same, technology is available to every country,

**Table 17.3** Illustrative input coefficients for three production processes

| Input | Process 1: Shoe production | Process 2: Computer production | Process 3: Shoe production |
|---|---|---|---|
| Labor | 2 | 5 | 1 |
| Capital | 0.5 | 5 | 0.5 |
| Technical personnel | 0 | 0 | 1 |

but some countries have larger supplies of technical and managerial personnel than others. This is a valid point that can be translated to a statement that human capital is the crucial factor in determining a country's production capability. I have some reservation on its general validity, because social and economic organization determine how well-trained Princeton PhDs, Harvard MBAs, and experienced and innovative entrepreneurs from Hong Kong can get such technology to work in China, a subject discussed at the end of chapter 16.

The choice to explain a difference in technology as a difference in the supply of technical personnel is also open when we discuss foreign investment, the second topic of this chapter. Foreign investment can be viewed as import of capital goods, import of technology, import of technical and managerial personnel, or a combination of these, all of which can help to improve the production transformation curve of the importing country. International trade of final products also improves the transformation curve facing a trading country, if the output combinations incorporate imports and exports.

## 17.3 The Determination of Foreign Exchange Rates

In section 17.2 we explained why and how a country gains from international trade. We have also explained how the country's production transformation curve is determined by technology (a set of available productive processes or productive "activities") and the supply of inputs, and how the production transformation curve can be extended through trade. We have not dealt with the financial aspect of trade. The theories of section 17.2 apply even when there is no paper money in each country and trade takes place through barter. These theories, like the theories of demand and supply in a competitive economy as expounded in any standard economics text, deal with the quantities of different commodities traded or consumed and their relative prices, but not their absolute prices in money terms.

To understand how exchange rates between currencies in different countries are determined by market forces, consider the factors affecting the demand for and supply of these currencies. To begin with, consider the trading of two goods, shoes and computers, between two countries, A and B. Given the production transformation curves of these two countries and their demand conditions, how are production and trading of the two commodities by the two countries determined by the analysis set forth in section 17.2? For example, in the situation depicted by the technology of table 17.2, country A produces 100 units of shoes and exports 50 units to country B; country B produces 20 units of computers and exports 10 units to country A. The relative price of shoes to computers is 0.20 in both countries. Let country A's monetary unit be the yuan and country B's be the dollar. Let the prices of shoes and computers in country A be 20 and 100 yuan, respectively. Let the prices of shoes and computers in country B be 4 and 20 dollars, respectively. Common sense tells us that in this situation one dollar must be worth five yuan, or the exchange rate of the yuan is 0.2 dollars.

The commonsense conclusion can be justified in the following way. If the exchange rate were otherwise, there would be an excess demand for one currency to alter the exchange rate to the above level. For example, assume that the exchange rate of the yuan is 0.3 dollars. Traders can exchange 100 yuan for 30 dollars to buy 1.5 units of computers in country B, and sell them in country A for 150 yuan for a profit. Such traders will be selling yuan to buy dollars in order to buy computers in country B. This increases the demand for dollars relative to the demand for yuan. As a result, the price of the dollar relative to the yuan will increase, or the exchange rate of yuan in dollars will be lowered. The exchange rate will cease to change when one yuan can buy exactly as much in country A as it can in country B after it is converted to dollars.

This analysis suggests that the exchange rate of yuan in terms of dollars is that rate, if used to convert one yuan to dollars, which will provide just enough dollars to buy the same amount of goods in country B as one yuan can buy in country A. This explanation of the exchange rate is known as the purchasing power parity (PPP) theory. According to this theory, the exchange rate between two currencies should equal the ratio of the prices in the two countries. Each currency should be capable of buying the same bundle of commodities domestically as it can buy in a foreign country after conversion to the latter's currency. We will show below that this theory is at best a first approximation to a satisfactory explanation of actually observed exchange rates. It makes many unrealistic assumptions including zero transportation and distribution costs for exporters and importers, zero tariffs and no restrictions on trade, etc. which we will discuss.

If the exchange rate depends on the ratio of monetary or absolute prices in the two countries concerned and if, as a first approximation, absolute prices in each country depend on its money supply, then, as a first approximation, the exchange rate is affected by the relative money supplies in the two countries. Recall that when we study a competitive market economy, we use the demand and supply conditions to determine the relative prices of different commodities, but not their absolute prices in money terms. In section 7.2 we point out that as a first approximation, the absolute prices are determined by the supply of money in relation to the total output of an economy. As a first approximation, if the supply of money in country A increases by 20 percent, its absolute prices will increase by 20 percent and its foreign exchange rate will be reduced by 20 percent. This analysis is independent of the analysis of the production transformation curves that determine comparative advantage and trading patterns between countries. A finer theory than a first approximation will be concerned with the interactions between monetary forces and the production and trading of commodities. For example, money supply can affect the rate of interest, which in turn affects investment, and thus the production of producer goods relative to consumer goods. We will not be concerned with such refinements here.

Even without such refinements, the purchasing power parity PPP theory of exchange rates should be modified or extended in several ways. First, the absolute prices in the two countries that determine the exchange rate should refer to the prices of only internationally traded goods and not to goods and services that cannot be exported. Prices of goods and services that are consumed only at home should not be included in the PPP calculation. For example, the price of labor services may be very low in China when converted to US dollars at the prevailing exchange rate, but China may not be able to export these services directly to the United States. It can export labor services indirectly by using them to produce labor-intensive products for exports. Such exports would tend to raise the wage rate in China if the wage rate were determined by the forces of demand and supply in the market.

Second, besides the trading of goods and services, other factors affect the demand for and supply of currencies of different countries. Besides the export of goods, one important source of supply of foreign currencies is the inflow of foreign capital. Foreign investment is one source of capital inflow. If corporations in the United States want to invest in China, they have to sell US dollars for Chinese RMB to pay for the cost of the investments in China. This will increase the supply of US dollars in China and, other things being equal, raise the exchange rate of RMB in terms of dollars. In the future, if the investments turn out to be successful, the investing corporations will receive Chinese RMB, which they can trade for dollars. The supply of RMB will increase, thus lowering the exchange rate of RMB in terms of dollars. Foreign aid is another source of supply of a foreign currency. It tends to reduce the exchange rate of the currency of the country extending aid.

There are other sources of capital inflow than foreign investment. For example, foreign currencies will flow into a country to earn a high return if the interest rate in that country is high. Such flows will decrease the exchange rates of the foreign currencies. Thus, because of banking regulations favorable to depositors, Switzerland receives large quantities of foreign currencies for deposit in banks. This tends to raise the exchange rate of the Swiss franc and to lower the interest rate paid by Swiss banks.

Third, the purchasing power parity theory, after the above two modifications are incorporated, can be applied to explain the exchange rates of many countries by considering the trading and capital flows between any one country and the rest of the world. The exchange rate of any country depends on the absolute prices of internationally traded goods in that country compared with world market prices, in whatever international currency. It also depends on the inflow of foreign capital compared with the outflow of its own capital abroad.

Fourth, because of the existence of transportation and distribution costs, which we have assumed to be zero in the above analysis, the purchasing power of one currency, measured in domestically produced goods, may be somewhat different from that measured in foreign goods. As a modification to the analysis of the last section on trade flows, when transportation costs exist, trade will take place to a lesser extent than predicted by the theory and relative prices between commodities may not be completely equalized in different countries. The effect of transportation and distribution costs on the PPP theory for the determination of exchange rates is that the actual rates may deviate to a fairly large extent from the rate determined by the PPP theory. In section 5.6 we convert Chinese GNP into GNP in US dollars based on PPP calculation as performed by the World Bank, by using a conversion rate of about 2 yuan per dollar in 1998 when the free-market exchange rate was about 8.3 per dollar. Although the bundle of commodities included in calculating the above conversion rate include more than just internationally traded goods (the relative prices of which determine the market exchange rate) the difference between 2 and 8.3 suggests that the PPP exchange rate determined by only internationally traded goods should be below 8.3 even if it is above 2. In section 4.4 I mentioned some reasons for the Chinese yuan to be valued at lower than the rate based on economic fundamentals including PPP, and suggest that in the long run, say before 2006, the Chinese currency will appreciate in the direction of its PPP rate.

Fifth, the theories of trade and exchange rate determination set forth above are based on free trade and free capital flows among countries. In reality, many trade restrictions exist, such as import quotas and tariffs. Furthermore, the governments of many countries, including China, set their exchange rates and do not allow the rates to be determined entirely by the forces of demand and supply. The analysis of the last section can assist the reader in evaluating the economic consequences of trade restrictions. The analysis of this section sets bounds to the exchange rate that a government can enforce and reveals the economic effects of enforcing an exchange rate which deviates from a market-determined rate.

As the tools of demand and supply are useful in explaining market prices and in studying the effects of government price regulation, the theory of exchange rate determination in this section is useful in explaining exchange rates in free markets and in studying the effects of government control of exchange rates. When the value of the home currency is set above the market rate as determined by the forces of demand and supply set forth above, people will try to sell home currency to buy more foreign currencies than the supply of foreign currency offered in the market. Further controls to limit the purchase of foreign currencies would be required. For example, in China before 1994, RMB could not be freely used to purchase US dollars because its official exchange was set too high. Through several successive steps of devaluating the overvalued RMB, from 2 RMB for one US dollar in 1979 to 8.3 RMB for one US dollar in 1994, the official rate finally reached the market rate. It can freely be traded at this 8.3 rate as any tourist could do in Hong Kong. The rates of buying and selling RMB in exchange for one US dollar are almost identical in Hong Kong, showing the small profit margin for the traders under competition.

It took the Chinese government some twenty years to reform its foreign trade and foreign-exchange system to become one that is qualified for membership of WTO. In the early 1980s, Chinese economic officials did not appreciate the rationale for free trade and the role of a market-determined exchange rate. They had the notion that because of the shortage of foreign goods – and foreign goods could be purchased only by using a hard currency like the US dollars – the government should control the supply and demand for dollars. This is the same as assuming that if steel is a scarce and valuable resource for industrial production, its demand and supply should be controlled by the government in the form of quotas allocated to state enterprises which use it and to suppliers which produce it. The corresponding users of foreign exchange are enterprises which require imports for production. The corresponding suppliers are the export companies controlled by the government. The official price of American dollars, or the official exchange rate, is set low in order to allow its users to have easy access to it, just like the low price of steel set under central planning. A student of economics cannot understand such logic. If foreign exchange or steel is scarce its price should be high enough to allocate its use to the most needy users. By "high enough" we mean that the price will equate demand and supply. To continue the logic of the Chinese economic planners, the price of foreign exchange was set low and there was a shortage in the sense that people could not buy dollars at the official rate because there were not enough available at that low rate.

In order to limit the consumption of imported goods by Chinese consumers, a system of "foreign-exchange certificates" was introduced. There were two kinds of Chinese currency, one ordinary and a second foreign-exchange certificates. Foreigners could obtain foreign-exchange certificates at the official exchange rate by trading dollars. Since the official exchange rate was unfavorable for the dollar (or below the rate set by the market if it existed) foreigners were given some benefits in return in being able to use the certificate to purchase imported goods which Chinese consumers could not buy using ordinary Chinese currency. Because of its higher utility than ordinary Chinese currency, one yuan of foreign-exchange certificates was traded in illegal markets (by resourceful foreign visitors) for more than one ordinary yuan, but in many local stores local currency used by foreigners was not accepted. Storekeepers had an incentive to insist on getting foreign-exchange certificates which were worth more. The whole system led to confusion: arguments between foreigners trying to use ordinary yuan and taxi-drivers, storekeepers, and Chinese merchants; bargaining in illegal trading of foreign-exchange certificates for the ordinary yuan, etc. It did not take a very sophisticated economist to know that the foreign-exchange certificate should be abolished and that China should set its exchange rate equal to the market rate to eliminate the shortage of foreign exchange. If the government wished to promote the development of certain industries, it could give enterprises in such industries fixed subsidies for a finite duration to enable them to develop. The enterprises could decide how best to use the subsidies, including the purchase of foreign imports at a market-determined exchange rate. This would eliminate the waste of using the scarce foreign exchange under the Chinese system of undervaluation of the dollar and restriction of its use to favored users.

In 1984, when I first met Premier Zhao Ziyang to discuss at length economic education and economic reform in China, I suggested to him to abandon the use of the foreign-exchange certificate. This suggestion was made at a time when such an idea was contrary to the accepted wisdom of the top Chinese economic officials described in the last paragraph. (I chose not to make such a drastic suggestion in front of other government officials present at our meeting, but in the form of a letter delivered to the Premier after our meeting the afternoon of July 5, 1984.) Two years later in the summer of 1986, after at least two more meetings with the Premier and several intensive meetings with top officials of the State Commission on Restructuring the Economic System, of which the Premier served as chairman, I was very pleased to read in a newspaper an official announcement that the use of the foreign-exchange certificates was to be terminated in September of that year. This did not happen on schedule, but actually about two years later. The setting of the official exchange rate to equal the market rate occurred in steps in a period of about 8 years from 1986 to 1994.

At the beginning of the twenty-first century, the value of the RMB against the US dollar was higher than the official rate of 8.3 yuan for one dollar; this can be explained by both the purchasing power parity theory and by the demand for and supply of the dollar in exchange for RMB. From the PPP theory, if the exchange rate was approximately in equilibrium in 1998, China had a slight deflation from 1998 to 2002, while the US had a mild inflation. This makes the purchasing power of the RMB larger relative to that of the dollar by 2002. From the viewpoint of the supply of the dollar in the foreign-exchange market (one such market has actually existed in Shanghai since April 1994), both the foreign trade surplus of China and the inflow of foreign investment to China created an excess supply of the dollar against the RMB. This means that the supply curve of the dollar, with the price of the dollar in RMB per dollar measured along the $y$-axis, moves to the right, leading to a decrease in the value of the dollar against the RMB. Yet, as of April 2005, the Chinese government had not raised the exchange rate of the RMB against the US dollar. The large excess supply of US dollars under the below-market exchange rate for the RMB was manifested in the accumulation of foreign-exchange reserves in China to over 600 billion dollars by the end of 2004, with an increase of about 200 billion in 2004 alone. Some of that increase was probably due to speculation, when dollars flowed into China in exchange for RMB in anticipation of an increase in its value.

This failure to raise the value of, or revalue, the RMB to its market rate as determined by the forces of demand and supply has had the following unfavorable effects on the Chinese economy. First, the large amount of foreign reserves was not effectively used for consumption or capital formation for economic development in China, while a part was used to purchase US Treasury Bonds yielding a low rate of interest. Revaluing the RMB would make imports cheaper and increase the amount of imports for consumption and capital formation. Second, the acquired foreign exchange has led to a rapid increase in money supply in China since the Chinese banks are obliged to offer RMB in exchange for the dollar. This increase in money supply is not a result of the monetary policy of the People's Bank. Rather, the People's Bank passively increases the money supply because of the inflow of foreign exchange. In section 7.3 I pointed out that the resulting rapid increase in money supply in 2002–3 led to a rapid increase in total output in 2003 and 2004 and to inflation in 2004. The Chinese government tried to increase the rate of interest to slow down investment activities, as well as using administrative means to control what it called an overheated economy. The administrative means included assigning quotas to development projects and imposing restrictions on bank loans. If the banks had not had money to begin with, there would be no need to restrict their credit expansion or to control investment activities financed by their loans. The inflow of foreign exchange to buy RMB for the purpose of speculation will continue as long as the RMB is undervalued and expected to be revalued.

One argument against revaluation of the RMB is that reducing Chinese exports would have adverse effects on output growth and employment. My response is that the macroeconomic control policies introduced by the government to slow down the overheated economy had precisely the same effects. This means that the government was already prepared to pay the cost of slowing down the economy and possibly reducing total employment. Under a correctly adjusted exchange rate, the overheating of the economy would not have occurred, and no macroeconomic control by administrative means would have been required.

In the period 2003–5 much pressure from foreign governments, especially the US government, was put on the Chinese government to revalue the RMB. The US was under political pressure from certain domestic manufacturers and trade unions to reduce imports from China. Such pressure from foreign governments, especially when openly expressed, was counterproductive, as the Chinese government could not be seen by its people to succumb to foreign pressure. In the last paragraph I presented reasons in favor of revaluating the RMB for the good of China's own economic development, and not for the good of other countries. At the same time there were suggestions that the Chinese government change its exchange rate regime to one closer to a free-floating rate, just as the exchange rates of the Euro and the Japanese Yen that are determined by market forces. This is different from the current regime in which the Chinese government can decide on the exchange rate of the RMB and adjust it upwards or downwards according to demand and supply conditions as it considers appropriate. In response to such suggestions the Chinese government has repeatedly stated that it would seriously consider reform of its exchange rate regime to suit the economic conditions of China and world trade. Since in the past the Chinese government has been slow in giving up control of what it considers to be important economic policy instruments, the reform of its exchange rate regime is likely to occur after the government adjusts the exchange rate of RMB upwards to prevent or reduce the unfavorable economic effects of an overvalued RMB as described above.

In the meantime there were foreign-exchange swap centers in Shanghai where importers could swap local currency for foreign exchange supplied by exporters at a rate determined by that swap market, and more favorable to a holder of US dollars than the official rate. Here again, China was practicing a two-tier price system in terms of exchange rates. One could get dollars more cheaply at the official rate but only in limited quantity and subject to official approval, in the same way that a state enterprise at the time could obtain materials at lower than market prices but only in limited quantity. At the same time, foreign traders could buy and sell foreign exchange at a market rate in a swap center. Marginal calculations by importers and exporters using the market price of foreign currency could thus be carried out to preserve economic efficiency in the use of scarce foreign exchange as an economic resource.

## 17.4   China's Foreign Trade Policy

Perhaps the most significant aspect of China's foreign trade policy in the 1980s was the drastic reversal from self-sufficiency to trade expansion. The ratio of the total value of foreign trade to national income increased from a low of 0.058 in 1970 to a high of

0.182 in 1981. According to Zhang (1982: 621), as of 1980 China had established trade relations with more than 170 countries and regions and had signed bilateral government trade agreements or protocols with more than 80 of them. One can only interpret the change as resulting from the realization among Chinese leaders of the gain to be achieved from international trade.

China was largely a planned economy. Foreign trade was directed by central planning. When construction projects were included in a five-year plan, some required the imports of foreign capital goods and materials. Certain consumption goods in the plan had to be imported, including food grain when the domestic supply was insufficient. All these projected imports required the use of foreign exchange, which had to be earned by the planned exports of domestically produced goods. Thus, exports, imports, and the supply of and demand for foreign exchange had to be incorporated in any central economic planning. Foreign trade plans were part of China's economic plans. In the State Council, the Ministry of Foreign Trade directed the affairs of foreign trade. It incorporated the Bureau of Import–Export Control and the General Administration of Customs, and was assisted by the General Administration of Travel and Tourism and the State Administration of Exchange Control (later part of the People's Bank).

In June 1979 the People's Congress adopted a policy for the modernization of China, which included a policy of foreign trade expansion. The ratio of the total value of foreign trade to national income increased immediately, from 0.118 in 1978 to 0.135 in 1979, 0.154 in 1980, and 0.182 in 1981. Following the shift in policy from an emphasis on developing heavy industry to an emphasis on developing light industry and agriculture, the composition of imports changed. The imports of machinery and raw materials for heavy industry were reduced, and imports of food grains, cooking oils, materials for agricultural use, and raw materials for textiles and light industry increased. As reported in the article on foreign trade by Zhang (1982: 622), in 1980 imports of grains, animal fats and vegetable oils, cotton, synthetic fibers, chemical fertilizers, industrial chemicals, and wood pulp were 51 percent higher than in 1979. Their combined share in the total value of imports rose to 52.8 percent in 1980 from 41.7 percent in 1979. Imports of steel, nonferrous metals, machinery, and instruments decreased by 3.5 percent from 1979 and together accounted for 47.2 percent of the total value of imports, as compared with 58.3 percent in 1979.

As for the composition of exports, in 1980 the proportion of exports of heavy industrial products went up, while that of agricultural and sideline products, textiles, and light industrial products declined. Agricultural and sideline products decreased from 23.1 percent to 18.7 percent, while industrial and mineral products increased from 44.0 percent to 51.8 percent. In particular, the value of exported machine tools increased from 65.56 million RMB in 1979 to 77.88 million in 1980, and the export of tools and instruments increased from 112.19 million RMB to 147.30 million. Although China increased the value of its exports of machinery and transport equipment by 44.6 percent between 1979 and 1980, its imports of machinery and transport equipment still far exceeded its exports in 1981, being 9.798 billion RMB as compared with 1.815 billion (*Statistical Yearbook of China, 1981*, p. 390). The quantities of major exported commodities from 1950 to 1980 are given on pages 372–84 of the *Statistical Yearbook of China, 1981*; the quantities of major imported commodities are given on pages 385–9.

Before and at the beginning of economic reform, China's foreign trade policy had three main characteristics. First, imports were controlled by the government so that essential consumer goods and capital goods from abroad could be acquired in the process of modernization. Second, to obtain the foreign exchange to pay for the necessary imports, the Chinese government tried to direct and encourage the expansion of exports. New government units were set up in the early 1980s for the purpose of increasing exports. Besides directing selected centrally run enterprises to expand their exports, the government encouraged provincially run and collective enterprises to obtain export licenses to compete in the world market. Third, to ensure that the foreign exchange obtained from exports was used to pay for essential imports, the government controlled foreign exchange by setting the exchange rate and monopolizing and regulating the trading of foreign exchange. Foreign exchange was not allowed to be traded freely in the marketplace. To obtain foreign exchange for a purpose approved by the government, an importer, an enterprise, or a tourist had to apply to the Administration of Exchange Control, which is a part of the People's Bank. Furthermore, a system of multiple exchange rates was practiced. To encourage certain exporters, the government paid them more RMB per US dollar earned than according to the standard official exchange.

Concerning import policy in the early 1980s, Zhang (1982: 623) wrote:

> During the period of economic readjustment, imports of agricultural and industrial materials needed for maintaining economic stability and developing the textile and light industries must be timely and orderly. Imports of technology and equipment needed for upgrading existing industries, for expanding energy production, communications and transportation facilities and for advancing science, education and culture must be organized in a planned way . . . In drawing up foreign trade plans, we must take into consideration our actual export capabilities . . . From the short-term as well as the long-term point of view, import controls will be necessary . . .
>
> We shall not import those items that can be produced domestically in sufficient quantity and with satisfactory quality. Items that we can make at home but are still importing now will eventually be supplied mainly by domestic production. In this way, we can save our limited foreign exchange for the most essential items and make the composition of our imports more reasonable.

To promote exports, the Chinese government took the following actions after 1979 (Yen 1982). First, exports were decentralized. While commodities of the first categories (defined in section 2.5), including coal, oil, food grain, steel, and others, were still exported by enterprises under the direct control of the Ministry of Foreign Trade, commodities of the second category could be exported by enterprises under other ministries, subject to the approval of the State Council. Other commodities could be exported by trading companies established under the jurisdiction of provincial governments. Export licenses were issued by provincial bureaus of foreign trade authorized by the Ministry of Foreign Trade, rather than directly by the ministry, as had been the case.

Second, trading companies were formed in cooperation with manufacturing enterprises as well as industrial enterprises specializing in the production of export products. These enterprises were responsible for their own profits and losses. Many provinces and cities set up areas specializing in the production of agricultural and related products for export.

Third, special treatment was given to exporting companies and enterprises to encourage them to export, including allowing them to retain part of the foreign exchange they earn and extending to them special loans in RMB or in foreign exchange for short-term financing or long-term capital expansion. After 1981 a more favorable exchange rate was granted to exporters in exchanging the foreign currency earned for RMB. For example, in 1981, while the official exchange rate was 1 US dollar for 1.6 RMB, the more favorable rate was 1 to 2.8 RMB.

Fourth, several coastal provinces, including Guangdong and Fujian, established export-processing zones. Foreign investors were encouraged to set up factories in these zones, independently or jointly with Chinese enterprises, to process imported or locally produced materials for export. No import duties were levied on materials processed for exports. A main purpose was to absorb Chinese labor while using the capital and technical knowledge of the foreign investors. The use of export-processing zones to promote exports proved successful in Taiwan, which established the Kaohsiung Export-processing Zone in December 1966. Also, joint ventures with foreign investors outside the export-processing zones were established. These developments were relevant not only to China's foreign trade but also to foreign investment in China, a topic to be treated in chapter 18.

As the Chinese economy grew at a rapid rate from the early 1980s to the early 2000s under the open-door policy, China's foreign trade volume reached 5.13782 billion RMB in 2002, as shown in table 17.1, while its GDP was 10.47906 billion, making trade volume 49 percent of GDP. From 2002 to 2004 trade volume was expanding at an annual rate of 30 percent, making trade volume close to 70 percent of GDP by the end of 2004. The *New York Times*, April 9, 2004, p. C1, carried an article entitled, "Made in China. Bought Everywhere," which reported that China had a trade surplus with the world of US$33 billion in 2004, but if trade with the US is excluded, China ran a trade deficit of $47 billion with all other countries combined. As China's exports were expanding at an annual rate of 36 percent in the first two months of 2004, it was running a surplus with both the US and the rest of the world. Its major exports included toys, clothing, furniture, and television sets, as well as newer products such as portable electric lamps, radio navigation equipment, steels, chemicals, cars, and machinery. The Chinese government is no longer concerned about not earning enough foreign exchange by exporting in order to pay for its imports. Rather it is faced with the large accumulation of foreign reserves which have caused rapid increases in money supply. The trade surplus generated much pressure from foreign governments to revalue the RMB, with threats from the US and European governments to impose import quotas or raise tariffs on Chinese products.

## 17.5   Problems in Implementing Foreign Trade Policies in the Early 1980s

While China's foreign trade has expanded greatly since 1979, it had several problems which were the subject of debate in the Chinese literature: I take as an example the articles on pages 1–2 of the August 22, 1983, issue of the *World Economic Herald*, a weekly journal in Chinese published in Shanghai and edited jointly by the Chinese World Economic Association and the Institute of World Economics of the Shanghai Academy of Social Science.

The first problem was how to decide what to import and what to export. In China, where imports and exports were subject to government direction to a large extent, by what means could the government decide what and how much to import and to export? In the preceding section we quoted from an article by Zhang Peiji (1982) of the Ministry of Foreign Trade indicating that imports were a part of the overall planning of production and investment. Foreign consumer and producer goods were needed to satisfy the needs of consumption and capital accumulation. The principles of planning were discussed in section 2.2, and we have nothing to add here.

A difficult question concerns the choice of the kinds and the quantities of exports to pay for the imports. Chinese government officials had some awareness of the principle of comparative advantage, as evidenced by their choice of labor-intensive products for export, such as handicraft products. Further study is required to establish whether officials violated this principle by increasing the export of certain machinery and machine tools produced by skilled labor and technicians in China. One guideline that they sometimes used in choosing a commodity for export was the ratio of the cost of the product in RMB to the net revenue from the product in a foreign currency, typically US dollars. If this "RMB cost per dollar" is 2.2, for example, it takes 2.2 yuan to earn a dollar of foreign exchange. If the exchange rate is 2.0, for example, this product is considered a poor candidate for export because it takes more RMB to exchange one dollar by exporting than by currency exchanging. Of course, whether the official exchange rate should serve as the cut-off point for the use of this ratio depended on whether the rate truly reflected the purchasing power of one dollar relative to that of one yuan RMB. If the purchasing power (in terms of internationally traded goods) of one dollar was in fact 3 times that of one RMB, while the official exchange rate was only 2, it would be worthwhile to export a commodity at a ratio of 2.2 for the "RMB cost per dollar." However, the most serious problem with using this ratio arose from the fact that the relative cost figures often did not reflect the relative trade-off possibilities or the marginal rates of substitution in production because of government regulation of prices. Prices of certain agricultural products, the cost of labor, and the cost of using land were set too low. This affected the numerator in the above ratio. In practice, the ratio was used merely as a guide and not as the sole determinant of a commodity for export, but no better criteria were available.

The second problem was that many exporting enterprises continued to expand their exports even when they were operating at a loss. They often competed with other Chinese exporting firms by lowering their prices or giving special commissions or kickbacks to foreign agents for handling their products, resulting in high ratios of RMB cost per dollar earned, or in actual losses in their operations. While the Chinese government set official export prices and guidelines for commission rates to foreign agents, the provincial exporting companies sometimes charged lower prices and gave higher commission rates as well as other kickbacks. The losses incurred in exports amounted to selling products below cost to benefit foreign consumers.

The third problem was how to determine an appropriate exchange rate or set of exchange rates. The official exchange rate of RMB in terms of US dollars declined after 1980, or the exchange rate of one US dollar in terms of RMB went up. The latter rate was approximately 1.5 in 1980, 1.7 in 1981, 1.9 in 1982, and 1.97 in 1983, eventually rising to 8.3 in 1996–2000. Thus, from 1980 on, the RMB was steadily devalued relative to the US dollar. Ordinarily, the devaluation of a country's currency has the effect of increasing its exports and decreasing its imports, because it makes that country's products cheaper to foreigners and makes foreign goods more expensive to its own citizens. If the elasticity of demand in the world market for that country's exports is larger than one, as is ordinarily the case because there are close substitutes for these products in the world market, increasing the quantity of exports (at a lower price in foreign exchange) will lead to a larger total revenue in foreign exchange. Whatever the elasticity of demand in the domestic market for imports is, increasing the domestic prices of imports due to devaluation (given constant prices of these products in the world market) will lead to a reduction in the total quantities purchased at home and thus in the total expenditures for imports in foreign exchange. Therefore, a devaluation of a country's currency will tend to increase a trade surplus or to reduce a trade deficit.

In the case of China, the steady devaluation between 1980 and 1983 was in terms of US dollars, while the US dollar was itself appreciating in terms of some other major currencies. The Chinese RMB was not necessarily devalued in terms of these currencies. Be that as it may, it is interesting to note that China ran a trade deficit (with the dollar value of its imports higher than that of its exports) of US$1.14 billion in 1978, $2.01 billion in 1979, $1.28 billion in 1980, a trade surplus of $1.41 billion in 1981, $4.7 billion in 1982 (*Chinese Statistical Abstract, 1983*, p. 74), and a likely trade deficit in 1983. The devaluation of the RMB in 1981 and 1982 contributed to the trade surpluses in these two years. The Chinese government probably devalued the RMB to correct the trade deficits from 1978 to 1980. (Not only the official exchange rate of the Chinese currency was devalued. Since 1981 some exporters have been able to get 2.8 yuan for 1 US dollar under the dual exchange rate system, which further encourages exports.) Trade surpluses and deficits are the signs used by the government to adjust the official exchange rate of its currency. However, even when foreign trade is nearly balanced and the official exchange rate remains unchanged, with government control of imports and regulation of exports, there is no guarantee that at the official exchange rate one Chinese RMB has the same purchasing power in the world market as in China. For example, in 1983 800 RMB when exchanged for $400 was sufficient to buy a good color television in the world market, but not sufficient to buy one in China. After overvaluing the RMB in terms of US dollars, the Chinese government avoided a trade deficit by restricting imports. In so doing, it prevented Chinese consumers from enjoying foreign consumer goods and Chinese producers from using foreign producer goods by trading their own products according to the principle of comparative advantage.

Readers of the last section understand how these problems are solved by market economies practicing free trade. First, the government has no difficulty in deciding what to import and what to export. As long as the marginal rate of substitution in production or the relative prices of two commodities at home are different from the relative prices in the world market (after transportation costs are absorbed), there is economic gain from trade and traders will automatically engage in trade to equalize the price ratios. Trade will stop when there will be no further gain. Government planning will require certain state enterprises to import foreign producer goods. However, to allow the state enterprises to purchase these goods cheaply by supplying them with undervalued foreign currencies, the government encourages inefficiency of these enterprises.

Second, in a market economy one need not be concerned with financially independent enterprises engaged in export expansion when the operations are unprofitable. They automatically stop producing for export if such operations become unprofitable. The reason Chinese enterprises allegedly continued to export their products at a loss must be that there were economic incentives for them to do so. These incentives might include the foreign exchange that the enterprises were allowed to retain and the special loans extended to exporting enterprises. If an exporting enterprise could obtain foreign exchange cheaply at the official exchange rate, the gain might more than offset the loss of an export operation. All special favorable treatments to exporters encouraged the expansion of exports even when the operations might be unprofitable. Furthermore, competition among Chinese exporters in the world market is not necessarily a bad thing if they produce in competitive conditions. American computer manufacturers compete with one another in the world market, as do Japanese automobile manufacturers. Competition in the world market ensures that domestic enterprises operate efficiently and that inefficient manufacturers cannot enter the world market, or even survive in the domestic market when world trade is free. More on this point near the end of this chapter, where I discuss China's entry into the World Trade Organization.

Third, as we have pointed out, the exchange rate is automatically determined in the market by the demand for and the supply of the currency in question, like the price of any commodity. We have witnessed how the exchange rate of a freely traded currency such as the Hong Kong dollar before 1984 is determined daily or even hourly by the forces of demand and supply. Living in a free-trade area, the people of Hong Kong enjoy all the consumer goods produced in different parts of the world and pay for them by exporting products and performing services according to the principle of comparative advantage. Almost no government control of imports and exports is involved. There is no shortage of foreign exchange, and the Hong Kong government does not have to control the supply of foreign exchange. In fact, levying taxes at low rates was sufficient for the government of Hong Kong to earn substantial foreign exchanges for remittance to the British government before 1997. More funds, including foreign exchange, can be obtained by taxing a rich economy at low rates than by controlling a small amount of foreign exchanges earned by an unproductive economy.

This summary of how the problems of foreign trade are solved by market economies practicing free trade is intended to highlight the difficulties facing the Chinese or any economic planners who control imports, regulate exports, set official exchange rates differing from market rates, and set the prices of labor, land, capital, materials, and consumer goods to suit special planning purposes. Just as an understanding of the functioning of a market economy increases one's appreciation of the working of a centrally planned economy (the subject of chapter 2), an understanding of the functioning of international trade as set forth in section 17.2 increases one's appreciation of the three problems of foreign trade facing the Chinese government. The problems associated with administrative decisions on economic affairs, compared with decisions by market forces, are as real in the sphere of international trade as in domestic production and trade. Once resources are not priced by the competitive forces of demand and supply, it is difficult for any planner to make economically correct decisions concerning what to produce, how much to produce, and what and how much to export and import, not to speak of the need to provide proper incentives to the economic agents to carry out their tasks. In the 1990s the Chinese government came to appreciate the usefulness of market forces in the regulation of the economy. It instituted reforms to decentralize production for the domestic as well as the foreign market. As of 1984 it did not decontrol the prices of labor, land, many important products and materials, and the price of US dollars (namely, the exchange rate). Accordingly, rational economic calculations could not be successfully carried out by enterprises engaged in production for domestic consumption, capital accumulation, and exports. This was the main hindrance to the achievement of economic efficiency in China up to the early 1990s.

One argument often advanced to justify import restrictions is the protection of infant domestic industries. The theory of comparative advantage discussed in the last section is based on a given technology. Comparative advantage changes as technology changes, through the import of either new technology or some scarce factors required to use the technology known to the world. In the process of economic development and technological change, a country's comparative advantage changes. For example, Japan did not have a comparative advantage in producing automobiles in the 1960s but it did have such an advantage in the 1970s. While infant industries are being developed, one might argue, they should be protected from foreign competition by tariffs or other restrictions on competing imports. This argument was advanced in Taiwan in the 1960s to protect a domestic automobile manufacturer from foreign competition. The manufacturing cost of producing an automobile was about two and a half times the world price. Such protection lasted for 15 years, and the production cost of this manufacturer was still about twice the world price. In the meantime, consumers in Taiwan incurred a great loss by paying more than twice the world price for their automobiles. The resources that they used up to pay for these expensive automobiles could have been used to purchase more than twice as many automobiles from abroad. In other words, the economy of Taiwan was using a very inefficient way of producing or acquiring its automobiles. By allowing free trade, it could have acquired twice as many automobiles, or it could have paid only half as much for the automobiles it actually acquired. Up to the 1990s, mainland China still protected its automobile industry by imposing high tariffs on imports of automobiles. In many developed countries, import restrictions have been imposed to protect not infant industries, but declining industries that no longer produce at a comparative advantage. Such restrictions may be good for the owners and workers of those industries, but they are bad in general for the consumers of the countries concerned. See Baldwin (1969) for a criticism of the infant-industry argument.

In mainland China, importation of many other consumer products such as cameras, television sets, stereos, and video equipment was also restricted. Consumers lost out by not being able to buy these products. Protection of domestic infant industries is not the only argument justifying this policy. The government may decide which products the consumers should consume and which are luxury items consumers should not consume. Furthermore, the purchase of foreign consumer goods uses up valuable foreign exchange, which should be saved for more important consumer items and for capital accumulation. The last argument is not easy to justify if the principle of comparative advantage is understood. If a consumer decides to buy a foreign-made color television (assuming it can be imported freely) for $380, he has to give up the consumption of $380 worth of other resources to acquire it. Under free trade, the latter resources could be traded in the world market for $380 US and there should be no problem of the shortage of foreign exchange. One might imagine that the resources the consumer gives up consist of two domestic black-and-white television sets that could not be exchanged for $380 in the world market. In that case, assuming the exchange rate of RMB to be market-determined, the conclusion must be that the two domestic television sets are overpriced at home and China should not produce them. Under free trade and market-determined exchange rates, there should be no shortage of US dollars in China. Any (internationally traded) good in China selling for 1 RMB must be worth approximately its US dollar equivalent in the world market. Trade is determined by comparative advantages. The exchange rates will adjust so that the relative supply of and demand for US dollars and Chinese RMB will be equal.

The main reason for failure to develop infant industries by import restriction is the resulting reduction of competition. Without foreign competition, the protected domestic producers have no incentive to improve their products or change their technology. In the meantime, the consumers are forced to buy inferior products at higher prices than necessary. To develop an infant industry, if such an industry can be identified, a better method than import restriction is to provide the enterprises of that industry with subsidies of fixed and declining amounts during a specified period of, say, 5 years. This alternative method has several advantages over imposing import restrictions. First, consumers would not be deprived of the better and cheaper foreign products. Second, domestic producers would have incentives to improve because of foreign competition. The availability of good-quality foreign products in the home market would also have a demonstration effect stimulating domestic manufacturers to produce better products. One reason the opening of China in the late 1970s has been beneficial to China's economic development is that it enables Chinese planners and managers to see what goes on in the outside world. Third, through the subsidies, the government knows exactly the cost involved in helping to develop the industry concerned. By imposing import restrictions, the government does not know this cost and therefore may not care about the economic loss involved; only the consumers suffer. Knowing the cost involved and having to pay for it from its own budget would enable the government to choose a sound policy for developing infant industry and would help to prevent an inefficient industry from being protected for an extended period.

However, it is still difficult for the government to identify a promising industry to develop. A well-trained staff is required to identify such industries and to devise appropriate means of continually upgrading their technologies. The development of new industries and the upgrading of existing industries are related to the subject of foreign investment, to be discussed in the next chapter. One important principle in carrying out these tasks is that the central government should not set up and run monopolies in these industries. The central government can promote the development of an industry by various means, including providing subsidies and technical assistance in the form of training programs to its managerial, technical, and production staff. It can even set up new enterprises in the industry, but to prevent enterprises at the provincial and local levels and those established under collective ownership from competing would be harmful to the development of the industry. Most important of all, in the process of industrial development, prices should be unregulated, so that accurate cost and benefit calculations can be performed by state-owned and collectively owned enterprises and by consumers and workers to ensure economic efficiency.

Foreign trade has enabled the low-cost and high-quality labor in China to produce goods to be sold at higher prices in the world market, thus increasing the compensation to Chinese labor. It has also enabled the import of technology and high-quality capital goods for use in production in China, as well as the import of high-quality consumer goods. The availability of high-quality capital goods improves productive efficiency. The availability of high-quality consumer goods not only increases consumer welfare directly; it also acts as an important competitive force in the Chinese consumer market and stimulates im-provement of the quality of domestically manufactured products. In the latter part of the 1990s the Chinese leadership recognized the need to introduce foreign competition to speed up reform of state enterprises which had been protected and subsidized. It also recognized the danger of opening China for foreign competition too rapidly, as there would be adjustment costs including unemployment, need for reallocation, and possibly political instability. Therefore, the opening up will be accomplished in steps, as we have described in section 4.5, on the conditions which China offered in joining the WTO. The effects of China's accession to the WTO on its trading pattern and on the incomes of other countries are discussed in Ianchovichina and Martin (2001). By 2005, the Chinese government no longer faces the serious problem of protecting domestic production from foreign competition, with agricultural production as a possible exception. Rather other countries are facing serious competition from Chinese exports, to the point of threatening the use of import quotas and higher tariffs on Chinese products, as we will discuss in the next section.

## 17.6   Protectionism in the United States

At the beginning of the twenty-first century, as China's foreign trade and economic power have expanded greatly, the United States may consider China an economic threat. If "economic threat" is defined as an increase in the economic power of China relative to that of the US, the threat is real and perhaps unavoidable, unless the relative economic growth of China stops in the near future. We will consider four aspects of foreign trade and investment which sometimes enter into the discussion of the threat: the large amount of imports from China, the outsourcing of jobs to China (and India), foreign investment to China, and technology transfer to China.

First, concerning imports from China, the Ricardian theory of comparative advantage as expounded earlier in this chapter applies. Both countries benefit from trade. Yet Chinese textiles will compete with US textiles and are not good for the US textile industry. Hence there is political pressure to impose quotas on the import of Chinese textiles. According to the Ricardian trade theory the US should specialize in other industries (including services) in which it has comparative advantage. Do not forget the benefits to US consumers, who are enjoying low-price and high-quality consumer goods from China, and the benefits to US producers, including Boeing and producers of cosmetics and pharmaceuticals, who can take advantage of the large Chinese market for consumer goods. Furthermore, about 60 percent of Chinese exports are produced by foreign-invested companies in China, and a high fraction of the costs of Chinese imports to the US consumers goes to US traders and distributors, so that the profits of selling Chinese products in the US market contribute to the US GNP.

Second, the outsourcing of jobs – which means the purchase of (skilled) labor services abroad, possibly through the internet or wireless phone lines – should be viewed in the same way as the purchase of a textile product, and the Ricardian theory of comparative advantage applies. The producers of the same kind of labor services in the US lose out, but one can argue that the US should instead sell to China goods and services in the production of which it has a comparative advantage.

Third, the possible loss of US jobs because a factory is moved from Cleveland to Shanghai is a case of foreign direct investment from the US to China. US GNP increases as capital moves abroad because its marginal product in China has to be higher than in the US, otherwise it will not be moved. Consider an aggregate production function for the US. If capital can be moved to China to increase its marginal product, the loss of output produced in the US must be outweighed by the gain in output it produces in China, which is a part of the US GNP. The demand for labor in the US will decline because of the move, causing higher unemployment or lower wages in the short run, and creating personal suffering and adjustment problems for the displaced workers. In the long run, however, the US labor market will adjust, so that the long-run trend in the aggregate unemployment rate is not changed. This has been demonstrated historically: the aggregate unemployment rate has not changed because of US investment abroad. In the meantime US GNP has grown because of the higher returns to US capital.

Fourth, the above discussion has omitted the economic effect of possible transfer of technology to China when the US factory moves to China. Common sense tells us that if the US economy benefits from having an industry which has monopoly power in the world market, it would lose if another country develops an industry to take over some of the US's monopoly power. A case in point is the US automobile industry, which had monopoly power in the 1950s and early 1960s, until Japanese automobiles took over a significant part of the automobile market. The US lost as a result. Samuelson (2004) made this point in the context of a Ricardian model of trade with two goods. The US has a comparative advantage in producing good 1 and China in good 2. Trade benefits both countries. If China's technology improves to the point where the US loses its comparative advantage in producing good 1, trade will not take place. The US economy left with no trade is surely worse off than when it has trade. Thus the advance of Chinese technology can hurt the US economy. This is the only one of the four cases mentioned above in which foreign investment, not trade, could hurt the US economy if advanced technology is transferred to China. Technology transfer could produce such a result, but does not necessarily do so if China's technological development is not fast enough or if US technology in the meantime develops faster. Technology transfer to China can also occur when China invests in the US.

In 2005, the China National Offshore Oil Corporation (CNOOC) tried to buy the American oil company Unocal for 18.5 billion dollars. At the time of writing, there have been objections from the US Congress. One objection is that Unocal has technology in offshore oil drilling and exploration that China needs in expanding its share of the global oil market. If China's advance in technology and in monopoly power in the global market is an economic threat to the US, there seems to be little that the US can do in the long run. In the short run it can prevent or slow down the transfer of technology, as in the case of the CNOOC–Unocal acquisition, but other countries also have similar technology to sell to China, and China can develop its own if given enough time. In this sense the economic threat posed by China is real and perhaps unavoidable.

## References and Further Reading

Baldwin, R. E. "The Case Against Infant-industry Tariff Protection." *Journal of Political Economy*, 77 (1969), pp. 295–305.

Heckscher, E. "The Effect of Foreign Trade in the Distribution of Income." *Economisk Tidskrift*, 21 (1919). Reprinted as chapter 13 of *Readings in the Theory of International Trade*, ed. the American Economic Association. Philadelphia: Blakiston, 1949.

Ianchovichina, Elena and Will Martin. "Trade Liberation in China's Accession to WTO." Paper presented before the International Conference on Greater China and the WTO, City University of Hong Kong, Hong Kong, March 22–4, 2001.

Kenen, Peter B. *The International Economy*. Englewood Cliffs, NJ: Prentice-Hall, 1984.

Koopmans, T. C., ed. *Activity Analysis of Production and Allocation*. New York: John Wiley & Sons, 1951.

Ohlin, B. *Interregional and International Trade*. Cambridge, MA: Harvard University Press, 1933.

Samuelson, Paul A. "Where Ricardo and Mill Rebut and Confirm Arguments of Mainstream Economists Supporting Globalization." *Journal of Economic Perspectives*, 18 (2004), pp. 135–46.

*Statistical Yearbook of China, 1981*. Beijing: State Statistical Bureau.

Yen, Tzung-Ta. "A Study of Export Performance in Mainland China" (in Chinese). Economic Paper no. 3. Taipei: Chung-Hua Institution for Economic Research, 1982.

Zhang Peiji. "Growth of China's Foreign Trade." *Almanac of China's Economy 1981*. Hong Kong: Modern Cultural Co., 1982, pp. 621–4.

## Questions

1  Assume that the technology given in table 17.2 applies to both countries $A$ and $B$, but the quantities of labor and capital available in country $A$ are respectively 180 and 50 units, and in country $B$ are respectively 100 and 80 units. Draw the production possibility curves for countries $A$ and $B$ when there is no trade. If the utility function is $u = x_1 x_2$ ($x_1$ denoting the quantity of shoes consumed, $x_2$ the quantity of computers),

mark the equilibrium outputs for countries $A$ and $B$ in the diagram. Let the prices of shoes and computers have a ratio of 1 to 12 in the world market. Show the new production possibilities and the equilibrium points for countries $A$ and $B$ that incorporate the possibility of trade. Hint: To find equilibrium points substitute an appropriate linear function of $x_2$ for $x_1$ in the utility function and maximize it with respect to $x_1$.

2   What is the meaning of comparative advantage? Using the answer to question 1, what does country $A$ have a comparative advantage in producing and what does country $B$ have a comparative advantage in producing? Explain. What is the range for the ratio of the price of shoes to the price of computers that will enable both countries to gain from trade?

3   Modify the technology given in table 17.2 by assuming that in addition to the (unskilled) labor and capital inputs specified, processes 1 and 2 require respectively 1 and 5 units of skilled labor. Assume that there are 60 units of skilled labor available. Write down the inequality required and draw the new production transformation curve. Assuming the quantity of skilled labor to be 40 units instead, draw the new production transformation curve.

4   What are the main differences between the Cobb–Douglas production function and the input coefficient matrix as exemplified in table 17.2 as an alternative method to specify the technology of a country? How is a production transformation curve derived from a Cobb–Douglas production function?

5   What are the reasons the Chinese currency could appreciate in the future?

6   What is the annual rate of change of the ratio of the volume of foreign trade to GDP in China in the last five years? What is the annual rate of change of the ratio of foreign investment to GDP in the last five years?

7   What were the important characteristics of China's trade policy in the early 1980s? What was wrong with the policy?

8   What is the infant-industry argument against free trade? Is the argument valid in your opinion? Explain.

9   What are the main restrictions on foreign trade in China that joining the WTO will liberalize in steps?

10  What was the Chinese government's rationale in setting an official exchange rate in the early 1980s that overvalued the domestic currency? What was the economic problem resulting from such an overvaluation? How did the Chinese government try to resolve the problem?

# 18

# Foreign Investment

This chapter begins in section 18.1 with a discussion of the role of foreign investment as perceived by the Chinese government. Section 8.2 reviews the government's program to promote foreign investment, while the state of foreign investment as of 1999 is reviewed in section 18.3. Policies for regulating foreign investment are summarized in section 18.4. Opportunities for foreign investors and how best to take advantage of them are the subject of section 18.5. Section 18.6 summarizes an econometric study to determine how attractive China's environment is to foreign investors. Although China attracted a large amount of foreign capital, the question is whether it could have attracted more given the economic factors determining foreign investment if not for institutional deficiencies such as corruption. (The answer is yes.) Section 18.7 discusses the possible impact of China joining the WTO on its foreign investment. Section 18.8 contains my proposal for increasing foreign investment from Taiwan.

## 18.1   The Role of Foreign Investment

A main motivation of Deng's open-door policy is to attract foreign investment. (Here and elsewhere in this chapter, "foreign investment" refers mainly to foreign direct investment, since foreign financial investment has been much more limited up to the turn of the twenty-first century.) That policy was a 180-degree turn from the previous thinking prevalent in the Chinese Communist Party that foreign capitalists came to China to exploit the Chinese people. Exploitation takes the form of using cheap Chinese labor and extracting Chinese natural resources at low prices. Foreign investors take over Chinese land to set up their business. Foreign factories pollute the physical environment of China. Foreign businesses make money from the Chinese people. The sale of their goods drives out domestically produced goods in Chinese markets. All these accusations of exploitation have some partial truth. Even educated people living in developed market economies today believe in them. Human rights advocates complain that capitalist investors exploit cheap laborers in developing countries because they pay the laborers at much lower wages than in the developed countries, although the wages are quite a bit higher than most domestic wages in those countries. Buying the right to dispose of waste on the cheaper land of developing countries is considered immoral. Polluting the environment is equally bad.

American pride was hurt when Japanese investors bought the Rockefeller Center in New York City and some well-known golf courses in California in the 1980s. Only when the real estate prices slumped did American businessmen feel relieved for having disposed of some expensive properties at high prices to the Japanese. Thus taking over domestic assets and creating business opportunities for themselves are signs of exploitation by foreign investors. From the viewpoint of the investing country, importing inexpensive Chinese goods to the United States produced by American enterprises located in China is said to hurt American workers.

The negative sentiments of critics towards foreign investment aside, the Chinese government sees it as beneficial to China if it is properly channeled and regulated. The "if" in the last sentence will be elaborated in the last paragraph of this section. With qualifications, it sees foreign investment as an important engine for China's modernization and economic development. It has encouraged foreign investment by setting up special economic zones and opening up 14 cities, as we described in chapter 3. Foreign investment has provided to China capital, new technology, managerial skill, and training for labor. It has introduced modern managerial systems, business practices, and a legal framework for conducting business transactions. In addition it has provided competition in the domestic market, and competition has forced domestic enterprises to become more efficient. China's entry into the WTO makes China's door even more open. Both foreign investment and foreign trade are expected to increase because of it. Foreign firms will begin to penetrate China's financial and telecommunications sectors. Trade will increase in both directions. The Chinese government has committed to lowering the tariffs on both agricultural and industrial products, which will lead to an increase in imports. Chinese exports will also increase because Chinese goods will have better access to world markets open to members of the WTO.

The Chinese government is well aware of the economic and social-political costs and benefits of joining the WTO. While the government is pursuing institutional reforms in state-owned enterprises and the banking and financial sectors, it is aware that reforms and the accompanying globalization of the Chinese economy have to proceed at an appropriate speed. If foreign competition enters China too rapidly, Chinese producers and enterprises subject to the competition may have to make adjustments that are too severe to be socially desirable.

While we note the enthusiasm of the Chinese government to promote foreign investment, we have to understand the restrictions on foreign investment. As in other areas of economic reform, including reform of state-owned enterprises, of the banking and financial system, and of foreign trade, many Chinese government officials do not view the market economy in the same way as economists who believe in the economic benefits of free trade and free capital flows. They see certain elements of the market economy as useful in promoting China's economic development and modernization while believing that the government should exercise an important role in regulating the market forces. We have discussed some of the restrictions on foreign trade. In section 18.4 we will discuss government regulations on foreign investment. Bear in mind that the government has the conception that certain industries need to be developed and it needs foreign investors to do the job. Hence the promotion of foreign investment in those particular industries.

This reasoning is different from the justification in terms of the economic benefits resulting from free capital flows. The latter reasoning is based on the idea that economic goods and resources should go where they can command the highest prices or returns. First, from the viewpoint of the foreign investor, he decides to invest abroad because doing so will enable him to yield a higher risk-adjusted rate of return to his capital than otherwise. Thus it is economically beneficial for him to do so, and is also beneficial to the GNP of his country. Second, from the viewpoint of the host country, capital flows in only because it supplies the need that domestic capital fails to supply, as the foreign investor must be able to compete successfully with other, domestic and foreign, investors. This supply of foreign investment must be good for the host country, just like any other investment project that can compete in the domestic market in supplying capital and technology. If this viewpoint is accepted, there is no need for the government to promote investment in particular industries, as the market can decide by means of demand and supply of capital in different industries. This difference in viewpoint should be clearly understood without having to decide which is correct and under what circumstances. Some of the issues in the role of government intervention will be discussed in the second half of chapter 20.

## 18.2   Historical Developments

Foreign investors began to go to China soon after the British took over Hong Kong in 1842. A study of foreign investment in China by Remer (1938) provided statistics and analysis of the situation as of the 1930s. In the period from 1937 to 1949, China was engaged in a war with Japan, in the Second World War, and in a civil war. Soon after the establishment of the PRC in 1949 the Chinese government took over all foreign enterprises in China. Except for Soviet aid received until the beginning of the 1960s, China's door was closed to the outside world. Soviet aid ceased because Chairman Mao and Stalin disagreed on Sino-Soviet relations and Mao was unwilling to be number two among Communist countries. It was not until Deng Xiaoping came to power in 1978 that China's door was open again.

Early in 1979, the Law on Chinese–Foreign Equity Joint Ventures was announced. At that time, Chinese society was not conducive to foreign investment. Laws to regulate business conduct and to protect the investor's interest were very limited. The supporting facilities of power supplies, transportation, and communication were inadequate. The government was considered hostile by many potential investors who were unwilling to put their money in China. Furthermore, many Chinese Communist Party members and government officials mistrusted potential foreign investors and still considered such business to be exploitation by capitalist imperialists.

To solve these problems, four special economic zones were established. They are Shenzhen, Zhuhai, Shantou, and Xiamen, the first three in Guangdong province bordering Hong Kong and the fourth in Fujian province, which is also along the sea coast northeast of Guangdong and across the strait from Taiwan. The zones provide infrastructure, special business laws, and favorable tax conditions for foreign investors. They also served as experimental stations for skeptical Party members and government officials to observe. If the results turned out to be good, they would be convinced of the virtue of foreign investment. Better policies for foreign investment could also result from the experience observed in the special economic zones. Later, 14 coastal cities were opened, including Dalian, Shanghai, and Guangzhou. Hainan province also became a special economic zone. One hundred forty counties were incorporated into open economic areas. In 1986, entirely foreign-owned enterprises were allowed, whereas previously only joint ventures with Chinese had been permitted. Both joint ventures and entirely foreign-owned enterprises took advantage of the inexpensive labor and engaged in activities including processing for exports, manufacturing, service and retail trades, finance, insurance, and foreign trade. As the Chinese economy expanded, investors saw the potential of a large Chinese domestic market. Foreign investment grew rapidly, as shown in the table 18.1. By 2004, about 80 percent of the world's top 500 companies had invested in China.

## 18.3  The State of Foreign Direct Investment (FDI) as of 2002

In 2003 China ranked second in attracting FDI among all the countries and regions in the world, next only to the US. Chinese statistics measure FDI by both the contractual value and actually utilized value. This section follows official reports in classifying FDI by its legal form, its country of origin, its geographical location, its industrial distribution, and its value added and tax contribution. In 2002, FDI in operation employed over 20 million persons, accounting for nearly 10 percent of the employment in China's urban areas; 34,171 new foreign investment projects were approved with a contractual value of US$82.768 billion. In 2002 the actually utilized FDI amounted to $52.743 billion, as compared with $46.878 billion in 2001 (see table 18.1).

### 18.3.1  Forms of foreign investment

In the *China Statistical Yearbook 2003*, table 17-14, on foreign direct investment, is classified into (1) joint venture enterprises, (2) cooperative operation enterprises, (3) foreign investment enterprises, (4) foreign investment share enterprises, (5) cooperative development, and (6) others. The contract values of these enterprises totaled US$82.768 billion, as seen in table 18.1, but the total value of investment actually utilized amounted to only $52.743 billion. These two totals were divided into the above categories respectively in the amounts of (1) $18.502 and $14.992, (2) $6.217 and $5.058, (3) $57.255 and $31.725,

**Table 18.1**  China's utilization of foreign capital (US$100 millions)

| Year | Total value of foreign capital actually used | Foreign loans | Foreign direct investment | Other foreign investment |
|---|---|---|---|---|
| 1979–1983 | 144.38 | 117.55 | 18.02 | 8.81 |
| 1984 | 27.05 | 12.86 | 12.58 | 1.61 |
| 1985 | 46.47 | 26.88 | 16.61 | 2.98 |
| 1986 | 72.58 | 50.14 | 18.74 | 3.70 |
| 1987 | 84.52 | 58.05 | 23.14 | 3.33 |
| 1988 | 102.26 | 64.87 | 31.94 | 5.45 |
| 1989 | 100.59 | 62.86 | 33.92 | 3.81 |
| 1990 | 102.89 | 65.34 | 34.87 | 2.68 |
| 1991 | 115.54 | 68.88 | 43.66 | 3.00 |
| 1992 | 192.02 | 79.11 | 110.07 | 2.84 |
| 1993 | 389.60 | 111.89 | 275.15 | 2.56 |
| 1994 | 432.13 | 92.67 | 337.67 | 1.79 |
| 1995 | 481.33 | 103.27 | 375.21 | 2.85 |
| 1996 | 548.04 | 126.69 | 417.25 | 4.10 |
| 1997 | 644.08 | 120.21 | 452.57 | 71.30 |
| 1998 | 585.57 | 110.00 | 454.63 | 20.94 |
| 1999 | 526.59 | 102.12 | 403.19 | 21.28 |
| 2000 | 593.56 | 100.00 | 407.15 | 86.41 |
| 2001 | 496.72 | | 468.78 | 27.94 |
| 2002 | 550.11 | | 527.43 | 22.68 |
| 2003 | 561.40 | | 535.05 | 26.35 |
| 2004 | 640.72 | | 606.30 | 34.42 |

(4) $0.739 and $0.697 and (5) $0.055 and $0.272. Of the newly approved foreign invested enterprises or FIEs in 2002, jointly funded enterprises numbered 13,830. Chinese–foreign cooperative ventures numbered 1,595. There were 22,173 entirely foreign-owned enterprises, and 19 foreign investment share enterprises. In the order of the value of actually utilized foreign capital, entirely foreign-owned enterprises ranked first and joint funded enterprises ranked second in 2002, while the order had been reversed in 1999. This is one indication of the degree of liberalization of foreign investment.

## 18.3.2   Countries/regions of origin

According to the *China Statistical Yearbook 2003*, table 17-15, in 2002, of the US$52.743 billion of FDI actually utilized, $32.57 billion was from Asia, including $17.86 billion from Hong Kong, $4.19 billion from Japan, $2.34 billion from Singapore, $2.72 billion from the Republic of Korea, and $3.97 billion from Taiwan. Africa accounted for only $565 million of the total, while Europe accounted for $4.05 billion, including $0.895 billion from the United Kingdom and $0.928 billion from Germany. Latin America accounted for $7.55 billion, and North America for $6.49 billion, with $5.42 billion from the United States. Thus Hong Kong ranked number 1, the US number 2 (just over one-third of Hong Kong's), Japan a close number 3, and Taiwan a very close number 4, in terms of the amount of FDI actually utilized in 2002.

### 18.3.3   Regional distribution of foreign investment

In terms of the geographical distribution, the eastern areas accounted for about 85 percent of foreign direct investment in 1999, but the central and western regions were catching up gradually.

The eastern area approved 13,953 foreign investment enterprises in the whole year, with a contractual value of $35.065 billion and an actually utilized value of $34.34 billion. These figures account for 82.47, 85.06, and 87.88 percent respectively of the nation's total. The central area approved 2,100 foreign investment enterprises with a contractual value of $4.118 billion, accounting for 12.41 and 9.99 percent of the national total, and growing by 0.11 and 1.54 percent respectively. The western area approved 865 new enterprises using foreign investment, with a contractual value of $2.04 billion and an actually utilized value of $1.138 billion. Compared with the previous year, the contractual value grew by 0.34 of a percentage point.

In 2002, according to the *China Statistical Yearbook 2003*, table 17-16, of the total $52.743 billion of FDI actually utilized, Guangdong province received $11.33 billion, Jiangsu province $10.19 billion, Shandong province $4.73 billion, Fujian province $3.84 billion, Zhejiang province $3.08 billion, Shanghai municipality $4.27 billion, Beijing municipality $1.72 billion, Tianjin municipality $1.58 billion, and Chongqing municipality (which was designated the center for western Chinese development) only $196 million (as compared with $256 million in 2001).

As of the end of 1999, of the cumulative number of approved enterprises, cumulative contractual FDI value, and actually utilized value, the eastern area accounted for 82.13, 88.13, and 87.84 percent respectively; the central area had 12.86, 8.00, and 8.94 percent, and the shares for the western area were only 5.01, 3.87, and 3.22 percent respectively. The shares of the central and western area in the country's cumulative contractual FDI value and actually utilized FDI value went up by 0.36 and 0.11 percentage points over those at the end of 1997.

### 18.3.4   The industrial structure of foreign investment

The actually utilized foreign investment of primary and secondary industry accounted for 1.76 percent and 66.63 percent respectively in the country's total in 1999, up 0.39 and 2.26 percentage points over the previous year. Tertiary industry had a share of 31.61 percent, down 2.65 percentage point from the previous year.

For the three years 1997–9, the proportion of agriculture, forestry, husbandry, fishery, and manufacturing industry in the total FDI absorption was on the rise year after year, while the share of real estate industry declined. The share of manufacturing industry was increased from 49 percent in 1997 to 61.5 percent in 1999. The proportion of real estate industry decreased from 19.7 percent in 1997 to 10.1 percent in 1999. In manufacturing industry, high and new technology, especially the manufacturing of electronic and communications equipment, enjoyed the biggest growth margin, its share in the total in 1999 being 9.6 percent, 3.8 percentage points higher than that of 1997 and accounting for 15.56 percent of the manufacturing industry. Besides, the share of synthetic material and new-type building material with high-tech content in manufacturing industry was on the rise. In manufacturing, oil processing, coke making, nonmetal mineral-ware, and general machinery building declined by a big margin, the actually utilized FDI value in 1999 going down by more than 50 percent from the level of 1997 for all these industries.

From 2000 to 2002 the actually used amount of FDI was $40.41, $46.88, and $52.74 billion US dollars respectively. Of the last amount, manufacturing accounted for $36.80 billion, real estate management $5.66 billion, social services $2.94 billion, electricity, gas, and water production and supply $1.38 billion, and farming, forestry, animal husbandry, and fisheries $1.03 billion, with all other 15 minus 5 or 10 sectors each accounting for less than one billion (see the *China Statistical Yearbook 2003*, table 17-18).

### 18.3.5   Industrial value added and tax contribution to the economy

In 1999, the industrial value added of foreign invested enterprises (FIEs) amounted to $420.1 billion, accounting for 20.69 percent of the national total and growing by 12.90 percent, up 0.74 of a percentage point over that of the previous year. During the same period, industrial output (constant price) of FIEs was valued at 1.769649 trillion RMB yuan, growing by 18.30 percent over the previous year and taking up 27.7 percent of the country's total. In 1999, the foreign-related tax takings of the country (tariff, land tax, and fees excluded) totaled 164.886 billion, growing by 33.78 percent over the previous year. Of this amount, tax from FIEs accounted for over 96 percent. The FIEs set up in 1999 had a growth rate for the industrial value added, for export volume, and for tax payment – all higher than the national average. The industrial added value of FIEs in 1999 grew by 12.9 percent over that of 1998, paid tax increased by 33.78 percent, export value went up by 9.47 percent, and a foreign-exchange surplus of $5.997 billion was realized through bank account settlement. The FIEs in operation had a total employment of over 20 million, accounting for nearly 10 percent of the employment in urban areas of the country.

## 18.4   Policies for the Regulation of Foreign Investment

As we pointed out in section 10.1, under China's open-door policy, foreign investment is welcome and even encouraged, provided that, in the view of the Chinese government, it is beneficial to China's economic development as the government sees it. Therefore, certain categories of investment are encouraged and other categories are discouraged and even prohibited. There are numerous regulations governing foreign investment.

## 1) Interim Regulations and the Industrial Catalogue

In order to direct foreign direct investments in compliance with the national industrial planning, the Interim Regulations on FDI Directions and the Industrial Catalogue Guiding Foreign Investment were formulated and promulgated in June 1995. For the first time, the industrial policies aiming at inviting foreign direct investment were publicized in the form of laws and regulations, which promote the transparency of policies. The Regulations and the Catalogue classify industrial projects into four categories – items to be encouraged, items to be permitted, items to be restricted, and items to be forbidden – which are absolutely clear for the investors.

In December 1997, the State Development Planning Commission and the State Economic and Trade Commission together with the Ministry of Foreign Trade and Economic Cooperation began to revise the Industrial Catalogue Guiding Foreign Investment and put it into enforcement. The revised text of the Industrial Catalogue Guiding Foreign Investment reflects an expansion in the investment scope encouraged by the state. According to the new version, 272 items, or 83 percent of the total, involving the importation of equipment may enjoy tariff exemption. The revision highlights priority industries for the purposes of structural adjustment, contribution to the introduction of advanced technology, and encouragement to invest in central and western areas. The revised Industrial Catalogue gives encouragement to foreign businessmen on establishing export-oriented enterprises. Items in the Category of Permission whose products are 100 percent exported are listed in the Category of Encouragement. The Catalogue is revised to suit the needs of economic development.

## 2) The items to be encouraged in foreign direct investments

The items to be encouraged in foreign direct investments mainly include: agricultural new technology and agricultural comprehensive development as well as industrial projects pertaining to energy, transportation, and vital raw materials; high-tech projects; export-oriented projects; projects comprehensively utilizing resources, renewing resources, and prevention and cure of environmental pollution; projects which can give play to the advantages of the western and central regions. Direct foreign investments are encouraged for the technological upgrading of traditional industries and of labor-intensive industries.

## 3) Foreign direct investment in services

China has launched pilot projects utilizing foreign investment in services. In commercial retailing, ever since 1992 when the State Council decided to launch trial operations of foreign-invested commercial retail businesses in Beijing, Tianjin, Shanghai, Dalian, Qingdao, Guangzhou, and five Special Economic Zones, the utilization of foreign direct investment in the commercial retail sector has been expanding gradually. In foreign trade, in September 1996, with the approval of the State Council, the Ministry of Foreign Trade and Economic Cooperation (MOFTEC) published the Interim Procedures on Establishing Pilot Sino-Foreign Joint Venture Wholesale Business, which is a major step toward opening up the service sector. In tourism, at the end of 1998, the Interim Procedures on the Joint Venture Travel Agent were promulgated, which enlarged the geographical areas for permitted joint-owned travel agents to the regions outside the tourism development zones. At the turn of the century, in addition to the fields of commerce and foreign trade, China expanded the opening of foreign investment in other areas such as finance, insurance, transportation, international freight forwarding, legal services, tourism, advertising, medical care and public health, accounting, assets appraisal, education, leasing, engineering design, consulting, and real estate. China's entry into the WTO should help promote further opening of the service sectors to foreign investment.

## 18.5   Opportunities and Problems for Foreign Investors

The Chinese government is eager to build infrastructure, including highways, ports, telecommunications systems, etc., that require capital and modern technology which can be supplied by foreign investment. Chinese state enterprises are also looking for foreign partners to upgrade their technology, management, labor, and marketing abilities. These needs are well known. Many foreign investors have taken advantage of such investment opportunities, which can be seen from the data in table 18.1. The Chinese consumer markets are being opened wider as import quotas and tariffs are being reduced, partly as a result of the Chinese government's desire to join APEC and the WTO, and partly as a result of the rapid increase in China's reserves in hard currencies which can be spent to increase imports. Besides selling to the Chinese market, foreign companies also take advantage of the cheap and skilled labor in China to produce for exports. To take advantage of economic opportunities in China, investors have to deal with the Chinese bureaucracy in the bureaucratic market economy. Dealing with the Chinese bureaucracy requires special attention to the following areas.

### *1) Finding the right partners*

Doing business in China is different from doing business in Western countries, mainly because in China economic power is to a large extent in the hands of bureaucracies at different levels of government, because China does not have a Western-style legal system, and because Chinese workers and managers have different habits, ethics, outlooks, and training from those found in the West. To succeed in China a foreign investor needs approval and help from the Chinese bureaucracies, in addition to assistance from Chinese labor and management, who are accustomed to their own manner of doing business in their cultural and social environment.

To set up a foreign-owned enterprise or a joint venture a foreign investor needs the approval of many levels of the government, possibly including the central government in Beijing, a provincial and/or local government, ministry A and/or bureau (a) as well as ministry B and/or bureau (b), etc. It sounds like an impossible task. At each step, the approval of a business agreement may take a long time and require patient negotiations. Many foreign companies have had the sad experience of believing that the agreement of one or two Chinese bureaucrats is sufficient to conduct their business, only to find that the approval of many more bureaucrats is needed. Some less relevant bureaux or people can simply make trouble in order to reap some profit from the investor. The reason for the existence of so many bureaucrats surrounding an investment project is that many bureaucrats are looking constantly for opportunities to make money in the same way that all Western businessmen are looking for opportunities to make money. The bureaucrats are working under a system in which economic power is to a large extent in their hands. Many of them utilize their power to make money.

Is there any rule that can be followed to find the right local contact for a potential investor? The local contact or partner must have the authority, or must be able to acquire sufficient authority, to do the business desired. If the person or the agency is the right one, he/she can get the approval, or can help the investor get the approval from all others that may be trying to extract some benefit from the investor. If the investor cannot find such a person, his investment is unlikely to succeed. The way to find such a person depends partly on what the investor's business is and how much he has to offer. If he is investing in an area that China needs to encourage, as listed in the last section, the task is easier because many Chinese bureaucrats would be interested in cooperating and the investor only needs to select the right partner among them. Choosing the right person requires knowledge of the Chinese bureaucratic system and its personalities. If the investor is knowledgeable in this regard, and has the right contacts, he can find the right people to work with.

## 2) Dealing with an imperfect legal system

Many Western businessmen and scholars point out that a Western-style legal system does not exist in China and that makes it hard to do business. An economic historian might be interested to explain why such a system has flourished in China, and whether and how it compares with the Western legal system. Suffice it to state here that such a semi-legal system has functioned in China for a long time and it has served Chinese society. To deal with the semi-legal system in China, an investor can try to develop a network, getting to know the right people and making the right friends. This is called "developing *Guanxi*" in Chinese. Interpreted in modern economic terms, *Guanxi* is a kind of human capital both in the sense of your knowing and having access to influential people in China and their recognition that you are useful to them. Establishing personal connections in order to do business is common in Western societies as well, but the degree to which one needs to rely on it compared with the formal legal system is much higher in China. The subject of *Guanxi* is discussed further in chapter 20, dealing with the Chinese legal system.

If an investor cannot depend on legal contracts, how can he be sure that his Chinese partner will keep his part of the bargain? One way to ensure it is to remain an indispensable partner in the project or to maintain a position such that his services will be needed in the future. If he has a contract to share profits in the future, how does he guarantee that his Chinese partner will honor the contract? When Mr. Roebuck presumably lost his usefulness to Mr. Sears, the company's name was changed from Sears-Roebuck to Sears. This can also happen in China. To maintain his usefulness, a foreign investor has to keep his other business connections and maintain his influence in the world business community so that his Chinese partner will continue to value a good relationship with him. The above remarks apply equally to a Chinese partner who wants to maintain a good relationship with his foreign investor – he must try to maintain a position in the business community so that his foreign partner will honor all agreements and the partnership. If one loses his usefulness as a partner almost no legal protection can keep the partnership for him. The same applies even to some marriage contracts. It is prudent for a potential investor in China to recognize the Chinese semi-legal system. However, from a historical perspective, China's legal system will gradually improve in the twenty-first century as the system has already improved to some extent in the last 15 years of the twentieth. The improvement is a part of the process of economic development, and is partly driven by the need to deal with foreign investors under the terms stipulated by the WTO since 2001. China's legal system is the topic of chapter 20.

## 3) Technology transfer to China

Somewhat related to the fact of an imperfect legal system in China is the lack of sufficient protection of patents and intellectual property rights in China. This issue has been discussed widely in the Western press. Within the informal framework of doing business, what prevents a Chinese partner who is producing some products in a joint venture from setting up a business of his own to produce the same products? Lacking sufficient legal protection, a foreign investor can hardly stop his Chinese partner from doing so. Western investors are aware of this and have tried to devise means to protect their interests, for example by keeping an essential part of the technology secret and known to only a limited number of people whom they can trust. If a certain technology or patent is difficult to protect from a technical point of view, the investor has to take this fact into account in investing in China, possibly by reaping enough profits in a short time before the technology can be copied, or by sacrificing a calculated part of the Chinese market while maintaining a large part of the international market which is protected legally. Even protection in international markets can be uncertain – newspapers are full of stories of Chinese manufacturers copying videotapes, compact discs, movies, and software packages for export into the international market. One story is that in October 2000 the Chinese national government itself had difficulty in preventing a popular film on corruption, which the government itself sponsored, from being illegally copied, sold, and shown in theaters all over China. The number of pirated products in China offered for sale in the world market is so large that it draws much attention in the world community.

There is no solution yet for the problem of pirating in China. This phenomenon is easy to understand from the historical and cultural background of the Chinese. Patents are a recent product of world history after the Industrial Revolution. There were not too many scientific inventions to protect in Chinese history. If a Chinese knew of certain ways to produce useful drugs, for example, he would try to keep it a family secret. Many products in China were protected in this way. If a product cannot be so protected it is publicly available. Such products include all the herbs that are sold in traditional Chinese drugstores and are therefore available to benefit the Chinese population. The lack of patent protection is said to be socially undesirable because it may discourage people from investing in new products. Such discouragement may have negative effects, but the negative effects have to be weighed against the benefits of having a perhaps smaller number of invented products available to consumers on the market at lower prices. Before legal protection can be effectively enforced in China, foreign businessmen have to recognize this fact, while trying to put pressure on the Chinese government to enforce the laws on intellectual property at the same time.

A related point is that some Western governments may also have to recognize this fact. In February 1996, the United States government registered a strong protest to the government in Beijing for the large number of Chinese pirated products being sold in the world market. This worsened the already tense diplomatic relations between the two countries at the time. This protest to the Chinese government had a small effect, similar to that of a protest to the government of Mexico for having illegal drugs produced in Mexico and sold in America. The difference is that some of the Chinese products were said to be produced by firms which are otherwise legal in China, in some cases allegedly firms affiliated with the Chinese military. The similarity in both cases is that there is simply so much money to be made that the central governments in both countries have found it difficult to stop the illegal operations. The protest to the central government in either country is unlikely to be very effective. The government itself wishes to stop the illegal activities.

## 4) Cooperation with Chinese state enterprises

There are a number of examples of successful joint ventures between a foreign investor and a Chinese state enterprise controlled by the central, provincial, or local governments. By successful, I mean both the Chinese and the foreign partners have made profits. Such joint ventures are still available and plentiful if the foreign investor is resourceful enough to find them. The advantage of cooperating with a state enterprise is that the Chinese partner is likely to have sufficient authority to produce and market the product and may even have sufficient power to protect the product from infringement by pirating. If the foreign investor can find ways to protect his share of the profits, as discussed above, there may be much profit to be made by both partners. A potential investor should study the successful cases to find out what makes such cooperation successful. In addition, he or she should look into successful cases of cooperation with township and village enterprises. These enterprises, in contrast with the slow-growing state enterprises, constitute a very important component of the rapid economic growth of China.

### 5) Corruption and related institutional problems

In addition to facing a different legal system, foreign investors also face the problem of corruption. The need to compensate government officials to get approval for an investment project is an example of corruption. The payment of bribes might be considered as just a cost of doing business that has to be included in the calculation of profit. However, the problem is not so simple. It may require the right method and the right channel to pay the bribes required. The investor may not know which bureaucrats have to be paid and how much to pay them. For US investors, though not Japanese investors, payment of bribes is illegal. How to handle such problems is an art. Chinese bureaucrats sometimes get free trips to the United States on business and sometimes get scholarships for their children to study in the United States at the recommendation of their US investors. Perhaps such favors are legal according to US law. A related set of institutional problems can be called regulatory burden. It includes foreign-exchange control, interest rate control, and domestic financial market imperfection, which make doing business difficult and costly for a foreign investor.

In spite of all the above-mentioned problems, there are profit-making opportunities. By producing what is needed by the governments at different levels or by the consumers in China, and by producing for exports, some foreign investors have made profits. It would be interesting to find out what fraction of foreign investors has made profits so far. Perhaps the number is small, but many investors are counting on making more profits in the future by exploiting the large domestic markets in China and by using China as a base for producing goods for export to other parts of the world.

## 18.6   How Attractive is China for Foreign Investment?

In the last section we pointed out some special conditions in China which make it difficult or unattractive for foreigners to invest in China. Have such conditions affected the amount of foreign investment in China? In 1999 China received the third largest amount of foreign direct investment. If such unfavorable conditions had not existed would China have received even more? To answer this question it is necessary to specify a relation between the amount of foreign investment and a set of important determining factors that is valid for many economies. Given the values of the determining factors prevailing in China, if the amount of investment in China is below the normal amount predicted by this relation, then China is said to have underperformed. Such an econometric analysis was performed by Wei (1999).

Using a set of cross-country data on the stock of cumulated foreign direct investment (FDI) from 17 important source countries to 42 host countries, Wei estimated a relation of the amount of inward FDI for a host country like China to a set of determining factors. The source countries include the United States, Japan, Germany, the United Kingdom, France, Italy, and Norway. The dependent variable is log ($FDI_{jk} + A$), where the subscripts stand for source country $j$ to host country $k$ and $A$ is a positive constant to prevent the value of log FDI from being too small. If $FDI_{jk}$ is zero, which can happen, the log of zero is minus infinity, not suitable as the value of a dependent variable. Among the explanatory variables are an index to measure corruption, an index for regulatory burden, an index of degree of domestic financial repression, a measure of foreign-exchange control, the marginal corporate income tax rate (all above variables for the host country), a measure of the distance between the economic centers of the source–host pair, log GDP of host country, log GDP per capita of host country, linguistic tie between the source–host pair, the source countries' fixed effects (measuring the extent to which each source country wants to invest). Corruption is measured by a perception index based on a survey of 2,827 firms in 58 countries conducted by the World Economic Forum in 1996. Respondents were asked to rank each country on a scale of 1 to 7. Regulatory burden is measured by a ranking of 8 minus the original rating, where the original rating is from the same survey from 1 to 7 with a lower number meaning a more pervasive regulatory burden. Domestic financial repression is measured by an index on interest rate control obtained from the same survey.

Before introducing the last three explanatory variables Wei used the other variables and a dummy variable for China. The coefficient of this dummy variable is estimated to be approximately −1. This means that China is considered an unattractive country to invest in after we have allowed for the effects of all other factors. The coefficients of all other variables have the right signs. Then corruption, regulatory burden, and financial repression are introduced as additional variables to replace the dummy variable for China. The results show that all three have negative effects on foreign direct investment. This study has provided a quantitative measure of the total effect of the unfavorable institutional characteristics on foreign direct investment in China using a dummy variable, and three measures of the separate effects of corruption, regulatory burden, and financial repression, after the effects of other relevant factors on FDI have been taken into account. It is a supplement to the discussion of the institutional characteristics which affect foreign investment presented in the previous sections.

## 18.7   The Impact of WTO Membership on Foreign Investment

Membership in the WTO opens China's economy further for foreign investors. China has promised to open telecommunications, banking and finance, insurance, commercial, and other service industries to foreign investors. It has allowed foreign investors to acquire business enterprises in China, besides setting up joint or cooperative ventures and wholly owned enterprises. It has agreed to eliminate restrictions on foreign investors such as export quotas on products and limited sales in domestic markets, by allowing them to set up domestic sales outlets. It will lower tariffs and thus the costs of production, but the advantage of production for domestic sales will be decreased by competition from imports. The net effect of the further opening is to increase foreign investment. The composition will also change towards more of the service industries opened up under WTO membership.

The effects on China's economy are essentially positive. Domestic industries will be subject to more competition. State enterprises will be under more pressure to restructure. It may affect the unemployment situation adversely. On the other hand, the state enterprises will improve by absorbing foreign capital, technology, and management methods. Some may become joint ventures or be sold to foreign investors. Multinationals are helping China develop high-technology industries which the Chinese are not able to develop for lack of capital and management skills. Thus the industrial structure will be more rapidly modernized. The economic infrastructure of China will be improved by foreign investment in telecommunication and financial services. The business legal system will improve by the larger presence of foreign corporations. These corporations will help promote a modern legal system in China.

A few years have gone by since the above was written for the first edition of this book. For an account of progress since China joined the WTO in 2001 I summarize an article in the *People's Daily* of December 6, 2004, as follows.

The general tariff level was lowered from 15.6 percent in 2001 to around 10.3 percent. Nontariff barriers have been lowered, with the number of quota-administrated commodities reduced to 52 in export and 8 in import. Quota, license, and special bidding administration were canceled for goods under 16 tax item numbers including some motorcycles and their key parts, cars and key parts, cameras and watches.

In the banking system, region and client limitations on foreign-funded banks conducting RMB business were removed, with such business sites extended from Shanghai and Shenzhen to 13 cities. Around 100 foreign-funded banking institutions were allowed to conduct RMB business, and the establishment of independent automobile mortgage agencies was also permitted. Regarding insurance, international life insurance companies were allowed to operate in more cities, and nearly 40 of them have opened 70 businesses in China. In retailing, by the end of June 2004, the number of foreign-funded companies neared 270 with more than 4,500 outlets. Transnational retailing giants like Walmart, Carrefour, and Metro all expanded investment in China, while the Law of Direct Sale will terminate at the year end. Some 40 laws and regulations conforming with WTO rules have been passed, which, in theory, open China wider to international operators in service trades by allowing market access and improving legal transparency. There were 10,159 newly established foreign-invested enterprises in service trades during 2003 alone, or one-quarter of the new foreign-invested enterprises in that period.

The Foreign Trade Law, revised on July 1, granted full foreign trade rights ahead of schedule, allowing all enterprises at home and abroad as well as individuals to engage in foreign trade on Chinese land. From July to September alone, more than 18,500 registrations were made, including some 200 individuals and 570 foreign-funded firms. As for IPR protection, a string of laws and related rules, including Trademark Law, Patent Law, Copyright Law, and Regulations on the Protection of Computer Software have been passed, and a large number of right-infringing cases investigated and prosecuted by departments of industry and commerce, customs and copyright administration.

The article provides three reasons for the smooth transition after WTO membership:

First, protective policies on related industries played an active role. Thanks to the screening effect of the transition period, domestic sectors have not been hit hard by outside competition. The automobile sector is a case in point. While fulfilling commitments, the Ministry of Commerce used WTO rules flexibly and insisted on orderly administration and proper control over automobile import quotas, and through a series of adjustments effectively cushioned the blow of imported vehicles. Currently, imported automobiles take less than 4 percent of the domestic market (less than 6 percent for sedan cars), while home autos grew rapidly during the period, with both manufacture and sales thriving. Another example is fixed-line service, which did not open until the year end, thus reduced the impact of foreign funds. This point confirms my prediction in the first edition of this book that administrative means would be used to soften the impact of foreign competition.

Secondly, some sectors were opened ahead of schedule, such as retailing business. The rivalry between domestic and foreign firms started much earlier. Home enterprises grew stronger under the competition pressure.

Thirdly, in recent years, economic globalization and a fresh round of manufacturing transfer to many countries made international competition less severe. Changes on the global market also served as a cushion. The relative stability of China's telecom sector, for example, is due to a sluggish global market which left many telecom operators cautious towards investing in China.

Although for most sectors the transition period will end in 2005, other commitments will remain afterwards. By 2005, the general tariff level will be reduced to 10.1 percent and all nontariff barriers removed. On January 1, 2005, China will eliminate automobile quota control and cut automobile tariffs to 30 percent (and finally to 25 percent in 2006). In agriculture, the general tariff level for farm produce will be lowered to 15.35 percent by 2005, one of the lowest in the world. In the service sector, regional and client limitations on foreign-funded banks conducting RMB business will be removed on December 11, 2006. Compulsory reinsurance will be cancelled after 2005 and solely foreign-funded insurance broking corporations will be allowed after 2006. In mobile sound and data service, the percentage of foreign funds will reach 49 percent by the end of 2004, and regional limitations will be removed by the end of 2006. In basic telecom services both at home and abroad, regional restrictions will be cancelled in 2007, with the percentage of foreign shares reaching 49 percent. In the sectors of construction design, tourism, and transportation, the establishment of enterprises solely owned by foreign funds will be allowed from 2005 to 2007.

The editorial raises concerns that there may be further adjustment problems in the long run if the Chinese government and businesses are complacent. "The three-year stable transition, however, has made some people take the current situation as a normal state after WTO. As a matter of fact, our government lags rather behind in its public service and social administration functions; key and sensitive industries lack the capability of sustained development, and enterprises urgently need to raise their kernel competitiveness."

## 18.8   A Proposal to Increase Foreign Investment from Taiwan

In 1997, the largest sources of direct foreign investment were Hong Kong, Japan, Taiwan, and the United States, in that order. The United States overtook Taiwan as the third largest investor in 1998. Foreign capital from Taiwan amounted to over US$3.5 billion per year on average from 1996 to 1999. Since there is no direct transport from Taiwan to the mainland, Taiwan investors have to travel through Hong Kong, Macao, or Tokyo and are greatly inconvenienced in the process. In a speech before the Foreign Investment Forum sponsored by the Ministry of Foreign Trade and International Cooperation held in Xiamen on September 8, 2000, I presented a proposal for the government of mainland China to allow Taiwanese ships and airlines to come to the mainland directly. The proposal was intended to increase investment from Taiwan and to improve economic ties between the two economies. The speech read in part:

> We are all aware that agreements to open direct postal and transport services between the two sides of the Taiwan Strait have not yet been reached, but the lack of agreement should not prevent the Chinese government from adopting this proposal. A major obstacle to the agreement appears to be that the Taiwan government is concerned about easy access to the island by travelers from the mainland. Whatever may be the reasons for the government of Taiwan to be concerned about the opening of the island to direct postal communication and travel from the mainland, it is in the interests of the Chinese people and the mainland government to allow Taiwan residents to come to the mainland directly without having to go through Hong Kong or Tokyo . . .
>
> I cannot think of any reasons why the Chinese government would decide not to allow residents of Taiwan to travel directly to the mainland. It has indeed been the government's policy to give special privileges to travelers from Taiwan, as we have witnessed the special passages and lines at airports and points of entry to China reserved for the convenience of Taiwanese residents. Allowing them to travel directly is simply to extend to them more convenience. The fact that the government of Taiwan might not reciprocate this convenience to residents of the mainland should not matter because the policy by itself is good for China. It is not a concession to the government in Taiwan because it is not directed to the government. It is a policy for the Chinese people . . .
>
> The proposal submitted here is good for China as a whole. The only part of China which may incur some economic loss from it is Hong Kong, but the benefits to the other parts of China and to promoting China's investment and trade surely outweigh the loss to Hong Kong. Historically the economy of Hong Kong has benefited from the port's being the only entry to China for many purposes. Under the open-door policy, Hong Kong's unique position cannot be maintained as direct access to other cities including Shanghai becomes easier.

To pursue the open-door policy further, other parts of China should be open to direct travel by residents from elsewhere, especially of Taiwan. In a sense the proposal being discussed is not a new policy because, ever since Hong Kong was returned to China on July 1, 1997, Taiwanese airplanes and ships have been allowed to land or anchor in Chinese territory already. In fairness to other ports and cities of China, they should be granted the same privilege that Hong Kong has, namely, the privilege of receiving airplanes and ships coming directly from Taiwan.

A major concern of the residents of China and of the entire world today is the relation between the governments on the two sides of the Taiwan Strait. The relation affects all aspects of life, including China's foreign trade and investment, the topic of this conference. If the relations can be improved, it will be of great interest to all of us. The proposal to allow Taiwan residents to travel directly to the mainland can only improve relations, in addition to promoting more investment from Taiwan. It is a win–win policy. Since this policy is one-sided, it could be terminated at any time if the Chinese government should find it desirable to do so. There is no risk in adopting this policy.

If the experiment with this policy is successful, the next step is to allow Taiwanese cargo ships to come to the mainland directly. An appropriate charge to the ship can be levied. This would improve trade across the Taiwan Strait. We all understand that direct shipping has been occurring through fishing boats. Why not make direct shipping by Taiwanese ships legal and collect the rightful dues? This would lower the cost of shipping and reduce the risk of shipping by fishing boats. Direct postal services are a byproduct of the policy. Once airplanes and passenger ships come directly from Taiwan they can carry mail, thus speeding up the postal service between the two sides.

Relations between the two sides of the Taiwan Strait are not making much progress at this time. The governments on both sides realize that it is a slow and gradual process to improve relations. One step forward is recognized to be the opening of direct postal services and transport. Even this step is being stalled indefinitely. Fortunately, the government in Beijing can take the initiative alone to accomplish this step as suggested in this proposal. I sincerely hope that it will take such a step without delay.

In January 2001, perhaps as a defensive move to prevent the rapid opening up of direct transport and trade nationwide, the Taiwan government took the initiative to open up direct trade and transport through the small island of Jinmen to Xiamen, a move considered by the mainland government as a delaying tactic. In 2001, we still await the mainland government making a bold move and the two governments coming to some additional agreements to promote trade and investment in China.

# References and Further Reading

*Foreign Investment Administration*, a section in the website http://www.moftec.gov.cn of China's Ministry of Foreign Trade and Economic Cooperation.

Remer, C. F. *Foreign Investment in China*. Ann Arbor, MI: University of Michigan Press, 1938.

Wei, Shang-Jin. "China as Host of Foreign Investment: Facts, Fallacies, and Prospects." Paper presented before the Conference on Policy Reform in China, Center for Research on Economic Development and Policy Reform, Stanford University, Nov. 18–20, 1999.

# Questions

1  List the most important laws and regulations on foreign investment in China and the years in which they were put into effect. (See Wei, 1999.)

2  Using data for 17 major source countries to 42 host countries in 1996 to explain the natural log of the dollar amount of cumulated foreign investment, plus a constant $A$, from source country $j$ to host country $k$ up to 1996, with some relevant variables and a dummy variable (= 1 if the host country is China, = 0 otherwise), Wei found a coefficient of about $-1$ for this dummy variable. What is the meaning of the value $-1$?

3  China had a cumulated foreign direct investment up to 1996 of about US$170 billion according to Chinese official statistics (lower according to foreign statistics). If the coefficient of the dummy variable representing China in a regression to explain the natural log of cumulated investment from other countries to China, plus a constant $A$, were zero instead of $-1$ as reported in question 2, i.e., if China had not suffered the bad effects of institutional factors like corruption, how would you calculate the country's cumulated investment from the regression?

4  List the most important variables which you would use to explain cumulated foreign investment in different provinces in China in the most current year for which you can obtain data. What is the appropriate dependent variable? Explain why each explanatory variable is important, and what the sign of its coefficient in the regression should be.

5  Why is foreign investment helpful for economic development in China? Name four of its contributions.

6  What are the special conditions in China that a foreign investor should consider in order to invest successfully?

7  How large was foreign investment in China in 1999 (or in a later year if you can find the data) as measured by the fraction of total gross industrial output value that it produced? What was the exponential rate of growth of actually utilized foreign direct investment from 1995 to 1998?

8  What are the three industries that account for the largest shares of foreign investment? Which five countries or regions account for the largest shares of foreign investment in 1999?

9  Explain the role of the special economic zones in attracting foreign investment. If such zones are good for attracting foreign investment, why not make the whole of China a large special economic zone?

10 What kinds of regulation does the Chinese government impose on foreign direct investment? Which of these regulations can be justified on economic grounds? Explain.

# Part V

# Studies of Economic
# Institutions and Infrastructure

# 19

# Corruption and Misuse of Assets

Starting with the fact that public ownership of physical assets and state control of human assets are prevalent in a socialist country, and a hypothesis that managers of assets try make the best use of the assets under their control to maximize their own gains, this chapter derives four laws of behavior in the management of assets. These laws are applied to behavior in China in the management of one's own person, in the management of physical assets, and of a collection of assets like a state enterprise. The laws explain many behaviors that are wasteful of economic resources, and the phenomenon of corruption. Waste in the use in existing human capital and especially in the investment in human capital is noted.

## 19.1  Introduction

A socialist economy is distinguished from a capitalist economy mainly by the high degree of state control of the economic assets of the economy. Economic assets or wealth consist of human assets and nonhuman assets. The latter include physical assets, intangible assets such as patent rights, and enterprises. All assets generate incomes and are therefore valuable. In a capitalist economy most nonhuman assets are privately owned and human assets are subject to only very limited restriction by the state. In a socialist economy, nonhuman assets are owned by the state to a larger extent, and human assets are subject to more restrictions imposed by the state than in a capitalist country. The Chinese socialist economy can be distinguished from a capitalist economy by the above criterion even when it is to a large extent a market economy.

Readers of this book realize that the Chinese economy has been changing substantially since economic reform began in 1978. The degree of state control over human and nonhuman assets has been declining. It is the purpose of this chapter to study economic behavior when the state exercises a high degree of control over the economic wealth of a nation. The basic idea underlying the analysis is that under the institution of state ownership and control all assets have to be managed by people, since the "state" itself cannot manage anything. In managing an economic asset in the name of the state, any person will have an incentive to maximize the economic gain to be derived from it at a minimum cost. This rule of behavior can explain much of what has been happening in China concerning the use of assets. In a socialist society the rights of people to manage the assets under their control, including their own persons, physical assets, and collections of assets, are different from the rights in a capitalist society with private ownership. The rule of behavior stated above is capable of explaining behavior in the management of all kinds of assets in different societies, although this chapter is confined to explaining the behavior observed in contemporary China.

I was motivated by some unpleasant experiences while traveling in China to write an essay, Chow (1992), on which this chapter is based. Travelers to China in the 1980s experienced poor services everywhere, in government-owned stores, in government-owned hotels, and in railway stations and airports. The Chinese people in general are friendly, but when you encounter them in situations where they have control over resources and hold the authority to grant you something that you need such as a visa, a train ticket, or a hotel room, they become unfriendly and bureaucratic. In these situations they tend to abuse their power and authority in dealing with someone who does not have anything to offer in return, since a traveler is not allowed to pay them service fees. They treat their friends well and offer good services to those who can offer them something useful in return.

Some of this behavior is described by Fox Butterfield, once a *New York Times* reporter stationed in China, in his 1982 book *China: Alive in a Bitter Sea*. In Butterfield (1982: 94–5) one can read interesting stories of how people managing assets in the name of the state or working in government establishments use their power to benefit themselves – how they trade through the back door tickets to public movie theaters, piano lessons offered by teachers in public schools, the privilege granted by bureaucrats of not being sent to the countryside during the Cultural Revolution, medical services provided by doctors working in government-run hospitals, good cuts of meat, or fish, or fruit available in government-run stores, transportation services from drivers assigned to drive state-owned automobiles, a good table in a popular state-owned restaurant, clothes from tailors working in government tailor shops, etc.

Such use of economic resources generates a lot of waste in the Chinese economy. If an automobile is not used as a taxi operated for profit to provide services to customers who are willing to pay for the cost, and, instead, the government pays for the costs of operating the car and the driver has it for the benefit of himself and his friends without charge, there is waste in the use of this car. The government has wasted resources in producing and operating the car, but the car has not generated income to pay for the cost, except when it is used for official business by the government, which is supposed to provide useful services to society. If a tailor is not allowed to operate his own business and charge for the services he provides, he will not do good work in a government-run tailor shop to serve customers who do not pay him directly.

The harmful economic effects of the misuse of labor in China cannot be overemphasized. We have just mentioned the lack of labor incentives while working at a government-owned unit that does not compensate laborers sufficiently for their additional effort. Two more harmful effects should be mentioned. The first is the effect in discouraging investment in human capital, a point already discussed in chapter 12. If young people cannot look forward to future rewards from studying harder in school or from getting additional training, they will invest less in acquiring knowledge and skill for themselves. Second, to live in a society where one has to deal with an unfriendly and even hostile bureaucracy to get things done is very sad. In economic terms this decreases the welfare of the Chinese people or makes them unhappy. The Chinese government sometimes justifies having bureaucrats to control the population because, it claims with some merit, society will become disorderly and chaotic unless the government controls the population properly – and controlling the population requires bureaucrats. I could present an argument to support the government's viewpoint, but it is the purpose of this chapter to study the economic effects of having people control assets in the name of the state and imposing restrictions on the use of and reward given for the use of the Chinese people's own labor.

The economic effects of state control of physical assets and restrictions on the use of and rewards for human capital will be systematically explored in this chapter. The method of our exploration is to start with a general hypothesis of human economic behavior, and derive from it certain economic laws governing the use of state-owned assets or the use of services provided by one's own person. These laws are then applied to explain economic behavior in connection with the use or misuse of physical and human assets in China.

I will adopt the following *hypothesis of asset management*: A person managing an asset will, to the best of his or her knowledge, try to derive the most benefit from it at the minimum cost or sacrifice to himself, in (a) utilizing its services directly to benefit himself or herself or (b) allowing others to use its services. In section 19.2 three laws of economic behavior will be stated which are immediate implications of this hypothesis. These laws will be applied to the management of one's own person in section 19.3 and to the management of an individual physical asset in section 19.4. Section 19.5 deals with collections of assets including enterprises and parts of enterprises. Institutional arrangements affect the objective function which the enterprise management seeks to maximize and the production function constraints to which it is subject, and hence the behavior of the enterprise. Sections 19.6 and 19.7 deal respectively with the misuse of publicly owned land and corruption in general.

## 19.2    Laws of Asset Management

Consider an asset manager who is given control over an asset and some limited rights in the use of it. Under socialism, the rights to use economic assets and to derive benefits from them are more limited than under capitalism, where the owner of an asset has more rights over its use. Our hypothesis is that an individual managing an asset will try to derive the most benefit from it at a minimum cost. Two assumptions are made. First, in order to produce service $S$ from the asset (which may be a physical asset or simply the human asset of the manager), labor $L$ from the asset manager is required, through a production function $S = S(L)$. This is just a special case of production with capital and labor as arguments, but the capital available is the asset controlled by the asset manager and is fixed. Imagine the manager of a government-owned apartment which produces housing services S, possibly measured by the market rent if the apartment could be rented out in a free market. It may require L units of labor on the part of the manager to maintain the apartment in order for its services to be rendered properly. Thus the amount of service S depends on the amount of labor L used to maintain the apartment. It is reasonable to assume that the more labor put in to maintain the apartment the better its condition will be and thus more service S could be derived from it. In mathematical terms we have the derivative $dS/dL > 0$. In the case of managing one's own person, the asset is the person himself. The service provided by the person, such as providing gardening work S, is simply measured by the amount of labor L he puts into gardening. In other words, $S = L$ as a special case of $S = S(L)$. In the case of managing a physical asset, labor from the manager is required to extract from it in the form of physical handling, supervision, maintenance, etc.

Second, there exists a utility function $u(S, L)$ which the asset manager tries to maximize, with $\partial u/\partial S > 0$, $-\partial u/\partial L > 0$. The marginal disutility of labor $-\partial u/\partial L$ is an increasing function of L. In simple English the assumption of the utility function $u(S, L)$ states that the asset manager derives benefit from the service S rendered by the asset under his management, and disutility from the amount of labor L he has to put in to generate the amount of service S. In a market economy where the asset is owned by the asset manager, S is the market rent that he can extract from the asset in combination with his labor L. In a socialist economy where the asset is not owned by the person who controls it, the asset manager cannot collect a market rent from the asset but he still can get something out of it. The socialist institution specifies $\partial u/\partial S$, that is, how much benefit the asset manager obtains by providing additional service.

The equilibrium condition resulting from the asset manager maximizing utility is obtained by setting the derivative of $u(S(L), L)$ with respect to L equal to zero, yielding

$$\frac{\partial u}{\partial S}\frac{dS}{dL} = -\frac{\partial u}{\partial L} \tag{19.1}$$

From this simple condition and our assumptions concerning $u$, three laws of economic behavior are readily deduced, depending on the institutional setup.

### 19.2.1   The law of supply of asset services

*When the marginal benefit from providing the service of an asset is smaller (larger), the asset manager will supply less (more) of its service.*

This law does not require any of the calculus used in deriving equation (19.1) to understand. Let us envisage the asset manager keeping control of an asset and adding her own labor in producing a stream of services which would yield her some benefit. If she can get more benefit by providing one unit of labor, she will naturally apply more labor in order to get more benefit. To think in mathematical terms, starting with equilibrium condition (19.1), when the marginal benefit $\partial u/\partial S$ is reduced, the marginal disutility of labor $-\partial u/\partial L$ has to be reduced by decreasing L to maintain equilibrium. This will lead to reducing service S through the production function. In the case of supply of labor service, $S = L$.

For those readers interested in understanding the relation between this law and the law of supply of labor which we discussed in chapter 12, let me point out that the latter is concerned with the relation between the quantity of labor supplied and the wage rate. Reducing the wage rate does not necessarily lead to a reduction in labor supply because of the possibility of a backward-bending supply curve of labor due to the domination of the income effect over the substitution effect of wage reduction. The present law is concerned with the relation between labor supply and the marginal benefit of supplying an additional unit of service. Both laws are consistent with condition (19.1); let consumption $C$ enter the utility function $u(C, L)$, with $S(L)$ replaced by $C = wL$, where $w$ is the wage rate. Maximizing $u$ with respect to $L$ yields the following equilibrium condition which corresponds to (19.1):

$$\frac{\partial u}{\partial C} w = -\frac{\partial u}{\partial L} \tag{19.2}$$

By our law, given $w = 1$, reducing $\partial u/\partial C$ leads to reducing $-\partial u/\partial L$ and reducing $L$. By the law of labor supply, reducing $w$ might not lead to reducing $L$, or the supply curve for labor might not have a positive slope. In terms of (19.2) the reason is that reducing $w$ on the lefthand side does not guarantee a reduction of $-\partial u/\partial L$ on the righthand side, or a reduction in $L$ that follows, because the other term on the lefthand side $\partial u/\partial C$ evaluated at $C = wL$ may increase as a result of diminishing marginal utility of consumption.

There is an important special case of the law of supply of asset services. If the asset consists of the right to deliver other assets to others, asset service refers to the delivery of assets. This special case can be called the law of asset delivery.

*When the marginal benefit from delivery or surrendering an asset to others is smaller (larger), the asset manager will be less (more) willing to deliver it, possibly reducing the qualities of delivery in the form of delays or lower product quality.*

Consider an asset manager whose task is to deliver the asset, such as a producer good or a certain raw material, to a potential user. Interpreting $S$ to be delivery service, one can use equilibrium condition (19.1) to derive this law in the same way as the first law. An obvious application of this law to the Chinese scene is the explanation of the quality of delivery service provided by the bureaucrats who control the supply of materials to state enterprises, or by the sales personnel in government-owned stores to consumers. What benefit would a salesman in a government-owned retail store get by providing good services to consumers coming to the store? Very little. Hence the quality of service in government-owned stores was very poor in China.

### 19.2.2 The law of asset maintenance

*When the benefit of managing an asset, either through the use of its service or through surrendering it to others, is smaller (larger), the manager will be less (more) willing to maintain it or to improve upon it.*

This law is a statement concerning the optimum maintenance policy for an asset. Maintenance expenditures for an asset and addition to the asset will be small if the asset provides little income in the future. Without introducing a dynamic framework explicitly, one can simply derive this law by defining $S$ in the equilibrium condition (19.1) to mean the service to maintain or to improve upon an asset.

### 19.2.3   The law of rent seeking

*When opportunities to extract payment or benefit from providing the service of an asset or from delivering it to others are available and not unduly risky, the manager will take advantage of them.*

Here we interpret the utility function to mean that higher utility or return can be obtained by using labor $L$ to extract bribes from the user of the service provided by the asset. This proposition then follows directly from our hypothesis of asset management. In terms of the equilibrium condition (19.1), there are choices of $\partial u/\partial S$ available to the manager. Some, such as taking bribes, may be risky and lead to punishment if one is caught. Often the rule of a socialist society assigns no extra benefit to an asset manager for providing additional services, and hence he requires compensation from the user for providing the services. Any illegal payment that he can extract from the user using his economic power can be considered an economic rent.

### 19.2.4   Welfare effects of restrictions on asset use

Besides the three laws of economic behavior in asset management, I would like to state the following proposition concerning the welfare effects of restrictions on the use of assets: When restrictions are placed on the use of an asset's service or on the delivery of an asset, leading to less benefit to its manager, the manager will reduce the quality of service or the quality of the asset delivered. The net welfare effect of such restrictions on society is negative unless the use of the asset is harmful to society, or unless the government is able to redirect the use of the asset for social gains which outweigh the loss to its manager and other benefactors of its service.

The above laws are now applied to explain behavior in the use or misuse of assets in China.

## 19.3   Managing One's Own Person

### 19.3.1   Eating from a large rice pot

As an application of the law of supply of asset services, consider the low quality of the services provided by the farmers under the commune system before 1978 and the workers in state enterprises. The poor performance is sometimes attributed to the "Iron Rice Bowl", the implication being that, given job security which guarantees sufficient food to eat from an unbreakable rice bowl, farmers and workers have no need to work hard. The real reason for poor performance is not job security alone, but rather the lack of additional remuneration when one tries to work harder. In mathematical terms the derivative of the utility function with respect to $S(L)$ is low. Under the commune system, when the farmer worked harder to increase output, he or she would get very little additional benefit because the output is shared by the entire work team, consisting of some 50 farmers on average. That Chinese farmers respond to material incentives has been documented by Lin (1988), McMillan, Whalley, and Zhu (1989), and Putterman (1990). Lin (1988) models the team with supervision as maximizing average net income per worker assuming each worker to maximize his own utility function of income and effort, with the return to effort differing according to institutional arrangements. McMillan et al. (1989) also employ a utility function of income and effort for the farmer and find that Chinese farmers responded to income incentives provided after reform. Putterman (1990) found that even working under the system of a production team, Chinese farmers increased their work effort when a larger fraction of the team output was distributed to them.

The remuneration system for the workers is also such that by working harder a person receives little additional benefit. The services of retail store clerks, waiters in restaurants, public transportation personnel, and all government officials dealing with people are known to be extremely poor in China. The problem of the Iron Rice Bowl is related to the problem of "eating from a large rice pot." People have the right to share without having to put in additional work, just like the farmers working collectively under the commune system.

### 19.3.2   Restriction of labor mobility

The lack of labor mobility has been recognized to be a serious problem in China, although the situation has continued to improve since 1978. The farmers in the communes could not move to other locations. The urban population needed residence permits to reside in a given city. Without the permit, one could not obtain rationed food items and clothing if he moved to another city. The situation improved in the 1980s as the commune system was abolished in 1983 and as market supplies of food and clothing became more abundant, and rationing was no longer needed. Opportunities became available for urban migration. Another aspect of the restriction is the power given to labor bureaux to assign jobs to the urban population, and to university administrators to assign jobs to college graduates. The restriction of opportunities for an individual to seek the best job and the best location has limited the usefulness of his services to himself and to society. This is an illustration of the negative welfare effects of restrictions on asset use.

### 19.3.3   Poor investment in human capital

When the opportunities to use human services are restricted, there is less incentive for students in schools and laborers in the workforce to improve themselves through education and training. In the meantime, one can increase the benefits from his labor by joining the

Communist Party or by establishing personal connections in order to obtain a better job assignment. Such efforts replace the efforts to study and to obtain additional training. This is an illustration of the law of asset maintenance.

# 19.4   Managing Physical Assets

## *19.4.1   Assets for own use*

Chinese urban residential housing deteriorated rapidly from the 1950s to the 1980s, partly because of the poor maintenance by its tenants. A tenant, in China and in the rest of the world, puts little effort into maintaining a rental apartment if the benefit from maintaining it is small.

Although some tenants in urban China may expect to stay in the same apartment for some time, many tenants try to move to better apartments through negotiations with administrators, and hence have limited incentive to maintain the current apartment. On the other hand, the rural population in China, especially after the introduction of economic reforms in 1978, was allowed to build its own housing. Rural housing was therefore of good quality and was well maintained. Farmers in China allegedly did not take sufficient care of the land assigned to them partly because the future benefits from farming the land were uncertain. The government, realizing this uncertainty, instituted policies to make the right to land use inheritable by children, although the credibility of this policy was questioned by the farmers. The limited care devoted to maintaining and improving the stock of housing, farmland (ceasing crop rotation), and other productive assets is an illustration of the law of asset maintenance.

## *19.4.2   Assets for use by others*

### *Poor quality of services*

A widespread phenomenon in China is the poor quality of the services rendered by persons controlling physical assets when the services provided yield no benefit to the persons rendering them. One example is the poor maintenance of residential housing by the staff of the housing bureaux. Other examples are the poor services provided by the personnel servicing publicly owned retail stores, restaurants, transportation facilities, etc. To illustrate this point from personal experience, when I was scheduled to give a lecture at a university in 1982, I asked my host, the chairman of the economics department, to show me the lecture room. He presented my request to the bureaucrat in charge of room assignment and was first rejected on the ground that he allegedly had not filled out the appropriate forms to apply for the use of the room. After pleading with the bureaucrat, my host finally obtained approval to use the room, which was empty most of the time. As a favor, the bureaucrat unlocked the door and showed us the room before my lecture.

The above story is typical of the way assets are managed by bureaucrats in China. Each bureaucrat abuses his right in managing assets and provides poor services to those requesting them if the services provided yield no benefit to him. Poor services are provided partly to reduce demand and thus to reduce the workload of the bureaucrat. This is an important reason why life in China is so miserable, especially before economic reforms. The people are humiliated continuously by bureaucrats who control the assets yielding services necessary for daily living. The same bureaucratic behavior is observed in other societies under similar circumstances, including, for example, that of the bureaucrats managing subsidized faculty housing at universities. Such bureaucratic behavior elsewhere is sometimes not as bad as in China, when there are alternatives provided by the market. Having to deal constantly with bureaucratic behavior for survival, the Chinese on the mainland have learned ways to beat the system and to fend for their self-interests. Such behavior is not looked upon favorably by foreign hosts when the Chinese practice it in foreign countries as visitors or immigrants.

### Rent-seeking behavior by bureaucrats

Examples abound to illustrate the law of rent seeking. When opportunity arises, the asset manager will try to extract rent, often illegally, for the services rendered.

Bribery in China and the rest of the world occurs when bureaucrats in charge of assets extract rents for their use, and the users are willing to pay for the services. Some of the assets being managed are rights to issue permits for engaging in economic activities, such as import and export licenses, inspection permits to build a house, etc. Bribery is widespread in China after the economic reforms. Economic reform increased economic opportunities and hence the demand for the services from assets managed by the bureaucrats mentioned above. The increase in demand raises the price of these services and the quantity supplied, if they are paid for by bribes.

### Poor quality of asset delivery

The poor services provided to nonpaying users and the desire to extract payment for using the service of an asset also prevail in the delivery of an asset to others. Without compensation, one finds poor quality in the delivery, in the form of delays or physical defects. This explains why the material inputs delivered by the bureaucrats managing the supply of materials to state-owned industrial and commercial enterprises are often defective in physical terms or in delivery time. It also explains the extraction of rent by the asset managers in the form of return favors or outright payments. The products being delivered include producer goods (physical capital and materials) or consumer goods (airplane tickets, train tickets, food and nonfood items distributed to consumers).

### Nonmarket trading of services and goods (guanxi)

The manager of an asset-providing service or for delivery can trade the service or the asset with managers of other assets. In a capitalist economy, the trade often takes place in the market for money. If the manager is not allowed to receive money for providing services or supplying goods under his control, he will try to extract services and goods in return. Spot exchange does not take place frequently because the user of the services or goods provided by the asset manager may not have something immediately useful to the latter to pay in return, if money payment is not allowed. Payment often takes the form of credit, not explicitly recorded, to be settled in the future in the forms of goods or services provided to the asset manager, or to a friend or a relative, or simply a third person who has an (implicit) account with the manager. Such an implicit trading relationship is called *guanxi* in China, literally meaning "relationship." One obtains a "relationship" with a network of people with whom one can trade services and goods (or even jobs and other favors).

*Guanxi* existed in China before the Communist rule began in 1949, because the market was not perfect and many assets were controlled by bureaucrats. Such trades became much more prevalent after the establishment of the PRC because the market became even more imperfect and more assets were controlled by bureaucrats. In Chinese societies including Hong Kong and Taiwan, as well as the mainland, people are accustomed not to settle accounts immediately by money. There is a tradition of nonmarket and nonmonetary trading which has existed for some time. When a friend provides you with a service in a Chinese society, he or she accumulates a credit in the unwritten account with you and expects you to remember it in the future in case they need something in return. Developing *guanxi* is very useful. It is like having credit in many banks on which you can draw in case of need. Confucius canonized this practice by advising: "Do not expect returns when you provide a service to others. Do not forget when others provide a service to you." The practice will last as long as the Chinese follow Confucius' advice.

## 19.5   Managing Collections of Assets under the Responsibility System

This section discusses the responsibility system introduced to improve the management of assets. The management of state-owned enterprises was discussed in chapter 15.

### 19.5.1   In agriculture

The success story of China's economic reform began in agriculture and was due to the initiative and ingenuity of local cadres managing the work teams in the communes rather than to the design of the central authorities in Beijing. Work teams under the commune system were required to deliver assigned quotas of agricultural products to the government purchasing units at below-market prices for redistribution. In 1977 some local managers of the work teams in Anhui province, recalling experiences in the 1950s, realized that a better way to obtain the required output for delivery was to distribute the land under collective ownership of the commune to the farm households and to require each household to turn over a given quota of output to the team, so that the latter could meet its own delivery quota (see Chow 1987: 55).

Although the farm households do not have ownership rights to the land, they have the right to use it for production. Any output above the assigned quota for delivery belongs to the farm household and can be used for consumption or for sale in the rural markets, which expanded rapidly in the late 1970s and early 1980s. The incentives are similar to those of the farmers in a market economy who lease a piece of land for a fixed rental. Since the marginal benefit of producing extra output belongs to the farm household, there are great incentives to produce. This illustrates the law of supply of asset service. Such an institutional arrangement was termed the responsibility system, with the farm household taking the responsibility of delivering the production quota and of using the land otherwise as it pleases. The success of this system led to its wide adoption and to the central authorities pronouncing it official policy in 1978. Except for the uncertainty concerning the right to use the land for long periods and the limited rights of transfer, both of which were improved in the early 1980s by government policy, China began returning to private farming in 1978–9 and abolished the commune system in 1983.

## 19.5.2   In small nonagricultural enterprises

In the early 1980s, as the rural population developed small enterprises for handicraft and other nonagricultural production, trade, and local transportation using the wealth accumulated from farming, the government tried to apply the idea of the responsibility system to urban economic reform. Many small public enterprises, including retail stores and small factories, were allowed and encouraged to adopt the responsibility system, with one manager leasing the enterprise, paying a fixed rental, and distributing the profit. In a very small establishment the profit goes to the manager, who may pay higher wages or bonuses to the workers to increase their incentives. In larger enterprises there is social and ideological pressure for the manager not to take too large a payment himself from the profit of the enterprise. I will return to this point later when discussing medium and large public enterprises. In any case, success stories abound, some reported in newspapers, concerning the increases in outputs, services provided, and profits of these small enterprises.

## 19.5.3   For parts of larger enterprises

A significant landmark of economic reform was the Decision of the Central Committee of the Communist Party of China on October 20, 1984 on Economic Reform. Among the major provisions of this Decision are reduction of the scope of central planning, development of a macroeconomic control system using the economic tools of fiscal and monetary policy, reform of the price system to arrive at a set of prices that are more reflective of the forces of demand and supply (with restrictions on price increases that would result in "abnormal" profits), reform of the management of state enterprises, encouraging the expansion of collective enterprises and the market sector, and the further strengthening of the open-door policy to encourage foreign trade and investment. As far as the management of state enterprises is concerned, an important component of the Decision is to encourage adoption of the responsibility system in parts of state enterprises. The responsibility is given by a state enterprise to the units within the enterprise to perform tasks with rewards for additional outputs or services. Workers and groups of workers within an enterprise can get paid by the quantities of their products, through piece rates and similar reward systems. Parts of an enterprise can keep or get paid for their outputs once a fixed quantity is delivered to the enterprise. The leasing arrangement is introduced to parts of state enterprises as much as possible, practicing the law of supply of asset services.

### 19.5.4   For entire state enterprises

1987 was the year when the "contract responsibility system" was introduced rapidly into Chinese state (central, provincial, and local government) enterprises. By the end of that year, over 95 percent of public enterprises were placed under this system. The central idea is that the management of an enterprise signs an agreement with the government unit supervising it which specifies a fixed annual tax for several years, with the enterprise management retaining all the profits after the tax payment. This idea can be interpreted as an intended application of the law of supply of asset services, the asset being the enterprise. In practice, a number of problems arise concerning the effectiveness of the contract responsibility system.

The first problem is concerned with the compensation for the enterprise manager. Because of the possibly large profits of a state enterprise and the ideological and social objections to high compensation, the relation between additional profits and the manager's compensation is very limited. In practice, the manager obtains consent from the staff and workers concerning his own compensation and the remuneration of employees, including wage, bonuses, and other benefits. The link between marginal benefits to the manager and additional efforts is not satisfactorily established. One consequence of the law of rent seeking is that parts of the extra profits are used for distribution to the management, staff, and workers in the form of bonuses. The bonuses may take the form of consumer goods such as color television sets and refrigerators. The funds of enterprises are often used to purchase consumer goods for distribution to staff and workers.

The second problem concerns the determination of the appropriate amount of tax which an enterprise is required to pay. The collecting unit of the government would like to extract a large amount from the enterprise, leading to bargaining and negotiations not unlike those taking place during the period of central planning regarding output targets and material supplies assigned to state enterprises. There is also uncertainty concerning the possible increase in the "fixed" tax when profit increases in the future, lessening the possible incentive from a truly fixed charge. The third, and related, problem is that profits do not necessarily reflect economic efficiency. State enterprises have monopoly power. Assets are assigned to state enterprises without appropriate rental charges; ideally the tax levied should reflect an appropriate rental for the capital under the enterprises' control. Finally, both output and input prices facing state enterprises might not reflect scarcity, invalidating the use of profits as a measure of enterprise efficiency.

Since the contract responsibility system is recognized by Chinese authorities and outside observers to be unsatisfactory for making state enterprises efficient, discussion inside and outside China continues on how to improve the functioning of state enterprises. To contribute to this discussion, I have provided in sections 15.3 and 15.4 two models explaining the functioning of state enterprises before and after the economic reforms. These models are very simple but, I believe, capture the most important features of Chinese state enterprises before and after urban economic reforms. As the rights to assets affect the cost–benefit calculation of people managing individual assets and thus their economic behavior, so will the administrative arrangements provided for the managers of state enterprises affect their behavior. Economic reform of state enterprises is modeled by a change in the objective function and the constraints facing an enterprise manager. While the assumption of his maximizing an objective function subject to constraints imposed by production and marketing conditions is maintained, changing these two components of his maximization problem will lead to different behavior.

One important aspect of the misuse of power in controlling state-owned enterprises and state-owned banks is the embezzlement of assets. This kind of corruption has been publicized in Chinese newspapers, and serious cases have been severely punished. It can take many forms, including the diversion of assets into personal accounts or the selling of assets at below-market prices to companies controlled by the same managers. State-owned companies have set up corporations with stocks traded in the Shanghai or Shenzhen stock markets to attract capital from the general public. It has been alleged that some parent companies have diverted funds from the publicly traded companies under their control for illegitimate purposes. Although the government has tried very hard to control corruption, it has had only limited success because the economic gains are too tempting. One way to reduce corruption is to reduce the economic power of managers of state-owned enterprises and of government bureaucrats. This can be accomplished by reducing the role of state-owned enterprises and the extent of government intervention in the market economy. Government intervention can be a part of government regulation to preserve order in the market system, but one has to balance the benefits and costs of regulation, the latter including the opportunity for corruption.

## 19.6 The Misuse of Collectively Owned Land

When the responsibility system was introduced into Chinese agriculture to allow the farmers to farm their own piece of land and profit from farming it, there still remained a large amount of land that was collectively owned and in effect controlled by city, county, township, and village governments all over China. Township and village government officials utilized such land to establish township and village enterprises for the benefit of the people and themselves. As China has become richer, the people have accumulated wealth for urban and rural development. Foreign investors also participate in such development. The government officials in areas where development takes place can benefit from the income generated, from the credit and recognition received for the development, and from the side payments for approving the development projects. Since the term of office of these officials is finite and uncertain they will tend to take advantage of their tenure to encourage development while they are in office. This is in contrast with a private owner of the land, who can make more long-term decisions about when to sell or lease the land to developers, and will not do so in a hurry in order to take advantage of possibly better opportunities in the future. In short, government officials who control land that is not owned by them do not have the right incentives to utilize it to generate the greatest economic benefits in the future.

In the early 2000s, there are urban development and construction projects in many cities of China. The former include the rapid development of Dongguan, near Hong Kong, into a modern city. The latter include many construction projects in the city of Beijing. Such developments contributed to what the Chinese government officials considered to be "overheating" of the economy in 2003–4. This is not only a short-term problem of macroeconomic fluctuations, but also a long-term problem of economic development, when land as a most valuable resource is misused. The misuse of land as a collectively owned asset is a serious problem in China.

In the revolution that established the People's Republic of China in 1949, all private land became publicly owned. Economic reform since 1978 partially solved the problem of misuse of public farmland by assigning the land to individual farm households, with rights to transfer. (Many economists are concerned about the fine line between the right given to the farmers and private ownership; even without private ownership the major incentive problem was in reality solved.) The very large amount of land remaining in the control of government bureaucrats is still an unsolved problem from the viewpoint of efficient allocation of resources. This problem will be difficult to solve as long as the Chinese Communist Party is opposed to the private ownership of land. The government has to some extent solved the problem of efficient allocation of resources controlled by state-owned enterprises under share ownership, as enterprise managers are not allowed to sell the assets of the enterprises; any exceptions to this arise from corruption. If land remains publicly owned and the government has the power to sell it, a system needs to be devised to provide the bureaucrats controlling the land with the right incentives to use it to yield the highest economic returns.

## 19.7   Corruption and Economic Reform

Chow (2006) summarizes the problem of corruption in the process of Chinese economic reform at the beginning of the twenty-first century as follows:

> Past economic reform of the state sector in China consisted mainly of privatization, of agriculture and of small and medium-size state enterprises, leaving large enterprises in the control of the state. Current reform consists of making state-owned enterprises and banks more efficient and making them function like private enterprises, and gradual privatization of some large state enterprises. Bureaucrats managing state assets and the selling of assets take advantage of such power to benefit themselves, including embezzlement of public funds and

taking bribes from citizens needing their help, as can be found in state enterprises, state-owned commercial banks and in government projects. Reducing the size of the government sector is a basic solution to the corruption problem in China, while attention should be paid in the privatization process, which can involve corruption.

In the case of large state enterprises, we find corruption of the following forms: (1) managers and staff taking bribes from those who need to do business with them, and (2) managers and staff taking resources from enterprises for their own benefit. Both (1) and (2) will affect economic efficiency, (1) by not making the best deal for the company in maximizing profit or carrying out optimal investment decisions, and (2) by taking away resources which should be used to benefit the enterprise.

Thus reform to change large state enterprises to corporations or share-holding companies by itself does not work. To the extent that modern corporations in Western developed economies are thought to work better, one might be tempted to trace the difference to defective "corporate governance" in the Chinese case. Can we change the "corporate governance" of the large state-owned Chinese corporations to improve their operation? This is a question worthy of much research. One pessimistic answer, before further research is completed, is that change in corporate governance may not be effective because the managers and staff do not follow the rules of the game.

China's banking system is said to have two major problems. One is the existence of the nonperforming loans which we discussed in section 13.6. The second is the institutional problem that the bankers do not behave like bankers working in modern commercial banks. This problem is due to the working habit inherited from banking practice beginning in the period of central planning, where there were no modern commercial banks, but only branch banks of the central monobank with responsibilities merely to accept deposits and provide loans to state enterprises passively. They had little need to exercise judgment in the granting of loans. After economic reforms that allowed more autonomy to the branch banks, which were renamed commercial banks, there were opportunities for corruption on the part of the banking officials, since they have discretion in the spending and the lending of money.

The bureaucratic behavior of banking officials cannot be easily solved by legislation or regulation. I can make this point simply by copying the relevant statements in discussing the corruption of state enterprises and changing "state-owned enterprises" to "state-owned commercial banks." Until recently the People's Bank was responsible for supervising commercial banks, but in 2001 this responsibility was given to a Banking Regulatory Commission, probably because the task was too difficult for the People's Bank to perform in addition to its other function of exercising macro-control (by setting interest rates, the reserve ratio, and other policy instruments, including administrative means such as imposing quotas to bank loans). The Banking Regulatory Commission has had some, but only limited, success in reducing corruption in the banking sector, as I have learned from talking to numerous Chinese citizens in a position to know, including those who seek loans from banks.

Hopefully bureaucratic behavior and corruption (including well-known cases of the embezzlement of large sums of money belonging to the banks) will be reduced by competition from foreign banks under the terms of the WTO, but the effectiveness of reform through regulation of the banking sector may be limited under the principle that economic behavior is not changed easily by legislation (see section 20.2) or by regulation.

Another source of corruption is the administration of the Western Development Strategy discussed above in chapter 10. The government spent a large amount of money on development in western China. An interesting question is how much of the government expenditure for this project is lost by corruption or otherwise inefficiently used as compared with allowing the nonstate sector to engage in western development based on profit motives. One form of corruption associated with this Strategy is the unpaid wages owed local workers who worked on projects such as road construction. A related example, aside from the Western Development Strategy, is the illegal levies on the farmers by local bureaucrats, against the regulations set by the central government, as discussed in section 4.6 above. These are just two of the many examples of corruption connected with government projects.

Why is the problem of corruption as a hindrance to economic reform more serious now than before? First, the environment has changed. Second, Chinese culture has changed.

A major first step of economic reform in the past is leasing, from the introduction of the "responsibility system" into agriculture, retail stores, small factories, and later to larger enterprises. There can be no corruption if a farmer or a manager of a small store or a small factory gets all the output after paying a fixed amount of tax. In a leasing arrangement there is no need to solve the problem of the principle–agent divide, as the agent who reaps the return from his own effort will have as much incentive to work hard as the manager of a private firm. Under the "contract responsibility system" introduced in 1987 large state enterprises retained all their profits after paying the government a fixed levy, but the management was obliged to distribute a fair share of the profits to the staff and workers, who consequently kept a close watch on their behavior. A second step was privatization of small and medium-sized state-owned enterprises through the transfer of ownership to the managers and workers in the restructured shareholding companies, or simply through the transfer of ownership to former government employees who had operated state enterprises by a leasing arrangement. By definition, the manager of a private enterprise cannot be called corrupt if he takes his own money.

In the current stage of reform for large state enterprises or state-owned commercial banks, the situation is different. We need to reform these corporations and require the bureaucratic managers and staff who exercise economic power in the name of the state not to use it for their personal benefit. In a large corporation owned by nongovernment shareholders there is also the problem of making sure that managers and staff do not embezzle resources from the corporation; but such embezzlement is more readily punished by law.

When the state-owned banks extended loans to state enterprises, the staff of state enterprises would not personally pay the bankers for the loans, since they had no personal financial interest in it. Now more loans are extended to private enterprises, and borrowers are willing to pay bribes to obtain the loans. The bankers have more discretion in extending loans. For the bureaucrats in control of state funds for large construction projects, there is now more money under their control, as the government budget has increased, and the government is spending more on projects under the very costly Western Development Strategy, as well as on the rapidly expanding universities. More money going through the bureaucrats' hands means more corruption.

The theory of misuse of assets under state ownership applies in all stages of reform, but now the opportunities available to bureaucrats are different, or the environment is different. In contrast with the previous leasing arrangement or with reform by privatization, the current reform requires the bureaucrats in state-owned banks to behave like private bankers; in state-owned enterprises to behave like businessmen in the private sector; and bureaucrats in charge of large development projects not to take any money going through them.

The second part of our answer to the reason why corruption is a more serious problem is historical-cultural. The practice of corruption is now more widespread because more people have been doing it; desire for money grows as one sees others having more of it. Since economic reform in the early 1980s there are more and more rich people in China, some very rich even by American standards. This is a good sign, indicating the success of a market economy which allows for relatively free entry, since the rich people are by and large able, hard-working, and resourceful. Of course there are also those who got rich as bureaucrats mainly through their control of state-owned economic resources and exploiting economic power for personal gains. It now appears that the Chinese, rich and poor, seeing that there is much money around and that many others have made a lot of it, want to get their share if an opportunity comes.

Chinese culture is influenced by the practice of money-making as a legitimate activity, with every one watching for an opportunity coming his way. If the opportunity takes the form of occupying an administrative position in the government or in government-owned enterprises or banks, the person can take bribes and embezzle public funds as much as the prevailing practice allows, and as much as the person's own conscience dictates. Many Chinese still uphold the old cultural standard of honesty and integrity, but the instances of violation in practice have increased, and it is partly up to the individual to decide, subject to the effectiveness of law enforcement. Chinese culture as evolved through economic deprivation under central planning and the failure of the Great Leap, the lawlessness of the Cultural Revolution, the "getting rich is glorious" attitude after market reform, and during a period of rapid increase in real income has fostered an attitude and a mode of behavior conducive to corruption. Of course other societies have also gone through historical periods that are conducive to corruption, and some of them are more corrupt than China, but this book deals only with the Chinese case.

In summary, the problem of corruption existed before, but its effect on economic reform is now more serious because the nature of reform has changed and because the culture has changed as reform and growth have occurred.

If much corruption is the result of state control of economic power, a solution is to reduce the domain of such power, including the public ownership of land. The last may be resolved by granting an almost permanent lease of land to private users under a transparent system of auction or transfer of right to use. This is only a solution in principle. In practice the administrative and political problems of reducing the government's economic, and in fact political, power are very difficult ones.

## 19.8 Concluding Comments

As I stated at the beginning of this chapter, the main characteristic of a socialist economy is the high degree of control of economic assets and restriction of their use by the state. These assets include both physical assets and human beings. The control and restriction take the form of state ownership or control of physical resources and enterprises, and limitation to the economic freedom of the citizens to pursue their economic activities or to derive gains from such activities. Mathematically, maximization subject to more constraints can only lead to a lower value for the maximum. The effect of such control and restriction on society is negative, unless the economic activity itself is harmful to society. China's economic reform can be interpreted as lifting controls of and restrictions to the use of assets. The household responsibility system in agriculture, the introduction of state-enterprise autonomy, the contract responsibility system, and later the restructuring of state enterprises, the increase in labor mobility and the freedom to choose jobs, the increased freedom to travel abroad to study, and the permission of nonstate enterprises to develop are all well-known examples.

At the beginning of the twenty-first century the degree of state control over economic resources under China's socialist market economy is still higher than under a developed capitalist market economy. The control takes two forms, the first affecting state enterprises even after restructuring to become shareholding companies, and the second with regard to the operation of nonstate, especially private and foreign-owned, enterprises, which are subject to government red tape and market controls. The restructured enterprises under a shareholding system have government units owning majority shares, as well as managers and members of the board of directors appointed by the government. The problem of how to monitor the government-appointed managers of these enterprises is still unresolved. The interference with the working of nonstate enterprises still exercises a negative effect on entrepreneurship and on China's economic development.

At the beginning of the twenty-first century, the amount of state control and restriction on economic assets and their use is still substantial in China. Not only are much of the land and important enterprises under state control, but also the freedom to organize and operate private enterprises is restricted by Chinese bureaucracy. It is difficult for private and foreign enterprises to compete with state enterprises because of the subsidies which the latter receive and of the bureaucratic restrictions on the former. Corruption is still prevalent, and the end of it is not in sight.

## References and Further Reading

Butterfield, Fox. *China: Alive in a Bitter Sea.* New York: Bantam Books, 1982.

Chow, G. C. *The Chinese Economy*, 2nd ed. New York: Harper & Row, 1987a; Singapore: World Scientific Publishing Co.

Chow, G. C. "Development of a More Market-Oriented Economy in China." *Science* 235 (1987b), pp. 295–9.

Chow, G. C. "Rights to Assets and Economic Behavior under Chinese Socialism." *Academic Economic Papers*, 20, no. 2, part I (1992), pp. 267–90.

Chow, G. C. "Capital Formation and Economic Growth in China." *Quarterly Journal of Economics*, 108 (1993), pp. 809–42.

Chow, G. C. "Corruption and China's Economic Reform in the Early 21st Century." *International Journal of Business*, 209 (2006), pp. 263–80.

Lin, Justin Yifu. "The Household Responsibility System in China's Agricultural Reform: A Theoretical and Empirical Study." *Economic Development and Cultural Change*, 36, 3rd Supplement (1988), pp. 5199–234.

McMillan, John, John Whalley, and Lijing Zhu. "The Impact of China's Economic Reforms on Agricultural Productivity Growth." *Journal of Political Economy*, 97 (1989), pp. 781–807.

Perkins, Dwight H. "Reforming China's Economic System." *Journal of Economics Literature*, 17 (1988), pp. 601–45.

Putterman, Louis. "Effort, Productivity and Incentives in a 1970s Chinese People's Commune." *Journal of Comparative Economics*, 14 (1990), pp. 88–104.

# Questions

1   Provide one example of your own from the Chinese economy to illustrate: (1) the law of supply of asset services; (2) the law of asset maintenance; (3) the law of rent seeking; (4) negative welfare effects of restriction on asset use.

2   Provide one example from an economy other than the Chinese economy to illustrate the four parts of question 1 above.

3   Illustrate one of the four parts of question 1 using the experience from the township and village enterprises in China.

4   Illustrate one of the four parts of question 1 using the experience from joint or cooperative ventures or foreign-owned enterprises in China.

5   Do you think that corruption in China can be stopped soon? Why or why not?

6   The discussion of this chapter seems to imply that state control and restriction on the use of economic assets are socially undesirable. Provide counterarguments to support the founding of a socialist economy.

   In 1992 the Chinese Communist Party declared the Chinese economy a "socialist market economy." Based on your observations, in what sense is it a market economy? In what sense is it a socialist economy?

7   In what ways can a Chinese bureaucrat in charge of state property use it for personal gain? Describe the ways in which a bureaucrat can benefit himself using state property or state authority. When a bureaucrat benefits himself, under what circumstances does it have a harmful effect on society? Under what circumstances is the effect desirable to society?

8   It seems to be the case that persons in charge of state property cannot derive sufficient benefit from it and therefore state assets are not efficiently utilized. The reform policies in China were partly designed to improve efficiency in the utilization of publicly owned resources. Can you name four reform measures that have corrected some of the inefficiencies in the utilization of state assets or generated by the restrictions on the use of human capital, and explain how the measures succeeded?

# 20

# The Legal System and the
# Role of Government

In sections 20.1 and 20.2, respectively, the legal system in China before and after 1949 is discussed. The latter includes the government's efforts to reform the legal system after economic reform started in 1978. The role of the legal system in the functioning of a market economy is the subject of section 20.3. The role of the government in a market economy is discussed in section 20.4, including six areas of possible government intervention. Section 20.5 discusses the role of government planning in China's market economy. How the government makes its decisions in relation to the form of government, be it a democracy or otherwise, is the subject of the last section. This chapter illustrates the importance of institutional factors in the functioning and hence the transformation of an economy.

## 20.1   The Legal System prior to 1949

When economic reform was discussed in chapter 4, the legal system and the education system were mentioned as two important elements of the economic infrastructure in the building of which the government plays an important role. This chapter discusses the Chinese legal system and other functions of the government. The education system is the subject of the next chapter. Both systems are important in discussing the process of transformation of China's economy.

Before discussing the formal legal system itself, it is useful to remind ourselves of the role of law in a society. Some standard or set of rules for behavior is essential for a stable society and the proper functioning of a market economy. The standard comes from two sources. The first is the moral tradition of the society as evolved through its history. In the Chinese case, Confucianism is an important component of the moral tradition. A person grown up in this tradition automatically follows certain codes of behavior such as honesty and responsibility to one's promises. The second is a set of formal laws built upon the moral tradition. Laws enacted by a legislative body cannot be effective unless they are consistent with the moral tradition. Under imperial rule in China, what the imperial system decreed was law, and there was no elected legislative body to enact laws, but the laws still had to be consistent with the moral tradition of the Chinese people.

After the founding of the Republic of China in 1911, imperial rule was formally abolished. Some form of legislature was required to enact laws, but the political institutions were not firmly established. A powerful political leader could change the legislature and the legislation at will. The legislature and its legislation followed political winds. For example, in 1916, or the fifth year of the Republic after the death of President Yuan Shikai, who was very unpopular for having attempted to become an emperor, the new President Li Yuanhong was under pressure from provincial governors who had declared independence but were willing to support the new President if the Congress elected in the first year of the Republic and its legislation were reestablished, and the Congress established in the third year of the Republic and the legislation enacted under the Presidency of Yuan were replaced. The arguments hinge partly on the desirable nature of the legislation and only partly on the legitimacy of the procedure. After listening to some heated debates and considering the political forces at work, Prime Minister Duan Qirui decided to retain the Congress and the legislation of the third year of the Republic. (See the *Annals of Mr. Liang Yansun of Sanshui*, vol. 1, pp. 346–9.) This example illustrates two very important points: (1) formal legislation itself is no guarantee of social and economic order because its own fortune is subject to political conditions, and (2) the Chinese people use its "moral correctness" perhaps more than the legislative procedure to judge whether a law is valid. The last point applied to the laws decreed under imperial rule as well. If an emperor was regarded as having conducted himself improperly, his orders would not be obeyed.

The modern legal system includes institutions for the enactment and the enforcement of laws. These are the legislative branch and the judicial branch of the government, the third being the executive branch. To describe them in the case of China prior to 1949 one needs to describe briefly the Chinese government. The American government consists of the above three branches. The Chinese government prior to 1949 had two more branches, the supervisory branch and the examination branch. To supervise the functioning of the executive branch of the government a separate branch was established, whereas in the United States such a function is the responsibility of the Congress. The idea of the supervisory branch was due to Dr. Sun Yat-sen who was influenced by the history of possible abuse of bureaucratic power under imperial rule. The bureaucratic tradition of China might lead to corruption. The examination branch originated from the examination system to select government officials in imperial China. The Chinese system under the leadership of the Nationalist Party, or Kuomintang, was designed by Sun Yat-sen, who borrowed from the American political system and added two more branches to suit the Chinese situation. Sun advocated "three principles of the people" consisting of nationalism, democracy, and people's livelihood. These three principles were inspired by the "government of the people, by the people, and for the people" in Lincoln's Gettysburg address.

The legal system was gradually formed after the Republic of China was established in 1911. Although in the early years of the Republic there were both an upper and a lower house of the Chinese Congress with representatives selected from the provinces, the legislature was unstable. Congress was dissolved and recalled again several times following the changing fortunes of political leaders, as the Presidency and the cabinet of the executive branch changed several times. A strong President coming to power could dissolve the Congress using some excuse to claim that it was illegitimate. Political instability was described above in section 1.3. It was not until Chiang Kai-shek succeeded in unifying China to a large degree in 1928 that some political unity was established. The Kuomintang had announced its *Principles for Establishing the Nation* on April 12, 1924, the year before Sun Yat-sen died. The *Principles* advocated the establishment of democracy but in three stages. The first was military rule. This stage was required to take over control from the warlords and other military forces in the provinces. The second was the stage of training the population in the rules and responsibility of democracy. Finally would come a government under a constitution to be written at the beginning of the third stage. Chiang was practicing military rule in the first stage.

Chiang was elected President in 1947 not by popular vote but indirectly by the representatives in the legislature, as under the British parliamentary system. The legal system appeared to function fairly well in the 1930s. Laws were enacted by elected representatives of the people. The courts were functioning. More importantly, the people were by and large law abiding, partly under the influence of the Confucian tradition. They respected the law and the courts. Lawyers were considered to be working in a respectable profession. There were law schools to train them. The functioning of the legal system deteriorated somewhat after the Sino-Japanese War started in 1937, during the Second World War and the civil war afterwards. When survival was threatened people were willing to disobey the law for the sake of survival if necessary.

It appears that the legal system prevailing in China before 1949 had merits, just as the economic system prevailing in China before 1949 had merits, which the current government in China can study and possibly incorporate. The six comprehensive Chinese law books [*liu fa quan shu*] developed during the 1920s and 1930s are still being used to some extent in Taiwan. Scholars and government officials on the Chinese mainland are looking into the legal system before 1949. Some Communist Party and government officials may be open-minded and pragmatic enough to adopt any features of the former legal system that are meritorious without being restrained by ideological considerations.

## 20.2   The Legal System since 1949

The legal system is a part of the political system. The nature of the political system affects the legal system. In the case of China, a guiding principle of the government is the supremacy of the Communist Party. The government rules under the leadership of the Party. The Party Congress makes the most important decisions and is represented by its Central Committee. The Central Committee of about 200 persons is led by the Political Bureau. A small number (about 9 in 2003) of people serving on the Standing Committee of the Political Bureau (consisting of 24 people in 2003) are the most powerful group of people in China. The Party rules by selecting the Premier and the Ministers in the executive branch, proposing legislation to the People's Congress, and influencing the decisions of the courts. It rules also by placing Party secretaries in various government organizations. To the extent that the People's Congress can be influenced, the Constitution can be changed to suit the policy of the Party.

A Constitution was passed by the People's Congress soon after the PRC was established. The Constitution guaranteed the basic freedom of citizens, including freedom of speech and of assembly, but in practice if the exercise of such freedom is considered a threat to the rule of the Communist Party, it will be prohibited. The Constitution was changed several times, depending on the needs of the nation at the time. This happened during 1981 when there was a need to carry out economic reform. In 1998 the Constitution was revised because of a need to guarantee the rights of private enterprises.

Before economic reform started in 1978, the legal system in practice was characterized by rule of the Communist Party and by the political leadership, in particular Chairman Mao Zedong, besides what was stated in the constitution and the written laws. I mention in the last paragraph that even though basic freedoms were guaranteed by the first Constitution, in practice the exercise of such freedoms was restricted. For example, no one could openly criticize the doctrine of Communism without being punished. Furthermore, during the Hundred Flowers campaign of 1957 Mao first encouraged the intellectuals to speak out and later punished them for criticizing the government. Other notable instances include the persecution of thousands of landlords and punishment of managers and staff in factories after accusations at mass meetings without proper trials; and the lawless behavior of the Red Guard during the Cultural Revolution. When I visited Beijing in 1980, friends and relatives did not dare to speak about the conditions in China in the hotel room for fear of being heard, and had to wait until we walked out of the hotel. These people had no intention of overthrowing or even criticizing the government, but only wanted to tell about the horror during the Cultural Revolution. During the period of the Cultural Revolution people lived in fear without being protected by law.

After recovery from the Cultural Revolution, democracy, in the sense of people's participation in the political process, is practiced in the following ways. First, within the organizations of the Communist Party, members of the Party Congress, members of the Central Committee, of the Political Bureau and of its standing committee are all elected by members in the level below. Second, members of Congress are also elected. All these elections are indirect. Lower-level party elections select representatives who in turn elect representatives in higher levels. Local elections choose representatives, who in turn elect representatives up to members of the People's Congress. Third, in the 1990s, partly because of need to provide public goods and take care of social welfare, village elections became widespread in China to select government officials for the villages. These are truly direct elections. Officials are selected to serve the people. Such elections have not yet reached the county level at the turn of the century. Fourth, the power of the People's Congress increased in practice through the 1980s and 1990s, and members began to exercise their own judgment in voting rather than automatically approving the draft laws represented to them by the Communist Party.

Given the nature of China's political system, leaders in the Communist Party and in the government decided to modernize the Chinese legal system as a part of the economic reform process. In the early 1980s the Ministry of Education began to establish cooperative programs with law faculties in the United States, including the Columbia University Law School faculty, in order to provide law training in China. This effort slightly preceded a similar effort to provide economics training which will be described in section 21.3.

The record of the government's effort to modernize the legal system has been impressive. The People's Congress has functioned more independently of political influence and has legislated a large number of laws required for the functioning of the market economy. Examples are the Central Bank Law and the Commercial Bank Law discussed in chapter 13. There are bankruptcy laws, other laws governing corporate behavior, laws governing foreign trade and investment, etc. The power of the People's Congress further increased in the late 1990s when Li Peng served as its Chairman, as Li was the second most powerful leader in China, next to President and Party Secretary Jiang Zemin. The judicial system expanded. The Supreme People's Court in Beijing has the power to give judicial interpretation of law. The Litigation Law allows citizens to sue the government. The courts are deciding more cases, including suits against the government. In 1998, the number of judicial personnel was over 300,000, including approximately 130,000 judges and 175,000 lawyers. All these developments signaled the modernization of the Chinese legal system.

The impressive record just described should not leave the reader the impression that the Chinese legal system is in good shape. How well the Chinese legal system functions today cannot be judged by the large number of new laws or by the number of lawyers, of judges, or of lawsuits that have been filed. As pointed out at the beginning of section 20.1, formal legislation itself is not sufficient to provide social and economic order. Laws have to be based on moral standards accepted by the population. Some observers suggest that the number of new laws passed by the People's Congress is too large and that the contents of many laws do not sufficiently take into account the moral foundation and historical tradition of social behavior on which any laws must be based. Besides this important point, there are three other possible limitations to the current legal system in China.

First, economic behavior is not changed by legislation alone. It is the result of cultural tradition and social institutions. There is inertia to be overcome in changing social and human behavior. Being law abiding is a habit that is difficult to get into. People have not yet developed the habit of going to court to settle disputes. Many do not have a high regard for laws and are not law abiding. The enforcement of laws in Chinese courts is not perfect. I mentioned in the previous section that in the 1930s the Chinese people were by and large law abiding. The behavior might have changed because of two factors. First is the Cultural Revolution, which caused people to lower their moral standards and respect for the law for the sake of survival. Second is the economic deprivation during the long period of central planning and political disruption described in chapter 2. Economic deprivation had made the Chinese people much more materialistic than otherwise, once they were given opportunities to make money after the economic reform. Sometimes money was made by illegal means such as smuggling and selling goods produced in violation of intellectual property rights. For the same reason, at the beginning of the twenty-first century there appear to be signs that, as the country has gotten richer, the Chinese people are becoming more law abiding. The government also deserves some credit in promoting orderly behavior in addition to the reform of legal institutions.

Second, in some respect the effort to introduce Western laws has affected orderly social relations adversely. In traditional Chinese society, such relations are based on the tradition of *guanxi*, or social networking. The Chinese consider ethical and moral codes more important than laws. They feel justified if they behave properly according to their conscience, which comes from family education and social values. To the extent that orderly behavior based on such values is disturbed by a legalistic attitude, it may be harmful to society. Master Zhu Xi, the leading Confucian scholar in the Song dynasty, who is regarded as the authoritative interpreter of Confucianism by many Chinese, and the founder of Neo-Confucianism by modern scholars, in his well-known *Admonitions of Master Zhu*, advised: "In conducting family affairs, do not quarrel or engage in legal disputes, for engaging in legal disputes will result in misfortune." The fact that the amount of litigation has increased rapidly does not imply that the social system is working better. The Western legal system in itself has its limitations. It is said that there are too many lawyers in the United States, and the US economy devotes too much of its resources to legal services.

Third, the Communist Party in its role of providing political leadership is in some sense above the law. There are two senses in which this statement is true. First, laws cannot be written to restrict the power of the Communist Party to rule the country, which is absolute. Second, in practice, even when the law applies, the courts might decide in accordance with the wishes of a government official or Party member who is involved in the dispute.

## 20.3   The Role of the Legal System in a Market Economy

A modern market economy requires the existence of a set of rules of the game for the economic players who compete in the marketplace. This set of rules is the set of laws that have to be suitably enacted and effectively enforced by a legislature and the courts respectively. When China started economic reform in 1978 its leaders were wise enough to allow the market economy to evolve without a blueprint at the beginning. They relied on experimentation and experience to choose the appropriate institutions. They realized that institutional changes take time. Legal institutions had to be developed gradually. Since 1978 the government of China has succeeded to a large extent in developing such institutions, but much remains to be done to make people more law abiding and to improve the judicial system. Western legal institutions have served as an important reference point for the development of Chinese legal institutions, but are not used as a model for China. To be a member of the international economic community, Chinese laws on business conduct and intellectual property rights have to satisfy world standards. On the other hand, Chinese enterprises have their own characteristics and may require a different set of laws governing their establishment and organization. Other countries in the world also have their own business laws while being a member of the WTO and participating in economic transactions in the global economy.

Legal institutions are different because the method of enforcement and the degree of enforcement may be different. In some eastern Asian countries, business agreements are partly enforced by a set of informal human relationships known as *guanxi*. *Guanxi* serves as a supplement to the formal legal system. Even in the United States, where the number of lawyers per capita is much higher than in the rest of the world, not all disputes are settled through the legal system because it is sometimes too costly to do so. To have informal human relations to settle disagreements can be an advantage over having a legal system alone. Sometimes it is better not to enforce a law too strictly, or to view the situation with one eye open and one eye closed, as a Chinese saying goes. A law is a universal rule of conduct applicable to all citizens. Since different persons have different opinions on what is right and wrong, having one universal rule is a restriction on human freedom. One of the most controversial issues in the United States is whether abortion should be legal or not. No matter what the law is, about half of the population would oppose it strongly. Perhaps a solution is to make abortion illegal but not enforce it strictly, as circumstances dictate. A related example is the one-child-family policy in China. This policy has been more strictly enforced in the cities than in the countryside. Farmers need to have children, and the cost of enforcement in rural areas is higher than in urban areas.

Once we have a set of legal institutions to enforce the rules of the game governing economic behavior in a market economy, we need to specify the rules. The People's Congress of China has worked very hard in the last 15 years to enact laws governing business organizations. The Bankruptcy Law of 1986 and the Commercial Bank Law of 1995 are important examples. One important issue is the definition of competition. What kind of competition should be protected and what kind of monopolistic practices should be prohibited? An issue in the United States is whether and to what extent Microsoft is engaged in illegal monopolistic practices by preventing users of its Windows operating system from easily accessing competing products and its competitors from developing new products. Another important issue is how to assess, and to impose charges for, damages to society and to the environment which result from the activities of individual enterprises. In short, we need continuously to specify and enforce the rules of conduct for individuals and enterprises in order for a free market economy to function properly.

Historically laws have been changed to satisfy the needs of social and economic institutions which are evolving. The evolution of these institutions is only partially the result of government intervention. In the last two decades in China collective enterprises in townships and villages have naturally emerged. As economic opportunities became available, state enterprises were slow to respond and private enterprises had insufficient human and physical capital to respond. The governments of townships and villages had sufficient human and physical resources to set up or promote their own enterprises, and these enterprises have become the most rapidly growing sector of the Chinese economy. The establishment of these institutions was not planned by the central government. Once they are in existence, they are part of the social institutions which the legal system has to take into account. The government has the responsibility of ensuring that the legal system functions properly. In addition, it has its own economic role, which we will come to.

Citizens in a market economy have to take responsibility for the consequences of their own actions. Freedom to take risks is a feature of the market economy. It allows the individual to take economic initiatives and to innovate. Where should the government restrict economic freedom when the consequences are not harmful to others? One example is gambling. Societies often do not have a consistent policy to deal with it. In the United States, casino gambling is in general prohibited, but allowed in certain cities. In Hong Kong, gambling is in general illegal but horse racing and buying stock warrants are popular. Should the government prohibit individuals from taking personal risks, like drinking alcohol, smoking, taking certain drugs, engaging in prostitution, and taking one's own life?

## 20.4   The Economic Role of Government

What kinds of economic activities should be left to the free market and what kinds to the government? In the twentieth century the world has performed some very costly experiments to answer this question. It was once suggested that central planning should dictate what products to produce, how to produce them, how to distribute them, and the prices to charge for them. After experiments in the Soviet Union from the 1920s to 1980s, in eastern Europe, China, North Vietnam, and North Korea after the Second World War, the world has learned that central economic planning is much inferior to the free market. However, there remains much disagreement concerning what kinds of economic activities the government should engage in. The answers vary among countries according to the stage of economic development and cultural tradition. Let us consider briefly six areas of possible economic activity for the government.

First is the building of physical economic infrastructure. Private enterprises are capable of building railways, operating airlines, and constructing toll roads. Even parts of a seaport can be sublet to private enterprises. Postal services are partly supplied by private companies. There are three sets of arguments supporting government participation in providing these goods and services. One is that a private company may not have sufficient human and physical capital or is not willing to bear the risk in undertaking a large project such as building a seaport or constructing a railway, especially during an early stage of economic development. In some developing countries the government has the financial resources and is in the position to hire qualified persons to undertake such a large project; and perhaps do it better than any group of individuals can. The second is that owning a railway or a seaport may give a private company too much monopoly power. The third is that the returns to a large infrastructure project such as a dam cannot be easily collected by a private enterprise. In general the provision of public goods is regarded as within the domain of the government. Granted this role of the government, however, there is no reason to prevent private enterprises from competing in infrastructure-building if they are willing.

Second is the building of social infrastructure, including in particular investment in human capital. One can imagine the government playing no role in the provision of education, with all schools being private. Such a situation prevailed to a large extent in imperial China, when the government administered an examination system but the scholars were trained privately. For historical reasons most primary and secondary schools in the United States are public schools. It is important to distinguish between government funding of primary and secondary school education and providing such education only in public schools. Some have proposed to let the government provide a voucher to the parent of each child of school age. The parent can use the voucher to pay for education in a private or public school of their own choice. Such a voucher system would encourage competition among schools and improve the quality of education. The American public school system is considered by many to be poorly run because there is not enough competition. Hong Kong's education system is almost entirely public at all levels. One wonders whether private schools, perhaps through the voucher system, should be encouraged to develop side by side with public schools to improve the quality of education. We know that private schools have done well in many parts of the world, including private universities in the United States and in China before the 1950s, kindergartens, some primary and secondary schools in Hong Kong, primary schools in some villages and perhaps a few part-time colleges in China. Why not give private schools a better chance to compete in Hong Kong's market economy?

A third area is the provision of welfare, including health and unemployment insurance and retirement pensions. In a purely market economy all such insurance could be provided by private insurance companies according to the law of demand and supply. One reason for government intervention is the alleged inability or unwillingness of some individuals to purchase such insurance for their own protection. If so, this is not a good enough reason to impose government insurance on all individuals in the society. Some or perhaps even most people may prefer to have their own insurance provided by a private company. If such insurance must be compulsory, it may still be better for the individual to choose his own insurance, such as the choice of automobile liability insurance in the United States. A compulsory insurance system, with government subsidy to the poor through vouchers, and leaving room for private insurance to supplement government insurance, may be preferable to having the government providing and administering one insurance system for all.

With regard to welfare provision one important area is public housing. As a supplement to public schools or public housing each family can be given tuition and rental vouchers to pay for the schools and apartments they choose, public or private. Such a solution would prevent economically inefficient housing authorities in the United States from providing poor-quality and high-cost housing to the poor. In Hong Kong the public servants are well trained and service minded. When large groups of poor immigrants arrived in Hong Kong in the 1950s and 1960s many did not have adequate shelter. Government housing was a successful social program. Today the situation has changed. Perhaps some form of a housing voucher system would be desirable and feasible. If such a system is adopted, during the transitional period a tenant of an existing public housing unit is entitled to a voucher of an equivalent rental value. The family can choose to stay in the same unit so that no one is worse off. The family can also use the voucher to pay for another public or private housing unit after adjusting for the difference in rental. This would reduce the waste in housing consumption in Hong Kong when well-to-do tenants of public housing hold on to their apartments, possibly for their relatives, and seek private housing elsewhere. These people would not hold on to the public housing unit if they could use the voucher to pay for another unit.

Fourth, a very serious consequence of exercising economic freedom in a market economy is economic instability. I do not mean to imply that under central planning economic stability would be a less serious issue, but that the government has the responsibility to promote economic stability in either case. Business investments are undertaken under conditions of uncertainty. There are times when many investors lose money. Investors in the Hong Kong real estate market have experienced several cycles in the last four decades. The real estate markets in the United States and Japan have gone through ups and downs in recent years. A more notable illustration is the financial crisis in several east Asian countries since 1997. The crisis in each country, though different, was characterized by many unprofitable investment projects and the resulting bad debts in the banking system, leading to a credit crunch. The government, perhaps with the help of the IMF, was asked to provide external funds and restructure the debts. Changes in financial institutions were also recommended.

Generally speaking, economic fluctuations are a characteristic of a market economy and the government has a role in providing macroeconomic stability. Economists disagree on what the best policies are. They do not fully understand how the macroeconomy works, or they disagree on the objectives, how important price stability is compared with reducing unemployment. Some economists do not even believe unemployment in a market economy to be such a bad thing, since people can decide for themselves whether to work or not, and, in their opinion, most unemployed people choose not to work voluntarily.

Fifth, the government may choose to set up large corporations to compete in domestic and international markets. The common arguments against monopolies when discussing the efficiency of competition within a domestic economy may be somewhat convincing, but as Schumpeter argued, large corporations with some monopoly power have introduced technological innovations and promoted economic development. Furthermore, national monopolies may be required to meet international competition in a globalized economy. The government may need to help private monopolies to be efficient and to manage government corporations so that they compete internationally. Government enterprises are inefficient when there is no financial incentive for the management and when there is no competition. Both shortcomings can be overcome in setting up a government corporation such as a national airline, which is subject to international competition. The government may own shares of the corporation and require it to be managed for profit and provide incentives for its management. Some state enterprises in China seem to be economically efficient when the government separates ownership from management and provides the manager with sufficient incentives. The situation may improve after current reforms to change large state enterprises to shareholding companies with the government holding controlling shares, if management can be provided with better incentives. The incentive problem for management exists in any modern corporation, whether its shares are held by the general public, by private financial institutions, or by government agencies. Government ownership of enterprises is consistent with the principles of a market economy provided that private enterprises can compete on equal terms. There is no need to specify which areas the government should not enter once effective market competition exists.

Sixth, in order to promote development of certain industries the government may provide assistance to the enterprises in those industries through subsidies or transfer of technologies. In so doing the government is presumed to have better knowledge of the future profitability or the social needs of such industries and to have more resources to promote them than the private sector does. This presumption is more likely to hold for a developing economy with highly trained government officials. Through an industrial policy a government can provide conditions for the development of selected industries. Even if the government is not willing to pick the winners it may have sufficient information to decide what basic technology to promote. At the most basic level the government can set up a university which has the capability to provide support in science and technology for industries to draw upon. At the next level the government can sponsor research in universities in particular areas of science and technology that are deemed useful for certain potentially promising industries. The establishment of the Hong Kong University of Science and Technology and the selection of particular areas of research to be supported by the Hong Kong government serve as outstanding examples. The United States government also supports both basic and applied research through the National Science Foundation, the National Institutes of Health, and other government agencies.

Examples of government institutions which transfer and develop technologies for industrial use are the science park in Hong Kong and the Hsinchu Industrial Technology Research Institute in Taiwan. Economists have asked whether the government assistance provided to certain industries may interfere with the rule of fair competition in a market economy. They do not agree on the efficacy of carrying out industrial policies. Two propositions seem less controversial. First, when government officials are better trained in economic affairs, the chance of success is higher. In developing countries, especially mainland China and Taiwan in its less developed stage, the government often has many officials who can make intelligent decisions. Second, the chance of success is higher when the policy is confined to the transfer of technology to the private sector and avoids choosing a specific industry to support.

In the case of China there has been a tradition of government officials helping to promote economic development. In imperial China, and under the influence of Confucianism, a scholar's main mission in life was to pass an official examination at the highest level to become a government official to serve the emperor and the country. The same ideal remains to the present day to some extent. Mr. Liang Yansun, whose *Annals* are quoted here and elsewhere, served the Qing government and the government of the Republic of China. As a government official he established a number of important economic institutions, including the Bank of Communications. Dr. K. T. Li of Taiwan, who served as Minister of Economic Affairs and Minister of Finance, played an important role in establishing the Kaosheung Special Economic Zone to attract foreign investment and the Science-based Industrial Park in Hsinchu for the training of technical personnel and development of hi-tech industries. In China many talented people are in the government. Often entrepreneurs in the private sector do not have sufficient capital or foresight to go into new industries which are subject to economies of scale. There is a need for the government to intervene, as in the case of developing the poor region of western China which I discussed in chapter 10.

## 20.5   The Role of Planning in China's Market Economy

### 20.5.1   Scope of planning

Although China's economy is essentially a market economy, the scope of planning is still quite broad, partly because some top officials still believe in the importance of planning and partly because the bureaucratic structure of planning persists. *The Outline of the 10th Five-Year Plan for Economic and Social Development of the People's Republic of China* passed by the National People's Congress on March 15, 2001, consists of 10 parts: I. Guiding Principles and Objectives; II. Economic Structure (chapter 3, on agriculture, chapter 4 on manufacturing, chapter 5 on services, chapter 6 on telecommunications, chapter 7 on economic infrastructure, chapter 8 on Western development, and chapter 9 on urbanization of rural areas); III. Science, Education, and Human Capital (chapter 10 on technological innovation, chapter 11 on development of education; chapter 12 on development of human capital); IV. Population, Resources, and Environment (chapter 13 on population policy, chapter 14 on protection of resources, chapter 15 on environmental policy); V. Reform and Opening (chapter 16 on reform of the market system, chapter 17 on further opening); VI. People's Livelihood (chapter 18 on employment and social insurance, chapter 19 on people's income and living standard); VII. Spiritual Civilization (chapter 20 on development of ethical ideals, chapter 21 on promotion of a socialist civilization); VIII. Democracy and the Rule of Law (chapter 22 on the promotion of democracy, chapter 23 on the establishment of the rule of law); IX. National Defense; and X. Plan Realization (chapter 25 on improvement of macro control mechanisms to promote economic stability and growth, chapter 26 on devising means to carry out the plan).

The scope of this Plan is broad and comprehensive. In section 20.4 I discuss six economic functions of the government in a market economy. If we go through all the chapter headings of the Tenth Five-Year Plan listed above, we can fit each of them into one of these six functions. In doing so we have to define "social infrastructure" in the second function to include the building of a spiritual civilization (Part VII) and the promotion of democracy and the rule of law (Part VIII). This means that, although the scope of the activities of the Chinese government included in the Tenth Five-Year Plan is broad, all activities are in principle within what a government should do in a market economy as one of its six functions. The main question is the extent to which the government should engage in each of the activities. I will try to answer this question in section 20.5.4 below.

## 20.5.2    The administration of plan formulation and plan implementation

China has two basic plans, including the Five-Year Plan and plans for urban and spatial developments, as well as a third plan which is a guidance plan. The following discussion will concentrate on the Five-Year Plan and include the other two plans as parts of its components, as the current Tenth Five-Year Plan does.

In the late 1990s the Commission for Restructuring the Economic System and the Planning Commission were combined into the State Planning and Reform Commission, later renamed the National Development and Reform Commission (NDRC), partly to reflect that China has a market economy and not a planned economy. The NDRC has the responsibility for drawing up the Five-Year Plan. In doing so it can seek inputs from all relevant ministries and organizations of the State Council. The latter can in turn solicit information from provincial and lower-level governments if necessary. There are two components in the proposal submitted by each ministry or organization, one requiring central government action and financing (to be included in its budget), and the remainder to be left to provincial governments (which in turn need to coordinate and direct local governments under their jurisdiction) or to market forces (as a part of guidance planning and requiring only limited government financing). Hence all three plans mentioned above are included.

The Minister of the NDRC and its staff will draw up a proposed plan taking into account all the inputs from the different ministries. As is well known, different ministries such as Agriculture and Education have a tendency to promote the development of their own sector. The resolution of conflicts given the limitation of economic resources is done first by the NDRC based on its knowledge and understanding of national priorities, and ultimately by the Premier in consultation with the relevant Vice-premiers and State Councilors at appropriate meetings. The same principle applies to the coordination of economic development plans and urban related plans, and of national and local plans.

Although China is a market economy today, much of the administrative process for plan formulation before 1978 is applicable. Only the content of the plan is different. In a market economy, many of the productive and distributive activities are no longer included in the plan. The number of industrial ministries in the State Council has been greatly reduced. Previously the State Planning Commission had to coordinate the outputs and inputs of state-owned enterprises, whereas in the current set-up the inputs of plan formulation are targets from ministries on projects under their control. However, the need to coordinate the demands from different ministries or from different provincial governments, to determine priorities and to come up with a final consistent plan, still remains. The NDRC needs to make sure that all parts of the plan are consistent. Since the other two types of plans for urban and spatial developments and for guidance planning are already embedded in the Five-Year Plan, there is an integrated plan. The administration for carrying out different parts of the plan, however, can be decentralized and left to different ministries of the State Council. Each can suggest or even make revisions based on changing circumstances, and at time intervals considered most desirable for the activities under its control.

In terms of plan implementation, the ministries or organizations which submit inputs to a proposed plan have the responsibility of seeing through its realization or its revision as circumstances may require. If provincial governments also have planning agencies covering a similar area (such as agriculture or education), the ministries at the State Council should have the authority to coordinate and direct their activities. One concern of members of the current NDRC is that its decisions may not be sufficiently respected by provincial and local officials. They have expressed a desire for new legislation to give the Commission authorities on specific planning matters, rather than relying merely on the Constitution that gives the State Council administrative authority to "draw up and implement the plan for national economic and social development," and to "direct and administer economic work and urban and rural development." (See Article 89, points 5 and 6.) Much of the difficulty in plan implementation may lie in the existence of local power and vested interests that are difficult for the central government to control. Two well-known examples in China are the difficulties of the central government in controlling certain provincial governments which traditionally behave fairly independently, and to control the local bureaucrats who tend to extract payments from farmers, or refuse to pay wages to local workers engaged in building national construction projects or to pay for farm products. There are sufficient laws and regulations to prohibit all these activities, but the abuse of power continues.

### 20.5.3   Methods of planning and of plan execution

Methods of planning and of plan execution are summarized in the last two chapters in Part X of the Tenth Five-Year Plan. In that plan, chapter 25 deals with macroeconomic control mechanisms for stability and growth; chapter 26 deals with mechanisms to achieve other plan objectives.

First, on the macroeconomic control mechanism, China has made much progress through the reform of its banking and financial system and of its fiscal system, partly for the effective execution of monetary and fiscal policies (as we discussed in chapters 4 and 7). The reform enables the Chinese government to carry out monetary policy through the control of money supply, the interest rate, and the foreign exchange rate. The latter reform provides revenue for the execution of fiscal policy. The Chinese government has tried to apply both monetary and fiscal policy to achieve price stability and economic growth. The term "macroeconomic control mechanism" includes administrative means to control specific investment or industrial projects in order to influence aggregate output as well as allocation of resources. The Tenth Five-Year Plan sets targets for GDP growth at a 7 percent annual rate, for a stable price level, an urban unemployment rate of 5 percent, and other targets. It is up to the State Council to achieve these objectives. In reality real GDP grew faster in 2001–4 than the 7 percent target.

Second, on mechanisms to enforce other planning objectives, the Chinese government uses a combination of administrative orders carried out by the responsible ministries of the State Council, directions to provincial, city, county, and local governments to fulfill certain parts of the plan, and solicitations of support from the Chinese people to cooperate. As an example, to improve the education system in China as specified by the plan, all three methods are employed. The last includes the encouragement and fostering of people-operated schools at all levels.

One unsolved problem in carrying out projects that involve large sums of money is to ensure that the money is effectively utilized. There are at least two sources of economic waste and inefficiency. One is the lack of rational planning. This aspect can be improved by applying the method of project evaluation, which provides a cost and benefit analysis to determine the economic worth of a project. Many projects are desirable if we consider only their benefits to society, without regard for the costs. In China many major projects, including the Three Gorges Project, have been decided mainly by political leaders, without careful deliberation by experts concerning their costs and benefits in the long run. The second is the possibility of corruption. Money is wasted when it goes through the hands of government bureaucrats. As examples, although many people think that the Three Gorges Project and the Western [China] Development Plan are good ideas, it is difficult to determine whether each is worth the money spent and how much of the spending goes to corruption.

One way to reduce corruption is to reduce the levels of government economic activities which can breed corruption. Another is to narrow the scope of government authorities in regulating the private sector, such as the granting of licenses and permits to operate private businesses, which provide bureaucrats opportunities for corruption. When the Chinese government has to carry out a project to build infrastructure, it has often auctioned the project to private entrepreneurs. Well-known examples include the building of a superhighway connecting Guangzhou and Hong Kong, the building of power plants, and the encouragement of foreign investors to participate in the Western Development Project. To the extent that government bureaucrats have authority to approve parts of each project, corruption can occur. Some local government officials may utilize every opportunity to extract payments from private investors. The central government has the legal authority to prevent them from doing so, but in reality finds it difficult to exercise this authority.

### 20.5.4  The coordination with market forces

Many officials in the Chinese government understand the coordination of government activities and market forces. There is no need to specify which economic activities belong to the government and which to the private sector. One major principle that the government has followed is to foster the market sector to supplement and to discipline government economic activities. The nonstate sectors of China's economy have grown rapidly to supply the output needed. In the meantime they provide competition to Chinese state-owned enterprises to make them more efficient and to force them to adopt new technology. Similarly, while the Chinese government has ownership of the majority of schools, it encourages the establishment or operation of nongovernment-operated schools to provide more educational services to the population and to provide competition to government-operated schools.

The same principle has been and can be applied to other aspects of planning. In developing any selected industry, such as a high-tech industry, or in promoting state enterprises in that industry as a part of an industrial policy, the Chinese government leaves room for and even subsidizes the simultaneous development of the private sector. The success of the privately owned Legend in producing personal computers and of Gus Tsao in developing the software Evermore Integrated Office to compete with Microsoft are outstanding examples. This principle is consistent with the Chinese planning system.

How large should the scope of planning be in China? The answer depends partly on the level of China's economic and social development. As China becomes more developed and its market economy becomes more mature, the private sector will become better informed and more resourceful in developing the economy and discovering new industries to go into, and there will be less need for government involvement. We do not have to answer the above theoretical question in the abstract. The answer in practice is to enforce the principle that all state enterprises subsidized under a planned industrial policy have to be disciplined by the market, financially independent, and subject to competition from nonstate enterprises on an equal footing. Any ministry requesting funds from a plan to develop new industries and enterprises needs to make a convincing argument to the NDRC that such funding is justified. In approving funds for each project, the ministry concerned should follow the principle that each enterprise only receives a fixed amount as start-up costs for the project and has to be financially profitable afterwards, and that state-owned and nonstate enterprises can compete for the initial subsidy to start the project on an equal footing. The past financial record of enterprises, state and nonstate, that are financed by any ministry can be used to determine the amount of funding they will receive in the next government budget and the next Five-Year Plan. Coordination of planned activities and market activities for economic and social development is achieved mainly by competition and by the limitation on the amount of subsidy provided to each enterprise in an industrial policy. Past records should be used as a guide for future appropriations under the plan. Of course the above principles sound good on paper, but are hard to put in practice when self-interested bureaucrats are required to carry them out. Again this speaks for narrowing the scope of planning and government control of economic activities.

## 20.6   The Government's Decision Process

We can discuss the pros and cons of government participation in specific areas of the market economy in principle. What the government decides in practice depends not only on economic principles but perhaps more often on the process by which the government makes its decisions. The government's decision process in turn depends on the form of government.

To illustrate by an example, Hong Kong is governed under the principle of "one country two systems." As far as the two economic systems are concerned there is much similarity between Hong Kong and China. Both are market economic systems. The Hong Kong economic system is more mature, as a free market and the associated legal institutions have been in existence for over a century. The two political systems are more different. China's is a one-party system. It is in the process of development toward a democratic government, as the leaders of China have repeatedly proclaimed and partially achieved. Witness the expansion of local elections and delegation of more power to the People's Congress. Hong Kong's is built upon a former colonial system and is also in the process of transformation to a democratic government. It is a local and not a national government. Because the people in Hong Kong are better educated and the rule of law has been practiced longer than in China, one can expect the development of democracy to advance faster in Hong Kong. The two democracies may turn out to be different in the near future. In both Hong Kong and China this development will take time. Progress toward a democratic government in Hong Kong will provide an important example for the development of democracy in China. Chinese leaders will not copy the Hong Kong model, but as always they will learn from the valuable experience in other parts of the world.

Before 1997 in both Hong Kong and China decisions were made by a government which was not democratically elected. Both economies functioned extremely well for two decades, and Hong Kong's for even longer. It is reasonable to surmise that under a democratic government neither economy could have done better. The question is, as democracy is being gradually introduced, will the government do worse in performing its economic functions? I raise this important question not because I believe that democracy will have harmful effects on the functioning of a free-market economy. After all, many free-market economies have been developed under or alongside democratic institutions. I raise this question to underline some possible developments which, if left unchecked, can adversely affect the free-market economic system under a democratic government. Awareness of these possibilities might help us prevent them from occurring.

One ideal of a democracy is to give political rights to its citizens. To exercise these rights public elections are held to select government officials who will make economic and other decisions. The election procedure is not without its shortcomings. The votes of poor or uninterested citizens can be and have been purchased. Even in the United States there are problems with improper campaign financing and money can unduly influence the outcome of elections. Once legislators are elected, decision by majority rule can be in conflict with minority rights. A simple example is a highly progressive income tax passed by a legislature which is inconsistent with the property rights of high-income citizens. Hong Kong's flat tax of about 17 percent levied only on wages above a certain level and not on capital gains is an important feature of its free-market system. This flat tax has probably contributed to the vitality of its economy through more savings and more investment. It is doubtful whether such a tax system would have been enacted if the Hong Kong legislature had been democratically elected and given authority on income taxation. One hopes that future legislation on income tax in China takes the negative effects of income tax into consideration, and that other forms of taxation such as a consumption tax or a flat tax similar to Hong Kong's will be seriously considered. The democratic political process has the tendency to redistribute income through taxation, perhaps without sufficient regard for the incentive effects. When income is earned, goods and services are produced. Why tax people for earning income or for producing? In lieu of an income tax, a tax on consumption encourages saving and makes possible a higher rate of capital accumulation.

Under a market system economic gains can be obtained mainly by competition in the marketplace. In a democracy, to the extent that the government has economic power to allocate resources, political forces determine the economic benefits to different members of the society. In the United States there are lobbyists to represent different economic interest groups. Tobacco farmers want and get government subsidies. The defense industry fights for more spending on defense. Laws are passed to satisfy these interest groups. In Hong Kong, now that both the chief executive and the legislators are elected, they are bound to be influenced by political pressure to make economic decisions not necessarily for the common good but for the benefit of special interest groups. Let us hope that they can resist such pressure.

Whatever the ideal lines to be drawn between government and private economic activities might be, and I have suggested that there might not need to be such lines, even a democratically elected government has a tendency to increase the sphere of government influence. This can be the result of political pressure from interest groups or of the desire of government officials to increase their power or simply to show their superior performance. A minister of education may wish to demonstrate his performance by setting up some new programs or even a new university, and the benefits of these initiatives often cannot be measured during his tenure. Given such temptations the Chinese government under Premier Zhu Rongji deserves much credit in the downsizing of the State Council by reducing the number of ministries from 40 to 29 in the late 1990s. We will all observe with interest future changes in the size of the Hong Kong government, especially those parts that deal with economic affairs, and find out whether the changes, if they occur, are justified.

An intrinsic problem in human society is to find the delicate balance between individual self-interest and the good of society. In schools in Hong Kong and China students are taught to give up self-interest for the common good. Individualism is sometimes identified with selfishness and treated as a bad thing. When we study economics we learn that under a free-market system we can all pursue our self-interest and at the same time benefit society. However, the harmony of individual self-interest and the welfare of society cannot be expected to operate automatically. In sections 20.3, 20.4, and 20.6 I have discussed the rules of the game which need to be specified and enforced properly for the market economy to function, the possible limits of the market economic system that justified government intervention, and the relation between the nature of government intervention and democracy.

# References and Further Reading

Alford, William. "Will the Rule of Law Really Rule?" Paper presented before the Conference on China at the Center for Research on Economic Development and Policy Research, Stanford University, Nov. 18–20, 1999.

*Annals of Mr. Liang Yansun of Sanshui*, 2 vols. (in Chinese). Hong Kong, private publication, 1939. Reissued as a Monograph in the "Modern Chinese Historical Series." Taipei: Wenxing Book Co., 1962.

# Questions

1   Describe briefly the legal system prevailing in China prior to 1949.
2   What are the main features of the Chinese legal system since 1949?
3   Describe the important elements of reform which the Chinese government has introduced to improve the legal system.
4   What are the limitations of reforms introduced to the legal system in China?
5   Name the major possible shortcomings in introducing a Western-style legal system to China.
6   Discuss the possible impact of China's joining the WTO on its legal institutions.
7   What is the role of the legal system in the proper functioning of a market economy?
8   What is the proper role of the government in a free-market economy?
9   Are there relations between the form of government, such as democracy or a one-party system, and the functioning of a free-market economy? Parts of the answer could come from the last part of chapter 16.
10   Is there any conflict between the leadership of the Communist Party and the idea that all people are equal under the law and no one is above it? Explain your answer.

# 21

# The Education System and Policy

After a brief review of the education system before and after 1949, this chapter discusses education policy in section 21.3. Economics education at the university level is discussed at length in section 21.4, covering the introduction of modern economics into Chinese universities, the current status, the choice of economics curriculum, possible ways to improve the teaching of economics, and the status of economists as a profession in China. Section 21.5 describes the important role of private spending in education, and applies demand analysis to explain why expenditure on education has increased dramatically from 1998 to 2002, and why tuition and other expenses per student have gone up. Concluding remarks are contained in section 21.6.

## 21.1 The Education System prior to 1949

Traditional Chinese culture has emphasized learning for over 2,000 years. Confucius stated before 500 BC, "knowledge is acquired through observations and knowledge is required to lead a disciplined life, to head a family and finally to govern a country." In the later part of the Han dynasty, Confucianism was adopted as the main school of teaching in China, perhaps to establish an orderly society, as he advocated, and one that is easy to govern. Later an examination system was introduced to select government officials. Studying Confucius and related classics and learning to write essays about ethics, philosophy, literature, and political ideas were necessary to pass the examinations. Government jobs were assigned according to grades on the examinations. Although scholarship was the activity of only a minority of the Chinese population that consisted mostly of farmers, all Chinese families, rich and poor, had a desire to provide education to their children so that they could get ahead in society. For most people, to get ahead meant to pass an official examination and get a government position. This was more important than to get rich through commerce because the social status of government officials was higher, and wealth came with government positions.

The Chinese are very proud of their cultural tradition until the Opium War of 1840, when they were defeated by the British. They also were defeated by and had to make concessions to other European countries between 1840 and 1895, including Japan after the Sino-Japanese War. During this period Chinese leaders began to reexamine the adequacy of traditional Chinese education in dealing with the Western impact. It was soon recognized that science and technology had to be incorporated into the Chinese education system for China to modernize and to compete with the powerful nations. Modern education was introduced into China through the effort of Western missionaries and through government policy. My own alma mater, Lingnan University in Guangzhou, was founded by American missionaries in 1888. Beijing University was founded in 1896 by the Qing government. Beginning with a mixture of traditional and modern education, by the 1930s the Chinese educational system resembled the American system, with six years of primary school, six years of junior and senior high school, and four years of university education available only to a small minority of high-school graduates. Besides public universities under the national or provincial governments, there were a number of private universities, many founded by American or French missionaries. Public and private primary and high schools existed hand in hand. The public schools were financed by local governments and charged a lower tuition. The well-to-do tended to send their children to better and more expensive private schools, which also had scholarships for students from poor families.

The Chinese education system in the 1920s and 1930s was remarkably good considering the political disruptions and instability described in section 1.3. After the war with Japan started in 1937, the Chinese government moved to the wartime capital of Chungking (now Chongqing) in Sichuan province. Many high schools and universities moved to the interior also. Teaching went on and students continued to study during the war, even when there was not enough electric light and students could hear the Japanese bombing. The education system soon recovered after the end of the Second World War in August 1945.

A description of the Chinese education system before 1949, however brief, should include mentioning the freedom of inquiry and the respect for scholars. Despite political disruptions in the 1920s and 1930s, education in science and engineering continued to improve and scholars continued to engage in public discourse on politics, literature, and philosophy. New journals were published to discuss ideas in the humanities. There was freedom to express and publish different ideas. Scholars were respected in the society. After the Second World War China had serious inflation and national output did not recover to the prewar level. Nor did compensation to teachers and scholars reach prewar levels. Low economic status probably had a negative effect on the psychological well-being of the scholars and on their position in society.

## 21.2 The Education System after 1949

Briefly speaking, university education was changed to the Soviet system in about 1952 and returned to the former system to a large extent, but under government control, during the latter part of the 1980s and the 1990s. Governments at different levels began to monopolize education in the early 1950s, but privately funded education conducted under the framework of state education flourished in the 1980s and 1990s. In 1952 all private universities were abolished and the university system was modeled after the Soviet Union. Higher education changed from a general, liberal education to a narrowly focused professional education. Universities were divided into different units with their own special fields of study. Some universities offered liberal arts courses while others offered engineering courses, and still others became colleges for special areas like agriculture. Specialized colleges were under the supervision of a ministry in order to train graduates in the disciplines required by the ministry. For example, the People's Bank had and still has its own graduate school. By the late 1990s, however, the system had been reversed back to something like the previous system. Specialized colleges and universities were combined so that they became large universities offering a variety of subjects.

## 21.3 Education Policy

Before going into the substance of education policy, it is useful to point out that the amount of public expenditure on education as a percentage of GDP is low in China compared with other countries. In 1995 the percentage was 2.5, compared with the world average of 5.2, and 5.4, 4.8, 5.4, 3.4, 4.1, and 2.8 for the United States, Germany, the United Kingdom, India, Thailand, and Pakistan respectively (see the *Statistical Yearbook of China, 1999*, appendix 3, table 3-17). Of the total expenditure on education of 226.23 billion yuan in 1996, only 24.587 billion was by the central government and the remainder by local governments (*Statistical Yearbook of China, 1997*, p. 670). Also, rural education is much more limited than urban: expenditure per student in urban areas is about four times that in rural areas. However, the role of nongovernment-funded education in China should be taken into account in evaluating the total resources devoted to education. In the last two decades up to 2002, nongovernment-funded education established through the government education system at all levels has flourished. The nongovernment-funded sector includes (1) certain public schools assigned to nongovernment operation and (2) private schools. Any public and privately operated schools can also collect tuition and fees under their own initiative. Such funding accounted for close to 50 percent of total education spending in 2002, while the ratio of educational spending to GDP had increased to 5.21 percent from 3.46 percent in 1997. This can be explained by the factors of demand for education, namely relative price and real income (see Chow and Shen 2005 for a discussion).

To measure the level of education attained by the Chinese people data are available from the *Statistical Yearbook of China, 1997* (pp. 76–9), based on a 1.028 percent sample of 1,246,243 persons taken in 1996. Among the population aged 15 and over, 17.82 percent were illiterate or semiliterate, 10.12 percent among males and 25.54 percent among females. The numbers of persons in the sample having had primary school education, junior secondary school, senior secondary school, and college and higher level were respectively 470,880, 358,780, 107,344, and 25,422. These absolute numbers can be converted into percentages of population reaching the corresponding graduating age. Of the 1,246,243 persons in the sample there were 322,330 persons aged 0–14, 837,470 persons aged 15–64, and 86,443 persons aged 65 and over. There were thus 923,913 persons aged 15 or over. This number can be used to divide the numbers of persons having primary school and junior secondary school education to yield respectively 50.97 and 38.83 percent. To estimate the number of persons aged 25 and over in the sample, let us subtract two-thirds of 322, 330, or 214,887, as persons aged between 15 and 24, from the 923,913 of persons aged 15 and over to yield 709,026. Using this as the denominator we find 15.14 percent having had senior secondary school and only 3.585 percent having had college-level education. (The 15.14 percent is an overestimate because the denominator should be population of age 18 and higher, and not 25 and higher.) Very few rural children go to senior secondary school. In 1998 only 4 percent of junior secondary school graduates in rural areas were enrolled in senior secondary school, compared with 29 percent in urban areas.

To summarize the education level of the population in China, the percentage of illiterate or semiliterate persons is about 18 percent, 10 percent among males and 26 percent among females. Attainment of primary school, junior secondary school, senior secondary school, and college was respectively 51, 39, 15, and 3.59 percent. Thus the degree of attainment dropped off rapidly for senior secondary school and even more rapidly for college level. The 3.59 percent of college-level attainment was low. The corresponding percentage was 46.5 in 1994 for the United States, 2.5 in 1981 for India, 5.1 in 1990 for Thailand, 7.6 in 1995 for Singapore, and 2.5 in 1990 for Pakistan (see appendix table 3-16 of the *China Statistical Yearbook, 1999*, data based on *United Nations Educational, Scientific, and Cultural Organization Statistical Yearbook, 1998*). Thus at this stage, with the people attaining a fairly low level of education, the Chinese government has been spending a relatively small amount of its expenditures on education.

Concerning the substance of education policy, four important areas can be discussed. First is the possible improvement of public educational institutions. Much improvement has been achieved since economic reform started. One contributing factor of this improvement is the willingness of Chinese educators to learn from the experiences of other countries. Foreign scholars have been invited to lecture in China on a large scale. Chinese students have been sent abroad by the government and have been allowed to study abroad through a liberal policy. The high and improved quality of graduate students from China has been witnessed by professors at foreign universities which Chinese graduate students attend. A second contributing factor is the moderately liberal policy in the administration of higher educational institutions in China. For example, although national university presidents are formally appointed by the Ministry of Education, in practice, representatives of the Ministry would visit the university to take a vote of the faculty members as the basis of making the appointment. Much flexibility has been given to university administrators in the administration of their respective universities. Perhaps even more flexibility is desirable, and it is being contemplated. It seems desirable to have more autonomy and flexibility in decisions regarding tuition, faculty salaries, student enrollment, and faculty allocation in different departments, and, most importantly, to have the ability to lay off staff and faculty members. Chinese universities are overstaffed. Staff and faculty members have in effect lifetime contracts; whereas in state enterprises this "iron rice bowl" system has been gradually broken down. The same reform needs to be carried out at universities in order to improve the quality and efficiency of educational services.

Second is the establishment of educational institutions initiated and financially supported by nonstate sources at the primary, secondary and higher levels (see Chow and Shen 2005). It is remarkable to see the flow of private funds to finance education at all levels under the state education system all over China in the last two decades under a liberal government policy. One can cite a number of successful nonstate and privately funded educational institutions at all levels. Since primary and junior high school education is compulsory and is the responsibility of the government, private kindergartens and senior high schools are allowed, as are cooperative ventures for higher educational institutions. One well-known example is the Nanjing University–Johns Hopkins cooperative program. Some of the nonstate financed schools charge very high tuition fees and provide very high-quality education. They are sometimes very profitable. The current government policy is to encourage the establishment of privately funded universities. These universities can help absorb some of the excess personnel of state universities, especially when the commercialization of university housing progresses to a greater extent. Perhaps more effort could be beneficially made to subsidize such universities, by providing them with land or some initial grant or low-interest loan in the formation stage.

Third, on the financing of education and research, the government has set a number of carefully considered policies and set up institutions such as the National Natural Science Foundation to carry them out. The policy to award research grants has been to concentrate on a small number of very promising projects. Peer review is being practiced. Under the same principle, the limited amount of government funds could be used to build up or support only a very small number of projects or research institutions. At the same time, government budgetary appropriation to universities can be made dependent on performance and market demand.

Fourth is the development and application of modern technology for education. An extremely promising area is the development and eventual widespread application of the internet for education at all levels. This could solve the problems of the small number of high-quality educational personnel and the need to educate the large number of students in many underdeveloped parts of China. China is in a position to develop the internet, and can use it to reach the forefront of education, as there is not much inertia to hinder its development as in an educationally more advanced country. At an international conference on "science, technology and education for the betterment of the national economy" held in Beijing in August 1999, Professor Binglin Zhong, Director General of the Department of Higher Education of the Ministry of Education, mentioned the development of the internet as an important project for the improvement of education. This is also potentially an area of cooperation with educators and researchers in other countries, including Taiwan.

One important development in the policy towards higher education at the turn of the century is the effort to raise the level of a few selected top universities by spending a vast amount of money, in the order of 50 billion yuan for one university. The idea that a few top universities can play an important role in leading research and education in the entire country appears to be a sound one. In science and education it is the quality of the top institutions that pave the way for the rest to follow. However, the means to improve the quality of the top Chinese universities in the short time of several years might not be appropriate and realistic. It takes a long time for a university with an existing faculty and tradition to change. The research ability of the incumbent faculty cannot be improved easily, and new faculty members of very high quality are very difficult to recruit from abroad. More money spent by one university to recruit faculty members from another university only leads to lowering of the standard of the second university. Simply spending a lot of money on the existing faculty members in China and on physical equipment cannot do much to improve research and education in China, at least not to the extent of being able to compete with the top American universities within a decade or two.

Since the above was written for the first edition, the development of a few top universities in China has been more rapid than I expected. By offering internationally competitive salaries and special working conditions, Qinghua University was able to attract faculty members on a full-time basis from Princeton University in 2004, in addition to a number of faculty members from top American universities to teach courses on a part-time basis.

Besides the improvement of the education system in China, one way to acquire talented people for China's economic development is the effective utilization of the existing personnel. A well-recognized source of such personnel is the large number of Chinese professionals working overseas. The Chinese government and many Chinese institutions have made various attempts to encourage them to return to China. The improvement of the educational system along the four aspects as discussed above will help provide more opportunities and a better working environment to induce more people to return. For example the privatization of housing, the flexibility of the salary scale (aided by the initiation in 2000 of some 200 distinguished professorships, each paying an annual salary of 100,000 RMB, followed by over 20 professorships in Qinghua University in 2002, each paying an annual salary of 1 million RMB), and the decrease in restrictions to travel abroad are all helpful. The flexibility mentioned could be further improved. On the right to travel abroad alone, the current restrictions in terms of approval by the university administration, the Ministry of Education, and the passport office are still much more severe than what is customary for someone used to living elsewhere. All this is a part of the working environment affecting the decision of overseas Chinese to return and of foreign scholars to work in China.

Overseas Chinese have also been invited to pay short-term visits to lecture, consult, and perform other duties. Perhaps an even greater effort could be made to identify such individuals who would be willing and are capable. Foreign nationals should also be included. Channels of communication with such individuals could be further developed. Cooperation could take various forms, including short-term or long-term appointments as consultants or as members of committees or advisory boards. Many more individuals would be willing to serve if opportunities were provided for them to realize their ideals, and if their work could make an important contribution.

## 21.4   Economics Education

This section provides a brief history of the introduction of modern economics education to China and discusses the current status of teaching the subject. It also deals with the choice of curriculum and problems in improving the current system. Finally, the practice of modern economics as a profession in China is assessed.

China opened its door in 1979 when only Marxian and socialist economics was taught at its universities. In the last two decades much progress has been made in reforming its economic institutions towards a market economy and reforming the teaching of economics towards modern economics. In the early 2000s perhaps about 70 percent of institutional reforms in both the economic system and in the teaching of economics have been accomplished. Of course this does not mean that the level of development of the economy or of economics teaching and research is 70 percent of the level of a developed country, but only the institutions. The success can be attributed to the government's open-door and market-oriented reform policy under Deng's leadership, the efforts of Chinese officials and scholars, and cooperation of foreign friends. Section 21.4.1 will review how modern economics was introduced in China. The current status of the teaching of modern economics is discussed in section 21.4.2. Problems in the choice of curriculum are the subject of section 21.4.3. Section 21.4.4 deals with issues in improving the current system, and section 21.4.5 with the use of modern economics or economics as a profession. Section 21.4.6 provides some concluding remarks.

### 21.4.1   How modern economics was introduced

To understand the rapid progress that has taken place in the teaching of modern economics in China one has to understand the way that it was developed. The main driving force for progress was the willingness and determination of government officials in charge of economics education and research to embrace modern economics. They first wanted to understand what it is, and then decided to adopt essentially all of it in the university curriculum and for the purpose of research. This was a consequence of the open-door policy under the leadership of Deng Xiaoping. Once given the opportunity to learn modern economics, teachers and students in China studied it eagerly. The rate of progress has been limited only by the financial resources required to invite qualified economists to teach or to conduct joint research in China. There has been no lack of willingness to learn and adopt.

When China established diplomatic relations with the United States in 1979, the teaching of economics was entirely Marxian and socialist in content and contained no modern economic theory and empirical analysis. Economics was treated as a philosophy rather than a science. There was no written material in university libraries on any aspect of the Chinese economy, and professors of economics did not conduct empirical research on China. An important landmark in the development of modern economics was a workshop on econometrics in the summer of 1980 sponsored by the Chinese Academy of Social Science, with its Vice-president Xu Dixin as host. Lawrence Klein was the organizer. He had visited China in 1979 to negotiate with Xu on this workshop. Six other lecturers including T. W. Anderson, Albert Ando, Gregory Chow, Cheng Hsiao, Lawrence Lau, and Vincent Su also participated. About 95 researchers and teachers aged up to the sixties attended. Econometrics was introduced first because it was considered politically neutral and input–output analysis had already been applied to economic planning in China. In 1980–5 there was a program to teach applied economics in Dalian, with 50 percent financing by the US Department of Commerce and the Asia Society and the remaining 50 percent by the Chinese government.

In 1983, a delegation from the Ministry of Education led by Wang Fusun and Wang Zenong, respectively Director of International Cooperation and Director of Law and Economics, visited the United States with the purpose of modernizing the teaching of law and economics. While the delegation visited Princeton University it was decided to have the Ministry sponsor three summer workshops for university teachers of economics in 1984–6 on microeconomics, macroeconomics, and econometrics respectively, with Gregory Chow as the organizer. During the 1984 workshop in Beijing, Premier Zhao Ziyang met with Chow and the report of their meeting in the *People's Daily* of July 6 signaled the official acceptance of the teaching of modern economics in China. The term "modern economics" was introduced to replace the prevailing term "Western economics." Later in July 1984, the Ministry of Education accepted Chow's proposal to select graduate students nationwide to pursue PhD degrees in economics in the United States and Canada. The students had to pass an examination in economics based on Chow (1985); most of them were majors of science, engineering, or mathematics. About 65 students so selected entered over 40 graduate schools in the US and Canada in the fall of 1985. The program continued till 1998. The students were selected entirely by merit with no regard for personal connections. By 2004, many of these students have established themselves professionally in the United States, mainland China, Hong Kong, and other parts of the world.

In 1985, with financial support from the Ford Foundation, the US Committee on Economics Education and Research in China was formed to cooperate with the Chinese Committee on Economics Exchanges with the US, appointed by the Chinese State Education Commission (the Ministry of Education until early 1985). The US Committee was co-chaired by Gregory Chow and Dwight Perkins, with Robert Dernberger, D. Gale Johnson, Lawrence Klein, Lawrence Lau, and Herbert Simon as members. The Chinese Committee was chaired by Vice-president and later President Huang Da of the People's University, and consisted of representatives of seven major universities. The programs supported by these Committees included a one-year graduate economics training center at the People's University from 1985 to 1996 and a similar center at Fudan University from 1988 to 1993, summer workshops, financial aid to Chinese visiting scholars and to graduate students studying abroad, and research grants to joint research projects with the Chinese Academy of Social Science. In 1987, a group of economists from the US, UK, Canada, Germany, and Japan visited China under the sponsorship of the World Bank to study the economics curriculum in China and made recommendations for reform. As a result, the State Education Commission adopted a number of core courses in economics to be taught at the major universities under its supervision, including microeconomics, macroeconomics, statistics, accounting, public finance, money and banking, development economics, and international trade. These courses would be taught in addition to Marxian and socialist economics. The adoption of these core courses was followed by the appointment of a committee of economists to write texts on modern economics similar to those used in the United States.

Thus through the willingness and efforts of both Chinese officials and educators and of foreign economists and organizations, the teaching of modern economics was firmly established in China by the second half of the 1980s. More details on the history can be found in Chow (1994, chs. 4 and 5).

### 21.4.2 Current status

The fact that modern economics is officially accepted and firmly established in China does not imply that its teaching is in a satisfactory state. The curriculum, the staffing, and the education system itself are not as modern as one would like.

Concerning the curriculum, although many courses in modern economics have been introduced, the degree of adoption is uneven and the contents of individual courses vary among universities. Some important courses are missing at certain universities and courses of the same title vary a great deal in content. The latter could be a desirable feature, as it indicates the freedom in teaching, but in the present case it reflects more the inability of the teacher to cover the relevant material. Traditional Marxian economics courses also take up the students' time at the expense of modern economics. As a general observation there are fewer theoretical courses such as game theory and mathematical economics being offered compared with the US departments, partly because of the lack of qualified teachers. In their place there are some very applied courses such as foreign insurance, operation of the US capital market, international marketing, and other management courses. Mathematics courses including calculus, linear algebra, and probability and statistics are required in the undergraduate economics curriculum, but mathematics is in general not effectively used and integrated in teaching and research in economics. The most up-to-date foreign texts are used to a limited extent, and the availability of computers is still limited, although China has placed great emphasis on the development and application of the personal computer.

The major factor affecting the curriculum and the quality of teaching is the availability of qualified teachers. This problem will take a long time to solve as it is difficult and time-consuming to train a large number of qualified teachers. When the State Education

Commission issued its decision to introduce the core courses in modern economics, it had to allow time for these courses to be placed in the announcements and for the quality of teaching to reach acceptable levels. There is also the personnel problem of retraining existing economics teachers and researchers and convincing them to accept modern economics and work with the new and often younger teachers of modern economics. There has been a natural resistance among some of these teachers, but this problem has been gradually overcome, as the acceptance of a market economy has gained momentum rapidly since the early 1980s. If the former economics teachers cannot teach modern economics, they can teach institutional and applied material concerning the current Chinese economy. Most of them retired by the latter part of the 1990s.

The education system itself is an important factor affecting the teaching of modern economics. In the 1950s, China adopted the higher education system from the Soviet Union. The system de-emphasized liberal college education and compartmentalized the teaching of different applied subjects in different schools under the control of different government units or ministries for technical training. Each of many industrial ministries and many of its branches at the provincial and city levels have their own schools to train the required personnel. The People's Bank of China and the Chinese Academy of Social Science have their own graduate schools offering training in economics. This has resulted in large differences in quality and content among different graduate schools of economics. Economics itself was not offered as a discipline, but under different specialties such as international economics, economic theory (having a different content from ours), and public finance which form different departments of their own, without the recognition that the same set of ideas and tools are applicable to all. In general students are loaded with course work, with over 20 hours of lectures per week compared with about 15 in the United States. Time is devoted to studying and memorizing lecture material and assigned reading, and less to problem-solving and creative thinking.

In China, a master's degree takes two and a half to three years as an official requirement. At the PhD level, the degree is granted at the discretion of only one faculty member. There is a lack of quality control exercised by PhD general or qualifying examinations and by other members of the faculty serving as thesis committee members. At the major universities under its control the Ministry of Education (transformed in 1998 from the State Education Commission) has approved only a small number of professors, usually from none to at most two in one department, to serve as PhD supervisors. The difference from the US system is due partly to the fact that having a master's degree is considered a very high and rare accomplishment, as it was in the United States over half a century ago.

The current trend of reform is toward a system closer, but not necessarily identical, to the system in the United States in the several aspects mentioned above. For example, many schools under the various industrial ministries were abolished in 1997 as a part of the effort to downsize the government bureaucracy. The universities have emphasized liberal education to a larger extent. Allowing undergraduates to choose their major after rather than before entering the university is a subject of current deliberation. Problem-solving and creative thinking are emphasized in discussions on the reform of education policies. Departments teaching different subjects in economics have been reorganized into one department. Economics departments are separated from newly formed or reorganized schools of business administration. The granting of master's degrees in one year and the change to a more US-like PhD program are being discussed, but adoption may take some time.

### 21.4.3  Choice of curriculum

As I have pointed out, the major limitation in the choice of curriculum is the availability of qualified teachers. There are no ideological limitations. However, this does not necessarily mean that the Chinese will and should adopt the typical curriculum in the United States.

Although the attitudes of Chinese economists and educators differ, the prevailing view is that much of modern economics that is taught at the best economics departments in the United States should be taught in China. If China had more qualified teachers, they would be asked to offer more up-to-date courses in modern economics. This attitude is evidenced by the fact that many politically conservative or highly theoretical economists have been invited to teach in China freely, without regard to the ideological inclination of the lecturer and the immediate applicability of the subject matter.

Regarding the issue of applied versus highly theoretical economics, Chinese economists and educators can easily see the relevance of the former, but some may not be equally appreciative of the latter. Yet they frequently are willing to keep an open mind, as there are many government officials and scientists in China supporting basic research in the physical sciences without seeing its immediate practical relevance. Therefore, the current trend appears to be that the economics curriculum in China will become more similar to that of the United States in having more theoretical courses, to the extent that there will be sufficient qualified teachers to offer such courses.

Should China have a different economics curriculum? A Chinese government slogan talks of developing a socialist market economy "with Chinese characteristics." Should the modern economics curriculum be developed "with Chinese characteristics?"

My answer is yes. Even assuming that the economics tools currently taught in the United States are exactly those suitable for China, no more and no less, the illustrative examples to teach the students should be drawn from Chinese experience and institutions to make the material more comprehensible and relevant. Attempts have been made in China not only to translate well-known textbooks from the US but also to write texts with Chinese institutions and examples (see Wang 1994). Second, the historical background, stage of development, and current economic problems would make certain topics in modern economics more important for China than for the US. Economics of transition, economic development, corporate governance, and financial institutions are subjects that are receiving more attention. Third, as teaching and research in modern economics progress in China, there will likely be innovations in modern economics which will affect the teaching of economics not only in China but in other parts of the world.

### 21.4.4   Improving the teaching of economics

The teaching of modern economics has been and is being improved continuously through institutional reform, the redesign of curricula, and the improvement in the quality of teachers.

In the reform of institutions, the teaching of economics was once mainly a part of management education. Schools of management covered both management subjects and economics. The gradual separation of the two has made economics a separate discipline for educational purposes, having a separate and independent department, budget, faculty, and student body. This change is beneficial to the development of modern economics. Changes in the administration of public universities in general are also beneficial. They include giving the universities more autonomy and flexibility in decisions regarding tuition, faculty salaries, student enrollment, and faculty assignment in different departments and mobility of faculty and staff members. Faculty mobility is facilitated by the change, initiated in 1991, of housing reform from publicly subsidized housing to private housing. The system of tenure provided to all faculty and staff, a part of the so-called "iron rice bowl," has made the education system inefficient and poor in quality. Proposals have been made to enable the university administrators to lay off staff and faculty, and to introduce termed appointments, a practice that is also being applied in the institutional reform of state enterprises. Nonstate and private (the official term is "people-operated" or "citizen-run") universities have flourished in China. They are getting even more widespread under the current government policy to encourage their establishment, and as the demand for them continues to increase. They compete with state universities and provide opportunities for the teaching of modern economics and other subjects.

The economics curriculum has been improved continuously. Many universities, including the People's University, Lingnan (University) College of Zhongshan University or Sun Yat-sen University in Guangzhou, Peking University, Fudan University, and Shandong University, to name a few cases familiar to me, periodically review their economics curricula and make changes as conditions permit. Zou Heng-fu, a PhD from Harvard now working for the World Bank, established an Institute of Advanced Economic Studies at Wuhan University to offer courses using the material and texts for the PhD program at Harvard. His effort has led to a new double major in economics and mathematics at Lingnan (University) College at Zhongshan and a similar program at Peking University. The Chinese Center for Economics Research was established at Peking University by Justin Lin, a PhD from the University of Chicago, and was staffed by over 10 economics PhDs from the US and UK. These and similar developments are changing the economics curriculum in China.

Efforts have been made to improve the quality of teachers, mainly through the effective utilization of economists overseas, especially those of Chinese origin, and the training of Chinese economists. A small number of Chinese economists who have obtained their PhD in the United States have returned. The improved working environment is motivating more to do so. In 1998 the Ministry of Education initiated a program to award about 200 distinguished professorships, each paying 100,000 RMB annually, or about four times the average salary for ordinary professors. Many of the overseas economists have been invited to teach on a short-term basis. The program in Wuhan is staffed by such economists who volunteer their time. Economists in China are constantly being sent abroad to receive training. American government and private institutions, as well as Chinese state and nonstate institutions and individuals, have supported the above efforts. The Chinese Economists Society, formed in 1985 by the initiatives of Dahai (David) Yu and Xiaokai Yang (then graduate students at Princeton), now has a membership of several hundred in the United States, and has contributed greatly in such efforts.

I should also mention the important contribution and influence of Hong Kong, before and after 1997 when it was returned to China. Hong Kong has universities staffed with economists better trained than those found in most universities in China. These economists, as individuals and through programs sponsored by their universities, have assisted the Chinese mainland universities in curriculum design and in teaching and research. The Hong Kong University of Science and Technology, established in 1991, is staffed mainly by American-trained faculty, many of whom have working experience in the US, and has an economics curriculum very similar to the ones in the US. Other universities in Hong Kong also offer good training in modern economics and are helping mainland Chinese universities in teaching and research in modern economics.

### 21.4.5  Economics as a profession

Economics is a popular subject in China, partly because there is a high demand for economics graduates. Besides going to graduate school, many can get offers to work in banks and other financial institutions, state and nonstate enterprises, and foreign corporations and joint ventures. Some may soon establish their own businesses. For people with graduate degrees in economics, there are both research and nonresearch opportunities in the above-mentioned organizations.

The quality of research using the tools of modern economics has continued to improve. Beginning with its non-existence in 1979, research using econometrics and micro- and macroeconomic analysis has progressed rapidly in quantity and quality in government institutions, research organizations, and universities. Econometric and economic planning models were introduced in the early 1980s in the Center for Social and Economic Development, which provided support for long-term economic analysis and planning in the State Council. At the same time, economists were employed in the State Commission for Restructuring the Economic System and the Institute of Economic Reform. The former was responsible for economic reform and was regarded in the 1980s as the most important Commission of the State Council, listed in the organization chart above the State Planning Commission and the State Education Commission. The latter provided staff support to Premier Zhao Ziyang. These economists are familiar with modern economics to various degrees, some having spent one to two years studying economics abroad. Modern economics affects their thinking. Economics research provides support for their policy recommendations.

In the Chinese Academy of Social Science, the Institute of Quantitative Economics under the directorship of Li Jinwen, and recently Wang Tongsan, has conducted research on many aspects of the Chinese economy, including a joint study on productivity changes in China with Dale Jorgenson, and the building of an econometric model with the co-operation of Lawrence Lau and as a part of Project LINK initiated by Lawrence Klein. Even in the early 1980s economists in China began building econometric models consisting of systems of simultaneous stochastic equations. Economics research at universities has been improving rapidly. One outstanding example is the research on mathematical finance conducted in Shandong University by Peng Shige and his colleagues, on the theory of backward stochastic differential equations and its application to financial economics; it has attracted international attention. Other examples of significant research in economics can be cited.

Good economists are in high demand in government, industry, and universities in China. Gang Yi, a PhD from the University of Illinois, returned to China in 1994 from an associate professorship at the University of Indiana and in 1998 became the Executive Secretary of the Committee of the People's Bank in charge of monetary policy implementation. Ming Zhu, a PhD from the University of Pittsburgh who returned to China in 1995 from a post in the World Bank, became the director of research of the Bank of China. Many universities are actively looking for economics PhDs from the US, offering them special housing, annual research grants of US$10,000 or more for two to three years, and freedom to travel abroad. The monetary compensation of economists working for financial institutions such as stock exchanges and in foreign enterprises can be higher than the above amount.

Economists, like other intellectuals and scholars, are highly regarded in China. There is a long tradition of respecting scholars, who, after an official examination on Chinese classics, once could become high officials in the imperial Chinese government. President Jiang Zemin and Premier Zhu Rongji were both trained as engineers, while the Premier and the Senior Vice-premier, Li Lanqing, have received training in economics. This high regard for scholars persists along with the fact that in the transition to a market economy, wealth confers social status as well. In this respect good economists have also done well, by consulting and teaching short-term courses to government officials at all levels and executives in state and nonstate enterprises and financial institutions.

### 21.4.6 Summary of economics education in China

China has made great progress in introducing the teaching of modern economics, mainly because of the willingness and determination of government education officials and educators, the cooperation of foreign economists and supporting institutions, and the efforts of Chinese economists. From non-existence in 1979, the teaching of modern economics was already well accepted in the late 1980s. It has become much more widespread and the quality has greatly improved in the 1990s, although it is not quite up to international standards, except for a handful of institutions including those in Hong Kong. The greatest obstacle to progress is the lack of qualified personnel. Both curriculum and institutional reforms are taking place. One can expect continued improvement in the future.

At the same time the spread of research using the tools of modern economics has taken place. The quality has been improving. It is used in various parts of the government as an aid to the reform of economic institutions and for economic policy formulation. Good economists are in high demand in government, industry, research, and academic institutions. They are also highly respected and well compensated. Economics is a good profession in China.

## 21.5  Demand for Education

In this section we describe briefly the important role of private spending in China's education system, and apply demand analysis to explain why total expenditure on education and expenditure per student have gone up so rapidly in recent years. The material is based on Chow and Shen (2006).

In 1978, educational services at all levels of schooling were provided by the government. Since economic reform started, nongovernment schools have sprung up rapidly at all levels (see also section 21.3). Nongovernment or "people-operated" schools consist of two kinds: those established and operated by nongovernment institutions ("social organizations") and the public schools turned over or leased to private operations. Both types of schools are "run by social forces in China." The development of a free market in education accelerated with Deng Xiaoping's "Southern Expedition" in 1992, in which the leader declared a policy of further opening the Chinese economy to the outside world, and urged the Chinese people to adopt market institutions to promote economic growth. This policy further encouraged the establishment of nongovernment-financed educational institutions. "Private funding" in China includes funds raised or spent by three types of schools: (i) private or nongovernment schools; (ii) public schools which are leased for private operation, or parts of which are operated and financed independently, or financially independent colleges or schools that are set up by public universities or their affiliated units; and (iii) tuition and fees charged by public schools.

In the *China Statistical Yearbook* total education funds (TEF) are divided into 5 categories: (1) "government appropriation for education" (a part of which is [1a] "budgetary"), (2) "funds of social organizations and citizens for running schools," (3) "donations and fund-raising for running schools," (4) "tuition and miscellaneous fees," and (5) "other educational funds." Government (central and local) appropriation is divided into budgetary funds and nonbudgetary funds. Budgetary funds include funds from both the education sector and other sectors. Nonbudgetary funds have the following major components: (1) taxes for education levied by local governments; (2) educational funds from enterprises; (3) funds from school-supported industries, from self-supporting activities (*qin gong jian xue*), and from social services; and (4) other funds that belong to government appropriation. While private funding can be defined as TEF minus government appropriation, we choose to define it as TEF minus the budgetary portion of the funding (TMB), since the former includes funds outside the government budget that are not restricted by government revenue, and we will use government revenue as the income variable in our demand analysis.

We adopt a theoretical framework and an estimation strategy as stated in assumptions A and B below.

**Assumption A**: No matter whether demand is from the government or the nongovernment sectors, there exist an income effect and a substitution effect that are constant in terms of elasticities during the sample period.

Government demand can be derived from a utility function with different goods and services provided by the government as arguments, provision of education being one. Maximization of that utility function would yield a demand function with price and government revenue as major explanatory variables.

Nongovernment demand by the parents or by the students themselves is assumed to be affected by relative price and real income, whether it is interpreted as demand for consumer goods or for investment goods. For primary and secondary school education, demand by parents can be derived by maximization of utility for the family. If higher education is viewed as investment in human capital for some of the college students, the rate of return would be an important explanatory variable, but price and income also have important effects, the latter due to capital-market imperfections. In our empirical analysis we have not introduced the rate of return explicitly, because for China as a whole during our sample period the expected rate of return to education can be assumed to be constant. For an individual investor, the expected rate of return depends on her future income stream; for the students in China as a whole, the average rate of return depends on the flow of future national income per capita. Since the annual rate of growth of per capita GDP or GNP during our sample period, 1991–2002, remained approximately constant at about 7.5 percent, we can assume a constant rate of return to education during our sample period and omit it as an explanatory variable.

Data are available on income, price, and quantity of education services demanded. Concerning the data generation process and the estimation strategy we adopt:

**Assumption B**:
1. The income effect can be estimated by using cross-provincial data.
2. While the time-series data satisfy a constant-elasticity demand equation the supply of education services is predetermined because the number of teachers and the available education facilities could only increase slowly relative to the increase in income or government revenue.
3. Given the income effect, the increase in price observed in time series can be used to estimate the price elasticity.

Let $q$ denote demand for education services measured by (quality-adjusted) school enrollment divided by an appropriate population figure, $y$ denote real income per capita, $p$ denote relative price, constructed by dividing education spending by the product of student enrollment and the consumer price index cpi, and $pq$ denote education spending in constant prices divided by an appropriate population figure. We assume a demand function of the following form in all applications

$$\ln q = c + a \cdot \ln y - b \cdot \ln p + u, \tag{21.1}$$

which implies

$$\ln pq = c + a \cdot \ln y + (1 - b) \ln p + u. \tag{21.2}$$

We use cross-provincial data to estimate income elasticity $a$ in equation (21.2) under the assumption that log relative price $p$ is uncorrelated with log per capita real income $y$ across provinces, so that we can regress $\ln pq$ on $\ln y$ with the $(1 - b) \ln p$ term absorbed in the residual. We realize that provinces with higher per capita income may spend more for each student enrolled, as the quality of education per student may be higher. This is similar to estimating income elasticity of demand for food by regressing log(food expenditure) on log income across individual families, where richer families tend to buy better-quality food; the estimated elasticity measures the effect of income on quality-adjusted food and not on pounds of food consumed, the latter corresponding to student enrollment without being adjusted for the quality of education. Given $a$ we estimate the price elasticity $b$ using time-series data. In time-series analysis we make the assumption that quantity of education services can be measured by student enrollment without adjustment for quality, as is customary in demand analysis for commodities that may have slow quality improvement through time.

If we subtract $\ln y$ from both sides of equation (21.2) we obtain an equation explaining the ratio of education spending $pq$ to $y$ or GDP as follows,

$$\ln (pq/y) = c + (a - 1) \ln y + (1 - b) \ln p + u \tag{21.3}$$

In the course of rapid economic development (the case in China), income increases rapidly, to shift the demand curve for education services upward, while the supply of education services cannot catch up, leading to an increase in relative price of education. According to equation (21.3) this increase in price will lead to an increase in the ratio of education spending to GDP, provided that the price elasticity of demand for education $b$ is much smaller than unity, and the income elasticity $a$ is not much above unity, both being found empirically to be correct.

Chow and Shen (2006) applied the above theoretical framework to Chinese provincial data for 2001 (in the estimation of income elasticity) and time series data from 1991 to 2002 to study the aggregate demand for education (the quantity being total student enrollment) and separately the demand at the three levels of primary, secondary, and higher education. The 10 important findings are the following.

First, although China's education system is under the direction of the government, it is guided by market forces to a large extent. The fraction of nongovernment education funding (defined as total spending minus government budgetary spending) has been increasing in recent years and rose to about 43 percent in 2002.

Second, from an institutional point of view, nongovernment funding can take a variety of forms. It can take place in public schools which collect fees, or which are operated by nongovernment organizations or individuals through a leasing arrangement. Some schools are privately owned and operated by nongovernment professional associations or by collections of individuals. The operation of privately financed educational institutions is guided by economic and financial considerations.

Third, the development of privately financed or privately operated educational institutions illustrates one important policy of China's government in transforming the economy into a market economy. While the government maintains an important role in many sectors in the economy, including the industrial, financial, transportation and communication, foreign trade, and education sectors, it has allowed and encouraged the development of nongovernmental institutions in these sectors. It is often the latter that were the driving force of economic growth and development in an environment of free entry and competition.

Fourth, as compared with parents in the United States, Chinese parents have more choice of schools for their children. They are not subject to paying a real estate tax to finance the usually only local public school available to their children. The Chinese schools are financed partly by general tax revenue and partly by tuition. There are several public and private schools available to most urban families. The schools are not obliged to accept any student below the standard they set, and thus have different academic standards. Parents have a choice of primary and secondary schools; and schools, public and private, can choose their students.

Fifth, the framework of demand analysis is applicable to explain spending on education, with real income and relative price as the major explanatory variables.

Sixth, when primary school, secondary school, and higher education are studied separately, we find income elasticity to be 0.42 for primary school and 0.81 for secondary school, and about unity for higher education. The price elasticities are respectively 0.31, 0.22, and 0.29, with the price paid by the government as the price variable in the demand for higher education.

Seventh, when aggregate spending of all three school levels is studied, income elasticity is 0.88 and price elasticity is between 0.43 and 0.48. When aggregate demand is decomposed into governmental (budgetary) and nongovernmental components, we find a government revenue elasticity of 0.66 and a price elasticity of 0.61 for the governmental component, and an income elasticity of 1.1 and a price elasticity of 0.45 for the nongovernmental component. (Note the possible overestimation of price elasticity due to overestimation of the increase in price as a result of proportionally more students enrolled in universities in later years.)

Eighth, our framework can explain the ratio of education expenditures to GDP very well. The increase in this ratio from 3.38 in 1991 to 5.21 in 2002 can be explained by the increase in real GDP and government revenue which raised demand. Given an inelastic supply of education services, this resulted in a large increase in price. Since demand is price inelastic, total spending increased as price increased. This mechanism, explicitly given in equation (21.3), can explain the increase in the ratio of education spending to GDP in other rapidly developing countries as well. Hence one should be cautious in criticizing a government for an apparent low ratio of education spending to GDP, without studying the influence of market forces on this ratio.

Ninth, on the relation between income inequality and education inequality (respectively measured by the standard deviation of log[per capita income] and log[per capita education spending] across provinces), to the extent that the demand for education is affected by income, income inequality will be reflected in education inequality. For primary school and secondary school education, the degree of education inequality is less than the degree of income inequality, indicating that education opportunities tend to be more nearly equal among families of different incomes. However, since other factors than income affect education expenditures as well, inequality in education spending can be larger than income inequality. This is the case for higher education, and to a lesser extent for aggregate education and for its governmental and nongovernmental components.

Tenth, the Chinese government places a strong emphasis on developing world-class universities, and has spent a large amount on higher education. In the meantime it has a policy of compulsory primary/secondary education for 9 years, though many children aged 15 or below do not receive the required education, because the central government has given the responsibility for providing it to provincial and local governments, which may have limited financial resources and resort to collecting tuition and fees from the students.

# 21.6   Concluding Comments

Since 1949 the Chinese education system has gone full circle, perhaps like other institutions which went through a period under central planning and then returned to a form suitable in a market economy. It changed to almost strictly public education and Soviet-style university education emphasizing professional training and compartmentalization. It then returned to the encouragement of privately funded and "citizen-run" education alongside public education, and the reorganization of specialized professional schools and liberal arts schools into multipurpose universities. The quality of education has improved a great deal since 1978, especially economics education, and much progress is expected in the future. Freedom of inquiry and discourse has also improved, especially in the social sciences and humanities, but perhaps not to the level in the 1930s. The strong influence of the government and of the Communist Party in their search for political stability under the status quo is a factor affecting the freedom of discourse. This has a much smaller effect on research and publication in the natural sciences and engineering, subjects that are politically more neutral.

From its recent trends, one can expect continued improvement in the Chinese education system as in the Chinese economic system. Both systems have shortcomings, some of which were pointed out in sections 21.3 and 21.4. However, both systems will improve slowly because of the fundamental driving forces at work. In the case of education, the forces include the intellectual curiosity and energy of scholars and students in China. In the case of the economy, the forces include the ingenuity and energy of the entrepreneurs and the working ethics of the labor force. The resourcefulness of the Chinese people has succeeded in increasing both the educational level and economic output in the years after economic reform, in spite of the shortcomings of the education and economic systems. One can expect that similar progress will be made in the future. The first part of the twenty-first century will witness a golden period of Chinese learning and scholarship, together with substantial growth in the national economy, as we have seen in chapter 5.

## References and Further Reading

Chow, Gregory C. *The Chinese Economy*. New York: Harper and Row, 1985; 2nd ed., Singapore: World Scientific, 1987.

Chow, Gregory C. *Understanding China's Economy*. Singapore: World Scientific, 1994.

Chow, Gregory C. "The Teaching of Modern Economics in China." *Comparative Economics Studies*, 17 (Summer 2000), pp. 51–60

Chow, Gregory C. and Yan Shen. "The Demand for Education in China." *International Economic Journal*, 20(2) (2006), pp. 129–47.

*Statistical Yearbook of China*. Various years.

Wang, Zeke. *The Market Mechanism: Cases in China* (*Shi Chang Ji Zhi: Zhong Guo An Li*), 1994. 2nd ed., Beijing: China Economics Press (Zhong Guo Jin Ji Chu Ban She), 1998.

## Questions

1  What are the main differences between the American and the prereform Chinese university education system? State two relative advantages and disadvantages of the Chinese system. Justify your answers.

2  Privately funded schools at all levels in China have flourished in the 1980s and 1990s. Why did this happen? Try to provide an answer using the concepts of demand and supply.

3  What fractions of Chinese youth in the corresponding school ages receive primary school, high school, and post-high school education? What are the corresponding fractions in the US? You may consult the *China Statistical Yearbook* and the *Statistical Abstract of the United States*.

4  Estimate a regression of the fraction of youth of college age attending a university on the natural log of income per capita using cross-section data for the provinces in the most recent year for which data can be obtained from the *China Statistical Yearbook*. Comment on the size of the regression coefficient. Can you use this regression to forecast the fraction of Chinese youth of college age who will attend a university in the future? If so, how? If not, why not?

5  What is Chinese government expenditure on education as a fraction of GDP in the last 10 years? What are the corresponding figures in the US in the same years? What can these data say about the adequacy of government expenditure on education in China?

6  In order to describe the growth of privately funded education in China since 1985 one needs to use appropriate statistics to measure the extent of private or "citizen-run" education. Possible measures are total tuition in billion yuan, total tuition deflated by an appropriate price index, total tuition as fraction of GDP, the number of students in privately funded schools, the number divided by population of school age, divided by the number in public schools, etc. Justify the measure you would choose.

7  Many educated Chinese are staying abroad, such as in the United States. Do you advise them to stay abroad or to return to China? What are your reasons?

8  Offer two important proposals to improve the higher educational system in China. Explain why they are important and effective.

# 22

# Taking Stock and Looking Ahead

This book has emphasized the transformation of China's economy as a dynamic process influenced by its social-political and economic characteristics. This concluding chapter summarizes the seven most important institutional characteristics of the Chinese economy and, based on their continued operation and influence, attempts to forecast the economy's future development. Some of these institutional characteristics provide challenges for further deliberation and research. To look ahead we will extrapolate from past trends by considering the momentum and inertia that have been affected by China's important social-economic characteristics and which are affecting the future development of the Chinese economy. At the end, we provide an overall assessment of China as a member of the future global economy.

## 22.1 Taking Stock

Living at the beginning of the twenty-first century, we are fortunate to have witnessed social changes in the second half of the twentieth century of an enormous scale. The changes include the rise and fall of Communism in Europe and the emergence of a market economy in China. Such dramatic changes in social institutions provide us with an opportunity for study, as I have done in examining the transformation of China's economy presented in this book. This section summarizes seven institutional characteristics of the Chinese economy that have influenced and will continue to influence its future development. The rapid economic growth in China, in the order of 9.5 percent annually from 1978 to 1999, suggests that China's current market economy, however imperfect, is a much better system than its planned economy existing before 1978. China's *is* a market economy, as about 80 percent (see section 16.1) of its GNP is produced by profit-seeking units and is subject to the law of demand and supply. It is a socialist economy, as the government plays an important role in economic activities, including the ownership of many public enterprises by different levels of the government. In 1992, the Central Committee of the Chinese Communist Party proclaimed that China's is a "socialist market economy." It has the following seven important characteristics.

### 22.1.1　Bureaucratic behavior of government officials

Bureaucratic behavior of Chinese government officials has existed in China for centuries. The word "bureaucracy" originated from China. There are positive and negative aspects of the behavior of Chinese bureaucrats, although the word "bureaucracy" often connotes the negative aspects more than the positive aspects.

On the positive side, Chinese bureaucrats in the Confucian tradition consider it a duty and an honor to serve the emperor and the country to the best of their ability. In modern times this behavior takes the form of promoting the development of market institutions. Examples are the establishment of the private Bank of Communications by the official Liang Yansun at the end of the Qing Dynasty, the establishment of the Science-based Industrial Park in Hsinchu, Taiwan, by Dr. K. T. Li, to foster the development of private high-technology industries, and the establishment of enterprises by thousands of township and village officials in China in the 1980s. It is a duty of a government bureaucrat to promote economic development and other social improvement in China.

On the negative side, bureaucrats can take advantage of their power for personal gains. Their power is derived from their authority to grant permission for an entrepreneur to operate his business and their right in controlling state assets. Anyone who needs permission to be granted by, or needs to use a state-owned asset controlled by, the bureaucrats is at their mercy. That is why bribery and corruption exist in China and other countries. When combined with the widespread ownership of economic assets by the state in China, a second characteristic to be mentioned below, the negative aspects of bureaucracy can be more damaging. As a familiar saying goes, "power corrupts, and absolute power corrupts absolutely."

Allowing the state to have more power under the government of the People's Republic of China is a source of corruption. In chapter 19 we discussed the misuse of state assets. On the other hand, more power in the hands of the central government can also help reduce the corruption of local officials. In China, anyone controlling some form of public assets can try to extract economic rent from it. Families living on either side of a country road leading to a tourist attraction can put up a road block to charge a fee for passing on the road, unless some government officials try to stop them. Local and provincial governments can extract charges from travelers using their roads (local airport charges of all kinds being accepted as normal) and from traders shipping goods to their territory (as a form of provincial tariff), unless the government above them can stop them. In a society where law and order are not firmly established, it requires welfare-minded government officials at a higher level to use their power to control the corrupt officials.

## 22.1.2    Extensive public ownership

While bureaucracy has been a characteristic of the Chinese government for centuries, also intensified since the establishment of the PRC in 1949, extensive public ownership of economic assets is a new institution introduced by the government of the PRC. A main distinction between capitalism and socialism is that the former accepts private ownership of the means of production as a basic principle, whereas the latter favors public owner-ship. China is an interesting experimental station for both public and private enterprises. In China, state-owned enterprises coexist with collectively-owned enterprises (many by townships and villages) and private enterprises. Private enterprises are owned by Chinese nationals, by foreign corporations, or jointly by Chinese and foreign corporations. Some state-owned enterprises, though a minority, appear to be efficient, as they are financially independent and are making large profits. Successful examples are easier to find in state enterprises which have joint ventures with foreign corporations. Many collectively owned township and village enterprises are successful in increasing output and making profits. The successful experience of the township and village enterprises in China is sufficient to challenge the proposition that only private enterprises in a capitalist economy can be efficient. Some public enterprises in China's socialist economy appear to be efficient. Theory to explain the efficiency of Chinese state enterprises can be found in Groves et al. (1994; 1995), and the efficiency of township and village enterprises is a subject of Weitzman and Xu (1994) and Che (1996).

At the end of chapter 15, which deals with state enterprises, I suggested two conditions for the efficient management of an enterprise whatever its form of ownership. These two conditions are that a manager should not be able to get rich through his position without working hard for the benefit of the enterprise, and, secondly, that if he works hard he should be rewarded. These two conditions are useful in the design of corporate govern-ance for an enterprise and would make the management efficient, but are not sufficient in themselves. In the design of a corporate governance structure, one should consider not only its merit on paper, but also whether the institutional and cultural setting of the country is ready for such a form of enterprise. This point is related to my repeated observation in this book that by passing legislation alone the government cannot change economic behavior and the extent to which citizens are law-abiding. A governance struc-ture that looks good on paper might not work in practice because the parties involved may not follow the agreed provisions and may act according to circumstances not easily specified or identified under the structure. Hart (1995) tries to allow for a contract not being honored and the possibility of renegotiation in discussing corporate governance, whereas renegotiation may not be the major issue in designing a governance structure to satisfy the two conditions stated above. The issue seems to be the assignment and limita-tion of the power of management, together with proper incentives, under a social system where there is a network of power relationships among the bureaucratic managers.

Returning to the issue of public versus private ownership, the reader will recall that most assets in China are publicly owned, by the central government, by provincial and local governments, and by villages as collectives. Incentive systems have been adopted to make the management of these assets efficient. The most prevalent is the leasing system, known as the responsibility system. Notable examples are the leasing of land by the village to farm households and the leasing of enterprises of all kinds by different levels of government. The terms of the lease include fixed rents and forms of profit sharing. In all cases there is a positive relation between the profits of the enterprise and the economic benefits of the management and workers. Providing incentives for the management of publicly owned assets is a key to the success of China's economic reform. The experience of restructuring enterprises as shareholding companies under the directions stated in Secretary General Jiang Zemin's report of September 1997 indicates that changing the form alone is not sufficient to improve performance. The new board of directors may consist of the same Party members and government officials that used to control the management, and the government still controls the majority shares of the new company.

Besides the management of existing assets, government units at different levels have created new enterprises. Even universities as public institutions have created and own enterprises, some selling research or consulting services and others selling products produced in factories run by faculty members. This is like having Mathematica, a private corporation started by faculty members of Princeton University, function as a Princeton-owned enterprise. Ownership by a public institution in China confers advantages to the enterprise, including the institution's reputation and physical assets, which the enterprise can share. A possible disadvantage of public ownership to the society is said to be the monopoly power engendered.

However, publicly owned enterprises in China are subject to competition from other public enterprises at different levels of government and in different regions, and from privately and internationally owned enterprises. More foreign competition will come when China becomes a member of the WTO.

Once management of an enterprise is separated from ownership, along the lines of a modern corporation in developed Western economies, we can call into question the incentive of management to pursue profits for the owners, in the short or long run. A large number of individual stockholders might not be able to influence the management to pursue their interest more effectively than a number of public agencies. In reality, Chinese government agencies holding controlling shares of state-owned enterprises do not seem to perform better than governing boards elected by share owners in the United States. Corporate governance issues related to the Chinese state-owned shareholding companies provide an important topic for research. The Chinese government has not found a way to make these companies work as efficiently as it wishes and is in the process of finding ways to improve their performance. One problem is not the governance but the assignment of the right managers for the largest state enterprises. Many of the managers are bureaucrats assigned historically and cannot be easily removed. They have been given vested interests through the bureaucratic system, as well as personal relations with top government leaders. Even a Prime Minister finds it difficult to change these incompetent and sometimes corrupt managers.

One important characteristic we have emphasized in studying the behavior of the Chinese state-owned and nonstate enterprises is the influence of the bureaucratic system. Managers of state-owned enterprises are bureaucrats who take advantages of their own power in dealing with bureaucrats in the government and in other enterprises and with people in the nonstate sector for their personal benefit. Government bureaucrats interfere with the operations of state and nonstate enterprises and prevent them from functioning effectively in a market economy. On the positive side, some bureaucrats serving as enterprise managers work for the interest of the enterprises. Those working in the government also want to help and foster the development of nonstate enterprises.

When discussing public ownership of economic assets in the first edition of this book, I did not realize the problem of collective land ownership by local governments. Perhaps the problem did not surface until recently. I concentrated my discussion on public enterprises and pointed out that the collectively owned land was used by bureaucrats to built economically beneficial township and village enterprises. At the turn of the century, a large amount of private capital in China has been accumulated in the process of rapid economic development. There is a high demand for urban development from the private sector all over China. A traveler in Beijing would discover new hotels and shopping centers along the main streets financed by private capital with the approval of Beijing government officials. The *New York Times* in the summer of 2004 reported the rapid building of a new city in Dongguan, a county near Hong Kong where the local government officials must have approved the use of land for development. Besides getting kickbacks and monetary benefits from the developers, the government bureaucrats have an incentive to approve the use of land for development during their limited tenure of office just to receive political credit. This short-sighted view of land use is in contrast with the case of private ownership, where the landowner would consider the opportunity cost of a future sale before allowing it to be developed immediately. Before 1949 most of China's land was owned privately. The government of the PRC took over control of all the land in China. Now the bureaucrats controlling it frequently are misusing it to their own advantage, and at the expense of efficient land use. This also contributed to the "overheating" of the Chinese macroeconomy in 2002–4, in addition to the rapid increase in money supply that we discussed in chapter 7.

### 22.1.3   The moral and legal system

A modern legal system as practiced in a Western developed economy is sometimes considered essential for the proper functioning of capitalism. The non-Western legal system in China is considered deficient by Western investors and economists. Some might prefer to call it a moral-legal system. It is a legal system if the word legal means "pertaining to law," as stated in *Webster's Dictionary*. Law has been practiced in China for over 2,000 years, but the legal system has been different from most current systems in the West, as we have discussed in chapter 20. One major difference is that in traditional China, social and economic order depended more on the social values and moral standards that the people followed than laws. Under this system a contract is enforced partly by an honor system of social values and partly by a set of informal social relationships known as *guanxi*, which play an important role in ensuring that a contract is honored. First, we observe that not all contracts should be strictly enforced from the social point of view. An economist calculates the cost and benefit of law enforcement to determine the optimal degree of enforcement. If the cost of hiring an additional policeman is higher than the benefit of the reduction in crime he can produce, the policeman should not be hired, resulting in a positive level of criminal activities. Similarly, there is some optimum degree for honoring contracts which can be derived from balancing the costs of enforcement with the benefits of enforcement. This issue is an interesting research topic.

Second, granted that it is advantageous to have a certain agreement or contract enforced, the effective means of enforcement may be legal or through moral values using *guanxi*. As I have previously mentioned, *guanxi* is a network of human relationships which set the rules of behavior among the parties concerned. When applied to two individuals in the case of certain business dealings, it is like a "handshake" accompanied by a verbal or written agreement for each party to do something in the future, contingent on the occurrence of certain events. The event might be the selling of certain merchandise to yield some amount of profit. The agreement stipulates how profits should be shared. The judicial system could not necessarily be relied upon to enforce such an agreement. It is rather a gentleman's agreement, which the "gentleman" members of the *guanxi* network would likely honor. The high cost of enforcement achieved entirely by legal means in the United States suggests that perhaps there is some advantage in enforcing an agreement partly by an informal network. In chapter 20 we suggest that replacing the traditional way of settling disputes through social values and social networks by litigation may not necessarily be beneficial. The displacement of the moral-social system by a modern legal system may have its drawbacks, but establishing a modern legal system that incorporates the traditional values as its foundations and allows for arbitration through socially accepted channels may be desirable.

It would be interesting to provide an economic explanation for the appearance of the moral-legal system (with the aid of social network *guanxi*) in China and for the appearance of the modern Western legal system after the Industrial Revolution. At the current state of knowledge one can only compare the characteristics of the two systems. The Chinese government has been trying to modernize its legal system to make it resemble that of a Western country, partly for the convenience of Western investors and partly to enable Chinese producers and traders to enter the world market. Perhaps incorporating some form of the legal system as practiced before 1949 may be beneficial to China to achieve the dual purpose of effective law enforcement in the Chinese environment and the smooth transaction of business with foreign investors.

It would also be interesting to study the economics of *guanxi*, which could be considered a form of human capital. Having *guanxi* amounts to having knowledge of which friend would be helpful when needed, having a personal reputation which is similar to a degree from Princeton and/or having a good credit rating, so that you can obtain help from others, material or otherwise, in future business dealings. The service from this form of human capital can supplement legal enforcement of contracts by moral enforcement or social pressure. It would be nice to have a formal model to explain the relative roles of legal enforcement of contracts and the enforcement through *guanxi*, what the optimum combination of the two is in a given social institution. In a capitalist society like the United States the number of legal contracts and the amount of resources devoted to legal services might be too excessive. By comparing the ratio of the number of lawyers to the number of engineers in the United States to the ratio in Japan, casual observers are tempted to conclude that the ratio in the United States is too high. Is the ratio in China too low, and if so why?

People in China are sometimes considered insufficiently law-abiding, especially in violating the patent rights of companies selling videotapes, music CDs, computer hardware and software, and other consumer products in China. The optimum enforcement of patents in any economy including China is an interesting question. Patent enforcement helps to encourage technological innovation. As a monopoly right, a patent discourages innovations which might infringe upon this right, and makes the invented products more expensive to consumers. Opinions on the economic effects of patents differ. For example, the view of Phillips (1964: 302) is "that a weakening of the patent rights of large corporations . . . would do little to hinder the 'Progress of Science and useful Arts' and, in some market situations, would be instrumental to these ends." One might argue that patents have been invented to serve the economic interests of industrial monopolies at the expense of the common people. Even if this statement is not true in general, it may be true in isolated cases. For example, patent protection for American pharmaceutical companies might have greater harmful effects in restricting the sales of drugs than possible benefits in encouraging the invention of new drugs.

There are situations in which a less than strict enforcement of a law might be better than a strict enforcement. An example is a law to make abortion illegal in the United States. The rationale of this law is to protect the lives of unborn babies, but this law is in conflict with the right to choose of the mothers. A solution might be to make abortion illegal and to enforce it less than strictly according to circumstances. Such a law would discourage unwanted pregnancy, but if unwanted pregnancy does occur, the right of the woman should be respected. A problem with strict law enforcement is that a law tries to apply itself uniformly to all citizens, who hold different opinions as a part of their freedom. A law imposes a uniform treatment on all persons. A less strict enforcement allows the coexistence of opposite viewpoints in a society. Both pro-life advocates who oppose abortion and pro-choice advocates who permit abortion would benefit from a less than strict enforcement of a law against abortion. One other example of difficulty in enforcement is the death penalty in the US. In the enforcement of the death penalty, the state governor has the authority to make an exception to weaken strict enforcement. This is an example to illustrate the possible advantage of less than strict enforcement. Once discretion is exercised by a person in enforcing a law, the law is not strictly enforced.

It is easy to understand the desirability of a Western legal system compared with the moral-legal system in China. The latter relies partly on informal relationship and is less strict in law enforcement. It is a generally accepted view that a modern legal system is an essential part of modern capitalism. In view of the successful experience of China's recent economic development under a different legal system, one might be led to reexamine the relationship between the Western legal system and the effective functioning of a market economy. What features of the Western legal system are essential and under what circumstances? Some light on this question might be shed by studying the legal system in China's history, especially during the Song dynasty, where some form of capitalism is said to have existed, and in the 1930s in the Republic of China. What features of the moral-legal system based on China's tradition should be incorporated in the development of China's modern legal system?

### 22.1.4    Emphasis on collective welfare

Individualism is an ideal under Western capitalism. This ideal is not generally accepted in Japan, an Eastern capitalist country. Individual rights may be in conflict with the common good. An example in the United States is the freedom of television stations to broadcast material which might be harmful to children. Freedom to smoke can be harmful to others. To what extent should an individual restrict her free action for the sake of the common good? Adam Smith has pointed out that under certain conditions the pursuit of individual self-interests in the marketplace can lead to a better economic outcome for the society as a whole. This idea lays the foundation for a market economy under capitalism and tends to make capitalism and individualism synonymous. In a socialist society, the common good is considered more important than in a capitalist society. That is partly the meaning of the word "social." Not only is individual freedom more restricted, but members of a society are encouraged and educated to serve the society for the society's sake.

A society is more than a collection of individuals. Hence the welfare of the society is more than the sum of the welfares of its individual members. Individuals exist not only for their individual self-interests but also to serve the society as an entity. The contract theory of government of Rousseau might not be entirely acceptable. If members of Chinese families do not choose their membership by a voluntary contract and still have to fulfill family obligations, it may be reasonable to think that the Chinese people do not choose their country and still have to fulfill their duty to the country. In addition, people in China, having gone through a period of domination and humiliation by foreign powers, may strive for nationalism. They may consider the common good and the economic and political status of their country more important than certain elements of their individual freedom and individual rights.

The issue of human rights is related to and perhaps derived from the ideal of individual freedom in a Western capitalist society. Many people in Western societies consider human rights to be violated in Singapore. However, people in Singapore love their own system, including the banning of the import of chewing gum. Some residents of Hong Kong before 1997 considered Singapore an ideal place to move to in case conditions in Hong Kong became unacceptable after 1997. China does not practice the same kind of human rights as the United States. With the consent of many, and perhaps even a majority, of its citizens, the Chinese government imposes restrictions on certain freedoms essential to preserving law and order in China. Granting too much freedom makes the enforcement of law and order more difficult. In this book, especially in chapter 12 on investment in human capital, chapter 17 on foreign trade, and chapter 19 on the use and misuse of assets, I have pointed out the downside of the restrictions on the freedom of Chinese citizens to utilize their human capital and their freedom to trade. There is a "golden mean," to borrow a term from Confucius, in designing the optimum amount of freedom for Chinese citizens. The Chinese people are not fortunate enough to have lived through periods of prosperity and political stability in the last two centuries. Many of them have not yet learned how to exercise restraint when freedom is given to them, including the students occupying Tiananmen Square for a period of two months, preventing the proper functioning of the government.

A related point to stress in this context is that the practice of Western-style human rights, however desirable, is not a necessary condition for rapid economic growth. This point is convincingly demonstrated by the recent rapid economic development on the Chinese mainland, Taiwan, Singapore, and South Korea. Whatever stand one might take on the extent of violation of human rights in these countries, successful economic development has occurred.

The welfare economics of a socialist market economy with emphasis on the common good is interesting to study. Much has been written about the welfare state in which the government provides for the economic welfare of individual citizens. After the Great Depression and the New Deal in the 1930s and the programs initiated under the Great Society of the Johnson administration, the US government has taken an active role in providing welfare benefits to members of American society. The pros and cons of these welfare programs have been extensively discussed. One topic of government intervention for the promotion of social welfare is government policy towards education not merely for the personal benefit of individual citizens. The policy takes into account the external effect of education on the welfare of society as a whole. From the viewpoint of studying the Chinese economy one should also recall an important government mission to promote science/technology and education for the betterment of the national economy.

There are three key questions in welfare economics. First, how is a welfare function defined, for an individual citizen, for a collection of citizens, and for any political entity? Second, how are these welfare functions formed, or how are social preferences determined? Third, by what process do the welfare objectives of these units affect the social-economic outcomes of concern to them? The last question is answered by the derivation of theorems if the problem is formulated as a welfare maximization problem. When the collective good is emphasized, answers to these questions may be different from those under a society with individualistic values.

Consider the case of determining the education levels of citizens, for example. For a purely individualistic society the welfare function of each citizen might be assumed to include her own level of education as the only argument, and the welfare function of the government may be assumed to be an aggregation of the individual welfare functions obtained by whatever weighting scheme. When collectivism is emphasized, the education levels of other citizens and perhaps some aggregates of the levels also enter the welfare function of each citizen. Furthermore, the welfare function of the government may depend not only on the individual welfare functions but on a certain measure of collective education. Second, traditional welfare economics takes all welfare functions as given. To the extent that a collective society tends to motivate its citizens to serve the common good, their welfare functions cannot be taken as given and the formation of welfare functions has to be explained. In the economic transformation of China, the government assumes an important role in guiding the development of education, as we have discussed in chapter 21. In the United States, the President may choose to motivate citizens to various degrees to achieve a certain national purpose, such as the achievement of a higher level of education. In a country like China, which emphasizes the collective good, government leadership or influence is stronger. Third, the process by which a given set of individual and government welfare functions affect the economic outcomes may differ according to the degree of individualism versus collectivism in the society. In the next section, possible differences in this process due to the institution of a one-party versus a two-party political system will be discussed. The discussion will be relevant for the effects of individualistic versus collective social welfare.

### 22.1.5    The one-party system under the Communist Party

What is the relationship between a multiparty political system and a market economy? The answer is not simple. A one-party political system is consistent with a market economy. This is evident from the one-party systems on mainland China, in Taiwan until the 1990s, as well as in South Korea and Singapore. In practice Japan had only one party that ruled during several decades of rapid economic growth. A multiparty democratic government is not required for an expanding market economy, as the above facts have demonstrated. This observation should not be construed as an endorsement of the one-party political system.

Second, we should distinguish a multiparty democratic system from the practice of human rights. Human rights were practiced in Hong Kong under British rule, but there was absolutely no democracy until the 1980s because government officials were not elected by the Hong Kong people and the Hong Kong governor was appointed by the government in London. It is interesting to observe that when Hong Kong was returned to China in July 1997, the Western press was very critical of the election of the new Chief Executive of Hong Kong by a Committee of 400 electorates appointed by the People's Congress under the Basic Law of Hong Kong. The Western press referred to the elected Chief Executive as Beijing-designated. The new system was in fact much more democratic than the previous system under British rule in several respects. First, the Chief Executive was not simply appointed but elected. Second, the electorates were democratically generated in a limited sense, since they were chosen by the People's Congress and members of the People's Congress were indirectly elected by members of congress a level below, members at the village or street level who are publicly elected. Third, all 400 members of the electorates were Hong Kong residents with social responsibility, including all the university presidents, and representatives from professional organizations, from workers' unions, and from the business community. Fourth, these electorates were not controlled by Beijing. They exercised their own judgment in voting for the candidate for Chief Executive of their own choice, and there were three leading candidates, all receiving a certain number of the votes. Beijing had no hold on these people. They are highly respected Hong Kong citizens who wished to select the best candidate to serve Hong Kong. One of the considerations could very well have been that a person with a good Beijing connection would be preferable to some members of the election committee, other things being equal. However imperfect this election process was, it was much more democratic than appointment of the Governor under colonial rule by the British government.

My third observation is that democracy in the sense of a government of the people, by the people, and for the people can be practiced at least to some extent under one-party rule. In the United States, the two-party system came after a long, slow process. The Democratic Party was largely the outgrowth of Andrew Jackson's popularity in his re-election in 1832, and the current Republican Party was founded only in 1854. Inspired by the American democratic system as expressed by Lincoln and with his understanding of the historical and cultural setting of China, Dr. Sun Yat-sen tried to form a democratic government in China under the rule of his Nationalist Party or Kuomintang. In the early 1920s Sun asked members of the Communist Party to join the Nationalist Party when Soviet help was needed, but the Nationalist Party alone was to be the ruling party. Former Communist Party members could participate only as members of the Nationalist Party. In 1924 the Kuomintang made a declaration on basic principles for the development of China, all under a one-party system.

In considering the possible introduction of a multiparty democratic system to China today, one needs to study the current political system and the social institutions of China. The question can be discussed in two respects, its normative aspect and its positive aspect. The first asks whether it should happen. The second asks whether it will happen or whether it can happen. The first question hinges on whether the Chinese people are ready for a multiparty democratic system given their average education level, their ability to take responsibility for citizenship under such a system, and their limited experience in participating in a democratic government. Some positive signs have been observed, in the widespread village elections all over China in recent years, of the people's ability to participate in a democratic process, although not under a multiparty system. Assuming that the Chinese people are ready, we explore the second question by asking whether in reality the Communist Party leadership is ready to give up one-party rule, and how it will attempt to introduce democracy in China, which is a stated objective of the Party.

To understand China's political system it is necessary to study its historical background, its rationale, and the thinking of the political leaders and the Chinese people, as I have tried to indicate in this book. After a very careful study along these lines, would one be able to come up with some informed judgment and recommendations for possible improvement? I would also stress the difference between informed judgment and useful recommendations. The latter are harder to come by because a good diagnosis may be far from a good prognosis. Useful recommendations have to take into account the political reality of the country as well as its cultural, historical, and institutional background.

It would be interesting to study the relation between an economic system and the associated political system (or between a political system and the associated economic system). The development of Western capitalism, together with the increase in the economic power of a large segment of the population, gradually led to a democratic government as the prosperous citizens demanded more rights to govern their own destiny. The same reasoning suggests that as the Chinese people become richer and more educated they will demand more political rights from the government. Under a one-party system, political representation of the people through elected members of the People's Congress has strengthened in the past decade. One may ask what forms of political institutions are likely to emerge from the current practice of a socialist market economy in China, and what forms of political institutions should or would emerge to be compatible with the changing economic institutions of this market economy.

The relation between a democratic government and economic behavior is an important area of research. To cite just one example in welfare economics, Dixit and Londregan (1998) have provided a model for the determination of the income transfers $(C - Y)$ to each group of voters who consume $C$ and produce $Y$ units of output under a two-party system. Social welfare for each voter or party is a weighted average of the means of $(C - Y)^2$ and $(C - \text{mean of } C)^2$; the former measures dead weight loss and the latter consumption inequality. The voter in each group maximizes her objective function which is a weighted (by a group-specific $a$) average of consumption of the group and individual social welfare. Each political party is assumed to maximize its objective function, which is a weighted (by a party-specific $b$) average of its vote share, and its social welfare function by choosing its transfer strategy. The transfer will produce a vector of final consumption for all groups. The final consumption vector is determined by a Nash equilibrium as each party maximizes by taking the other party's strategy as given. If we wish to study economic behavior under a one-party system we could ask how redistribution takes place under such a system in which elected representatives in a Congress can enact laws on tax and transfers. One might model the economy as having the government maximize an objective function similar to that of one political party stated above, while the voters can vote "no" to a government strategy. Or the one party can propose two candidates who function like the two parties above. It is necessary to study economic behavior under a one-party democratic system to find out its performance characteristics.

Another interesting question concerns the effects of democratic politics on economic growth. Some members of the business community in Hong Kong are concerned that democratic politics might affect the level of government expenditure as a percent of GNP, resulting from the introduction of social welfare programs and the tax system at the expense of entrepreneurship. Some economists in Taiwan have expressed the view that the recent introduction of a multiparty system has made rational government economic decision-making more difficult and thus hinders economic growth. Can economic analysis shed light on these questions?

### 22.1.6   An intelligent and pragmatic government

Whatever the merits or demerits of the current Chinese political system, the Chinese government since 1978 has been very successful in transforming the Chinese economy into a market-oriented economy, in spite of the remaining shortcomings of the economic system. One should take it as a characteristic of the Chinese government that it is served by intelligent and pragmatic officials. This characterization is demonstrated by the government's record in guiding the economic transformation of China in the last two decades of the twentieth century. (I would say the same about the government of Taiwan, which

started promoting economic development through market forces two decades earlier.)
The government in China still follows its belief that state ownership of some essential
parts of the economy is essential, and hence the role of the market forces should be
limited. Its thinking is that market forces are useful for promoting the nonstate sectors as
an important supplement of the state sector and to stimulate the state enterprises to be
more efficient, without giving up the important role to be played by the state sector itself.
This thinking is subject to slow change as Chinese leaders gain more experience
in guiding economic reform and the economic development of China. The freedom
unleashed by the current system is sufficient to enable many Chinese entrepreneurs
to exercise their ability to establish and operate nonstate enterprises for the promotion
of economic growth. If not hindered by government bureaucrats and the restrictions
imposed on their operations, these entrepreneurs would be doing much better.

### 22.1.7   Abundance of human capital

An important characteristic of the Chinese economy is the abundance of human capital
inherited from its long history. In chapter 1 I discussed the human capital in the Sheng
dynasty beginning 1900 BC in the form of skilled artisans and workers. The market
economy was already functioning in the Han dynasty, as was well understood and described by the great historian Sima. Trade through the silk route with the Romans flourished
in the Tang dynasty. Chinese entrepreneurship has been demonstrated in countries in
southeast Asia, in Hong Kong, in Taiwan, and in mainland China before 1949 and after
1978. Human capital in China serves as the most important engine for growth, whether in
the form of skilled and hard-working labor, in entrepreneurship, or in knowledge in science and technology. Compared with many other developing economies, China appears
to have plenty of human capital. Compared with some developed economies, China is
still in need of able managers for state and nonstate enterprises and for the commercial
banks.

   In this section I have discussed seven important characteristics of the Chinese economic, legal, and political system that have affected and will affect China's economic
development. Our next task is to use these characteristics as a basis to assess the past
performance of China's economic growth and to forecast its future growth. The past
growth process based on these characteristics provide a basis to study the dynamics of the
Chinese economic system, just as a system of differential equations enables one to derive
the time paths of economic variables given suitable initial conditions.

## 22.2   Prospects for the Chinese Economy up to 2020

In this section I will discuss the future of the Chinese economy in the first two decades of
the twenty-first century by the conventional method of extrapolating historical trends. The
extrapolation is based on three forces at work that are the result of the seven institutional

characteristics summarized in section 22.1. In the last section of chapter 5 I provided a forecast of China's economy in 2020 based on projections of the World Bank in connection with the model of China's economic growth described in that chapter. As a check on the previous forecast based on econometrics, I am here forecasting simply by informally extrapolating historical trends. Such a method of forecasting is valid if two conditions are met: first, the basic forces driving economic change in China can be identified correctly and, second, there are no unexpected events seriously disrupting the trends. Our first task is to identify the important characteristics of the development of China since reform started in 1978, and the important forces at work. We will then discuss future prospects and important areas that have received the attention of policy-makers.

Many observers have characterized the reform process by the words "gradualism" and "experimentation" (i.e. to seek truth from facts). I would like also to emphasize "continuity," "market incentives," and "inertia," the latter two asserting opposite influences on the economy. The continuity of the reform process was due to the existence of a bureaucratic system, the important share of state-owned industrial enterprises and banks, the traditional moral-legal system, the important social objective of promoting economic development for China as a nation, the important role of the government under one-party rule of the Communist Party, and the pragmatic attitude of government officials. These are the first six characteristics summarized in section 22.1.

The declaration of the Fourteenth Party Congress in September 1992 that China's economy is a "socialist market economy" was a natural result after the economy had been changed sufficiently to a market orientation, and when the policy-makers were sufficiently convinced after experimentation that a market economy is the correct institution to adopt. The important "Decision on Issues Concerning the Establishment of a Socialist Market Economic Structure," adopted by the Third Plenum of the Fourteenth Party Congress in November 1993, the important report of Jiang Zemin in the Fifteenth Party Congress of September 1997, and the Constitutional Amendments of March 1999 can be viewed as natural consequences of the decision in 1992 to adopt a market economy. This is true for the later reform measures, including the foreign-exchange liberalization of 1994, the tax and fiscal reform of 1995, the monetary and financial reform with the two important central bank and commercial bank laws of 1995, the state enterprise reform, and the government and legal reform.

To understand the basic forces driving the Chinese economy in order to forecast the future economy, I would like to mention (1) the role of the government, (2) incentives generated in the market sectors, and (3) inertia inherent in economic institutions. The experience of the last 20 years has demonstrated that the government has played and can play a positive role in promoting economic growth. Its main achievement is to adopt institutional changes which allow market forces to operate for the benefit of the economy. The household responsibility system created incentives for the farmers at the beginning of the reform. The energy of township and village enterprises accounted for much of the growth in the 1980s and early 1990s. The open-door policy allowed foreign investment to contribute to growth through the import of capital, technology, and managerial training. Foreign and domestic competition forced state enterprises to improve their efficiency. It is true that the government has made some mistakes in macroeconomic policies, accounting for the inflation in 1988 and 1994. Yet through years of experimentation and learning, government leaders have reached a better consensus about the efficacy of the market system and government officials have learned more about how the Chinese market economy functions. Such consensus and experience will help promote further growth. In addition the government is engaged in infrastructure-building and other growth enhancing activities which will be discussed.

Second, concerning the market forces we can expect that private enterprises, under better legal protection, and foreign investment and joint ventures, in the context of a more open economy with China entering the WTO, will contribute positively to growth up to 2020. These enterprises will play the role of township and village enterprises in serving as the most dynamic sector of the economy. They also will provide competition to the state and collective enterprises, making them more efficient.

Third, there will be continued inertia in economic institutions, including in particular the state enterprises, the banks, the legal system, and in general in ways to operate an economic institution. Economists who believe in the rationality of economic behavior as a general principle operating in all parts of the world should not overlook the inertia due to lack of information, lack of knowledge, social and political pressure affecting economic decisions, and simple persistence of customs and habits. Some economists would suggest that once economic incentives are provided under a private ownership system, economic production will be efficient. They can point to the success of the responsibility system in Chinese agriculture as an example. Overnight, the Chinese farmers' behavior changed under a new incentive system. It has been suggested that the same reform could not have worked in Russia because the Russian farmers had forgotten about private farming and only knew how to work in a collective farm. Whether this difference is true or not, in the Chinese case some credit has to be given to the old institution of Chinese farming prevailing before the Great Leap of 1958, which had been developed through centuries of experience. Incentives alone without high-quality human capital are insufficient for high productivity.

The first five characteristics of the Chinese social-economic system that we summarized in section 22.1 provide the institutional setting for this inertia. Recognizing the role of inertia, one can understand the difficulties encountered in the reform of state enterprises and the banking system. One most important problem facing the reform of both institutions is the lack of well-trained managers and staff to run a modern enterprise or a modern bank. There are examples of very successful state enterprises in China. The reason for success is often traced to the unusual ability of the general manager. Even if the economic institutions in China are perfect in any sense that one wishes to define, unqualified managers in state or nonstate enterprises cannot make the enterprise profitable. The same applies to commercial banks, where well-trained staff members are also important and lacking in China.

The second element of what I called inertia is the tendency to retain the old ways of doing things. One manifestation is that in many state enterprises which had been changed to shareholding companies, the shareholders still elect the same people, including the Party secretary, to the governing board of directors, and there is no change in management. One can explain this partly by political and social pressure, another element of inertia which I have mentioned. In August 1999 one enterprise manager in Beijing complained to me that the restructuring of his enterprise to a shareholding company had not changed the practice of running the enterprise, except that he had to deal with more bureaucrats on the board and to waste more time in meetings than before, when he was accountable only to the person appointing him. At the same time, workers were forced to purchase shares in medium-sized enterprises against their will, although in some enterprises restructured in this fashion profits increased and the workers benefited greatly.

Inertia can prevent economic institutions from changing rapidly, just as it can prevent political institutions from changing rapidly. Because of inertia it is not possible for Chinese state enterprises and banks to be changed to modern institutions in a few years simply by enacting new laws. In chapter 15, on the behavior of state enterprises, and in chapter 16, on the nonstate sectors, I emphasized bureaucratic behavior as a hindrance to the efficient operation of both state and nonstate enterprises. Therefore we can expect the reform of state enterprises and of the banking and financial system to be a slow and gradual process, as it has been in the past; but continued progress to a limited extent will likely be made, as in the past.

The balance of the three sets of forces at work – the positive role of the government, the energy unleashed in an essentially market economic system with an abundance of human capital, and the resistance from institutional inertia – is that the economy will continue to grow at a substantial rate, say over 7 percent annually, in the first decade, and perhaps over 6 percent in the second decade of the twenty-first century. I have come to this judgment by observing the data of the past 20 years. The negative factor, namely institutional inertia, has not prevented the economy from growing at an average rate of about 9.5 percent per year. This fact demonstrates that there is no need to have "perfect" institutions to grow rapidly, as long as important market incentives are allowed to operate in important parts of the economy. In the future, the role of state enterprises in producing total national output will be even smaller than in the past, making further reform in this sector less essential for economic growth. Even with slow reform, the banking sector is unlikely to collapse, as the Western media were expecting during 1997–9, the years of the Asian financial crisis. The large fraction of nonperforming loans is not as serious as it might appear, because the Chinese people have faith in the banks as a government institution, their deposits being implicitly guaranteed by the government. They have continued to deposit their savings in the banks, making serious bank runs unlikely. There should be sufficient time for the government to restructure bank credit, especially now that the Asian financial crisis is over.

I have discussed the fundamental forces which have contributed to the rapid growth of the Chinese economy in the past 20 years, and predicted that they will continue to operate in the next two decades to produce substantial rates of growth. This prediction would be incorrect if there were new developments to interfere significantly with these forces at work. One such development may be political instability, though it is unlikely to be a major disruptive force affecting the economic trends I have described. As of 2001, the majority of the Chinese people appear to be satisfied with the government. With people getting richer and having more economic freedom, there will likely be gradual change towards a more democratic political system. To achieve a democratic system is a stated objective of the government. In connection with economic progress one can also expect change towards a larger degree of human freedom, continuing the trend of the last twenty years. A second possibility is that income inequality among regions, created during the growth process, may lead to social instability. This problem is unlikely to be serious enough to affect the basic economic trends, and the government is making a serious effort to assist the poor in its program for western development, which we discussed in chapter 10.

Given the optimistic forecast for the Chinese economy, are there any important policy options which will affect China's future development? In general the economic officials in China know much more about the available policy options than an outside observer. While institutional and market forces are the determining factors for continued growth, the government is aware of its important role in creating an environment suitable for growth. As an example of government awareness, consider the signing of a set of agreements between China and other countries on the terms under which China will enter the WTO. These agreements indicate that top government economic officials, especially Premier Zhu Rongji, consider the further opening of the Chinese economy to world market competition as a major government policy. Chinese economic officials also understand that the financial market should be opened step by step, for example with current account transactions to be opened before capital account transactions. After the Asian financial crisis occurred in July 1997, I began to appreciate the decision to allow foreign investors to buy only B shares traded in the Shenzhen and Shanghai stock exchanges, with A shares reserved for domestic Chinese investors. Under this rule, price fluctuations in the B shares could only affect the fortunes of foreigners and would not create as much instability in the Chinese financial market as it would otherwise. In March 2001, the Chinese government allowed Chinese citizens to buy B shares using foreign currency. This illustrates the strategy to open Chinese markets in steps. In the present case the majority of Chinese stockholders who did not buy B shares using foreign currency were still partly protected by the insulation, although the prices of A and B shares tend to fluctuate together.

A second area, besides opening China's market, is the building of economic infrastructure, including highways, railroads, power plants, water conservancy and flood control projects, environmental protection facilities, and communication networks. Some projects were constructed during the Asian financial crisis of 1997–9 to increase aggregate demand in order to achieve growth targets of 8 percent and 7 percent in those years. Some may not be cost-effective, but the building of infrastructure is a responsibility assumed by the Chinese government. In a more developed market economy there may be more capable entrepreneurs to help build infrastructure. In fact China is quite liberal in allowing private entrepreneurs to participate, including the construction of superhighways connecting Hong Kong, Guangzhou, and many other cities.

Third, Premier Zhu Rongji stated that "science/technology and education for the betterment of the economy" was to be a main theme of his tenure when he responded to a question raised during his first press conference in March 1998. On August 18–20, 1999, with the support of the Premier, an international conference on this topic was held in Beijing involving over 30 Chinese participants from the five sponsoring organizations (the Chinese Association of Science and Technology, the Ministry of Education, the

Academy of Science, the Academy of Social Science, and the Academy of Engineering) and some 18 outside experts. Several days later top government officials held a conference on this topic. The government is aware of the importance of basic science as well as the need to promote technology. It has adopted a policy to encourage the privately financed education which has flourished in China at all educational levels, and to make the administration of public universities more flexible, including the determination of tuition, personnel policy, and curricula. The use of the internet for educational purposes is being seriously considered.

There are other important areas to which the government is paying serious attention, including the improvement of technology in agriculture, environmental protection, the social welfare system, healthcare, income inequality, and housing reform. These topics, except for the improvement of agricultural technology, have been discussed in this book. Government efforts in these areas should have a positive effect on the national economy, although government programs in these areas might not always be cost-effective, and waste and corruption will be observed in many cases.

Undoubtedly, there have been economic policy mistakes in China. While the ability of Chinese government economic officials is high on average, they face difficult problems in setting policy while Chinese economic institutions are continuously changing. The policy-makers are facing a new environment continuously. One example of failure is the macroeconomic policies contributing to the periods of inflation in 1988 and 1994. After inflation was successfully put under control in 1996, perhaps monetary policy could have been more expansionary in 1997–9, especially when China was affected by the Asian financial crisis. Such a policy could have prevented the deflation in 1998–9 and might have helped increase the rate of economic growth in these years. By choosing a more expansionary monetary policy, the government could have financed a part of its expenditures for building infrastructure through the increase in money supply. Moreover, the failure to revalue the RMB upwards in 2001–2 contributed to the very rapid increase in money supply in 2002. That increase in money supply led to a large expansion of bank credit, an investment and construction boom in 2003–4 (referred to as "overheating" in the Chinese press), and inflation in 2004 in the order of 5.5 percent (as compared with zero percent in 2001) (we discussed this at more length in chapter 7).

In June 1989 I was scheduled to speak to a group of Princeton alumni in Hong Kong on the prospects of economic growth in China, a topic agreed upon before the Tiananmen tragedy. I forecasted continued growth (see chapters 6 and 7 of my *Understanding China's Economy*, 1994) based on the fundamental economic forces at work. My forecast was very unpopular among the audience, who were extremely upset by the Tiananmen tragedy. Some ordinarily friendly newspapers in Hong Kong and Taiwan described me as a spokesman for the Chinese government in making such an optimistic economic forecast. They changed their opinion later when the forecast turned out to be correct. My forecast, then and now, is based only on the evaluation of the fundamental economic forces at work under Chinese institutional conditions.

The above forecast for the first two decades of the twenty-first century could turn out to be inaccurate, but the method of forecasting appears to be valid: to make a medium-term forecast one first examines the economic fundamentals and then considers other factors which might alter the course of events determined by the fundamentals. The above forecast will be correct if the most important fundamentals have been identified and if no unexpected factors can seriously affect past trends.

In chapter 3, where I discuss economic reform in China, I provide in section 3.10 reasons for the success of the reform, and ask whether the success was inevitable. My answer was yes. In section 22.1 I provided seven important characteristics of the Chinese economy. We can now ask whether the continued rapid growth of the economy is inevitable. My answer is also yes. This answer is based mainly on the combination of the market economic institutions already established and the high quality of human capital in China, the last of the seven characteristics. The other six characteristics only describe the special nature of the Chinese market economy, which I have called a "bureaucratic market economy" based on the first two characteristics. Communism itself is mentioned only as a part of the fifth characteristic, and has affected the first and the second characteristics. If China had not had its Communist Party ruling the country, characteristic 1, the bureaucracy, would be different, there would be fewer state enterprises (characteristic 2), and the one-party rule (characteristic 3) would have been different or might already have been changed. Given the stage of economic development at which China is today, I would still predict continued growth based on the combination of market institutions and Chinese human capital. Thus Communism is not a major factor in this forecast.

The section 5.6 cited forecasts contained in the World Bank's *China: 2020*, and contains some rough calculations to reach the conclusion that by 2020 the Chinese economy will overtake the US economy in total real GDP in terms of 1998 dollars. Even if the rough calculations turned out to be off by one decade, the emergence of a powerful China on the world scene will occur in the lifetime of most readers of this book. Just witness the extremely remarkable growth of Shanghai. Such an economically powerful China will share the economic dominance of the United States in the world economy. To understand China in order to develop a constructive US–China relationship is a most important task in shaping future world peace and prosperity. This book is partially dedicated to the purpose of promoting such an understanding.

## References and Further Reading

Che, Jiahua. "Township Village Enterprises: An Organizational Approach in Investment Finance." Department of Economics, Notre Dame University, 1996, mimeo.

Chow, Gregory C. *Understanding China's Economy*. Singapore: World Scientific Publishing Co., 1994.

Chow, Gregory C. "Challenges of China's Economic System for Economic Theory." *American Economic Review*, 87 (May 1997), pp. 321–7.

Dixit, Avinash and John Londregan. "Ideology, Tactics, and Efficiency in Redistributive Politics." *Quarterly Journal of Economics*, 113 (May 1998), pp. 497–530.

Groves, Theodore, Yongmiao Hong, John McMillan, and Barry Naughton. "Autonomy and Incentives in Chinese State Enterprises." *The Quarterly Journal of Economics*, Feb. 1994, pp. 183–209.

Groves, Theodore, Yongmiao Hong, John McMillan, and Barry Naughton. "China's Evolving Managerial Labor Market." *Journal of Political Economy*, 103, no. 4 (1995), pp. 873–92.

Hart, Oliver. *Firms, Contracts and Financial Structure*. Oxford: Oxford University Press, 1995.

Kornai, Janos. *The Socialist System: The Political Economy of Communism*. Princeton: Princeton University Press, 1992.

Lange, Oscar. "On the Economic Theory of Socialism." *Review of Economic Studies*, 4, no. 1 (Oct. 1936), pp. 53–71; 4, no. 2 (Feb. 1937), pp. 123–42.

Phillips, Almarin. "Patents, Potential Competition, and Technical Progress." *American Economic Review*, 66 (May 1966), pp. 301–10.

Weitzman, Martin L. and Chenggang Xu. "Chinese Township-Village Enterprises as Vaguely Defined Cooperatives." *Journal of Comparative Economics*, 18 (1994), pp. 121–45.

# Questions

1  What are the major institutional characteristics of the Chinese economic system?
2  What characterizes the Chinese reform process? Why are these characteristics conducive to successful reform?
3  What were the three sets of forces driving the reform process? And how?
4  What are the basic premises on which the forecast of the future of the Chinese economy presented in this chapter is based? Do you believe that these premises are reasonable?
5  What are the main lessons that you have learned from studying the Chinese economy using this book?

# Conclusion: Lessons for the Study of Economic Transformation

Chapter 22 serves as a concluding chapter of this book as far as the study of the Chinese economy is concerned. In the Introduction of this book four important features in the study of the process of economic transformation are stated. It is only fitting to end the book with lessons that we have learned from the case study of China regarding both the method and the substance of the study of economic transformation.

In section 1 below, the Chinese experience is briefly reviewed in the light of the four main features in the study of the process of economic transformation. Section 2 raises the question of whether unique historical events are inevitable or predictable, and gives three examples of inevitable or predictable historical events. Section 3 discusses a method for forecasting unique historical events as a generalization of the econometric method for forecasting. Section 4 provides six substantive economic propositions that are drawn from the Chinese experience. Section 5 concludes.

## 1 A Brief Review of the Chinese Experience

The four features in the study of the process of economic transformation are the important role of the government, the initiative of nongovernment sectors and their interaction with government policies, the influence of cultural and institutional factors, and the treatment of institutional changes as unique historical events.

In the light of these four features, the following characteristics of China's economic transformation should be noted. First, the reform process has been a combination of the effort of the central government to modernize China and the natural desire of the Chinese people and lower-level government units to improve the economic institutions for their own benefit. For example, it was a combination of the efforts of the farmers and the government which changed the commune system. While reform of the state enterprises and the banking system was mainly directed by the government, collective enterprises in towns and villages and in urban areas grew by themselves. The Chinese people's support for government reform efforts and their own energy and initiative contributed greatly to the success of the reform.

Second, as far as the role of central government is concerned, the process has been a gradual and experimental one and has proceeded in steps based on experience from the previous steps and on prevailing circumstances.

Third, institutional and cultural factors affected both the nature and speed of reform. The factors included bureaucracy in the government and state-owned enterprises and banks, the practice under the former system of economic planning (including the entitlements given to consumers and to state enterprises), as well as China's cultural traditions. The nature of reform in the education system and the legal system is affected by these factors. The legal system has to be based on the moral values of the society. The speed of reform in state-owned enterprises and banks was affected by practices and the bureaucratic tradition developed under the planning system. Bureaucracy affects the speed of formation and growth of private and foreign invested enterprises. With the bureaucrats restricting the free entry and operation of these enterprises, China's market economy could be called a "bureaucratic market economy." Entitlement affects the speed of price reform, reform towards private housing for urban workers, and the speed of restructuring of state enterprises to downsize their staff and workers.

Fourth, the strategy adopted in the process of economic transformation consisted of several elements that have parallels in the transformation of Taiwan's economy two decades earlier. These are the promotion of market forces, reliance on the agricultural sector in the initial stage, encouragement of exports, emphasis on price stability, and the gradual decontrol of foreign exchange.

During the two decades after reform started in 1978, economic growth took place at a phenomenal rate of 9.6 percent per year on average. Five reasons for the success of reform are: (1) the pragmatic approach of the economic reform officials, who "seek truth from facts," as Deng advised, by the use of experimentation; (2) the support of the party and government officials as well as the population; (3) political stability; (4) the high quality and large quantity of human capital in China and the contributions of overseas Chinese and foreign friends and investors to the success of the reform process, not so much by helping in its design as by promoting economic growth to push reform forward once it got started; and (5) the ability of Chinese leaders, especially Deng Xiaoping.

## 2    Three Examples of the Predictability of Unique Historical Events

In observing the occurrence of a historical event one may ask whether it is inevitable. If the answer is yes, that means that the historical conditions at the time are sufficient to predict the occurrence of the events. I have given three examples of inevitable historical events in this book which will be briefly reviewed below. I will present in the next section a general method for forecasting.

### *Why reform started*

Given the four reasons for the initiation of reform stated in section 3.1, was economic reform in 1978 inevitable? My answer is yes, as stated in that section. The first two reasons alone were sufficient for the government to initiate reform. The Cultural Revolution had made the government so unpopular that both it and the people wanted to change eagerly. The direction of change was clear because economic planning was recognized to be a failure. Given these two conditions there was no other way for China to go.

### *Why reform succeeded*

Was the success of China's economic reform inevitable? My answer is yes, as stated in section 3.10. Given the pragmatic attitude and the ability of Chinese leaders and government officials, the use of experimentation, and the support of the Chinese people, there was no way for the reform *in China* toward a market economy to fail unless a market economic system does not work better than a planned economy (which no economist believes). Besides pragmatism and gradualism, the open-door policy allowing international visits and exchanges between foreigners and the Chinese helps change the attitude of the rank-and-file members of the Communist Party to a new mode of thinking in support of a market economy.

### *Predicting the continued growth of the Chinese economy*

Will China's economy continue to grow rapidly until 2020? Yes, because the combination of the existing market institutions and the high quality of Chinese human capital are sufficient to produce rapid growth in the future. Chapter 5 provides an econometric model to forecast China's real GDP up to 2010, and section 5.5 contains forecasts up to 2020. Chapter 22 discusses three sets of forces at work to push China's economy forward. These forces are the government's attempt to modernize the country under an open-door policy, the energy of the Chinese people, and the inertia of bureaucracy and existing economic institutions, some inherited from the period of economic planning. The first two are positive while the third slows down the process of growth. The combination of these forces will lead to a substantial rate of growth, as they did in the last two decades of the twentieth century. The institutional weaknesses of the Chinese state enterprises and the banking system are not so serious as to affect the positive forces driving future economic growth.

## 3   A Method for Forecasting Unique Historical Events

As for a general method to predict discrete historical events, such as the occurrence of a new economic regime or a war, one cannot rely on applying the experience of one single historical event unless all the important conditions surrounding the past event were identical with the current event to be forecasted. As Aldous Huxley has put it, the most important thing we learn from history is that we never learn from history. This statement is correct if by "learning from history" is meant using only one event to predict the future simply by analogy without analysis of the most important conditions. To predict the future, it is necessary to apply knowledge from social sciences, analyze institutional and cultural factors, study the motivations of policy-makers, and, in short, examine the important social-economic-political variables present in that moment of history when the forecast is to be made.

The forecasting method I propose is more general than the method of using an econometric model. Both require the selection of the important variables and knowledge of how the variables affect the outcome. Econometrics is a special case when the variables can be conveniently measured and when the effects can be formulated in mathematical equations. For example, the degree of competence of particular leaders and the quality of human capital in China need not be quantified in the general method. The effects need not be embedded in mathematical equations. Doing either will not help for two reasons. First, the measurements themselves are subject to errors. The ability of certain political leaders, the quality of the human capital of a country, and the degree of belief in Confucianism are difficult to measure. Any measurements constructed are likely to be so arbitrary as not to be able to yield better predictions than the use of common sense and intuition. Second, it is difficult to specify a set of predictive mathematical relations that would give correct weights to different factors that interact in a complicated way. The computer has not yet surpassed the human brain in processing information for making important decisions, such as whether to marry a certain person. Neither can the use of mathematics for the above reasons.

However, certain steps in the use of econometrics for forecasting are applicable in general. First, specify the major "variables" relevant to the historical situation at hand, even if these "variables," like the ability and character of a certain political leader, are not measured quantitatively. Second, write down how each factor may affect the outcome in history, such as whether a war will start. Political scientists, historians, and especially political leaders do forecast such events. What has just been said about forecasting applies to business forecasting also, since business executives in making decisions need to predict the future outcomes under different policy options, although the qualitative variables and their relationships may be different.

One example is to forecast the future of Hong Kong's economic and political system before its return to China in 1997. A pessimistic forecast was based on the judgment that the government in Beijing would interfere with the free-market system. This judgment could be derived from the history of the PRC government in destroying the capitalist system in Shanghai in the early 1950s. An optimistic forecast was based on the judgment that the government in Beijing would honor its commitment to "one country – two systems" and allow Hong Kong to maintain its existing capitalist system. This judgment could be made based on the more recent record of the PRC government in economic reform and the honesty of the government since reform started. The major variable in this case is the behavior of the government. One person may assign a large negative value, and another person a positive value. Given the value, the prediction can be made by a characteristic function that maps a large negative value for the character of the Beijing government into an outcome of zero, meaning no more free market for Hong Kong, and a large positive value into one, meaning preserving the Hong Kong market economy.

When more factors are considered, the forecasting process will be more complicated. These variables may include the opinion of the world community, possible international interventions, and the reaction of the people of Taiwan, which the Chinese leaders would like to be a part of China under the same "one country, two systems" formula, etc. A forecast based on a negative assessment of the government in Beijing may have to be modified if the Taiwan factor is taken into account. To do so may turn a negative forecast of Hong Kong's future into a positive one. Whether this will happen depends on how severe the negative judgment of the PRC government is, and how much weight is given to the Taiwan factor. A forecast can incorporate such factors without quantitatively measuring the negative value for the PRC government, the weight it gives to the Taiwan issue, the possible influence of the international community with which China wishes to trade and from which China wishes to obtain investment, etc. All these considerations can be incorporated in a forecast without using a set of mathematical equations. Even in the use of econometric models for forecasting, judgment plays an important role. Judgment is sometimes incorporated by changing the intercepts of equations that have been estimated by statistical methods. In the forecasting of unique historical events, judgment in the framework just described can be supplemented by mathematical analysis, rather than the other way around.

The general method to forecast unique events and the quantitative method for economic forecasting have three other common features. First, not all events can be forecasted. The knowledge of economics or the limited knowledge of the person doing the forecasting may be insufficient to forecast certain events. The short-run changes in the prices of stocks are an example. Second, to the extent that certain events can be forecasted, such as the demand for automobiles 10 years ahead (see Chow 1960), past data can be utilized to produce the forecast. In the case of an econometric forecast, statistical data and statistical analysis are applied. In the general case, one collects information on the behavior of the relevant important decision-makers, on the quality of the labor force and the entrepreneurs, on the cultural traditions affecting social behavior and the legal system, etc. A Bayesian statistician combines qualitative and quantitative information into a quantitative model. A forecaster of unique historical events combines qualitative and quantitative information into a qualitative framework for prediction. Historical information is utilized to predict the future in both cases. Important possibilities or possible states of the world should not be left out of the analysis in both cases. Third, applying a valid method for forecasting, two persons may end up with different forecasts depending on the variables they have chosen and the models they have assumed. It is the sound judgment and knowledge of the forecaster that determine the accuracy of a forecast in either case.

Given the method of forecasting that we have just outlined, we may apply it to the three forecasts discussed in section 2 as a review of the method. First, given the conditions prevailing in 1978, economic reform was inevitable. The conditions included the need for the Party to change, the recognition of Communist Party leaders, and especially

Deng Xiaoping, that central planning was not a good way to achieve China's modernization, and the support of the Chinese people for change. Second, the success of economic reform, given that it had started, was inevitable. The sufficient conditions were a set of market institutions, though imperfect, and Chinese human capital. In addition, the reform process was pushed forward by the open-door policy. The third is the forecast of continued rapid growth for China into the first and second decades of the twenty-first century. This forecast is based on the momentum of the past. The sufficient conditions are continued government effort for reform, the existing set of market institutions, and (again) the high quality of human capital in China. Hence, substantial economic growth will continue into the future. We assume that great political disturbances will not occur, which appears to be a reasonable assumption.

# 4   Six Economic Propositions from China's Reform Experience

Besides methodological issues, the study of China's economic transformation has provided six propositions on substantive issues in economics.

1) *Private ownership is not necessary for management efficiency.* There have been efficient state-owned and collectively owned enterprises in China. This demonstrates that private ownership in a market economy is not necessary for economic efficiency. One important factor accounting for economic efficiency is the existence of competition from other enterprises. Private ownership is not as important as the following two conditions, which are sufficient for enterprise management to work hard for the enterprises. The two conditions are, first, that the manager should not be able to benefit economically without working hard for the enterprise and, second, that by working hard he or she will be financially rewarded. The first condition can come about if there is competition and if the manager can be held financially accountable. The second condition will result if the manager is allowed to share a part of the profit of the enterprise. These two conditions can serve as the basis for the design of corporate governance.

2) *Market incentives are insufficient for rapid economic growth.* The heading of this section is not a new insight, but should be emphasized following the experience of China's economic development in the last two decades. The high quality of human capital is a necessary condition for rapid economic growth. It is not sufficient if there is no market institution to allow the able people to work for their self-interest and thereby for the economic welfare of the society under the guidance of the invisible hand of the market. Market institutions and high-quality human capital are necessary and sufficient for rapid economic development given political stability.

3) *The form of government is irrelevant to the rate of economic growth.* As a corollary to the last statement of the last paragraph, the form of government is irrelevant to rapid economic development as long as there is sufficient political stability, provided that market institutions and high-quality human capital are present. Rapid economic growth can take place with or without democracy, as Hong Kong and Singapore have demonstrated.

Rapid economic growth can occur under a one-party political system, as in Taiwan from the 1960s to the 1980s and in mainland China in the last two decades of the twentieth century. The form of the political system, such as Communism, is also irrelevant.

4) *Alternative economic institutions can serve a market economy.* An interesting phenomenon was the blossoming of township and village enterprises operating without clear property rights, and the protection of a well-functioning modern legal system. A market economy can flourish under different legal systems and different forms of ownership structure. The study of a variety of legal systems and of ownership arrangements provides challenges to economists accustomed to observing the functioning of private enterprises under a Western legal system.

5) *Political feasibility is an important factor in economic transformation.* Political feasibility affects both the general direction of economic reform and the particular steps to be taken in particular areas and at particular times. It was not possible to introduce reform towards a market-oriented economy while Mao was alive or when the Gang of Four, supporters of the Cultural Revolution, were still in power. The entitlement of certain people to certain privileges made rapid decontrol of prices and urban rents politically unfeasible in the early 1980s.

6) *Bureaucratic economic institutions under central planning are difficult to abolish.* Agriculture was privatized overnight, but state enterprises and state banks could not be changed rapidly. The success of reform in agriculture seems to favor "shock therapy" as a strategy for reform, but the failure in reforming state enterprises and banks seems to raise doubt about the possibility of a quick transformation. In general it is difficult to change any institution that is staffed by bureaucrats who are accustomed to old ways of doing things and to an entitlement to certain economic benefits. The farmers in a household farm are not such bureaucrats. The commune leaders did not lose anything by allowing the farmers to farm separately, as long as they could collect the same amount of output from the farmers. The managers of state enterprises and state banks would lose their privileges and would not know how to manage after privatization. Some of these bureaucrats could not easily be dismissed because they had political support from certain top government officials. The successful state enterprises were run by bureaucrats who were not given vested interests, could be dismissed if profits were low, and were allowed to share a part of the profits. These enterprises were usually subject to competition from other enterprises in the sale of their products. This proposition should be qualified by the condition that the Communist Party remains in power. If it loses political power a new group of people might take control. Even in this case, as in Russia, former members of the Communist Party may still retain their political and economic power after a change in party membership.

# 5  Concluding Remarks

In this book I have tried to broaden the theoretical framework of economics and its method of analysis. The transformation of economic institutions is an important topic in economics. To study this topic, the existing theoretical framework and methods of analysis have to be broadened. In the theoretical framework, the roles of the government and nongovernment institutions and their interactions, the importance of historical-institutional factors, and the consideration of important aspects of the transformation process as isolated events have to be taken into account. For the method of analysis and forecasting, more than mathematical models and statistical data are required. The data and "variables" may not all be quantitative. The "models" may not be confined to being mathematical. Yet both are equally important concepts. Some phenomena may not be subject to forecasting because of the lack of knowledge on the part of the profession or the individual making the forecast. Data, quantitative or qualitative, should be collected and are useful for forecasting.

Economics as a subject of inquiry can evolve and has evolved by the application of existing economic tools to study social problems that are traditionally the domain of other social sciences. It can also evolve and improve by extending its method of inquiry and incorporating noneconomic factors in the deliberation. Just as cost and benefit calculations can explain many social phenomena, noneconomic factors do affect economic decisions for individuals and for a nation. It has been constructive to advance the use of mathematical and quantitative methods in economics and to try to apply them to new areas. It is counterproductive to confine economics to the use of such methods only, by giving up other means of acquiring knowledge. Besides proposing a more general method of analysis and forecasting of unique events, I have also provided six substantive economic propositions based on the experience of China's reform process. The reader may challenge some of these propositions, and should treat them as working hypotheses for further investigation.

Nothing in the above remarks precludes the use of existing economic tools to study the process of economic transformation with its special theoretical and methodological characteristics. In both broadening the method of inquiry and the application of existing tools, there are possibilities for the development of new tools to study the dynamic process of transformation. The important case of China may provide a setting for such a study.

# References

Chow, Gregory C. "Statistical Demand Functions for Automobiles and their Use for Forecasting." In A. C. Harberger, ed., *Demand for Durable Goods*. Chicago: University of Chicago Press, 1960.

# Index

acceleration principle, 112–
13, 114, 115, 117–18
adaptive expectations
hypothesis, 116–17
administration
economic planning, 41–4,
270–1, 378–9
expenditure on, 138
aggregate demand, 110,
111–12
fiscal policy, 139–40
monetary policy, 129, 130,
131
western development
strategy, 184
aggregate output
dynamic optimization
model, 143, 144, 146,
151–7
fiscal policy, 139
human capital, 208–9
neoclassical growth model,
93–4, 96–9, 110–11
agricultural areas *see* rural
areas
Agricultural Bank of China,
54, 73, 235–6
Agricultural Development
Bank, 73, 244
agriculture
asset misuse, 352–3, 354,
356–7
environmental damage, 188

foreign investment, 332,
333
geography of China, 66
government revenue from,
137
gross domestic product,
287
historical background, 18,
19, 25, 26
marginal product of labor,
194
output data reliability, 95
planned economy, 30,
34–6
production function
estimation, 104
reform, 2, 49–50, 58, 60,
63, 64, 65
birth rates and, 201
demand for labor, 215
healthcare, 228, 229, 230
problems and prospects,
85–7, 184–7, 431
responsibility system, 49,
58, 85, 86, 229,
356–7, 408, 419
in Taiwan, 58
three-farm policy, 184, 187
western region, 180, 184–7
WTO membership, 78, 79,
80, 81, 341
air pollution, 188, 189,
190–1, 227

American International Group
(AIG), 250
apprenticeship system, 223
Asian financial crisis, 4
acceleration principle and,
118
economic instability, 375
economic reform, 72,
74–8, 88
fiscal policy, 139
monetary policy, 130–1
nonbank financial
institutions, 247–8
stock market interventions,
264
asset management businesses,
250
asset management companies
(AMCs), 75, 245–6
asset misuse, 347–64, 406
asset management
hypothesis, 349
collectively owned land,
359–60, 409
corruption, 348, 352, 355,
359, 360–3, 406,
409
laws of asset management,
349–52
asset maintenance,
351–2, 353–4
rent seeking, 352, 355,
358, 406

asset misuse (*cont'd*)
   supply of asset services,
     350–1, 352–3, 357
   welfare effects, 352, 353
   personal assets, 352–4
   physical assets, 354–6
   responsibility system,
     356–9
automobile industry
   protectionism, 320, 323
   WTO membership, 79–80,
     81, 84, 341
autonomous regions, 43, 66,
   179

Baldwin, R. E., 320
Bank of China, 73, 236, 245,
   289
Bank of Communications, 73,
   289, 406
banking and financial sector,
   235–54
   Asian financial crisis, 4,
     74–5, 88
   bad loans, 72, 73, 74, 75,
     245–7, 420
   corruption, 237, 242, 361–2
   foreign investors, 247–8,
     250–1, 340, 421
   historical background, 18,
     247, 288, 289
   insurance companies, 247,
     250, 251, 340, 341
   monetary policy, 129, 130,
     131, 132, 235–6,
     237–41, 242, 243,
     244, 246
   pension funds, 247, 251
   reforms, 54, 62, 64, 186,
     235–6, 239
     government role, 251–3,
       264–5
     problems and prospects,
       72–6, 80, 88, 242–7,
       420, 421, 431
   regulation, 252–3, 264,
     361–2, 372
   stock markets, 18, 247,
     248–9, 250–1, 253,
     255–65

trust and investment
   corporations, 247–8,
     253
   WTO membership, 78, 80,
     81, 340, 421
barefoot doctors, 227, 228
Barsky, Robert, 258–9
Becker, Gary S., 204–5, 207,
   208, 213, 219–20, 223
behavior
   asset misuse, 347–64, 406
   democracy and, 416
   legal system and, 370–1
   in a planned economy,
     33–6, 40–1, 117,
     275–8
   *see also* bureaucracy;
     corruption
Binglin Zhong, 389–90
birth rates, 195, 196, 197–8,
   200–2, 203, 204–6
brain drain, 222–3
bribery *see* corruption
Britain, 16, 294, 386, 414
Brzybyla, Heidi, 80
Buck, John L., 18, 104
budget constraints, 276–7,
   289
bureaucracy/bureaucrats, 5,
   406, 408–9
   asset misuse, 348, 349,
     351, 354–5, 356,
     362–3, 406, 409
   banks, 242, 246, 361–2
   foreign investment, 334–5,
     338
   reforms and, 59, 70–1, 80,
     84, 87, 88, 89, 296–7,
     431
bureaucratic market economy,
   89, 289, 296–7
Butterfield, Fox, 348

Campbell, John, 258–9
capital, 207–8
   Heckscher–Ohlin theory of
     trade, 304–7
   human *see* human capital
   in a planned economy, 31
   regional development, 182

township and village
   enterprises, 288, 289
   *see also* capital flows,
     capital stock
capital flows
   foreign investment, 328
   purchasing power parity,
     309
capital stock
   dynamic optimization
     model, 143–4, 146,
     151–6
   multiplier-accelerator
     model, 112–13
   neoclassical growth model,
     93, 94, 96–9, 102,
     103–4, 105–6, 107,
     110, 111, 208
capitalism
   asset use, 347
   collective welfare, 412
   consumption function, 112
   experimentation with,
     54–5, 61
   financial institutions and, 247
   history of in China, 14–15,
     18, 22, 24–5, 288
   socialism distinguished
     from, 407
central bank *see* People's Bank
centrally planned economy
     *see* planned economy
Chairman Mao *see*
     Mao Zedong
Che, Jiahua, 407
Chen, Guidi, 86–7
Cheng, C. Y., 267
Chiang Kai-shek, 17, 21, 25,
   57, 368
children, cost–benefit
   analysis, 204–6
   *see also* one-child-family
     policy
China Banking Regulatory
   Commission, 238,
   246, 361
China International Trust
   and Investment
   Corporation (CITIC),
   247–8, 253

China National Offshore
    Oil Corporation
    (CNOOC), 324
Chinese Communist Party *see*
    Communist Party
Chow, Gregory C., 58, 60,
    95, 96, 98, 101, 103,
    104, 113, 115, 116,
    120, 132–3, 135–6,
    146, 149, 150, 166,
    168, 229, 256, 258–9,
    261, 264, 280, 348,
    360–1, 392, 399, 401
cities *see* urban areas
city governments, 43–4, 202
civil war, 21
classical literature, 11
clothing consumption, 166,
    167–72, 173
Coale, Ansley, 201
Cobb–Douglas production
    function
    demand for labor, 214
    dynamic optimization
        model, 143–4, 150
    human capital, 207, 208, 209
    neoclassical growth model,
        93–4, 96, 101–4
    population, 194
    state enterprises, 280
Cochran–Orcutt procedure,
    101–4
cointegration relation, 135
collective enterprises, 55, 64,
    70, 286
    coexistence with public, 407
    competition from, 71, 290
    conditions for growth,
        288–91, 431
    demand for labor, 215
    efficiency, 291–2
    future of, 296
    gross industrial output, 55,
        56
    legal system, 372–3
    regional development, 185,
        187
    tax revenues from, 137
collectively-owned land,
    359–60, 409

collectivism, 412–14
colleges *see* universities and
    colleges
colonial period, Hong Kong,
    294, 414
command economy *see*
    planned economy
Commercial Bank Law, 54,
    73, 236, 251, 372
commercial banks
    corruption, 237, 242, 361–2
    functioning, 236–7, 242,
        245–7
    macroeconomic policy,
        131, 132, 237, 240,
        243, 246
    pre-1949, 288
    reforms, 54, 75–6, 78, 88,
        235–6, 243–4, 252
    supervision, 253, 361
commercial law, WTO
    membership, 81–2
Commission for
    Reconstructing the
    Economic System, 50,
    53, 60–1, 174, 378,
    397
commune system, 27, 34–6,
    43, 44
    asset misuse, 352–3, 356–7
    data reliability, 95
    healthcare, 227, 228
    reform of, 49, 82, 85, 86
Communist Party
    agricultural development,
        185–7
    banking and financial
        system, 236
    democracy, 82, 83–4, 85,
        369
    economic reforms, 47, 51,
        52, 54, 57–8, 61, 69–
        70, 88–9, 236, 357–8,
        431
    education, 216, 218
    family planning, 198–9
    foreign investment, 326,
        328–9
    historical background, 3, 4,
        17, 21, 24–5, 26, 28

legal system, 368–70, 371
one-party system, 414–16
the planned economy, 41,
    44, 270–1
political indoctrination, 216
regional income equality,
    178
rural development, 185–7
socialist market economy,
    295–6, 418
township and village
    enterprises, 288, 296
WTO membership, 82,
    83–4, 85
comparative advantage
    theory, 302, 305, 317,
    319, 320, 321, 322–3
computable general
    equilibrium model, 81,
    122
Confucianism, 5, 11–12, 21,
    289, 356, 366, 371,
    385, 406
Constitution, 369
construction projects, 360,
    362–3, 380
consumer behavior, 34
consumer demand theory,
    145
consumer goods
    pirating, 336–7, 411
    trade policy, 320–1, 322
    as work incentives, 358
consumption
    by province, 172–4,
        178–9
    durable goods, 165, 175
    dynamic optimization
        model, 143, 146, 147,
        149–50, 151–7
    effect of Cultural
        Revolution on, 119
    effect of Great Leap
        Forward on, 119,
        151–2
    healthcare, 229
    household expenditure
        patterns, 165–72
    housing, 166, 167–73,
        174–5

consumption (cont'd)
  multiplier-accelerator
    model, 111–12, 113,
    114, 115, 116,
    117–19, 147
  in a planned economy, 30,
    31–3, 37, 117
  regional inequality, 178–9
  rural per capita
    expenditures, 162,
    163, 164–5, 172–4,
    178–9
  social insurance system,
    294–5
  trends in per capita, 161–5
consumption function,
    111–12, 125
  see also consumption,
    multiplier-accelerator
    model
contract responsibility system,
    48–9, 52, 243, 281,
    358–9, 362
cooperation, nature of in
    China, 290
  see also guanxi
Cooperative Medical System
    (CMS), 227–8, 230
cooperatives, joint stock, 291
corporate governance, 71,
    245, 281, 282, 361,
    407, 408
corruption
  asset misuse, 348, 352, 355,
    359, 360–3, 406, 409
  banks, 237, 242, 361–2
  collectively-owned land,
    360, 409
  economic reform and, 59,
    62–3, 355, 359, 360–3
  foreign investment, 338,
    339
  major infrastructure
    projects, 380
  in a planned economy, 40
  privatization of state
    enterprises, 72, 281–2,
    359, 361
  regional development
    strategy, 187, 362

rural poverty, 86–7, 185
stock exchange admission,
    259
township and village
    enterprises, 291
county administration, 43–4,
    87, 187
credit
  bad debts, 72, 73, 74, 75
  monetary policy, 129–33
credit cooperatives, 244
credit quotas, 244–5
cross-section analysis, 165
cultural development
    expenditure, 136, 138
cultural factors
  asset misuse, 356
  bureaucracy, 406
  corruption, 363
  economic transformation, 2,
    5–6, 426
  education, 385–6
  legal system, 366, 371
  major historical dynasties,
    10–12, 21
Cultural Revolution, 28
  economic effects, 142, 143,
    146, 154–7, 119
  economic fluctuations, 119
  economic growth, 96
  economic reform, 47, 48,
    49–50, 61, 427
  education, 28, 218–19
  legal system and, 369, 370
currency exchange rate see
    foreign exchange rate
currency supply see money
    supply

Daoism, 11
Dasgupta, Susmita, 189–91
data, reliability of, 94–6, 140
De Haan, Jacob, 243
death rates, 195–6, 197, 198,
    226
decision processes,
    government's, 381–3
decollectivization, 49
  see also household
    responsibility system

defense expenditure, 136,
    138
DeLong, J. Bradford, 258–9
demand
  birth rate and, 204–5
  for education, 219–20,
    399–403
  elasticity of
    consumption patterns,
      166–74
    exchange rates, 318
    for money, 246
  for labor, 211, 213–16
  labor supply and, 211–12
  marginal productivity
    theory of, 213–15
  multiplier-accelerator
    model, 110, 111
  see also aggregate demand
democracy
  government's decision
    processes, 382–3
  historical background, 3, 4,
    20, 22, 367, 368
  Hong Kong, 294, 382,
    414–15
  legal system, 367, 368, 369
  one-party system and,
    414–16
  prospects for, 420–1
  WTO membership, 82–5
Deng Xiaoping
  assumption of leadership,
    4, 28–9
  economic reforms, 47, 49,
    61, 63, 64
  education, 391, 399
  foreign investment, 326,
    328
  monetary policy, 129–30,
    240
  Tiananmen Square
    demonstrations, 63
  township and village
    enterprises, 290
  western region, 180, 183
deterministic trends, 144,
    149–50
disease, 226, 227
dissidents, 3, 4–5

distribution costs, PPP theory, 309–10
Dixit, Avinash, 416
Donaldson, R. Glen, 258–9
Duan Qirui, 367
dynamic optimization model, 142–57
dynasties, history of, 10–16, 21–2, 289, 293

eastern region, 179–80, 181, 182, 184, 331
econometric modeling, 120–2, 392
  computable general equilibrium model, 81, 122
  dynamic optimization, 142–57
  foreign investment, 338–9
  future historical events, 428–9
  household expenditure patterns, 166–72
  industrial pollution, 190–1
  monetary policy, 133–6
  multiplier-accelerator model, 110–19
  neoclassical growth model, 93–4, 99–107, 110–11
  state enterprises, 275–81, 291–2, 359
  township and village enterprises, 291–2
  vector autoregression system, 119–20, 135–6
economic asset misuse see economic behavior, asset misuse
economic behavior
  asset misuse, 347–64, 406
  democracy and, 416
  legal system and, 370–1
  in a planned economy, 33–6, 40–1, 117, 275–8
  see also corruption
economic data, reliability of, 94–6, 140

economic development
  characteristics affecting, 406–17
  consumption, 161–75
  environmental policies, 177, 187–91
  government officials' role in, 376–7
  human capital, 194–5, 207–30
  policy statement in 1997, 69–70
  population, 193–206
  western China, 177–87, 362
economic fluctuations
  dynamic optimization model, 143
  government role, 375
  multiplier-accelerator model, 110–19
  vector autoregression system, 119–20
economic freedom, 3, 20, 293, 294–5, 373
economic growth
  dynamic optimization model, 143
  fiscal policy, 139–40
  forecasting, 104–8, 422–3, 427, 430
  human rights and, 413
  market incentives and, 430
  neoclassical model, 93–107, 208
  political system and, 416, 430–1
  population policy, 203–4
  predictability, 427, 430
economic infrastructure see infrastructure
economic instability see economic fluctuations
economic institutions
  inertia, 419–20
  macroeconomic policies and, 124
  natural evolution, 253, 288, 290, 293, 295, 372–3, 431
  planned economy, 41–4

reform see economic reform
regional development, 181
role in economic transformation, 1, 2
  see also agriculture; banking and financial sector; education; foreign investment; foreign trade; legal system; state enterprises
economic planning see planned economy
Economic Planning Commission, 29–31
economic reform, 47–67, 425–6
  consumption and, 162, 163, 174–5
  corruption, 59, 62–3, 355, 359, 360–3
  demand for labor, 215
  planning in China's market economy, 377–81
  predictability, 427, 429–30
  problems, 69–87, 417–23
  propositions from China's experience, 430–1
  prospects for, 87–9, 417–23, 427
  see also specific economic institutions
economic transformation, study of, 3–4, 425–32
economic zones, 54–5, 61, 329
Economics Commission, 41–2
economics education, 391–9
economics profession, 397–8
education, 56, 385–403
  attainment levels, 388
  bank personnel, 236–7
  demand for, 219–20, 399–403
  determining levels of, 413–14
  economics, 391–9
  expenditure on, 136, 138, 387, 402
  future prospects, 421–2

education (*cont'd*)
    government policy,
        388–91, 403
    government role, 374, 376
    historical background, 18,
        26, 28, 218–19,
        385–7
    Hong Kong, 294
    human capital, 208–9, 210,
        216–26
    medical, 227
    regional development, 181,
        186
efficiency, TVEs, 291–2
    *see also* total factor
        productivity
Eijffinger, Sylvester C., 243
elasticity of demand
    consumption patterns,
        166–74
    exchange rates, 318
    for money, 236
elections, 382, 414–15
emigration *see* migration
emperors, 10, 12, 13, 15, 16,
        20, 21
endogenous variables, 113,
        114, 120
energy conservation, 188,
        189
Engel's law, 165, 168
Engle, Robert, 134, 135
enterprises *see* collective
        enterprises; foreign-
        owned enterprises;
        individual-owned
        enterprises; state
        enterprises
entrepreneurship, 13, 290,
        296–7, 417
environmental policies, 177,
        187–91
Epstein, Joel, 250
error-correction equations,
        134, 135
Europe, 301, 331
exchange rate *see* foreign
        exchange rate
expansionism, 15, 22
exploration, 15, 22

Export/Import Bank *see* Import
        and Export Bank
export-processing zones, 316
exports, national income
        determination, 113
    *see also* foreign trade

factories, in a planned
        economy, 30, 35, 43–4
    *see also* First Lathe Factory
        of Beijing
Falun Gong, 3–4
family decisions, labor
        supply, 212–13
family planning, 194, 197–202,
        205
family policy
    economic growth, 105, 106,
        107
    population control, 198–204,
        205
family size, household
        expenditure, 168–9
family values, 11, 12
famine, 27
farm economy *see* agriculture
female:male ratio, 199–200,
        201
financial crisis, Asia *see*
        Asian financial crisis
financial repression, 339
financial sector *see* banking
        and financial sector
First Lathe Factory of
        Beijing, 268–75
fiscal policy, 125, 136–40,
        244–5, 379
Fisher, R. A., 263
Five Year Plans, 26, 38, 41,
        44, 125, 177–8, 187,
        271, 377–81
food, consumption patterns,
        165, 166, 167–72, 173
food supply, population and,
        193–4, 203
forecasting the Chinese
        economy, 104–8,
        417–23, 427
forecasting historical events,
        427–30

foreign-exchange certificates,
        311–12
foreign exchange rate
    Asian financial crisis, 76,
        77–8
    determination, 307–13
    economic reforms to the
        mid-1990s, 59
    monetary policy, 132, 240,
        422
    trade policy, 315, 316, 317,
        318, 319, 321
foreign-invested companies
    *see* foreign-owned
        enterprises
foreign investment, 326–43
    Asian financial crisis, 75,
        76–8
    conditions for, 334–9,
        340–1
    countries of origin, 330–1
    exchange rate and, 309
    export-processing zones,
        316
    forms of, 329–30
    from Taiwan, 331, 342–3
    government perceived role
        of, 326–8
    historical developments,
        328–9
    industrial structure, 331–2
    nonbank financial
        institutions, 247–8,
        250–1
    protectionism, 323–4, 341
    reforms to the mid-1990s,
        54–5, 59–60, 64
    regional development,
        181–2
    regional distribution, 331
    regulation of, 332–4
    state of FDI at 2002,
        329–32
    stock trading, 248, 249
    WTO membership, 78,
        79–80, 327, 339–42,
        421
foreign-owned enterprises, 55,
        70, 286
    Asian financial crisis, 76

banking and financial
    sector, 244, 247, 251,
    340
  historical development, 329
  industrial value added, 332
  setting up, 335
  state of at 2002, 329–30
  WTO membership, 78, 80,
    339–40
foreign trade, 299–324
  Asian financial crisis, 76,
    77
  China's policy, 301,
    313–22
  exchange rates, 307–13,
    315, 316, 317, 318,
    319, 321
  fiscal policy, 140
  free trade principles,
    301–7, 318–20, 322–3
  government interference,
    297
  historical background,
    13–14, 16, 22
  infant industries, 320–2
  monetary policy, 131, 132,
    240
  population and, 203
  reforms to the mid-1990s,
    54, 58–9, 64
  see also foreign trade,
    China's policy
  relations with Taiwan,
    342–3
  statistics, 299–301, 314,
    316
  US protectionism, 322–4
  WTO membership, 78–85,
    322, 327, 339–42, 421
Foreign Trade Law, 340–1
fortune-telling, 11
free-market economy, 293–5
  see also market economy
free trade, 297, 301–7,
    318–20, 322–3
freedom, 3–5, 20, 293, 294–
    5, 369, 373, 412–13
freelancers, 216
Friedman, Milton, 111–12,
    120, 125–6, 131

Frisch, Ragner, 114
fuel consumption, 166, 167,
    168–9, 172
fund management joint
    ventures, 250
future Chinese economy,
    104–8, 417–23, 427
future historical events,
    427–30

geography of China, 65–7,
    180, 182
globalization, 341
Goldfeld, Stephen M., 276
Gordon, Myron, 258
Gordon, Roger, 136
governance, 71, 245, 281,
    282, 361, 407, 408
government, 3–5
  bureaucracy rationale, 349
  decision processes, 381–3
  economic planning
    structures, 29–30,
    41–4, 270, 378–80
  see also planned
    economy
  economic transformation
    role, 1, 2–3, 425–6
  see also government,
    market economy role
  education policy, 218–19,
    220–2, 387–91, 403
  environmental policies,
    187–91
  exchange rates, 310–13,
    315, 316, 317, 318,
    319, 321
  expenditure, 125, 126, 136,
    138, 139–40
  foreign investment, 326–9,
    332–4
  foreign trade policy, 301,
    313–22
  form of see political system
  healthcare policy, 230
  Hong Kong, 294
  imperial dynasties, 10,
    16–17, 289
  infant industry development,
    320–2, 376

labor policy, 214–16
legal system, 367–70, 410
macroeconomic policies,
    124–40, 237–41,
    242–3, 244–5, 246,
    312–13, 375, 379, 422
  market economy role, 29,
    288, 290, 293, 294–5,
    373–7
    economic reform, 57, 59,
      87, 88, 295–6, 359
    financial system reform,
      251–3
    future prospects, 418–19,
      420
    planning and, 377–81
  People's Republic of
    China, 20–1, 26–9
  population policy, 193–4,
    197, 198–204, 206
  Republic of China, 17,
    20–1, 367–8
  revenues, 136, 137, 139
  stock trading, 250–1, 253,
    264–5
  streamlining of, 186–7
  township and village
    enterprises, 289, 290–1
  western region policy,
    182–4
gradualism, 61, 65, 84, 322
Granger, C. W. J., 134, 135
Great Leap Forward, 27, 28,
    40
  economic effects, 119, 142,
    143, 146, 150–7
  economic fluctuations, 119
  economic growth, 95, 96
  education, 218
  First Lathe Factory during,
    272
  population, 197
Griffin, Keith, 224
gross domestic product (GDP)
  Asian financial crisis, 76
  bad loans, 245
  data on, 19, 95–9
  economic growth analysis,
    95–9, 102–3, 104–7,
    111

gross domestic product (GDP)
(*cont'd*)
  economic reforms to mid-
    1990s, 60, 62, 63–4
  education expenditure, 387,
    402
  effect of Great Leap
    Forward on, 151–3
  fiscal policy, 139–40
  Five-Year Plan targets, 379
  forecasting, 104–7
  foreign trade, 299, 316
  government expenditure,
    136, 139–40
  government revenue, 136,
    137
  monetary policy, 127–8,
    131, 132
  nonstate sector, 287, 289–90
  pollution, 189
  WTO membership, 79, 81
gross national product (GNP)
  nonstate sector, 287
  projecting to 2020, 107–8
  protectionism, 323
Groves, Theodore, 407
Guangdong International
    Trust and Investment
    Corporation (GITIC),
    247–8, 253
*guanxi* (social networking), 2,
    5, 335–6, 356, 371,
    372, 409, 410

Hall, Robert E., 116, 117
Han dynasty, 13, 22, 293, 385
Han, Jun, 87
Hart, Oliver, 407
healthcare, 186, 216, 226–9,
    230, 294
Heckscher–Ohlin theory of
    trade, 303–7
Hicks, J. R., 211, 212
higher education *see* universities
    and colleges
highways, 181–2, 183, 380
historical background, 2–3,
    5–6, 9–10
  Communist Party rise to
    power, 24–5

corruption, 363
education, 18, 26, 28,
    218–19, 385–7
foreign investment, 328–9
legal system, 366–8, 410,
    411–12
major dynasties, 10–16,
    21–2, 289, 293
People's Republic of
    China, 15, 21, 22,
    26–9, 267–8
the planned economy,
    29–44, 267–71
pre-1949 private enterprise,
    17–20, 288
the Republic of China, 15,
    16–21, 22, 367–8
historical events
  forecasting, 427–30
  predictability, 426–7
Hong Kong
  after 1997 return to China,
    4, 16, 294, 428–9
  banks, 244
  cession to Britain, 16
  decision processes, 381–2
  democracy, 294, 382,
    414–15
  economists, 397
  exchange rate, 319
  free-market system, 293–4
  government-sponsored
    research, 376
  housing, 374–5
  human capital, 222
  investment in China, 330,
    331, 342
  investment in, 328
  share trading, 249
    *see also* Hong Kong
    Stock Exchange
  social security, 294, 295
  Taiwan and, 342–3
  taxation, 382
  trade with, 301
Hong Kong Stock Exchange,
    261, 262, 263–4, 294
household behavior
  expenditure patterns,
    165–72

labor supply, 212–13
per capita consumption,
    162–5, 172–4
household responsibility
    system, 49, 58, 85, 86,
    229, 356–7, 408, 419
housing
  asset misuse, 354
  commercialization, 174–5
  consumption, 164–5, 166,
    167–73, 174–5
  government role, 374–5
  policy statement in 1997, 70
  two-tier price system, 53
  urban–rural gap, 86
  village planning, 187
Houthakker, H. S., 165, 168–9
Hsiao, William, 227, 228
Hu Yaobang, 61, 62
Hua Guofeng, 4, 28
human capital, 5, 207–30
  abundance of, 417, 420
  dynamic optimization
    model, 155, 156
  economic reforms, 62, 63,
    64, 87, 88
  education, 208–9, 210,
    216–26
  government role, 374
  healthcare, 216, 226–9
  Heckscher–Ohlin theory of
    trade, 306–7
  historical background, 11,
    12, 14, 18, 21, 417
  investment in, 194–5, 208,
    216–26, 349, 353–4,
    374
  misuse of, 349, 353–4
  population policy, 203
  quality index of, 209
  rates of return to schooling,
    224–6
  regional development, 181
  township and village
    enterprises, 288
human rights, 412–13, 414
Huxley, Aldous, 428

Ianchovichina, Elena, 322
Ichimura, Schinichi, 121–2

immigration *see* migration
imperial rule
 major dynasties, 10–16,
 21–2
 moral tradition and, 367
imperialism, 5–6, 16, 22, 25
Import and Export Bank, 73,
 244
imports *see* foreign trade
impulse responses, vector
 autoregression model,
 120
incentives
 asset misuse, 348–9, 353,
 356–7
 banking and financial
 sector, 237, 239, 242
 environmental protection,
 188–9
 joint stock cooperatives,
 291
 in a planned economy, 32,
 35, 36, 40, 49, 276
 public ownership and,
 407–8
 *see also* responsibility
 system
 rapid economic growth and,
 430
 regional development, 185,
 187
 state enterprises, 49, 50,
 51–2, 280, 281–2,
 283, 284, 358–9,
 375–6, 407
 two-tier price system, 53
income, national *see* national
 income
income–consumption relation,
 111
income effect, labor supply,
 212, 213
income tax
 democracy and, 382
 government revenue from,
 137
incomes
 democracy and, 382, 416,
 421
 education inequality, 402–3

healthcare, 229
household expenditure
 patterns, 165, 168
 in a planned economy, 30,
 32–3
 population and, 203, 204–6
 regional inequality, 178,
 179, 180–1
 urban–rural gap, 85, 86
 *see also* wage rates
indifference curve analysis,
 211–12
individual-owned enterprises,
 55, 70, 286
 asset misuse, 357
 national output, 55, 56, 60
 regional development, 185
individualism, 12, 383, 412,
 414
Industrial Catalogue Guiding
 Foreign Investment,
 333
Industrial and Commercial
 Bank of China, 54,
 72–3, 235–6
industrial development
 foreign investment, 331–2,
 333
 government role, 376
 historical background,
 16–17, 18–20, 26, 27,
 288
 People's Bank and, 244–5
 trade policy, 320–2
 western region, 180
industrial output, by
 ownership type, 55–6
industrial pollution, 188–91
industrial reform, 50–1, 63–4
industrial structure
 foreign investment, 331–2
 western development, 183
inertia, economic institutions,
 419–20
infanticide, 199
infectious diseases, 226, 227
inflation
 civil war, 21
 economic reform, 59, 62–3,
 73

exchange rate and, 312
 monetary policy, 126,
 127–36, 239, 240–1,
 246, 422
 in a planned economy, 33
 quantity theory of money,
 126, 132
infrastructure
 fiscal policy and, 139
 foreign investment, 334, 340
 future prospects, 421
 government role, 373, 421
 Hong Kong, 294
 institutional *see* education;
 legal system
 project evaluation, 380
 regional development, 181–
 2, 183–4, 185, 186
 traditional Chinese market
 economy, 18
institutional factors, 406–17
 economic transformation,
 2–3, 88, 426
 inertia, 419–20
 WTO membership, 82–5
 *see also* economic
 institutions; economic
 reform
institutional infrastructure *see*
 education; legal system
insurance companies, 247,
 250, 251, 340, 341
insurance system
 health, 229, 230
 social security, 229–30,
 294–5, 374
intellectual property, 81–2,
 336–7, 341, 411
intellectuals
 control of/attacks on, 26,
 28, 181, 218
 education reforms, 56
 *see also* scholarship
interest rates
 exchange rates and, 309, 312
 money supply and, 129,
 130, 131, 132, 240,
 244
 People's Bank objectives,
 239, 243, 244

international relations
  Chinese nationalism, 6, 16
  historical background, 13,
    15, 16, 22, 28–9
international trade *see* foreign
    trade
internet, 389–90
investment
  credit cooperatives, 244
  dynamic optimization
    model, 143–5, 147,
    149–50
  economic growth model,
    93, 94, 98, 105, 106,
    107, 111
  economic reforms to the
    mid-1990s, 57
  fiscal policy, 139, 140
  foreign *see* foreign
    investment
  in human capital, 194–5,
    208, 216–26, 349,
    353–4, 374
  "iron rice bowl", 71, 214–15,
    352–3
  in a market economy, 29
  multiplier-accelerator
    model, 112–13, 114,
    115, 117–19, 147
  in a planned economy, 29,
    32
  *see also* stock market

Japan
  comparative advantage, 320
  investment in China, 330,
    331, 338, 342
  political system, 414
  role in Chinese history,
    5–6, 15, 20, 368, 386
  trade with, 301
Jefferson, Gary H., 291
Jefferson, Thomas, 1
Ji Hua, 221
Jiang Zemin, 28, 52, 61,
    69–70, 77, 398
job creation, 215
job outsourcing, 323
job security ("iron rice bowl"),
    71, 214–15, 352–3

Johnson, D. Gale, 200
joint stock cooperatives, 291
joint ventures, 250, 328, 329,
    334, 335, 337–8,
    339–40

Kamstra, Mark, 258–9
Keynes, John Maynard, 111,
    112, 125, 139, 143
Klein, Lawrence, 121–2, 392,
    398
Koopmans, T. C., 303
Kornai, Janos, 276
Kunming Lake, 187–8
Kuomintang (Nationalist
    Party), 17, 368, 415
Kwan, Y. K., 146, 149, 256,
    261, 264

labor, 207, 208
  demand for, 211, 213–16
  dynamic optimization
    model, 143–4, 147,
    149, 150
  employee numbers in state
    sector, 287
  foreign investment, 326–7
  foreign trade policy, 322
  health workers, 227
  Heckscher–Ohlin theory of
    trade, 304–6
  marginal product of, 194,
    213–14, 215
  misuse of, 348–51, 352–4
  mobility of
    asset misuse, 353
    human capital, 222
    regional development,
      182, 185
    rural migrants, 85–6,
      185, 186, 222
  neoclassical growth model,
    93, 94, 96–9, 102,
    103–4, 105–6, 107,
    208
  outsourcing of jobs, 323
  protectionism, 323
  state enterprise reform, 70,
    72, 282, 283
  supply of, 209–13, 351

Keynes' theory, 111
  law of asset services and,
    351
  marginal output, 104
  in a planned economy,
    30–1, 35
  technological
    development, 14
  township and village
    enterprises, 289–90
  *see also* unemployment
labor camps, 4–5
labor participation
  birth rate, 198, 205, 206
  family decisions, 213
  per capita consumption,
    163–4
land development, asset
    misuse, 359–60, 409
land reform, 26, 27, 49, 50, 58
  asset misuse, 354, 356–7,
    359, 409
  rural poverty, 85, 86, 87
land resources, western
    region, 180
Langlois, John D., 245
language, written, 11, 12
leadership, state enterprises,
    270–1
learning *see* scholarship
leasing system *see*
    responsibility system
least-squares method, 99–100,
    115–16, 118–19,
    148–9
legal system, 366–73
  collective enterprises, 55,
    64
  executive branch, 367–8,
    369
  foreign investment, 328,
    335–7, 340–1
  *guanxi*, 2, 5, 371, 372, 409,
    410
  intellectual property, 81–2,
    336–7, 341, 411
  judicial branch, 367, 370
  legislative branch, 367
  in a market economy, 293,
    371–3

post-1949, 368–71
    *see also* legal system,
        reform of
    pre-1949, 366–8, 410,
        411–12
    reform of, 2, 3, 5, 12,
        56–7, 89, 368–71,
        372, 426
    in a socialist market
        economy, 409–12
    township and village
        enterprises and, 290
    WTO membership, 81–2,
        84, 297, 340
legislation and regulation
    banking and financial
        sector, 54, 73, 236,
        242, 243, 251,
        252–3, 264, 361–2,
        372
    environmental protection,
        188–9
    foreign investment, 328,
        332–4, 338, 339,
        340–1
    legal system modernization,
        370
    marriage, 201–2
    stock markets, 248
    WTO membership, 81, 82,
        340–1
Leibenstein, Harvey, 276
levies
    agricultural, 86–7, 185, 362
    pollution, 189, 190–1
Lewis, W. Arthur, 194
Li, K. T., 58, 376–7, 406
Li Kaixin, 37–9
Li Peng, 370
Li Shantong, 81
Li Wei, 136, 246–7
Li Yuanhong, 367
Liang Shiyi, 289
Liang Yansun, 376, 406
likelihood function, 149
Lin, Anloh, 96, 103
Lin, Jonathan, 256, 261, 264
Lin, Justin Yifu, 353
linear stochastic equations,
    115–16

liquidity trap, 131
Liqun Jin, 245
literature, Zhou dynasty, 11
Litigation Law, 370
Liu Shaoqi, 27, 218
Liu, T. C., 19, 57
Londregan, John, 416
Long March, 17

Ma Hong, 176, 268
Ma Yin-Chu, 194
McMillan, John, 353
macroeconomic analysis
    economic fluctuations,
        110–22
    economic growth, 93–108
    macroeconomic policies,
        124–40
    political events' effects,
        142–57
macroeconomic control
    mechanism, 379
macroeconomic policies,
    124–40, 375
    exchange rate and, 312–13
    fiscal, 125, 136–40, 244–5,
        379
    future prospects, 422
    monetary, 120, 125–36,
        235–6, 237–41, 242,
        243, 244, 246, 379
maintenance of assets, 351–2,
    353–4
male:female ratio, 199–200,
    201
Malthus, Thomas R., 193,
    194
management efficiency,
    private ownership and,
        430
managers
    misuse of assets *see* asset
        misuse
    state enterprises, 70–1, 80,
        407, 408–9
        after initial reform,
            278–81, 358
        asset misuse, 358, 359
        banks, 236, 237, 242, 245
        inertia, 419, 420

late 1990s reforms, 282,
    283, 284
planned economy,
    270–1, 275–8
manufactured goods
    export, 301, 305
    protectionism, 320–1
manufacturing sector
    foreign investment, 332
    WTO membership, 79–81,
        84
    *see also* automobile
        industry; state
        enterprises
Mao Zedong, 4
    control of intellectuals, 26
    Cultural Revolution, 28,
        218
    environmental damage, 187
    first Qin emperor and, 12
    Great Leap Forward, 27, 95
    legal system, 369
    planned economy, 35
    population growth, 193–4
    Sino-Soviet relations, 328
    unification of China, 12,
        20–1
marginal product of labor,
    194, 213–14, 215
marginal productivity theory
    of demand, 213–15
marginal revenue product,
    213–14
market economy
    characteristics of free,
        293–5
    China as, 88–9, 286, 289,
        295–7, 373–7
    characteristics, 406–17
    demand for education,
        399–403
    government's decision
        processes, 381–3
    misuse of assets,
        347–64, 406
    planning and, 377–81
    prospects, 418–23
    reforms for *see* economic
        reform
    role of planning, 377–81

market economy (*cont'd*)
    free trade, 297, 301–7,
        318–20, 322–3
    history of in China, 11–12,
        13, 14–15, 17–20, 22,
        288, 289, 293
    legal system, 293, 371–3
    planned economy
        compared, 29, 30–2
    social security, 294
market incentives *see*
    incentives
marriage age, 201–2, 205
Martin, Will, 322
Marx, Karl, 126
Marxian economics courses,
    391, 392, 393
material balancing, 37–9, 41,
    43
maximization problems, 145,
    146, 277, 359
maximum likelihood method,
    149–50
medical care *see* healthcare
Meiselman, David, 125–6
migration
    human capital, 222–3
    labor mobility, 85–6, 182,
        353
    regional development
        policy, 185, 186
Mincer equation, 208, 224
Ming dynasty, 15, 22
missionaries, 386
misuse of assets *see* asset
    misuse
modernization
    education, 386
    foreign trade, 314, 315
    historical background,
        18–20, 27, 47
    legal system, 370, 419
    western region, 180, 183
    *see also* economic reform
monetarism, 126
monetary policy, 120, 125–36,
    235–6, 237–41, 242,
    243, 244, 246, 379, 422
money, quantity theory of,
    125–6, 132

money flow, in a planned
    economy, 39
money supply, 62, 126–36,
    235–6, 238, 240–1,
    244, 246, 312, 322
monopolies, 375, 411
moral system, 366–7, 370–1,
    409, 410
    *see also* Confucianism
multiplier-accelerator model,
    110–13
    dynamic properties, 113–15
    estimating for the Chinese
        economy, 116–19
municipalities, 43, 66, 67

National Development and
    Reform Commission
    (NDRC), 378, 379
national income, 95–6
    dynamic optimization
        model, 144
    Friedman's theory, 111–12,
        125–6
    Keynesian theory, 111,
        112, 125
    multiplier-accelerator
        model, 111–19
    *see also* gross domestic
        product
nationalism, 5–6, 16, 20, 21,
    22, 89, 367
Nationalist Party
    (Kuomintang), 17,
    368, 415
Neary, J. P., 34
neighborhood administration,
    43, 44
neoclassical growth model,
    93–4
    data for, 94–9
    GDP forecasting, 104–7
    human capital and, 208
    multiplier-accelerator
        model compared,
        110–11
    production function
        estimation, 101–4
    regression analysis and,
        99–101

New York Stock Exchange,
    261, 262, 263–4
nonstate sectors
    economic reforms, 55–6,
        64, 65, 69–70, 89, 253
    future of Chinese market
        economy, 295–7
    health insurance, 229
    pre-1949 private enterprise,
        17–20, 288
    relative efficiency, 291–2
    relative growth, 286–7
    role in economic
        transformation, 1, 2
    WTO membership, 79, 297
    *see also* collective
        enterprises; foreign-
        owned enterprises;
        individual-owned
        enterprises

Ohlin, B., 303
oil companies, 324
old-age insurance system,
    229–30, 294–5
on-the-job training, 223
one-child-family policy,
    198–204, 206
    economic growth, 105, 106,
        107
one-party system, 414–16
one-tail test, 292
Opium War, 16, 386
optimization model, 142–57
output, aggregate *see*
    aggregate output
output planning, 36–41, 271,
    272–3, 278
outsourcing of jobs, 323
overseas Chinese, 63, 65, 390
overseas exploration, 15, 22
overseas-funded enterprises
    *see* foreign-owned
    enterprises

parameter estimation, 99–100,
    115–16, 118–19,
    147–50
Pareto optimality, 175
patents, 336–7, 341, 411

peasants *see* rural areas
pension funds, 247, 251
pension system, 229–30, 294–5
People's Bank, 237–9
  bad loans, 246
  commercial banks and, 236–7, 243, 253, 361
  economic reforms, 54, 64, 72, 73, 75–6, 235, 244–5
  independence, 242–3
  monetary policy, 129, 130–1, 132, 235–6, 237–41, 242, 243, 244, 246
People's Bank Law, 54, 73, 236, 242, 243, 251, 253
People's Congress, 4, 41, 50, 82, 187, 199, 314, 369, 370, 377
People's Construction Bank of China, 54, 73, 235–6
People's Insurance Company of China, 251
People's Republic of China (PRC), history, 15, 21, 22, 26–9, 247, 267–8, 369
  *see also* government
permanent income hypothesis, 111–12, 116–17
Phillips, Almarin, 411
pirating, 336–7, 411
planned economy, 29–33
  behavior of economic units, 33–6, 40–1, 117, 275–8
    *see also* asset misuse
  dynamic optimization model, 146, 147, 156
  foreign trade, 314, 319–20
  organizational structures, 29–30, 41–4, 270–1
  output planning, 36–41, 271
  People's Bank, 239
  quantity theory of money, 126

reform of *see* economic reform
  state enterprises, 267–78
planning, role in China's market economy, 377–81
policy banks, 73, 244–5, 252
political discontent, 62–3, 240
political dissidents, 3, 4–5
political events,
    macroeconomic effects, 142–57
  *see also* Cultural Revolution; Great Leap Forward
political feasibility, 431
political indoctrination, 216
political power, 5
  abuse of, 86–7, 185, 187
  major dynasties, 10, 12, 15, 16
  Mao Zedong, 12, 27, 28, 218
  the planned economy, 41, 44
  Republic of China, 17, 367–8
  transfer on Mao's death, 28
  WTO membership, 82–3, 85
political pressures
  exchange rate policy, 313, 316
  government's decision processes, 383
  monetary policy, 239, 242
  trade policy, 322, 323
political rights, 382
political stability, 420–1
  economic reform, 62–3, 82
  WTO membership, 82, 84–5
political system, 414–16
  Chinese market economy, 296
  decision processes, 381–3
  economic growth, 430–1
  legal system, 367–70
  WTO membership, 82–5
pollution, 188–91

population, 193–206
postal services, 342, 343
poverty, 85–7
  healthcare, 229
  regional inequality, 178, 180–1, 184–7
power, abuse of, 86–7, 185, 187, 335, 406
  asset misuse, 348, 354–5, 359
pragmatic government, 416–17
predetermined variables, 113, 114, 116, 120
prefectures, 43
present-value model, stock prices, 256–9, 264
prices
  comparative advantage theory, 302
  determination of for stock, 255–65
  economic reforms, 49, 51–3, 59, 65, 86
  foreign trade policy, 317, 318–19, 321, 322
  Heckscher–Ohlin theory of trade, 305
  infant industry development, 322
  inflation *see* inflation
  market economies, 37
  monetary policy, 126, 127–36, 240–1, 246
  planned economies, 30, 31–3, 34, 39–40, 41
  purchasing power parity theory, 308, 309
  quantity theory of money, 125, 126, 132
  vector autoregression model, 119–20
  WTO membership, 78
private ownership, management efficiency, 430
private sector
  coexistence with public, 407
  education, 221–2, 386, 387, 389, 399–403

private sector (*cont'd*)
 future prospects, 419
 land use, 360, 409
 physical infrastructure
  projects, 373
 planned economy
  coordination with, 381
 pre-1949, 17–20, 288
 *see also* collective
  enterprises; individual-
  owned enterprises;
  nonstate sectors;
  privatization
privatization
 agriculture, 49–50, 58, 86,
  201
 healthcare, 228, 230
 state enterprises, 71–2, 250–
  1, 281–2, 359, 361
 township and village
  enterprises, 291
 urban housing, 174–5
production
 economic reform to the
  mid-1990s, 49, 51,
  280–1
 in a market economy, 29,
  30, 31–2
 in a planned economy, 29,
  30–3, 35–9, 40–1,
  43–4, 271–5, 278
production functions
 demand for labor, 214
 dynamic optimization
  model, 143–4, 150
 Heckscher–Ohlin theory of
  trade, 303
 human capital, 207, 208–9
 neoclassical growth model,
  93–4, 96, 98, 101–4,
  107, 110–11
 population, 194
 state enterprises, 280
production transformation
  curves (production
  possibility frontiers),
  36–7, 40–1, 302,
  303–5, 307–8
productive efficiency *see* total
  factor productivity

profit incentives, 408
 asset misuse, 358
 late 1990s reforms, 282,
  283, 284
 in a planned economy, 32,
  274
 reforms to mid-1990s, 50,
  51–2, 53, 60, 278,
  280, 281
 *see also* responsibility
  system
profit maximization, demand
  for labor, 215
prospects for the Chinese
  economy, 104–8,
  417–23, 427
protectionism, 320–1, 322–4,
  341
provincial governments
 geography of China, 66–7
 planned economy, 43, 44, 379
 trust and investment
  corporations, 247–8,
  253
public ownership, 407–9
purchasing power parity
  (PPP), 308–10, 312
Putterman, Louis, 353

Qin dynasty, 12, 21
Qing dynasty, 16–17, 22, 289
Qualified Foreign Institutional
  Investors (QFII)
  scheme, 250
Quandt, Richard E., 276
quantity theory of money,
  125–6, 132

random residuals, 99, 114–15,
  119
random-walk process, 143, 144
rate of exchange *see* foreign
  exchange rate
rational expectation
  hypothesis, 117
rationing, 30, 34
Rawski, T., 291
Red Guard, 28
reduced-form equations, 114–
  15, 118–19, 140, 147

Rees, Albert, 213
regression analysis, 99–101
 dynamic optimization
  model, 147–50
 of monetary policy, 133–6
 multiplier-accelerator
  model, 115–16
 nonstate sector, 291–2
 production functions for
  China, 101–4
 rates of return to schooling,
  224–6
regulation *see* legislation and
  regulation
regulatory burden, 338, 339
religious freedom, 3–4
Remer, C. F., 328
remuneration *see* incentives;
  wage rates
renminbi (RMB)
 exchange rate *see* foreign
  exchange rate
 first issue of, 126
 monetary policy, 132
rent seeking, 352, 355, 358,
  406
Republic of China, 16–21,
  22, 367–8
 in Taiwan, 15, 22
research
 economics, 398
 education policy, 390
 government-sponsored, 376
responsibility system, 408
 asset misuse, 356–9
 banks, 243, 252
 future prospects, 419
 household, 49, 58, 85, 86,
  356–7, 362, 408
 state enterprises, 48–9, 52,
  61, 281, 357–9, 362
retail sector
 asset misuse, 351, 357
 investment, 333–4, 340,
  341
Ricardian theory of
  comparative
  advantage, 302, 305,
  317, 319, 320, 321,
  322–3

Roberts, K. W. S., 34
Roosevelt, Franklin, 125
rural areas
    agriculture *see* agriculture
    asset misuse, 354, 356–7
    consumption of housing,
        174, 175
    credit cooperatives, 244
    demand for labor, 215
    expenditure patterns,
        166–9
    healthcare, 227, 228–9,
        230
    migration from, 85–6, 185,
        186, 222
    per capita consumption,
        162, 163, 164–5,
        172–4, 178–9
    population, 195, 196, 202,
        205
    poverty, 85–7
        healthcare, 229
        regional development
            strategy, 178, 184–7
    rates of return to schooling,
        225–6
    social welfare system,
        230
    *see also* township and
        village enterprises

Samuelson, Paul A., 114, 115,
    323
Schiller, Robert, 258–9
scholarship
    education reforms, 56
    history of, 11, 12, 14, 376,
        385–6, 398
    *see also* intellectuals,
        control of
schooling *see* education
Schultz, T. W., 207, 219
science
    education, 389–90, 421–2
    regional development,
        183–4
service sector
    foreign investment, 333–4
    GDP data collection, 96
    job outsourcing, 323

rural areas, 185
WTO membership, 78, 79,
    80, 341
*see also* banking and
    financial sector
services, asset misuse, 348,
    350–1, 352–3,
    354–6
Shang dynasty, 10–11, 21
Shanghai stock market,
    248–9, 250
    stock price determination,
        255–65
Shantou economic zone,
    329
Shapiro, Judith, 187
share trading *see* stock
    markets; stock price
    determination
shareholding companies, state
    enterprises as, 71, 72,
    80, 229, 250, 259,
    282–4, 361, 364, 408,
    419–20
Shen, Yan, 120, 133, 135–6,
    399, 401
Shenzhen economic zone,
    54–5, 61, 329
Shenzhen stock market, 248,
    249, 250
shipping, 342–3
Silk Route, 13
Sima Qian, 13, 31, 293
Sims, C. A., 120
simultaneous equation model,
    111–19, 120
Sino-Japanese War, 15, 17,
    20, 386
Smith, Adam, 209, 412
Snow, Edgar, 25
social development
    expenditure, 136, 138
social infrastructure
    government, 374
social networking (*guanxi*),
    2, 5, 335–6, 356,
    371, 372, 409, 410
social stability, WTO
    membership, 84
social welfare, 229–30, 413

birth rate and, 206
government role, 374–5
healthcare *see* healthcare
Hong Kong, 294, 295
Pareto optimality, 175
policy statement in 1997,
    70
as a principle of the people,
    20
rural migrants, 86, 185,
    186
rural residents, 85, 186
state enterprise reform,
    282, 283
urban–rural gap, 85, 86
socialist market economy, 54,
    63, 89, 295–6
    asset misuse, 347–64, 406
    bureaucracy, 406
    collectivism, 412–14
    human capital, 417
    legal system, 409–12
    one-party system, 414–16
    pragmatic government,
        416–17
    prospects for, 418–23
    public ownership, 407–9
society, collective welfare,
    412–14
soft budget constraints,
    276–7, 289
Solow residual, 208, 209
Solow, Robert, 93, 146, 208
Song dynasty, 14–15, 22,
    411–12
Song Jian, 201
Soviet Union
    aid to China, 328
    Chinese communism and,
        24, 25
    Chinese economic reform,
        65
    education system, 394
"Spring and Autumn" period,
    11
standard error of estimate, 99,
    100
state banks, 54, 72–3,
    235–6
    *see also* commercial banks

State Council of China
  agricultural development,
    184–7
  economic planning, 30–1,
    38, 39, 41–3, 44, 271,
    378–9
  economic reform, 50, 60–1
  foreign investment, 333–4
  People's Bank, 238, 239,
    242, 243
State Development Bank, 73,
    244
State Economic and Trade
    Commission, 71, 282,
    333
state enterprises
  Asian financial crisis, 72, 76
  asset misuse, 348–9,
    352–3, 357–9, 364
  bad debts, 72, 73, 74, 75,
    245–6
  banks see commercial banks
  central planning, 267–78
  coexistence with private, 407
  demand for labor, 215
  economic importance, 286,
    287
  economic planning see
    planned economy
  foreign investment, 334,
    337–8
  governance, 71, 245, 281,
    282, 361, 407, 408
  government tax revenues
    from, 137
  gross industrial output
    value, 55–6
  healthcare, 228–9
  historical background, 26,
    267–8
  monetary policy, 129
  reform, 5, 48–9, 50–2,
    57–8, 61, 64, 65
    econometric models,
      278–81, 291–2, 359
    problems and prospects,
      69–72, 80, 88, 89,
      281–4, 358–9, 364,
      375–6, 431
  relative efficiency, 291–2

responsibility system,
    48–9, 52, 61, 281,
    357–9, 362
  as shareholding companies,
    71, 72, 80, 229,
    250–1, 259, 282–4,
    361, 364, 408, 419–20
  social welfare, 229–30,
    282, 283
  vocational training schools,
    223
  WTO membership, 79, 80,
    340
State Planning Commission,
    41, 44, 50, 378
State Planning and Reform
    Commission, 378
State Statistics Bureau, 94–5,
    96
statistical data, reliability,
    94–6, 140
stochastic dynamic
    optimization problems,
    145
stochastic equations, 114–16
stochastic trends, 144, 149–50
stock markets, 18, 247,
    248–9, 250–1, 253
stock price determination,
    255–65
structural equations, 114–16,
    118, 140, 146–7
student demonstrations, 5,
    62–3
subsidised industries, 321, 376
substitution effect, labor, 212
Sun Shangqing, 161
Sun Yat-sen, 17, 20, 25, 367,
    415
supply
  of asset services, 350–1,
    352–3, 357
  of educational services,
    219–20, 221–2
  of labor see labor, supply of
  neoclassical growth model,
    110, 111
supply management, 37–9,
    41, 43, 51, 272,
    273–4, 278

Taiwan
  birth rate, 197
  death rate, 196
  economic growth, 103–4
  economic reform, 57–60, 64
  export-processing zones, 316
  government-sponsored
    research, 376
  historical background, 15,
    21, 22
  human capital, 223
  investment in China, 331,
    342–3
  legal system, 368
  one-party system, 414
  protectionism, 320
  stock market intervention,
    264
  trade with China, 301,
    342–3
Tang dynasty, 13–14, 22
tariffs
  government revenue from,
    137
  protectionism, 320
  WTO membership, 78, 79,
    80, 81, 340, 341
taxation
  abolition of on farmers,
    185
  asset misuse and, 358
  banks, 245–6
  democracy and, 382
  fiscal policy, 136
  foreign invested
    enterprises, 332
  free-market economy, 293
  government revenue from,
    136, 137
  illegal agricultural levies,
    86–7, 185
  per capita consumption,
    162
  pollution levies, 189,
    190–1
  reform, 136
teachers, 393–4, 395, 396–7
technology
  comparative advantage
    theory, 320

for education, 389–90
foreign investment, 332,
    333, 336–7
future prospects, 421–2
government role, 376
Heckscher–Ohlin theory of
    trade, 303–4, 306–7
history of development of,
    14–15, 18, 22
protectionism, 323–4
regional development,
    183–4, 186
telecommunications
    democracy, 83
    WTO membership, 78, 79,
        80, 340, 341
tertiary industry see service
    sector
Thailand, financial crisis, 74, 75
Three Gorges Project, 380
Tiananmen Square, 5, 21,
    62–3, 240
Tibet, 3–4
time-series analysis, 165
    stock price determination,
        259
total factor productivity (TFP)
    dynamic optimization
        model, 143, 144, 145,
        149, 150, 151–2, 153
    neoclassical growth model,
        101, 103, 105, 106,
        107, 111
    state enterprise reforms,
        280–1, 291–2
    township and village
        enterprises, 291–2
tourism, 334
towns see urban areas
township governments, 87,
    186–7, 288
township and village
    enterprises (TVEs),
    55, 64, 286
    coexistence with public,
        407
    conditions for growth,
        288–91, 431
    demand for labor, 215
    efficiency, 291–2

future, 296
legal system, 372–3
regional development, 185,
    187
trade see foreign trade
training
    bank personnel, 236–7
    government role, 376
    health workers, 227
    human capital, 208, 216, 223
transition economics, 65
transportation
    between Taiwan and China,
        342–3
    government role, 373
    historical background, 19
    purchasing power parity
        theory, 309–10
    regional development,
        181–2, 183–4
treasury bonds, 251
Treaty of Nanking, 16
trust and investment
    corporations, 247–8,
    253
Tsiang, S. C., 57
two-stage least-squares
    method (2SLS), 116
two-tail test, 292
two-tier price system, 53, 313

unemployment
    demand for labor, 214–15
    Keynes' theory, 111
    protectionism, 323
    social welfare system, 230
    state enterprise reform, 70,
        72, 282, 283
    WTO membership, 84
unification of China, 12,
    20–1, 25, 368
universities and colleges, 56
    demand for education,
        399–402
    economics education, 391–9
    government policy, 388–91
    government role, 376
    historical background, 26,
        28, 218, 221, 386, 387
    labor supply, 210

medical, 227
ownership of enterprises, 408
urban areas
    asset misuse, 354, 357,
        359–60, 409
    consumption of housing,
        174–5
    credit cooperatives, 244
    demand for labor, 215, 216
    healthcare, 228–9, 230
    household expenditure
        patterns, 169, 172
    labor welfare, 282
    per capita consumption,
        163–5
    pollution, 188, 189, 190
    population, 195, 196, 197,
        202, 205–6
    rates of return to schooling,
        225–6
    social welfare system,
        229–30
    tensions with rural, 85–6
    see also township and
        village enterprises
urban development, 359–60,
    409

USA
    central bank, 239, 242
    Chinese economic growth,
        107, 108
    Chinese economics
        education, 392–3, 395,
        396, 397, 398
    Chinese nationalism, 6
    Chinese students in, 220–1,
        222, 223
    democracy, 415
    dollar–RMB exchange
        rate, 312–13, 317,
        318, 321
    foreign investment in, 327
    investment in China, 331,
        338, 342
    investment in human
        capital, 208, 216
    labor supply, 209–10
    legal system, 372, 410–11
    macroeconomic policy, 125
    medical services, 227

USA (*cont'd*)
  migration to, 222–3
  New York Stock Exchange,
    261, 262, 263–4
  population, 194
  protectionism, 322–4
  social welfare, 294–5, 413
  trade with, 301, 316,
    322–4
  utility functions, 145, 204–5,
    213

value-added tax (VAT), 136
vector autoregression (VAR)
  system, 119–20,
  135–6
village enterprises *see*
  township and village
  enterprises (TVEs)
village governments, 82
  abuse of power, 86–7, 185,
    187
  financial resources, 288
village planning, 187
vocational schools, 223
voucher systems
  education, 374
  housing, 374–5

wage rates
  demand for labor, 214
  failing state enterprises, 72
  human capital, 208–9, 212,
    224–6
  labor supply, 212, 213
  law of supply of asset
    services, 351
  per capita consumption,
    162, 163–4
  in a planned economy, 30,
    32–3, 35–6, 275
  privatized housing, 174–5

rates of return to schooling,
  224–6
rural poverty and, 86
state enterprise reform,
  283
*see also* incomes
Wang Donglin, 216
Wang, Hua, 189–91
Warring States period, 12
water pollution, 188, 189–91,
  227
Wei, Shang-Jin, 338–9
Wei Zhi, 226–7
Weitzman, Martin L., 407
welfare, collective, 412–14
  *see also* social welfare
welfare effects, asset use
  restrictions, 352, 353
western China
  development, 177–87,
    362
  foreign investment, 331
Western imperialism, 5–6,
  16
Whalley, John, 353
Wheeler, David, 189–91
worker behavior, in a planned
  economy, 34–6
World Trade Organization
  (WTO)
  impact of membership of,
    78–85, 106, 297, 322
  foreign investment, 78,
    79–80, 327, 339–42,
    421
written language, 11, 12
Wu, Chuntao, 86–7

X-efficiency, 276
Xiamen economic zone, 329
Xu, Chenggang, 407
Xu Dixin, 121, 392

Yao Yilin, 50
Yeh, K. C., 19
Yen, Tzung-Ta, 315
Yi Zhenqiu, 175
Yin, K. Y., 57
Young, Leslie, 13
yuan, 4, 77–8
  exchange rate *see* foreign
    exchange rate
Yuan dynasty, 15, 22
Yuan Shih-kai, 17, 367

Zhang Peiji, 314, 315
Zhang, Xiabo, 87
Zhao Renwei, 224
Zhao Ziyang, 57, 61, 135,
  174, 180, 311–12, 392
Zheng He, 15
Zheng Ji, 223
Zheng, Y. X., 291
Zhou dynasty, 11–12, 21
Zhou Enlai, 17, 27
Zhou, Kate Xiao, 49
Zhu, Lijing, 353
Zhu Rongji
  economic development
    tasks, 177–8, 184,
    228, 421
  economic reform, 44, 61,
    72, 77, 80
  education policy, 421–2
  financial reform, 251–2
  GITIC bankruptcy, 248
  macroeconomic policy,
    130, 139, 240, 241
  scholarship, 398
  State Council downsizing,
    383
  western development, 183,
    184
Zhu Xi, 371
Zhuhai economic zone, 329